THE
MBA HANDBOOK

Visit *The MBA Handbook, sixth edition* Companion Website at **www.pearsoned.co.uk/cameron** to find valuable **student** learning material including:

- Learning logs, checklists and activities
- Study and revision planners
- Answers to questions in the book
- Links to relevant sites on the web

We work with leading authors to develop the strongest educational materials in business, finance and marketing, bringing cutting-edge thinking and best learning practice to a global market.

Under a range of well-known imprints, including Financial Times Prentice Hall, we craft high quality print and electronic publications which help readers to understand and apply their content, whether studying or at work.

To find out more about the complete range of our publishing please visit us on the World Wide Web at: **www.pearsoned.co.uk**

THE
MBA HANDBOOK

Skills for Mastering Management

Sixth Edition

SHEILA CAMERON
The Open University Business School

Prentice Hall
FINANCIAL TIMES

An imprint of **Pearson Education**
Harlow, England • London • New York • Boston • San Francisco • Toronto
Sydney • Tokyo • Singapore • Hong Kong • Seoul • Taipei • New Delhi
Cape Town • Madrid • Mexico City • Amsterdam • Munich • Paris • Milan

Pearson Education Limited
Edinburgh Gate
Harlow
Essex CM20 2JE
England

and Associated Companies throughout the world

Visit us on the World Wide Web at:
www.pearsoned.co.uk

First edition published 1991 in Great Britain under the Pitman Publishing imprint
Second edition published 1994
Third edition published 1997
Fourth edition published 2001
Fifth edition published 2005
Sixth edition published 2008

ISBN: 978-0-13-613873-0
ISBN: 978-0-13-613874-7 (Open University edition)

British Library Cataloguing-in-Publication Data
A catalogue record for this book is available from the British Library

10 9 8 7 6 5 4 3 2 1
11 10 09 08

Typeset in 9½ Stone Sans by 3
Printed by Ashford Colour Press Ltd, Gosport

The publisher's policy is to use paper manufactured from sustainable forests.

Contents

Supporting resources

Visit **www.pearsoned.co.uk/cameron** to find valuable online resources

Companion Website for students
- Learning logs, checklists and activities
- Study and revision planners
- Answers to questions in the book
- Links to relevant sites on the web

For more information please contact your local Pearson Education sales representative or visit **www.pearsoned.co.uk/cameron**

Guided tour of the book

Learning outcomes introduce topics covered and summarise what you should have learnt by the end of the chapter.

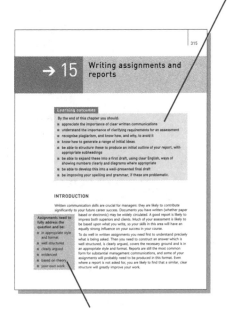

Activities feature throughout the text to reinforce learning by prompting thought and application to real life.

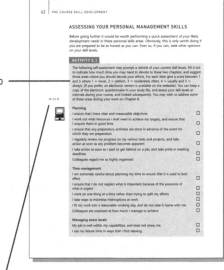

Information boxes appear throughout the text offering either guidelines on how to tackle an issue, or a summary of key points from a section of text.

Chapter linking arrows highlight the connections between chapters and indicate where you can find further details about a topic or concept.

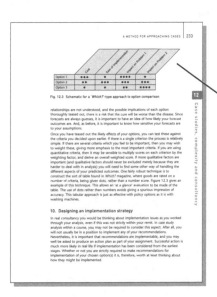

Figures and **diagrams** feature throughout the text to illustrate key points and clarify topics discussed.

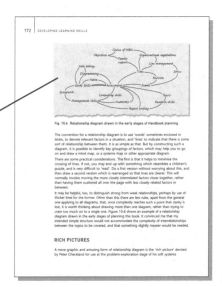

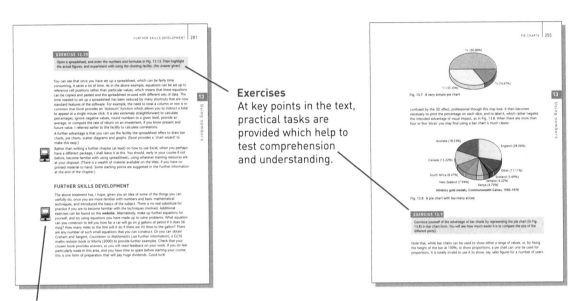

Exercises
At key points in the text, practical tasks are provided which help to test comprehension and understanding.

A **website icon** in the margin highlights where checklists, additional exercises, and other useful resources are available on the book's companion website (**www.pearsoned.co.uk/cameron**) to further help you with your MBA studies.

Helpfiles offer 'back to basics' guidance to mastering key skills such as maths, grammar, and examination terms.

Summaries pull together the key points addressed in the chapter to provide a useful reminder of topics covered.

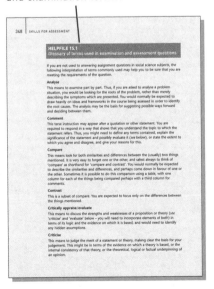

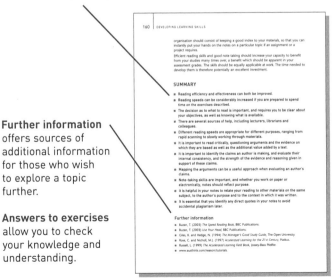

Further information
offers sources of additional information for those who wish to explore a topic further.

Answers to exercises
allow you to check your knowledge and understanding.

Acknowledgements

Among the many people I should like to thank are Penelope Woolf for persuading me to write this book in the first place, The Open University as an institution, and close colleagues, in particular, for giving me the space to write, and my students for being an endless source of challenge, stimulus and ideas. Last but definitely not least, I should particularly like to thank Hester, Neill and James for their research, comments, suggestions and general support throughout.

INTRODUCTION

→ 1 Management, learning and the role of this book

Learning outcomes

By the end of this chapter you should:

■ appreciate the nature of the learning needed by today's managers

■ have considered your own development needs and career goals

■ understand how the skills developed in the book can contribute to meeting these needs and achieving your goals

■ have identified those sections of the book which will be of most use to you

■ be planning your work on priority chapters.

INTRODUCTION

Managers today face more challenges than ever before. Most organisations now operate in highly competitive, rapidly changing environments. To build a successful career in this context, managers need a wide range of skills. 'Knowledge management', sense making, and virtual teamworking have been added to more traditional skills such as time management, problem solving, report writing and statistical analysis. 'Leadership' is in frequent demand. Continuing professional development is seen as crucial, and 'learning skills' are perhaps the most important of all.

Increasingly, managers are seeing postgraduate study as a route to career success, and this book is designed to help you choose – if you have not already chosen – a suitable programme, and then to study it successfully. Most of the skills you will need for successful study are highly transferable to managerial work. Thus, even if you choose to defer, or even reject, formal study, you will be able to use the book to develop a range of skills directly relevant to your career as a manager.

A glance at the contents pages will show you the breadth of the coverage of this book. Better communication, time and project management, teamworking, complex problem solving, writing, IT and number skills should make you far more effective at work. And above all, the ability to operate as a 'reflective practitioner' and learn continually from your experience should mark you for success. In an attempt to remain ahead of the competition, organisations are restructuring, delayering and resizing, merging, acquiring or being acquired. They are continually redefining their processes, adopting new technologies, seeking to alter their corporate culture, and adopting whatever change initiative is the current 'flavour of the month'. To thrive amidst this constant change, you need flexibility and the ability to respond to new situations in a creative and effective manner.

If you decide to seek a qualification, this book will help you to gain high marks. But far more importantly, it will help you to exploit your studies to become a more effective manager. Managers often see obtaining a qualification as all-important: I would argue that the impact on your effectiveness at work is even more valuable. It is this, not the letters after your name which will do most to accelerate your career and lead to success.

The following comments by past students give a flavour of some of the benefits of management study:

> 'My MBA course has altered the whole way I approach my job.'
>
> 'I am now far more creative in the way I approach problems.'
>
> 'I am now good at seeing what we need to do to fit in with overall strategy.'
>
> 'I find I am far better at coping with complexity – I no longer try to over-simplify situations in order to make them manageable.'
>
> 'I have become far better at setting priorities and managing my time.'
>
> 'My communication skills have improved enormously.'
>
> 'I feel far more confident when talking with our finance specialists.'
>
> 'I have become more aware of the range of stakeholders in my organisation, and of the ethical issues this raises.'
>
> 'Above all, I am a better manager as a result of this course – and I have already been promoted twice!'

An MBA was once a rare qualification: this is no longer the case. MBAs are now widely available, and have been joined by a broad range of Master's degrees in management-related subjects. A Master's qualification is becoming almost a prerequisite for success as a senior manager. If you have already enrolled on such a programme, and want to prepare yourself for it, this book will help you assess which skills you need to develop to benefit fully from the course. These same skills should immediately transfer to your work situation.

If you are still considering whether to study, and which course to choose, the book will help you address these questions. Working through the next two chapters may make it clear that it is not yet the right time for you to enrol on a course. If so, decide which chapters will help you develop the skills that will make you more effective at work, and accelerate your career. They will also prepare you for eventual study. Obvious candidates are chapters which address improved time management, better team-working and networking, and more effective spoken and written communication. Developing these skills can help you to reach a position from which an MBA or similar programme is an appropriate goal.

Perhaps you have decided to do a Master's degree and are thinking seriously about choice of course. It is an important choice. Formal management study at this level is a significant undertaking, and a major investment. It will not be easy – it would not be worth it if it were – and it will not be cheap. There will be personal as well as financial costs. Some students will inevitably fail or drop out before completing the course. Others will gain a qualification, but little else. Most, however, will find that their studies are fascinating in themselves, and lead to a transformation of their work experience and of their subsequent careers. The right choice of course will make this more likely, as will appropriate study skills.

The book helps you to choose a course which best suits your needs, and having chosen, to develop the learning skills to maximise the benefit from your study. It shows you how to manage your time effectively, how to deal with stress and how to gain organisational support for your study. It covers basic skills (numeracy, written communication, use of IT, teamworking) which may be rusty or new to you. It explores common aspects of management programmes such as learning from case studies, and doing projects or dissertations. It looks at how to approach the sorts of assessment you are likely to meet, and how to get good grades. It looks at how to go on developing your skills, and your career, once you have gained the qualification.

Although written primarily for the manager who is studying while working (in Europe, the majority of postgraduate management students are in this position), large parts of the book have proved useful to full-time students, particularly those with an academic background unrelated to management.

When the first edition of this book appeared, MBAs were the predominant management qualification at Master's level. Now enrolments on generalist MBAs have stabilised (though as I write there are signs of a slight upturn again). At the same time the number of specialist management-related Master's programmes is expanding rapidly. For continuity, I have kept the title as 'The MBA Handbook'. But the book serves equally well as support for a wide range of other management-related programmes at Master's level.

This Handbook is *not* a textbook – it is not designed to be read passively nor is it full of facts. It is closer to an interactive distance learning text. To gain full benefit you need to work through the activities and exercises provided as well as reading the words. Note that you are unlikely to need to use *all* chapters. Management students come from a wide range of backgrounds. Some have PhDs, others left school at 16, and have gained professional qualifications while working. Some are engineers, others studied arts subjects. Their needs with respect to learning skills therefore cover a wide range. Your own needs are likely to be some subset of these. To gain full value from the book it is suggested that you work out your needs, and actively manage your learning in order to meet them. Keeping a file devoted to your personal development can be a great aid in this.

If you have already chosen a course, you do not need to work through the chapter on choosing. Engineers will probably find the numeracy chapter completely unnecessary. If you have an English degree, you are unlikely to need the revision section on writing clear English. You therefore need to select those parts of the book which *are* relevant to you. This short introductory chapter aims to help you understand how the book is structured, to relate this to your own particular needs and thence to work out how best to use it.

HOW THE BOOK IS STRUCTURED

→ Ch 2, 3

If you refer to the contents list, you will see that the book falls roughly into three main parts. Chapters 2 and 3 deal with the period before you commit yourself to a course of study. What does postgraduate management study entail, and what benefits can you expect? Given your own particular set of goals and circumstances, is a Master's an appropriate goal, or is some other qualification more desirable? If so, which available course is most likely to suit your needs? Is part-time or full-time study better for you? If opting for part-time, do you need the discipline of regular class attendance, or would the flexibility of distance learning be better? Could you cope with a purely on-line course, or do you want some face-to-face component? Having decided on a type of course, what questions should you ask of possible colleges or other providers? Clearly, if you have already enrolled on a course, you have answered these questions to your own satisfaction, and do not need to work through the early chapters.

→ Ch 4, 5, 6

The next three chapters deal with preparation you could usefully do if you have time available before starting your course. There are several possible reasons for not starting a course immediately. Many programmes run only once or twice a year. It may take time to obtain sponsorship. Your life may be too full at present to allow study. But if you have decided that you will study at some future point, you can start *now* to prepare yourself. This part of the book covers broad preparation – preparing the context in which you will study, and developing necessary personal management skills. These include planning and time management that will help you to make effective use of what will be your scarcest resources, time and energy. Also important are the assertiveness and negotiation skills you will need to protect that time, and the stress management techniques you will need for the times when the conflicting pressures of work, home and family become greater than is ideal. You will also need information-management skills to acquire and organise the large volume of information likely to be involved, and the ability to use IT to suppport your studies.

→ Ch 5, 6

If you are planning a full-time course, the contextual issues will be different. But you may still need to develop the personal skills covered in Chapters 5 and 6.

Even if you decide not to proceed with a qualification at this point, many of the skills addressed in this 'preparatory' part of the book are likely to be relevant to your job as a manager.

→ Ch 7–13

Chapters 7–13 deal broadly with developing the more specific learning skills you will need for postgraduate study. This could be seen as a further part of your preparation, usefully done before your course starts. But the skills addressed are in a different category from the more general preparation of earlier chapters. If you have already started your course, you may be hard pressed to find the time to develop these skills. However, they are so important that you might perhaps select two or three chapters likely to be of most use, and focus on those. A key aim of this part of the book is to help you develop the habit of reflective learning. A personal development file will help you to manage your learning and capture insights gained. Because of the importance of continuing development at work, the skills involved will be relevant even if you are not at present studying.

Again, these skills are highly transferable. Organisations and their contexts are changing so rapidly that the ability to learn and adapt is a vital management skill. This is why course *learning* usually has a far greater impact on work performance and career success than being able to put MBA (or MSc or whatever) after your name. This part of the book should help you to maximise that learning, and the benefits it brings. Gaining a qualification is of course an important goal, and a valuable incentive to exerting the necessary effort. In order to pass the course, and certainly if you are seeking a distinction, it is necessary to do *more* than 'learn'. Unless you can *demonstrate* this learning, via whatever assessment is used on your course, you will not gain the qualification. Assessment is not the same as performance evaluation at work. It will probably involve a selection of written assignments, assessed group work, examinations and a substantial thesis or dissertation. You therefore need to develop a separate set of

→ Ch 14–19 skills related to this aspect. Chapters 14–19 deal with this. Even if you have already started on your course you should find this part of the book helps you to improve your grades.

The final chapter is intended to help you consider your career goals after you obtain your qualification, and how you can continue to develop as a manager. In a changing environment continuous professional development is essential for success as a senior manager.

PLANNING YOUR WORK ON THE HANDBOOK

You are unlikely to need to study every chapter. And as time is likely to be scarce, you need to target your efforts. To do this you need first to identify your development needs. There will be more on this as you work through the book, but it will be helpful to do a first rough pass now. This will start a thought process that will make the more detailed work in later chapters easier. Use the book chapter headings, together with any information you have about the course you have enrolled on, or courses you are considering, as prompts. It will be helpful to start a file for any rough jottings you make in association with the following activities. There will be suggestions for developing and organising this into a more systematic personal development file later.

ACTIVITY 1.1

Think in broad terms about your preparedness to study, and areas which concern you. List these, noting down reasons for your concern. You will need to do this as a document which you can file for later reference.

Figure 1.1 shows how work on the various chapters might relate to milestones in an MBA or similar course. You should now study this diagram, and highlight those chapters which you think you will wish to use.

ACTIVITY 1.2

Spend some time skimming through one or two of the chapters which seem most relevant to your needs. Try to assess how long they would take you to work through if you were to do all the activities thoroughly. Then think about how long you can afford to spend working on them, either before your course starts, or while you are at the same time doing coursework. Try to be realistic in your estimates. If you have focused on more chapters than you know (being honest) you can find the time for, then be ruthless. Discard the least pressing. It is better to set yourself an achievable task, than to attempt too much, become discouraged and achieve nothing. You can always revise your targets later if you are getting on more quickly than anticipated.

Now decide on target completion dates for the chapters you have selected. Complete the chart below, or devise a more extended one. Be sure to note your target dates in your diary, too, to ensure that you do not forget to check your progress. You will need to bear your course timetable in mind, if you are already registered for a course, or your anticipated course start date if not.

Chapter	Target completion date	Notes
_____	_____	_____
_____	_____	_____
_____	_____	_____
_____	_____	_____
_____	_____	_____

Comment

The above activity should have introduced you to one of the key ways in which you are intended to use this book, that is, to write on it! By the end of your course you should have absorbed all you need from the book, and need to make only limited reference to it thereafter. So there is no need to keep it in pristine condition. Deface it as much as you like, provided this will help you. Indeed, it will be suggested that you deface other printed materials, too (provided that they belong to you, not the library), so you might as well start now. (If you prefer working with a computer rather than on paper, an electronic version of this and other activities is available from the Web page.)

You should not be locked into your plan above. Course demands and other experiences will almost certainly cause you to revise your priorities and assessed needs. When this happens you should revise your plan too. You may sometimes wish to look at parts of the book you decided were not important, in order to check that your decision was right. The fact that your plan will probably change considerably does not invalidate it. Such changes should constitute improvements. It is difficult to make such improvements without an original plan to improve on. The key thing is that you *have a* plan, and that you follow it, modifying it only to make it *more* effective. Because you will need to revisit the plan it helps to keep it on file, either paper or electronic. There

→ Ch 4, 7, 8 is more on planning in general in Chapter 4, on study planning in Chapter 7. Chapter

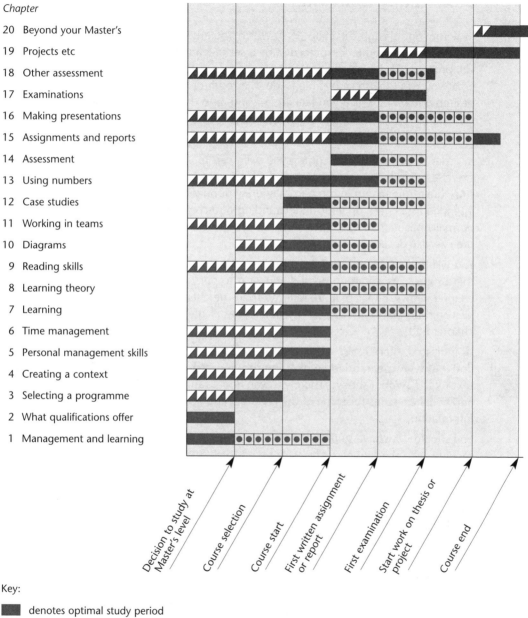

Key:

■ denotes optimal study period

◨ denotes scope for bringing study forward

●● denotes period into which study could be postponed if unavoidable

Fig. 1.1 Optimal study times for Handbook chapters in relation to course milestones

1

Management, learning and the role of this book

8 looks at development more generally and suggests keeping a personal development file. Your plan for using the book could be your first study planning entry.

CHAPTER STRUCTURE

In skimming through the chapters in which you are interested, you will see that each starts with an introduction preceded by a set of learning outcomes for the chapter. You will probably find it helpful to think about these outcomes, and see whether they are what you would wish to be able to do as a result of reading the chapter. If there are desired outcomes which you feel are missing, add these with a question mark. And at the end of your work on the chapter, check whether these have been met as well. (Write to me c/o the publishers if you find significant omissions.)

In order to achieve the outcomes, you will need to work through any activities and exercises included in the chapter. Activities do not have answers, though the subsequent discussion in the text may draw upon what you have written. Exercises are intended as a check on your understanding of techniques or concepts, and will normally have an answer. These answers are printed at the end of the chapter in which the exercise occurs.

You will find suggested sources of further *information* at the end of most chapters. Use these sources as a starting point if you wish to pursue a subject in more depth than the chapter allows. Books that are referred to in the chapter, but which may not be the best starting point, are listed in the references at the end of the book rather than at the chapter end.

 As indicated, there is also a **companion website** associated with this book. You will find it at **www.pearsoned.co.uk/cameron** and items on this website are shown in the text by the symbol shown. There you will find a range of proformas for activities, additional exercises for some of the chapters and links to other useful sources of information.

You should now have sufficient grasp of the book's structure to start working through sections with the highest priority for you. I trust that this will prove a useful and enjoyable exercise.

SUMMARY

- Postgraduate management-related study is increasingly important for managers, but represents a major investment of time and money.
- This book can help maximise the return on that investment, while at the same time developing skills that transfer readily to managerial work.
- This book is intended to be used selectively, but relevant sections should be worked through, rather than merely read.
- Although chapters divide roughly into choice, preparation, learning skills and

assessment skills, much of the book can be worked through in preparation for the start of a course.

■ Your plan for working through the book should depend on your priorities, and the timetable of the course you intend to study. It is important that this plan be realistic.

■ There is a companion website for this book at **www.pearsoned.co.uk/cameron**.

1

Management, learning and the role of this book

BEFORE DECIDING ON A PROGRAMME

→ 2 Differences between Master's qualifications

Learning outcomes

By the end of this chapter you should:

- understand the original rationale for an MBA syllabus and subsequent expansion of specialist Master's programmes in management-related topics
- appreciate the range of stakeholder perspectives on Master's-level study, and the potential benefits of such study from both student and employer perspectives
- be aware of the range of possible qualifications and key dimensions of variation
- appreciate the different costs likely to be involved in different programmes.

INTRODUCTION

There are now well over a thousand management Master's programmes on offer, with huge variation between these. Choosing a programme which meets your particular needs is crucial. The right one might transform your career, and indeed have a major impact on your life as a whole. The wrong one may leave you with a sense of failure, or no more than some letters after your name and a hole in your bank account.

Before choosing a course it is important to understand the range of potential benefits that different programmes may offer: you can then decide which of these are most important to you. You also need to understand the other dimensions of variation between programmes, such as length of course, academic level, degree of specialisation and the pattern of time commitment needed. These are likely to be equally important factors in selecting a programme.

This chapter looks at how provision has developed from the original US MBA model to the wide range of programmes now available, and at the way in which both student and employer perspectives on MBAs have changed, in the UK, and Europe more generally. This historical digression is not strictly necessary, but if you have the time you may find that it helps you to understand the current situation.

Change in provision has been – and continues to be – dramatic. Forty years ago Master's-level management study was rare in Europe. Although MBAs were popular in the USA, few European employers had more than a hazy idea of what 'MBA' even stood for, and were probably unaware of any other qualifications at this level. Only a handful of young, ambitious managers pursued an MBA, and on gaining it risked being thought of as expensive, arrogant and generally useless.

This is no longer the case. A formal management qualification is now almost a prerequisite for management success. Key stakeholders in the management education process include managers seeking such qualifications and their employers, the universities and colleges providing such education, and the government who partly funds it, and has an interest in the impact on the quality of management within the economy. Some 500 European business schools produce more than 20 000 graduates a year, most of whom already have substantial management experience behind them. (This is still a small number in relation to the 80 000 or more MBA graduates annually in the USA, together with increasing numbers of managers gaining specialist management qualifications.)

The reasons for this expansion, and its consequences, may help you to consider what you want to do. Costs and benefits of study have changed markedly, and you need to evaluate both when deciding, first, whether or not to seek a qualification of this kind, and, subsequently, which qualification to pursue.

MBA ORIGINS

The prototypical MBA originated at Harvard around a century ago. Programmes following this model are highly selective, highly pressured, and normally involve two years of full-time study. The first year concentrates on the basic management disciplines: control, managerial economics, finance, marketing, organisational behaviour, human resource management, production and operations management. It also covers factors influencing the business environment, such as government and the international economy. During the second year there will be scope for organisational placements, perhaps in the form of consultancy projects, and for study of a range of electives.

Teaching on such programmes is heavily case study based – a method pioneered in the Harvard Law programme. Harvard MBA students report being expected to analyse two or three substantial case studies per night – each requiring two to four hours' study – in preparation for class presentations and discussions the next day. The academic level is extremely high, and the atmosphere highly competitive, placing considerable pressure on students.

This distinctive approach to teaching management has many benefits. The first and obvious one for students is the prestige attached to the qualification itself. The top business schools are highly selective: merely being accepted suggests something special. The competitive nature of the programme ensures that successful graduates are likely to thrive in competitive business environments.

Until fairly recently employers would compete vigorously for the graduates of these business schools, offering 'golden handshakes' on starting, and salaries two or more times the size of those offered to non-MBA graduates. The MBA graduates were valued because they had gained a highly analytical approach to managerial problem solving, and the ability to approach new problems in a structured and rational fashion. From the 800 or so case studies they had analysed, they had a 'vocabulary' of types of problem, and a degree of familiarity with a wide range of business contexts. They had a clear grasp of finance, and the ability to use financial models. The competitive approach to teaching developed a high level of confidence in students who survived it. These qualities made graduates particularly attractive to management consultancies and investment banks, the subsequent employers of the majority of graduates.

The first European business schools modelled themselves upon Harvard, but several important changes took place from about 1980 onwards. These significantly influenced what managers and employers wanted from a qualification, and how they wanted to achieve it. As a consequence, the 'Harvard' model is no longer the dominant one in Europe.

THE CHANGING MANAGEMENT DEVELOPMENT CONTEXT

The factors which brought about this change are somewhat interrelated. They include government interest in management education, growing employer interest, concern for more relevant and practically oriented programmes, a massive increase in the number of 'MBA' courses being offered, particularly via distance learning or other part-time modes, and a change in the type of manager choosing to study. The organisational context has also changed significantly. Figure 2.1 tries to show how these factors led to the current provision. It uses a convention (multiple cause) described in Chapter 10. This section is written from a UK perspective, but broadly similar factors have operated, albeit on slightly different timescales, elsewhere in Europe and indeed around the globe.

→ Ch 10

Government influence

To the extent that they fund education, governments are significant stakeholders in the process. During the 1980s the UK government, concerned with industry's apparent competitive weakness, started to wonder if the solution lay in better management training, and commissioned several reports on this. It emerged that management training was seen by employers as an overhead, rather than an investment. Of the 90 000 or so who entered managerial roles each year, most had no prior formal management education, and subsequently received on average only one day of training per year. The USA had only four times the population of the UK, but produced forty times as many management degrees and diplomas.

Some of the suggested reasons for this disparity were employer confusion over available qualifications, and worries that courses were over-academic and non-vocational. One response to this was the development of a framework of management competences, and qualifications based upon these. While these are successful at lower levels they have not supplanted the more academic and knowledge-based programmes available at Master's level – though application of knowledge is strongly emphasised in

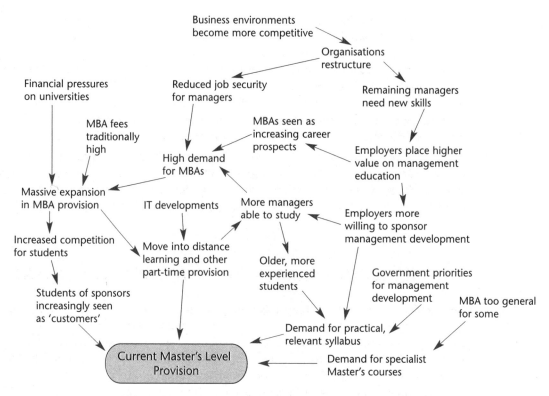

Fig. 2.1 Factors contributing to the current range of management courses on offer at Master's level

many such programmes. The development of critical and analytical skills is generally agreed to be crucial for senior managers.

Indeed, the Quality Assurance Agency for Higher Education (QAA) completed a benchmarking exercise for Master's awards in business and management which lays down the expected standards for an award, and the attributes and capabilities expected of possessors of this award. The full set of standards can be accessed at: **http://www.qaa.ac.uk/academicinfrastructure/benchmark/masters/mba** (accessed 13/01/2007). In summary, they outline the purpose of all such Master's programmes as:

- *the advanced study of organisations, their management and the changing external context in which they operate;*
- *preparation for and/or development of a career in business and management by developing skills at a professional or equivalent level, or as preparation for research or further study in the area;*
- *development of the ability to apply knowledge and understanding of business and management to complex issues, systematically and creatively, to improve business and management practice;*
- *enhancement of lifelong learning skills and personal development so as to be able to work with self-direction and originality and to contribute to business and society at large.*

The university perspective

By the 1980s, concerns were surfacing in the USA about the MBA syllabus. There were complaints from employers that the focus on 'hard' quantitative and analytical skills neglected other areas crucial to success – interpersonal skills, for example, or creativity. The *Harvard Business Review* itself addressed this issue (*see* Lataif, 1992). One view expressed therein, by a leading management writer, Professor Mintzberg, went so far as to suggest that business schools such as Harvard were seriously damaging US business. He claimed that the process of case study analysis fostered a willingness to pronounce on complex issues from a basis of dangerous ignorance! Thus, the method favours the ambitious, glib and quick-witted, rather than those committed to the good of their organisation. (More recent discussion of topics, such as 'emotional intelligence', leadership, 'social capital', the importance of teamworking in organisational structures, and recognition of the complex and 'wicked' nature of organisational problems, has continued to reinforce such doubts about a glibly rational approach.)

By 1990, many UK universities were coming under considerable financial pressure, and saw management courses, for which premium prices could be charged, as an important new source of income. There was therefore a big expansion in provision: many institutions with little track record in management started to offer a range of management courses, up to Master's level, often 'retraining' redundant staff in other disciplines to teach on these. During the 1990s this extended to quasi-franchise arrangements, with colleges of further education offering courses under the auspices of (usually new) universities in the region. Undergraduate management programmes also expanded massively during this period.

Because of the prestige attached to the MBA qualification, and the high prices that could be charged, almost every college wanted to provide such a qualification, thereby threatening that very prestige. To fill all these new courses, entry qualifications were lowered, sometimes to the point of non-existence. Staff with limited academic background were pulled in as lecturers. It could be argued (indeed, I would argue quite strongly) that the best management teachers are those with current experience of senior management allied to a strong academic background in the subject and experience in, and a love of, developing managers. But many of those sucked into this expansion of provision as part-time lecturers did not fit this pattern.

Another major influence was the move away from full-time courses for managers. In the 1980s, the Open University, the major undergraduate distance learning provider in the UK, realised that many managers could not afford the luxury of full-time study and experimented with adapting their well-tried undergraduate methods to postgraduate management study. Because distance learning students are working while studying, they can instantly apply what they are learning to real life. This approach proved so effective for managers that distance management learning, and the emphasis on 'improved management practice' and transferable skills that it allows, have become the most widespread form of formal management education.

Such courses normally equate to little more than a year of full-time study. They take students with no formal management education, and cover the full range of subjects 'management' embraces. Considerable variation in quality of provision still exists: you can still find fairly undemanding (and correspondingly fairly unrewarding) programmes, and need to choose very carefully in order to be sure that the course is well taught, sufficiently challenging, and well regarded by employers.

Because the marketplace for MBAs is now highly competitive, many universities have expanded into the provision of specialist degrees in management-related subjects. Thus, you can find, for example, an MSc in Human Resource Management or International Finance or Marketing or Development Management. Usually much of the teaching is shared with the generic MBA programme, but the coverage of the area of specialism will be greater, and the breadth less. This allows universities to expand their range of 'products', and staff to gain the satisfaction of teaching their favourite subjects in greater depth than an MBA allows.

The current situation can be summarised as:

- A highly competitive marketplace, which has forced universities to become more customer focused.

- Heavy emphasis on part-time provision, which allows managers, typically in their early 30s, to bring considerable experience to their studies: study can be designed to build on this experience, rather than relying exclusively on case studies, and can focus on application. This is consistent with government (and employer) emphasis on the importance of transferable skills.

- Provision of a range of programmes from generalist MBAs to a variety of more specialist Master's programmes, which usually give the same basic understanding of the management context, but will then have a narrower focus on a specialist area.

The employer's view

There is, of course, considerable variation in employers' attitudes towards Master's programmes, and in what they seek in their managers. The following general trends suggest themselves, but treat them with caution!

There is still a residual caution in some quarters about MBAs in particular, with some employers still associating the qualification with arrogance, unrealistic salary demands and lack of both practical experience and common sense. This is now, however, a minority view. The rapid pace of change has made the possession of the analytical skills associated with Master's-level study far more important, and most employers now welcome such a qualification.

Organisational environments have become far more turbulent in recent years, with fierce new competition, and major impacts from developing information and communication technologies. One response has been to 'delayer', stripping out whole layers of management. Another has been to outsource non-core areas of work. Managers who have survived such restructuring are likely to have greater and more varied responsibility than previously, and may need to be very flexible in the way they operate. A formal management course which can increase the ability to operate in such an environment is therefore desirable. With delayering, all levels of management may need to be able to operate autonomously, flexibly and with an understanding of strategic issues, not just the 'high-fliers'.

I quote but one employer, Nokia's head of human resources, writing in one of the many publications (in this case Hobsons MBA Casebooks) designed to help you choose/sell you an MBA. As a rapidly growing international organisation, in one of the most turbulent markets of all, Nokia is well aware of the importance of good managers. They value MBAs because they give graduates a strategic perspective and wider vision so that they are not seduced by short-term advantage into avenues that will threaten longer-term success. They value the interpersonal skills which allow total relationship management with customers, seen as crucial. They appreciate a high level of cultural awareness, which will enable managers to operate across the globe (I spoke recently to a Nokia manager whose team was spread across three continents, and many more countries). Lateral thinking, willingness to take early responsibility and ability to work under pressure were other advantages cited.

Employers tend to prefer their existing employees to study part-time, rather than sending them on a full-time programme. Apart from the obvious benefit of not needing to replace the manager, they fear (not without reason) that if they sponsor someone on a full-time course there is a real risk that that person will leave soon after completing the qualification.

When considering job applicants with a Master's degree on their CV, the selection panel's questions are likely to concern the reputation of the awarding institution, the nature of the programme and the level of marks gained. More importantly, potential employers will want to know how the learning has been used subsequently.

Many employers feel that their management development needs are unique, and can be met only by a specially designed organisation-specific programme. While such 'corporate MBAs' can be of a very high standard, they may fail to develop the breadth of view that is one of the advantages of an open programme, where you will probably learn as much from the varied organisational experience of fellow students as you will from the teaching staff. A middle ground is the consortium MBA, specifically designed for a small number of different but collaborating organisations.

The manager's view

In the next chapter you will be exploring your own objectives in seeking a Master's-level qualification. Suffice it to say here that part of the growth in Master's courses in business and management was driven by the job insecurity that has followed the radical organisational restructuring of the last 20 years or so. This forced many managers to realise that 'a job for life' no longer exists. Instead, they were likely to need to seek a new position several times during their career, against fierce competition. A qualification that would both help them compete for good jobs, and enable them to operate for periods of self-employment, therefore became very important.

The increased availability of part-time and distance learning courses made pursuit of a qualification a realistic possibility for many whose commitments meant that full-time study was simply not an option. This goes a long way to explaining the increasing age profile of management Master's students, already described.

2

Differences between Masters qualifications

KEY DIMENSIONS OF VARIATION

The first questions managers wondering whether to join a Master's programme tend to ask are:

- How long will it take?
- How much will it cost?
- Will I get a place?
- Will I be able to cope?
- How do employers rate this particular qualification?

While these are extremely important questions, there are others equally important, if slightly less obvious, which should influence your choice. These concern the suitability of the delivery mode to your particular circumstances (dealt with in the next chapter), the approach to teaching and the focus of the content – how strategic is it, how international, how practically oriented?

Length of programme

Few students can afford the traditional two-year programme, so most full-time courses now take between 12 and 18 months. While some of the reduction in time can be at the expense of vacations and industrial placements (less important for those who already have management experience), some will inevitably be at the expense of learning. For those who can afford it, or have willing sponsors, a two-year programme at a top school is likely to offer significantly more learning than a shorter programme.

Part-time programmes are designed to spread study over a longer period. The duration will depend upon the expected commitment per week. You need to check how many hours you are expected to devote to your studies each week. In choosing a programme you need to think about what time you can commit, and assure yourself that the coverage offered is of sufficient breadth and depth to be useful.

Delivery pattern

Full-time programmes are now in the minority, and there are many variations in 'part-time'. Traditionally, part-time study involved regular weekly attendance either in the evening or a mix of daytime and evening attendance. This is still widely available. However, because many managers have jobs which do not allow of such regularity, either because of frequent travel or because of irregular working hours, two other variants of part-time study have become common.

The first is the 'executive' model, which requires blocks of attendance at perhaps monthly or two-monthly intervals. This is only feasible for managers working in organisations which support this form of development. It has many of the advantages of full-time study – intensity of study, ability to concentrate wholeheartedly on the course, interaction with fellow students, the ability to study overseas for some of the programme, or with managers from other cultures. These are combined with some of the advantages of part-time study – the ability to apply what is learned almost immediately to work, and continuity of employment and salary.

The second variant is distance learning, which removes, or at least greatly reduces, the need to study in a particular place or at any particular time. The flexibility of this mode, the opportunities now offered for electronic interaction, and the lack of any logistical reasons to limit numbers, together with the high quality of the teaching on some distance learning programmes, have made this the dominant method at present. (The Open University had over 6000 MBA students in its programme during 2003, with nearly half its intake coming from continental Europe or beyond.) You do need to beware, however. The quality of provision varies enormously. Choosing between these variants is addressed in more detail in Chapter 3.

→ Ch 3

Cost of programme

Costs can vary quite significantly, and are not always fully transparent. The obvious costs to consider are course fees, the cost of travel, accommodation costs, living costs if full-time, the cost of books, PC and any other materials and equipment. You may also need to budget for the cost of getting into the school of your choice. You may need to take the GMAT test (at your own expense), an English language test if you are not a native speaker, and to travel for interviews. There may be costs for processing your application. There may be examination fees, and perhaps additional costs for studying overseas. You will be able to find information about fees fairly easily from the Internet or one of the MBA guides listed at the end of the chapter, but may need to ask specific questions to elicit the full picture.

As a rough guide to the variation in cost of study in 2007, you could pay in excess of US $120 000 if you include two years' tuition, living expenses and loss of salary, £30 000 or more for an executive MBA programme, or about £12 000 for a good distance learning programme. The latter two allow you to continue earning so tuition fees are the main cost. Part-time face-to-face courses may cost even less, with a few specialist Master's courses available from as little as £4500.

You may be lucky enough to persuade your employer to pay your fees and/or allow you time to study. After all, the organisation should benefit considerably from your improved efficiency. If not, it may be possible to obtain a loan to cover your study. A very few scholarships are also available. Business schools, banks and the World Wide Web are the best starting point for up-to-date information on current sources of finance.

Entry requirements

Requirements for entry vary enormously, with the top business schools requiring a high GMAT score (*see* Further information at the end of the chapter for books and other sources that cover this), together with a strong academic record and evidence of other achievements (as well as the ability to pay high fees). Indeed, there are organisations devoted to helping you (for a fee) make a successful application to one of these schools. At the other end of the spectrum you may find programmes which will accept you with any class of degree, a professional qualification, or failing that, evidence of management experience. Sometimes this is out of a desire to attract sufficient students to make a programme economically viable, but low entry requirements do not always imply a low standard of teaching.

Three factors allow programmes to be flexible over entry qualifications. The first is that an academic background in *management* is usually not required. Unlike a Master's degree in, say, mathematics, where you would be expected to start with a high level of knowledge of the subject, MBA courses assume the general intellectual level of a graduate, but no subject-specific academic knowledge, though the better programmes will expect substantial management experience. Successful managers are likely to be able to operate at this level, even if for some reason they do not hold a BA or BSc.

Some specialist Master's programmes will build on a professional qualification in the area, but some require neither prior specialist knowledge nor management experience. The assumption is that this is a good qualification for recent graduates seeking to start their management career in a specific functional area.

Second, there is a different cost to failure on a part-time programme. It would be highly irresponsible to accept someone who was unlikely to succeed on to a full-time programme, particularly if they were giving up their job in order to study. Failure would, for them, be a disaster. For the manager who continues to work while studying, failure may be painful to the ego, but is less catastrophic. Part-time programmes can therefore afford to take risks with students lacking the normal qualifications (though they should make it clear to applicants in this category that they *are* perceived to be at risk, so that they can decide whether it is a risk they wish to take).

Third, whereas on face-to-face programmes large classes are undesirable, and limits therefore need to be set, the reverse is true of distance learning. The larger the student body, the more likely students are to find others on the programme living near them, and for local tutorial provision to be feasible. Distance learning materials are costly to produce, too, and if the cost can be spread over a larger number of students, fees can be kept lower. Thus, there are good reasons for distance learning programmes in particular to be more relaxed about academic entry requirements.

Many, however, do set entry requirements relating to management experience, particularly for an MBA. This is linked to the shift in emphasis that has taken place in most European programmes. Once an MBA is seen as an active learning process, rather than mere passive absorption of information, then a student needs to have experience of management to gain full benefit. There are still MBAs which do not presume management experience, and more specialist Master's programmes tend not to require any. If you do not yet meet your preferred institution's experience requirement, you can either wait until you do, or select a programme elsewhere which is designed not to need it. (I must admit to a preference for the former option. While purely academic study in a management subject can be intellectually challenging, and good preparation for an academic career, there is little to match the excitement of studying a subject you have already *lived*, in the active learning mode – described later – that this allows.)

Degree of specialism

The prototypical MBA, although allowing limited specialisation via second-year electives, was essentially a generalist management qualification. Many (including some of the major accrediting bodies) still feel that all MBAs should remain generalist qualifications. It is a contradiction in (their) terms to talk of an MBA in Marketing, in Technology, in International Tourism or in the Music Industry. But these, and many other specialist 'MBAs', are currently available: you can find many MBAs specific to a particular industry or sector. There are now also a great many specialist Master's programmes that are not described as MBAs, but which do contain a varying degree of general management content in addition to the specialist material.

Obviously within any given 'size' of programme, only so much material can be covered. There will be trade-offs between breadth and depth, specialism and generalism. This is clearly a factor you will need to take into consideration, selecting a programme that covers what you think you are likely to need most for the next few years. Content specialisation is one dimension, contextual specialisation is another. Such programmes are, by definition, of more restricted applicability. Their relevance to your needs will depend upon your future career plans as well as your current job.

Degree of strategic focus

Traditionally, a distinguishing feature of an MBA programme was its strong strategic focus, this being perceived as essential for senior or would-be senior managers. Managers at lower levels could study for certificates, diplomas or specialist professional qualifications. These concentrated upon developing the functional skills such managers were deemed to need. (Specialist Master's programmes vary in their strategic emphasis.)

Organisational restructuring has blurred the distinction between junior and senior management in many organisations. A substantial proportion of intending MBA students do not expect rapid promotion to Board level. Most MBA programmes today offer a mix of functional skill development and strategic understanding. There is, however, considerable variation in balance between these. Indeed, a clear divide seems to be emerging between institutions offering a highly strategic traditional MBA, frequently to younger full-time students, and those offering a more practical, less strategic programme, often to slightly older, more experienced part-time students.

In the flatter, more flexible organisations in which many managers currently work, all managers need an appreciation of strategy. This is something that employers value (*see* the views of one employer mentioned earlier in this chapter). But they also need practical skills. Given size constraints, this is a difficult balance to achieve. Consideration of where a programme lies on this dimension, and how this relates to your current and likely future job situation, will clearly be important.

Internationalisation

Given the global nature of much business today, most MBA programmes will claim to prepare graduates to operate internationally, through international faculty, an international student body and/or a curriculum which is deliberately international. Language teaching may be included, as well as visits to, or work experience in, another country.

If this is an important variable, you need to look carefully at the likely effectiveness of a programme in meeting your needs. Benefits may be surprisingly limited, particularly if you are studying part-time. Language skills are indeed important, but difficult to develop. An extended placement where you operate in another language will be invaluable, if you already have the basic skill level to take advantage of it. But at the other extreme, it is unlikely that the minimal language teaching some programmes offer will take you beyond the point of being able to order a beer or ask the way to the station. Similarly, a one-week 'field trip' abroad with a group of fellow students, while enjoyable, is likely to do little to improve your understanding of how managers operate in another culture.

Students generally claim to learn as much from fellow students as from the curriculum. If the student body is international, and there is a lot of time for interaction, this can be invaluable. But again there may be limitations. If the overseas students are recent graduates, they may contribute little in terms of cross-cultural management experience. On part-time programmes outside the major cities there may be few non-local students.

Many distance learning programmes now operate over a wide geographical base. But this will only provide benefits if students who live far apart have opportunities to interact, perhaps electronically or at residential schools. Although such contact is far less than a full-time programme would offer, many remote students find it to be extremely helpful.

Programme credibility

All of the above factors, and others, will influence the credibility of a particular qualification. Given the diversity of MBA and related Master's programmes, their different content and the variation in standards expected, concern over 'whether this Master's is a good one, which employers will respect' is justified. In the USA 'rankings' of business schools are published by both *Business Week* and *US News and World Report*. Although there are arguments about the validity of the methods used, such rankings are influential. Some European schools feature in such lists, but European listings are more recent, and at present exclude distance learning provision, which is a major shortcoming, since this is the largest sector.

In the USA, business schools also need to gain accreditation. The main body performing this is the AACSB. In the UK, all universities are deemed to be of an acceptable standard, so accreditation has been seen as less important, although non-universities *will* need to have programmes validated. Because of the variability of programmes, accreditation *is* valued by potential students, and therefore increasingly sought by universities, particularly if they operate outside the UK as well. The best-known UK body is AMBA. This also accredits some programmes elsewhere in Europe. AMBA has stringent criteria, and provides networking opportunities and other services to those with an AMBA-approved MBA through an active alumni association.

Accreditation is a developing field within Europe. The US-based AACSB is substantially expanding its operations in Europe. Perhaps in response, the European Foundation for Management Development (Efmd) has launched EQUAL, an international association of quality assessment and accreditation agencies in the field of European management development. EQUAL has developed a European Quality Improvement System (EQUIS), which has developed a system of quality benchmarking which can be used for audit, or as a 'stamp of approval' through an accreditation process.

In the UK, intending students can gain information about the general credibility of a business school by finding how it scored in the most recent Research Assessment Exercise, and how it was rated in the Higher Education Funding Council's assessment of teaching. Schools that have received high scores will tend to include this information in publicity material. You need to treat such information with a degree of caution. The research will not necessarily inform the teaching you receive, although academics may argue strongly to the contrary. And while schools receiving bad teaching assessments are best avoided, given that the assessment teams vary from school to school, and it is difficult therefore to calibrate assessments, the difference between very good and satisfactory ratings may be elusive.

Indeed, you need to use all 'official' information about credibility with a degree of caution. A business school with a high US ranking, or a top research ranking, while undoubtedly credible, may still not be the best programme for you. A school with a lower, though still good ranking might offer a programme more suited to your situation, or provide more of the sort of support that you need in order to do well.

Employers, too, may have their own preferences with respect to MBAs. Those which influence sponsoring decisions may be different from those which influence hiring ones. It is impossible to predict what these will be – there is no alternative to doing a little research. In-company values, preferences and prejudices should be fairly easy to elicit. If you are aiming at an eventual job in another organisation or sector you may need to do some investigating for yourself.

Teaching approach

The approach to teaching will depend greatly upon the type of programme. If it is highly academic there may be a strong emphasis on the relative merits of different theories and different methods, with a strong reliance on input from lecturers or textbooks. If there is a more practical orientation, the programme may focus more on the application of such theories to the real world, and on the development of transferable skills. Discussion of students' own experience will be important, and assessment is more likely to be based on real situations encountered by the students.

There is an increasing emphasis on transferable skills in higher education generally. A possible list of such skills which any MBA programme might develop, albeit in different proportions, is:

- numeracy and analytical skills – through case studies and projects;
- written presentation skills – through assignments and project reports;
- oral presentation skills – through presentations on group work;

2

Differences between Masters qualifications

- team skills – through group work on cases and projects;
- leadership skills – through group work and through consultancy or similar projects;
- IT skills – through use of word processing and graphics, spreadsheets, databases, the World Wide Web, and electronic conferencing;
- negotiation and other consultancy skills – through an in-company project;
- personal skills (self-organisation and time management) – through meeting programme demands;
- learning skills and self-awareness – through a continuous process of challenging personal assumptions and reflection on practice;
- critical thinking skills – through research and writing on this.

Your own needs with respect to these skills will form an individual profile: an ideal programme will match this fairly closely.

Another element of teaching approach which will be important is the degree of 'spoonfeeding'. There are two aspects to this, one good, one bad. If you are told what to think, and what to reproduce in exams, this is not good. Study at Master's level should be developing your ability to think for yourself. But some institutions are very much better than others at providing you with the information and materials you need in order to study efficiently, and this sort of 'spoonfeeding' is all to the good for the majority of pressured students.

Teaching media

Although in one sense a subset of teaching approach, the use of media in teaching is so important it warrants a separate section. Information and communication technologies (ICTs), in particular, have become a transforming force in management and management education, the full effects of which have yet to be envisaged. These developments have had an effect on the curriculum, with e-commerce and knowledge management courses highly popular at present. More importantly, they have impacted upon almost all the basic components of conventional teaching.

Consider the traditional 'building blocks' of education. Information was transmitted by a lecturer or textbook. Understanding was increased through questions to the lecturer and seminar discussion, and tested in examinations. The physical presence of students in lecture room or library was essential.

Distance learning has allowed this physical presence to be dispensed with. 'Lectures' are transformed into printed workbooks and/or video and audio tapes, or delivered via a CD-Rom. Necessary readings may be compiled into books and mailed to students, or web links provided to them. Telephone or e-mail allows students to receive answers to specific questions or to discuss things in 'virtual' tutorial groups. Web pages can hold tests which you sit at your leisure, and from which you receive automatic feedback. You can submit substantial assignments electronically and receive tutor comments almost immediately. Via the Internet you can attend 'lectures', and access not only the equivalent of a first-class library, but also an almost infinite variety of more transient and current (albeit often less reliable) materials.

Opinions are at present divided on how best to exploit the technical options for teaching. The latest ICT developments can be sources of frustration as well as excitement. Equipment or software incompatibilities may waste hours or even days of valuable time. Searching the World Wide Web without some guidance can positively devour time, and produce results ranging from amazingly good to worthless. Trying to study quantities of material directly from a screen is for many far more difficult than working from good quality print. Conferencing with fellow students round the globe can produce fascinating insights, but on the whole is less exciting than a good face-to-face debate followed by a visit to the pub.

Because your own situation and preferences are important here, and things are changing so quickly, this is another dimension which you will need to research carefully when making your choice. Bear in mind the quality of materials and interaction in the media used, the likely learning efficiency, and whether you will feel comfortable with, and enjoy using, the different media on offer.

SUMMARY

- MBAs and other management Master's programmes vary in length (duration and size), degree of specialisation and strategic focus.
- The original US MBA was generalist, analytical, strategically focused and highly competitive.
- In Europe a clear split has developed between programmes like this, normally offered full-time, and more practical skills-oriented programmes, aimed at slightly older, more experienced managers, and normally offered via distance learning or other part-time mode. The latter type is now dominant.
- Increasing numbers of specialist MBAs and other specialist Master's programmes are now available.
- ICTs are transforming management education in many ways, but not all of these are universally perceived as improvements upon more traditional media.
- Transferable skills you can reasonably expect an MBA to develop include: learning skills, critical thinking, numerical and analytical skills, written and oral presentation skills, problem-solving skills, leadership and teamworking skills, IT skills, consultancy skills, personal management skills and perhaps entrepreneurial skills.

Further information

- Bickerstaff, G. (ed.) (2006) *Which MBA? A Critical Guide to Programmes in Europe and the USA* (18th edn), The Economist Publications/Pearson Education.
- Frost, V. (2006) 'Can Your Manager Manage?', *Guardian*, Work 2, pp. 1–2.
- Kelly, F.J. and Kelly, H.M. (1986) *What They Really Teach You at the Harvard Business School*, Grafton Books.

2

Differences between Masters qualifications

This is an entertaining read, giving a good flavour of a traditional programme and introducing many of the concepts you are likely to encounter.

■ *The Official MBA Casebook 2006/2007* (19th edn) (2006), Financial Times Prentice Hall, with the Association of MBAs.
This is the guide to business schools produced by AMBA, and, again, has useful editorial content.

■ Robinson, P. (1994) *Snapshots from Hell: the Making of an MBA*, Nicholas Brealey.
This is also entertaining, though it may risk discouraging you from pursuing a traditional programme.

■ **www.abs.ac.uk**
The UK Association of business schools.

■ **www.mba.hobsons.com**
For information on a variety of courses.

■ **www.mbaworld.com**
The site for the Association of MBAs, which has extensive information on choosing an MBA and easy links to AMBA accredited institutions' MBA websites.

■ Additional links are provided on the book's **companion website**.

→ 3 Selecting a Master's programme

Learning outcomes

By the end of this chapter you should:

- see the extent to which a Master's-level management qualification could help you achieve your wider life objectives
- understand the constraints limiting your freedom of choice concerning management courses
- have identified the most important features, from your particular perspective, of a management course
- be in a position to make an informed choice of course in the light of your analysis.

INTRODUCTION

If you have already registered for a course of study, skip this chapter. If, however, you have not yet decided whether Master's-level management study is a good idea, read on. You need to think hard before reaching a conclusion. A management qualification requires a substantial investment of effort. Unless your employer supports you financially, it represents a large cash investment too. Before investing you should think very carefully about your objectives in seeking a qualification, and the type of course which is most likely to enable you to meet these objectives.

You will need to decide, first, whether to study for an MBA or a more specialist Master's degree and then to decide between full- and part-time study. If the latter, you then need to compare the relative merits of face-to-face or distance learning. If studying at a distance looks more attractive you will need to consider the type of support you need for this type of study. Once you have decided on the mode of study, you need to compare institutions, to see which offers the course and support best suited to your needs.

ASSESSING YOUR PRESENT POSITION AND GOALS

The previous chapter discussed some of the shifts taking place in the management development environment, and the wide range of programmes that have developed in response to these. Choice is now far from straightforward. However, if you think carefully about *why* you want to study it will help you decide upon what is best for you. Most of the rational problem-solving and planning techniques taught on an MBA are elaborations on the simple theme of:

- establish where you are now;
- decide where you want to be;
- identify possible routes from the first to the second;
- select the best route;
- follow it.

A final step of checking progress is often added. So common is this model, and so frequently does it appear wearing but slightly refurbished clothing, that I have come to think of it as the 'Universal Management Paradigm' (the UMP). You can use this model to help you reach a decision.

In this case 'where you are now' does not mean merely what job you are in, though this is probably an important element. It encompasses *all* relevant aspects of your life, your management experience, qualifications, knowledge, strengths and weaknesses, family environment, sources of finance, leisure interests, and anything that could affect, or be affected by, your proposed studies.

ACTIVITY 3.1

→ Ch 10

Take a large sheet of paper and find some way of representing your current situation as it relates to management study. The diagramming chapter (Chapter 10) of this Handbook gives some ways of mapping information if you feel this request is difficult, or Fig. 3.1 shows one potential student's attempt, which may get you started if you do not know where to begin. But make sure that you look at your particular situation, and the factors that are important to you. (File your map in your study file, when you have finished working on it. You may wish to refer to it as you work through the book.)

Drawing up an objectives tree

Having mapped features of your current situation, think about what it is important to you to *achieve* in the medium term, say the next five years. Think about every important aspect of your life not just your career. You may find that some of your objectives can be broken down to show sub-goals which need to be reached in order to achieve the higher-order objective. A useful technique for representing such hierarchies of objectives is the *objectives tree*. Such trees look like the familiar organisation chart, but show goals instead of management roles. They are drawn from the top downwards. You start with what seems to you an important goal and put it at the top of the tree. Then you think about all the things that you need to achieve in

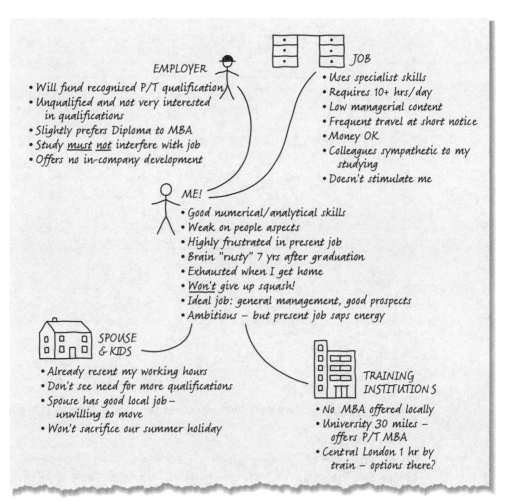

EMPLOYER
- Will fund recognised P/T qualification
- Unqualified and not very interested in qualifications
- Slightly prefers Diploma to MBA
- Study _must_ _not_ interfere with job
- Offers no in-company development

JOB
- Uses specialist skills
- Requires 10+ hrs/day
- Low managerial content
- Frequent travel at short notice
- Money OK
- Colleagues sympathetic to my studying
- Doesn't stimulate me

ME!
- Good numerical/analytical skills
- Weak on people aspects
- Highly frustrated in present job
- Brain "rusty" 7 yrs after graduation
- Exhausted when I get home
- _Won't_ give up squash!
- Ideal job: general management, good prospects
- Ambitious — but present job saps energy

SPOUSE & KIDS
- Already resent my working hours
- Don't see need for more qualifications
- Spouse has good local job — unwilling to move
- Won't sacrifice our summer holiday

TRAINING INSTITUTIONS
- No MBA offered locally
- University 30 miles — offers P/T MBA
- Central London 1 hr by train — options there?

Fig. 3.1 Student map of factors relevant to choice of a Master's-level programme

order to realise your main goal, and put them in at the next level down. For each of these you consider necessary sub-goals and so on downwards until you have gone as far as it makes sense to go. Figure 3.2 gives an example.

You will probably have a number of different objectives in life, and for each of these you can construct a different tree.

ACTIVITY 3.2

Take more large pieces of paper, and draw objective trees for all the major goals in your life. Highlight any conflicts between sub-goals, either on a single tree or between trees. Think about any barriers to achieving your goals and note these. (More potential entries for your file.)

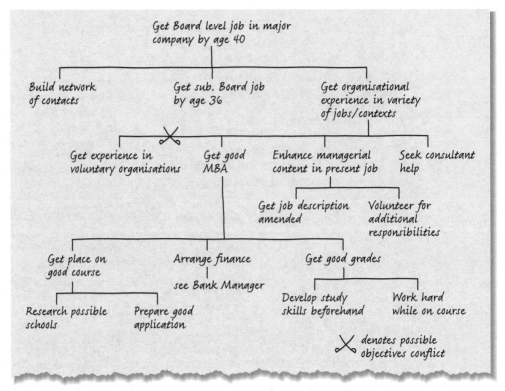

Fig. 3.2 Hierarchy of career-related objectives for an intending Master's-level student

Conflicts between objectives are common. For example, you might have one goal of getting into the squash club's first team, which would require a lot of practice and coaching, and another of obtaining a part-time MBA which would also be very time consuming. If a third objective is to write your first novel, and you already have a job which requires you to put in long hours if you are to be considered for promotion, conflicts could be impossible to resolve!

You will need to think about how to handle such conflicts, even if they are somewhat less extreme. One whole set of objectives may need to be put aside until another is achieved. Figure 3.2, for example, showed an example of an objective tree related only to career.

Mapping objectives is a highly rational approach. You may wish to experiment with a less rational way of thinking about what you want as a useful complement to your objectives tree. This involves developing a personal vision.

Mapping onto your personal vision

Visioning is a pictorial technique which can be extremely useful in working out steps which you can deliberately take to progress your life in the way that you want it to develop. It requires you to think about a desired future and gain a clear picture in your mind of this future. This technique has much wider uses than deciding on your future study. Many writers on leadership see developing and communicating a vision for the organisation as the defining characteristic of great leaders. 'Shared vision' was one of the other four disciplines which Senge (1990) considered essential for a learning oganisation, and he saw the ability of key people to build their personal visions as crucial to this. Organisational visions, he says, are rooted in personal visions. Personal vision is frequently seen as a key component in leadership, as well.

Visions can be surprisingly powerful in creating changes in your life, even if you do not deliberately plan to achieve them. It is as if you have set up an instruction to your subconscious, and without further effort on your part it will gradually move you towards your vision. Research on US undergraduates showed that those who had visions as undergraduates were far more successful 20 years on than those who did not. (If you want to explore more about how this might happen, doing some reading about neuro-linguistic programming – NLP – is a good way to start). Because of their power, it is important to ensure that your vision is indeed your personal one, not what other people want for you. Also that you 're-vision', building a new vision at regular intervals – as your understanding of what might be available, and what is important to you develops. The following activity can be done alone, or with a listener (it is a good exercise for practising attentive and sometimes active listening – a technique that can improve working with others as individuals or team members).

→ Ch 11

ACTIVITY 3.3

Imagine that it is some time into the future and you have just come to the end of the best day you can imagine. Indeed it has been the best week, the best month, the best six months. 'See' where you are, what sort of room you are in, where you are living, who you are with, what work you have been doing, how you have spent your leisure time during this period. Try to make this 'vision' as vivid as possible. Add colours, sounds, smells. A listener can be helpful in noting down what you see, and in prompting you with questions such as: Where is the house? What sort of people are you working with? What did you do last night?

When the vision is as clear as you can get it, use your listener's notes, or your own memory, to write/draw/perhaps even collage the picture. Put it somewhere safe and make a diary note for a set date each month to look at your vision, remind yourself of its contents, and make any changes necessary.

You may like to compare your objectives tree with your vision, and revise the latter if there are major discrepancies between your vision and where your objectives will lead.

CHOOSING THE BEST ROUTE

Having constructed your objectives trees, ask yourself how central a postgraduate management qualification is to your most important objectives, and whether it will conflict with some of these. Other routes to your objectives might be more direct and generate fewer conflicts. For example, if the main block to achieving your objectives is the attitude of your current employer, a judicious change of jobs might be a quicker path to advancement than two or three years of study. If you are unsure about your academic abilities, it might also be safer.

Any management qualification, and this is particularly true of Master's-level study, demands a certain amount of pain and self-denial. It is likely to take over your life for the duration, allowing little space for food and sleep, let alone the higher pleasures. Choose this path only if you are absolutely sure that the qualification will justify the sacrifices required. If this book causes you to realise that you do not really want a Master's, it will have saved you hundreds of times its purchase price!

Factors influencing choice:

- academic background
- professional role
- career aspirations
- management experience
- preferred study mode.

Of course, my livelihood, and that of many of my friends, depends on large numbers of managers being convinced that they really do want a management qualification, so I hope that you will wish to proceed. Naturally, I cannot claim to be unbiased in this, but the vast majority of my students claim that the effort is indeed enormously worthwhile. Since there are far easier ways of earning a living, I continue in my own job only because I believe that management education really can transform people's lives.

If you *are* convinced that a management qualification will help you achieve your longer-term objectives, you need first to decide whether to start with a certificate and/or diploma, to obtain a professional qualification or to enrol on a direct entry MBA or a specialist Master's programme. Relevant considerations are described below.

Your academic background and ability

If you have not studied at university level before, you may find it difficult adjusting to the pace of study. You will need to develop new learning skills at the same time as you engage with course content. This is particularly likely if you choose one of the more academically focused programmes available. Even if, by heroic effort, you gain the qualification, you may not gain full value from the programme in terms of self-development. An MBA which offers the alternative of a more practically based diploma as its first part might take a little longer or be less strategically focused, but you might gain far more from the experience. During the more skills-based early part of the programme you would be developing a wide range of transferable skills, including learning skills that will make the remainder of your MBA courses much more rewarding. And if you decide that you do not want to go beyond a diploma, you will still have gained a useful qualification.

If your background already includes a Diploma in Management Studies (DMS) or a management-related professional qualification, you will obviously want to explore the extent to which this will gain you exemption from parts of your chosen course. This will vary from institution to institution, and will depend on how long ago you gained your qualification, as well as the structure of the programme you are considering. Exemptions will be less likely for the more strategically focused MBAs than for those that themselves build on a diploma.

You may know that your background includes specific areas of weakness. (Mathematics is one such area which bothers many potential students, though this Handbook will attempt to convince them that this concern may not be justified.) If so, you will wish to explore the extent to which compulsory components of possible MBAs will require you to be competent in the areas about which you are most worried.

Your current role

If you are in a specialist management role, such as finance, human resources or marketing, and planning to continue in that area for several years, one option is to gain a relevant professional qualification. For some professions such as accounting or HR this is virtually essential. Many of the professional bodies have revised their syllabuses, expanding their general management content. Where this is the case the qualification may not only serve to meet the entry requirements for an MBA programme, but also, if overlap in content and teaching method is sufficient, count for some credit exemption, thus reducing the time needed to gain a subsequent Master's. If you are not sure whether the professional route would be best for you, check with your own organisation as to which they would find most useful. At the same time, check the views of likely business schools about recognition of your intended professional qualification. Much of this information is now readily available on business school websites.

An alternative to a professional qualification may be a specialist MBA or an MA or MSc in your specialism. Some such programmes are recognised by relevant professional institutes.

Your managerial experience

If you have *no* managerial experience (note that job title is not a reliable guide here – many managers are not labelled as such, but still perform a managerial function), you may wish to defer your studies until you have spent a year or two struggling with the problems that constitute a manager's job. While you can study management as a theoretical subject – indeed, undergraduate management degrees now attract large numbers of students – it can be far less exciting, and less developmental, than study based on some managerial experience. Conceptual tools are far more meaningful if they help you make sense of problems you have personally experienced. To someone who has never faced the issue, the concept may be seen merely as one more thing to learn. This is particularly the case with MBAs. If you have no management experience yet, you may be better suited by a specialist Master's in an area which interests you. Many of these are designed for recent graduates without experience.

If you *do* decide that an MBA is the best route out of a non-managerial job and into the career you always wanted, you would probably find that, paradoxical as this may seem, a more theoretical and strategically based MBA will suit you better. Practical skills development on an MBA is most effective if you can practise the skills in parallel with the course. Part-time and distance courses offer splendid opportunities for practice for those already in managerial jobs. These are rather wasted on students who are not in a position to take advantage of them. Full-time institutions, especially the longer-established ones, also tend to offer more help with finding jobs after the course, an important consideration in times when management openings are restricted, even for MBA graduates.

Your career objectives

If you see your future lying within a specific function, organisation or sector, then one of the more specialised MBAs, or a management-related MA or MSc, may be your choice. The price you will pay in terms of reduced 'portability' may be more than compensated for by the added depth to which an area can be studied. Generalist MBAs are strong on breadth, and excellent for those who do not know in which ways their career is likely to develop, or who are in a generalist role. However, those with specialist interests may find that their favourite areas are necessarily covered somewhat superficially in generalist MBAs.

If you are strongly ambitious you will need to look seriously at the small number of 'prestige' MBA institutions, and may need to consider going overseas. Although there is a fair degree of consensus as to the 'best' MBAs, different employers may have slightly different orders of preference, and you might wish to find out the prevailing views of the organisations which you would most like to join. You would certainly wish to ensure that your chosen MBA had a strong strategic focus.

Your preferred mode of study

The three main options, full-time; part-time face-to-face; and distance learning, also part-time, were outlined in the previous chapter. In the following discussion 'part-time' will normally be used to refer to the face-to-face variety, unless indicated to the contrary.

Full-time study has major advantages in terms of allowing you to immerse yourself single-mindedly in the course. Library, computing and other facilities will be provided. There will be frequent contact with faculty members, and even more contact with fellow students. Their backgrounds will depend on the admissions policy of the institution, but they are likely to constitute an enormously rich resource in terms of information and organisational experience, they may come from many different countries, and there should be plenty of scope for you to benefit from this. (In the UK some full-time programmes are filled almost exclusively with overseas students, the majority of whom have little if any management experience. You might wish to check this out if you are hoping to share management experiences from different cultures.)

Traditional teaching methods of lectures and case study discussion can be used, and you may be seconded to a cooperating employer for some part of the course, sometimes overseas. This allows you to gain valuable insight into how another organisation operates, and to make a good impression on a potential employer. If the course emphasises skills development, there will be ample scope for role play and other simulations.

You will get to know many of your fellow students well, and may form a network that will serve you throughout your career. Indeed, Japanese companies started to sponsor employees on US MBA programmes specifically in order to improve their spoken English, and to develop networks and contacts with potentially influential Americans. Networks may traditionally have been less central to business in the European culture, but they are now becoming increasingly important.

Employers will normally advertise opportunities within the school or visit to interview potential graduates. Or your secondment may develop into a job offer.

Full-time courses can be very hard work, but are usually stimulating and rewarding, and some types of learning can be highly effective on this type of course. There are, however, some fairly obvious disadvantages.

The first is the high cost involved. Even large employers finance no more than a handful of their highest-fliers on full-time courses. You are therefore likely to have to take leave of absence or resign. Loss of a year or more of income has to be added to the substantial fees charged. Loans can be obtained fairly easily, but if you have dependants the decision to take such a step can be a difficult one. It is no longer as easy as it once was for new MBA graduates to find suitably challenging and rewarding jobs. And the expected salary premium for UK MBAs has dropped from almost 100% (i.e. you could expect to double your salary on qualification) to a more modest, if still healthy, 30–50%.

Even if financial considerations do not deter you, you may not wish to leave a job that you really enjoy, and suffer the upheavals to family life that it will entail. Although a year is not long, it can seem an eternity to a partner or child left at home with little support while you are having an exciting, stimulating, developmental experience elsewhere.

Less obviously, while full-time study lends itself admirably to the gaining of theoretical knowledge, it does not allow you the opportunity to experiment with concepts and techniques in a real working environment, so skills development is likely to be less. Case studies are a poor substitute for on-the-job experience as a vehicle for developing the more competence-based aspects of the course. Full-time students find it very difficult to *apply* their learning as they acquire it. Indeed, managers who studied full-time often say that most of what they learned they have *never* put into practice. This will to some extent reflect the relevance of their syllabus. But even potentially relevant techniques, if not practised while 'fresh', are unlikely ever to be applied. By the end of a year's full-time course, a student's head may feel completely stuffed with all that has been covered. It is not surprising that much of this material may be pushed to the back, never to appear again.

Thus, although full-time study has many advantages, it is not *necessarily* the best route, even for those with indulgent employers or for whom money is not a major consideration. To decide whether this route is the best for you, you will need to reflect on how well the characteristics of full-time learning match your personal situation, and your most important objectives, as mapped in the earlier activities.

Part-time face-to-face teaching is a method adopted by many business schools with established full-time programmes. It allows them to increase the accessibility of their courses, attracting students within reasonable travelling distance who are not in a position to give up their jobs in order to study. The teaching approach is normally similar to that on full-time courses. However, lectures will be concentrated into a shorter period, perhaps one afternoon and evening a week, so there will necessarily be less opportunity for group working and discussion.

Advantages are that regular attendance imposes its own discipline, and allows a reasonable amount of contact with faculty and other students. Library, IT and other facilities will be available, although opening hours are not always suited to part-time students. The fact that you can continue to perform your normal job protects your income and allows tremendous advantages in terms of making possible the immediate application of what is taught on the course. (This advantage obviously applies equally to distance learning.)

Disadvantages are that your job must allow regular attendance, usually at least some of this during normal working hours. Many employers are unwilling to allow this, or your job may be prone to crises or require frequent travel. In either case, it may be impossible to ensure that you will be free on a regular basis. The need for regular attendance may involve considerable travel time.

Less obvious disadvantages include the possibility that the course may not be taught by the same lecturers as the full-time course, as they may be unwilling to work the unsocial hours required. While the alternative lecturers may be excellent, this is not always the case. You would need to find out about the quality of teaching if at all possible.

Executive programmes are a variant of part-time face-to-face provision. Such programmes concentrate the teaching into longer, more widely spaced blocks than the normal weekly part-time offering. There is wide variation in the length of the blocks. They might be two days, or a month, or occasionally even longer. Between the face-to-face blocks you are expected to study alone, while continuing with your normal job. Obviously, the disruption to your regular job means that this form of provision is not feasible without full employer support. The disruption is less than with a full-time course, however, and does allow some of the advantages of full-time study. There is more room for intensive contact with faculty and other students, and students from a much wider geographic base can be assembled. It is possible for a UK manager to study on a French executive programme, or for an Italian manager to study on a UK programme.

The limited face-to-face teaching on either form of part-time course will need to be supplemented by considerable private study, which will require self-discipline, and will be prone to disruption by conflicting demands from the job and elsewhere. If the main focus of an institution is full-time teaching, there may have been little thought given to the support part-time students need to ensure that their private study is effective. The 'give them a reading list and let them get on with it' approach is still all too frequent. But part-time students have little time to chase books that are not readily available. Often if the book *is* located, it turns out that only a small part of it was relevant after all, and that part not particularly good. There may, too, be little attention given to study skills development. (It was precisely this identified need that led to the production of this Handbook.)

One of the biggest disadvantages is, of course, the continual conflict between course and job demands. Part-time students *cannot* be single-minded in their studies. Good time management can help, but the problem will never go away entirely. The other inevitable problem is that the course will necessarily take longer than a full-time course covering the same ground, so motivation will need to be sustained over several years.

If you are fairly sure that part-time study *is* the most appropriate route to satisfying your objectives, you will obviously want to check out the syllabuses of possible courses. You might additionally wish to ask possible institutions any of the following questions which are not clearly answered in their brochures:

- What attendance is required? (Not just for classes, but for any residential component, examinations, etc.)
- What additional costs will any residential requirement incur?
- What additional study time is likely to be needed over and above class attendance?
- Who actually teaches the courses?
- What flexibility is there if you hit a prolonged crisis at work or home?
- What support is there if you find any part of the course difficult?
- How many books, etc. are you likely to need?
- Will these need to be bought, or are there sufficient copies in the library?
- Will you need your own PC and modem? If so, what software will you need to run and how powerful a machine do you need?

 As a check on the answers you receive, you might also enquire about dropout rates, and pass rates in previous cohorts of students. (You will find a checklist for questions you might ask on the **website**.)

Distance learning has been the most dramatic development in management education in recent years. Or developments, as there have been two major waves. The first was the mixed-media (print/audio/video/software) plus support version pioneered by the Open University in the early 1980s. More recently, purely on-line versions have been developed and are currently being marketed strongly, particularly by 'for-profit' organisations. A number of 'consortia' have been formed to exploit on-line opportunities. However, many of these have had a short life.

The majority of part-time MBA students in the UK are now on distance learning programmes, and a growing number of specialist Master's programmes are delivered in this way. If full-time study is unattractive or not feasible, and no suitable part-time course is available, or perhaps feasible, you should think seriously about the possibilities of a distance-taught programme. For many managers, job demands are unpredictable or variable, or involve substantial travel, and distance learning is the only mode flexible enough to accommodate these.

Distance learning programmes vary enormously in what they provide. You do need to look carefully at what is offered, in terms of both learning materials and support while you are learning. Some on-line programmes are particularly limited in this respect. Electronic delivery of materials is cheap for the provider, and the 'search' facility is a big plus for students. But many find study from a screen is tiring, and incur substantial costs in printing materials themselves.

A good distance learning course will provide you not only with all the materials you need for your study, saving you hours of time wasted in chasing elusive references, but with substantial support as well. Materials will be written specifically for the course, and designed in such a way as to make individual study as easy and rewarding as possible. They will be well laid out, to avoid eye-strain, and learning outcomes will be clear so that you know what should be achieved by the end of the part of the course being worked upon. Material will be broken up into 'chunks' which can normally be studied at a single sitting, and a study calendar provided so that you know what should be achieved by each point of the course. Most importantly, the material itself will be interactive, asking you at regular intervals to think about what you have just read, and apply it to your own job context. There should also be regular exercises and self-test questions, with answers provided, so that you can ensure that you understand each part of the material before progressing to the next.

Written text will be supplemented by video and audio materials, either to allow 'expert' lectures (a video has the advantage of allowing replay of any difficult bits!) or as a vehicle for providing case study materials. There will probably be software provided, and there may be CD-Rom based materials. You may also have access to on-line databases via the Internet, and the opportunity to participate in computer conferences with other students and teaching staff.

In addition to teaching materials, a good distance course will provide substantial personal tuition. A designated tutor will provide extensive written teaching comments on assignments you submit and someone, ideally that same tutor, will be available by phone and e-mail to help you with any difficulties encountered, either with course content, or with more general study problems. Ideally there will be deadlines for the submission of written work. Flexibility is great in theory, but without interim deadlines many students fail to complete the course.

While some courses may be capable of being taught solely at a distance, in many areas of management education there is much to be gained from at least some face-to-face teaching. It would be difficult to learn how to interview, for example, with *no* face-to-face component. And any business policy course which did not provide opportunities for discussing options with other students would be greatly impoverished. While such interactions can take place electronically, most students prefer at least some of this discussion to take place in groups. Good distance-taught courses will therefore include a limited face-to-face component, in the form of either one-day workshops or shorter tutorials, with probably a small residential component as well.

The most obvious advantage of distance learning is its flexibility. You are not tied to regular class attendance, and can pursue your studies whether on a plane to the States or sitting on an oil rig in the North Sea.

A major advantage for your employer (and for you if your employer doesn't believe in management development or qualifications) is that no time off work is required, except perhaps for examinations and any residential course component. Distance learning should be compatible with any job that does not make totally unreasonable demands on your time, and you can do extra course work at slack work times, to allow you to do less when things are busy.

There is also the major advantage, shared with other part-time courses, that you are instantly able to put into practice what you learn. In this way new ideas and techniques will become part of your way of working as you go through your course, rather than mere theory to be learned for an exam and then forgotten.

Potential students sometimes worry that they will lack the necessary self-discipline, but motivation is seldom a problem if materials are designed well. And some distance learning programmes offer a surprisingly high level of interaction with tutors and other students. Frequent tutorials and residential occasions help sustain momentum. On larger programmes there may be many students living in the same area, and they can meet informally outside the official tutorial programme. On-line interaction offers further interactive possibilities, with web-groups, blogs and shared areas increasingly used. However, on some programmes interaction may still be fairly restricted, so this is an aspect to investigate.

As noted earlier, distance learning courses may not be ideal for students who are not currently working as managers. Assignments may require you to analyse aspects of your own organisation, difficult if you do not work in one, or if your position in it is such that access to information is difficult. If you are in this situation you should discuss requirements carefully with any intended distance provider, to see whether you would be at an unreasonable disadvantage.

You may find the following questions useful if considering different distance learning programmes, to supplement those listed for part-time face-to-face programmes:

- What proportion of the materials are specially written?
- What is the quality of the specially written materials? (Inspect some of this if at all possible.)
- How many students are enrolled, in what area? (This will determine whether you will have a chance of working informally with students living near you.)
- How much face-to-face contact is there?
- What use is made of electronic communication?
- How much feedback is given on written assignments?
- Do you have access to telephone, fax or e-mail help in cases of academic difficulty?
- Is there any local support available, and if so, what?

CHOOSING BETWEEN INSTITUTIONS

Once you have a clear idea of what you are looking for in general terms, you will need to decide which institution offers you the best programme. Syllabuses and prospectuses can give some information, but they are primarily written to sell you the course, rather than to convey detailed information. And while prospectuses are not dishonest, they are unlikely to go out of their way to highlight possible disadvantages. Some 'guides' to business schools, while telling you what programmes are available in a range of institutions, are little more than collections of promotional material. As all the schools featured sound wonderful, they may not help you choose between them.

Websites now offer quite a lot of information, though they may share some of the drawbacks of prospectuses. Most institutions will be happy to answer questions by phone if the site does not address the issues that concern you. (Note, you may need to persist in order to go beyond the routine enquiry clerk and speak to someone who can answer the more detailed, less administrative, questions that you wish to put.) Present and past students can be an excellent source of information. See whether there are any within your own organisation, or ask the institution how you might contact students.

It *is* important to check on the credibility of your intended course. While rankings are available for US business schools, such rankings are fairly recent in Europe, and often exclude distance learning. European business schools do vary widely in the quality, as well as the nature, of what they offer. Qualifications from some will be highly regarded, whereas those from others will be deemed worthless by the majority of informed employers.

There are two key sources of information in the UK. The Higher Education Funding Councils, via the Quality Assurance Agency for Higher Education, review business schools on their teaching quality (across all the programmes they offer). You can ask schools for information on their assessment or access the information via www.qaa.ac.uk. This will provide some guidance, but is a fairly blunt instrument. Employers are not greatly concerned with quality of teaching, though it may impact significantly upon your experience of the course, and upon quality of graduates, so it does have an indirect effect upon credibility.

You can also ask for information about their research rating – again this is assessed at intervals. A high rating in research *does* tend to be associated with business school credibility, though it may not be associated with quality of teaching! Teaching and research may be done by different people.

Another useful source of information is the Association of MBAs (AMBA). This accredits some programmes, and employers may ask if your MBA was from one of these. Furthermore if studying on such a programme you will have access to certain loan schemes not generally available, and on graduation will be eligible to join AMBA and attend local meetings. However, AMBA has tended to accredit only generalist MBAs. Non-accreditation by AMBA of a specialist programme does not imply poor quality.

Others accrediting programmes in Europe include the AACSB, the primary US accrediting body, and EQUIS, the quality improvement arm of the European Foundation for Management Development (Efmd).

Useful information sources, including the guide produced by AMBA, are listed at the end of the chapter. Because this is an area where information changes fairly rapidly you will find it invaluable to seek information electronically. Guides will give links to home pages of programmes featured, so that you can be sure that your information is as up to date as the information currently being shown by the institutions concerned.

In choosing between institutions, quality and credibility will be as important as the nature of the programmes offered, and therefore something you need to research carefully. The 1990s saw a major expansion in the number of institutions offering postgraduate management courses, MBAs in particular, often under franchise arrangements from other institutions. Not all of these arrangements have yet settled down. Some overseas 'universities' award qualifications on very dubious authority. Given the significance of the investment you are considering you really do need to investigate possible course providers thoroughly. This will ensure that the course you choose will be an exciting developmental experience, and the qualification you gain will be widely respected.

SUMMARY

- You should think carefully about whether postgraduate management study is the best route to your own personal objectives.
- You should decide whether you want a more traditional, academically based course, or one emphasising competence development.
- You should decide whether a professional qualification, specialist Master's or more generalist MBA will best meet your needs.
- You should consider the relative merits of full-time, part-time face-to-face or distance learning before coming to a decision.
- The experience, reputation and track record of any institution should be an important consideration.

Further information

Most of the sources of information in the previous chapter are relevant here too, but particularly:

- Bickerstaff, G. (ed.) (2006) *Which MBA? A Critical Guide to Programmes in Europe and the USA* (18th edn), The Economist Publications/Pearson Education.
  This gives a broad, albeit expensive view.
- *The Official MBA Handbook 2006/2007* (2006), Financial Times Prentice Hall with the Association of MBAs.
  This gives detailed information on AMBA-accredited MBAs, and includes a CD-Rom.
- Bryon, M. (2007) *How to Pass the GMAT*, Kogan Page.
  If you are applying for a programme which uses the GMAT for selection you may find the test questions and answers with explanations useful.
- **www.mba.hobsons.com**
- **www.mbaworld.com**
- **www.qaa.ac.uk/reviews/default.asp** for reviews of academic institutions.
- Useful websites are given on the **companion website**.

3

Selecting a Master's programme

→ 4 Creating a suitable learning context

Learning outcomes

By the end of this chapter you should:

- have explored the relationship between the course and your job and how best to exploit this
- have explored the resources and support available to you and taken steps to secure them
- have estimated how much time you have available, and how much you will need
- understand your current pattern of time usage and have worked out how this will need to change
- be starting to make the necessary changes.

INTRODUCTION

It is important to understand the context within which you will be pursuing your studies, and do what you can to make it as favourable as possible. If you are studying full-time, the context should not be problematic, and you may not need to read this chapter. But if, like the majority of Master's students, you are combining work with study, contextual preparation may be the single most important factor for your success: you should work your way through this chapter carefully.

Master's study requires money, time, space, energy – mental and emotional – and access to information. Cooperation from those around you can help to secure these, and you will require skills to protect resources once secured. These necessary skills are

→ Ch 5, 6 addressed in the next two chapters. Here you will be 'mapping the context' and identifying the areas where skills will need to be exercised.

Key factors in your context will be your job and your family (or other personal commitments). You need to explore how your studies will interact with your job and your other commitments, and what you need to do to secure the 'space' needed for a major new commitment.

→ Ch 7   In addition to the obvious physical space (addressed in Chapter 7), you need emotional and mental space. And most of all you need to 'make' time. The most frequently quoted cause of dropout or failure is 'not enough time'.

This is not altogether surprising. Few busy managers (and it is the busy ones who sign on for courses) have the hours required for Master's-level study currently uncommitted. Are *you* sitting doing nothing for up to 15 hours each week? Or are you already finding it difficult to fit in the gardening, decorating or socialising that those around you demand? Somehow time has to be 'found', whether by ceasing to do some things you are presently doing, or by doing some things more efficiently, or both. You need to work out a strategy, and negotiate it with work colleagues and family, if you are to avoid divorce, dismissal or physical and mental decline while still gaining your qualification.

Developing such a strategy is a significant task. Some of the time will be released from your leisure. Some will probably have to be found through more effective time management at work (dealt with in Chapter 6). Some may be through a 'negotiated'

→ Ch 5, 6   reduction in duties whether at home or at work, which may need you to practise the assertiveness skills addressed in the next chapter.

'I haven't time to improve my time management.' If you, like many busy managers, feel like this, then you should regard your work on this aspect as a test of your commitment to your future success. If you cannot find the time *now* to make the changes needed for study in future, what are your chances of making the time you will

→ Ch 4, 6   need – over a period of years – in the future? Working through all the aspects covered in Chapters 4 and 6 may take you up to 15 hours. (Time management, in particular, is not improved easily.) But the time invested will have a profound influence on your success. (Note that it is not enough merely to read this part of the book. You *must* work through the associated activities carefully if it is to have an impact.)

GAINING ORGANISATIONAL SUPPORT

A key contextual factor is your employer's attitude to your studies, and it is worth devoting some time to gaining organisational support. This can make your path far easier. The advantage of financial support is obvious, but other forms of support are equally important. If your organisation allows you protected time for study, access to information about your organisation and opportunities to apply your new skills through increased responsibilities at work, this can transform your learning experience.

It is not unreasonable to seek such support. Your motivation for studying is likely to include a desire to improve at your job, which is of equal benefit to your employer. And your desire to apply course ideas to organisational problems for assessment purposes, and probably to undertake a work-related project as the culmination of your programme, can obviously be harnessed to good effect by an enlightened employer.

Managing your workload while you study is one important issue. If the combination of overload at work and demanding study generates intolerable stress, you will do poorly at both, and your employer will suffer twice over. So if your organisation is supporting you, it is worth discussing workload issues with them. Can your workload be reduced, or at least not increased, while you are on the course? What other organisational support might be made available?

Of course, you may be studying secretly, with a view to changing jobs as soon as possible. Or your study may be known, but attract no support from your employers. If so, you may be unable to follow many of the suggestions in this section. But if your employers are not supporting you because you have not told them, do think carefully about why you have not done so, and whether your silence is necessary. I was phoned at work one day by a manager part-way through an MBA. He had been nervous about admitting to study because he felt it might be seen as either presumptuous or threatening by his employers. But following the advice given in an earlier edition of this book, he did approach them. He was delighted (so much so that he had rung me to tell me, and thank me) that they had not only agreed to pay his remaining fees and allow time off for study, but also given him a new project to manage that allowed him to apply his newly acquired skills.

Potential sources

There are several obvious sources of organisational support:

Sources of organisational support:

- the HR or training manager
- your own manager
- a mentor
- your team.

HR managers are likely to have an interest in management development in the organisation as a whole, and should be in a position to support you in many ways, so discuss your plans and progress with them. They may be able to arrange contacts with organisational information sources, discuss possible project topics, take your part if your line manager starts to overload you once the course has started, help you to obtain any resources you may need, or put you in touch with other past or present students. They may suggest supplementary short courses which might help you with parts of the course you find particularly difficult.

Your immediate boss is another important source of potential help. S/he can both protect you from overload and help you to see how what you are learning relates to your organisation. A perspective from slightly higher up the organisation may help you to understand better how strategy is formed in your organisation.

If your boss is sympathetic to your study, you may be able to schedule regular discussions on your progress, as well as get help with particular queries as they arise. There are several potential benefits to your boss. First, this should help you to gain more from the course and thus increase the contribution you can make. Second, the discussions about how to apply the course should be beneficial to both of you. If your boss has a qualification, supporting you may act as a useful reminder of previous learning, and a stimulus to its continued application. If not, there is scope for shared learning.

A mentor is a third source. If you have a mentor, involve them from the start in your thinking about a Master's. If you do not, it may be possible to set up such a relationship even if your organisation does not have a formal mentoring scheme. Discuss this with your training manager. Mentoring means that you are linked to a particular senior manager, who will have the responsibility for advising and supporting you in your career. The mentor should be at least one level above you, but not in a line relationship so that they cannot directly influence your progress. Thus, you can discuss your personal and career development freely.

Because of their senior position, mentors can be expected to have a better understanding of the organisational context, and of policy development issues, than you do yourself. A mentor from a slightly different part of the organisation can offer a wider perspective on the organisation, and increase your own understanding of organisational issues. Again, because of their relative seniority, mentors are often able to arrange access to other senior people in the organisation if you need this.

Regular discussions with a mentor about how your course relates to your organisation, and how you might apply what you are learning to your job, can enhance your learning and help your career. It can also be of benefit to the mentor, who may learn from your different perspective. Some organisations now formally recognise this two-way learning with co-mentoring schemes, where long-serving senior managers deliberately seek to benefit from the fresh perspective of recent recruits. You may find that, even if the concept is new, it is welcomed.

Your team is the final major source of organisational support. Many managers find that they can usefully reinforce their learning by involving those they work with. One of my students used his own MBA as a framework for developing the team he managed. He shared course concepts with them as he learned them, and then made opportunities for all to use them. He said it was the most cost-effective form of staff development he had ever encountered!

ACTIVITY 4.1

Consider the potential sources of organisational support for your studies. List those which are important, and the support that ideally they would provide. Draw up a plan for negotiating with them for this support, once you have worked through the next chapter which addresses some of the skills required. Put a note in your study log to revisit this activity when you have worked on these skills.

GAINING FAMILY SUPPORT

Gaining the support of your family, or others with claims on your non-work time, is as important as gaining organisational support. Study is for the most part a solitary activity. You will be shutting the door, metaphorically and quite probably literally, on those used to enjoying your company. If this is resented, you may find the resentment expressed in a wide range of ways, all of them destructive to your study, and many destructive to your relationships. ('I've asked your best friend to lunch on Sunday', 'I've got us tickets for that show you wanted to see', 'I've poured you a glass of wine, and we can watch that video', 'How many times do I have to ask you to fix that socket?', 'If you don't want to spend time with me I'll find someone who does . . . ', 'Either you stop studying or I go...') As a tutor, it is heartbreaking to see someone near the end of their MBA studies, yet having to withdraw from the programme because it is 'my marriage or my degree'.

4

Creating a suitable learning context

As you work through this chapter you will gain a clear idea of the magnitude of the likely impact of study on those around you. I cannot stress too strongly how essential it is that you do all you can to gain the support of important people in your life for something that will affect them profoundly. Such support is far more likely if the decision to study is a shared one, and your partner feels that they too will benefit from your endeavours. So start talking to your partner about what study will mean, in terms of all the costs as well as the potential benefits as soon as you *start* to think about the possibility.

Note that advantages which seem 'obvious' to you may be less obvious to those around you. Once you are enthusiastic about something it is easy to assume that this enthusiasm is shared. You need to be very careful about such assumptions. Study can be intellectually exciting, the sense of personal growth can be exhilarating. You can make new friends who share your new enthusiasms and bond through shared adversity. It is easy for a partner to feel excluded. And the benefits may be genuinely unequal: it is *your* career that benefits while your partner takes the major share of keeping the family going, perhaps at the cost of their own career. If this is the case you may need both to explicitly appreciate your partner's contribution and to negotiate some compensatory rewards – for example promising to fund and support your partner through a relevant qualification once you have gained your own. There will also be ways of minimising some at least of the costs to partners, for example by a shared approach to planning the leisure you will need to survive. This is addressed later in the chapter.

ACTIVITY 4.2

If you have not yet done so, sit down with your partner and others close to you and talk through your current thinking with respect to study – the pros and cons as you anticipate them and the different ways in which these are likely to impact, short- and long-term, on family life. Ask, without trying to 'persuade' them, for their views on the decision, what they see as important factors, and what they would ideally preserve in your family life though your period of study. Try to come to a shared decision that takes their views into full account.

OTHER USEFUL RESOURCES

Explore other resources and sources of support that you may be able to access. Do friends or colleagues have particular expertise (or books) that might be useful to you? Perhaps you know people who have studied a similar course before? They may be a valuable source of coaching, notes and moral support. Are others in your organisation on the same course? If so, can you meet sometimes to discuss progress?

If you work in an unusual organisation, can you arrange the cooperation of friends in more mainline contexts? It may be extremely useful to discuss with them how things work in their organisations when course ideas do not easily match your own situation. What other information sources are there? Are management journals or other useful publications circulated at work? If so, are you on all the mailing lists? Is there a good management library to which you could gain access? Would it be useful to join a professional association in order to use their resources? It is likely that there will be reduced student rates, and this may be a useful investment. Indeed, if you are seeking a professional qualification this may be a requirement. Local meetings of such an association may give opportunities for networking, as well as provide interesting speakers. Check whether your organisation has corporate membership. If you have time, it is worth investigating possible sources of information before the pressures of the course begin.

EMOTIONAL SUPPORT

Implicit in much of the above is emotional support. This is so important that it is worth highlighting. Undertaking a significant course of postgraduate study is a major commitment, particularly if you are working at a challenging job, and have family to care for as well. There will be times when you will be exhausted, wonder how you can continue, and doubt the wisdom of your chosen course. It is at such times that emotional support can be invaluable. You will need people to reinforce your original choice, give you back your faith in it and generally help you feel you can cope.

Such support can come from family, colleagues, friends, fellow students and tutors. Some of these sources of support will become available to you once you have started studying. But before your course you can increase your likelihood of emotional support when necessary by making sure that family, friends and colleagues do understand your goals, and support your chosen way of achieving these. Such preparation, and continued involvement of such people in your progress, will make it far more likely that emotional support will be available when you most need it. (If you wait until you are pleading with them to support your decision to give up, it will be too late!)

SPACE

Space to study is crucial. One important element of context is the place in which you will study – you will be spending a lot of time in this place, and it needs to be as conducive to learning as possible. This is addressed more fully in Chapter 7, as a key component of effective learning. If you are not planning to look at that chapter in detail, you might like now to consider briefly the physical context in which you plan to study. If you do not have an obvious study, or other suitable location, at least read the

→ Ch 7   part of Chapter 7 addressing 'place'. There may be things you can do before your course starts to ensure that your chosen location provides a good context for study. Whether this means having a grand clear-out of a junk room, or installing bookshelves in the dining room or a work table and heater in your garden shed, it would be good to have completed the necessary work before the course starts. This is something which clearly impacts upon those with whom you live, so you need to involve them in your planning.

ACQUIRING TECHNOLOGY

It is hard to find a management programme that does not make heavy use of IT and you will need to ensure that you have access to a suitable machine and, almost certainly, modem and Internet link. Be careful if buying or upgrading a PC for use at home. It usually makes sense to buy the highest specification you can afford to allow for updating of requirements during your studies, but seek advice from expert friends as well as from your intended institution.

ASSESSING THE TIME REQUIREMENT

By far the most important dimension of your study context, and the 'space' in which you will be working, is that of time. Freeing the time needed for study is likely to be your biggest challenge. If you fail to do this, you will fail the course. As with any managerial problem-solving exercise, it is important to explore the nature and size of the problem facing you before you consider the options available for responding.

How much time do you need?

Do you have a time problem?

- How much time will you need?
- How much time will you have?
- Can you bridge the gap?

The time needed will depend on the demands of your chosen institution and on your own capacity for getting through the work at speed. This may vary, with some parts of the course proving far more time consuming than others. Some people find accounting and finance hugely time consuming, while others find they need to put in little effort for these subjects. Projects and dissertations are notoriously demanding of time for most people.

If you are already studying, you will be well aware of the time needs. If you have not yet started your course, try to make a rough estimate. Your chosen institution may have suggested the study time requirement. If not, they should be happy to provide a figure on request. Make sure that this includes *all* likely activities: attendance at face-to-face sessions; work on study materials provided with the course; any additional required reading or Internet use; preparation of assignments; any residential periods; any computer-based conferencing or other work; use of any audio and video materials; and any other time needed for completion of the course.

'Official' and 'real' time demands can vary significantly. I have come across several managers who have had to drop out of programmes because quoted study times were unrealistic. It is therefore worth checking the official estimates against the experience of several current or past students, if possible.

As a rough guide, many students on full-time MBA courses claim to work for up to 70 hours a week during a one-year course (and some courses take more than a year). If a part-time course were to aim to cover the same ground in two years, you could find you needed up to 35 hours' study a week to reach the same standards. (The Open University estimates that honours graduates taking its direct entry MBA will need to study some 12 hrs per 50-week year over three years.)

All mentions of study hours in contexts such as this refer to the mythical 'average student'. The extent of variation from this average is demonstrated by a survey I did on a distance learning course I had developed. The course was rated as 100 hours, and the average was indeed close to this, but student estimates of the time actually taken ranged from 70 hours to 150 hours.

How close you are to 'average' will depend on how fast you can assimilate material, how quickly you can write assignments, how much of a perfectionist you are, and how much you are wanting to gain from the material itself. (You may choose to devote more time to subjects which interest you and/or are highly relevant to your current job.)

Your previous studies may have given you some idea of whether you are faster or slower than 'average'. This estimate will be more reliable if you were studying a similar subject. Modify your assessment according to whether you are merely trying to pass, or aiming to be the best student ever, and take into consideration the extent to which you are in the habit of engaging with the more serious management literature.

Once you have come to a first estimate of your time need (and you can always revise it later), the next stage in exploring the problem is to estimate how much time you can fairly easily free for study. This will require careful thought on your part, and checking of estimates against reality, and may take you some time.

How much time do you have?

Whatever your 'time required' estimate, freeing this time is likely to require major reorganisation of your life. Some of the things you do at present will need to be sacrificed altogether for the period of your studies, some may need to be reduced, and some might perhaps be done more efficiently. Others may be capable of being combined with your study. In order to decide which activities fall into each of these categories, it is necessary to conduct a rough time audit.

The first step to this is to produce an instant estimate of time usage. Complete Activity 4.3 on pp. 55–6 before reading further.

Estimates of this kind are notoriously unreliable. It is better, if you can, to work from observations of actual behaviour. If you have a while before your course starts, keep a *time log*. Concentrate on your non-work time. Working time will be analysed later if this proves necessary.

How much time can you free?

Cutting down on watching television or leisure reading are obvious routes. A more painful necessity for many is significant reduction in their social life. But there is also room for some creativity. Fairly minor changes in habits can free significant slots for study. Taking a slower but less crowded train could yield three hours a day of ideal study time for the extrovert commuter who works best with a degree of external stimulation. Leaving for work an hour early when traffic is lighter may save significant driving time, and give you ideal study conditions in an empty office. Flying time provides many students in mobile jobs with hours of potential time to work on their course materials. Replacing a meal by a (healthy) snack can be good for the figure, as well as freeing a worthwhile total of hours per week.

When planning how to save time, you must be realistic. People you live with need, and have a right to, some of your time. You probably have a similar need to spend time with them. If you do not allow for such time in your plans, you will lose their emotional, and often practical support. This is why it is crucial to involve those close to you in preparations for your studies. So make finding time for study a shared problem. Your family need to feel that your solution is their solution too, and takes account of their needs as well as yours. If not, they may well indulge in effective (though perhaps unconscious) sabotage of your efforts to work on your course.

Many of the world's most successful people claim to manage on four hours of sleep a night, but do not assume that this will work for you too. It is worth experimenting with *gradually* cutting back on sleep; you may find that your brain still functions and you feel well. But many people feel dreadful on such a regime, and say they 'cannot think properly or remember things'. If you experience this, it is clearly not going to help your study. Experiments with cutting back on sleep should be carried out prior to the course start if at all possible. And remember that, if you routinely cut sleep to a minimum, there will be less room for burning the midnight oil as an emergency measure. If you feel overtired or irritable on reduced sleep, it is probably not worth persevering with the regime. A Master's in management is above all a test of endurance. It is not worth risking your ability to last the course.

What time do you need to maintain your effectiveness?

To complete a significant programme of study successfully you need to sustain your mental and physical health, and your energy levels. For this you need to protect some time at least for things that make life worth living (at least in your view). *Schedule* some relaxation and treats for yourself. These need to be actively planned. Otherwise their effect will be destroyed by guilty feelings that you should really be working. Knowing that there is a treat coming up may make it easier to stick to a piece of difficult work. So make sport and active relaxation (yoga, meditation, or your favourite television comedy) a positive part of your strategy for effective study. Even if you do not actively exercise at present, you might like to think about building some form of exercise into your schedule. If you are reasonably fit you may well find that you can use study time more effectively.

ACTIVITY 4.3

Jot down estimates of time spent per week, using the categories given as prompts. They are in no sense intended as a definitive list, and you should add any other significant categories at the end. An electronic version is available on the **companion website**.

(Ignore the right-hand column for now. You will need this later.)

Work	Hours	Revised hours
Time at work		
Time travelling to and from work		
Time spent on work brought home		
Time on physical maintenance		
Sleeping		
Eating and other necessities		
Exercise		
Other		
Time on mental maintenance	Hours	Revised hours
Leisure (list activities)		
Meditation, etc.		
Time spent on social activities		
With partner and children (if any)		
Other social activities (list)		
Time spent on 'environment' maintenance	Hours	Revised hours
House		
Garden		
Car		
Other maintenance (list)		

4 Creating a suitable learning context

Other activities (List any significant other use of time, e.g. TV)	Hours	Revised hours

Comment

Having provided this instant estimate, you must next, a more demanding task, check it. There are several possible checks. The first is to ask your partner, if you have one, to do a similar estimate of your time usage, and then to compare their estimate with yours. You may find some interesting discrepancies. Then go back over your diary for the last few weeks, and see whether this is consistent with what you have written. Finally, think carefully about last week. How did you spend your time then? In what ways was this atypical? Modify your estimates in the light of these checks.

Confirming your estimates

You are now in a position to develop a more realistic estimate of time availability, and identify whether there is indeed a serious problem to be addressed. This will require two more activities.

ACTIVITY 4.4

Log your usage of time when not at work, for a period of at least a week, preferably two weeks. A simple format to use is that of the large office diary (an electronic version is available on the **companion website**), which divides the day into periods, though in this case for times outside normal working hours. Log waking time and activities until arriving at work. Log your time of leaving and activities thereafter until you go to bed. You can record either *events*, i.e. the start time of each new activity, or *time usage*. For this you will need to make an entry each hour, estimating use of time within that hour.

Depending on the imminence of your course start, you may wish to sample random days, or even random weeks, for time logging. Watch out, however, for seasonality effects. If, for example, your course has a summer break, and you are working through these activities during the summer, ask whether your time patterns will be sufficiently representative to be worth the effort of logging.

Do not continue beyond the point at which you feel you have sufficient information about actual time usage to progress. If your log differs significantly from your instant estimate, you might like to highlight areas of difference and reflect on these.

You should now work from a combination of your estimate and log. Categorise the activities listed, and start to estimate how much time could be fairly easily freed.

ACTIVITY 4.5

Use the spare right-hand column on your list of time estimates to write down a realistic estimate of weekly time that could be freed for study without detriment to health, relationships or time spent at work. Total these, and check against your estimate of time needed.

If you are still well ahead of your course start, you can check your estimates for feasibility. Draw up the sort of timetable you will need to fit in the level of work you think your course will require, using the time that you have estimated could be freed. Then for a period of about two weeks, use these times to do activities similar to study. These might consist of working through the preparatory sections of this Handbook, doing suggested remedial work, for example on your mathematical skills, or reading and taking notes on relevant management literature, doing exercises to increase your reading speed, or even getting ahead on personal business (tax, letters, or similar) so that you will not need to devote time to this once your course starts. You will find it useful to keep any plans and comments on their effectiveness in your study file.

Comment

Obviously, the closer your chosen activities are to the sort of mental activity your course will demand, the more reliable the test. Getting ahead with gardening or DIY might save time later, but would not test your ability to keep to the timetable you propose. While you may be able to slap paint on walls at 1.00 am, your ability to read, absorb and evaluate management literature at that time might be much reduced.

This trial will indicate whether your estimates of available time are realistic. Discuss them with your partner. Ask whether they see the time allotted to them as enough. Ask whether there are other activities on your list they would like to share. I was humbled to hear from a tutor on a Scottish island that an earlier edition of the book had 'changed the life' of one of her students. Such is the power of print. As a result of this part of the book, for the first time ever he discussed with his wife whether she was happy with the time they spent together, and how they might do things together in the little time he would have free. As a result, they stopped spending most of their 'shared' time silently in front of the television, and despite his studies, she felt they were doing far more together, and more enjoyably, than they had in years.

IF THE TIME IS NOT THERE

If your work above suggests that you cannot free sufficient time for study without doing serious damage to your life, you have two options. You can give up the idea of study, or you can reduce the time you spend at work.

If you wish to explore the latter, there are at least three possibilities. You may be able to negotiate time off for study, or a more general reduction in workload (as discussed earlier). Or you may be able to do your job effectively in less time by more effective time management at work (*see* Chapter 6).

→ Ch 6

4

Creating a suitable learning context

Beware promises of time off work for study if they are not associated with reductions in workload. Training managers may make generous promises that are not honoured by those who allocate your work. If any leave taken involves putting in the equivalent amount of time either before or after the leave, in addition to any normal work, it is of dubious benefit. Many managers are in this position. Work does not go away, but merely awaits their return. While a promise of time off during working hours for attending any classes or residential component is a prerequisite, and revision or thesis-writing time can be a great advantage, you do need to consider whether any promised study leave will involve you in excessive overtime to compensate.

If you can see no way of bridging the gap between your estimate of the time needed and the time that you can make available, you should think seriously about the viability of your study plans. There is little point in committing yourself to a course knowing that you will not be in a position to benefit from it to the full. Overcommitment can seriously damage your personal life, your job performance and even your health.

However, before you abandon your plans, do see how much time you *can* make available by more effective time management at work. You may be surprised at how far this can reduce the number of hours you need to achieve the same (or better) results. Even if you still feel unable to continue with your study, you will benefit from the improved time management skills at work.

SUMMARY

- Ensuring your context is favourable can significantly increase your chances of success – time, space, information and emotional support are all important.
- Organisational support can be invaluable for successful study, and is worth pursuing if at all possible.
- Family support is crucial and most likely to be obtained if planning for study is a shared enterprise, recognising the needs of all involved.
- Freeing sufficient time for study is a major challenge, and insufficient time is the most common contributor to failure.
- To estimate the size of this challenge it is necessary to analyse your current time availability and compare this with the time which you estimate will be needed.
- You may need to reduce some non-working activities, make creative use of potential time such as that spent commuting, and/or negotiate a reduction in the demands of your job.
- If you cannot see how you can free the time you need, you should seriously question the viability of pursuing a course at present.

PRE-COURSE SKILL DEVELOPMENT

→ 5 Personal management skills

Learning outcomes

By the end of this chapter you should:

- have assessed your personal management skills and have identified those where pre-course development would be useful
- have started to improve your planning skills
- recognise the symptoms of stress and know how to start reducing your own stress levels
- be aware of the distinctions between aggression, avoidance and assertion, and have a plan for developing your own assertiveness
- have assessed your information management skills and started to address any inadequacies.

INTRODUCTION

Studying for a Master's is a major project: it needs the same management skills as other projects if you are to succeed. These skills, importantly, include the ability to plan and manage a range of disparate activities, and the ability to protect resources against competition by a combination of planning and assertiveness. You also need the ability to monitor and control your own stress levels, as study will create potentially stressful situations. A further essential skill is the ability to manage large amounts of information, inevitably with the help of IT. The relevance of these skills to your work as a manager is clear: all are highly transferable.

→ Ch 6, 7, 8   You can usefully start to develop these skills before your course starts: this chapter suggests how. Another essential personal skill, time management, is the subject of the next chapter. (Learning skills are addressed in Chapters 7 and 8.) Time spent working through these chapters can markedly increase your chances of success by helping you to extract the maximum learning from the experience, and to gain good marks on your course.

ASSESSING YOUR PERSONAL MANAGEMENT SKILLS

Before going further it would be worth performing a quick assessment of your likely development needs in these personal skills areas. Obviously, this is only worth doing if you are prepared to be as honest as you can. Even so, if you can, seek other opinions on your skill levels.

ACTIVITY 5.1

The following self-assessment may prompt a rethink of your current skill levels. Fill it out to indicate how much time you may need to devote to these two chapters, and suggest those areas where you should devote your efforts. For each item give a score between 1 and 5 where 1 = never, 2 = seldom, 3 = moderately often, 4 = usually and 5 = always. (If you prefer, an electronic version is available on the **website**). You can keep a copy of the electronic questionnaire in your study file, and assess your skill levels at intervals during your course, and indeed subsequently. You may wish to address some of these areas during your work on Chapter 8.

→ Ch 8

Planning

I ensure that I have clear and measurable objectives ☐

I work out what resources I shall need to achieve my targets, and ensure that I acquire them in good time ☐

I ensure that any preparatory activities are done in advance of the event for which they are preparation ☐

I regularly review my progress on my various tasks and projects, and take action as soon as any problem becomes apparent ☐

I take action as soon as I start to get behind on a job, and take pride in meeting deadlines ☐

Colleagues regard me as highly organised ☐

Time management

I am extremely careful about planning my time to ensure that it is used to best effect ☐

I ensure that I do not neglect what is important because of the pressures of what is urgent ☐

I work on one thing at a time rather than trying to split my efforts ☐

I take steps to minimise interruptions at work ☐

I fit my work into a reasonable working day, and do not take it home with me ☐

Colleagues are surprised at how much I manage to achieve ☐

Managing stress levels

My job is well within my capabilities, and does not stress me ☐

I use my leisure time in ways that I find relaxing ☐

I fall asleep easily, and sleep well ☐

I eat healthily and do not drink more than I should ☐

I do not worry about something if I cannot influence it ☐

Colleagues regard me as a calm and balanced person ☐

Assertiveness

If someone tries to exploit me, I tell them what I feel about this ☐

If there is a conflict of opinion, I express my views firmly ☐

If people disagree with me, I do not get angry ☐

My needs are as important as those of other people ☐

Other people's needs are as important as my own ☐

My colleagues regard me as reasonably assertive ☐

Knowledge management

I routinely search for information relevant to work ☐

I find my computer invaluable for word processing, spreadsheets and databases ☐

I read widely on management topics ☐

I file anything of interest so that I can easily find it ☐

I routinely review and organise information on key topics ☐

Colleagues regard me as someone who confidently exploits IT, and a source of help with their own problems ☐

Comment

Obviously the above gives only a rough indication. But if your assessements are reasonably honest and accurate, and you score 24 or more on a section, you should be well prepared in that area. However, it is always worth checking colleagues' assessments of your skills. And if an area is not important to you at work at present, you might want to work through the relevant material in case you did not have enough evidence on which to base a judgement. You will find it useful to file your responses – there will be similar questions on other areas, and your responses will inform your reflections on personal development in Chapter 8.

→ Ch 8

5

Personal management skills

PLANNING SKILLS

Planning means establishing clear and appropriate objectives, working out what is required to achieve them and then ensuring that these requirements are met. Effective planning needs to include a process of monitoring progress, and adjusting efforts to stay on track, even if circumstances change so that the original plans are no longer effective. You were introduced to the elements of the planning process in working through Chapter 1, and they will be dealt with in more detail in Chapter 19 in the context of planning a project. You can now, however, usefully start to improve your skills.

→ Ch 1, 19

Planning has long been seen as central to effective management. Fayol (1916, 1949), perhaps the first management 'guru', listed *forecasting and planning* as the first elements of management. The others were *organising* the necessary resources, *commanding*, i.e. instigating the activities needed to implement the plan, *coordinating* activities to meet goals and *controlling* activity to ensure it is done properly. More recently Luthans (1988), in a study of a range of managers in different settings, found planning, decision making and control to be a major part of their jobs.

Planning may already be one of your strengths. If, however, you know that you tend to be disorganised, and as a consequence often waste your own (and others') efforts and fail to achieve goals, this should be a priority area for you to address. Such skills will be essential if you are trying to balance work and study demands. You will need to be very clear about your objectives, and about the activities and resources needed to achieve them, both at work and for your course. Otherwise you will find yourself with impossible clashes of demands.

If this is an area on which you feel you need to work, you might try the following:

Guidelines for effective planning

- When accepting a new task, check that you are clear as to the objectives, and know how progress will be assessed. Your organisation may already insist on SMART (i.e. specific, measurable, achievable, relevant and time-defined) objectives. If not, it is a useful mnemonic.

- For each major objective, work out the hierarchy of subordinate objectives needed (again these need to be SMART) and the actions and resources they will require if they are to be met.

- Set aside 15 minutes at the start of each day for planning. Consider the tasks that you intend to work on. Check that your objectives and success measures are clear, and that you have all the resources necessary. Prioritise tasks and plan the order for addressing them.

- Set aside 15 minutes at the end of the day to review progress on tasks, and any action needed to compensate for deviation from plans. (Note any learning points.)

- Draw up your list of intended tasks for the next day.

- Every month, set aside at least an hour for thinking about longer-term objectives, both for your job and for you personally. Check that your shorter-term goals are contributing to satisfactory progress towards longer-term goals. If not, work out what to do about this.

- Keep a work diary in which you record objectives, progress towards them, notes of any 'corrective action' needed if objectives are starting to look unlikely to be achieved, and notes on learning points.

If you can improve your planning at work before your course starts, you will find it easier to plan for the increased volume and complexity of demands that study will bring.

MANAGING STRESS

Work is a major source of stress – in 2006 the CBI estimated that workplace stress was costing industry in the UK £9.6 bn a year! (Frost, 2006) According to the CIPD, stress may affect 20% of the workforce, be one of the main causes of sickness absence, and pose the biggest threat to businesses in the near future. Workplace stress may be caused by overload, by the lack of resources or skills or information to do what is required, or even lack of understanding of what *is* required. It may be caused by having no say on how work is done, by work that involves a fast pace, by the need to resolve conflicting priorities, by lack of recognition, understanding and support from their managers or colleagues, sometimes even by bullying. Sometimes underload may be stressful. Managing stress is a popular (and important) topic for authors and trainers to address.

Stress can:

■ impair concentration

■ affect judgement

■ damage your health

■ impact on your team

■ damage other relationships.

While definitions of stress vary, a useful way of looking at it is to say that stress occurs when pressures on an individual are such that health and/or performance are impaired. Note that there is substantial variation between individuals in the level of pressure that constitutes stress, and that stress may be caused by pressures that are too low as well as too high. (One of the most stressful periods in my life occurred when I started a new job: for weeks I was given nothing to do except 'familiarise' myself with a heap of files. For surprisingly many people, holidays are very stressful!)

Individual variation in what is 'appropriate' pressure may make it difficult to predict and detect stress.

If demands are too low, an increase in pressure is welcomed. It is seen as a challenge: the job becomes more exciting, and the satisfactions to be gained from doing the job increase. Even very high levels of pressure can be positive, provided they are short-term. If you work through the night to meet an impossible deadline, and succeed, you feel great. There is tremendous satisfaction in having achieved something where others might have failed.

If the short-term crisis is extended, however, the positive aspects are rapidly overtaken by negative. Similarly, if there is a gradual increase in pressure over time, there will come a point where, if you stop to think, you realise that your job is no longer an exciting challenge, but rather something to be endured, and which is having a negative impact on your enjoyment of life in general.

Causes of stress include:

■ sustained overload (or underload)

■ role ambiguity

■ conflict of objectives

■ emotional pressure.

The trouble is that one of the many bad effects of stress is to make us less able to stop and think: we no longer have the time, and besides, our thought processes have become impaired. Because the process is gradual, we may never be aware of it. We go home a little later, and a little later. We cut back our running to twice a week, then once, then miss it altogether. Our partners are no longer keen to go out to dinner with us because we are too tired to be good company.

The fact that stress sets in at different levels for different people makes the situation worse. If we see others thriving on more work than we are coping with ourselves, we feel that we should not be stressed. Organisations may have cultures demanding that all managers exert the same superhuman efforts as their exceptional chief executives. Admitting to what might be seen as weakness is unacceptable in many working contexts.

The first stage, as with any problem, is to look in more detail at the situation. But how can you see whether you are stressed or not, given the difficulties described? The surest guide is how you feel. Supplement this, if you can, with assessments by others close to you.

ACTIVITY 5.2

Think of the last time you felt really good about your job: you woke each day looking forward to the challenges ahead, and arrived home at night looking forward to the leisure activities you had planned. Now think about how you felt this morning, and how you felt when you got home after work. It can't be *too* bad, or you would not have felt up to working on this chapter, but is the difference significant? Ask your partner, if you have one, if they think that you are under more stress than they think is ideal. Ask your colleagues if they think that you are ever irritable, or perhaps make errors of judgement, because of pressure. Think about your health. Do you have a number of minor ailments, perhaps more than you used to? Headaches, respiratory and digestive disorders, sleep problems, asthma and eczema are among ailments which can be made worse by stress. What is your alcohol intake? If you need a couple of drinks when you get home to help you relax, this suggests a fairly high stress level. Can you turn off thoughts of work when you are at home? Or do you continue to toss problems around half the night? Do you tend to eat too much, or find difficulty eating enough to maintain a reasonable weight? (A questionnaire is available on the **website**.)

Comment

Your answers to the above questions, and if you have time, to the further questions on the **website***, should make it possible for you to assess your own stress level, and to be fairly honest with yourself as to whether this is something you should be tackling even before the course starts. Even if stress is high but not excessive, you should perhaps be thinking about developing techniques for handling the increased levels once your course starts.*

If there is no problem, skip to the next chapter (remembering that this chapter exists should you need it in future). If there is a potential problem, more analysis is needed. This should focus on the **causes** *of the stress levels you are experiencing, and on the possible ways open to you for* **coping** *with stress when it is unavoidable.*

One common cause of stress is simple overload, a workload higher than is reasonable over a sustained period. If you feel that this is the source of most of your pressure, work carefully through Chapter 6. More effective use of your time at work, together with clear thought about your objectives, should do much to reduce your problems.

→ Ch 6

Another common reason is role ambiguity. Perhaps it is not clear what you are being required to do, or what your boss sees as a reasonable effort. Maybe the goalposts

→ Ch 6 seem to shift every time you are in a good position to shoot. Again, Chapter 6 will be of some help here, but if the fault lies in ambiguity further up the organisation, a solution may be beyond your grasp. You may either need to look for another job, itself a source of considerable stress, or set your own objectives.

A simple clash of objectives can be almost as stressful as ambiguity. This may be between yourself and someone higher in the organisation, or between you and your subordinates, or between you and your family, who feel your priorities do not include family life sufficiently high on the list. Some clashes have moral overtones, for example if your company starts to operate in a way that is inconsistent with your personal value system.

ACTIVITY 5.3

Assess the major sources of stress in your life. Divide them into those that you can reduce, and those which you can do nothing about. (You will probably want to list these privately.)

Reduce stress by:
- controlling workload
- resolving conflicts
- re-evaluating priorities
- accepting the inevitable
- relaxation and exercise.

The next step is to find ways of reducing stressors which *can* be reduced. This will depend so much on your personal situation that discussion here would be inappropriate. In order to think as creatively as possible about options, you may find it helpful to discuss your situation with a good friend.

Once you have thought of action you could take, set yourself deadlines for actually *doing* something. Check regularly that you are keeping to your deadlines. If you have involved friends in this, they will be helpful as progress chasers. This can be an exercise in planning skills. You may wish to file your plans and record of future progress as an example.

COPING WITH UNAVOIDABLE STRESS

The remaining action needed is to find ways of coping with unavoidable stress. Actions fall into three main categories: attitude change; relaxation techniques; physical change.

Attitude change

An old prayer asks for the strength to change what can be changed, the patience to accept what cannot and the wit to know the difference. This is, in essence, what you need. There is no point in wasting energy trying to change the immutable. The knack is to find a way of thinking about it that allows you to work at an acceptable and safe level, without loss of self-respect. To achieve this, you need to *value yourself* sufficiently to accept your own definition of what is reasonable, even if this is at odds with what goes on around you. You may lose your job, but this is unlikely. It is far more likely that, if you do not recognise your own limitations, your performance will gradually

→ Ch 6

decline to the level that your job is threatened anyway, with additional detriment to your health. This topic is developed further in Chapter 6.

The following technique drawn from neuro-linguistic programming (NLP) (Andreas and Faulkner, 1996) might help you reduce negative feelings. It uses visualisation to reduce the intensity of feelings about a situation or event which has happened to you. While it may seem strange at first if NLP is new to you, it is worth a try if the 'patience to accept' is proving difficult.

Think of such a situation, trying to see it unfolding as a film, complete with images and sounds. Next, deliberately select theme music which *mismatches* the prevailing mood of the 'film' – perhaps a ridiculous or joyful tune. Replay the film in your mind with the new music sounding loud and clear. If you then revisit the images *without* the music you are likely to find your unpleasant feelings have greatly diminished. (To neutralise them completely, repeat the exercise a few times more, each time using different, but still inappropriate, music.)

A simpler (though not at all easy) technique, drawn from cognitive therapy (*see* Neenan and Dryden, 2004, for an introduction), may be to try to note the negative automatic thoughts (NATS) and the assumptions underlying these which may be driving you to undervalue yourself. A NAT is something that pops unbidden into your mind – e.g. 'Colleagues are going to think I'm rubbish because I can't handle this workload'. There may be a range assumptions underpinning this. Some may relate to the world – 'This level of workload is reasonable'. Some may relate to deeper beliefs about yourself – 'I'm incompetent', 'I'm not worthy of this job'. Identifying and questioning these assumptions may be an important step to changing your attitudes about the situation.

Another may be to strengthen yourself by focusing not, as is common, on your weaknesses, but on your strengths. Try listing each day what you have done well. Ask your friends what they *like* about you. Keep a 'warm fuzzy file' for e-mails which thank you for things you have done well and other evidence of your strengths as perceived by others, and read its contents at regular intervals. All this may seem fairly tangential to reducing overload and stress, but you may be surprised at its impact.

Relaxation techniques

Such techniques need to be *learned*. You cannot suddenly relax on demand if you have not developed the necessary skills. Popular techniques include yoga, meditation, or relaxation using a CD as a prompt. Different techniques suit different people: ask friends what has worked for them, see what classes are available or seek a good book or CD.

If you wish to start practising basic relaxation without further help, sit or lie in a quiet, dimly lit room. If the room is not warm, wear warm clothes. Spend a little time letting your body go soft; think of it melting into the floor like warm fudge. Relax your face muscles, and although your eyes should be shut, imagine you are looking towards a far horizon. Start to think about your breathing, trying to keep this fairly slow and regular. Gently discard any other thoughts that intrude, returning to your breathing each time. If you prefer, you can concentrate on a visual image, such as a blue water lily or rippling water. The image must be one which you can visualise clearly, and which conveys a sense of peace. Or repeat a short phrase over and over in time with your breathing. Choose a phrase with peaceful overtones, although the exact content is not important. With the image or the phrase you should again try to put aside other thoughts as they occur, gently, and without irritation. Practise for about five minutes at a time to begin with, gradually building up to 15 or 20 minutes. You should find that with practice you will be able to keep your thoughts increasingly focused on your chosen object, and that you will feel greatly refreshed at the end of the period. At the end of your time, move around gently before getting up, and rise slowly to avoid dizziness.

As an alternative or supplement to such approaches, increase the time you devote to activities you find relaxing. Listening to music, reading poetry or flying kites: the possibilities are extensive. A major source of stress is often friction from those with whom we live, so see whether a shared form of relaxation can be found. 'Relaxation' which increases friction will not reduce your stress levels. Something which is relaxing *and* companionable may reduce stress in two ways at once.

Physical exercise

The merits of physical exercise will be referred to on a number of occasions in the Handbook. If you are not already an exercise convert, or doing a physically demanding job, think seriously about building more exercise into your routine as part of your pre-course preparation. If you have not developed the habit *before* your course starts, your chances of doing enough exercise during your course will be extremely slim. The type of exercise is unimportant, provided it raises a sweat for half an hour or so, and you do it at least two or three times a week. The effects on your health and your ability to study should be significant.

You are unlikely to stick to regular exercise if you do not *enjoy* it. Unaccustomed exercise is hard work and can feel more like punishment than enjoyment, particularly if you demand too much of yourself. Always start gently, stopping before it becomes a trial. Within a couple of weeks enjoyment should start to seem possible, at least, provided you have chosen an activity which suits you. Within a month you should be actively enjoying it.

Think about what you *used* to enjoy as a guide, or something you like the idea of. Your chosen activity should be convenient. You will seldom have time or energy for exercise requiring major planning and complex arrangements. Your time will be at a premium during your studies, so time devoted to exercise needs to be spent actually exercising. This is why jogging is so popular. Almost no preparation or other non-exercise time is needed: you can set aside 25 minutes, and spend 20 minutes actually running. It can be done in most weathers, and little cost is incurred. You can usually find a friend to run with you, too, which will increase the chance of your making the effort when you do not really feel up to it. You may be able to involve your partner.

You may be surprised how much difference even 20 minutes' exercise, two or three times a week, can make to your chances of success. This is not a sales pitch, although it may sound like one. Some people *hate* running, but love swimming, or squash, or fast walking. Some swear by dancing (privately) to a fast CD. Choose an activity to suit your circumstances. But do choose one, unless there are health reasons for not doing so.

If you are new to exercise, *force* yourself to set exceedingly modest targets to begin with. There is always a challenge to run farther or faster, or play squash against a better opponent than is ideal. But if you injure yourself, it will set back your plans considerably. Even if muscles and tendons survive, over-exercising can build up a psychological resistance to further exercise that no amount of willpower will overcome. Starting *below* your capacity, and increasing your exercise only very gradually, will be both more enjoyable and more effective overall.

ACTIVITY 5.4

Decide on a plan for introducing a modest amount of exercise into your life, if you do not already exercise. Set targets, and review your progress against these. Again, involve a friend or member of your family if you can, as this will increase your motivation significantly.

DEVELOPING ASSERTIVENESS SKILLS

How assertive did the earlier activity suggest you to be? If you tend to acquiesce with the demands of others, even when you would prefer not to, you are likely to encounter difficulties while studying. You will be prone to overload at work if whenever you are asked to take on more work you say 'Oh, all right. I suppose I can do it'. This will lead to problems with finding time for your studies. If you tend to keep quiet when you disagree with what others in your group are saying, or stop defending a particular point as soon as there is any dissent, you will probably not enjoy the group work on your course. Nor will you make a very positive contribution to it.

Avoiding conflict at whatever cost has a *high* cost. You may already be aware of some consequences of your lack of assertiveness. But equally, if you have absolutely no inhibitions about telling people they are wrong, or about telling them precisely what you think, you may still have a need to become more assertive. Aggression is not the same as assertion, and may create as many problems as avoidance. Figure 5.1 explores the relationship between the three strategies.

The essence of assertion is to stand up firmly for your own rights while giving due regard to the rights of others. (The exercises earlier on valuing yourself are highly relevant here.) Avoiding conflict may 'respect the rights of others', but at the expense of your own rights. If so, you are likely to suffer, as your needs will not be met. You may end up working on a weekend when you had other, more attractive plans. Colleagues may assume that you will do all the jobs that no one else wants: you will then be so busy that more interesting projects are given to others. Your boss may not see you as MBA material, and fail to support your request for sponsorship. In the long term your mental or physical health may suffer.

There are other, less obvious costs. If your reticence means that you contribute less to a group than you could, whether at work or on your course, the group is missing out.

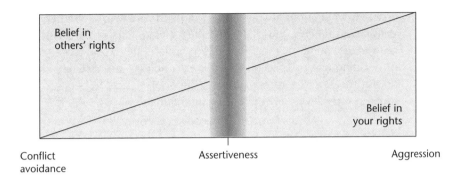

Belief in
others' rights

Belief in
your rights

Conflict
avoidance

Assertiveness

Aggression

Fig. 5.1 Assertiveness – the balance of rights

You may disagree with the others because you have information that no one else possesses. Or you may have interpreted information differently from others – and perhaps better. Even if your disagreement stems from a misunderstanding, perhaps because your background is different, it may point to an area where careful explanation is needed in any presentation. If you fail to express your disagreement, and to persist until people hear what you are saying, your potential contribution will be lost.

If your response is aggressive rather than assertive, you may be being less effective than you think. Aggression tends to arouse either matching aggression or defensiveness in others. Neither is likely to lead to constructive problem solving, nor to future positive relations between the parties concerned. If you are aggressive to a superior, he or she will be equally aggressive in response. If so, the communication will become a contest, and your superior is likely to emerge the victor. You will have gone down in your superior's estimation in the process.

With subordinates the damage may be less obvious, as a defensive response is more likely. This may mean that you never find out why the conflict really arose – there will be excuses rather than a genuine attempt at finding reasons – so things are unlikely to be better next time. Furthermore, subordinates will find their own, possibly counterproductive, ways of avoiding future conflict. Longer term, your aggression can damage their health, as well as your own.

In a group, if you tend to dominate through aggressive behaviour such as interruptions, sarcasm or put-downs directed at other members or similar behaviour directed at ensuring that your point of view is accepted whatever others think, you will do more than prevent the group from coming to the best solution. (It may seem impossible, but the best solution may not necessarily be the one that you are convinced is right!) You will find that if the group does not become demotivated – to the detriment of everyone's learning – it will find a way of controlling what it sees as the damage you are doing, and this can be very uncomfortable for you.

The benefits of assertion, rather than aggression or avoidance, go far beyond helping you to control your workload and to make a positive contribution to group work on your course. At home, as well as at work, assertiveness can lead to constructive outcomes rather than conflict in a wide range of situations. Whether it is a matter of coaching your subordinates (and giving and receiving praise benefits from assertiveness skills just as much as does giving and receiving criticism), discussing how to handle a crisis, negotiating an expansion of your role to allow you to use newly developed skills, or deciding on where to go for your next holiday, assertiveness skills are relevant. You do not therefore need to wait until your course starts to begin to develop them. Indeed, such development can start immediately.

EXERCISE 5.1

Classify each of the following responses as **aggression, assertion** or **avoidance**:

(a) 'You always blame me when things go wrong. It was Fred who accepted the contract.' _____

(b) 'That's all right. I'll see if I can find something for you to use as an ashtray.' _____

(c) 'I find it very difficult to feel I am making a contribution when I am never allowed to finish any sentence.' _____

(d) 'Well I suppose I could go to the meeting, though I am a bit busy at present.' _____

(e) 'I need to work on my report this afternoon if I am to meet our agreed deadline. Do you think that the meeting is so essential that I should go despite this?' _____

(f) 'Why are you always so critical?' _____

(g) 'Never mind. If you all think the main problem is cash flow I'll go along with that.' _____

(h) 'It seems to me that we are focusing exclusively on the financial aspects of this case, and ignoring fairly important human resource implications.' _____

(i) 'You are right. The first section is unclear, though I don't think this criticism applies to the subsequent analysis. Perhaps next time we could discuss what is needed in a background section in a bit more detail before I start the report.' _____

(*The correct classification is given at the end of the chapter.*)

In developing your assertiveness skills you need first to appreciate the nature of assertiveness – that it is an adult, self-confident, rational rather than emotional, straightforward and constructive response in a situation. The discussion thus far should have made this somewhat clearer. You can reinforce the message by observing interactions around you, at work and at home, and classifying responses in the same way as you did in the above exercise.

5

To become more assertive:

- believe in your rights
- express these calmly but firmly
- prepare, if possible, for any likely conflict.

Believing in your rights

You first need to work on your own confidence, and think about your rights in any situation. It is easy to say that assertiveness is about respecting your own rights, but too many of us undervalue those rights, and underestimate the worth of our own contributions. If you wish to become more assertive, you need to *believe* that you do have rights in a situation. These could be described as:

- **The right to ask for what you want, or to make clear what you do not want**. Your wants and needs in a situation, whether a desire for time off, for recognition for what you have achieved, or a chance to use valued skills, are valid information. If you do not make your wants clear, others may be totally unaware of them, or fail to appreciate their strength. Even if aware of them, they will find it easier to ignore your wants if you leave them unstated.

- **The right to be listened to and respected**. There is no reason why you are not worth as much as anyone else. If you are not being respected as a person, this reflects badly not on you but on those who are failing to respect you. In any situation, a key element may be the difference between the various perspectives that interested parties bring to bear upon it. By representing part of this diversity you are making a valuable contribution. You may feel that your experience is inadequate and your view in a debate therefore worthless. This is likely to be far from the truth. You can be more analytical about a discussion if you are coming to it fresh. You are less contaminated by preconceptions and assumptions which may be widely held but not necessarily right. A problem may seem insoluble precisely because the shared view of it is so strong that no one can escape from it to a creative solution. So value your own contribution, particularly if it *is* different from those of the rest of the group. And stand up for your right to make it.

- **The right not to know, or not to understand**. You have a perfect right not to be omniscient. The trouble comes when you are reluctant to admit to a lack of knowledge or understanding. In consequence, you may fail to make a contribution, or misdirect your efforts. If you do not know or don't understand, admit to it and ask for help from those who do. Sometimes you may be the only one who has seen a flaw in a line of reasoning, and they may not understand either. Sometimes once you have clarified something you may be able to use that knowledge more effectively than those to whom it was already familiar.

- **The right to make mistakes**. There is, of course, a corresponding duty to learn from your mistakes, but no obligation to be infallible. Again, it is usually far more damaging, and takes far more effort, to attempt to conceal mistakes than to face up to them and learn from them. In some organisations mistakes are recognised as evidence that you are trying to push back the boundaries.

- **The right to change your mind**. All too often it is seen as a sign of weakness to move from a position once you have adopted it. But if subsequent exploration of a problem shows it in a new light, it is only by changing your mind that the best solution can be found. A group will never reach its full potential if any position is defended to the death by its original protagonists, regardless of what emerges in subsequent debate. Sometimes the most significant contribution you can make to a group discussion is to say that you have changed your mind about something and explain why. At work you may have taken a decision in the light of imperfect knowledge (the normal condition for taking decisions) and subsequent events may have shown that a better course of action would be better. Again, it is a sign of strength rather than weakness to revise your decision, though again information about the reasons for this will be useful to others who are involved.

ACTIVITY 5.5

During the next two weeks observe those around you. Note any situation where assertiveness might be appropriate. Think about whether those involved in the situation are acting as if they believe they have the above rights, and whether they are respecting similar rights in others. Observe your own reaction in such situations. Which of your own rights do you have the most difficulty in respecting? (It is important to be honest with yourself here.) Discuss with someone whom you trust reasons why this might be, and why the right is important. Keep any notes in your study file.

Expressing assertiveness

You will have noted from the earlier exercise that the words in which you express yourself are important if you are to assert yourself effectively. Once you have started to work on believing in your rights, you will need to practise using assertive forms of words.

The essence of assertiveness is clarity, objectivity (though your own wants and feelings are valid data), calmness rather than emotion, firmness, a refusal to be sidetracked and the pursuit of a positive and constructive solution rather than a victory. The words you use will therefore be characterised by at least some of the following:

- use of phrases such as 'I prefer . . .', 'I think . . .', rather than 'You . . .', 'He . . .'
- use of phrases such as '. . . could . . .', 'choose' and '. . . might . . .' rather than '. . . can't . . .' or '. . . shouldn't . . .'
- checking that you have understood before responding – 'I think your argument is . . .'
- asking for more detail if you are not clear – 'Could you give me another example . . .'
- acknowledging the other person's feelings – 'I know that you have been hoping . . .'
- saying what you feel – 'I feel very frustrated . . .'
- calm repetition, possibly using the same words each time, when it is clear that you are not being listened to
- the absence of apology (unless justified).

ACTIVITY 5.6

During the next two weeks write down the words you have used in any context where you might have been more assertive, and then 'rewrite the script' using more assertive forms of words. If you can, act out these rewritten scenarios with the help of a friend. This should make you more comfortable with using the words, and more likely to use them in a real situation.

Body language is as important as the words you use. If you avoid all eye contact, speak with your hand over your mouth, cower into your chair or lean as far away from the other person as possible, you will find it harder to use assertive phrases, and their effect will be diminished even if you succeed. If you raise your voice, clench your fists, stare the other person down and get *too* close to them, the effect will be aggressive, whatever you say. So get into the habit of observing first the body language of those around you and then your own, and of ensuring that your body language is reinforcing your words, rather than giving a conflicting message.

Preparation

The final important step to assertiveness is to prepare for any anticipated conflict situation. Think about what you want to achieve and why. If you feel in danger of undervaluing your rights, discuss the situation with a supportive colleague to reinforce your beliefs. Think about the other person's likely response. If your colleague, or a friend, is willing to cooperate, act out the scenario in a range of possible ways, trying always to be calm and assertive, rather than avoiding issues or becoming aggressive.

If a situation is thrust upon you with no warning, it is often acceptable – and extremely useful – to ask for thinking time, so that you prepare yourself at least a little rather than trying to respond while in a state of mild shock. A response such as, 'This is a complete bolt from the blue. I had no idea you were feeling like this. Could you give me five minutes to think about it . . .' may lead to a much more constructive outcome to the encounter.

Assertiveness skills take time to develop. So too does the skill of knowing when to be assertive. Aggression has its (limited) place, and there will be times when avoidance will be an appropriate response. You can, however, become considerably more effective in a wide range of situations where assertiveness *is* appropriate through preparation beforehand, use of the sorts of phrases that are most effective during the encounter, and reflection as to your success afterwards, with a view to further development of your skill in this area.

The above discussion is necessarily no more than a brief introduction to the subject. If you want more help, there are good books on the subject (*see* Further information at the end of this chapter). Even better is to go on a good course. If you start developing your skills now, and review your progress at intervals, your job performance, your studies and your relationships outside work should all benefit.

If you have developed the ability to be assertive you will be well on the way to being an effective negotiator, particularly in the context of the sorts of negotiations necessary to protect your time, and gain any other resources necessary to your study. The essence of successful negotiation is to understand your opponent, and their likely objectives, to be equally clear about your own objectives and to identify if at all possible a solution that is acceptable to you both, and as favourable to yourself as possible, within that shared area of mutual acceptability.

KNOWLEDGE MANAGEMENT AND INFORMATION TECHNOLOGY

During the 1990s the impact of developments in ICT started to produce dramatic changes in the ways organisations handled information, related to their customers and did business. When the first edition of this book appeared (1991) few students were familiar with on-line interaction. It is now so common that it is likely that most readers will be using e-mail, and chat rooms, and blogs, though possibly not in a learning or business context. The emphasis in this book has therefore shifted towards maximising opportunities for learning and more formal collaborative work. It is commonplace now for work teams to have members around the globe, who hold regular 'virtual' meetings and exchanges of information. Spreadsheets and databases are almost universal. Statistical packages are relatively easy to use and offer great power. And it is hard to imagine a presentation that does not use PowerPoint® overheads. But while basic competence is now widespread, many people are less skilled than they might be – if you are better than your colleagues at exploiting the potential of ICT you will be at a substantial advantage at work.

The concern in organisations has moved beyond mere use of ICT to a more sophisticated concern with knowledge as a key organisational resource, and knowledge management as a major concern if this resource is to generate maximum competitive advantage.

The impact of technological developments on education has been almost as great. If you are on a distance learning programme, you will be probably be operating within a 'virtual learning environment' (VLE) which is your campus equivalent. Face-to-face universities increasingly require electronic submission of assignments to allow plagiarism checking. Even if they do not, the ease of producing an impressive document, which incorporates a range of graphics, puts those who are still using pen and paper at a disadvantage.

If you fear that you are in the small minority who lack the necessary IT skills it may be worth devoting some of your preparation time to ensuring that you have the necessary technical skills for your course. Whatever your IT skill levels it will be worth thinking about the sorts of information you will need and how you can best manage this information.

A book like this cannot be a crash course in IT. There is too much to cover, and the software is continually being updated: my version may not be yours. However, it does try to help you understand the uses you are likely to make of IT as a student, and identifies some of the general areas that you might usefully address before the course starts. Areas which are specific to a topic elsewhere in the book are addressed there. For example, information search is addressed in the context of projects, and the use of PowerPoint or similar software when considering presentations.

Why courses require IT use

IT skills are essential for management success, and a core competence for a programme to develop. But many requirements for ICT use stem from the fact that it offers a wide range of practical advantages for universities, allowing them to make substantial savings, improve the student learning experience and expand their geographic range. Student registration can now be done on-line, assignments can draw on a wide range of information from the Internet and be submitted electronically. Resources in university libraries are often 'virtual'. Many teaching materials may be presented in electronic form, and notes and slides from lectures may be made available via a lecturer's website. Distance learning institutions such as the Open University have sophisticated 'on-line environments' in which students from around the globe can easily interact with each other and with teaching staff.

Although the obvious impact of IT has been on distance learning, it has transformed conventional courses almost as much. Full-time students will still rely on e-mail to contact tutors, rather than waiting for 'office hours', and will find it invaluable when working on group projects. Libraries will have many resources only in electronic form. Notes and materials for courses may well be distributed electronically. And students increasingly (though not always wisely) incorporate materials found on the web into their essays and project reports.

As with the other skills addressed, IT skills are highly transferable. Managers need to be able to make full use of IT in their jobs. Intranets and the Internet are the source of much of the information managers use. Such information needs to be stored in readily accessible form. It is expected that if you write a report it will look professional and include tables and diagrams. In many contexts, a presentation without sophisticated computer-generated visual aids is unlikely to be taken seriously.

Furthermore, organisations increasingly use IT for communication. E-mail has eclipsed 'snail mail'. Teams are often widely separated geographically; conferencing and virtual meetings are an essential element in effective working.

Finally, with e-commerce a major growth area, some of your programme is likely to address strategic issues relating to this growing market. It will be essential for you to be familiar with the medium if you are to appreciate these issues.

The following sections address some of the issues above in more detail. Others are addressed at appropriate points later in the book.

Preparing documents

You are likely to need to prepare a number of substantial written documents for submission during your course and will need to use your PC for this. It is relatively easy now to produce a report of an extremely high quality, incorporating sophisticated graphics, and analyses of data. The transience of the medium reduces 'writer's block', as discussed in Chapter 15, while 'cutting and pasting' from notes or other sources is

→ Ch 15

5

Personal management skills

also easy (though you do need to be extremely careful not to commit plagiarism – more on this in Chapter 15).

Improving wordprocessing skills

If your current use of a keyboard is restricted to e-mails, you may be content with the biblical approach to typing (seek and ye shall find. . .). However, this is expensive of time if you are regularly preparing substantial assignments. You may want to use some of the time before your course to practise touch typing. Many print and electronic 'tutors' are available, and it is well worth investing some time in developing your typing skills. It will pay off at work, as well as in your assignment writing.

Reports demand:

- keyboard skills
- familiarity with frequently used edit and format commands
- awareness of tools available
- good filing habits.

In addition to basic keyboard skills, you need to be familiar with the main wordprocessing commands and the basics of filing. A brief summary of these basics is given in Helpfile 5.1 at the end of this chapter.

If you cannot easily produce an impressive document, checked for grammar and spelling and incorporating all the diagrams and other graphics that will support the case you are making, you should work through this helpfile. Doing so may significantly improve the quality of your work, then therefore your grades, as well as saving you many hours of unnecessary work.

Accessing information

Your library will almost certainly provide extensive access to information presented electronically. Indeed for 'distance learning' students this provision may be a major benefit of study, overcoming one of the major difficulties they experienced in the past if they did not live near a suitable university library.

→ Ch 19

You will be able to access all sorts of non-library information via the Internet, as well. You will have found this already if you used the suggested websites as the start of a search for information about suitable MBA programmes. Later in your course you are likely to find Internet searches invaluable when researching projects or for a dissertation (*see* Chapter 19).

Communicating with students and tutors

Even if you are studying full-time, you may find e-mail is the most convenient way to communicate with tutors. If you are a part-time student, particularly if you are studying at a distance, then it may be far superior to other routes. To make effective use of e-mails for communication follow the guidelines outlined below – despite the widespread use of e-mail, they are not always observed!

Guidelines for effective e-mails

- Use a descriptive title: some tutors may receive hundreds of e-mails and open them selectively.
- Use the high priority marker if the matter is urgent (but only if so).

- Be concise.
- Make clear why you are communicating and what response you want/need.
- Give all the information your tutor needs to respond appropriately.
- If replying, do not assume your tutor remembers exactly what s/he originally wrote – quote the relevant part of the e-mail, or otherwise make clear what you are replying to. The message should be complete and not require reference to earlier correspondence.

Communication possibilities go far beyond simple e-mail. A distance learning programme is likely to use a web-based conferencing system that will allow you to 'discuss' with other students, and perhaps tutors as well, issues related to the course. Indeed you may be required to work collaboratively on some of your assignments, exchanging thoughts, data and drafts electronically. While much of this work may be 'asynchronous' – as with e-mail, messages are posted, to be read when someone else logs on – some systems allow real-time interaction, through voice and/or video links, together with 'shared screens', where changes one person makes to the image on the screen are seen by all taking part. The scope here is considerable, and the technology may significantly alter the nature of distance learning. There is more on this in Chapter 11.

→ Ch 11

You are likely to be given training in any system used on your course. Such communications are mentioned here only to alert you to the sorts of possibilities, and to strengthen your resolve to ensure that you have the necessary machine and communication links operational well before the course requires them. Installing software and connecting to systems from home may take longer than you expect. It can be a real setback if this means that you miss an on-line tutorial or cannot submit your first assignment on time.

OTHER USES OF IT

As I said, other uses of IT will be developed during the book. If you feel you want to continue developing your skills now, rather than wait until you reach them, refer to Chapter 11 for electronic communications, Chapter 13 for using spreadsheets, Chapter 16 for PowerPoint presentations and Chapter 19 for searching the Internet.

→ Ch 11, 13
→ Ch 16, 19

SEEKING INFORMATION: PREPARATORY READING

Using technology to find and communicate information is only part of knowledge management. Print is still important. Many intending students feel that as soon as they sign on for a course they should rush out and obtain the textbooks they will be using, and start to read them. While it is often helpful to do preparatory reading, textbooks are not always the best starting point. Without the supporting lectures or distance teaching materials, they can be unrewarding. Other forms of preparation may be preferable.

First, it is most important that you develop the study skills that you will need, so you should give priority to working through those parts of the Handbook that are relevant. Second, your course will be more stimulating if you have started to develop a strategic perspective, that is, to think about the higher-level decisions taken by organisations, and the context in which they are taken, and their implications. Ask your chosen institution what preparation they recommend. Rather than reading textbooks, you may find this contextual information more accessible via the business section of your newspaper, in the *Financial Times*, in a variety of management publications and in radio and television programmes devoted to the subject. You may find your local main library takes relevant business publications, or that they are available within your organisation. Reading these, perhaps in conjunction with the chapter on effective study, should be useful preparation. There are also many good management-related websites. Develop your Internet search skills by seeking some of these.

You can also usefully start to explore your own organisation's policy and strategy formulation. Use this to see the organisation from the perspective of those who are developing policy, rather than merely cursing the effects of that policy when it starts to impinge on your job. Find out from colleagues, your manager, your mentor, your training officer, or anyone else in the organisation who might know, what information is available, and where.

If you do wish to read books, then there are countless general management books. Some of these are excellent, some of little value. Again a library should have a reasonable supply (few of them stand re-reading, so it is probably not worth investing other than in paperbacks). Autobiographies of senior industrialists, although needing to be taken with a pinch of salt, can be enjoyable reading and give you the perspective of a decision maker. You will probably find the array of management books available in a good bookseller rather bewildering. It is easier to shop at airports, or the larger railway stations, which often have an excellent, though not too large, selection of management books. Some suggestions are listed under 'Further information' at the end of this chapter, but this list is by no means exhaustive. It is merely a starting point. Of course, all the books listed under 'Further information' elsewhere in this book would also be good preparation.

In addition to reading relevant materials, you need to capture the essence of the important ones in a way that you will be able to access during your studies. Start to experiment with the electronic equivalent of a card index, some way of taking notes and filing them that will enable you to access those notes from a variety of different routes.

As you will discover later in the book, it is not usually a good idea to be too ambitious. Think about your priorities in preparing yourself for the course, work out a realistic plan that will enable you to meet at least the highest of these, and follow the plan. It is far better to decide that you will work through two chapters in detail, talk to your training manager, and start reading the business pages, and *do* these, than to buy a heap of books, and decide that you also need a lot of study skills development, and sit there never doing anything because the whole task seems so forbidding. So opt for preparation that will not be too onerous, and enjoy it.

SUMMARY

■ You can usefully devote time before a course to developing relevant personal skills.

■ Planning skills will make you more effective at work, and will be essential if you are to meet learning objectives without compromising work objectives.

■ Assertiveness skills will help you to resist unreasonable demands on your work time, and help you contribute effectively to team activity at work and on your course.

■ Stress will normally be increased by your studies. You need to think about the sources of stress in your life and reduce what can be reduced. Techniques for coping with inevitable stress should be developed *prior* to the course if at all possible. They will probably include attitude change, relaxation techniques and regular exercise.

■ Useful preparation can also include developing a more strategic perspective.

■ Developing basic wordprocessing skills will enable you to use study time more effectively once your course starts.

■ Rather than reading textbooks, you can exploit media business coverage, material on the Internet, more general management books and resources within your own organisation.

Further information

There is a wealth of books on the personal skills covered in this chapter. Some are very superficial, some rather irritating. Those that follow are my personal choice. You are advised to browse and find one that suits you. Different things irritate different people!

■ Adair, J. and Allen, M. (2003) *The Concise Time Management and Personal Development*, Thorogood.

■ Andreas, S. and Faulkner, C. (1996) NLP. *The New Technology of Achievement*, Nicholas Brealey.

■ Back, K. and Back, K. (1999) *Assertiveness at Work* (3rd edn), McGraw-Hill.

■ Bishop, S. (2000) *Develop Your Assertiveness* (2nd edn), Kogan Page.

■ Clegg, B. (2000) *Instant Stress Management*, Kogan Page.

■ Kellaway, L. (2000) *Sense and Nonsense in the Office*, Financial Times Prentice Hall. A strictly non-academic book that could arm you with a healthy degree of cynicism about what you will meet on your course.

■ Lifeskills International (1999) *Staying Healthy at Work*, Gower. This addresses stress, physical health, interpersonal relations and lifestyle planning.

■ Neenan, M. and Dryden, W. (2004) *Cognitive Therapy: 100 Key Points and Techniques*, Routledge.

5

Personal management skills

- Roberts, B. (1999) *Working Memory: Improving Your Memory for the Workplace*, London House.
- Thompson, G. (2005) *Stress Buster*, Summersdale Publishers.
- http://www.cipd.co.uk/subjects/health/stress/stress.htm
  For a good overview of stress in the workplace.

If you have time and wish to read for more general awareness raising, starting to develop your mental fitness and preparing for the finance part of your programme (if this is the part that terrifies you), the following are recommended.

- *The Economist.*
- *Financial Times.*
- The 'business pages' of any quality newspaper.
- Butler, G. and Hope, T. (1995) *Manage your Mind: The Mental Fitness Guide*, Oxford University Press.
  This covers stress, study skills and memory.
- Cramer, S. (2000) *The Ultimate Business Library: 75 Books That Made Management*, Capstone.
- Drucker, P.F. – just about any of his books!
- Gibson, R. (ed.) (1998) *Rethinking the Future*, Nicholas Brealey.
  A set of highly accessible contributions 'from today's most highly regarded thinkers' – which will provide a good preview of a range of issues and 'names' that you are likely to encounter in your course.
- Glynn, J.J., Murphy, M.P. and Perrin, J. (1998) *Accounting for Managers* (2nd edn), International Thomson Business Press.
- Greising, D. (1998) *I'd like the World to Buy a Coke. The Life and Leadership of Roberto Gorzueta*, Wiley.
- Handy, C. (1999) *Inside Organisations*, Penguin.
  Plus any other of his management books.
- Huczinski, A. (1996) *Management Gurus. What Makes Them and How to Become One*, International Thomson Business Press.
- Israel, R., Whitten, H. and Shaffran, C. (2000) *Your Mind at Work: Developing Self Knowledge for Business Success*, Kogan Page.
  This includes some excellent examples of diagrams relevant to Chapter 10, as well as material useful in preparation.
- Kakabadse, A., Ludlow, R. and Vinnicombe, S. (1987) *Working in Organisations*, Penguin.
- Kind, J. (1999) *Accounting and Finance for Managers*, Kogan Page.
- Nutz, K. and Freiberg, J. (1997) *Southwest Airlines Crazy Recipe for Business and Personal Success*, Orion Business Books.
- Pizzey, A. (1998) *Finance and Accounting for Non-Specialist Students*, Financial Times Pitman Publishing.
- Stutely, R. (2003) *The Definitive Guide to Managing the Numbers*, Pearson.
  Useful information on spreadsheets and finance for those who are worried about this part of a programme.

HELPFILE 5.1
Edit and format commands

If you are not comfortable with anything other than basic typing, the following is a rapid and very basic introduction to what you can easily do. In what follows, I have described what works in most versions of Microsoft Word. If using something different, you will still be able to find out what it is useful to do, and ask someone for the appropriate commands. If you click on 'Edit' on the toolbar (usually at the top of your screen), you will see a list of options, some dark (active), some light. To perform that command, either press the key combination shown (e.g. 'Ctrl' + 'z', i.e. both 'Ctrl' and 'z' keys pressed at once), or press your left mouse button (called 'left click' hereafter) while the cursor (the thing that moves when you move the mouse) is over that command. To activate the pale items you need to select some text for them to operate on. Thus, if you want to copy something, you first need to select what to copy. To do this, put the cursor at the start of the text you want to select, and hold down the left mouse button while you move the cursor to the end of the text. This should black it out. Then 'Edit' as appropriate. Experiment with what you can do.

Beware of hitting either 'Enter' or 'Del' when text is highlighted. It will all be deleted. To undo the selection, you need to mvoe the cursor to another part of the document with the mouse unclicked, and then left click. The black should vanish. Although mistakenly deleting without noticing you have done it is a disaster, the text can be easily retrieved if you realise it by pressing 'Ctrl' + 'z'. These two keys combined have the miraculous power of undoing the deletion. Even better, if you keep pressing them they will undo the deletion before that, and the one before that. . .

Undoing is probably the most useful thing to be able to do. Cutting and pasting is next. Select text as above. If you want to select a whole document, 'Ctrl' + 'a' does this much more quickly than scrolling down with the mouse. Then 'Cut' using 'Ctrl' + 'x' or the menu on the toolbar. This puts all the text on to the machine's clipboard, where it waits until you decide what to do with it (provided you do not exit the program first). Then move the cursor to the point at which you want the text to appear, and press 'Ctrl' + 'v'. The text is pasted into the document at that point. You can select text from e-mails, or from materials found on the Internet in this way, and paste into reports you are writing. 'Ctrl' + 'c' will copy rather than cut, but remember to delete the text from its original position, either while it is still highlighted, but on the clipboard (the quicker method), or after it has appeared in the desired position (safer?).

Improving appearance

You can easily improve the appearance of a document by the use of appropriate formatting (see the format key on the toolbar for options). To have these options always visible and easily available ensure that you have your formatting subsidiary toolbar switched on. (Go to 'View' on the main toolbar, and left click. Put the cursor over 'Toolbars' on the menu that drops down, and left click again. Then click on 'Formatting' if it does not have a tick against it. The toolbar should then appear, and next time you look at the Toolbars menu it will have a tick beside it. To remove, go through exactly the same process (or click on the 'X' button to the top right of the toolbar which will close it, in the same way that clicking on the 'X' will close any window).)

Use the formatting bar to alter the size of highlighted text, or of the whole document by selecting before you start. The standard is 10, but is rather small for many purposes. You may also want to use a larger font for headings, and larger too for a title. To alter this, move the cursor to the arrow beside the number on the bar, left click for menu, and left click again on the number you prefer. This will change the size of everything you type from wherever you left the cursor in the text, or of the text which is highlighted. To switch back, select the original font. As well as changing font size, you may find it a help to use a different font. A huge variety is on offer – Times and Arial are most common. Arial has the virtue of being clearer if a document is to be read electronically. The current font will be shown on the formatting toolbar, again left click on the arrow beside it for options, click on one to select, and see whether you like it!

Another useful formatting device is paragraph spacing and indentation – you click on 'Format' on the main toolbar and then 'Paragraph', or hold the cursor over the interesting symbols on the formatting toolbar to see what they mean. It can improve appearance to introduce a small space between paragraphs (it is obvious how to do this from the paragraph options). You can also indent selected portions of text, or indent first lines of paragraphs, or create a 'hanging indent', where the first line is aligned with the rest of the text, but subsequent lines in that paragraph are indented. Again, experiment with the appearance these formats create.

'B', 'I' and 'u' allow you to embolden, italicise or underline selected text in a similar fashion. Highlighting text and then clicking on the picture of a pen with a yellow line will highlight selected text (useful in notes). You can change the colour of the highlight by clicking on the arrow. And you can change the colour of the text itself by clicking on the A with a coloured underline for that colour, or the arrow beside it to change the alternative colour.

Filing documents

Think carefully about how you want to organise your files. It is best to design a structure of folders so that things are easy to find – for example you might want a folder for each course on your programme, another for 'personal development' in which you keep your personal development file and associated logs and plans. Within your dissertation folder you might want sub-folders for notes on relevant references, interview data, correspondence or whatever. In addition to a good file structure, you need to think about giving each file a clear title, so that you will be able to find it months later. (When you open a new blank file, use 'File', 'Save as' to indicate the title you want, as well as the folder in which you want to store it. To create a new folder, click on the symbol on the toolbar at the top of the window which opens when you click 'Save as', once you have clicked on the major folder within which you want the new folder to appear. Time spent thinking carefully about file structure will save time later.)

Other useful tools

Spelling and grammar checks are extremely useful. When you are typing you will find a red wavy underline if the machine doesn't like your spelling. This may be because it prefers US spellings, or does not know the word you want (it may be a name, or an uncommon word). But often the machine is right! Green wavy underline is a grammar warning. Check in either case that you are correct. To spell check a completed document, go to 'Tools' then 'Check spelling and grammar'. This will highlight the first dubious instance. Correct (it will suggest options) or click on 'Ignore'. It will then move to the next dubious word.

You may be writing to a word limit, in which case the automatic word count is useful ('Tools', then 'Wordcount').

Pagination is also useful if a document is to be presented in hard copy ('Insert' on toolbar, then 'Page numbers').

Drawing diagrams

There are many sophisticated diagramming packages, but you may like to start, if you are unfamiliar with them, with the basic drawing facility Microsoft Word offers. (Go back to 'View', 'Toolbars' and check that 'Drawing' is ticked. Click on it if not.) As with editing, some commands require something to work on. So create a rectangle. Make some space in a document, put the cursor in the space, left click on the picture of a rectangle on the toolbar to get 'Create your drawing here', and then click within the outlined space to get a square. This will have nice little circles at corners and mid-points. When the cursor is over one of these you get a double-headed arrow. Hold the left mouse key down and move the mouse to change the shape and size (experiment). Corner points allow two sides to move at once. Mid-points allow you to move just one line. Holding the cursor in the middle (crossed double-headed arrows) allows you to move the entire diagram. You can do the same with the oval symbol to draw circles and ellipses. If these are boring, click on the arrow by 'Autoshapes' and choose a cloud, or something else more interesting.

To colour an outline, use the symbol which looks like a highlighter. To fill in with another colour, use the button with a colour and a square arrow as symbol (hold the cursor over it to check that it means fill colour). As with text, you can change the colours used.

To create a duplicate shape, select the object (i.e. left click within it) and then press 'Ctrl' + 'D'. The duplicate can then be moved to wherever you want it. To delete any shape, first select it then press 'Del'.

You will frequently need to join shapes by arrows, and will see line and arrow keys on the toolbar. Draw two squares, and separate them. Then click on the arrow key. Move the cursor to a point on one rectangle, then drag (i.e. move the mouse while left-clicking) to the other. Release the button when you get there. You need to get the crossed arrows exactly centred on your desired start and end points. If a simple arrow is boring, go to 'Autoshapes', 'Block arrows' for variants. You can duplicate arrows in the same way as other shapes. And rotate them by clicking on the arrow beside 'Draw' for options. Again, experiment.

The other thing you need to incorporate is text. Create the shape you want, click on the text box (text, in a box) button, and then insert text.

Once you are happy with the above commands, you can amuse yourself in quiet moments at work by finding what diagrams you can induce your machine to produce.

→ Ch 16 PowerPoint (*see* Chapter 16) can produce more sophisticated diagrams, so many students prefer to cut and paste diagrams prepared in PowerPoint into their reports.

→ Ch 13 Graphs, bar and pie charts can easily be drawn from spreadsheets (*see* Chapter 13).

Answers to Exercise 5.1

(a) aggression

(b) avoidance

(c) assertion

(d) avoidance

(e) assertion

(f) aggression

(g) avoidance

(h) assertion

(i) assertion

→ 6 Time management at work

Learning outcomes

By the end of this chapter you should:

- know the principles of good time management
- have identified key objectives of your job
- be allocating your time according to established priorities
- be directing your efforts towards the efficient achievement of your objectives
- have reduced ineffective use of your time by others
- be monitoring your time use and adjusting plans accordingly.

INTRODUCTION

If you are aiming to study while working you will almost certainly need to improve your time management if work is not to spill over into time you need to protect for study. Similar skills will help you make effective use of study time. Many managers work extremely long hours. Chapter 4 should have shown you how much working time *you* need to free for study. Read the relevant part now if you skipped it earlier.

→ Ch 4

'Eight out of ten managers work late at the office and 47 per cent take work home', according to a 20-year-old survey by Philips Dictation Systems. 'Very few were prepared to say "no" to their bosses about taking on extra work', says the survey. 'Taking work home and working late at the office are symptomatic of the late 1980s culture . . . these practices are unnecessary and caused by poor time management, failure to set priorities, setting unrealistic targets – or all three.' Thus spoke *Personnel Management* in January 1989 (p. 9). Evidence from my own students suggests that managerial workloads have actually *increased* in the 20 years since then.

You might wish to argue about whether bringing work home *is* a sign of poor time management, but it is fairly incompatible with part-time study. If you regularly work late, and/or bring work home, then you will probably need to change your habits or abandon thoughts of a qualification by this route.

If you have by now successfully negotiated a reduction in workload, all may be well. But if this was not possible, either because your employer was unsympathetic, or because fear of the effect of raising the subject on your job prospects kept you silent, you will need another solution.

This may well lie in learning how to achieve the same results in less time, by becoming more efficient. Someone recently told me that the most valuable benefit of his own part-time MBA did not stem from the course content, useful though this had been. Far more significant was the fact that combining study with work had *forced* him to practise good time management. By the end of his course the habits were so well established that they remained, and he continued working far more effectively than had been the case prior to his course.

This chapter will tell you little that you do not know already – you are probably well aware of ways in which you *could* make better use of your time. The problem is that breaking old habits and establishing new ones is not easy, as you will know if you have ever tried to stop smoking, overeating or drinking too much, or to substitute running for watching television. (I met someone on a time management course a few years back who often attended such courses. He claimed he needed 'booster shots' at regular intervals! One is put in mind of the man who was 'an expert on giving up smoking' – having done it so many times.)

If you want to do something badly enough, it can usually be achieved. Your previous analysis should have established the need. This section will provide a framework for starting to change your habits now that the need to do so is more pressing. Nothing can make the process *easy*. New ways of working will inevitably be uncomfortable at first. You can expect a difficult period while you are consciously trying to do things differently, perhaps to the surprise or resentment of colleagues. But the difficulty will be temporary, and eventually you will wonder why you ever functioned in your old

→ Ch 5   fashion. Assertiveness skills (developed in Chapter 5) will be an essential component.

You are more likely to achieve significant change to your ways of working if you can work on this chapter with a small number of colleagues. This will bring the experience much closer to that of going on a short course, and will considerably strengthen your motivation to do the necessary work. It will also provide you with a wider range of ideas, and improve your colleagues' performance as well as your own. You may find that you can talk your employer into regarding the exercise as an in-house course, allowing you to get together during working time.

This chapter requires you to carry out a series of activities. Merely reading is not enough. The answers to the activities will often be fairly lengthy, so you may find it helpful to start a time management section in your file for your work on the topic. Proformas are available on the **website**.

BASIC TIME MANAGEMENT PRINCIPLES

As I said, the principles of time management are simple and make good sense. But this does not make it easy to change ingrained habits and start putting these principles into practice!

Guidelines for good time management

- Direct your effort *appropriately*, i.e. towards the things that are most important.
- Direct your effort *efficiently*, i.e. maximise your achievements for time and energy expended.
- Stop *wasting* time.

To achieve the above, you will need a continual awareness of time as a scarce and non-renewable resource. It is necessary to plan all your use of time, and to monitor this usage on a continuing basis to ensure that bad habits are not creeping back.

ACTIVITY 6.1

Start your time management file by thinking about your last full working week, and writing down answers to the following questions below or use the electronic version on the **website**:

- Were you absolutely clear what objectives you were trying to achieve? _____
- To what extent did you achieve them? _____
- How many hours did you work? _____
- How many of these hours were directly spent on work towards your objectives?

  _____

- What proportion of your desk surface was clear when you arrived at work each morning? _____

  _____

- Of the time directed towards objectives, how much was spent working as effectively as possible? _____

- What prevented full efficiency? _____

  _____

  _____

- How often were you working on something when you knew there was something more important that should have been tackled? _____

In addition to the above, think about how your time was divided, and write down estimates of the percentage of your working time devoted to different activities:

Reading _____ Writing _____

Formal meetings _____ Informal meetings _____

Travelling _____ On the phone _____

Other activities _____

_____

(add all those which are relevant to your job).

Direct your effort more appropriately:

- understand why you overcommit
- plan more effectively
- concentrate on important work
- delegate
- do things 'well enough'
- stop doing unimportant things.

Directing your effort appropriately

To direct your effort appropriately, you need to allocate your time according to the importance of the different tasks facing you. Spend more time on those crucial for success, less on those which are less significant, and none on work that is unnecessary. This may sound obvious, but it is surprising how often some managers work on low-priority jobs (perhaps because they are ones they like doing) while a high-priority job is waiting. They may supervise subordinates far more closely than is necessary, or indeed desirable, or do work themselves which could be delegated. They may aim at perfection when something far less would be 'good enough'. They may read documents in close detail when a quick scan would suffice, or spend hours composing an e-mail. Another inappropriate use of effort is to take on more work when you are already fully committed.

ACTIVITY 6.2

Identify your own key job areas. Think about your job, and list up to seven key objectives. If you find this difficult, refer to your job description, and discuss it with your boss. Your last appraisal report might also be helpful. For each objective identify the tasks needed to achieve it. These may be ongoing or one-offs. Place your list of objectives and tasks somewhere convenient for easy reference – in your desk diary, in your newly formed time management log, or on the wall. You will need it for future reference.

ACTIVITY 6.3

Identify your current misdirections. Look back at your answers to the previous activities, and think about your time usage in relation to the objectives you have just identified as important. List those aspects of your own behaviour which contribute most strongly to misuse of time.

_____

_____

Remedial action if you suspect misdirection of your effort

The action needed will depend on what you have identified as your most pressing faults, but some or all of the following will probably be helpful:

- **Plan your time.** When you next get to work, and daily thereafter, review your key objectives, and think about how you can best use the next working day to achieve progress towards these. It will be necessary to allow time for such routine as is inevitable, and to plan a margin for the unexpected, but aim to make some progress towards at least some key objectives each day. When you do your planning depends on your job and your preference. Many managers find it helpful to spend 15 minutes or so at the *end* of each day, reviewing progress and planning the next day's work, so that they arrive at work with a clear idea of what they will be doing. Indeed, they may find it helpful to leave themselves a note of this on their desks. Others find early morning, before they have read the post, better. Others use travelling time. Palmtop computers make it very easy to set, review and revise objectives no matter where you are. Experiment to find the time of day that makes it easiest to build this planning session into your daily routine, and then do it regularly.

Managers commonly underestimate the time required for task completion. This often stems from a genuine and confident belief that *this* task will proceed without the delays and other glitches experienced in the past with similar work. This type of optimism is typical of poor time managers. If you suspect yourself of this fallacy, log your estimates for tasks, and the actual time taken. The stark evidence of a mismatch may help you improve your estimating.

■ **Delegate more.** Delegation requires an initial time investment in training your subordinate(s). Perhaps even more of a hurdle, it requires absolute clarity on your part as to the objectives of the work, a reasonable final deadline, and suitable points at which progress should be reviewed. All this must be clearly communicated to the person who is to do the work, together with an idea of how the work relates to other departmental work and objectives. This understanding of the context in which the work is required will make the job far more meaningful for the subordinate, and will make it likely that any discretion needed will be exercised in an appropriate way.

'Busy' managers often cannot find the time to develop their subordinates. They do not *think* clearly enough about what is required for successful completion of a piece of work, let alone communicate this to the subordinate. As a result, the work is poorly done; the subordinate learns nothing; and the manager's view that 'It's quicker to do it myself', or even 'I'm the only one who can do it properly', is reinforced.

ACTIVITY 6.4

Within the next week, identify at least three areas of work which could be delegated. Plan any staff development necessary for this delegation to be successful, and take steps to set this in motion. Once it is complete, start to delegate work. Ensure that objectives are understood, and agree targets and review points. Leave the subordinate to get on with it between reviews. Log plans and progress in your file, and put a note in your diary for six weeks hence to review the success with which you are delegating.

■ **Understand why you overcommit.** We nearly always connive at our own overload by agreeing to do more than is reasonable. Perhaps, as suggested above, we underestimate either imminent demands from our current workload, or the requirements of the new task. (This underestimation is so common as to have earned the title 'planning fallacy'.) Or we may be insecure, feel afraid of being left out, and want to prove that we are essential to the organisation. Being busy, and involved in everything, reduces this anxiety. Sometimes the new task may simply have looked too interesting to refuse. If there is a culture within the organisation of saying 'yes' to every piece of work assigned, agreeing to overcommitment avoids adverse notice. Or sometimes it may be that non-working life offers few rewards, and working long hours is preferable to facing the demands of the family, or being alone.

Whatever the reasons, overcommitment is seldom a solution. It can lead to high levels of stress, which may be physically damaging. Chronic fatigue leads to less efficient, low-quality work and missed deadlines. This negates many of the reasons for taking on the work in the first place!

ACTIVITY 6.5

Identify the reasons for your own overcommitment, and make a private note of any personal weaknesses they reveal. For each of these, think of at least one step which you could take in the near future to improve the situation. Decide when you will act, note review dates in your diary, and log progress in your file.

→ Ch 5

■ **Practise saying 'no'.** Assertiveness skills, as discussed in Chapter 5, are necessary for many of the remedial actions listed in this chapter. They are of particular importance here. You need to know what is reasonable, and to accept that you have a right to this. You then need to be able to persist calmly, and with explanations, in asserting your rights. Calmness and persistence are likely to succeed where anger and defensiveness will not. If you do wish to accept an interesting new assignment, then you will need at the same time to say 'no' to some of your existing work, i.e. negotiate a reduction in existing load.

ACTIVITY 6.6

From now on keep a record of all new tasks which you are asked to do. Try to refuse them unless you are not currently fully occupied or they are accompanied by a reduction in existing work. Set a suitable review date in your diary to assess progress in this.

■ **Renounce perfection.** Much of our early training encouraged thoroughness, and doing things as well as is possible. As a result, you may feel dissatisfied with anything less. Sometimes it is essential to achieve a result as close to perfect as you can manage, but there are many more times when this is totally unnecessary. Brief minutes of a meeting, noting action points and not much more may actually achieve more than something approaching a verbatim record, and will save other people's time, as well as your own. Current definitions of quality emphasise fitness for purpose, and it is worth heeding this.

ACTIVITY 6.7

Think of the last four pieces of work that you completed. Consider whether a lower standard would have been equally effective. If so, identify what was unnecessary. Was there excessive detail, or better presentation than is strictly required? Set review dates in your diary at monthly intervals to assess your progress away from unnecessary perfection, and log progress.

Do be careful in the above to preserve the *necessary* perfections. You must, for example, be fully prepared before conducting a disciplinary or appraisal interview, and cannot afford to skimp if you are drawing up a project contract, or entering into negotiations with a trade union!

- **Stop doing things.** Think carefully about how you described your use of time in the previous activities, particularly about the way in which you spend the largest fractions of your time, and those jobs which are routine. How many jobs could be omitted without disaster? Are you filing things which you will never need to refer to again? Are you routinely circulated with, and reading, materials from which you gain little? Are you attending meetings at which your presence contributes little? It is all too easy to accept demands on your time, particularly those which are part of the accepted routine, without ever questioning their necessity.

ACTIVITY 6.8

During the next month check at the start of each activity whether it is really necessary. Omit it if not. And take steps to avoid ever doing it in the future. Ask your secretary to bin some types of material directly, or to remove your name from mailing lists. Withdraw from working groups or regular meetings, and so on. List any activities you already know to be unnecessary, and add to the list as the month goes on.

_____

_____

Make your effort more effective:

- organise your working space
- organise your computer files
- avoid procrastination
- use prime time for prime jobs
- clarify objectives
- set deadlines
- do one thing at a time.

Effective effort

Once you are sure that you are directing your efforts towards the right things, you need to work at making those efforts as effective as possible. One common problem is procrastination, leading to effort being wasted worrying about what things you have to do, rather than actually getting on with it. Another is lack of organisation: time is wasted looking for things, important deadlines may be missed, or delays caused by failure to do preparatory activities. You will not work effectively when you are tired, or if you are frequently interrupted. Trying to do two things at once is another common problem.

ACTIVITY 6.9

List six factors which you feel contribute most to your own reduced efficiency at work.

1 _____   4 _____

2 _____   5 _____

3 _____   6 _____

Remedial action if your efforts are not fully effective

Again, the remedial action you take will depend on your particular weaknesses, but it is likely to include at least some of the following.

- **Organise your working space.** It is extremely hard to concentrate when surrounded by a mess, so aim to keep your desk and floor clear. A simple but effective system for this is to use files for 'Do today', 'Do this week', 'Awaiting information' and (if files are hard copy) 'Out'. You will also need a system for keeping together all documents and notes you are ever likely to need when working on each of your key job areas. (Electronic 'clutter', while less obvious to the casual observer, may be as great a threat to your effectiveness as physical disorder: pay as much attention to your virtual working space as to more concrete aspects.)

  The system you choose is unimportant. That you *have* a system is vital. And a major component in any system will be your wastepaper baskets, real and virtual. If you are not sure where to put something, put it in the bin. If it does not need action, and does not relate to a key area of your job, you probably do not need it. If you are daunted by the magnitude of the task of organising yourself (and I can sympathise – recently someone who uses the same 'horizontal' filing system as I favour gave me a beautiful sign for my wall which read, in magnificent gothic script, 'A tidy floor is a sign of a sick mind'), then enlist the help of a good secretary or personal assistant. (Secretaries usually understand the principles of filing, whether paper or electronic, far better than managers.) Once you *are* organised, you may be pleasantly surprised by the time you save by instant access to the information that you need, and how much better you feel, working at a clear desk.

- **Stop devoting effort to *not* doing things.** As my grandmother was irritatingly fond of pointing out, 'Procrastination is the thief of time'. Certainly it uses an enormous amount of energy, not only in thinking of reasons for not starting a piece of work and finding alternative activities, but in coping with the feeling of doom and oppression induced by work hanging over you. Even work which has been put off for excellent reasons can absorb effort, particularly if you keep thinking about it while working on something else. To avoid this, you need to decide when you *will* start the work, note this in your diary or work planner, put it in the appropriate file, and then forget about it until the scheduled time. The simple act of 'booking work in' to some future date makes it much easier not to worry about it in the meantime, as well as easier to start it when the scheduled time arrives. David Allen (2001) has made a substantial fortune largely out of this simple principle.

Procrastination is usually associated with tasks which are either distasteful for some reason, or so big as to be rather frightening. If a task is one you are *not* looking forward to, it can help to supplement the 'booking in' by scheduling a reward for tackling it. You could arrange lunch with a congenial colleague on the day you have set aside for budgets, or a trip to a part of the organisation you enjoy visiting on completion of a major report, or even a stiff whisky after work when you have done that disciplinary interview (provided you are using public transport).

For large tasks, a 'divide and conquer' approach may be effective. Split the larger task into sub-tasks which are more manageable, set deadlines for these, and book them in individually. You will see that this is the approach recommended in a later chapter for your thesis. One of the pioneering organisations in training managers in this area, Time Manager International, classifies such jobs as 'elephant' jobs, using the splendidly graphic, albeit distasteful, image of eating an elephant. This would be impossible to achieve at a single sitting, but might eventually be accomplished if you sat down to a plateful each day.

Indeed, there is considerable value in tackling some part of larger jobs on an almost daily basis. The anticipation is usually far worse than the reality, and increases as time passes, until resistance to the work may become so great that 'booking in' is no longer sufficient remedy. Even a small amount of work each day or two will prevent the build-up of this negative anticipation.

Another form of 'not working' which can be a drain on energy is 'not working at home', i.e. taking work home and then not doing it. This can cast a blight over the entire evening or weekend. You will have enough study to do at home, so should get out of the 'taking work home' habit *now*. If extreme circumstances force you to break this rule, 'book in' the work to a specified time slot in the evening or weekend, and do your best to forget it for the remaining time.

■ **Use prime time for prime jobs**. All time is not equal. The time between 7.00 am and 8.00 am is likely to have a *different value* from, say, that between 2.00 pm and 3.00 pm, and that between 11.00 pm and midnight. We all have daily biorhythms: alertness and energy levels fluctuate throughout the 24 hours with individual patterns varying considerably.

The value of the 'time that you have' thus depends upon *when* you have it. You may be able to increase its value by identifying your 'good' times and rescheduling to take advantage of these. You may already be aware of your own good times – I know that mine are early morning and late afternoon. (If you have not yet identified your own rhythms, you might like to jot down at regular intervals how alert you are feeling, and how well you think you would be able to cope with study at that particular time.) For many managers there is a tiredness factor building up as the day goes on, and superimposed upon these rhythms.

It is not good use of your prime time to fritter it away on routine activities. These should be reserved (if they cannot be omitted altogether) for times when you are less effective. In planning your work, schedule demanding work for your personal 'prime time', even if this means saving all but the most urgent items in your in-tray until after lunch. Block this time out in your diary, ignore your e-mail, close your door and redirect phone calls in order to make best use of this valuable time.

6

Time management at work

→ Ch 5

ACTIVITY 6.10

Unless your work on Chapter 4 allowed you to identify your own prime times, do this now. During the next two weeks note down all times at which you have a feeling of working really well, and those when you seem to be minimally effective. From this identify your own 'prime times'.

- **Make sure that you know what you are meant to be doing.** If you are at all unclear about the objectives of any activity, it is highly likely that you will waste effort. If you are writing something, you need a clear idea of who will read it, and exactly what you wish to communicate. When you ask a subordinate to come and see you, it is essential to work out what you want to achieve by the meeting, and to jot down beforehand the points that you wish to cover. If you are making a phone call, a similar checklist should be made, and unless developing your relationship with the person called is one of your objectives, extraneous conversation should be curtailed.

  It is essential to spend time at the start of each task thinking about your objectives, and how best to achieve them. This will enable you to plan all the resources that you need, thus saving considerable time later. You can also save time by thinking *around* the task, about the possible effects of other factors upon it, and the implications of the likely outcome of the task itself. Planning for these at the outset can reduce the chances of this job creating further work later on.

- **Work to deadlines**. Deadlines tend to concentrate the mind wonderfully and to focus effort. You will find out how necessary they are in your studies, as well as in your job. Harness this effect by creating your own deadlines for tasks that do not already have them, and interim deadlines for tasks with a long time-span. Treat these deadlines as *real*. They will indeed *be* real, as your time planning and 'booking in' systems will disintegrate if work spills over into time allowed for other activities. Your deadlines may need to be in advance of external deadlines on some pieces of work, in order to balance workload. Few managers can write four major reports in a single week, for example. In such cases your personal deadline will be more important than the external one: if you fail to meet the first, you are likely to miss the second. You must, therefore, resist any temptation to see the more distant external deadline as a reason for taking your own shorter-term deadline less seriously.

- **Work on one thing at a time, aiming to finish it.** Too often a feeling of being rushed makes us flit from one job to another without finishing any, or to work on more than one thing at once – for example, trying to write e-mails while on the phone. Split attention is tiring, and almost never effective. Discipline yourself to concentrate on one thing at a time. It is a good idea to keep a notebook to hand, so that any ideas about other jobs, which surface while you are working on something else, are not lost. This will help you resist the temptation to drop what you are on and start working on the job to which the idea relates. You will know that you can ignore the idea until the end of the present job without losing it.

■ **Write 'morning pages'.** The above are all fairly obvious and logical remedies, but if they are not working there is one, possibly less logical approach you may wish to try. It is the technique devised by Julia Cameron as an aid to creativity (Bryan, Cameron and Allen, 1998) and subsequently applied to the work context. It is very simple. Every morning you wake a little earlier and write (longhand) three A4 pages continuously. Just keep writing, putting down anything that occurs to you. It doesn't matter what. Thoughts about work (or anything else), to-do lists or whatever. It is *intended* to be messy, disorganised, chaotic. Do not stop to think. Do not re-read. Do not show to anyone else. When you have finished, put them to one side. Do not re-read them. Or not for now. You may want, much later, to revisit them and look for patterns, or progress, but not for some months.

It is claimed (and it works for me) that the act of writing creates a safe psychological space, and starts a process of reordering: goals and aspirations emerge from the chaos, you will find that you get more done, are more focused, and although writing these pages takes time (20–40 minutes at first, though you will speed up with practice) it also *creates* time at work, and frees up a great deal of energy. The result is not instant, but should be felt within a matter of weeks. If you have time before your course starts, this technique is something well worth experimenting with. (It has the added bonus of giving writing practice, so that you will answer exam questions much more fluently!)

Reduce time wastage

Many managers act as if everyone else has more right to their time than they have themselves. Keep reminding yourself that your working time is *yours*. It is your scarcest resource, and the responsibility for its effective use lies with you. You should not allow others to cause you to use your time in non-productive ways. It will make a nonsense of your time planning, and considerably reduce your effectiveness. Meetings may be one of the greatest thieves of your time. It is a salutary experience while sitting in a meeting to calculate the cost of that meeting, and consider whether it will achieve enough to justify this. If your mind is wandering sufficiently to do this calculation, the chances are that your contribution is not justified, for a start! I heard of one organisation which had a special clock for meetings. When the number and status of participants were entered, the clock showed not the time, but the cost of the meeting so far. Apparently meetings became much shorter following its introduction.

Reduce time wastage:

■ cut down on meetings

■ keep control of your diary

■ reduce interruptions

■ shorten informal meetings.

Another source of 'stolen' time is casual conversation with people who drop in, or are encountered when you are on your way somewhere. Such informal communication can be invaluable, a part of the networking that tends to be associated with management success, or a way of showing that you value team members as individuals. But you need to ensure that only productive conversations intrude on your time. If very busy you may need to curtail even these.

ACTIVITY 6.11

During the next week, without consciously trying to reduce lost time, log all time devoted to activities not contributing to the direct achievement of your key objectives. Identify the major sources of time loss, and plan action to reduce these in future. Log non-productive time for the following fortnight, and file this. Aim for a steady reduction throughout the period. Thereafter, check non-productive time on occasional days, to ensure that you are not slipping back.

Remedial action if time wastage is a problem

Again, you will need to suit the remedy to the disease, but the following prescriptions are available:

■ **Reduce meeting commitments**. For all meetings you chair, think carefully about the objectives of the meeting, and whether the meeting could be run differently to achieve these. Do the objectives justify meeting with this frequency, and for this duration? Is the attendance of all the participants necessary? Although your main effect in this is likely to be saving others' time, there will be some effect on your own as well. For meetings which you do not chair, ask whether your attendance is really necessary. Could someone else represent you, if representation is needed? Could you persuade the chair to schedule meetings less frequently? Are the meetings well run?

For any meeting you attend, you should know well in advance when the meeting will start and finish, its purpose, and what you need to do in order to be prepared to contribute effectively. The meeting should be well chaired, so everyone can make appropriate contributions, and discussion is orderly. Decisions need to be reliably recorded, and someone needs to take the responsibility for ensuring that action is taken to implement decisions. If these conditions are not met, then everyone's time has probably been wasted. You could argue that you have a right to leave a meeting at its stated finish time, and to stay away if papers are not sent to you in advance.

■ **Keep control of your diary**. One common problem is an electronic diary which allows others to have access to your schedule and the *right* to book time in it. You need to find out how you can retain control over your time. While it may be very helpful to others to be able to set up meetings without the need to consult participants, the right to your time should remain with you.

ACTIVITY 6.12

Review your time for the last two weeks and the next two. How much of your time is scheduled for meetings? How reasonable is this?

■ **Reduce interruptions**. It has already been suggested that you protect your 'prime time' from interruptions, but you may also need to cut down the total volume of interruptions. By breaking into your concentration, and requiring you to spend time afterwards picking up the lost threads, interruptions can cost you far more time than their actual duration. Use your secretary as a filter. A good secretary may be able to deal with many of the interruptions, perhaps with a little training, or to direct people to someone who can help them at least as well as you could. If not, your secretary can at least ensure that you are disturbed only during whichever part of the day you have set aside for this.

You will obviously wish to remain accessible to your staff in the case of real problems, so you need to make sure that they do not feel 'distanced' by your change in practice. If they understand *why* you are trying to alter your schedule, this is less likely to happen. If you compensate by encouraging contact at times when it will not be disruptive, such as coffee breaks, or a *short* regular meeting to discuss ongoing concerns, you may even achieve better communication than previously. Perhaps your subordinates could be encouraged to apply the same principles of time management to their own jobs.

Bosses may present a greater problem, but again careful explanation of what you are trying to achieve should go a long way towards bringing about improvements.

■ **Shorten unavoidable interruptions**. You may not wish to go so far as those managers who ostentatiously start an egg-timer when a visitor walks into their office, but you should make sure that those who interrupt you for informal meetings make their objectives clear at the outset. Ask them what it is that they want to talk about, and how much of your time they think they need. If you anticipate a visitor staying longer than you would wish, do not invite them to sit down, and prime your secretary to ring you after, say, five minutes. If you feel that the meeting would be more efficiently conducted if you were better prepared, arrange a time to meet later.

PUTTING PRINCIPLES INTO PRACTICE

The activities in this section should have started you on the route towards improving your time management, but it is essential that you make time *now*, not next week or some time after that, to plan a systematic approach to better practice. Unless you at once set a deadline for completing the planning phases, and commit yourself firmly to meeting that deadline, all that this section will have done for you is to provide something else about which you can procrastinate, and thus constitute a further drain on your energy!

Your plan will depend on the particular weaknesses that you have identified, and upon the demands of your job. Only you know what you need to do, and when you can realistically expect to have done it. Do discuss your plan with someone else if you can. This could be the colleagues who have been working through this chapter with you, your boss or your partner. Such discussion will strengthen your commitment to your plan, and increase the likelihood of your putting it into action.

If you have not done so yet, start a time management file for use at work. This can be electronic, or paper based. You will need a section for each major job objective, with subsections for each task within it. You will also need an overview chart at the start, which can show all the deadlines you are working towards, and review pages for regular completion. These will help you to monitor your time usage, and its effectiveness, using the sorts of points covered in the above discussion. A simple file can be more effective than a specially designed leather portfolio organiser because you

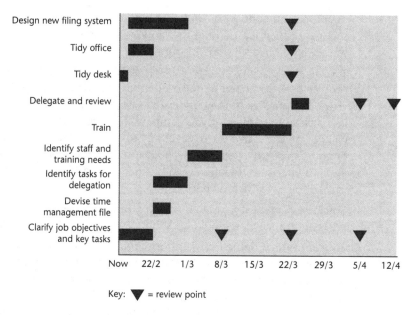

Key: ▼ = review point

Fig. 6.1 Part of one manager's planning process for improving time management

can design its contents and format to suit your particular needs. An electronic organiser is both flexible and portable.

An example of part of one manager's planning process for implementing the principles described is shown in Fig. 6.1.

ACTIVITY 6.13

Drawing on the work you have done in all the other activities, draw up a complete action plan for improving your time management at work. You will probably need about six weeks to implement this fully, but choose a timescale to suit your circumstances. Build in review dates for all planned changes.

Whatever approach you adopt to implementation, it is important that you adopt the following habits:

■ *think* each day, before post, telephone and unscheduled visitors start to intrude upon you, of what it is that you wish to achieve;

■ *check* at some point each day that you are progressing satisfactorily towards deadlines;

■ *review* your time effectiveness at intervals;

■ *alter* future plans or ways of operating if your review shows this to be necessary.

It is also important that you do not become obsessive about time management, and make your subordinates feel that they can no longer look to you for support, or that they have no call on your time. Nor should you miss out entirely on the informal communications that are one of the most valuable sources of information in an organisation, generate some of the social rewards that help make a job enjoyable, build the contacts that you may need in the future and keep people loyal to the organisation. In planning your strategy you should value these factors, and make sure that you find a way of retaining them. Remember, time management is an aid to better **management**, not an end in itself.

SUMMARY

- Time is a scarce resource which must be managed.
- All time must be planned for, and effectiveness of time usage monitored.
- Improving your time management means breaking ingrained working habits, both your own and your colleagues'.
- It therefore requires considerable discipline, a plan devised to help you make necessary changes, and frequent reviews to assess progress.
- Working with others to develop your time management skills can generate better ideas, and sustain motivation.
- Time management depends on three key elements:
  - effort needs to be directed *appropriately*
  - effort needs to be directed *efficiently*
  - time-wasters must be eliminated.
- Action needed is likely to include clarifying objectives, setting and meeting deadlines, planning to use your best time for your most demanding work, controlling interruptions, organising office, desk and diary, delegating more and avoiding needless perfection.
- A secretary can be a great asset in helping you manage your time better.
- Assertiveness skills are important for effective time management.
- It is important to start improving your time management *now*, and to monitor your progress continually.

Further information

- Allen, D. (2001) *Getting Things Done*, Piatkus
- Bird, P. (1998) *Teach Yourself Time Management*, Hodder & Stoughton.
- Bryan, M., Cameron, J. and Allen, C. (1998) *An Artist's Way at Work: Twelve Weeks to Creative Freedom*, Pan.
- Caunt, J. (2000) *Organise Yourself*, Kogan Page.
- Clegg, B. (1999) *Instant Time Management*, Kogan Page.
- Forster, M. (2006) *Do It Tomorrow: and Other Secrets of Time Management*, Hodder and Stoughton.

6

Time management at work

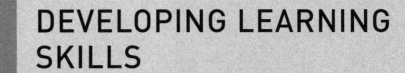

DEVELOPING LEARNING SKILLS

→ 7 Effective learning and reflective practice

Learning outcomes

By the end of this chapter you should:

- have considered the practicalities of study
- be able to develop a study plan
- appreciate the importance of developing good study habits
- know how to use breaks, etc. to increase the efficiency with which you study
- have developed techniques for focusing your study of a set of materials, and for learning more effectively.

INTRODUCTION

Despite your improved time management skills, time is likely to be your scarcest resource. It is important to think about how to use it to best effect. There are two aspects to this. The first concerns very practical considerations of when and where to study, and how to develop a study plan. This may seem absurdly basic, but such issues can have a significant impact on the effectiveness of your study. Careful planning may make the whole process far easier than it might otherwise be.

It is also important to think about what is meant by 'learning' in a management context. This chapter introduces different sorts of learning that may be important to managers, and appropriate study techniques for each. In the next chapter ideas about management learning are developed further, and some relevant theory is introduced.

Taken together, the two chapters should help you to become a much more effective learner both on your course and in your job. The advantage for your studies is obvious, but developing your learning skills may have an even more significant impact upon your whole career.

FINDING A PLACE

If study can become a regular habit, you will find the process relatively easy. But if each study session involves prolonged debate with yourself as to whether you work now or later, and where to do it, enormous amounts of energy can be wasted before you even *begin* to achieve anything. Have you have ever sat down in front of your books, got up to do something, sat down again, decided to move elsewhere, decided that some books you need are back where you were to begin with, and then decided that the whole thing would be better left until tomorrow? If so, you need to develop your study habits! Otherwise you will often find that an hour or more has passed, leaving you frustrated and exhausted, and having achieved nothing.

A study location needs:
- peace and quiet
- storage facilities
- comfort for reading and PC use.

The first step towards making study a habit, if possible, is to establish a habit of place. This is something which you can usefully do as part of your preparation, prior to the course start. For part-time students in particular, there are obvious practical advantages to having a place devoted to study. You will be accumulating a significant volume of materials, and will be working on substantial assignments that may take weeks to complete. You need to be able to store your materials and your 'work in progress' in an organised fashion, readily accessible so that you do not need to spend time searching for, or shuffling through, heaps of books and papers. Work materials need to be safe from the attentions of dogs, cats, children and cleaners. Unless you are wireless, for on-line work you will need a phone point near your PC. The place needs to be one in which you can work without being subjected to too many distractions. As you will be spending a lot of time reading and at a PC, ergonomic considerations are important. Check that you have adequate lighting for reading and PC work, that chairs are the right height for you, and that screen and keyboard are in the right positions to avoid eye and wrist strain.

The ideal is a room of your own, used exclusively for studying, and with the layout designed for your particular requirements. If, however, such exclusivity is impossible, time separation can be a good second best. Provided your study time does not overlap with other usage, and there is a cupboard or something similar for easy storage of materials, a kitchen or dining room can work perfectly well.

Some students prefer to study in their office, provided they have access outside normal working time. An hour before everyone else arrives can be excellent study time. Others have found more creative solutions, using garden sheds, spare rooms in friends' houses, and even in one case adapting the back of their van and working in the office car park for an hour or two early in the morning and again through their lunch hour.

Pin your study plan to the wall where you can see it from your desk (study plans will be discussed shortly). This will enable you to check your progress easily. If no suitable wallspace is available, keep a copy in the front of your working file. Either way, make sure that you can check the plan regularly.

ACTIVITY 7.1

Spend 15 minutes designing your ideal study. Now think of what is available to you in reality. Note the ways in which your best available option departs from the ideal. Think of as many ways as possible in which you can improve your proposed location, and set the improvements in motion. Once completed, use this location for further work through this book, so that you start to develop the place habit.

Studying is easier with:
- scheduled times
- clear cues
- family cooperation
- sustained discipline.

Having a place where you normally study is a tremendous advantage. But if you travel frequently, you may have chosen part-time study, probably of the distance variety, precisely because it allows you to vary your study location. In this case it is worth thinking about how you can gain some of the advantages of a habitual study place while on the move. The first advantage, that of having everything to hand, can be approximated by careful packing before you leave, and perhaps having a special 'course briefcase' in which you keep current materials, in order to make the packing easier.

The second advantage of a dedicated study place, that you instantly slip into 'study mode' on entry because it has become a habit, is harder to duplicate, but a comfortable 'study jumper', or a special mug for coffee, or other visual cues that 'this is study time' can be surprisingly helpful. If the sight of your materials is not sufficient to trigger your study mode look for a convenient portable cue.

THE ADVANTAGE OF STUDYING AT REGULAR TIMES

Possibly even more important in developing the study habit is to study at regular times. Again, this may seem to contradict the advantages of flexibility claimed for part-time study, but where regularity *is* possible, students find that it takes away much of the pain of deciding whether or not to study on a particular occasion. It becomes automatic, after a time, to go to your study on Tuesdays, Thursdays and all of Sunday, or whatever pattern you have chosen. No decision is necessary. Family and friends know the pattern and what to expect, and that you will be available to them at other times. Indeed, if family and friends helped you devise your study pattern, and feel part-ownership in your plan, they may act as 'police' rather than 'saboteurs'.

→ Ch 6

If regularity is impossible because your life just isn't like that, then follow the practice recommended in the section on time management at work, and 'book in' your study time. This will have the same advantages that it had there. You need not worry about the work when you are not doing it, because you know it is under control, and when the scheduled time arrives, no decision is needed as it has already been taken.

Of course, with either approach you will need to be prepared to adjust your schedule when study is genuinely impossible. If you have a temperature of 105 °F, or the cat has just been run over, or an old friend has dropped in en route from Alaska to Zaire, then it would be unreasonably obsessive to insist on continuing to study. Lesser interruptions should, however, be firmly resisted. You will *often* feel a bit tired and disinclined to study. If you start to make such common occurrences an excuse you will never complete your course. Similarly, you can see your next-door neighbours on another night, and if you forgot to feed the cat it will probably not die of starvation before you finish your scheduled study session.

A schedule which you stick to under all reasonable circumstances, whether it is a regular weekly schedule or one which you draw up each week or fortnight to suit prevailing circumstances, will considerably reduce the effort required for study. Procrastination is probably the greatest threat to successful course completion, and scheduling should help you to avoid it.

In drawing up your schedule, you will need to make sure that you do not make unreasonable demands upon yourself. It is highly unlikely that you will be able to study effectively for six hours at the end of a demanding day at work. Shorter sessions during the week are far more likely to be effective, with longer sessions reserved for weekends or any study leave. Even then, arrange for breaks to keep your mind fresh.

→ Ch 6

Think, too, about the best times of day for you to study. The concept of 'prime time' was introduced in Chapter 6. You may already have used it to improve your time management at work. It is equally applicable to study time. If you are a 'morning person', getting up early to study may be 'prime', but if you sometimes need to use late evening slots they may not be! Try to devise your schedule so that you maximise 'prime' periods, and reduce the others. Reserve the best periods for your most intensive work.

ACTIVITY 7.2

Devise a study schedule for the period between now and your course start, aiming to work through relevant sections of this book or to do other preparatory work in the slots you identify. This need not be as heavy a schedule as you will need once your course has started, but it will help you to get into the habit of working regularly, and in at least some of the periods which you intend to devote to your course. If the course has already started, draw up a schedule and start working to it straight away.

DEVELOPING A STUDY PLAN

The study schedule you draw up, whether it is made up of regular study times for an extended period, or is a variable weekly schedule matched to other demands in your life, provides the framework within which you will construct your study plan. The process involved, not unnaturally, is very similar to that of work planning described earlier. Note: although it is possible to think about your schedule in the abstract as part of your preparation for the course, you cannot draw up your *plan* in advance: it depends upon specific course requirements – you may therefore wish to omit this section if you have not yet started your course. If so, make a note in your diary for the time your course begins, reminding yourself to revisit this section and draw up a study plan as soon as you have the necessary information.

Study planning involves deciding, for each study topic, what material you will need to cover as a bare minimum, and how long this is likely to take. It is also helpful to know

Plan for:
- time
- materials
- achievements
- motivation.

what additional material would be worth studying if time allows, and how much time would be required for this. You then need to plan which scheduled study sessions you will devote to which work, in order to do all that is necessary before any submission deadlines, or any deadlines that you set yourself in order to balance workloads. Your planning must include ensuring that you acquire any materials not already in your possession in time for their anticipated use.

This may all sound blindingly obvious, but it is surprising how many managers, excellent though they may be at scheduling tasks and resources at work, fail to 'manage' their studies. They seem victims of a particularly seductive optimism – a belief that somehow, shortly before a deadline, time will miraculously expand to allow the necessary work to be fitted in, and that all the references they require will be sitting in the library ready for their use, despite the fact that everyone else on the course is wanting to borrow them at the same time. Whenever you feel this nice, warm feeling of security creeping up on you, stamp it out fast. It is particularly common for work

→ Ch 19   with a distant deadline. (Chapter 19 on managing projects, theses and dissertations offers techniques for handling it.) Sit down at once, and draw up a realistic schedule, making sure you have included *all* the interim tasks that will be needed in order for you to meet the deadline with a good piece of work. Beware the planning fallacy referred to earlier. And remember to build sufficient slack into your plan to allow for the unexpected.

If you are a distance student, much of the scheduling may have been done for you. The course I teach for the Open University Business School, for example, provides students with *all* the materials they need, and divides the work into study sessions for which rough time indications are usually given. A printed study calendar is provided showing exactly what the student should have achieved by each week in the course, though students may still need to modify the calendar to take account of the demands of their particular job or lifestyle. Other programmes vary in the extent to which they do the organising for you: if yours leaves most of the planning to you, it is especially important that you tackle this task carefully.

Devising, or adapting, an overall study plan is perhaps the easy part. Planning each individual session to ensure that it is effective is harder. You need to be very clear about your objectives in covering the material. Focusing on what you aim to *achieve* in each session, rather than merely on how long you plan to spend, is crucial. There are many

→ Ch 8   ways in which you can learn, and many things that can be learned. The next chapter looks at some of the simpler ideas about how managers learn. These may help you to improve further the effectiveness of your own study. In the meantime, consider the advantages of keeping a study log.

One of your challenges will be sustaining your motivation through many study sessions. A useful motivational technique (though it has many other uses as well) is to keep a study log. For each of your study sessions, log date and duration, and the material on which you have been working. Make notes on the significant points absorbed, and the sources from which they were derived. Note any queries raised which you will need to pursue at a later date, and any interesting points you might wish to raise with your tutor, or in class discussion. Make a particular note of anything

7

Effective learning and reflective practice

that looks potentially relevant for forthcoming assignments. Comment, too, on any difficulties encountered in maintaining concentration, and on how accurate your time estimates are turning out to be.

CLARIFYING YOUR STUDY OBJECTIVES

→ Ch 8

At this point, it is worth starting to think about the 'what' of learning: the next chapter will take this topic further. You might be learning facts, such as the content of a particular piece of employment legislation, in which case memorising is appropriate. Some students try to learn *all* their course materials by rote – particularly if their earlier education has been within a system which emphasises recall of 'the facts'. But this is not appropriate to a subject like management. Some things will indeed have to be learned by heart, but there are many different sorts of learning which are more important.

Techniques

Study objectives may include:
- learning and practising techniques
- understanding and evaluating theories
- learning and evaluating methodologies
- learning about context
- developing your ability to be critical.

Learning to *apply techniques* will be central to your study. You may need to know, for example, how to calculate the weighted average cost of capital or the net present value (NPV) of possible projects to allow you to choose between competing potential investments. In these cases, you need to know what to include in the calculation, and how to do the mathematics. Some of this comes fairly close to rote learning. But also, you will need to *practise* doing the calculations until you know which buttons to press without thinking. You also need to know what the answer *means*, and when you would need to calculate it, and how you would use it in decision making, and when it may give you a misleading impression. You need to know, too, what alternative approaches might be considered and when they might be preferred. All this requires that you understand what you are learning, and its significance. To achieve this sort of understanding requires much more than learning by heart. It requires you to *think* about what something means, to try it out against things which you already understand, to think about some of the things which it implies if you have understood it correctly, and to see if these make sense. If not, you need to work out where you have gone wrong. A colleague told me that the difference between the USA and the UK in their approach to management study is neatly demonstrated by the different approaches to net present value (NPV) calculations. In the US approach, it is the resulting *value* that is deemed significant. In the UK it is the *process* of arriving at that value that is of interest: one could plausibly arrive at almost any desired value by making the appropriate assumptions. Apart from suggesting caution in using this book outside the UK, this neatly illustrates the richer type of learning that your course may aim for, and the different time requirements likely for the different types. When you are trying to learn techniques, your study plan should therefore allow for you to practise them until you are confident in their use. If you are trying to understand their application, or indeed anything else, then you need time for thought, for experimenting with the consequences of your thought, and ideally discussing them with others.

Theories

You will often need to study *theories*. These are ways of describing complicated sets of phenomena more simply, in a way that will allow you to make sense of what is happening, and predict what is likely to happen if you make certain changes. One theory that you may well have already encountered on short courses (if not, you will probably meet it soon) is the Herzberg 'two-factor theory of job satisfaction' (Herzberg, 1966). In a nutshell, this asserts that there are two sets of job-related factors. The first, which includes items like pay and working conditions, contributes to employee job *dissatisfaction*. He calls this set the hygiene factors. The second set, including responsibility, achievement and the work itself, contribute to employee *satisfaction*, and he refers to these as *motivators*. The essence of Herzberg's theory is that, while *dissatisfaction* can be reduced by improvement of hygiene factors, such improvements will not generate job *satisfaction* or motivation. To achieve this, it is necessary to make changes to motivator factors. The most frequent change made by adherents of the theory is to increase responsibility levels, a process referred to as *job enrichment*.

In learning a theory, merely learning the 'facts', i.e. what the theorist is asserting, is of limited value. You also need to know the *significance* of the theory. What is it explaining that is not explained by other theories? What new predictions would it cause you to make? (In the case of Herzberg's theory, that attempts at improving motivation by altering pay are doomed to failure.) What sense would this enable you to make of things that concern you in your own job? (Perhaps your own subordinates show such low levels of motivation because they have so little responsibility.) Where does the theory contradict your own experience? (Perhaps you have just introduced a payment by results scheme which has had wonderful effects on output, and by inference, motivation.)

Also relevant is the *evidence* on which the theory is based. If it is merely the result of armchair pondering, or (as in the example above) based on a fairly limited questionnaire study capable of other interpretations, it needs to be viewed differently from a theory based upon extensive observations and varied tests of its predictions.

Theories can be enormously useful in helping you make sense of a complex situation, but they *are* only theories, not God-given truths. Herzberg's may be famous, but there are other theories which make more sense of motivation at work. For any theory you will need to go beyond learning, and into thinking about believability and usefulness. Is the theory logically consistent? Does it fit all the data the author quotes? Are all its predictions plausible? Asking questions such as these develops a key postgraduate conceptual skill, that of critical thinking. This will be discussed shortly, and explored in → Ch 9, 14 more detail in Chapters 9 and 14.

You will find your own managerial experience offers plenty of scope for applying the theory, and thinking about whether it is useful. You should get into the habit, even if course materials do not demand this, of testing everything against your own experience. You will find that your study is much more interesting if you do so. You will also find theories, or other concepts, much easier to learn if you have already linked them to your personal reality. You should also aim to start *using* the ideas to help you function better at work. This may take a little working time, but apart from improving your job performance, it will mean that you do not have to *learn* them when you come to the exam. They will already have become part of your personal conceptual toolkit.

Methodologies

Another category of learning to which you will be exposed will be that of methodologies, or ways of approaching problems. (Strictly, methods, as 'methodology' means the body of knowledge about methods, but the everyday usage of the word in the above sense is widespread, so used here.) Again, this will be far more rewarding, and interesting, and have more effect on your managerial practice if you go beyond rote learning of content, and into an understanding of why the methodology is offered, what it can and cannot do, what advantages and disadvantages it has compared with alternative approaches, and when it would be suitable. This applies whether you are talking about a simple approach, such as the framework for looking at a competitive environment via analysis of social, technical, environmental and political (STEP) factors, or a more complex approach such as the Checkland Soft Systems Methodology, a set of stages designed to help you address organisational problems from a systems perspective. Again, you should, if at all possible, go beyond understanding, and start using the methodologies whenever suitable opportunities present themselves in your job.

Understanding context

Gaining an understanding of *context* and its importance is crucial at Master's level. The STEP factors just referred to constitute a simple classification of factors in the *external* environment which are likely to be important. For departmental-level problems the wider organisation will constitute an important *inner* environment. Much of your learning will involve coming to appreciate the importance of both types of environment, understanding their likely impact and becoming more sensitive to all the relevant factors in any particular problem which you may have to face.

Rote learning will have little part to play in this. Instead, you will need to think about what is happening in the cases with which you are presented, and start to become more aware of general trends, such as political ones, which influence business. You will need to concentrate particularly upon those environmental factors to which your own organisation is especially sensitive. This sort of learning should be a continuous process, once you are sensitised to the issues involved.

Becoming critical

Most MBA programmes would see the development of your critical faculties as *the* most important learning outcome. During your career you can expect to encounter all sorts of new fads and theories. You will be faced with many reports from consultants or others, arguing for various investments or changes. You will need to be able to evaluate these critically. Some may be worthless, others highly significant. Much of what appears in the management literature is of limited usefulness. The ideas may be old ones, thinly disguised in new jargon. Or the content may be primarily the author's opinions and prejudices, even wishful thinking, rather than based upon hard evidence or sound reasoning. It is important that you approach all your study materials critically: do not assume that anything in print is automatically worth reading. Otherwise you may replicate their errors in your own thesis, and finish the course without developing the important transferable skill of being able to critically evaluate papers written by → Ch 9, 14 either academics or consultants. Chapter 9 gives more detail on how to read critically, and Chapter 14 discusses how to demonstrate critical thinking in work you submit for assessment.

Objectives and planning

In planning any single session, you should be clear first of all about your objectives. Are you aiming to learn this material by rote, or is it theoretical, needing evaluation, or a technique which you wish to become competent at using? Is the material intended to change your perspective? If you are working on a paper in a journal, for example, it is a good idea to set down at the beginning what you would ideally like that paper to tell you about the topic it addresses. Then when you have finished it you can check what it *did* tell you (if anything). Be clear as to how this fits into course requirements. How much detail are you expected to absorb about something? What assignments does this material relate to? What other courses might it be relevant to? You will often find interrelationships between the concepts in different courses, and it is worth noting these in your study log.

If you plan your work for each session, noting your objectives and the extent to which these are achieved in your study log, together with any insights gained from testing the ideas against your work experience, you will find your study time exciting and productive. This is unlikely to be the case if you regard your study periods as something to be endured (as many children see their music practice), during which something of value may, if you are lucky, rub off in a passive sort of way. You can gain further benefit by using your log to record the effects of your attempts to apply course ideas and techniques while at work.

USING TIME EFFECTIVELY

The principles of good time management at work are important if you are to make effective use of study time. Strong time and place habits should reduce any tendency to procrastinate. You can further reduce the risk by making a point of *always* starting to work exactly when you scheduled yourself to do so, thus preventing any bad habits from starting to develop. This means making that cup of coffee *before* your study session is due to start. And it means completing, or postponing for the duration, all those other tasks like fixing the shelf, or cleaning the oven, that have a way of becoming terribly urgent just when you are about to start work.

Just as you need a time management file at work, you need a study log and working file to help you manage your studies. Instead of key objectives, you will have *courses* as your main dividing categories, subdivided by learning objectives and study tasks. Your study plan should schedule these tasks so as to ensure that all course deadlines are met, and workloads kept even, or fitted in with other conflicting demands. Again, regular review of your effectiveness is crucial. Your study log, by recording what you have achieved, difficulties encountered and thoughts about future tactics, will enable you to gain insight into your own study skills and their development. It helps motivation because of the satisfaction derived from recording achievements on each occasion.

Another important factor, if you are to be fully effective, is to take account of your own body rhythms, and plan your work in accordance with your personal good and bad times. Even if you were able to schedule most of your sessions to take advantage of 'good' times, as suggested above, there will almost inevitably be occasions when you have to study even though you are not at your best. In this case, as at work, you should make sure that you schedule demanding tasks for your better times, leaving more routine work for times you are not at your peak.

Even at your better times you should not try to force your concentration too far. For most people an hour is about as long as concentration can be maintained without strain. You are likely to make far more effective use of your time if you schedule short (five- to seven-minute) breaks every hour or so, using this time to have a drink, move about or get some fresh air. A few brisk exercises, or even a very brief walk can do wonders for concentration, as well as easing the strain caused by sitting still. You may have your own favourite exercises already. If not, friends who do yoga could give you suggestions. Alternatively you can simply experiment by yourself to find movements that make you feel good. If you are short of ideas, you may like to try the following exercise suggestions. Remember, the point of the exercises is to make you feel good, not to cause pain. Stop at once if there is any discomfort. And if you have back or other physical problems, consult a doctor first.

EXERCISES WHICH CAN BE USED DURING STUDY BREAKS

Stretch

Stand with feet slightly apart, and reach as high as you can towards the ceiling. Hold this position for 10 deep breaths.

Hang

Keeping feet in the same position, and legs straight, hang forwards from the waist, with head and arms loose. Only rest your hands on the floor if this is totally comfortable. Aim for a slight pull behind the knees. Hold for up to 10 deep breaths, then unroll upwards slowly, from the small of the back, imagining that you are putting your vertebrae back in place one by one.

Shrug your shoulders

Do this up to 10 times, exaggerating the movement as much as possible, perhaps including a circling motion.

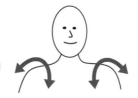
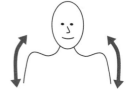

Circle your head

Drop chin on to chest, then let your head roll in a large circle towards your shoulder, backwards, over other shoulder and back to chest. Repeat in the reverse direction.

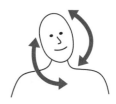

Massage your back

Lie on your back on the floor, knees drawn up loosely towards your chest, hands clasped above them. Pull your knees gently towards your chest five times, feeling your lower back pressing slightly into the floor. Then place one hand on each knee and move knees in small horizontal circles, keeping them joined, again feeling the movement of your back against the floor.

Twist your spine

With knees still drawn up, let legs flop apart slightly (think of a baby lying in a pram) and wriggle a bit. Then stretch arms out to each side, along the floor. Keeping both shoulders firmly on the floor, flop both knees over to the left, so that your left leg is on the floor, the right resting gently upon it. Increase the twist by turning your head to look along your right arm, and gently sliding your right leg a little further down and across your left leg. Hold for up to 10 deep breaths, then do it in the opposite direction.

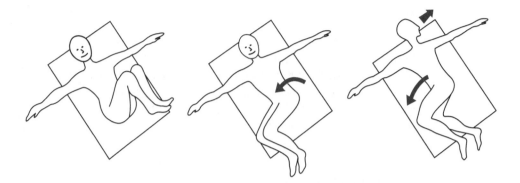

Relax

Spend about a minute deep breathing, and trying to keep all your muscles relaxed, and your mind as clear as possible. Get up slowly after this, taking at least five deep breaths to become vertical.

ACTIVITY 7.3

If you have been working on this book for at least 40 minutes, try the above exercises, or others, now. Otherwise wait until you have been working for 40–60 minutes and try them then. Before you start, note any parts of your body where you are aware of tension or discomfort. Check to see whether any remains after the exercises. If so, experiments with other movements to relieve it.

Try to do exercises after each of the next five hours of study you do. Only then can you feel justified in abandoning them if they still seem not to be working.

It is important that you schedule the end of any study sessions, as well as the beginning. This allows you to enjoy the time afterwards, and relax properly. If you finish your planned task in less time than you anticipated, you might even stop early.

→ Ch 9

In addition to scheduled breaks, you should stop if you are finding it totally impossible to concentrate at any point. It is a waste of time to sit in front of a page without registering it in any way. If you have clarified your study objectives, are taking notes as suggested later and having regular breaks, you should not find this problem arises, unless you are ill or overtired, have serious worries or the material is extremely badly written. Take 10 minutes to explore possible causes. If no obvious reason can be found and remedied, try some exercise or fresh air, and try again. If concentration is still lacking, try a different activity. If that fails too, admit defeat and terminate your study session rather than wasting time. Log the problem in your working file. If it recurs, look for a pattern that might help you identify the reason. Before stopping, remember to reschedule the missed time.

The above fairly practical points, combined with good planning techniques similar to those which you should by now be using at work, should help you to make effective use of the study time that you have freed, perhaps at considerable sacrifice. The following chapters on more specific study skills should further enhance your effectiveness.

SUMMARY

- It is important to develop habits of time and place if at all possible, as this will reduce the effort wasted by procrastination.
- Study periods should be broken by brief scheduled rest periods in order to improve concentration. Exercise may be helpful here.
- Time management techniques are as applicable to study as to work. In particular, you should actively plan your study in order to achieve objectives and meet deadlines. And you should plan non-study time too.
- Part of this planning should be done with a clear understanding of what it is that you are trying to learn, and why. Different approaches will be needed for facts, techniques, theories, methodologies or material intended to broaden your perspective, or heighten your awareness.
- Your study will be more effective if you adopt a critical approach and make a habit of testing ideas against your prior work experience, trying to use as many course ideas, techniques and methodologies as possible in the practice of your job.

→ **8** Learning from learning theory

By the end of this chapter you should:

- understand what is meant by learning styles, and the learning process
- have an idea of your own preferred learning style and its strengths, and how to develop less preferred styles
- have a deeper appreciation of how learning can be made far more effective through integration with work experience
- be starting to develop the habit of reflection on practice.

INTRODUCTION

This is not a psychology textbook, and cannot give you an exhaustive treatment of learning theory. But the previous chapter referred briefly to different sorts of learning that you might need, and this can usefully be expanded. Ideas about management learning have shifted some way beyond earlier ideas of managers needing to *absorb* knowledge imparted by tutors. Competences, or the ability to *do* things, have come into the frame. The importance of learning through reflection is now widely seen as crucial to professional practice. Ideas from knowledge management suggest that managers' ability to *construct* meaning and knowledge is at the heart of management learning in a complex and rapidly changing organisational world. An understanding of how this type of learning is best achieved will enable you not only to benefit from your course, but to continue learning from the experiences that you have thereafter.

WHAT IS LEARNING?

Long, long ago I went for an interview for a job at the Civil Service College. It was a typical Civil Service panel interview, with – I think – seven panel members. About halfway through the interview, the then head of the college, a middle-aged, middle-European man, asked me rather aggressively what I thought I had learned from my experience as an Open University tutor that might be relevant to the job in question. I enthusiastically replied that the one thing it had convinced me of was that, if you wanted to change the attitudes or behaviour of adults, learning needed to be participative. He looked at me disdainfully, and said, 'But Mrs Cameron, we are not trying to change people's attitudes or their behaviour.' At that point I stopped wanting to work there (I'm still not sure why I accepted the job!) as I couldn't see what on earth they *were* trying to do in the name of training.

Management development, as other education, originally aimed to transfer 'knowledge' from lecturer to student (the 'jug and mug' metaphor is often used to describe this – the lecturer being the jug, and the student the mug to be filled...). I suspect, in retrospect, that this was where the Civil Service College was at the time. In the 1980s there was a shift (in the UK) of focus towards management *competence* (although the jug/mug approach seemed to persist in many countries until much more recently). Subsequently there have been further shifts. One has been towards emphasising knowledge management and sense making. Another has been an increasing emphasis on leadership rather than management. Indeed the two are linked, as leadership can be seen as making sense of the situation, and moving from this to creating and communicating a compelling vision for the organisation.

The knowledge management argument runs thus. The role of management is changing, and changing rapidly. The world in which managers operate is fluid – prediction is difficult, competition often fierce. 'Information' proliferates as IT becomes ever more sophisticated. Senior managers need more than 'facts' and 'competences'. In such an environment the ability to 'make sense' of a complex and rapidly changing world, and to learn continuously from experience, is crucial. Learning is seen as going beyond the absorption of facts and theories into developing the ability to actively *construct meaning*.

The leadership argument often places more emphasis on the role of emotion and vision in inspiring others to act. A distinction is made between management (primarily about control) and leadership (winning 'hearts and minds'). 'Leaders' are said to motivate and empower people to act via a shared vision of the organisation – derived from the sense-making process described above. Control is associated with maintaining the status quo, leadership with developing shared meanings, which generate flexibility and learning. Thus, the argument goes, leadership is crucial in times of rapid change.

The integration of theory and experience is crucial to the sense-making process. One of the advantages of part-time study (noted earlier) is that it ensures a continuing supply of experience to be interpreted. Kolb, Rubin and MacIntyre (1984) developed a simple framework suggesting how this integration might be achieved, and Honey and Mumford (1986) built on this to provide suggestions for practical steps which students could take to make their own learning more effective.

KOLB'S THEORY

Kolb *et al.* suggested that learning should be viewed as a circular process, whereby experience was followed by attempts to make sense of that experience through reflection and conceptualisation, followed by experimentation with the concepts so developed, followed by further experience, reflection, and so on, as shown in Fig. 8.1.

8

Learning from learning theory

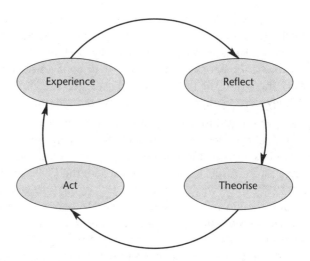

Fig. 8.1 The learning cycle (adapted from Kolb)

There are a number of points to derive from Kolb's theory. First, learning is very much an *active* process involving thinking: experience by itself is not enough. You can do something wrongly for years, if nobody has told you to the contrary. You can continue to do something poorly indefinitely, if you do not reflect on what you are doing, try to understand it, and experiment with ways of doing things better. In either case, experience is likely to teach you almost nothing. Similarly, purely theoretical knowledge, if not related to experience, and itself experimented with, is unlikely to produce useful learning.

Your course is likely to help you to use all the stages in the cycle, thus accelerating your learning. You are likely to be encouraged to reflect on your own experience (or that of others as described in case studies). You will become more aware of the 'theories' that you have, perhaps unknowingly, been using, and will be offered a wide range of alternative frameworks which you will be encouraged to use. Your 'reflection' will therefore become a more deliberate, and much richer, process of making sense of what happens in organisations. It will also become established as a habit which will remain with you throughout your career, and a key element in your continued learning post-qualification. 'Reflective practice' is now seen by many professional institutes as a crucial element in continuing professional development: it will be discussed in more detail shortly.

Unfortunately some programmes, particularly the more academic, have yet to adopt this approach fully. If this is the case with your chosen course, you can make your learning much more effective by consciously seeking links even when not prompted, and *always* testing concepts against your experience.

Doing this in informal study groups will enable you to draw on a wider range of experience for the testing process. Something may not seem particularly useful to you because your own experience has been limited. Hearing others discuss how the concept helps them will make you more aware of its possibilities and uses.

Improve your learning:

- test concepts against experience
- discuss your 'sense making' with others
- seek feedback from colleagues on how you are perceived
- reflect continually on experience
- keep a learning log
- develop less preferred learning styles (see later).

As well as testing each concept you encounter against your experience, Kolb's theory suggests that you should get into the reverse habit of becoming more reflective about your experience. If something *always* seems to go wrong, try to analyse why. How does it differ from fairly similar things that go right? Is there anything in your studies that can throw light on this? Can you gather constructive feedback from colleagues to indicate whether you are unwittingly contributing to problems?

What about aspects of your job performance with which you are fairly satisfied? Think about what is actually happening and try to understand it. This may suggest ways of building on your strengths and reducing your weaknesses. Such reflections do not need to be limited to ideas from your studies, although such links should be sought out and built upon.

Both your superior and your mentor can aid your attempt to undertake active learning. A formal appraisal system may offer opportunities, but you will probably achieve more, and do so more flexibly, through informal discussions. Discuss problem areas of work with colleagues. Perhaps they understand aspects of the situation better than you, in which case you can benefit from their insights. Experiment with their ideas to see if they work for you too. If they, too, are uneasy as you are, discussing the issue from your different perspectives may help you all come to a clearer understanding of the real problem, and to find ways of being more effective. Subordinates are a further source of ideas.

In organisations which take learning seriously, review sessions are a regular feature. Through these, teams working on a project can take time to learn from what is happening, both from what is going smoothly and from hitches, and can discuss ways whereby practice might be improved in future. You may be able to introduce course concepts into these discussions (though you may need to tread carefully so as not to antagonise people in the process), but it is not essential. A particular concept may provide a short cut to understanding. Or the more general approach developed in your course may help. If your organisation does not currently encourage review sessions, you might think about whether they would be an advantage in your context. If so, think about what you could do to encourage their introduction.

For learning to be effective, people must be confident enough to acknowledge their imperfections. Many organisations now accept that learning involves getting it wrong: they may have slogans such as 'It is OK to make a mistake – once!' The important thing is to take the risk and then learn from the experience. But if review sessions turn into ways of shifting blame away from each person on to others, this learning will not take place. Instead, the process will be highly counterproductive. But if nobody is expected to be perfect, and it is seen as a sign of *strength* to be able to recognise possible areas for improvement, then active review with the aim of learning from experience can be extremely useful.

For your own individual learning, you will need to be prepared to admit to yourself that there are areas where you could improve. Even this may be slightly uncomfortable.

We often hate to admit, even to ourselves, that we might not be perfect. To admit it to a boss is even more difficult, to subordinates, worse still. But if handled positively, such admissions can increase your standing in others' eyes, rather than diminish it. (If this is not normal behaviour in your organisation, you should be cautious when adopting this approach – thorough groundwork may be needed to ensure that everyone involved understands, and agrees to, this change.) (An example of student reflection in which development areas are confronted is given later in this chapter.)

By involving others in your organisation you may be moving it towards a more learning-oriented approach, which is likely to have major benefits in the increasingly fluid situation of the twenty-first century. Employers are increasingly becoming aware that continuous development of staff is the only way in which the organisation can remain competitive. One of the benefits from your course of study might be a move towards developing a culture in which this continuous development can more readily take place.

LEARNING STYLES

Kolb's cycle involves phases of activity, reflection, conceptualisation and application of those ideas. Honey and Mumford (1986) have suggested that different individuals prefer to learn in different ways, broadly related to Kolb's four phases. They have developed a learning-styles inventory to help people identify their own preferred learning style.

ACTIVITY 8.1

Tick the statement most characteristic of your own reaction to a learning situation.

1. 'I'm game to try it, let's get started.' ☐
2. 'I need some time to think about this.' ☐
3. 'What are the basic assumptions?' ☐
4. 'What's this got to do with my job?' ☐

The above statements give only the broadest of indications. If you are really interested in your learning style you should obtain, and work through, the full learning-styles inventory. But the above gives you a flavour of what is meant. The following descriptions relate to the four learning styles identified.

- **Activists**. These are open-minded, and involve themselves fully in new experiences. They are not noted for their caution, nor for their tolerance of boredom. They love short-term crisis fire-fighting, and the challenge of new problems, brainstorming and finding solutions. They are weaker on implementation, consolidation and anything requiring sustained effort. They are highly sociable and like to be the centre of attention. If this sounds like you, and if you favoured Statement 1, you are probably an activist.

- **Reflectors**. These are thoughtful and cautious, preferring to consider all possible angles, and collect as many data as possible before coming to a decision. They prefer to observe others rather than take an active role themselves, and will adopt a low profile in discussions, adding their own points only when the drift of the discussion is clear. If this sounds like you, and you preferred the second statement, you are probably a reflector.

- **Theorists**. They approach problems logically, step by step, and adapt and integrate their observations into complex but coherent theories. They like to analyse and synthesise, and to establish basic assumptions, principles, theories and models. They are often detached, and dedicated to rational objectivity. They are uncomfortable with anything that doesn't fit into their theoretical framework, and hate subjectivity, uncertainty, lateral thinking and a flippant approach. If this sounds like you, and you chose the third statement, you may well be a theorist.

- **Pragmatists**. These thrive on new ideas, provided they can put them into practice. They like to get on with things, and are confident about trying to apply new ideas. Open-ended discussions are seen as highly frustrating 'beating about the bush'. Problems and opportunities are seen as a challenge, and they are sure that there is always a better way to do anything. If this sounds like you, and you preferred the fourth statement, you could be a pragmatist.

As with most simple categorisations (and you will encounter a lot of them during your studies), this is an oversimplification. Examples of 'pure types' may exist, but you are likely to have found elements in more than one category that you felt applied to you. The analysis is useful, however, because it is clear from each of the 'styles' that every strength has associated weaknesses. By being alert to these, you can take steps to minimise the effects of weaknesses, and arrange your learning activities so as to build on your strengths.

If you have *activist* tendencies, your open-mindedness, energy and creativity will be enormous assets. But you will need to find ways of sustaining your motivation during the course. You will also need to discipline yourself to plan adequately for assignments, and to ensure that you are meeting requirements fully. Your tendency will be to get excited about something, and leap in without exploring all the other possibilities. You will thrive on new and diverse experiences, and on short exercises such as role-playing, competitive team activities and business games. You will love learning in groups, and volunteer to chair meetings, give presentations or lead discussions.

But other group members may resent your leading role, and feel they are prevented from making a full contribution themselves. Lectures will strain your concentration. And you will find it hard to learn from other people's experiences. You will also be unlikely to think sufficiently about your learning objectives before a task, and may be poor at assessing what you have learned afterwards. Dissertations are potentially a major problem, as they require both careful planning beforehand, and sustained work thereafter to carry them through. Neither of these comes easily to an activist.

If you are a *reflector*, your strengths will be in careful analytical work, and detailed, painstaking research. You will consider the full picture, never neglecting important background features. You should find a dissertation the most enjoyable part of your course, provided you do not spend too long planning, thereby leaving yourself insufficient time for data collection. You will be excellent at observing groups in action.

8

Learning from learning theory

However, many characteristics of Master's work will be uncomfortable for you. You will hate to be asked to reach conclusions on the basis of insufficient data, will hate being forced into chairing groups or making presentations, and will find the conflicting demands of work and study particularly hard to reconcile. Indeed, you may hand work in late, because you spent too much time perfecting it. If you fail an exam, it will probably be because you used the time to produce excellent answers to rather fewer questions than were required.

If your strongest tendency is as a *theorist*, you will thrive on the more academic aspects of a course, such as evaluating competing theories, perhaps even coming up with improvements, organising data into neat frameworks, and looking for interrelationships between factors in a situation. You may indeed prefer a more academic specialist Master's to an MBA. If your programme includes a course on Systems Thinking, you will probably enjoy this enormously. Provided objectives are clear, and the situation well structured, you will be able to handle complexity well. Concepts will excite you, whether or not they are relevant at the time.

You will be highly uncomfortable, however, if you are asked to participate in activities without the context or purpose being clear, and particularly if you have to take part in situations where emotions or feelings are significant factors. In a dissertation, your methodology section will probably be brilliant, but you may risk adopting a more complex methodology than was strictly necessary, and will find it hard to cope if you are forced to work with less than the perfect data you had planned. You will also be reluctant to include qualitative information. In group work you will be infuriated by the less considered approach of the activists in your group, and may find it difficult to work effectively with them.

If you are mainly a *pragmatist*, and the majority of MBA students seem to tend this way, you will find your course enormously exciting provided you can see how to use it in your job. If choosing an MBA, you should seek a programme which has embraced the 'competence' approach to the full. You will enjoy any skills development parts of the course, provided you get good feedback on your performance, and will do well at learning any techniques which will help you do your job better. Part-time and distance learning are particularly suited to pragmatists, because of the opportunities they offer for practising skills and applying concepts to their job as soon as they are learned.

You will be highly frustrated by any lecturers with no practical managerial experience, or indeed by any material presented without guidelines on how to put it into practice. In project work or dissertations you will leap into solving a problem, probably coming up with excellent and practicable solutions, but a lack of emphasis on the conceptual underpinning of what you are doing may cause you to receive low marks. You will also tend to apply solutions from one situation to another, preferring something which has been shown to work to something totally innovative. This may limit your options on occasion. Creativity is not usually your strong point in any case.

Whatever your preferred style, and however strong your preference, you will on occasion be required to take part in learning activities unsuited to your natural style. It is possible to increase your capacity to benefit from these by developing aspects of those styles which do not come easily to you. This will have potential benefits at work, as you will be better able to go through all the stages in the Kolb cycle, as well as helping with your course. A 'fully competent learner' operates comfortably at *all* stages of the cycle, and you may need to work on your less preferred styles to become one.

ACTIVITY 8.2

From the following list of activities designed to develop aspects of the different styles, choose at least six which you feel would be useful to you, and practise them. Write a note in your diary one month from today to review progress.

To develop activism

1. Do something totally out of character at least once a week (e.g. talk to total strangers, wear something outrageous, go somewhere totally new).
2. Force yourself to fragment your day, switching deliberately from one activity to another.
3. Force yourself to be more prominent at meetings. Determine to make at least one contribution in the first 10 minutes. Volunteer for any chairing or presentational role.
4. Practise thinking aloud. When you are trying to solve a problem, bounce ideas off a colleague without thinking before you speak.

To develop reflection

→ Ch 11

1. At meetings practise observing behaviour and interactions, and analysing what is happening (Chapter 11 will help).
2. Keep a diary, reflecting each evening on the day's events and what you have learned, or enter this in your development file.
3. For your next piece of written work aim for perfection, doing more drafts than normal, and polishing it as best you can.
4. Undertake to research a topic of concern at work, investigating in as much depth as possible.
5. Before actions or decisions, force yourself to draw up a list of pros and cons, looking as widely as possible for potential results and effects.

To become more of a theorist

1. Spend at least 30 minutes daily reading something heavy and conceptual, trying to analyse and evaluate the arguments involved.
2. Find a complex situation at work and analyse how it developed, and what might have been done differently.
3. Before acting, clarify your objectives, and try to structure the situation to make the outcome more certain.
4. Look for inconsistencies, dubious assumptions and weaknesses in others' arguments.
5. Practise asking probing questions, persisting until a clear, logical answer is received.

To become more of a pragmatist

1. When discussing problems, make sure that you do not conclude before devising action plans for yourself and any others involved.
2. Put as many techniques as you can into practice (e.g. time management, forecasting, making presentations, drawing up budgets).
3. If possible, seek feedback from experts on the above task.
4. Tackle some DIY project (but not if you have already started your course!).

Whatever your preferred learning style, there are advantages in making active links between your studies and your work experience, and you should do all that you can to ensure that you get into the habit of doing this. Discussions, whether with fellow students, colleagues or interested others, will be very helpful in this.

THE ROLE OF REFLECTION IN LEARNING

The activity above provides a start to becoming more reflective. However, this is so important that you will probably need to do rather more to develop your skills as a reflective practitioner. Reflection is now seen as absolutely crucial to professional development. It is therefore worth looking in rather more detail at the role that reflection plays in learning. This will help you to use the process to full effect both for your own development and to meet course requirements for evidence of reflection as part of your assessment. This section therefore looks at how reflection 'works' to strengthen learning, and at why it is important to develop a lifelong habit of reflection. It also covers some of the main reflective tools.

Deep or surface learning?

Much of the argument for reflection rests upon the idea of 'levels' or 'depths' of learning. You might, for example, learn five key theories of motivation, their authors and the textbook diagrams in order to regurgitate them for an examination. This is one level of learning. But it is unlikely that you would then be able to go into a situation where staff seem to be demotivated, find out why and do something to improve the situation in the light of this analysis. Being able simply to reproduce material from the textbook seldom helps you sort out real life problems – to do this you would require rather more understanding than is implied by mere reproduction, and a deeper level of learning.

Suppose that you get really excited about the idea of motivation and go on to do some more reading, comparing what different authors said and deciding the relative merits of the different theories you encountered, and their weaknesses, perhaps with a view to writing a new paper. Again, this level of learning is different from the simple ability to reproduce material. It is different, too, though in a slightly different way, from learning to apply ideas in a work situation.

Now imagine yourself to be the manager whose behaviour may be contributing to lack of motivation. You may think you are an excellent manager: you are firm with your team, you stand no nonsense. Then you learn that there are different styles of managing, and that the rather authoritarian way you have managed all your life may not be appropriate for your current team, which is made up of highly creative people tasked with finding new ways of doing things. It may be very difficult to come to terms with this, to set aside your long-held beliefs and assumptions and to start to think about people and their needs in a very different way. This is learning on a different level still.

In an educational context, Entwistle (1996) suggests that a *surface approach* is directed merely towards meeting course requirements, often when there is a feeling of being under pressure and/or worried about the work. Study is done without regard to its purpose, beyond that of passing the course. The material is approached as a series of unrelated 'bits'; there is an emphasis on routine memorisation, without making sense of the ideas presented.

In contrast, a *deep learning approach* is driven by the desire to understand the ideas for yourself, and is associated with an active interest in the subject matter. Thus, you try to relate each new idea you come across to your previous knowledge and to any relevant experience. You look for patterns and any underlying metaphors. You look carefully and critically at the author's evidence and logic. Material approached like this is far more likely to be remembered. And if ideas are related not just to other ideas but to relevant experience, your learning is far more likely to lead to improved practice. It is thus particularly important for any study of vocational relevance.

You might think that if you adopt a deep approach you will inevitably get better marks than by taking a surface approach. Usually you will. And you are more likely to be able to remember what you have learned after the course, and incorporate it into your practice as a manager. But it is possible to get so carried away by passion for a subject that you forget the course requirements altogether and actually do worse! It is therefore suggested that a third type of approach, the *strategic approach*, is important. This is directed towards doing as well as possible on a course, being always alert to course requirements and the need to use time and effort to best effect in meeting them. It involves balancing deep and surface learning in order to achieve this. Much of this handbook is devoted to enabling you to do just that.

Rather than making a simple 'surface-deep' distinction, Moon (1999) suggests a series of levels of learning with increasing changes to the way you perceive and think about the world. These are shown in Table 8.1. The division between surface and deep would occur around level 3. She indicates how your tutor or lecturer would detect this in your work. Note the presence of 'reflective' at the two deepest levels.

Although this book is trying to improve your ability to be an effective strategic learner, and to get really good grades, I firmly believe that it is deep learning which is of importance for your career as a senior manager. The emphasis in many of the activities will therefore be to deepen your course learning towards the 'working with meaning' level. This is where you are really engaging with ideas and questioning – and perhaps improving – the mental models with which you make sense of the world. Moon

Surface learning	1.	**Noticing** – represented as 'Memorised representation'
↓	2.	**Making sense** – represented as 'Reproduction of ideas, ideas not well linked'
↓	3.	**Making meaning** – represented as 'Meaningful, well integrated, ideas linked'
↓	4.	**Working with meaning** – represented as 'Meaningful, reflective, well-structured'
Deep learning	5.	**Transformative learning** – represented as 'Meaningful, reflective restructured by learner, idiosyncratic or creative'

Table 8.1 Levels of learning
Source: adapted from Moon (1999), p. 138.

describes this as 'a process of "cognitive house-keeping", thinking over things until they make a better meaning, or exploring or organising the understanding towards a particular purpose or in order that it can be represented in a particular manner'.

This form of learning is more exciting than surface learning, and has a far more profound impact upon your ability to go on learning from the many experiences you will have throughout your life. Many professional organisations now require evidence of such ongoing reflective learning and practice as a condition for continued membership. (If you already have a habit of 'reflective practice' you will need no convincing of its worth.)

The reflective process

You will remember that Kolb *et al.* suggested that for learning to take place experience needs to be followed by reflection, and then conceptualising, or theory building. Thus, you move from action in the real world to a process of detached observation, taking place somewhere inside your head. Clearly, this is not surface learning. But the nature of this process was relatively unspecified, and there are still differences of opinion as to how best to reflect. It is something many students struggle with. If you are finding the Kolb cycle a bit too abstract, you may prefer to use a simpler cycle. This was shown me by one of the best management teachers I have ever met, Dr Reg Butterfield. It has three stages in the cycle:

- Wot?
- So wot?
- Wot next?

(He draws a lovely cartoon face by each.) This is as 'simple' as can be, and with the mis-spellings and faces, totally memorable. At its centre is the essence of the whole process, the 'so wot?' 'So what' is the key question in almost any analysis, followed by the equally important question of what, therefore, to do in the light of your analysis.

8

The basic elements for successful reflection include:

- time to reflect
- something to reflect upon
- medium for capturing reflection
- skills in reflection
- honesty
- feedback.

What follows is what seems to work for me and for many of my own students. If your own course has already given you tools for reflection, ignore it. But if it has not, and you do not quite know where to start, you may find it helpful.

Successful reflection depends first and foremost on making time to reflect. You should by now be managing your time better. Once you are convinced of the value of reflection making time for it will become a priority.

So what to reflect upon? Kolb suggests 'experience'. If you are studying while working, you will have daily experiences to reflect upon. But experiences gained during your studies are equally relevant to reflection. For example, you might be working on a group project. After a meeting you might ask yourself whether it went well, and if so why? Was there anything that might have gone better? How did you feel during the meeting? Was this how you expected to feel? Why? How did your own behaviour influence others in the group, and contribute to the progress you made? Were there ways in which you might have been a more effective team member? What might you do differently next time?

You might reflect, individually or better still as a group, upon how well the team as a whole is progressing towards its objectives, and ask yourself whether there are ways in which this might be improved. Your reflections on your own and others' behaviour in the light of theory – perhaps motivation theory or what you have learned about

→ Ch 7, 11   effective group working – might also help you to realise the significance of parts of that theory that you had not appreciated before. It might make you aware of shortcomings in a particular theory in terms of its ability to cast light on your experience. You might reflect on the content of the project work in the light of theory you have been taught which is potentially relevant to the project itself, and whether you might make fuller use of that theory, or seek other theories.

Some of your reflection might be prompted by reading or lectures. After the event you can usefully deepen your learning (and make it far more likely that you will remember the material) by thinking about how what you have read or heard relates to what you already know. Does it contradict other theories or support them? Does it suggest different interpretations of data on which they are based? Does it relate to your own experience, or to things you have read about business in the paper? What light does it shine upon things that you didn't fully understand before? Does it make you realise the importance of something that perhaps you previously disregarded? Does it make you doubt something that you had previously assumed might be true?

→ Ch 9, 14   Much of this more abstract reflection on the relation between different ideas, and the extent to which they are based on firm evidence relates to the '*critical thinking*' that has already been highlighted as important. This will be discussed further in the context of critical reading and writing answers to assignments which demonstrate critical thinking skills.

Perhaps most important of all, since your primary objective during your course is to *learn,* is to reflect upon the learning process itself. For any 'learning event', whether reading, lecture, other course work or work experience, ask yourself questions such as:

- How did that go?
- How did I feel about the experience?
- What did I learn from it? What did I fail to learn?
- How might I have learned more effectively?
- What will I do differently in future to help me learn better?

You can see from the above that reflection is about asking yourself (or yourselves if doing this in a group) a whole lot of different questions and thinking hard about the answers. It is about being prepared to think about how your own thinking is affecting your actions. It is about realising how your thinking is affecting what you are observing in a situation. You are more likely to be able to 'think about your own thinking' if you are working with one or more other people: this way you can find out that others see things differently from you, and then start exploring both the reasons for these differences, and their implications.

The role of feelings in reflection

You may have been surprised to see the 'How did I feel' question above, but exploring your feelings is an important part of reflection. Often they will highlight areas of concern that you have yet to put into words and signal profitable areas for reflection. Suppose after a job interview you ask yourself 'How did I feel' and get the answer 'somewhat uncomfortable from the very beginning'. If you try to work out the source of this discomfort you may learn a lot. Ask yourself questions like 'When did it start? Was it before I even walked into the room?' Such reflection might show that you felt unprepared for the interview, with obvious implications for future action. Or perhaps you weren't sure about whether this was a company you wanted to work for – maybe you have ethical concerns about their product or way of working. This might affect your choice of companies to apply to in future. Perhaps you felt 'unworthy' of the job? If so, assuming you were honest on your application and they decided to interview you does this suggest that perhaps you undervalue yourself? Or did the discomfort start with a particular question that you were asked early on? If so, what was the question and why did it make you feel uncomfortable? I could continue, but you should see by now where exploring feelings might lead you.

Feelings can also be important when you are thinking about things you have read or which someone has said. They tend to be driven by your non-conscious, non-rational brain, which has far more processing capacity than the conscious part. Discomfort here may mean that there is a mismatch that you have yet to access consciously. It may be that assumptions which form a central part of your way of looking at the world are being challenged. It is very easy, and feels comfortable, to dismiss such challenges as rubbish. Our very identity stems from the set of assumptions, values and beliefs about ourselves which act as a filter through which we see and interpret what happens to us. We tend to be very protective of our identities. It can be unsettling, even painful, to have them challenged. But it is through such challenges that 'cognitive housekeeping' – or even an extension to our cognitive house – is achieved.

One of my most profoundly disturbing experiences as a very young trainer in the Civil Service occurred during an interviewing course I ran for people working in the equivalent of 'Personnel'. I went through some of the relevant theory, and guidelines for effective interviewing, and then had the course members role-play interviews. Nothing very innovative. But a large number of the participants, mainly women in their middle years, who had been interviewing for decades, burst into tears. I had not said anything about their performance. But by reflecting on what they had done in the role plays in the light of the material we had covered, it had dawned on them that for years they had been really bad at interviewing. Part of their identity was 'expert interviewer', and they had been sure that 'their way' was the best, indeed the only way, of going about it.

There are three morals to this story. Firstly, that they needed to change their way of thinking not only about what they did, but also about themselves, as a step on the way to doing it better. Secondly, it took honesty with themselves to bring about this change. In order to protect themselves, they could have decided that the material I was teaching was wrong, or that any feedback they received was useless. Honesty in answering reflective questions is an essential component in learning from reflecting. The third message is that such change can be seriously painful, and support may be needed. I was totally unprepared and unqualified to give such support, and failed those women really badly. You are probably much younger than they were, but still need to tread carefully when exploring your own assumptions, particularly about yourself, or when working as part of a group which is reflecting.

ACTIVITY 8.3

Think about something you have read or experienced, or perhaps received feedback on, which occasioned some discomfort. Think about your feelings in more depth, and try to explore why you felt like that. Note any learning points from this exercise.

TOOLS FOR REFLECTION

You should by now be clear that the main item in your toolkit is a good list of questions. A number of such questions are given above. A slightly longer set is available on-line, but this is still far from comprehensive. You need to select those questions that work for you, in the contexts in which you are reflecting, adding any which are missing from the list and which you feel are important.

Personal reflection is essentially an internal dialogue based around these questions – and honest answers to them – so you need a medium within which this dialogue can take place. One category of tools for reflection consists of formats for recording the dialogue. Key among these are learning logs, learning diaries, learning journals, development records, development plans, audio diaries, and blogs.

I have referred already to the need to create a Personal Development File as an aid to capturing, evidencing and managing your learning. You should by now have a number of responses to activities that are worthy of filing. The other important component is likely to be some form of ongoing reflection such as a learning journal.

This is a relatively new area, and the terms used do not yet have universally agreed definitions. However some distinctions are worth noting. The first is between a simple record and writing with more reflective content. The second concerns the extent to which you move on from your reflection to planning further learning. The main forms are described below.

Simple recording

A learning log might be a simple record of what you learned and when. You could for example note key learning points from each lecture, and each occasion when you did some course-related reading. A simple format would suffice: the following is but one example (adapted from Open University MBA resources for students in a distance learning context).

Event and date	Reason for doing	What I learned from this
2.11.2006 Read first part of course introduction	Required reading	Key management roles, current management challenges (ICTs, globalisation, etc.), Kolb's learning cycle.
14. 11. 2006 Attended first tutorial	Get better idea of course (and tutor) requirements	Need to make explicit reference to key concepts in assignments, need to submit on time, word-limit penalities, value of web-groups.

Such a factual record can be useful both to sustain motivation and for quick reference after. Professional institutes may require a similarly basic record of continuing professional development. Thus, the Chartered Institute of Personnel and Development (CIPD) requires members to keep a record of their development and suggests the following continuing professional development (CPD) recording format (www.cipd.co.uk, accessed 19/03/07) – though they say they are happy for any reasonable format to be used. (I've included an extract from my own record to show how this might reasonably be used.)

Key dates:	What did you do?	Why?	What did you learn from this?	How will you use this? Any further action?
May 05	Attended London seminar run by Bioss on their consultancy model	Wanted to see whether this model would be appropriate for inclusion in new course 'The HR Professional'	How Jaques's ideas on levels have been developed into a full consultancy model – this would be a useful example of theory-driven consultancy	Incorporate into new course unit. Need to visit Bioss website for more detail and contact them re collaboration

You will probably find it convenient to keep such core records on-line, both for ease of updating and because you may be required to use electronic means to submit your learning log for assessment or your CPD record for approval.

Learning journals – a reflective record

Learning logs and development records have their uses, but are directed more towards demonstrating that learning has taken place (or at least, towards claiming that it has). They do little to encourage reflection.

If you want to create a forum for the sort of dialogue – with yourself, or with others – that constitutes effective reflection, then slightly less structure may be helpful. Indeed, you may find it helpful to have almost no structure. This is where the idea of a learning journal comes in. Reflection is probably most effective if it happens soon after the event upon which you are reflecting, and in a way that is easy for you to use. Many of my students use either their PDA or a very small notebook which they keep with them at all times. Some make an audio recording – it is important that the medium is one that suits your way of thinking and which is convenient to carry around. You need to be able to note what it was that struck you, and any thoughts about 'so wot?' and 'wot next' as soon as possible after the 'wot' happened to you, or you read about it in the business pages, or whatever. Thus, in my own example above, on the train on the way home I noted in my little book (I'm a paper person):

> This felt really weird – why? Think it was mainly time travel element. Last time I was in this room was 30 years ago – when I worked for the DE just around the corner and was doing my MPhil research on Jaques and his levels! Comforting that some ideas endure, though they seem to have developed it quite a lot. The 'flow' idea from Csikszentmihaly really resonates with my own experience of being over- and under-stretched. Someone mentioned this the other day as relevant to some other research. Wonder if/how it relates to coaching. Need to get his book and read more about it. If we want to demonstrate some HR consultancy underpinned by sound theory this would be a really good example to pursue. Need to contact Bioss to see if they would be willing to provide a case study.

The following is a reflection (at the end of an MBA) on how reflection has altered the way that the manager 'makes sense' of organisational situations.

> A good example . . . is that during my project design phase, I worried about the Knowledge Inventory (KI) being the 'definitive' repository and having to be an accurate representation of our knowledge. Reflecting on this had shown it to be almost impossible, and using Pareto's 80:20 rule, attempting to make it 100% definitive would take huge amounts of time compared to it being 80% definitive and still very useful. My revised perspective is one of accepting a state of not exactly satisficing, but a realisation that the KI can never be 'wholly accurate', but a better representation of our organisational knowledge compared to where we are now. I now think in terms of moving a problem along a continuum towards a better state, rather than always seeking a 100% solution. I consider this is linked to the over-analysis issue outlined above – previous over-analysis was the result of attempting to find the perfect solution.

> The beauty of the continuum model is that it creates a sense of a timeline over which we can continue to make improvements and refinements – once again showing the iterative nature of the model of planned change. Each iteration moves us further along the continuum, progressively improving the situation.

Overall, a substantial change in my mode of engagement is that my perceptions of and reactions to problems has 'moved', and I am now almost regarding them as opportunities to apply my learning to see 'what sort of a fit' I can make, and what this application of theory is telling me about the problem.

Another example of narrative reflection, again on a final project, shows how self-perceptions can change through reflection on feedback from colleagues, interpreted in the light of concepts gained through reading:

This [project] has provided me with an opportunity to leap from a position of learning through theory and knowledge to gain significant understanding and insight into my own personal behaviour and style and that of other people.

The human interplay and how to read the power structures and influences that people, including myself have, has been a powerful learning experience. It is almost as though I have stepped outside of my skin and looked at myself through a new window.

By doing this, I could see my strengths and achievements through this [project]. I could view my weaknesses without being defensive, but examine their effect upon other people and test concepts for more effective communication.

Eight months ago, I found critical feedback very difficult to take and had become rather hung up about people thinking me 'too passionate and enthusiastic'. I could not see what they meant, after all wasn't that a good thing? I now understand, that the feedback was in respect of the effects of the passion and enthusiasm, not passion and enthusiasm itself. I can see with clarity that my exuberant style can make people feel railroaded into agreeing with me and unable to stop me and raise important questions.

Last year, I truly felt let down that people had waited 40 years to tell me the truth about my style and the effect that it has, even though I had never actually asked them. Through this course, I have learned and understood that only I am responsible for my behaviour and it is my responsibility to reflect on the how that impacts on other people and to make and implement plans for self improvement.

Towards the end of the [project], I had a significant moment of dawning enlightenment. I had been through a very traumatic time at work, almost losing months of work that I was very committed to. I was working very long hours and was tired. I had a very heavy workload with tight deadlines, and felt that I may not get through this [project] which would mean I had to start again. I was not being supported by my line manager and felt very alone.

During a literature search, I found an article, just released, 'Bridging the Gap between Stewards and Creators' (Robert, Austin and Nolan 2007). The article felt as if it had been written for me and my situation. It explained so many events and suggested that the conflict and struggle that I had experienced was inevitable.

I started to understand and was able to not only live with it, but see the positives that the different style of my colleague could bring to balance my own work. I was able to think about how we might start to more fully appreciate each other and ask for help to bridge the gap between our opposite traits. Help is not something that I commonly ask for; but suddenly it seemed to be acceptable and necessary.

The more I searched though the research literature about innovation, the more I found that conflict and struggle between different personalities in the innovation process was experienced by others around the world.

It was a moment where I no longer felt ostracised or alone in my quest for innovation.

I cannot describe the significant step change in my understanding and the ensuing calm that I have developed for dealing with situations, but feel that I must continue to develop this understanding above all else. I need to develop my 'innovator' strengths to reach their full potential, and continue to understand my own behaviour and its effects on individuals and teams. By adopting more open strategies for public (Raelin 2001), group and individual reflection in action (Johnson 1998) I will be able to build on my new understanding and continue to develop my personal effectiveness at work.

Johnson (1998) describes reflection on action as 'making the difference between having 20 years of experience, and one year's experience 20 times'. I know that I am still in the early stages of my development and that I have to develop further before I can even think of myself as having experience that builds year on year. My new understanding has caused my to reflect much further back than this [project], probably as far back as five years, finding clarity about past successes and difficulties, including times where I have had problems influencing other people or have found myself in conflict.

The penny feels like it has dropped which is a very empowering and energising experience. I now feel confident that I have just gained five years' experience, rather than one year's experience five times.

This was a major project and it has been hugely successful for the organisation. Furthermore, a whole new network of partnerships has been created and these are continuing beyond this particular initiative. The success on this project can be easily replicated and the organisational learning has been good.

More significantly, I believe that I have gained even more value from understanding myself and my impact on others. My learning from my interactions with just one person has led me to a paradigm shift in my thinking.

I hope that these two examples give a flavour of the reflective process, and of its potential power. Although they were written at a particular point in time, summarising the reflective learning over a year, they summarise a 'reflective conversation' which took place over a period of time. You will find it useful to have such an ongoing conversation with yourself as your thoughts develop and also as you are able to distance yourself more from the original event and your reactions to it. If you use a small notebook it is therefore useful to transcribe your jottings to a slightly more permanent location, whether paper-based, on your PC or online. If you have made an audio recording you might want to copy it onto your computer.

It is this rather more permanent record that is normally referred to as a learning journal. While a diary would normally have daily entries, the essence of journal keeping is to record things fairly often, and fairly soon after they happen, but not necessarily daily. Crucially, this record incorporates a strong element of reflection, and captures this in a way that is easy to come back to and add to. It is easy to come back to and modify an electronic record, and for this reason transcribing to your PC is strongly recommended. You can usefully print off your entries to date at any point when you want to peruse them in leisurely fashion in the bath or by a river.

If you prefer the tangibility and portability of a paper journal it is worth leaving alternate pages blank. You can then revisit entries and add further comment on how your thinking has developed subsequently, or how this item relates to subsequent experience or reading.

Construct a journal entry on your learning from this chapter thus far. Choose your medium. Label your entry 'work on Chapter 8', date it, and write a fairly free-form entry. Possible questions to address, if you are unsure how to start, are:

■ What is the most interesting thing I have read in this chapter and why was it interesting?

■ What are the three main things I have learned from it?

■ What, if anything, that I previously thought was true now seems as if it may be wrong?

■ What was new or surprising in the chapter?

■ Was there anything missing that I expected to find? Can I find this some other way?

■ What am I still unsure about?

■ What did I dislike about this chapter and why?

■ Was there anything that particularly interested me? Can I find out more about this?

■ What do I intend doing differently as a result of reading this chapter?

■ What do I need to do to make it more likely that I will actually carry out this intention?

Keep this entry in your learning file and revisit and update it at intervals. From here on, make reflective entries for each chapter as you work through it, as part of a more general learning journal.

The questions above suggest a journal based purely on words. However, reflection is likely to be far richer if you extend your recording to include diagrams such as mind-maps or rich pictures (*see* Chapter 10). One of the key elements in reflection is looking at relationships between things, and diagrams are normally far better for this than are words. If you are doing comparisons between different ideas, say, you may also find it useful to use a table. The golden rule is to use what works for you, and what works for the particular sort of thinking which the learning event requires.

→ Ch 10

Reflecting in a virtual learning environment

Many universities are creating 'virtual learning environments' (VLEs) for students. These can have many purposes, and for some distance learning institutions they may be the place where most of the learning takes place. Face-to-face institutions may make more limited use of them, but one really useful function is to allow students to construct an 'ePortfolio'. This term is still used in a variety of ways, but it is useful to think of it in terms of an on-line space which is personal to you. In it you can have an area for constructing and storing your assignments, evidence of competence, an area for storing resources you have gathered, study and/or development plans, your reflective writing, your CV, and anything else that you will find useful to have easy access to.

Items in these various storage areas can be collated for different purposes. Thus, you could easily extract a relevant part from your learning journal and insert it into an assignment and extract it again for a portfolio needed for accreditation by a professional institute. Furthermore, while parts of your ePortfolio may be private, other parts may be accessible by your tutor, or, say, other students who are working with you on a project. This ease of access – both for you and for others – can be a great advantage. Another advantage is that back-up becomes the university's problem not yours.

Formats for planning

Chapter 1 showed a simple planning chart which can be used to manage your studies as a whole. But your learning journal may throw up things which are more complex than the 'learn X' or 'complete assignment Y' which such a chart easily accommodates. A slightly more complex format may thus be a useful supplement to an overall planning chart. Such a chart is trying to capture the further learning element of the 'wot next' in the Butterfield version of a learning cycle. You can simply extend your log or record to include a 'what next' column, and a column for target dates and for checking when action is complete. But a separate action plan, preferably driven by a combination of your course and your reflections from experience, may work better for you.

Again, a very simple format may serve. The example overleaf uses a format derived from that suggested by the Chartered Institute of Personnel and Development (www.cipd.co.uk, accessed 19/03/07) for demonstrating continuing professional development – a condition for remaining a member. (You will find that most professions now require members to show evidence of continuing professional development.) The CIPD version has five columns.

A portfolio 'exhibit' for a professional institute to demonstrate that you are competent at managing your learning area would have to include not only your action plan (and annotations if you chose a brief format), but also evidence that you have carried out the plan and monitored its success.

→ Ch 1, 6   I hope that you now have a fuller understanding of earlier references to logging and diaries. Chapter 1 suggested that you start a file for such activities, and Chapter 6 contained frequent references to action planning as part of improving your time management. A work diary with a learning log helps you map out your main and sub-objectives, programme tasks for the day, monitor progress and note learning points, barriers to achieving your ends, and steps that may be needed to help you overcome these barriers.

→ Ch 7   Chapter 7 suggested that a study log could be a useful aid to study planning and sustaining motivation while working on your course. Again, logging objectives and charting progress and learning points can help both motivation and consolidation of learning. Logs are simple, practical and highly effective tools – provided you establish the habit of writing them, and the habit of reviewing them at regular intervals. But higher education is increasingly emphasising the importance of a fuller 'Personal

What do I want to learn?	What will I do to achieve this?	What resources and support will I need?	What will be my success criteria?	Target dates for review and completion
How to reflect more effectively	Experiment with the formats provided in this chapter to see what works for me Discuss with tutor whether I could get some feedback	Notebook Time Input from others in my learning set Feedback	To have actually kept journal for a month and submitted for feedback To feel I'm learning more effectively To have used output from reflection to drive further learning via plan Feedback from tutor to say this approach is acceptable as evidence	Review: 1/7, 8/7, 15/7 Submit 22/7

Development File' which will be a richer record of both your reflections and your active management of your learning in the light of your reflections.

Such a file will involve you in a consideration of your objectives and your strengths and weaknesses. It will require you to identify your main career, and perhaps life, objectives, and chart a path towards these. You were starting this process in Chapter 2 when considering what form of study to pursue, if any. Your work diary relates to managing your job, and your learning log relates to managing your studies. Your Personal Development File (PDF) relates primarily to *you*, and to developing yourself in ways that will enable you to achieve your life objectives. Your career will probably feature largely in these. And your studies are presumably directed towards meeting life objectives via advancing your career. But this final file will help you to take a strategic view of both, and relate work and study to the longer-term path you seek to take. You can keep your study log as a subsection.

→ Ch 2

→ Ch 2

To start to compile such a file, revisit your work on your objectives in Chapter 2 and try to identify your major life goals. Then look at your work log and consider how your current job is helping you to achieve these goals. Are there 'barriers' at work that are acting as barriers to progress in this wider sense? If so, think carefully about them and try to plan a set of actions that will overcome or circumvent these barriers. These may involve learning, change of role, communicating your feelings to others in your organisation, or something completely different.

It is fashionable at present (to judge by the volume of books on the topic) to apply marketing concepts, and think of yourself as a brand. What are your identifying characteristics? Why might an employer 'buy' you? What are your current strengths and weaknesses, and the opportunities and threats that life is likely to present? (You will encounter such 'SWOT' analysis on almost any management programme.) If you are finding it difficult to see how your aims may be achieved, looking at yourself in this way may help. And it will be a useful framework, too, when you are starting to think about what you want to do after your course is finished.

Thus, you could start your file with a statement of your main objectives, and key stages to be reached en route to these. Then develop a page for each of these sub-objectives, outlining the actions which will help you achieve them. In order to plan how to reach these key milestones, you need to take an honest look at where you are now. What are your current strengths? Which skills do you need to develop? Consider the full range of skills and other abilities which are involved, not just narrow job skills. Aspects such as interpersonal awareness, social skills, flexibility, clarity of thought, willingness to be wrong and energy levels may be important, as well as more obvious characteristics. If strengths give you a problem think of your last four major achievements, work or otherwise, describe them, and think about what abilities you demonstrated in achieving them. For weaknesses try a similar exercise with things that have gone less than well.

As you develop your work diary and study log, update your personal development file, amending strengths and weaknesses in the light of work experience and course learning. Once a quarter, revisit your overall objectives. You may find that you now feel that these were unnecessarily modest, or the reverse. One area of development which is important, but hard to log, is self-awareness, but your course should help by giving you feedback on various aspects of your performance. It will also help with that other notoriously difficult area of 'making sense' more effectively of situations around you.

As you log your daily learning experiences in your work diary and study log, writing comments on how your way of *making sense* of work situations has altered as a result of your study will be particularly useful. What assumptions have you become aware of? Which of these have you deemed unhelpful and changed? What additional factors/relationships have you become more aware of? What are you doing differently as a result of such changes in thinking? Your note taking should always highlight links between theory and practice and in assignments you should be actively seeking to use theory to inform your analysis. At regular points, update your PDF in the light of these notes.

Throughout the book the importance of linking theory to experience, and of becoming a reflective practitioner, will be stressed. But it is worth taking time now to think about how you can develop the habit of making linkages, and actively interpreting experience in the light of theory or concepts (developed by yourself or offered as part of the course), until it becomes second nature. And start to capture this experience in your logs. This will ensure that you gain more from your study than specific learning. You will have developed the capacity to learn from everything that you do and experience, throughout your working career. This could be of far more benefit to you than anything else that you learn on the course itself.

8

Learning from learning theory

SUMMARY

- Learning can be viewed as the active construction of meaning.
- Such 'making sense' is a central component of exercising leadership.
- Learning is usefully seen as a continuous cycle of experience, reflection on experience, and the development and testing of concepts.
- Individuals vary in their preference for activist, reflector, theorist or pragmatist learning styles.
- Each style has strengths and weaknesses.
- Aspects of non-preferred styles can be strengthened.
- For optimal learning you need to be comfortable with all four styles in order to use the four styles in the learning cycle.
- Reflection is now recognised as a crucial element in learning, and a habit of reflective practice as essential for any professional.
- Reflection involves a dialogue, with yourself and/or others in which you question your experiences and responses to them with a view to developing the way in which you think about them, and improving your future practice.
- Learning to learn, whether from theory or experience, is perhaps the most valuable outcome of MBA studies.
- Keeping a work diary and a learning log, and a more reflective learning journal, and combining insights from these into A Personal Development File, will help you to learn effectively from experience, and contribute substantially to career success.

Further information

- Bolton, G. (2001) *Reflective Practice: Writing and Professional Development*, Sage.
  This is a fascinating, but moderately dense book showing how creative writing can help with developing reflection. Although aimed mainly at teachers, it would be applicable to any professional.
- Butler, G. and Hope, T. (1995) *Manage your Mind: the Mental Fitness Guide*, Oxford University Press.
- Buzan, T. (2003) *Use Your Head*, BBC.
- Entwistle, N, (1996) 'Recent research on student learning and the learning environment', in '*The Management of Independent Learning'*, J. Tait and P. Knight (eds), SEDA, Kogan Page.
- Honey, P. and Mumford, A. (1986) *The Manual of Learning Styles*, Peter Honey.
- Lucas, B. (2001) *Power Up Your Mind*, Nicholas Brealey.
- Moon, J.A. (1999, reprinted 2005) *Reflection in Learning and Professional Development*, RoutledgeFalmer.
- http://www.cipd.co.uk
  For frameworks for planning and recording continuing development as a Human Resource practitioner and examples of completed forms – these can be easily generalised to general management, or management within other functions.

→ 9 Improving reading skills

INTRODUCTION

Studying for a Master's degree will almost inevitably involve many hours of reading. This chapter suggests three ways in which you can cut down on these hours while increasing the benefit gained. Since most people read inefficiently, one way of saving time is to read more efficiently. This can greatly reduce study time, while improving your understanding and retention of what you read. The second way of reading more effectively is to think differently while you read, by becoming more critical in your reading. This will deepen your learning and develop the critical skills expected of someone with a postgraduate qualification. A third set of skills is to take effective notes on what you have read. Reading efficiently and effectively and taking useful notes on what you have read will be useful in a wide range of work contexts, as well as helping you to study more effectively.

This chapter explores the reasons why reading is normally slower than it might be, and suggests exercises which will enable you to improve your own reading speeds if you so desire. Although there is a common perception that speed reading can achieve miracles, the benefits for management study are more limited. There is an old Woody Allen joke, where he stated that after a speed-reading course he was able 'to go through *War and Peace* in 20 minutes. It's about Russia'. Obviously, you will wish to retain rather more than this from many of the materials that you read. But there will be times when rapid scanning will be useful, perhaps in deciding which of the hundreds of theses in the library would merit serious attention, and techniques for this will also be covered.

Management study makes many students, particularly those with a background in the sciences, feel as if they are drowning in a sea of paper. Electronic materials may present even greater problems than paper. It is difficult for many people to absorb large amounts of information from a screen. (Some people resort to printing quantities of it themselves, which rather negates the intended benefits of electronic transmission.) Increasing your reading speed can be a tremendous help in dealing with the volume.

Reading skills go far beyond the mere mechanics of reading efficiently. As you read you need to be able to think about what you are reading and evaluate it against several criteria. The ability to read critically is crucial to study at postgraduate level. The principles of critical reading can also be usefully applied to what you yourself write, in assignments, examinations, and any end of programme dissertation or project report.

EFFICIENT EYE MOVEMENT

ACTIVITY 9.1

Before reading further, look at your watch and note the time _____. Now read the next section quickly but carefully, without stopping, aiming to remember significant pieces of information contained in the text (there will be a short quiz on these) until you are told to look at your watch again.

Most readers are unaware of their eye movements while they read, and assume that their eyes are moving steadily along each line before moving to the next. If this were the case, and if you read at one line per second, which most people who are asked assume to be a reasonable speed, you would be reading at 600–700 words per minute. At this pace, you would find you could easily cope with the volume of materials you are likely to encounter on an MBA or similar programme. Eye movements when reading are far more complex, however. The eye makes a series of extremely rapid jumps along a line, with a significant pause, 0.25 to 1.5 seconds, between each jump. Furthermore, many readers do not move, albeit in this jerky fashion, straight along a line. Instead, as Fig. 9.1 shows, they indulge in frequent backward eye jumps, fixating for a second, or even a third time on a previous word, and at intervals their eye may wander off the page altogether. With erratic eye movements like this, and forward jumps from word to adjacent word, many readers achieve reading speeds of only 100 words per minute. At this rate of reading, the volume of work for an MBA is likely to prove an impossible task.

At the purely technical level, it is possible to achieve reading speeds of up to 1000 words per minute by:

■ reducing the number of fixations per line, stopping every three to six words rather than every one;

■ eliminating backward movement and wandering;

■ reducing the duration of each fixation.

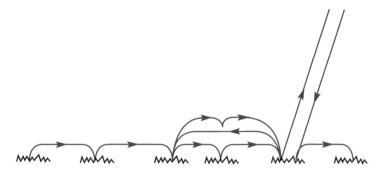

Fig. 9.1 Typical unskilled eye movements when reading

Such improvement will require substantial concentration and considerable practice. But benefits will include: improved ability to get through your course materials; reduced eye fatigue because of the reduction in eye movements; faster reading at work, contributing to better time management. The investment will therefore pay off handsomely. Also, far from being reduced by faster reading, comprehension may be improved. The pattern of a sentence, and its meaning, may emerge much more clearly, and be more readily absorbed, if the sentence is read in phrases, rather than one word at a time. Your interest will be sustained if ideas are coming at you more quickly, and your motivation will be higher if you feel you are making rapid progress. Improved reading techniques offer a wide range of benefits.

If practice is what is needed, why we are all reading so slowly? Surely we have been 'practising' reading most of our lives. Unfortunately, we have been practising our existing bad habits (in the process establishing them more firmly), rather than practising rapid-reading techniques. You will find that it takes much *more* effort, at least at first, to read at increased speed, and improvement will be made only through the practice of exercises specifically designed for that purpose. Even when you have developed efficient reading techniques you may still find that you have to make a point of consciously practising them at intervals, to prevent yourself from falling back into less efficient habits.

ACTIVITY 9.2

Look at your watch again and note the time _____. Now note how long it is since you last noted the time _____. There were approximately 700 words in that piece of text. Divide that figure by the number of minutes elapsed in order to find your reading speed in words per minute. Write this down _____.

EXERCISE 9.1

Now check your comprehension by answering the following questions, saying whether each statement is true or false according to the preceding text. Do not glance back at the text.

9

Improving reading skills

	T/F
1. Poor readers fixate once per word.	_____
2. With practice a poor reader can increase from a speed of 100 to 1000 words per minute.	_____
3. A speed reader will fixate only once per line.	_____
4. Once you have mastered speed-reading techniques they will become second nature.	_____
5. The only drawback to rapid reading is that it tends to reduce comprehension.	_____
6. The duration of each fixation can range from as little as 0.25 of a second to as much as 1.5 seconds.	_____

Comment

Answers are at the end of the chapter. If you got more than one wrong, you should be aiming to improve your retention skills since you were specifically instructed to try to retain the information in the passage.

A reading speed of 250 or more words a minute, with reasonable retention, is an adequate basis on which to start your course. If your speed was significantly less than this, or at your present speed you are not absorbing enough, you may find the following exercises useful.

INCREASING READING SPEED

The following practice activities are developed from those suggested by Tony Buzan. They will enable you to make significant improvements in your reading speed, *provided you are prepared to invest the necessary time and effort in your practice.* You will need to spend 20–30 minutes a day for several weeks if you wish to reach the full speed of which you are capable. This will allow you to do some of the activities several times per practice session. To keep up your motivation, and to see when your rate of improvement is beginning to level off, keep a graph of your progress. Using a single book, to control for ease of reading – material varies enormously in difficulty – set a timer, and read for five minutes, noting start and finish points. Then count the number of words read. Aim to remember significant points in each piece of text. Check your speed during your first practice session, then every five to seven sessions thereafter. Plot your speeds on a graph, so that you have a visible record of progress. If you choose to use this book, then you can use your earlier speed as the first point on the graph. When you have reached the speed you want, or progress seems to be minimal, cut back to one practice session per week for a while, and then one per month. Check your reading speed monthly thereafter, and resume more frequent practice sessions if your speed starts to fall off.

Many of the practice activities which follow require a way of measuring speed. Counting chimpanzees, or whatever you usually do in the absence of a clock, will interfere with your reading. A metronome, which will allow you to vary the speed of your cue, is ideal. If you do not have one, it may be possible to borrow. Failing that, your phone, PC or watch may be able to emit regular beeps. A kitchen timer that can be made to ring at intervals of from one to five minutes can also be used.

You will also need suitable practice material of various density of text. This Handbook could be regarded as medium density on average, although there is variability between sections. A light novel would be low density, an academic management textbook heavy density.

For all the activities you will need an 'eye guide'. You will use this to coax your eyes to fixate less often and more rapidly, by pointing with it to where you wish to fixate, and moving it after the duration of fixation you require. A finger will do, but since the comprehension exercises which follow this section suggest highlighting key points, you might prefer to get used to reading with highlighter in hand, moving this, just *above* the surface of the page, to indicate stopping points.

Reading practice activities

1. Muscle exercise

Fixate alternately between the top left-hand and right-hand corners of the page, moving your eyes between them as quickly as possible. Then alternate between top and bottom, and between diagonals. Aim to speed up slightly at each session.

2. Page turning practice

Practise rapid page turning. Turn pages at a rate of three seconds per page, increasing to two seconds per page after about 10 sessions. Move your eyes rapidly down each page, aiming to absorb *something*, though it will not be much at first. Do this for two minutes at a stretch.

3. Reducing fixations

Practise fixating less often. Start by pointing at every third word, or every second one if you find three too difficult, and moving your pointer every 1.5 seconds. After a few sessions gradually increase both the speed at which you move the pointer, and the distance you move it, until you eventually can fixate once per line, for one second only. Once you can do this quite easily (and this may take some time), experiment with more than one line per fixation. It is unlikely that you will be able to read many of your course materials at these higher speeds, though.

4. Speed reading

Still using your eye guide, practise reading as fast as you can for one minute, regardless of comprehension. Mark start and finish points. Then read for a further minute aiming for comprehension of significant points, noting your end point. Count and record words per minute. This exercise can be done several times per session, varying the density of the material.

5. Progressive acceleration

Using light- to medium-density material, and starting with your fastest comfortable 'reading with comprehension' speed, increase your speed by about 100 words per minute, and read for a minute, then by a further 100 words per minute for a further minute, until after four minutes you are reading for a minute at approximately 500 words per minute faster than your starting speed. Calculate the speed at which your eye guide must move to achieve these speeds. Then read for a further minute, aiming for the fastest 'with comprehension' speed you can achieve. It should be higher than in Exercise 4.

6. Pre-scanning

Using fairly light-density material, start at the beginning of a chapter. Estimate approximately where 10 000 words will take you, and put a marker there. Scan read to the marker, taking two to four seconds per page. Then go back to the beginning and read for *some* comprehension, at a minimum of 1500 to 3000 wpm. (Use the lower speeds in early sessions, increasing with time. You might also increase the density of material over time.)

The above exercises, if practised regularly, should increase your speed of reading without loss of comprehension. It was suggested that it might even increase comprehension. You can, however, make a more direct attack on improving the effectiveness, rather than merely the speed, of your reading. In parallel with the fairly mechanical exercises described above, you need to develop study strategies that will enable you to read more *effectively*. To do this you need to know *what* to read, what speed it is appropriate to read it at, how to absorb and think about significant points, and how to take good notes to supplement recall. It is also helpful to index these notes for later reference.

These ideas were briefly introduced in the last two chapters, but will be developed further here.

SELECTING READING MATERIAL

Knowing what to read is critical. Even if you are a distance learning student and provided with everything you need in carefully measured packets (and this is not the case on all distance courses), you will need to make some decisions about what to omit if short of time, or what additional reading to do in areas which really interest you.

For most other part-time students there are fairly major decisions to take. There may be huge reading lists, and selection will be essential, especially if there are several texts on a single subject, any one of which looks as if it would do. On projects and dissertations *all* students are faced with major choices of what to read.

→ Ch 3 This Handbook can do no more than suggest a systematic approach to an answer that will suit your particular circumstances. It is, naturally, a variation on the 'Universal Management Paradigm' (UMP) described in Chapter 3.

Define the problem

What are your objectives? Why do you want to read something in this area? What do you *really* need to know? Is it facts, ideas, alternative approaches, background information, or something else that you are seeking? Is the information a requirement for an exam, necessary or potentially useful for an assignment, or just for your own clarification or interest? Refer back to the discussion of the different types of learning in Chapter 7.

→ Ch 7

Identify options

What sources exist? Look at references at the end of recent or key papers on the topic. Seek a librarian's help in identifying and searching relevant databases. Use the same keywords to search the Internet more generally. Look at reference lists in recent theses on the topic. Ask teaching staff and other students or knowledgeable colleagues for ideas. Check government publications and websites, in-company resources, etc. Browse in a good bookstore. (Note: there is more guidance on literature searching in Chapter 19.)

→ Ch 19

Identify your measures of effectiveness

Coverage relevant to your purpose is obviously crucial. Availability is important, with price and order time also significant. Reputation is crucial. The level at which something is written is also a factor to consider. You do not want something trivial, but nor should it be so specialist that it is impenetrable. It helps if something is well written. Has the author used substantial evidence, or extensively surveyed published material, or is the piece written on the basis of opinion and prejudice? When was the work published? You will need to consider in each case which of these factors are most important for you. If using material 'published' electronically be particularly cautious. It may not have been subjected to the scrutiny given to papers in refereed academic journals.

Selection

Selection will be difficult unless you have access to possible materials, and can inspect them. With even brief access you can scan materials rapidly to gain an idea of their likely usefulness. Otherwise you will need to accept advice, or use other clues. Always ask a tutor or project supervisor for as much help as you can get in the vital area of identifying materials which are worth the effort of obtaining and reading. In evaluating possible materials, check whether the author's objectives are compatible with your own. Particularly in North America, where academic tenure depends largely on the length of a lecturer's publication list, there is enormous pressure to publish, regardless of whether the person has done any research or had any ideas worth reporting. Whole books may be written around a single, fairly basic idea, filled out with anecdotes drawn from the author's consultancy experience. These may be interesting, but may not score highly on relevant measures of effectiveness.

Going through the stages of the UMP should help you to make a sensible choice of materials. Having done so, you need to consider the appropriate reading speed for the materials selected.

9

Improving reading skills

Searching the Internet

Increasingly you will be searching for your reading materials electronically, either via electronic resources in your library or directly on the Internet. Extreme caution is necessary if you are to avoid wasting hours of your time on material of little worth. Because this is a real hazard with literature searches for projects and dissertations, this subject is dealt with at length in Chapter 19, and web references are given for on-line training in search skills. You might, if you have time, like to refer to that now, and start to practise your search and selection skills.

→ Ch 19

CHOOSING YOUR READING SPEED

Sometimes you will be looking for a highly specific piece of information. Did this research use a particular technique? What sample was used? What does this author say on a particular point? If your purpose is to find something like this, a full reading of the book or article, at whatever speed, will be unnecessary. Instead, use the index, plus rapid scanning of the material to identify the part you need to read in detail. Just as you can hear your name being mentioned at the other side of a crowded room (the so-called cocktail party effect), so can you bring selective attention to bear upon written materials. You can scan the page too rapidly to read it, but still notice the word or phrase that you are seeking. In the photo-reading technique you will be scanning pages even *more* rapidly. Scanning requires concentration, and a determination not to be sidetracked by interesting points irrelevant to your purpose. Of course, if you *can* spare the time, such digressions can be rewarding; indeed, some would say they are what study is all about. Alas, they will often be a luxury.

The next-fastest type of reading after scanning is that aimed at getting a picture of the overall pattern of a book, chapter or article. To obtain this kind of mapping of material, you need to focus first on any contents lists, then introductions and summaries, and main headings and subheadings. Diagrams and tables of results are also useful. You may find that several rapid passes through the material will help you to map it better than will a single, slightly slower pass. It is useful at this stage to note any specific questions you would like the material to answer, together with any aspects which arouse your curiosity more generally.

Slightly slower again is speed reading, using your fastest comfortable speed. This may be suitable for lengthy materials, where the level of relevant content is fairly low, or for background reading. You will be aiming to absorb the author's main arguments and the extent to which these are based on relevant and reliable evidence.

Much of your study will need to be at a slower rate. This is not to say that speed-reading techniques are a waste of time. You will still benefit from eliminating redundant eye movements, and from more rapid reading of any non-critical parts of the texts. But there will be materials where there is little redundancy. Almost every word will be important, and concepts will require active thought, particularly to assess the extent to which they fit, and help make sense of, your own experience. For this type of study you will need to take notes, both to aid comprehension, and for later recall, and you may need to stop reading to think, or even to consult other sources, before coming back to the main materials. You may need to practise working something out, if it is complicated. If you are trying to understand the basics of linear programming, for example, speed reading will not be appropriate.

Slowest of all is reading to learn by heart. If you need to be able to reproduce an equation, or a diagram, or a set of categories, you will need to spend time on the item itself, committing it to memory and ensuring that you fully understand every detail, and its significance, particularly in relation to the sorts of things you are likely to use it for. You will probably need to practise applying the thing learned, preferably to a variety of situations. It has already been argued that there is little point in learning something if you do not at the same time learn how, and when, to use it.

You may find that, once you have gone over all the details, relationships and possible uses, you will have *learned* the material in question. But other things may prove more elusive. If so, try to devise a mnemonic. I still recite the colours of the rainbow, on the rare occasions when this is requested, by remembering the phrase from my childhood, 'Read out your green book in verse', and go through the entire 'Thirty days hath September . . .' rigmarole to feel sure that August really does have 31 days. In either case, this is a fairly long-winded procedure, and you might feel that the learning by rote, or constant repetition, in the way that tables used to be taught, is more efficient. If speed of recall is important, such as when you need to know what 7×9 is in the middle of some mental arithmetic, then indeed straight learning may be preferable. But mnemonics are extremely useful for information that you might not need for several months, as they will enable you to drag from the recesses of your memory material that would otherwise be inaccessible.

An alternative to devising a phrase is to make the initials into a pronounceable word. (Remember 'SMART' objectives?) Many authors help, by going out of their way to come up with things that are in themselves memorable. The uncharitable might say that this, rather than the merit of what it is that they are enabling you to remember, is what has made them so popular. You will almost certainly encounter the 7 Ss, the 4 (or more) Ps, and many more of that ilk. Rhyming is also popular. The 'form, storm, norm, perform' sequence is used in Chapter 11 on working in teams, and there are several other such formulations in different areas. If authors have not been so helpful, you can have fun devising your own mnemonics.

→ Ch 11

Guidelines for effective reading

- Establish purpose in reading.
- Select appropriate material.
- Scan entire text rapidly to establish structure and coverage.
- Refine purpose – what key points/questions are of interest?
- Read relevant parts of text at fastest appropriate speed.
- Capture understanding by diagramming structure of arguments, highlighting text and/or note taking.
- Review against purpose.
- File notes carefully.

9

Improving reading skills

PHOTO-READING FOR ACCELERATED LEARNING

One system claiming to enhance your ability to learn from printed materials uses an ultra-rapid scanning stage called photo-reading, incorporated into an approach similar to that already described. In (very) brief outline, this requires that you first clarify your objectives in approaching the text, as you should with any study. Then, again as suggested, you preview the text, getting the gist of it, looking for trigger words that catch your attention, looking at a contents list. Then the method departs slightly, in an attempt to put the brain into a receptive state and to absorb material without being aware of it. To achieve this you need to 'enter an accelerated learning state' through relaxation and visualisation. Music may also be helpful (they suggest Mozart or similar – not all music is appropriate). While in this state you 'photo-read', with your eyes focused on something behind the book (if you can vaguely see two lines between the pages, not one, you have it right). With this 'fuzzed' focus, breathing evenly and maintaining your relaxed state you turn the pages steadily, once per second or so. On finishing, set the text aside for a while, then deal with it through normal effective reading and note taking. It is claimed that you will absorb far more because of the photo-reading stage.

If you want to experiment with this, you probably need to read more about it: achieving the relaxed state is not particularly easy. As with other techniques, this will require practice, but it may be something you wish to try if you are going to have to read a lot during your course.

READING CRITICALLY

→ Ch 8

The idea of questioning the material you read was introduced in the last chapter in the context of reflection on what you learned from reading. There, the focus was very much on how what you read related to your existing mental models, and whether it suggested that you might be able to enhance or improve them. This is closely related to the process of reading critically, and indeed depends upon it. But here I want to look in rather more detail at the 'critical' element, with a focus shifted more towards the material read and its author.

Critical thinking is a key skill, and one increasingly emphasised in learning outcomes for postgraduate courses. So it is important to get a clear idea of what is meant. 'Critical' is not used in the sense of saying disparaging things about an author. Rather it means engaging with the materials at a 'deep' level, making sure that you understand the claims which are being made and the arguments and evidence which the author is using to support these claims. It means understanding how these claims relate to those made by other authors, and understanding, too, the context within which the author is writing. There may be cultural, discipline-based or other assumptions which are never made explicit, but which underpin the claims made. (As a psychologist I have always had immense difficulty coming to terms with papers written by those with a sociology background: the agendas and the vocabulary and the assumptions made seem to me to differ radically from those with which I am familiar.) When you read critically you need to be alert to such assumptions, and prepared to question them. It is also helpful to know when the author was writing. Some older books and papers offer splendid insights, but it is important to be aware of possible differences in organisations and their contexts at the time of writing, and of the implications of these if drawing conclusions about the present.

The nature of claims

Having established the context in which something was written, the next step to becoming a critical reader is to understand the sorts of claims being made. By claim I mean any idea which someone says is 'true'. Usually they give reasons for this claim. The claim plus its associated reasons constitutes an argument. Before looking at arguments and how they are constructed, it is helpful to understand some of the terms used. In particular I should like to look at possible differences between concept, model, metaphor, framework, and theory. I say 'possible', because these terms are used in different ways by different authors. Even though these words are distinguished differently on occasion, the distinctions themselves are worth noting.

A *concept* is any abstract idea. 'Motivation' is a concept. 'Learning' is a concept. 'Hidden agenda' is a concept. Such concepts can be really helpful in making you aware of an aspect of a situation and helping you to understand it. I can still remember my excitement when I first came upon the idea of hidden agendas and started to look for the *real* objectives of people in meetings, something it had never occurred to me to consider before. In the last chapter I mentioned 'cognitive housekeeping': adding a new concept is one of the ways you can improve your 'cognitive house'. When you are reading something it is important to understand any concepts which the author uses which are unfamiliar. Be particularly alert to 'everyday' words or phrases that seem to be being used in a non-everyday manner. ('Critical' is one such example in this chapter.) If you do not understand the specialist sense in which the word is being used, your reading will be of little benefit.

A *model* in everyday language is a simplified representation of something. Thus, the map of the London Underground is a model of one aspect of the system itself, namely the relationship between lines and stations on a line. An architect's 3D representation of a building he has designed is another sort of model. When you are diagramming a situation you are creating a model of it, often concentrating on only one aspect of the situation. It is important to remember this uni-dimensionality when dealing with models, and not to confuse them with the reality: 'the map is not the territory'.

A *metaphor* is the use of a familiar term to describe something probably less familiar. It carries with it the suggestion that understanding the former will help you understand the latter. Examples include talking about an organisation as a 'well oiled machine', or 'a tight ship'. Metaphors can usefully highlight key features of a situation. Morgan (1986) uses the spider plant as a striking metaphor for one form of organisational structure. But they are only as useful as the similarities contained. The comforting feeling of understanding that they give can be a dangerous illusion if you draw too many conclusions. As with models, you need to remember that metaphors only partially resemble the thing you are applying them to. Metaphors can be a great aid to creativity.

Framework tends to be used to indicate a rather more organised abstraction. Frameworks are extremely common in management 'theory'. Thus, you may well encounter the 4 (or 7) Ps in your marketing studies, and you have seen the SWOT framework in this book. Such frameworks tend to provide useful checklists for analysing a situation. If you wanted to look at the environment in which you were operating you might use STEEPLE (and look at sociological, technological, environmental (in the physical sense), economic, political, legal and ethical factors surrounding the organisation). You have already tried SWOT and SMART as frameworks for examining yourself and formulating your objectives.

'Management Theory' is often used as a loose collective term to refer to any of the above, but it is more useful to think of *theory* as being an organised set of assumptions which allow you to make predictions about a situation. The STEEPLE framework alerts you to a lot of things to look for, but does not in itself allow you to predict anything. In studying motivation you will probably encounter *Expectancy Theory* (a brief explanation is given in the box below). You can see that this allows you to make a number of predictions. For example it suggests that if you reduce the value of outcomes, or link them less closely to performance, or make it appear less likely that effort will produce performance, then less effort is likely to be made. Management theories in this sense are rather less common than frameworks.

Box 9.1

Expectancy Theory (Lawler and Porter (1967))

Expectancy Theory suggests that there are three major linked elements that need to be understood in order to predict the effort that someone will put into their job. The first is the likelihood, *as they see it*, of that effort resulting in the desired performance. The second is the likelihood that *as they see it* that this performance will result in some sort of outcome. (Outcomes might be positive or negative and intrinsic (e.g. a sense of achievement) or extrinsic (e.g. a bonus).) The third is the value *to them* of the expected outcomes. Note that all these things are *subjective*. The person concerned may over- or under-estimate their chances of successful performance, and may misperceive the link between performance and reward. And it is the value *they* put on the outcomes that matters, not some general value – not everyone values money particularly highly.

To work out motivation, you need to multiply the two perceived probabilities by the perceived value of the outcomes likely to follow performance.

The theory predicts that motivation would be strengthened by an increase in the strength of the perceived effort–performance link. The real probability might be increased by additional training or resources, or the subjective probability might be increased by increasing someone's confidence in themselves. Motivation would also be strengthened by an increase in the perceived performance–outcome link by actually linking rewards more closely to performance or by clarifying perceptions if there is a link but the person doesn't understand it. Motivation could also be increased by increasing the value of the outcomes to the person concerned – some organisations offer a 'menu' of incentives in recognition of variation in such values.

Management writing varies greatly. Sometimes the author is proposing a new theory or a new framework, sometimes critiquing an existing theory, sometimes describing a case study. Some less academic publications may seem to be proposing the answer to life, the universe, and everything! When you are reading critically it is helpful to be clear whether the author is proposing – or drawing on – a theory or framework, or using metaphor. Some of the questions you would ask while reading will depend upon the nature of the claim.

Analysing the argument

In most papers you read, the author will be claiming that one or more statements are justified/true/useful, and providing arguments from evidence (which might be other theories, or research data or even armchair observations) to support this case. So before going further you need to work out the main claim that the author is making, and indeed any secondary claims. As an example of this sort of thinking I'll take another classic motivation theory, Herzberg's (1966) 'Motivation-Hygiene' theory: you are likely to encounter this at some point in your studies and I have already introduced another theory of motivation so it allows comparison. I shall abbreviate the argument here, for simplicity.

Box 9.2

Herzberg's (1966) theory of motivation

Herzberg claims that man has two sets of needs: one set concerns the need to avoid pain and the other concerns the specifically human need to grow psychologically. This claim is supported by the results of interviews with 200 engineers and accountants 'who represented a cross-section of Pittsburgh industry'. Interviewees were asked to think of a time when they had felt especially good about their jobs, and then to answer questions about why they had felt like that, and its impact on their performance, personal relationships and well-being. This process was then repeated for a time when they had negative feelings about their job. Five factors stood out as strong determinants of job satisfaction: achievement, recognition (for achievement), work itself, responsibility and advancement. Dissatisfaction was associated with company policy and administration, supervision, salary, interpersonal relations and working conditions. Thus satisfaction was associated with the person's relationship to what they do, while dissatisfaction was associated with the context within which they do it. Herzberg provided a chart showing how responses were distributed. This broadly supports the 'two factor' idea. Although most factors receive mentions in the context of both satisfaction and dissatisfaction, they appear in the 'wrong' category much less frequently than in the 'right' one.

Now look at this theory critically. Remember the original claim: there are two categories of human need operating. The evidence to support it appears plausible. Different circumstances seemed to cause feeling good about your job, and feeling bad. But consider the evidence: is it actually adequate? No detail is given about whether the 'theory' was already known to the person categorising the responses, or whether this was done blind. There is room for subconscious bias in any subjective judgements: the paper I was reading (an extract from a book) did not make this clear, so I would need to go back to the original research paper to check the method. (At this point you would make an action note to do this.) Then what about the sample of people interviewed? You could argue that two professional groups in a single US city is not really a representative sample. Would blue collar workers respond in the same fashion? Would poor people in other countries be similarly unmoved by money?

Then what about the reasoning? Is the conclusion inevitable from this evidence? Would you get these results *only* if people had two different sets of needs? There is quite a lot of evidence to suggest that in other contexts we tend to take personal credit for good things that happen to us, and blame others for the bad. Herzberg's results could be explained equally well by this human tendency. Alternatively, as indeed Herzberg points out, the 'motivators' tend to be associated with performing the task, the dissatisfiers with the context in which it is performed. Would not Expectancy Theory, which was being developed at around the same time, predict exactly this? And in a way that enabled further predictions to be made about ways in which strengthening the effort–outcome link could increase motivation?

The next question is the 'so what' one. At the time, Herzberg's theory had a profound influence on organisations. Out of it came a new approach to improving employee motivation called 'job enrichment'. Instead of offering pay rises, organisations sought to motivate staff by increasing responsibility. A whole industry grew up, offering the highly prescriptive approach Herzberg developed. (Indeed, increasing responsibility levels is still the thrust of many job redesign exercises, although because the underpinning theory is less simplistic, the chances of success are arguably higher.)

Did it work? Sometimes. But in other cases the effort–performance link was already weak because the staff concerned lacked the necessary skills to do what was required of them. As Expectancy Theory would have predicted, the effects of job enrichment and giving additional responsibility were catastrophic in such cases! It might have saved a lot of money in some of the organisations concerned if a more critical reading of Herzberg had been undertaken before job enrichment was embarked upon.

Mapping the argument

In looking at Herzberg's much quoted and, at the time, highly influential piece of writing, I was trying to do three things:

- identify the claim being made
- evaluate the evidence being used in support of the claim
- evaluate the reasoning used to link the evidence to the claim.

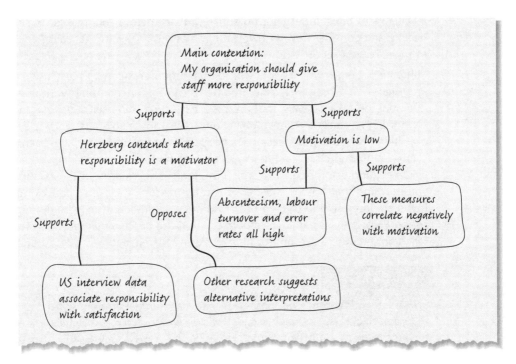

Fig. 9.2 Example of an argument map

It can be really helpful to approach this graphically. You can use an argument map – a development of the more generalized form of a mind map (described later in this chapter). In an argument map each branch represents a single 'reason' with the twigs being the pieces of evidence that together form that reason. Figure 9.2 shows an example of an argument map. (*See* Fig. 9.3 for an example of a more generic mind-map.)

Branches might be in the form of different logical links. Such links might be:

■ A proves B

■ A suggests that B is likely

■ A is consistent with B

■ A is inconsistent with B

■ A disproves B.

There might be a set of twigs that would establish one of these main links. You could write the nature of the link on the branch. When you have a complex argument, unless there is actual proof – rare in management research – you will be faced with working out how much weight to give to the different reasons. This will depend upon the strength of the evidence itself, its consistency, and the strength of the evidence–claim links.

Although we have been talking about mapping other people's arguments, the technique is really valuable for mapping your own reasoning when you are planning an essay answer. If you are planning a research project or dissertation it can also be

→ Ch 14, 15, 19
invaluable to think about your potential evidence before you finalise your research design, and consider how – however it comes out – it relates to claims you might hope to make in your report.

Software packages which allow you to map arguments can be really useful if the argument is at all complex. And arguments can be *very* complex, with many reasons operating on several levels. In these cases each twig is in itself a claim, and has supporting reasons (premises), objections to reasons (rejoinders) and objections to objections (rebuttals). By teasing them apart it is possible to evaluate each chain of claim–supporting claims–evidence, by looking both at the logic involved and the evidence (and assumptions) to which this logic is applied. As in the example above, you may find that both the evidence and the reasoning leave something to be desired. If you are interested in this, you can find material on-line. It may be designed to support – or sell – a particular product, but in the process may provide more detailed teaching than there is room for here (try www.austhink.com/reason/tutorials).

ACTIVITY 9.3

Select an article from a business or management journal or professional. Try to identify: the principal claim and any secondary claims. If applicable, it may help to decide whether theory, framework and/or metaphor is involved. Define any new concepts. Ask 'so what'? If the claim is true, what does it imply? If the implications are important enough to justify the effort, try to tease apart the arguments involved. What claims and/or evidence are used to support the main claim(s)? What if any evidence is used to support any intermediate claims? What are the logical links used? Do they add up to a valid argument provided the evidence is sound (i.e. is the conclusion drawn the only possible one)? Is the evidence adequate? Are there any hidden assumptions being made? If so, how valid are these assumptions?

Hidden assumptions are difficult to identify, but may be absolutely critical to an argument. There was a hidden assumption in the Herzberg case which you may have seen once the alternative explanation was pointed out. This was that 'no other explanation is possible'. Once this assumption was queried, other possible explanations were looked for, and some found. So when a reason is offered it is always worth asking whether this reason is sufficient in itself to support the claim.

The other real difficulty in business research is the complexity of most of the issues addressed, and the variety of contexts in which these issues arise. This makes it very difficulty both to obtain convincing evidence, and to know how far to generalise from it. Even if the evidence and argument was adequate in its context, would it be reasonable, for example, to draw conclusions about all employees from two professional groupings in one city? It was clear in the example above how difficult it was to interpret the subjective responses given by the professionals concerned. There is a real dilemma faced by many authors between seemingly 'scientific' quantitative data and the richer, → Ch 19 but harder to interpret, qualitative information. More of this in Chapter 19.

There are many other useful questions to ask when reading critically. A basic selection, including those already covered, is given in the guidelines below.

Guidelines when reading critically

- When/where was this written and what was the author's purpose?
- What claims is the author making?
- What new concepts are introduced, and what do they mean?
- Are they really new or merely 're-badging' of existing ideas?
- How/when might they be useful?
- What new frameworks are introduced?
- What do they add to existing frameworks?
- How/when might they be useful? Are there limitations to their application?
- Is there any new theory introduced?
- Do the 'organised assumptions' that make up the theory 'hang together' logically?
- Does it extend an existing theory? (Sometimes quite small additions can be surprisingly useful.)
- Is it consistent with other theories that you already know? If not, what are the inconsistencies? Are they explained/justified?
- How/when might the new theory be useful? Are there limitations to its application?
- Are there ways in which this new theory might usefully be amended?
- Was the author arguing a case to which s/he was personally committed? (This can indicate potential for bias.)
- How good is 'the argument' supporting the claim? Are there any shortcomings in the evidence or the logic, or any hidden assumptions which might be questioned?
- If there are inadequacies, is this because the paper is a shortened version of something else? If so, could you find more of the evidence by looking at other sources?

9

Improving reading skills

TAKING NOTES

There are several reasons why note taking is important. If you are working with borrowed books, then apart from the parts that are so important that you photocopy them, you will need something that you can refer to once the book has gone back to the library. If you are working with your own materials, then taking notes can be helpful *while* you are studying, as it can maintain your concentration, can help you to sort out the essence of what an author is saying, and can give you something that is much easier to use for revision than the full volume of materials.

Furthermore, your notes can be *more* helpful than the original materials, as they may be easier for you to understand. You may have managed to represent the original materials in a way that makes more sense to you, and included relevant other material, such as cross-references to key parts of other courses that have a bearing on the point, or comments on how the material relates to your own experience. Because they are briefer than the originals, your notes may be easier to refer to, and to revise from. Indeed review and revision is one of the most important uses of notes.

The most useful type of notes will depend on the purpose for which you are taking them. Notes on borrowed materials will normally need to be more detailed than those on materials you own. For borrowed materials you may well need to copy out the most quotable phrases and diagrams, as well as any references that look potentially useful, and may need to go into detail on the actual content.

With materials that are electronically available there may be a strong tendency to copy huge chunks, because it is so easy. While this may provide you with material for future reference, you still need to be able to extract and absorb key points, in the same way as with printed material, if you are to make effective use of the ideas and information contained therein. So even if you have saved the material intact, notes on it can be useful.

The most basic form of note taking with your own printed (or electronic) materials is to highlight key points or concepts. This will in itself ensure that you are *thinking* as you read, continually striving to extract the main ideas. This form of interaction with the text helps you to absorb more, and to maintain your concentration more easily, than with passive reading.

Also, when you return to the materials you will be able to extract the key points very quickly by reading the highlighted text. If you have made brief notes in the margin to supplement the highlighting the process will be even easier. Such notes might be brief 'labels', explanations of points that took you some time to grasp, examples from your work which exemplify the idea, or cross-references to other materials.

If your course does not provide one, you may wish to construct a glossary, or other digest of the course, defining and explaining each major idea, and cross-referencing or adding relevant notes from your reading. As you will need to add to this glossary continually, it has to be in flexible form. A palmtop which you can take to libraries is ideal, or you can transfer rough paper notes to your PC. Either way the material will be readily accessible for future assignments.

Avoiding plagiarism is essential. This is including work that is not your own, without attributing it, and is discussed in more detail in Chapter 15. You can inadvertently put yourself at risk of plagiarising someone by careless note taking. Whenever your notes include direct quotes it is **essential** to make this very clear, so that when you come to use the notes for an assignment or report you know which parts are the author's words and which your own. Firstly this allows you to *deliberately* quote exactly what someone said when you are writing an essay or dissertation, giving the full reference for the original. To do this you need to know which words are a direct quotation. (With this in mind it is always a good idea to note beside such quotations the page number from which the quote is taken – you may be asked to give this when quoting.) More importantly, if you quote without giving credit to an author, you will be plagiarising,

→ Ch 15, 19 and risk severe penalties if discovered). If your notes do not make make clear what is a direct quotation, you are in serious danger of accidental plagiarism when you come to use these notes for an assignment.

In all your notes, paper or electronic, it will be very important to note relationships between ideas in different sources, whether used for the same course, or different ones. Although most Master's courses are taught as a series of discrete modules, the problems you encounter as a manager are unlikely to fit within such boundaries. In your work, in analysing general case studies, and in your final project, if there is one, you are likely to need to draw on a range of different courses for relevant concepts and techniques. This will be much easier to do if you have made a practice throughout your studies of noting how different topics interrelate, or have the potential for interacting. The best way of ensuring that you do this is to highlight such relationships in your notes.

Notes in diagram form

If possible, take notes in as many forms as possible. The value of argument maps has already been discussed, but in general it is helpful to use notes in the form of diagrams to support your more 'wordy' notes. They can be helpful not only for establishing the structure of arguments but also for showing other relationships between components. Diagrammatic notes can also help you remember what you have read. The process of drawing a diagram forces you to *think* about the structure of text in a way that a précis of points made may not. The resulting picture may be much easier to remember than

→ Ch 10   words. A useful type of diagram for such note taking is described in Chapter 10, but Fig. 9.3 gives you an example of what you might have produced if taking diagrammatic notes on note taking itself. (This is an example of a mind map – free software is available that will produce basic diagrams of this form very easily; more sophisticated packages are not expensive, and many students find them a useful investment.)

Whatever the form of your notes, disciplined filing is essential. A series of organised notes can be invaluable. A collection of scruffy pieces of paper scattered all around the house, or of randomly titled files scattered about your computer, is useless. Part of this

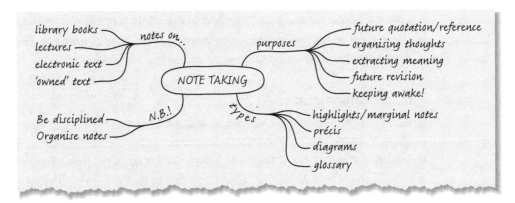

Fig. 9.3 Diagrammatic notes on note taking

organisation should consist of keeping a good index to your materials, so that you can instantly put your hands on the notes on a particular topic if an assignment or a project requires.

Efficient reading skills and good note taking should increase your capacity to benefit from your studies many times over, a benefit which should be apparent in your assessment grades. The skills should be equally applicable at work. The time needed to develop them is therefore potentially an excellent investment.

SUMMARY

- Reading efficiency and effectiveness can both be improved.
- Reading speeds can be considerably increased if you are prepared to spend time on the exercises described.
- The decision as to what to read is important, and requires you to be clear about your objectives, as well as knowing what is available.
- There are several sources of help, including lecturers, librarians and colleagues.
- Different reading speeds are appropriate for different purposes, ranging from rapid scanning to slowly working through materials.
- It is important to read critically, questioning arguments and the evidence on which they are based as well as the additional value added by a text.
- It is important to identify the claims an author is making, and evaluate their internal consistency, and the strength of the evidence and reasoning given in support of these claims.
- Mapping the arguments can be a useful approach when evaluating an author's claims.
- Note-taking skills are important, and whether you work on paper or electronically, notes should reflect purpose.
- It is helpful in your notes to relate your reading to other materials on the same subject, to the author's purpose and to the context in which it was written.
- It is essential that you identify any direct quotes in your notes to avoid accidental plagiarism later.

Further information

- Buzan, T. (2003) *The Speed Reading Book*, BBC Publications.
- Buzan, T. (2003) *Use Your Head*, BBC Publications.
- Giles, K. and Hedge, N. (1994) *The Manager's Good Study Guide*, The Open University.
- Rose, C. and Nicholl, M.J. (1997) *Accelerated Learning for the 21st Century*, Piatkus.
- Russell, L. (1999) *The Accelerated Learning Field Book*, Jossey-Bass Pfeiffer.
- www.austhink.com/reason/tutorials.

This gives detailed explanation of argument mapping and of practice in constructing such maps.

Answers to Exercise 9.1

1. False. Poor readers fixate more than once on some words. This backtracking is a major cause of slowness, and you should have remembered this.
2. True, provided it is specially designed practice.
3. False, according to the text, which claimed three to six fixations per line, although it may well be true, as later text will show. You may have *known* that the statement was really true, but it is often necessary to note what is actually in a piece of writing, even if it conflicts with what you think is true.
4. False. You would still need to practise the techniques at intervals to maintain high speeds.
5. False. Rapid reading may increase comprehension. This was another very important point.
6. True.

9

Improving reading skills

→ 10 Using diagrams

INTRODUCTION

In analysing management situations you are frequently dealing with a large number of interrelated factors, and the interrelationships will be as significant as the factors themselves. It is extremely difficult to represent such a situation other than by the use of diagrams. (By a diagram I mean any representation where position on the page is significant, and lines and possibly symbols are used to add further meaning.) Words are inadequate for describing multi-directional relationships. The pattern of those relationships is unlikely to emerge without the use of diagrams.

Diagramming is an essential study skill with several uses. As you saw in the last chapter, diagrams can be used to sort out an argument, whether your own or one you read, and can form a useful part of the *notes* you take in lectures or on things you read. Diagrams can be used to help you *clarify your thinking*, for example to explore the factors involved when you are analysing case studies or other problem situations. They are an invaluable *aid to communicating* your thoughts to others involved in the analysis, and your findings when you write an assignment or report on your work. Thus, they help your learning and can improve your grades. Diagramming skills are highly transferable, too. You can use the techniques in project groups at work to aid problem solving, and diagrams can improve the effectiveness of your written reports and oral presentations to others in your organisation. (You have already encountered a range of diagrams in this book, drawn in the interests of communication.) The visual

→ Ch 13 presentation of numerical information in graphs and charts is dealt with in Chapter 13. The present chapter concentrates on other forms of diagramming for clarifying, exploring and communicating key aspects of a situation, whether for study purposes or at work.

THE IMPORTANCE OF DIAGRAMS

Speech, especially when written, is characteristically linear. Word follows word in a one-dimensional sequence. But management situations are extremely complex, and *relationships* between factors are of crucial importance. It is extraordinarily difficult to describe multiple interrelationships using only words. Understanding such descriptions is even more difficult! Imagine trying to describe the London (or other) Underground network without recourse to a map of it. And then consider how much more complex managerial situations tend to be than the Underground.

Diagrams use symbols and spatial relationships to supplement words. (On the Underground map, the use of colour is significant, as is the relationship of one station to another, though distance between them on the map is not significant.) Patterns between elements can be readily shown and understood on a diagram, though there must be an agreed convention between 'artist' and reader as to the meaning of patterns. Similarly, symbols will increase the information which can be usefully conveyed only if the meaning of those symbols is agreed beforehand.

Diagrams, whether bar or pie charts, maps, or those using other agreed conventions, can be an invaluable aid to communication, whether incorporated in reports, or used as visual aids to a spoken presentation. They can be drawn so as to make clear those relationships you wish to emphasise. Extraneous material is omitted. From a large table of figures, for example, it is possible to draw a bar chart of monthly or annual values for a key variable, so that any trend is readily apparent. This would be totally obscured by all the other figures on the table if the raw data were presented. An organisation chart can clearly represent reporting relationships: these would be confusing if described in words alone, particularly if the organisation is structured on matrix lines. In all these cases, diagrams are being used to communicate something which has been worked out beforehand, and is understood by the sender, in such a way as to be easily understood by the receiver.

Simplifying situations

Even more powerful is the role diagrams can play in helping you to understand a situation or an argument, and to work out by yourself or in a group the complexity of relationships contained therein. In trying to understand a lecture or article, you will find that diagrams can be an invaluable aid to teasing out its structure, as well as providing a form of notes that will be useful for future reference or revision. In case study analysis, where complexity can be considerable, diagrams can help you explore how situations arose, and represent the complex dynamic of interrelationships that will need to be taken into consideration if the likely results of a possible solution are to be anticipated. In planning a report or a presentation, you can use diagrams to clarify and structure what you want to say. When planning your dissertation you will find you can use diagrams to move from an original vague idea of your intended topic to a detailed series of questions to be answered and approaches to answering them. Other diagrams such as bar charts and networks will help you schedule your research activities and monitor progress. In group work, the construction of joint diagrams can be an

10

Using diagrams

Diagrams can:

- clarify perceptions
- develop understanding
- emphasise relationships
- simplify situations
- show different perspectives
- aid communication.

excellent way of developing a shared understanding of the situation, and of highlighting differences in perception between the various group members.

Diagrams can be used in a divergent or a convergent fashion. They can be used to tease out all the possible strands of a single theme or topic, as in dissertation planning, or when representing your first ideas of what *might* be relevant in a report you are going to write. Or they can be used in a more convergent way, to impose structure on something where structure is not immediately apparent, such as your first ideas on a topic, or a somewhat convoluted argument in an article.

Presentation

Diagrams can be rough working tools, in which case the rougher the better. You will want to feel free to modify them repeatedly as your ideas develop. Students are often inhibited from using diagrams because they doubt their artistic skills. But when you are using diagrams for analysis, artistic skills can be a positive disadvantage. The more finished a diagram looks, the less it invites modification. Yet, diagrams are extremely powerful analytical tools precisely *because* they can be regarded as tentative, disposable models. Your diagrams are a way of making explicit your current perceptions and of making it easier thereby to examine those perceptions and improve them by experimenting with variations. So the inartistic are at an advantage when using diagrams for analysis. If you *are* an artist and using diagrams to help develop your thinking, you should resist the temptation to make them too beautiful!

There will, of course, be occasions when a polished finished product is called for. When you are using your diagrams for communication, you will want them to be as clear and attractive as possible. If you are writing a report for the Board, or even a dissertation, high-quality graphics can contribute considerably to the overall impression of the quality of your work. But artistic skills are no longer necessary. Computer graphics can be easily incorporated in a report, or if you are giving a talk they can be incorporated into a PowerPoint presentation.

→ Ch 16

However, a caution concerning 'art' is in order even here. I have had many heated discussions with graphic designers who have 'beautified' diagrams I have produced for use in texts. Their versions were indeed more attractive and professional looking than mine, but by making things symmetrical that were not intended to be, or changing the diagram so that it no longer followed an accepted convention, they often reduced the diagram's clarity and sometimes even altered its meaning. Computer graphics present almost irresistible temptations to elaborate and beautify. You may have been exposed to stunningly complex PowerPoint slides that were either illegible or impossible to interpret in 30 seconds while at the same time trying to listen to the speaker.

Your first goal should always be to communicate *clearly*. If you have sophisticated techniques at your disposal, you should think very carefully before you sacrifice clarity or meaning to appearance. The whole point of a diagram is that it enables you – or your audience – to grasp a pattern, or gain an instant picture. If this pattern is obscured by spurious symmetry or over-elaboration, the communication value of the diagram becomes zero.

Symbols and conventions

Symbols and conventions are an invaluable aid in diagrams. Conventions are rules about what sort of symbols to use, what they mean, and how to combine them. They are the 'language' in which a particular diagram is drawn. An example of a convention for the London Underground map is that stations on a line will be shown in the right order, but that the distance between them on the map does not relate to actual distance. If a convention exists, and your reader is likely to be familiar with this, then all that is needed is to say what convention you are using, and stick to it resolutely. If no suitable convention exists, then devise one, give a clear key as to what arrows or other symbols mean in your diagrams, and stick to your usage so that your reader can become familiar with it. As an enthusiastic walker, I can just about manage to nagivate using a map. I have come to 'read' it almost intuitively, so that if the hills and woods ahead don't look quite what I was expecting from the map I start to feel uneasy, and pay more attention. But imagine how impossible this would be if each UK Ordnance Survey map used its own symbols and in its own way. With a key to symbols on each map, you *could* use them. But the process would be much more laborious than with the standard convention which allows you to become familiar with the symbols used, and to understand them at a glance without frequent reference to the key, regardless of whether you are in the Lake District or at Land's End.

As well as increasing the amount of information that can be easily communicated, conventions serve a further purpose for the diagrammer. In drawing a diagram, you are trying to produce a useful model of a situation. Models are characterised by being simplifications of a situation, and by being capable, normally, of manipulation. The simplification is where the increase in your own understanding may first arise. The situation is almost always very complex. By using a particular diagramming convention, say one that focuses on causal links, or one that looks at flows within the situation, you are being forced into a particular kind of simplification.

It may be difficult to represent the situation in just this way, and you may be tempted to take liberties with the convention. But the discipline of keeping within the rules can generate a creative tension between your understanding of the situation and the needs of the diagramming convention. This may in fact advance your understanding in a way that using the convention less rigorously would not. If you find, therefore, that the conventions described here are frustrating, stick with them despite this.

It is worth remembering that every way of seeing is a way – or indeed a multitude of ways – of *not* seeing. This is as true of diagrams as of anything. But by drawing a *series* of diagrams from different perspectives, and looking at different aspects, you can gradually accumulate understanding. If a series of conventional diagrams still seem inadequate, you can always draw additional diagrams to a less rigorous convention. In this way you should gain full benefit from the diagrams in terms of increased understanding, as well as generating diagrams readily understood by others familiar with the convention. Indeed, although you may need to persevere for a while to get to this stage, particularly if you are not used to thinking spatially and are diffident about your drawing skills, there should come a time when you find diagrams indispensable. You will find yourself reaching for paper and pencil whenever you are talking to someone, or trying to sort out a problem at work, and using diagrams as a matter of course to improve your assignments.

THE MAGIC MANAGEMENT BOX

By far the most common 'diagram' you will encounter is the two by two matrix, as shown in Fig. 10.1. The heading above refers to the fact that many authors (and particularly students writing assignments) seem to think that producing such a box is the answer to everything. Think of some catchy labels, and then decide which cell your example fits, and you have somehow made progress . . .

If you are familiar with drawing graphs, you will know that it is conventional to have 'zero' at the bottom left-hand corner, with increasing numbers as you go up the left-hand vertical for one value, and increasing values as you move right along the bottom axis for the other value.

Such 'boxes' are derived from the idea of a graph, but with two interesting variations. First, rather than having a numbered scale on each axis they simply split dimensions into 'high' and 'low' or some other two-way categorisation. Second, there seems no obvious convention for deciding on the direction of the scales.

Consider two commonly used frameworks, familiar to most management students. The first is the Boston Consulting Group Matrix, or Boston Box, which you are almost certain to encounter on any introductory marketing course. This classifies a firm's products according to market growth and relative market share. As you would expect, market growth, the vertical dimension, has 'low' in the lower row, and 'high' in the higher row. However, the horizontal dimension is not as you would expect. The left-

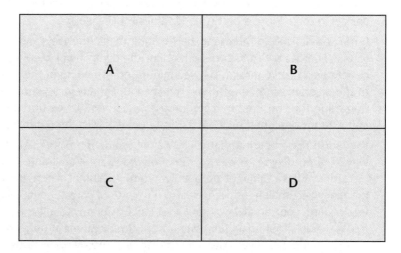

Fig. 10.1 The classic box

hand column is high relative market share, and the right-hand one is low. Thus products in cell A have a high share of a high growth market (they are labelled 'st<u>A</u>rs'), those in B have low share of a high growth market ('pro<u>B</u>lem children'). Those in C have a high share of a low growth market ('<u>C</u>ash <u>C</u>ows'), while those in D have low share of a low growth market ('<u>D</u>ogs'). The mnemonic capitals and underlining may help you remember for exams. The Boston Group suggested that an organisation needed to look at its products, drawing each as a circle which lay within the matrix. The circle need not be in the centre of the cell, and its size could represent the value of sales of that product. From this it would be possible to think about current profitability, cash flows and likely future prospects. Dogs, for example, have few prospects, so should be discontinued when their contribution ceases to cover overheads, or they compete for other resources.

Another classic framework you may well encounter when studying organisations classifies organisational environments according to the degree of risk they present, and the speed of feedback they provide (Deal and Kennedy, 1982) and suggests appropriate cultures for each box. This reverses the horizontal axis in the same way. Thus, if risk is the vertical dimension, it goes from low to high, and if speed of feedback is the horizontal, it goes from quick to slow. A (quick feedback, high risk) needs what they call a 'tough guy/macho' culture, B (slow feedback, high risk) is called 'bet-your-company' where decisions *have* to be right, C (low risk, quick feedback) produces a 'work hard/play hard' culture, while D (low risk, slow feedback, characteristic of bureaucracies) is called a 'process' culture.

ACTIVITY 10.1

Label the dimensions on Fig. 10.1 for a Boston Matrix, and label the cells appropriately.

Label the dimensions on Fig. 10.2, and the cells, to construct Deal and Kennedy's culture matrix. Think about how you would position your own organisation's products on the first, and its culture on the second.

It is obvious that the world does not split neatly into four discrete boxes. Markets can grow at many different rates. You might have 1% or 49% of a market, or any other percentage. Where do you draw the line? Sometimes, this complication is ignored and things are 'put in boxes' and everything in that box is treated according to the resulting label. But often it makes sense to locate positions anywhere on the grid to reflect just how high or how low on a dimension it is, and although a 2 × 2 box is drawn, elements are located at different points within a box to indicate their relative positions on the two axes. Either way, management writers have found this simple device, together with suitably attention-catching labels, a convenient way of communicating important points about complex ideas, and students find them a useful way of remembering the points.

When using 'magic boxes' always remember that such figures *are* diagrams – a particular way of modelling a limited aspect of reality – one way of mapping a far more complex territory. Treat them with caution. But look for what they *can* communicate, as well as what they do not.

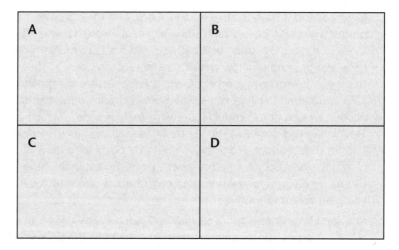

Fig. 10.2 Deal and Kennedy model (blank – to be completed)

BRAIN PATTERNS OR MIND MAPS

A highly versatile diagramming technique in the 'helping you to think' category, and one that is invaluable for note taking, is that of mind-mapping – the brain patterns described by Tony and Barry Buzan (2003). Variants of this form of diagram appear in a variety of contexts, variously described as mind maps, spray diagrams, relevance trees and fishbone diagrams.

In constructing a mind map (the catchiest general title), you normally start in the *centre* of the page with a word or phrase indicating your main idea or central theme, and then branch out, with each sub-theme taking a separate branch. These branches divide further into sub-sub-themes. Software is readily available to make it easy to draw mind maps on a PC.

Figure 10.3 shows a Buzan-type mind map for the possible uses of diagrams as described in this chapter. (Figure 9.3 was also an example of a mind map.) You can often 'illustrate' your diagram with small sketches to make it more useful/memorable. Colour may help to distinguish different types of element, too. Buzan highlights the following advantages for this type of diagram over linear note taking:

■ the central idea is more clearly defined;
■ position indicates relative importance – items near the centre are more significant than those nearer the periphery;
■ proximity and connections show links between key concepts;
■ recall and review will in consequence be more rapid and more effective;
■ the structure allows for easy addition of new information;
■ patterns will differ from each other, making them easier to remember;
■ when using the patterns creatively (divergent use), the open-ended nature of the pattern helps the brain make new connections.

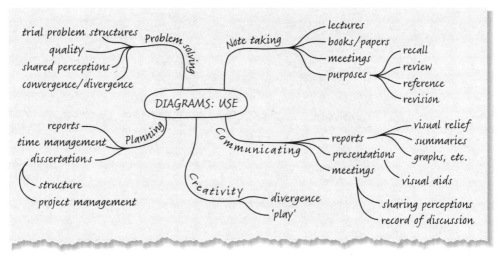

Fig. 10.3 Mind map showing uses of diagrams

The above list comprises a convincing argument for the use of such diagrams in note taking, although if taking notes in a lecture you may wish to supplement your mind map with more narrative notes, perhaps using one page for diagrams, the facing page for narrative.

But an even more powerful use of diagrams is to clarify your thinking about a complex situation. When doing this it is normally helpful to start with simple diagrams preferably with few limiting conventions. This keeps your thinking 'free' as you are starting to grapple with the problem situation. Once you have a clearer idea of the full range of potentially important factors you can choose diagrams which focus more narrowly on specific aspects of the situation. To focus too early may lead you to ignore a whole range of relevant factors simply because they do not feature on the form of diagram you have chosen to use.

Mind maps are useful for clarifying your thinking in a variety of contexts, from early analysis of a problem situation to generating a thesis topic. Because of their deliberately divergent form, they can lead you out from a central idea into a variety of subsidiary ideas that you might not otherwise have thought of, and at the same time can form the basis of the structure of anything you might write on the topic.

An alternative format with many of the same advantages as mind maps is the relevance tree. These were developed primarily for research and development management (Jantsch, 1967) but are applicable on as broad a front as mind maps, to which they are functionally equivalent. Figure 10.4 gives an example of a relevance tree for the early stages of a research project.

The main advantage of the relevance tree format is that you avoid the 'budgie syndrome' incurred by having to tilt your head at every conceivable angle to read the various twigs. Disadvantages are that the width of the page will rapidly limit the number of 'twigs' possible, and that the more formal, less playful appearance is less likely to stimulate creativity.

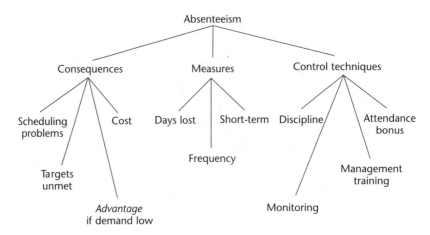

Fig. 10.4 Relevance tree for the early stages of a research project

The fishbone diagrams widely used in Quality Circles (an approach to generating suggestions for quality improvement through the use of voluntary groups of employees meeting to discuss problems reflecting the quality of output) are also devised to have parallel twigs, and are therefore similarly tidier than mind maps. Again, the tidiness places constraints on the branching that is possible, and makes it harder to add to the diagram, thus reducing its usefulness for creative purposes. Figure 10.5 shows a diagram of this kind.

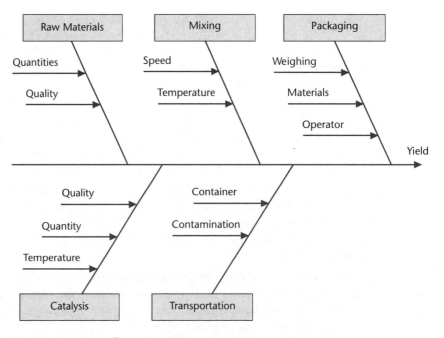

Fig. 10.5 Ishikawa-type 'fishbone' diagram used in quality analysis

Although, as Buzan emphasises, 'messy-looking' diagrams are a positive advantage at the note-taking or thought-clarification stage, they can be quickly 'tidied up' into something fairly respectable. If you *are* using them as a note-taking device this is worth doing, as it is hard to sort out a lecture structure while listening to it, and you will probably have needed to modify your diagram somewhat as you went along. Making a tidied-up version will have two benefits. First, the tidying-up process will consolidate your learning. Second, you will find the tidier version easier to use for reference or revision.

Even in their tidy form, such diagrams are best seen as primarily for your own consumption. Unless your audience knows and loves the technique, it can be dangerous to include mind maps in written work. In any case, once your ideas have become clearer through drawing the diagram, most of the information can usually be translated into the major and minor headings of a report. If you do wish to use a diagram showing your structure, then one of the parallel versions is most likely to communicate effectively to an uninitiated audience.

Despite the above reservation, Buzan does make one interesting suggestion about possible public use of this kind of diagram. In planning or problem-solving meetings, he says, points are often lost, and the chair may have difficulty in keeping discussion to the point. If the person organising the meeting uses the mind map structure as a basis for running the meeting, such problems may be avoided. A board should be presented to the meeting, with the central theme shown, and perhaps two sub-themes. As each member concludes a point, he or she is asked to summarise it, and show how it fits into the map. This ensures that all contributions are recorded, keeps speakers more to the point, means that a shared perception of the structure of the discussion will be built up, and allows participants to have a copy of the resulting pattern to take away as a record of the meeting. Use of magnetic write-on shapes, or more prosaically 'Post-it® notes', allow structure to be revised as the meeting develops. Some conferencing systems allow participants' PC screens to be used in a similar fashion during 'virtual' meetings.

You might like to experiment with this approach during group work on your course. Once convinced that the method works, and once you feel comfortable operating in this way, you might try it with colleagues. Remember, though, that you should gain participants' agreement to this method of working *before* the meeting, rather than spring it upon them when they arrive.

RELATIONSHIP DIAGRAMS

Mind maps are useful in the early stages of your thinking about a topic. A similar technique, also useful in the early stages of analysis because it has few limiting conventions, is the use of relationship diagrams. These differ from mind maps in that they do not require you to start with the main idea. This can be a considerable advantage if you are not sure which *is* the central theme (e.g. when you first meet a case study).

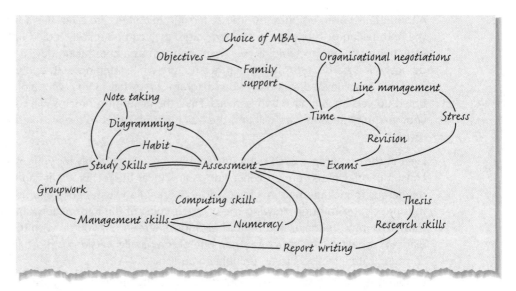

Fig. 10.6 Relationship diagram drawn in the early stages of Handbook planning

The convention for a relationship diagram is to use 'words' sometimes enclosed in blobs, to denote relevant factors in a situation, and 'lines' to indicate that there is some sort of relationship between them. It is as simple as that. But by constructing such a diagram, it is possible to identify key groupings of factors, which may help you to go on and draw a mind map, or a systems map or other appropriate diagram.

There are some practical considerations. The first is that it helps to minimise the crossing of lines. If not, you may end up with something which resembles a children's puzzle, and is very difficult to 'read'. Do a first version without worrying about this, and then draw a second version which is rearranged so that lines are clearer. This will normally involve moving the more closely interrelated factors closer together, rather than having them scattered all over the page with less closely related factors in between.

It may be helpful, too, to distinguish strong from weak relationships, perhaps by use of thicker lines for the former. Other than this there are few rules, apart from the general one applying to all diagrams, that, once complexity reaches such a point that clarity is lost, it is worth thinking about drawing more than one diagram, rather than trying to cram too much on to a single one. Figure 10.6 shows an example of a relationship diagram drawn in the early stages of planning this book. It convinced me that my intended simple structure would not accommodate the complexity of interrelationships between the topics to be covered, and that something slightly messier would be needed.

RICH PICTURES

A more graphic and amusing form of relationship diagram is the 'rich picture' devised by Peter Checkland for use at the problem-exploration stage of his soft systems

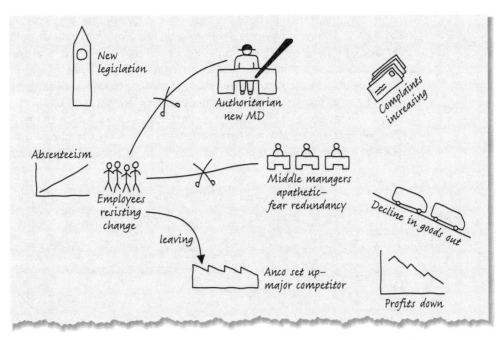

Fig. 10.7 Start of rich picture constructed in the early stages of case study analysis

methodology. This supplements the words and lines of the basic relationship diagram with cartoon-like pictorial symbols to show both the nature of the things the words represent, and the relationships the lines indicate. This type of diagram is particularly suited to group work during the early stages of investigating a problem. Using large sheets of paper such as flipcharts or wall boards, everyone can join in drawing the diagram, and there is usually much discussion of the relevance of possible items and relationships. There is no fixed convention as to symbols, though crossed swords are often used to indicate conflict, ££s for money, and sketch graphs to indicate trends. Stick men abound, with bowler hats for the managers, cloth caps for the workers. Beyond that, part of the fun is devising the symbols. Figure 10.7 shows a rich picture drawn in the early stages of a case study analysis.

Whether or not your syllabus includes a course on systems, and you learn how to use the other stages in Checkland's approach, rich pictures have many advantages. They can be a great aid to individual analysis (I know one student who at the planning stage of his project lined his downstairs loo with flipchart paper, laid out some pens, and added to his rich picture on each visit). Drawing rich pictures in a group is even better. The pictorial element encourages participation and creativity and is *fun*. And it allows you to share perceptions, and develop a much fuller and more complex set of potentially important factors than either a written description or a simple relationship diagram would permit. While you may later choose to disregard some of these factors, it is always easier to narrow down than to broaden your base once you are halfway through. In general, breadth at the outset will be an advantage, though selectivity will be necessary as your analysis proceeds.

As with mind maps, rich pictures are best seen as for authors' eyes only. You will risk being seen as eccentric or worse if you include them in a report addressed to those unfamiliar with the method, although Fig. 10.8 shows a splendid example of a rich picture successfully included in an MBA dissertation. If you have the personal presence you *may* be able to use rich pictures successfully face to face. Indeed, because rich pictures have so many strengths, and because they are easy to explain and use, you will usually find that you can introduce the concept to a group which has never used them before, without any need for expert guidance. Try it in your syndicate group, or when you are in a group at work that is finding difficulty in coming to grips with a problem.

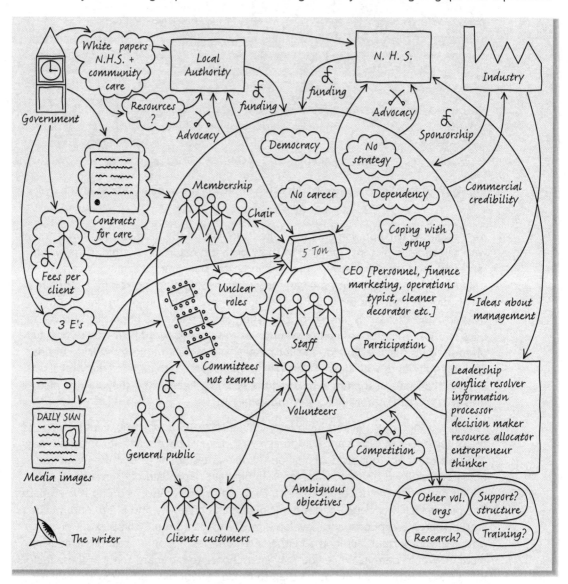

Fig. 10.8 Rich picture used in a successful MBA thesis (with thanks to C. Bolton and de Montfort University)

SYSTEMS MAPS

You cannot expect to gain full benefit from systems maps unless you have been exposed to basic systems concepts, but since many management courses include systems teaching, and since students find these diagrams far more difficult than the simplicity of the convention warrants, they are included here. Skip them if you do not need to use them now: you can come back to this section if they turn out to be necessary later.

Systems maps are a variant of the Venn diagrams now taught as part of primary school maths. Venn diagrams are blob diagrams where the blobs represent classes of things, so that where they overlap it shows that items are members of both sets concerned, and when one blob is totally contained within another, all members of the first set are also members of the second. Figure 10.9 shows an example. Think about what might be represented by the overlap in this case.

Although systems maps look like Venn diagrams, the convention is slightly, but significantly, different. In a systems map a blob represents a *system*, i.e. a group of components that have in some sense a group existence. Components in a system are interrelated to such an extent that if a component were to leave the system both component and system would be altered in some way. Thus, a battery full of chickens would be a system if all the parts which contributed to chicken production, such as food supplies, temperature regulation, etc. were included. The mass of chickens might be seen as a component of that system, though not as a system themselves, as they do not by themselves constitute a viable unit. This is in contrast to a Venn diagram, where chickens might well constitute a class of objects deserving of a blob to themselves. (You might have white and brown blobs within this, or male and female, for example, and all might be a subset of the category 'farm animals'.)

On a systems map, any elements grouped within a blob should be a system. They could be the system you are looking at, or a subsystem of it, i.e. something which could itself be regarded as a system if the level of analysis changed, but in this case is contained within the system you are choosing to explore. The line around the blob is the system boundary, a rather more complex concept than a physical or geographical boundary. It is better thought of as a rule for deciding on inclusion, and could have a number of dimensions.

Figure 10.10 shows an example of a simple systems map drawn at the stage of planning a move into distance education for a business studies department. Below the first simple map (a), there is an elaboration of this (b), showing what the author felt would be needed for successful delivery of such education.

Points to note about these diagrams include:

1. As just described, they are *not* simple Venn diagrams. Many students asked to draw a map would have shown staff, buildings, students, etc. as components. Indeed, they would not be wrong; at one level this is important information. But if we look at the system *structure*, particularly subsystems and the relationships between them,

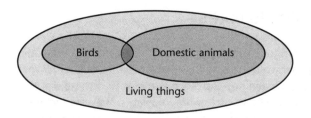

Fig. 10.9 A simple Venn diagram

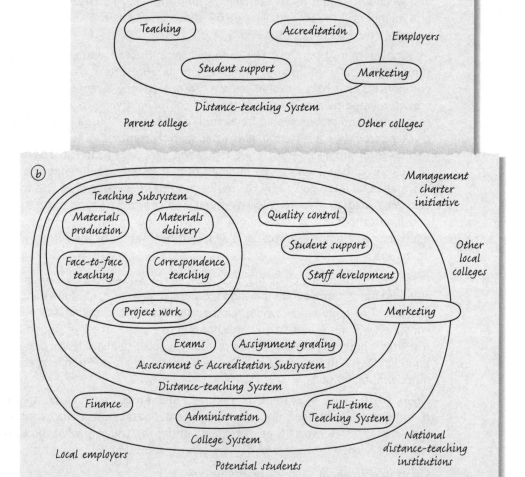

Fig. 10.10 Systems maps: (a) Simple map for a distance-teaching system; (b) a more complex systems map

Systems maps should include:

- system boundary
- any subsystems
- factors in the environment
- system title(s).

a much more enlightening picture emerges. It is all too easy to draw a systems map of an organisation showing every sort of employee, for example in the above case to show lecturers, administrators, students and so on, as components. But this is unlikely to add to the author's or the reader's understanding of how that organisation functions. Indeed, it may show *less* than an organisation chart. It is the effort of *imposing* a new structure, in terms of functional systems and subsystems, systems to *do* various necessary things, that aids conceptual development.

This element of 'does it *do* something?' (and if so, what?) is perhaps the strongest test of whether something should be regarded as a system. Indeed, the system title should reflect what it is that the system does, and should be clearly indicated on the diagram. In deciding whether or not to include a particular component, the acid test should be 'will this system do what its title suggests without the inclusion of this component?'

2. A simple diagram usually communicates far better than a complex one. While you may wish to go far beyond even the level of complexity in the second diagram for your own purposes, for communication you should always aim to keep your diagrams as simple as possible. If complexity is essential, start with a simple diagram first, showing the basic structure, following this with more elaborate versions.

3. Overlaps are used sparingly, as they reduce clarity. Whereas on a Venn diagram you *should* overlap in the case of shared membership of sets, on a systems map there is no such compulsion. In the example given, in the case of project and assignment work, learning and assessment functions may conflict, so it is important to highlight this. Also the fact that marketing of the courses is under the control of the wider college system is important. But the relationships between student support and teaching and assessment, or quality control and staff development, do not need to be indicated by overlaps. Because these are all shown as system components they are by definition interrelated, and overlaps do not need to be used to emphasise this point.

4. Things which the system cannot control, yet which have the capacity to influence it and therefore need to be taken into consideration in planning, are shown as in the system *environment*, i.e. outside the boundary of the system, but still there. It is not necessary to draw a further line around the environment. It is unlikely that the set of factors capable of influencing the system will themselves constitute a system, although sometimes your target system will be a subsystem of a wider system, and so can usefully be shown as totally contained within it. In this case, there will often be environmental factors outside the wider system which will also need to be included.

MULTIPLE-CAUSE DIAGRAMS

All the diagram types so far described are representations of things, and of the relationships between them. But when you are analysing a problem situation you usually want to understand *events* and why they happened. Multiple-cause diagrams are a powerful tool for this. In drawing a multiple-cause diagram, you use phrases and arrows. Starting with the event you wish to understand, you move backwards, looking at factors contributing to that event, factors contributing to these factors, and so on. Figure 10.11 shows an example of a first analysis of factors contributing to quality problems in an organisation. It is fairly easy to draw such diagrams electronically using no more than ellipses, words and arrows.

Provided that you remember to start with the end event and work *backwards* (and it is surprising how many students forget this simple point), and that you look for contributory *events* or states, not things (in the example it is not management that is

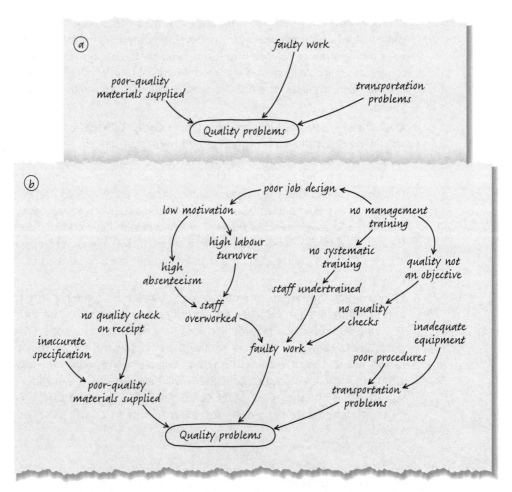

Fig. 10.11 Multiple-cause diagram showing factors leading to quality problems in an organisation

the contributory factor, but its untrained state), then you should have no problems. Even weak causal factors may be worth featuring. An arrow leading from A to B need not mean that A *causes* B, merely that it is one of the factors contributing to it.

OTHER DIAGRAMMING TECHNIQUES

There are many other techniques which you will encounter in your studies if you are not familiar with them already. Various forms of flow charts, algorithms or other engineering diagrams are commonly used. Systems maps may be elaborated into influence diagrams by the addition of arrows from major influences to the things influenced. You will almost certainly be taught the use of networks and bar charts for

→ Ch 19, 13   planning and project control, and Chapter 19 gives an example of their use in theses and dissertations. Chapter 13 shows how diagrams such as histograms and graphs can be used to represent numerical information. This chapter has concentrated on those diagramming types most useful for note taking, the preparation of assignments and general problem solving. Once you become competent in the diagramming types described, you will also find the use of other diagrams easier. It is partly a matter of confidence, partly the development of the habit of looking for patterns and the skill to represent these diagramatically, using space, convention and symbol to advantage. This skill applies to all types of diagram.

DIAGRAMMING HAZARDS

Note that many authors use diagrams poorly. A well-presented diagram can *look* extremely impressive, but be a logical mess. It is easy to assume that it is your fault if you feel you are missing the point. Instead, look carefully at the diagram, and apply the sort of critical thinking described in the previous chapter. What is it trying to show? What do the symbols represent? Are they being used consistently? Are any links logically sound? Are they based on evidence, or merely hypothesised by the author? Is

→ Ch 9   the title appropriate? The diagram may be riddled with shortcomings that obscure its meaning, or even conceal the fact that it is essentially meaningless.

Has the diagram been restricted by using IT? Many diagrams in reports are thus restricted. It is easy to draw tables, or to use the basic drawing facility in Word (*see*

→ Ch 5   Chapter 5) or the 'ready-made' diagram shapes offered by the 'Insert' and then 'Diagram' menus. But often insight depends upon a richer or more free-form diagram. Better to scan in something more appropriate, than to be restricted to the ready-made forms.

If you get into the habit of critiquing every diagram you encounter you will gain more (or justifiably less) from the diagram than if you accept it uncritically. And you will look critically at your own diagrams, thereby developing your diagramming skills.

10

Using diagrams

General diagramming guidelines

- Working diagrams should always be spaced out as much as possible. Take large sheets of paper, and use the whole sheet. Space will allow easy addition and modification, and will make your result much clearer. When using diagrams for communication, you should also avoid cramped diagrams. Again, space will aid clarity.
- Try to avoid mixing types of diagram. Avoid events on a 'thing' diagram such as a systems map, or 'things' on a dynamic diagram like multiple-cause.
- Start with simple diagrams, developing more complex ones from these only if the complexity is necessary. The simpler the diagram, the clearer will be the pattern.
- Always give each diagram a title to say clearly what kind of diagram it is and what it represents, and use a key if necessary.
- Experiment with different versions of diagrams, and different diagram types, to develop your thinking about a situation. Remember, diagrams are models, and their full value is apparent only when you play with them.
- If you are communicating diagrams electronically, remember that the whole diagram needs to be capable of being clearly read from a single screen – a diagram which needs expanding to more than a screen in order to read the words loses almost all its impact.

ACTIVITY 10.2

During the next month, each time you encounter a problem situation where the solution is not immediately obvious, try using different diagrams to clarify your thoughts. If possible, once you have drawn your diagrams, ask a colleague to 'read' the diagrams back to you, i.e. to translate them back into words. When the words do not match your intent, think about how you could have made your diagrams clearer. Note below, or in your learning log, points learned in the process.

_____

_____

_____

ACTIVITY 10.3

Also during the next month, use mind maps when planning reports or presentations, or as a method for taking notes on any presentation you attend or article you read. Again, note any learning points below or in your log.

_____

_____

_____

EXERCISE 10.1

Identify as many faults as you can with the following diagrams. (Answers are given at the end of the chapter.)

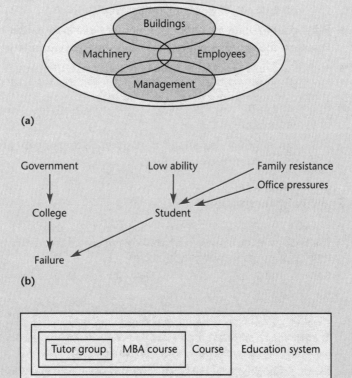

SUMMARY

- Its non-linearity makes diagramming a powerful analytical tool, better suited to representing complexity than is text alone.
- Use of position, symbol and conventions allows patterns to be explored, and increases the amount of information which can be easily handled.
- Similarly, diagrams can be a useful supplement to more linear narrative notes.
- Diagrams are also a useful vehicle for communication, developing shared understanding and encouraging creativity when working together as a team.
- Diagrams can also usefully communicate the results of your thinking to others who were not part of the team. Good diagrams can give an impression of overall quality.
- Diagrams may be convergent or divergent, dynamic or static. It is best to avoid mixing types on a single diagram.
- Mind maps are particularly good for note taking and for exploring the structure of arguments, or developing your own structure.
- Relationship diagrams and rich pictures are also useful for early exploration of problem situations, system maps for slightly later analysis.
- Multiple-cause diagrams are particularly useful for understanding how events or states of affairs came into being.
- Space and simplicity aid clarity. Titles are essential, and consistency in the use of symbols is important.
- Although you may find an initial resistance to using diagrams, with practice you will come to find them invaluable.

Further information

- Bryson, J.M., Ackermann, F., Eden, C. and Finn, C.B. (2004) *Visible Thinking*, Wiley.
  This shows a range of ways in which diagrams can be used to make sense of situations and develop strategies for dealing with them.
- Buzan, T. and Buzan, B. (2003) *The Mind Map Book: Radiant Thinking – Major Evolution in Human Thought*, BBC Publications.
- Carter, R., Martin, J., Mayblin, B. and Munday, M. (1984) *Systems, Management and Change: a Graphic Guide*, Harper & Row in association with the Open University.
  This paperback provides an excellent and entertaining introduction to the use of systems ideas, and includes many examples of diagrams.
- Morris, S. and Smith, J. (1998) *Understanding Mind Maps in a Week*, Institute of Management.
- Pidd, M. (2003) *Tools for Thinking: Modeling in Management Science* (2nd edn), Wiley.
  This offers a wide range of approaches, including additional diagramming conventions, for dealing with complexity.

Answers to Exercise 10.1

(a) Both the system shown and the diagram lack titles. This is a serious omission. There is nothing shown outside the boundary. It is highly unlikely that a system is not susceptible to influences outside itself. There is no attempt to break the system down into functional subsystems, i.e. subsystems that *do* something. This is essentially a list, not a systems diagram. It is unclear what grouping the components within a boundary add. The overlaps add nothing but confusion.

(b) Words on a multiple-cause diagram should be *events* or *states*. Student, college and government are *things*, not events. Arrows should mean 'this event contributes to this event'. Office pressures don't 'cause' a student!

(c) You can see why blobs are preferable to squares. It is much easier for the eye to distinguish them. Lots of parallel lines are very confusing. Nesting these 'systems' *might* be helpful, though it is hard to imagine why. It would be more informative, I suspect, to look at fewer levels of system in more detail.

→ 11 Teamwork and leadership

Learning outcomes

By the end of this chapter you should:

- appreciate the contribution communication skills make to working with others
- be developing your own skills in talking and listening
- be aware of the importance of teamworking
- understand what makes teams effective
- be able to differentiate between task and process management
- recognise behaviours helpful and unhelpful for task and process
- be able to record and analyse group activity
- be able to give constructive feedback on group behaviour
- understand the importance of different team roles
- understand the stages teams go through in becoming effective
- appreciate how a chair can help (and hinder) a team
- realise your own strengths and weaknesses in a group, and how to work with these
- be developing your own leadership skills in a team context
- understand the dangers group work presents
- appreciate the specific requirements for effective 'virtual groups'.

INTRODUCTION

A key management skill is to be able to work effectively with others. Building good working relationships with colleagues at all levels is important. At job interviews you will frequently be asked to demonstrate that you are an effective team member or have exercised leadership. Current organisational structures rely heavily on teamwork. In a challenging and rapidly changing context leadership is seen as crucial for organisational success.

During your course you are likely to need to work with others on many occasions, and some of your marks may depend upon work that you prepared as part of a team. Syndicate work forms a large part of many full-time programmes, and will feature in the residential component of many distance learning courses. Such courses often require students to work as part of a 'virtual' team, interacting electronically, a form of working which is now central to the operation of many organisations. While many of the general principles of teamwork apply to virtual working, the chapter considers additional factors which are particularly helpful for virtual working.

Developing your team working skills can thus help you to learn effectively as part of a team and to score well on group assignments, as well as being highly transferable to the work context. This chapter looks at the interpersonal skills upon which successful team working depends, at the elements which contribute to effective teamwork in general, and at ways in which you can exercise leadership within a group or team. While you can benefit from studying the chapter on your own, you will find it even more helpful if you can do some of the activities with others.

11

Teamwork and leadership

KEY COMMUNICATION SKILLS

Effective teamworking depends upon effective communication between team members. You need to be able to express yourself clearly, and more importantly you need to be able to listen effectively to what others are saying. You may feel that this is something you have been doing all your life, and that you have nothing more to learn. You *may* be right. But I know many people who have been *failing* to communicate fully for much of their lives without being aware of this. It is much harder than it sounds! Our assumptions about the world act as a filter on what we perceive in the first place. They then exert a strong influence on how we interpret whatever it is that we *have* perceived. Because of this, *genuine* communication – i.e. for a listener to fully understand what it is that a speaker intends to communicate – is difficult. If you look back to the examples of reflective writing by MBA students in Chapter 8 you will be able to see how assumptions were interfering to some extent with perception. To make things worse, much of the time a 'listener' is not actually listening at all, but instead is thinking about what to say next and looking for the first opportunity to say it.

→ Ch 8

A high proportion of work interaction depends upon effective talking and listening. By becoming a better communicator, you will become more effective in many aspects of your work. The following activity may help you decide whether you need to spend time addressing these highly transferable skills.

ACTIVITY 11.1

Answer the following questions as honestly as you can in order to gain a rough indication of your current skill levels. Score each item 1 if it is usually the case, 2 if quite often, 3 if sometimes, 4 if seldom the case, and 5 if almost never.

When talking with new people, much of my attention is on planning my reply rather than really listening to what they are saying _____

People I talk to are rather boring _____

I find it quite difficult to take a full part in any group discussions _____

In a group, I don't feel that my contributions have much impact _____

I get into arguments if people don't see my point of view _____

If people give me negative feedback, I defend myself by explaining
why I acted as I did _____

I focus more on a person's words than their non-verbal signals _____

I have no hesitation in telling people they are bad at something _____

People seem not to hear what I am saying _____

I feel uncomfortable in a social or group work situation _____

I find it hard to create a good impression in an interview _____

I interrupt if something someone says prompts a really good idea _____

Total _____

Note, this is a very crude questionnaire, but it will act as a starting point for thinking about these skills. Few people, if they are strictly honest, will score much above 50. (A very high score might mean you are unaware of your shortcomings.) Above 40 is good, but shows room for improvement. If you have any doubts about your skills in this area, file your current score, then reassess yourself at the end of the chapter and thereafter at intervals (a version of the questionnaire is available on the web) and develop an action plan for developing your skills.

ACTIVE LISTENING

There are many signals that indicate that someone is not really listening to you. They may look around the room while you are talking, forget or misremember what you have said, or interrupt you in mid-sentence with some non-sequitur or something about themselves. Now, be honest with yourself and think about how often you give out these signals yourself!

ACTIVITY 11.2

Think of a recent social and/or work situation at which you were present and at which people were clearly not listening to each other. Why do people persist in such non-communication? List as many reasons as you can for the talker continuing to talk, and for the listener not to listen, in the situation(s) you have just identified. If you are working through this chapter with others, compare your lists with theirs and discuss any similarities and differences.

You may have listed some or all of the following reasons for the speakers's behaviour. They may:

■ want to be seen by others to be talking – to create a good impression;

- fail to realise that the other person is not actually listening;
- enjoy the sound of their own voice;
- believe that the other person finds their words fascinating;
- be working out what they think by talking, even if they are having no effect on the thought processes of the other person;
- wish to stop the other person from saying something;
- talk to avoid an uncomfortable silence.

You may have come up with many of the above, plus a variety of other reasons. Some reasons represent more or less sensible behaviour, such as trying to avoid boredom or exploring your own thoughts and where they lead. Some are defensive, such as preventing the other person from saying something they do not wish to hear. Some are aggressive, such as exerting power over others. Some represent lack of perception. Some have to do with communicating something other than the message contained in the words spoken.

The skill of actually *being heard* when speaking, rather than having your words fall on unreceptive ears or minds, will be dealt with shortly. First, we shall look in more detail at the motivations for not listening.

Your list of possible reasons for 'non-listening' may have included:

- lack of interest in the speaker as a person or in what they are saying at the time;
- fears about how to respond blocking out what is said;
- inability to concentrate;
- inability to understand what is being said, or to perceive the emotions leading to its expression;
- desire *not* to hear because the subject is uncomfortable or unpalatable or challenges strongly held beliefs.

Active listening helps you:
- build relationships
- learn
- develop ideas
- develop colleagues
- work better together.

In addition to the above list, there are all the possibilities for 'hearing wrongly' because what is perceived is distorted by assumptions. 'Not listening' and hearing wrongly waste time and energy – both the speaker's and yours – and can create negative feelings between you. It may cause you to miss a real opportunity to learn something useful or interesting. It can reduce the speaker's self-esteem. In group situations 'not listening' wastes the entire group's time and energies if useful contributions go un-noticed.

In contrast, active and effective listening has the power to benefit individuals, relationships and shared tasks. The first major benefit of being listened to is *satisfaction of our own social needs* – we are social animals with a need to interact with others, and to feel valued by them. The second is effective *information transfer*. We learn a great deal from conversations with other people. This is one of the reasons that networking is so important. The information could include simple facts such as a problem that customers seem to be encountering, or names of useful contacts. But more tenuous information can be just as useful. For example, really listening to someone may give you a better idea of what is important to them, and of their potential to take on additional challenges.

The third category has to do with *developing ideas*. While much of this can be done in a solitary fashion, most people enjoy testing ideas against other people. Apart from the fun, this is an important way of identifying unconscious assumptions which you have made. These may seem so obviously true to you that you do not question them. They may be far less obviously true to others, and exploring areas where you differ, and the reasons for your difference, may make you realise the assumptions you are unconsciously making.

The fourth category has to do with *task planning and management* for a team. Communication is clearly essential for this, whether at work or in relation to study. For shared tasks the need is obvious. For solitary ones, you will still almost certainly need to communicate – often by talking – to make sure that you understand the task fully and have the resources you need. You may at some point need to renegotiate deadlines or resources if circumstances change or objectives turn out to have been unrealistic.

A final category has to do with developing social capital. It is now recognised that developing relationships that mean that others trust you and that you trust them can have a measurable impact upon any future performance where collaboration of some form is important. Indeed, the importance of social capital may be far wider reaching than the workplace (you might like to search the web for some of the different areas in which the idea has been applied). Effective face-to-face interaction is often seen as crucial to developing social capital.

Listening skills – active listening

Listening skills are of particular importance when interviewing or coaching, though necessary to any verbal communication. To communicate effectively *both* participants need to be skilled listeners. If you are listening actively and effectively you will do the following.

To listen better:

- suspend judgement
- concentrate on the speaker
- watch body language
- avoid interruptions
- seek clarification
- acknowledge feelings
- allow silence
- encourage and prompt
- avoid opinions
- don't offer your 'solutions'
- show you value the speaker.

Suspend judgement – keep an open mind while you are listening. If you have already judged a situation and come to an opinion, you are likely to hear only those things which are consistent with your existing opinion. Instead, try hard to approach the situation as one where what the other person has something important to say, based on information and a perspective different from yours.

Concentrate on the speaker – on what they are saying and how they are saying it – with your full attention. You need to think critically when listening, just as much as when reading. Is there a logical thread? Are there inconsistencies? If something sounds wrong to you, is it because you and the speaker have different basic assumptions? If the speaker is giving 'facts', what is the evidence for these? Similarly, what underlies opinions? What feelings are being expressed?

Watch their body language – this can tell you as much as the words. Do restless hand or body movements, looking away or inappropriate smiling suggest unease? When speakers are having a good conversation you will often find that their body language becomes similar, so that one mirrors the other. One way of building rapid rapport with someone else is actively to mirror their body language.

Demonstrate your interest – eye contact, smiles, and an 'open' posture help. Don't cross your arms or legs – this shows a degree of 'closedness' to the other person. Nods and expressions of agreement from time to time help to demonstrate interest. Reinforce these general cues by more specific ones. Paraphrasing what the other person has said at key points shows that content has registered with you. 'So what you are saying is . . .' or 'It sounds as if . . .' shows that something has registered and allows you to check that you are receiving the message intended. Sometimes the speaker may not have realised just what they *were* saying, or perhaps were unaware of some of its implications so this can help raise their awareness.

Avoid interruptions – if you are interested, you will interrupt only when the thing said is so interesting that you cannot control your excitement. But interruptions are such a frequent way in which listening fails that they are worth separate mention. Note that talking into a silence, but still breaking the speaker's 'train of thought', is a form of interruption.

Seek clarification – if you are not sure what someone means, or if it seems inconsistent with something said earlier, ask questions exploring this. Use questions such as 'Do you mean . . .?' or 'How does this fit with . . .?' or 'I don't quite understand why . . .' to help clarify things.

Recognise feeling – these are an important component in communications. It can be useful to show the other person that you are aware of how they feel. 'I can see how angry this makes you . . .' can convey that you have heard, and accepted, the feelings that are being communicated as well as the words. If, for example, you are trying to support someone who is worried it is very important to accept, and show that you have accepted, their feelings.

Allow silence – if the speaker is trying to say something difficult, or using talking as a way of developing their thoughts, they may need time to think. It is important that you do not rush in because you find silence uncomfortable. Instead, show by your body language that you are comfortable with the silence, and allow the person the thinking time they need. (You can usually see that they are indeed thinking, as their eyes will wander round the room rather than looking at you.) A good interviewer will always allow a candidate this thinking time. In a group, try to avoid leaping in as soon as someone stops for breath rather than having come to the end of their intended contribution.

Encourage and prompt – this can help when a person *is* finding things difficult, and appears stuck. A gently probing question: 'That's really interesting. What happened next?' or 'How did you feel about that?' or 'So what options do you think you have?' may help move their thinking on.

Avoid directing the conversation – if you are trying to listen, to learn and perhaps to help the speaker, then taking charge of the conversation should be done only with caution. Being too directive will carry the message that you are more concerned with your perspective than that of the speaker. Of course, in a more formal interview, where you have a clear agenda, you *will* need to be rather more directive. And in a group that is straying from the agreed task it may also be important to summarise or redirect the discussion.

Avoid expressing your own views – there is another important reason for suspending judgement. It stops you expressing opinions. If someone feels that you are making negative judgements they will soon stop talking. Praising them may direct the course of their thinking, which may not always be helpful. We almost all have a strong need to be approved. Expressing judgement will slant the conversation even if it does not stop it. The speaker will start to say things in order to gain your approval, which is unlikely to be helpful. This is particularly likely if the listener has a higher status than the speaker, for example, if you are listening to someone who reports to you at work.

Be wary of suggesting solutions – if the conversation is a joint problem-solving situation there will be a time when suggested solutions may be helpful. Even then it is possible to start looking for solutions too soon, before the problem is fully understood, as will be discussed shortly (*see* Fig. 11.3). Whether talking to an individual or in a group it can be unhelpful to suggest solutions before a situation has been fully explored and understood.

Show that you value the speaker – one of the results of a 'good' exchange is increased self-esteem. You will be going some way to showing the speaker that you value them by your active listening, your concentration on what they are saying, your efforts to understand their exact meaning and your encouragement when they find it difficult to put something into words. You can go further in helping their self-esteem, and in building a positive relationship with them, by showing your appreciation of their input.

You can see from the above why listening is a full-time job. It should also be clear that becoming a proficient listener is not something that you are likely to achieve overnight. You will need to overturn at least some habits of a lifetime unless you are exceptional and blessed with the skills already. Breaking habits is extremely difficult. To make progress you need first to become much more aware of the dimensions of listening and then to start reflecting actively on how well you are listening.

Attentive listening

There is a variant on active listening that can be useful in a range of situations from resolving conflict to developing your thoughts by 'thinking aloud' while someone listens. It can also give you useful 'listening' practice. This variant is *attentive listening*, and relies on attending very closely to the talker, rather than prompting, clarifying, or in any other way directing the conversation. At its simplest, the talker talks, and the listener listens, all the while looking at, and concentrating fully on the talker. The listener does nothing but listen.

This technique can be extremely useful when people cannot agree over something. In such a case it can be useful for the two who disagree to take two- or three-minute turns, and alternate talking and listening as many times as is necessary. If you are part of a group trying to work something out, you can similarly split into pairs and each have a timed talk and listen before feeding any new thoughts back into the group. (This technique has been fully developed into a technique for a wide range of applications in organisations. *See* Kline (1999).)

TALKING

The simple act of talking to another person is one in which a huge range of skills can be observed. Many of the dimensions will have been implicit in the discussion of listening, but briefly you can improve your success in communicating if you:

- **ensure that people can hear what you say** – self-evidently, if you speak too softly, in incomplete sentences or too quickly, people are less likely to hear what you are saying, and may therefore not grasp your meaning.

- **ensure that people can understand you** – content fairly obviously needs to be clearly organised. If your message is muddled, it has little chance of communicating anything. If the point of the conversation is to clarify your thinking, this is not an issue. But if you are attempting to make a specific point to an individual or group, muddle is a serious impediment – make sure that you have sorted out just what you want to convey before starting. Make sure, too, that you use language that your audience will understand.

- **check you are being heard** – watch your listener's reactions. If there are signs that their attention is wandering, try to find out why and adjust your talking accordingly.

- **consider your listener's objectives and likely perspective** – even when conveying straightforward information, your success will depend on the other's desire to receive it, and the sense it will make to them. If their assumptions or objectives are different from yours, they may take a different meaning from it than you intended. Explicit verbal 'strokes' (such as genuine compliments which make a person feel good) and other social rewards may be helpful in creating desire to understand.

Good 'talkers':

- speak clearly
- check listener reaction
- meet listeners' needs
- listen.

The above points mean that listening is crucial even when you are leading an exchange. It is unlikely that you will be able to see how a person is responding, adjust what you are saying accordingly, perceive or meet your listener's objectives very well or achieve anything at all if you do not listen carefully.

TEAMS THAT WORK

A group can be any set of people that interact more or less frequently, more or less formally, and with goals that may be unclear to the members. A *team* is usually seen as a particular sort of group – one that has a specific membership and has been formed to achieve specific goals. If you are required to work to achieve a shared goal as part of a group, your aim should be to be part of an effective *team*. This team/group distinction is not one that is universally made, and indeed many of the points about teamworking will apply equally to looser groups, such as a group of students who are asked, during a single class, to discuss a particular case. However, teams that work together over a longer period to carry out an assigned task are more important in a work context, and it is this sort of teamwork that this chapter primarily addresses.

The basic talking and listening skills discussed above form the foundation of effective teamwork. If team members are skilled communicators, the team is well on the way to being effective. But there are other features that need to be considered too. An effective team is one in which all members understand, agree, and are committed to achieving the task for which the group was formed. It is one in which all members feel enabled and motivated to contribute to their full ability, and have between them the necessary abilities and other resources to achieve the task. Its members feel comfortable working together, and it works in an efficient manner to achieve the task. This will include active management of the work undertaken, and normally regular interactions between members. This chapter will discuss how task and process management can be achieved, the ways in which team formation influences effectiveness, and some of the potential hazards of working in groups.

TASK AND PROCESS

Teams can be formed for many purposes. These days teams may seldom meet face to face; indeed, members may be on different continents, linked by video and/or computer conferences. Fortunately, the same basic principles apply to both face-to-face and remote group work.

ACTIVITY 11.3

Think about a group which you have belonged to recently, which you enjoyed belonging to and felt was effective, and another which was much less satisfactory. Try to think of at least three ways in which the groups concerned differed, and list these below.

'Good' group   **'Bad' group**

_____   _____
_____   _____
_____   _____
_____   _____

Comment

There could have been many reasons why your identified groups differed. Size might have been a factor, or the compatibility of the individuals concerned, or quality of leadership, or clarity of task, or any number of different factors. But it is likely that ultimately the factors you listed affected you either because they interfered with the group's achievement of its task, or because somehow they stopped the group working well together. Perhaps members were not in sympathy with each other, did not feel valued by the group, or even true members of it, and so did not work together effectively. If so, the process was wrong, with consequent detrimental effect on the task.

For a group to work as a *team*, that is, to achieve synergy, and to be in a sense *greater* than the sum of its parts, the social needs of members must be met. (In this context 'social' does not mean pleasant if aimless chatter over coffee, but the satisfaction gained from feeling that you are making a contribution to a group task, and that you and your contribution are recognised and valued by other group members.) Unmet social needs can drive people to act in non-helpful ways. You have probably encountered colleagues at work who insist on talking for a far larger proportion of any meeting than the value of their contribution warrants. The less the group appreciates their input (and the signals can be crystal clear) the more determined they are to monopolise the floor. If the group refuses to reward them for membership, they can at least claim the reward of forced attention, even, in extreme cases, the perverse satisfaction of annoying their colleagues. Action in pursuit of one's own social needs can disrupt group process. Behaviour which recognises and supports the social needs of others tends to help group process.

In considering aspects of group effectiveness, think in terms of a variant of the 'Universal Management Paradigm' for problem solving that you met in Chapter 3. As with any task, the group is likely to need to:

- define the problem
- clarify and agree objectives
- generate possible options
- evaluate options and select one.

The group may sometimes need to go on to:

- implement that option
- monitor implementation.

Managing the *task* requires that each of the above stages is gone through systematically. The first two stages are of course crucial. Unless all members are committed to an agreed set of objectives, they will not function as a team. Nor will they be motivated to progress the task. (Naturally, if the agreed problem definition is *wrong*, effort will be misdirected.)

It is equally important that the group *process* is managed well. If it is not, motivation is unlikely to be sustained, and many members may be unwilling or unable to make their full potential contribution to the task. When working remotely it is easy to forget process issues, but they are even more important when members do not physically meet.

Many classifications of group behaviour have been proposed; you will doubtless encounter several during your studies. The following is not intended as definitive in any way, though it is fairly widely used. Take it as a starting point, if you like, for developing your own classification, if you wish to explore this area thoroughly.

BEHAVIOURS SEEN IN GROUPS AND TEAMS

Behaviours serving task needs

These are as follows:

- **clarifying objectives** – essential if work is to be effectively directed;
- **seeking information from others** – they may be part of the team because of their knowledge or particular perspective;
- **giving relevant information** – the same is true of your inclusion;
- **proposing ideas and actions** – necessary if the team is to have any impact;
- **developing ideas or proposals suggested by others** – vital if synergy is to be achieved;
- **disagreeing** – it is important to express any disagreement with a point, rather than keeping quiet to avoid conflict or because you feel you must be wrong;
- **summarising progress** so far – helpful if discussion is tending to become repetitive and needs to move on, and helpful in giving members a sense of achievement;
- **evaluating progress** against objectives – again gives a sense of achievement, and additionally shows what still needs to be achieved;
- **timekeeping** – essential if there is a deadline, but useful in all circumstances;
- **assigning responsibilities for action** – decisions are more likely to result in action if someone is identified as having responsibility for that action;
- **setting up a review mechanism** – it is important to check that implementation is progressing as intended and to take corrective action if not.

Behaviours serving process needs

These are as follows:

- **encouraging** members to contribute – particularly important if some find it difficult to speak in a group;
- **rewarding individual contributions** – praise or agreement will make someone feel good about belonging and wanting to contribute further;
- **checking that you have understood** – it is important to do this before expressing disagreement, as your disagreement may stem from assumptions which are affecting your interpretation of what has been said – indeed, when you understand them you may actually agree with what the person intended;
- **resolving conflicts in a positive way**, without either party feeling rejected – this is helped by valuing disagreement because it serves to highlight important differences in information or interpretation;
- **changing your own position** – it is helpful to be open to different ways of seeing things in the light of discussion, and being prepared to question your own views and alter them if convinced;

- **controlling 'over-contributors'** – it may be necessary to ask some people to put a point aside or let others express their views but, again, if possible, this should be done in a positive way;
- **praising team progress** – again, members will feel motivated by realising how they are progressing towards achieving objectives;
- **discouraging unhelpful behaviours** – *see* below.

Behaviours interfering with task or process needs

These are as follows:

- **contributing too much** – or otherwise seeking attention;
- **reacting emotionally** – rather than considering points raised calmly and rationally;
- **defending** one's own position excessively;
- **attacking** the position of others by ridicule, or other unreasoned statement (e.g. 'You always make impractical suggestions') – such attacks are normally directed at the person not their point;
- **interrupting** or 'talking over' another group member – this stops them making their intended contribution;
- **de-railing a discussion** by raising a totally different point or even a totally irrelevant red herring when discussion is in full and productive flow;
- **holding private conversations** during the meeting;
- **not listening** – failing to concentrate on others' contributions so that ground has to be re-covered;
- **using excessive humour** – while some humour can defuse difficult exchanges, too much can interfere with the task;
- **withdrawing** ostentatiously from the group (the pushed back chair, crossed arms and determined silence . . .) – this can make other members feel uncomfortable.

Try observing some meetings, whether at work or on your course, with these behaviours in mind, recording your observations. The simplest method is merely to chart interactions. In meetings members often address their remarks to individuals, rather than to the whole group. One aspect of process can be recorded by mapping these interactions. Figure 11.1 gives an example. Each arrowhead represents a separate interaction. Arrowheads to the centre mean remarks addressed to the group as a whole.

If you wish to get more sophisticated, you can categorise the behaviours involved, and record each instance against the person generating it. There are too many categories in the list above for easy recording. The specimen chart in Fig. 11.2 gives an example of a possible recording form (a version is available on the **website**). With either approach it is worth looking at those who contribute little, and asking whether this level of contribution is appropriate. With the second method you will be able to see whether there is a lot of interrupting by other members, perhaps causing a more diffident member to cease in mid-contribution. You can also see whether the unhelpful

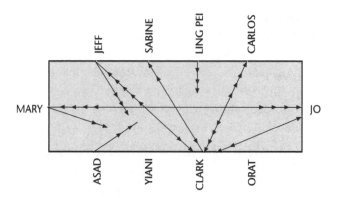

Fig. 11.1 One way of recording group interaction

behaviours are contributed by a limited number of members, or more widely distributed. If you notice a change in the proportion of unhelpful behaviours at some point, you may also be able to think back and consider what could have caused this.

A simpler recording method focuses on capturing how the task is progressing through the main stages of the problem-solving paradigm, logging the time at which each stage is started and completed. There is unlikely to be a single pass through. Stages are

	JEFF	SABINE	LING PEI	ASAD	YIANI	CLARK	JO
Clarifying objectives							✔✔✔✔
Giving/seeking info.						✔✔✔✔✔	
Proposing/developing			✔✔✔	✔✔✔		✔✔✔✔	
Summarising	✔						✔✔✔✔✔
Timekeeping	✔✔✔						✔
Encouraging/rewarding							
Conflict reduction		✔✔✔✔					✔✔✔
Gatekeepi ng'							✔✔✔✔✔
Interrupting/overtaking			✔✔✔✔ ✔✔✔	✔✔✔✔✔✔		✔✔✔✔	
Attack/defence			✔✔	✔✔✔			
Changing the subject					✔✔		
Excessive humour		✔✔				✔✔	
Withdrawal		✔			✔		

Fig. 11.2 Example of a simplified form used in recording behaviours in a group

often 'revisited' several times, sometimes effectively, because understanding has deepened, sometimes merely because of poor task management. You may find that some stages are omitted altogether, or undertaken surprisingly late. I have often observed student groups who, after much heat and little progress ask each other plaintively, often in the last 10 minutes of an exercise, 'What are we really meant to be doing?'

Such failures properly to define the task and clarify objectives are not uncommon in real life, either. Perhaps the most dramatic I encountered was a meeting to discuss the commissioning of research. Several fairly senior civil servants were present, together with a large number of more junior specialist advisers. Many proposals were discussed in great depth, with impressive intellectual skills being brought to bear. After about two hours I finally summoned up the courage, as a very new and junior member of staff, to ask the size of the research budget remaining, as this would rather determine how many of the projects under consideration could go ahead. (I assumed everyone but me knew this, but was bored by not being able to contribute because of my ignorance.) After some rather embarrassed debate, it emerged that almost none of the budget remained: it had all been committed many months previously!

Kepner and Tregoe (1965) found similar results in their classic work, *The Rational Manager*. They charted the progress of discussions on problems, and found patterns similar to that shown in Fig. 11.3. You can see how little attention is given to diagnosis, and how 'disorderly' is the flow of discussion.

While I hope that your observations will show nothing as dramatic as this, it can be enlightening to see which stages of the approach are habitually rushed, which laboured over, and how many loops indulged in, and to relate this to the quality of decision reached. From your various observations, you should become much more sensitive to the dynamics within groups, and to how these could possibly be altered for the better in order to arrive at better outputs.

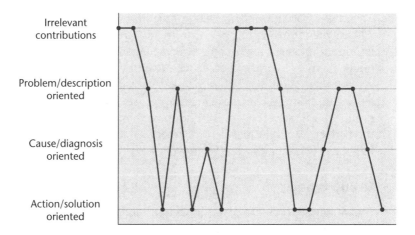

Fig. 11.3 Kepner–Tregoe-type chart of discussion flow

CHOOSING TEAM MEMBERS

You may find yourself assigned to a group, in which case you will have to work within the constraints imposed by your particular group's composition. But if you do have a choice, or indeed are putting together a team at work, there are several factors you may wish to consider.

Team size

Size can have a powerful influence on effectiveness. The optimum size will depend on the task, but four to eight will usually be the best range. A larger group gives you potentially greater resources of knowledge and experience to draw upon, and allows for division of labour on large tasks. However, the compensating drawback is that, the larger the group, the smaller the scope for individual participation. Larger groups can also present logistical problems as it may be difficult to find meeting times convenient for all members. More formal approaches tend to be necessary to manage a larger group. Parkinson, in addition to formulating his famous 'law', suggested that maximum inefficiency was reached in a group of 21, as once this size was reached, a group member had to stand to be heard, and once on his feet found the temptation to make a speech irresistible.

Expertise

The range of expertise contained within the team is important. While you may find it comfortable to work with a group of similar background, and therefore similar perspective, to your own, many tasks demand a range of expertise, as indeed do many tasks at work. Teams with complementary skills tend to be more effective. Aim to include as many different management disciplines as possible and ensure that those essential to the problem are represented.

Objectives

This one is really important. Being graded on work you have done as part of a team with different goals and priorities from your own can be deeply frustrating. It is important to realise that people seek management qualifications for many different reasons. When it comes to objectives, and how hard you are prepared to work to achieve them, similarity rather than variety is desirable. If you are highly ambitious, and aiming to do as well as possible in the course, you will find it frustrating to be in a group whose main concern is to do the minimum necessary to pass. If you have taken the perfectly valid decision to be one of the latter category, you will find a bunch of high-fliers equally unrewarding to work with.

Group type

People tend to prefer to play a limited number of roles within a group. Belbin (1981, 1993) suggested that for a group to be productive nine team role types need to be present. Different individuals will be stronger in some roles, weaker in others.

The best teams consist of a mixture of such preferences. It is helpful therefore that, as with expertise, you aim for a variety of preferred group types if possible. At the start of your course you are unlikely to know other course members well enough to be aware of their preferred role type in groups, and their strengths and weaknesses in this way. You may, however, have the opportunity during your studies to take various psychometric tests in order to become aware of your own characteristics. If so, the results can be helpful. The behaviour categories listed below can in theory be performed by any group member, but there will be a strong tendency for people to revert to their preferred roles if they are not concentrating on deliberately adopting less preferred ones.

The types (or roles) Belbin suggested for effective group functioning are:

- **Coordinator.** The coordinator clarifies goals and promotes decision making, is a good communicator and social leader, and a good chairperson. Coordinators may, however, be seen as somewhat manipulative, and too prone to let others do the work.
- **Plant.** The plant comes up with original ideas, is imaginative and usually very intelligent. But others may see plants as careless of detail, and prone to resent criticism.
- **Shaper.** Shapers are task minded and dynamic, and stimulate others to act. But they may be impulsive, impatient and intolerant of vagueness.
- **Monitor-evaluator.** These assess the qualities of ideas or proposals, being good at dispassionate, critical analysis. They may, however, be seen as lacking warmth and imagination, and have a damping effect on others' enthusiasm.
- **Resource investigators.** These are good at bringing in resources and ideas from outside. They tend to be extroverted and relaxed, but not overly original. The team will usually have to pick up their contributions and run with them, as their enthusiasm wanes rapidly.
- **Team worker.** Such people are very important in holding the team together through focus on the process side. Sensitive, good at listening and at defusing friction, they may be indecisive and too keen to avoid conflict.
- **Implementer.** Their strength is in practical organisation, and turning ideas into manageable tasks. They bring method to the team's activities, but may be inflexible, and resist changes to plans.
- **Completer-finisher.** They are good at checking details and chasing deadlines, so are essential for group performance, although they may make themselves unpopular in the process.
- **Specialist.** Specialists provide rare skills and expertise and are focused and self-motivated. But they may see only a narrow segment of the situation, and lack communication skills.

Although the above may read like a list of stereotypes, it is firmly based upon Belbin's work with groups within organisations, and his finding that groups with a mix of roles consistently performed better than groups that were more homogeneous (in role terms). Although Belbin's work is still widely used, there are now many other 'typing'

11

Teamwork and leadership

products commercially available – these typically have their own psychometric instruments to classify people into a roughly similar set of types.

Several things are worth noting. If you think about the above in terms of personality types it may seem depressing – at work in particular you are often stuck with a particular group. But if you think of it in terms of roles to be performed for effective group working (and you will readily see the links to useful group behaviours in Fig. 11.2) then it can give you another route into thinking about why a group is, or is not, working well.

If you do have a free hand in choosing a group to work with, it may be worth seeking to form a group where preferred roles are balanced. If not, you might wish to discuss how to handle the imbalance and deliberately allocate roles which do not come naturally to any members. This will help you all to develop your less-preferred roles, and therefore become more versatile group members.

If you are in a group where some of these functions are not being carried out, it may be helpful to comment on this, and for some members deliberately to adopt the missing roles.

TEAM FORMATION

It is rare for a team to be effective from the moment of its formation. Members are unsure of each other at first, and do not know what will turn out to be acceptable and unacceptable behaviour within the group. How formal will it be? Will disagreement be acceptable? Is everyone going to be far better informed, more confident, more experienced and a great deal more intelligent than they are? Different groups have different 'norms' of acceptable behaviour. And members fit into groups in different ways, playing different roles and having different status depending upon the circumstances. A popular (because easy to remember?) description of the stages of group formation was formulated by Tuckman in 1965. It suggests that groups go through four stages.

- **Forming.** This is when individuals try to establish their identity within the group. Behaviour is often tentative at this stage, and extreme politeness may prevail. A leadership pattern may emerge.
- **Storming.** All the positions established at the earlier stage are now challenged. There may be considerable conflict. Personal agendas emerge. Status battles may ensue. A group can disintegrate at this stage. Alternatively, if the conflict is constructive, it can generate greater cohesion, a realistic commitment to objectives and trust.
- **Norming.** This is when the group develops norms for how it will operate. Acceptable behaviour within the group is established.
- **Performing.** Only when the earlier stages have been passed through is the group in a position to operate effectively.

If members are aware of the need for the earlier stages, they are less likely to be disturbed or discouraged by them, as might be members who join the team expecting instant 'performing'. Instead, they will pay attention to managing the group process through the early stages, so that conflicts are used constructively, appropriate norms emerge, and the performing stage is reached as painlessly as possible.

'Adjourning' is sometimes added as a fifth category to highlight the need for attention to be paid to the way in which a team is disbanded. If members have worked closely together there may be feelings of sadness or dissatisfaction if this stage is ignored.

The need for a chair

Many groups which have floundered are likely to say at the end of the exercise 'If only we'd had a chair'. The advantage of having an agreed chair is that there is someone in the group with the *designated responsibility* for achieving progress towards objectives. It is accepted that it is the chair's job to manage both task and process issues, and behaviour directed towards achieving this will be accepted by the group. The chair has the *right* to silence an over-verbose member, to push people towards expressing agreement with what seems to be emerging as the group view, to instruct individuals to carry out follow-up work, etc.

With a chair who is skilled in managing groups, and good at both task and process issues, a group can be highly effective. Indeed, with a newly formed and temporary group, which will not have time to go through the processes of group formation, a designated chair is essential. This is also the case for most groups larger than about eight, and any formally constituted group. However, as with most benefits, there are associated costs. A good chairperson can be a tremendous asset, but a poor one can be a powerful liability. Because it is the *chair's* responsibility to manage the group, members take no responsibility for this themselves. Few chairs are equally good at managing task and process (indeed, you will note that Belbin saw the chair's role as primarily coordination, rather than the combination of many of his roles commonly expected).

Some chairs are singularly poor at *both* aspects. Perhaps they use the position to satisfy their own social needs for attention and the exercise of power, and monopolise the meeting, driving their own preferred conclusions through regardless of the views of other group members. Under such a 'tyrant chair', group members rapidly cease to feel any commitment to the group and see no point in trying to make a contribution. Instead, they gain what little satisfaction they can from criticising the chair behind his or her back.

Perhaps more common is the 'willing but weak' chair who would *like* to help the group to be effective but lacks the skill to do so. They may know they *should* control the over-wordy, but lack the ability to do this. They may not have sufficient grasp of the arguments flying around to be able to summarise effectively. Under such a chair, members will be equally frustrated, if less angry.

In either of the above cases, group members will usually see the group's failures as the chair's responsibility. They will not see that they have failed to assert their own rights as group members to effective chairmanship. Nor will they recognise their own responsibilities for managing aspects of task or process clearly beyond the reach of the chair.

If a group genuinely chooses a chair because they think the person is capable of filling the role, then problems are likely to be few and those that arise can be discussed openly because the chair knows that she or he has the group's support.

Hardest is the case when a chair is forced upon a group, perhaps by virtue of seniority. This used to be standard practice in the Civil Service, and it was clear that chairmanship skills were *not* necessary for promotion. With an imposed chair, group members feel far more inhibited about taking on aspects of the role which the chair cannot handle. Yet, there is no real reason why they should not assume these roles. If done skilfully this can be a great relief, both to the chair and to the other group members, and can turn an ineffective group into one which feels it is getting somewhere.

If the chair is self-assumed, the situation may be very difficult to resolve. Members sometimes volunteer to chair because they know they have the necessary skills. More often it is because they are very task-oriented, and want to start 'getting on with the job, rather than wasting time talking about how to tackle it'. Such chairs, while strong on task management, tend to be weak on process. Worst of all, the volunteer may be an incipient tyrant, with strong needs to dominate, and equally strong, though not necessarily right, views on what 'the answer' is. Such a chair will not allow group members to play a role in managing the group, or indeed any role at all other than that of audience.

In such circumstances, group members will have the choice of allowing the chair his or her head, or voicing their unhappiness, and expressing the need for a change of style. The one sort of poor chair who is not necessarily a liability is the chair who knows his or her limitations. If, for example, you very much wish to develop your own skills at chairing because you know these to be weak, let the group know that you would like to play the role. With their help, and with feedback on your performance, this can work very well.

By offering your weakness as material for analysis, you can help the whole group to learn from how you handle the role. Because you have admitted to your shortcomings before you start, and have asked for help, the group will be happy to take some of the responsibility for ensuring that the task is progressed. The comments about the dangers of a poor chair should not therefore make you reluctant to take this opportunity for skills development in a relatively protected environment.

Because of the risks associated with vesting all the management roles in one individual, some working groups choose to share roles between members. With a long-established team, well into the performing stage, this may be done informally. Indeed, if the team is small, and all members are taking responsibility for achieving the objectives this may work very well. Less assured groups, or those with a complex task, may prefer more formal allocation of roles, with individuals agreeing to take the main responsibility for timekeeping, or for making sure that everyone has a chance to contribute, or for summarising at intervals or checking against objectives. If your course involves much group work, or if you can become a member of an informal study group, you may be able to experiment with different ways of working, sometimes having a chair, sometimes designating and allocating different roles, sometimes trying to be completely informal about it. Eventually you should be able to choose the best approach for any given task and set of members; both will be important considerations.

PRACTICAL ASPECTS OF TEAM EFFECTIVENESS

There are some very practical factors which can have a marked influence on how well a team works. Seating arrangements are critical. Members tend to interact with those with whom they can have eye contact. With a rectangular arrangement they will therefore talk to those opposite, rather than adjacent to them. Circular arrangements are often, therefore, to be preferred (unless you wish to *discourage* interaction between certain members).

Physical comfort can help. If a room is stuffy or cold, or members are hungry or thirsty, the quality of the meeting is likely to suffer. Indeed, chairs have been known to gain agreement to unpopular decisions by making sure that they are low on the agenda, and are discussed at 1.20 pm, when the strongest concern is with getting lunch before the canteen closes rather than fighting a particular decision.

Stamina is limited. Full involvement in teamwork requires intense and sustained concentration. After about two hours, sometimes less, effectiveness is likely to diminish if there is no break for relaxation. It is important, therefore, to have an agreed end time for the meeting, and to have a number of interim deadlines so that the business is progressed at a rate which will allow this end time to be adhered to. With practice it will become clear how much can be attempted within a two-hour (or other length) meeting.

Just as a group goes through a series of stages over time, any single meeting has a number of identifiable stages which need to be understood if the meeting is to be fully effective. The first is *nurturing*, a slightly off-putting term for making people feel welcome and valued. Offering coffee, and encouraging members to talk to each other, having greeted them on arrival, can help this stage. Then there is the *energising* phase, when members gradually get 'up to speed'. It is inappropriate to tackle major tasks in this phase, though fairly routine items, on which easy decisions are possible, can speed the energising process. *Peak activity* occurs in the next stage, when major work should be undertaken. The final stage is *relaxation*, when the group unwinds, and achieves a feeling of completeness, having finished. It is important not to omit this stage, or members will feel slightly dissatisfied, and the sense of achievement generated in the earlier stage can be somewhat diminished.

Meetings go through stages of:

■ nurturing

■ energising

■ peak activity

■ relaxation.

If you are setting an agenda for a meeting, you should bear in mind the stages highlighted in the margin when doing so. If you are working in a case study syndicate, it can still be helpful to steer the group towards finding small but useful activities that can act as energisers, and trying to manage to include a relaxation phase at the end.

11

Teamwork and leadership

THE DANGERS OF GROUP WORK

Beware:
- groupthink
- scapegoating.

Can a team work *too* well? This may seem a silly question, but it is important to be aware of just how powerful an effect a group can have on its members. Being approved of by the group may come to be enormously important, while being rejected by them may be psychologically damaging, or at best very painful. If the team is firmly agreed on something, members feel that it *must* therefore be true. These aspects of membership lead to some of the potentially unproductive outcomes of teamworking.

The first such negative outcome is called *groupthink*. Often this involves extreme optimism and a willingness, because of the feeling of group invulnerability, to take undue risks. The group disregards any external evidence which contradicts its view, and any member rash enough to suggest that there *is* evidence of a problem will receive a clear message from the group that the suggestion is unacceptable. The person making the suggestion realises that if he or she wishes to remain in the group then he or she should stop acting in such a disloyal fashion. In such circumstances, the desire for group cohesiveness and sense of belonging are acting counter to task needs. If you find yourself in this position, you will start to think that you were wrong rather than insisting on your point of view.

This phenomenon is very common within organisations facing serious problems. Boards may refuse to accept that they have a problem, long after it is glaringly obvious to everyone else. They will question the understanding of anyone who suggests otherwise, and refuse to believe the clear implications of any sets of figures with which they are presented. If members are aware of the possibility of groupthink, they *may* be better able to resist it, although the tendency is a strong one. The rejected member can at least suggest that they examine the possibility that groupthink is taking place.

Another form of group behaviour which interferes with group learning is *scapegoating*. If a group performs poorly it will seek an individual to act as scapegoat and accept all the blame for the failure. ('Blame the chair' is a mild version of this game, 'blame the tutor' another.) This can be a painful experience for the group member concerned. It also removes from the group any perceived responsibility for what happened. There is, therefore, no felt need to look at how *the group* contributed to what happened, to learn from this, and to make changes that will increase the chance of future success.

BECOMING A MORE EFFECTIVE TEAM MEMBER

To work on your personal effectiveness, you need to know your own strengths and weaknesses.

ACTIVITY 11.4

Think about your own behaviour in the last two groups you were a part of at work, either as chair or member. Use the behaviour categories listed previously as a basis for identifying your own strengths and weaknesses in groups, and list these below.

Strengths

_____

_____

_____

Weaknesses

_____

_____

_____

If possible, check your perceptions with those of someone you trust. Ask them to observe you in a meeting soon, and give you feedback on aspects of your behaviour which they feel contributed to the meeting, and aspects which reduced your effectiveness. Indeed, if you are in a group of students who work reasonably well together, members might agree to nominate an observer for each meeting for a while, so that you all get feedback on your behaviour, and can support each other in increasing your personal effectiveness, as well as the effectiveness of the group as a whole.

Knowing your strengths and weaknesses helps you to work out ways of improving. Simple changes to the way you phrase your contribution might help. Perhaps you have strengths, for example in summarising, that you are not exploiting fully.

Many people, whether as chair or as member, are less effective than they might be because they are insufficiently assertive. Either they do not realise the difference between assertiveness and aggression, and avoid the former for fear of the latter, or they have never developed assertiveness skills, so the phrases that would help do not come readily to their tongues. They may simply never have thought about their rights in a meeting. If you recognise yourself in this description, and have not already done so, work through the section on assertiveness skills in Chapter 5.

→ Ch 5

Giving and receiving feedback on effectiveness

Supportive feedback is an essential tool in helping a team (and individual members) to improve. It is very easy to give feedback in a 'holier than thou' fashion, which carries the message that the observer is infinitely superior to the observed, and in possession of secret knowledge of all the observee's faults. As many of us feel vulnerable in social interactions, such feedback can be highly destructive. The group needs an agreement beforehand on how it wants feedback given, and a commitment to supporting its members in their efforts to improve in the light of feedback. If this works, it can provide one of the most important developmental aspects of your whole course. In our jobs we are seldom allowed scope for detailed feedback on this important area of performance. This is odd when you consider the enormous potential for organisational damage caused by poorly managed meetings and task groups.

If personal feedback is to be positive, and not cause psychological damage, you *must* pay attention to developing feedback skills. This means getting feedback on your feedback. In the USA I was exposed, back in the 1960s, to one of the rather nasty 't' groups then in fashion (also called encounter groups). Fairly typically, it was run in a totally non-directive fashion, and members seemed to think that the purpose of the group was to be as unpleasantly truthful as possible about each other's shortcomings. I certainly learned nothing about my performance from the experience, apart from the need to keep quiet in that group. Those less cautious will, I am sure, carry the scars to this day. But I did learn how important it is for feedback to be positive if it is to be effective.

Good feedback:

- focuses on behaviour not person
- emphasises the good more than the bad
- is constructive
- is collegial not superior.

It is easy to focus review and feedback on what is *not* working. While it is obviously important to identify such things, and to do something about them, it is equally important to look at what *is* working well. Indeed, there are many who would argue that you are likely to learn far more if this is your main focus. If at the end of a meeting, for example, you review the progress you have made as a group, and highlight achievements, the group will feel 'rewarded', and be motivated to future effort. They will be more likely to use any behaviours identified as contributing to that success on future occasions. And if there are a few 'areas for improvement' they will find it easier to recognise these if they are starting from a position of feeling good about themselves.

Giving feedback is a skill, and you cannot learn it from a book. That is why it is important to obtain feedback on your feedback. The following points should be remembered:

- Feedback is less threatening if it focuses on the behaviour shown, not on the person behaving: 'That remark about . . . might have been interpreted as an attack on . . .', rather than 'You were very aggressive'.
- Feedback should focus on good aspects even more than bad ones. This will reinforce strengths as well as making the recipient feel strong enough to face up to a limited number of weaknesses without becoming instantly defensive.
- Feedback which is given as between equals tends to be more acceptable, especially feedback that you give to fellow students. If you are giving feedback to a subordinate, you may draw on greater experience or knowledge, but it is normally best if the feedback is clearly based on such things, rather than mere position.

At the end of each meeting there should be, in addition to a review of individual effectiveness, a short period devoted to thinking about group effectiveness, which may prove useful in pointing out areas of potential improvement.

Guidelines for effective teamworking

■ Select members with appropriate skills, knowledge and, if possible, a mix of preferred team roles.

■ Ensure that all members understand and accept the objectives.

■ Pay attention to both task and process.

■ Accept that feelings may run high during early 'storming'.

■ Value all contributions.

■ Review both task progress and group process at regular intervals.

■ Reward success.

DEVELOPING YOUR LEADERSHIP SKILLS

One way of becoming more effective as a team member is by developing your leadership skills. Organisations are increasingly focusing on leadership potential, so these are highly transferable. Leadership is commonly defined in terms of the exercise of influence, often with the focus on influence that derives from other than power or authority. So you do not have to be acting as chair to exercise leadership. Developing confidence in taking the lead in a group without a formal chair, and knowing how to increase the chances that others will want to follow your lead will help you show leadership in work and other contexts.

A vast amount has been written on leadership (Amazon listed over 160 000 such items at the last count) but there is still substantial confusion as to what constitutes leadership and how it differs from management. You will often find the words used interchangeably, although increasingly the distinction highlighted earlier is adopted – management stems from position, and has to do with conformity and control, leadership comes from other sources and has to do with inspiring people to change.

So what skills does leadership demand? Goleman (1998) claims that his research 'clearly shows that emotional intelligence (EI) is the *sine qua non* of leadership'. (Note that he is clearly taking 'leaders' to mean senior managers, here, but the points are more generally applicable.) He identifies five components of EI at work:

■ **self-awareness** – the ability to recognise your own emotions and drives and their impact on others, and to be honest with oneself and others;

■ **self-regulation** – the ability to control impulses and moods, to suspend judgement, to think before acting;

■ **self-motivation** – a passion for the work itself, and energy and enthusiasm to pursue goals;

■ **empathy** – ability to treat people according to *their* emotional reactions (rather than your own);

■ **social skills** – proficiency in managing relationships and building networks.

→ Ch 8

→ Ch 1, 8
→ Ch 10

If you are working through this book, you should be developing most of these components. Reflective learning, as outlined in Chapter 8, should be increasing your self-awareness, and if you are including reflection on feelings, will also impact upon self-regulation. Your work on study planning and on motivation will help with self-motivation more generally. So too will ongoing emphasis on the need for clarity of objectives. This chapter and the previous one, together with the feedback you manage to gather on your own impact, will help with developing communication and other social skills – indeed you should be able to see close parallels between Goleman's factors and the characteristics needed for effective talking and listening described earlier.

If you have the emotional sensitivity Goleman describes, you will be well on the way to being able to influence people and make them want to follow your lead. I would argue that understanding their motivation is also important for this, and being able to make them feel good about the group task. (The process-oriented group behaviours are a big help here, while being able to listen attentively and/or actively, as appropriate, will help greatly in both one-to-one situations and groups.)

A number of writers on leadership emphasise 'authenticity' as a key component. This is a combination of the self-awareness that Goleman lists, and the willingness to be honest with other group members about your own feelings, possible inadequacies and mistakes. This kind of honesty can help to build trust with other team members. If you are all honest about your shortcomings, and your worries about being able to do a task well enough, or to meet deadlines, the group will be much better placed to exercise control. You will be able to re-plan to cope with any problems so that objectives are still met.

→ Ch 12

But there are other dimensions to leadership too, which concern the task and the environment. In the sorts of groups that you will be part of as a student, using the task behaviours listed earlier will help you to exercise an influence on a group. At work, the other key dimension will be to do with being the one who has the clearest idea of what will be needed to meet changes in the wider organisation, or its competitive or other wider environment. Chapter 12 will be particularly relevant here, though of course most of your Master's studies will be directed towards making you good at this.

ACTIVITY 11.5

Consider the extent to which you currently influence a team of which you are a member. What are your 'leadership strengths'? List those factors which you think are helping you to exercise leadership – perhaps you are good at making others feel part of the team and wanting to contribute to the task, or good at organising meetings. Make an action plan to become even more effective through these strengths. Look at any possible reasons for your influence being less than it might be. (Feedback from fellow team members can be really useful here.) Make an action plan to develop your skills in these areas too.

THE ROLE OF INFORMAL GROUPS

Well-managed groups can generate powerful learning experiences, as well as being a source of support, information and expertise. If your course offers few official opportunities for group work, perhaps because you have chosen a distance course, or a part-time one heavily based on lectures, it is important to create unofficial opportunities.

Distance learning students have for many years been exploiting the possibilities of self-organised study groups. Some operate very formally, with a coordinator, regular meetings, agendas circulated beforehand and minutes afterwards. Others are much less formal, meeting 'at the pub, every other Friday', or merely ringing each other for support or encouragement when they feel the need.

Such groups, formal or informal, can be a rich source of ideas, help with course material, and moral support. Although part-time students may feel slightly less need for such groups if they meet regularly at classes, they may be underestimating the potential benefits of self-help. If you are in this position, you should see whether there are others with whom you could meet, even if only occasionally, for additional discussion. If there are, try having a few meetings before rejecting the idea.

When there are several people from the same organisation enrolled on a course they can form their own group, perhaps meeting for lunch if they work on the same site. At their meetings, some of the time can be devoted to discussing how to apply course ideas to their own organisation. Indeed, this is such a powerful way of 'tailoring' a course to a specific organisation's needs that many employers deliberately arrange such meetings, perhaps with an in-house trainer as facilitator. If your employer is sponsoring several from your organisation and has not yet realised the value of such a provision, you might suggest it. That way you may be able to have your self-help group meetings in working hours.

Whether your group is in-company, or you all come from different organisations, and whether working face to face or remotely, you may find the following guidelines helpful. They are derived from various sets of guidelines available within the Open University for use by students and tutors, but are potentially of use in a wide range of collaborative learning situations.

Guidelines for running study groups

■ Nominate a meeting coordinator. This need not be permanent – the role may rotate, but someone needs to take the initiative for the first few meetings.

■ Decide where and when to meet, and for how long, and ensure that everyone knows how to get there.

■ Decide on an agenda. This need not be formal, but everyone needs to know the purpose of the meeting, what they should bring, and what preparation, if any, would be useful beforehand. Possible topics include discussion of the next assignment, comparing members' experience of organisational practice on a particular issue, role plays and so on. Start with fairly simple objectives for your first few meetings.

- Remember the nurturing; arrange a comfortable meeting place, where refreshments are available (not possible for remote meetings).
- Check your objectives at the start of the meeting, and review the extent to which they have been met at the end. Consider whether this has implications for the way future meetings will run.
- Bear in mind all the information in this chapter about effective group working.
- Fix your next meeting before you leave.
- Share phone numbers and e-mail addresses so that interactions can go on outside meetings.

VIRTUAL TEAMS

Increasingly, work groups are dispersed geographically, and need to 'meet' electronically. (Not long ago I met an MBA student who managed a team with members on four continents.) Since travel is expensive of time and energy, as well as money, such teams need to find ways of working effectively in an on-line environment. The widespread use of blogs and on-line discussion groups has gone far to develop the relevant skills, but you may find it helpful to spend a little time thinking about the particular challenges posed by virtual teams, and ways in which you can address these, particularly if your course requires this sort of interaction.

→ Ch 8 Distance learning programmes in particular make heavy use of e-mail and on-line discussion groups, and are now starting to expand their virtual learning environments, as discussed in Chapter 8. Conferencing (both synchronous and asynchronous) via the Internet, perhaps with a video element, is becoming increasingly common on such programmes, as well as in many work situations.

Effective working in a virtual team requires even more attention to task and process management than a group which can meet in real space. Even with a video element there is less information available to members. If you are relying on an audio link or text alone, you are working with a very narrow 'channel' indeed, having lost body language, and in the case of text only, being without even tone of voice. You can't make someone feel better with a smile! Contributions may be much less natural, and it is far harder to manage interaction without the normal cues involved in making eye contact.

Perhaps the greatest challenges are posed by on-line text-based forums, so these will be addressed here, as they are widely used as the basis for group working on courses where students are widely scattered. Such groups can work asynchronously, which is a great advantage both to students with demanding jobs and to those working in different time zones.

You will remember that effective teamworking required attention to both task and process – members needed to feel committed to achieving the team's goals, and enabled and motivated to make a full contribution to achieving these. Teams needed to go through stages of forming, norming and storming before they could perform effectively. And there were various behaviours which contributed to progressing both task and process. The following addresses some of these issues in the context of a text-based virtual group. I have categorised the issues slightly differently from the earlier discussion, hoping thus to reinforce it while at the same time fitting the challenges of virtual working. These challenges include:

Establishing a sense of membership. If you have been allocated to an on-line group and do not know the other members, this presents a real challenge. If you are going to be working together on a significant project, and it is at all possible, it is worth making a substantial effort to meet face to face at least once. If meeting is not possible, then try to create a virtual social space in which you can get to know the other team members. Post a more detailed résumé than you otherwise might, and start the discussion by posting messages that are about yourself and your current concerns – you might want to alert members to key aspects of your résumé, and also make clear what you can bring to the discussion by way of knowledge, experience and perspective. If there will be constraints on your availability, it is worth highlighting these, too. For a student group you might want to strengthen your on-line identity by signing your messages in a memorable way, e.g. 'Finnish Frederika', and adopting a particular font for your messages (though make sure that it is easy to read and will not be a distraction).

To help others feel part of the group, respond to their contributions in a personal way, and one which will make them feel comfortable about membership, and valued as an individual, e.g. 'Great to have a perspective from Finland, Frederika. There must be some major differences in perspective on [this issue] so your view will be really interesting. I went to Helsinki a couple of years ago – loved the food!'

Establishing rules of engagement (norming). It is important to establish how the group will operate, how much time people might expect to put into the exercise, how often they are expected to log on, how contributions are going to be summarised or otherwise organised, whether there will be different sub-areas for different sub-groups or tasks, whether there is someone who will be taking responsibility for managing such aspects and for archiving or editing contributions.

Agreeing objectives. It is really important that the group agree what they are trying to achieve and objectives need to be SMART so that progress can be checked. It is worth setting aside a specific time period at the beginning with the aim of ensuring that everyone agrees and has expressed commitment to the objectives.

Planning how to achieve these objectives. Because of the asynchronous nature of interaction in many virtual groups, particular attention needs to be paid to defining specific tasks, allocating responsibilities for any sub-group working, and setting clear target dates for sharing of sub-group outputs. Time management is extremely important when working asynchronously. The plan needs to take into account members' availability and frequency of logging on. It is all too easy for substantial time to pass with no progress because key individuals are not contributing quickly enough, and frequent milestones can reduce the risk of this.

Contributing effectively. One of the advantages of asynchronous working is that you have time to think before responding. Unfortunately not everyone takes advantage of this. On-line discussions that are interspersed with short messages which do not actually make sense because they are too brief, do not make clear what they refer to, or ignore much of what has gone before can be very hard indeed to follow. A message like 'Don't agree with Fred' is unlikely to be helpful if Fred was making three points, two of which build on a series of thoughtful previous messages. You do not have to display the wisdom of Solomon to make a useful contribution. Nor do you need to be *right*. So don't let this caution prevent you from contributing at all. But do try to ensure that you have read the full argument as it has developed thus far, and thought about it before responding. Make it clear what you are responding to – replying to the most recent message in the string, with the same heading will help (provided you first read the earlier messages in the string). Quote any particular points that you wish to respond to. Make clear the evidence or reasoning that underlies your response. Ensure that you have expressed your thoughts clearly (another advantage over real place meetings is that you can 'say' something, think about it, and 'say it differently' before sending). And remember the process issues – 'Fred, I think you've made a really interesting point here, and it has made me think about my own assumption that [. . .] But your suggestion that [. . .] is inevitably the case doesn't fit with my current experience. In my company we [. . .] I'd really like to know from others whether my company is unique in this, or if you have similar experiences'.

I hope that this example shows how you can value a contribution – and its contributor – while still disagreeing with content. It also ends with a question to other team members, which may make it easier for them to join the discussion.

It may be helpful, when appropriate, to give the URL of relevant evidence so that others can check your interpretation. Another useful feature of on-line working is that you can share materials very easily, so take advantage of this by attaching copies of relevant articles, or of your notes upon them, drafts of reports, or any other resources that may help your colleagues. If file titles are clear, and there is a brief explanation of the reason for an attachment, colleagues can decide whether or not to download it. (Without a clear explanation there is a risk of 'death by information' which can reduce the effectiveness of an on-line team.)

When you want to start a new point, start a new 'string' with a different (and descriptive) message heading to avoid confusion and to make it easier for a moderator or discussion leader to summarise the messages relevant to a particular point.

Monitoring progress and 'adjusting' effort. It can be depressing to feel you are the only person contributing to a 'discussion'. The group needs to agree how progress will be monitored and non-contributors 'encouraged' to play their part. While it may be fine for a member to read a general discussion and contribute but rarely (this is common in real space groups too), it may seriously reduce the quality of output for collaborative work towards a specific task. Summarising discussion at intervals and assessing how far there is still to go in order to complete the task can be invaluable in saving other people's time and in motivating the group as a whole.

Working in realtime. Even if a conference is mainly asynchronous, it can be helpful to set some time windows during which everyone tries to be on-line at the same time.

This can speed up discussions greatly, and is one way of 'energising' a discussion that is not moving along fast. It can also be useful when finalising one task and agreeing how best to more forwards to the next.

The following guidelines summarise points of good practice when interacting asynchronously.

Guidelines for asychronous conferencing

- Meet face to face if at all possible, in order to get to know group members and start to build trust.
- If you cannot meet, allow some 'social' time in the conferences for people to feel comfortable together.
- At the same time, post résumés so that people can check who you are if they forget. Include a photo if you can.
- Obtain members' explicit agreement on what is needed to achieve the group task, and on the most effective way of operating (times of logging on, deadlines for contributions and so on).
- Break tasks down into constituent parts with deadlines, and be absolutely clear who is responsible for doing what.
- Ensure that someone accepts responsibility for reminding people of incipient deadlines.
- Be particularly careful to give feedback in a constructive and supportive way and pay attention to making people feel their contributions are valued.
- Summarise discussion at regular intervals and check on progress.
- Set aside some short periods when people will all try to log on at once and respond quickly to each other – this can be a useful antidote to the more disconnected and 'measured' asynchronous communication.

Synchronous virtual working

Synchronous working has many advantages in terms of immediacy and speed of interaction which for many outweigh the potential disadvantage of needing to make a firm diary commitment to the meeting. If your system allows a group to talk while sharing screens, 'meetings' can proceed almost as if you were in real space. But in such systems managing contributions can be a real challenge and attention needs to be paid to ensuring that 'airtime' is fairly shared: gatekeeping is essential, and even if this seems sometimes to create a more stilted 'conversation' you may find it more effective to give one member particular responsibility for signalling who is to speak next.

In any form of group work it is important to stop at regular intervals and check on how well you are progressing with the task, how well you feel the process is being managed, and what behaviours are helping and hindering the exercise. To avoid groupthink you need to be brutally honest about how well the group is progressing. If it is not doing well, then it will take considerable skill, and a lot of process management, to ensure that people can take this as a learning point, and get back on track, rather than feeling unhappy about themselves and the group and therefore withdrawing. If you can learn how to do this you will be even more valuable as a team member at work.

SUMMARY

- Effective communication and talking and listening skills form a basic building block for working in a team (as well as being important in many other contexts). Such skills are far from universal.

- Effective teams need to pay attention to managing both the task itself and the process by which it is carried out if members are to feel motivated and enabled to contribute fully.

- In managing collaborative *tasks* it is vital to start by agreeing the team's objectives: the 'Universal Management Paradigm' can be a useful framework here.

- Behaviours concerning clarification, information giving and seeking, proposing, summarising, evaluating, timekeeping and identifying further action are important for task management.

- In managing *process*, behaviours of agreeing, encouraging, praising and resolving conflicts are important.

- Observation, and feedback based on that observation, can give valuable insights to members on their individual effectiveness, and can help the group to consider how to become more effective.

- Teams will work best if they include the necessary range of expertise and have members whose preferences include the full range of team roles.

- Groups normally go through stages of 'forming', 'storming' and 'norming' before 'performing', and a single meeting will need to go through a cycle of 'nurturing', 'energising', 'peak performance' and 'relaxation'.

- A good chair can manage both task and process issues, but these need not all be the chair's responsibility, and not all groups need chairs.

- Teams will usually be more effective if members exercise leadership outside of the formal chairing role. Leadership skills are increasingly valued by employers, and teamworking gives you an opportunity to develop these skills.

- Key tasks for leaders include identifying requirements, task management, process management, particularly making individuals feel valued and motivated. 'Emotional intelligence' and conceptual skills for problem identification and clarification contribute to effective leadership.

- Groups can exhibit negative features, such as groupthink and scapegoating.

- Informal groups can usefully supplement groups or teams which are formally required.

- Virtual groups need to pay even more attention to task and process management than face-to-face ones.

Further information

- Baguley, P. (1992) *Teams and Team-Working*, Teach Yourself Books, Hodder & Stoughton.
- Barker, A. (2002) *How to Manage Meetings*, Sunday Times/Kogan Page.
- Belbin, R.M. (1993) *Team Roles at Work*, Butterworth-Heinemann.
- Hardingham, A. (1995) *Working in Teams*, Institute of Personnel Development.
- http://www.helpself.com
  For a wide range of materials including a free (basic) EQ test and (linked from the leadership section) an electronic book on leadership.
- http://www.similarminds.com/personality_tests
  For a range of free personality tests.

→ 12 Case studies, complexity and consultancy

Learning outcomes

By the end of this chapter you should:

■ understand the strengths and weaknesses of case studies as a vehicle for learning

■ be prepared for the main difficulties encountered in working with cases

■ be able to approach case study analysis in a systematic and effective way

■ appreciate the importance of the 'diagnosis' stage

■ be aware of the need to use a range of models to handle complexity

■ appreciate the relevance of case study work to consultancy.

INTRODUCTION

The central role of case study analysis in traditional MBA programmes was discussed earlier. First used at the Harvard Business School in 1869, case studies are still widely used in postgraduate management study, as vehicles for both learning and assessment. In studying management, familiarity with a range of concepts, theories, frameworks and techniques is only the start. What is important is the ability to apply these techniques to the complex and 'messy' situations that make up the stuff of management. Successful application depends upon appreciating the *context* of the application, and being able to unravel the complexities in the situation. Case studies, which are representations of organisational situations, provide that context and usually a degree of complexity too.

By working through a number of cases you will become better able to recognise types of problem situation, more skilled at extracting key features in these, and better able to work out root causes and possible actions. This process of diagnosis is absolutely crucial and often underemphasised in real life. There are never 'right answers' to organisational problems, but through cases you may become better able to understand the nature of the problem, and avoid the 'obvious', but totally wrong, solution!

As well as providing the context for you to use concepts from the course, cases offer the opportunity to practise a wide range of transferable skills. These include reading and note taking, diagramming, analysing information, coping with complexity and ambiguity, working in groups, time management and written and oral presentation. They also place more of the responsibility for learning on the student than do lectures or seminars.

Given this, it is not surprising that case study work poses considerable challenges. This chapter is directed at helping you make full use of the learning opportunities that case studies present. It will also help you to do well in case-based assessment. It first outlines key features of case-based learning, and then offers a method for approaching cases. Although you cannot apply the method in full until you have studied the concepts to use in analysing the case, a quasi-case concerning problems facing a student is available on the **website**. This will allow you to practise analysis using concepts introduced in this Handbook.

Your course may include a consultancy project, or you may be involved as an internal consultant at work. If so, the analytical and critical skills, the ability to cope with complexity, and the broader understanding of a wide range of organisational contexts that case study work develops will be invaluable to you. The skills addressed in this chapter are highly transferable.

THE PLACE OF CASE STUDIES

Looking at how (and why) cases are used goes a long way to explaining their popularity. More importantly, if you understand *why* you are being asked to work in a particular way, you are more likely to benefit from that work.

The case method

Case studies:

■ are interesting

■ introduce 'real' situations

■ allow *use* of concepts and techniques

■ give practice in handling complexity

■ develop team and communication skills.

In the case method of teaching you are presented with information about an organisational situation, often a mix of written description of the situation, 'exhibits', and some quantitative information. Some cases are very brief – a few pages outlining events in the organisation and what was problematic, together with, say, financial information in the form of tables. Others are more extensive, and include 'original' information such as press cuttings, copies of internal memos, survey reports – the possibilities are endless. There may be video or audio material, perhaps including interviews with key protagonists. Some cases run to 60 or 80 pages.

Whatever the nature of the case with which you are presented, you will be required to 'analyse' it. This means working out what seems to be happening, and why. You might be asked merely to explain a situation, you might be asked to evaluate actions that have already been taken or you might be asked to consider possible future actions and compare the likely effectiveness of these. In doing so, you will be expected to use ideas that you have been taught in your courses, thus exploring the usefulness of theories and techniques in different contexts and gaining practice in linking idea to situation.

You may be asked to analyse the case single-handed (particularly for a written assignment or exam, where your analytical skills and conceptual grasp are being tested). More commonly, the case will act as a focus for group learning. In this case you will typically be asked to stand up and present your analysis and conclusions to the rest of the class (assuming a face-to-face context). The following discussion assumes a group context, but most of it will be relevant to individual case study analysis.

Intended learning

Cases use a different style of learning from other methods, thus adding to the variety of the learning experience. They give the impression of 'reality' and therefore of validity, of access to privileged information, of learning what *really* goes on. Particularly for students with limited organisational experience, this can be seen as highly valuable. However, early encounters with cases can be stressful.

When faced with a case study, your first reaction may be panic – 'Help! What am I supposed to do with this?' This may be followed by the feeling of drowning in a sea of so-called information that seems to tell you nothing you really want to know. By now you may be barely speaking to some of your group, who are not pulling their weight, and wanting to inflict serious physical damage on others who seem to be deliberately obstructing your work. The whole thing may seem a total waste of time.

However, if you think about your objectives in studying, it may become clear that case study work is useful *precisely because of* its capacity to generate this frustration. If you are studying in order to become more effective as a manager and accelerate your career, rather than merely acquire letters after your name, you need to develop the skills that will achieve this. Many of these skills will be conceptual ones, and of a fairly high order at that. Others will be interpersonal skills.

Managing is not easy. You are continually faced with new and complex situations, with many interrelated factors, and different views both on what is happening and on what should happen. Some important factors may be unknown, perhaps unknowable until it is too late. Ready-made answers seldom work. Someone may sound impressive when they say, 'We had this problem at X and solved it by doing Y, so we should do Y' but this can be highly dangerous. The chances are that at X there were key differences: what worked there will not work here. Indeed, they may not really have had 'the same' problem at all. In many situations it is difficult to know just what the problem *is*. Frequently a situation will be construed as a particular type of problem when deeper investigation identifies something completely different. One of the most valuable skills a manager can have is the ability to diagnose a situation, identifying the underlying factors which are creating symptoms of a problem.

In order to take appropriate action as a manager or consultant faced with a complex, unfamiliar and uncertain problem situation, you need to be able to:

- identify those with an interest in the problem situation – the stakeholders – and their different perspectives;
- understand the wider context within which the situation is located – how it links to other problems (and other non-problems), what is changing outside the area of

immediate concern that may impact upon it, what constraints will be imposed by the context;

■ figure out what information you have, or can obtain, that will cast light on the situation, and how reliable this information is likely to be;

■ become aware of assumptions that are being made about the situation – by yourself and by fellow group members, as well as by key actors in the case; these may be leading to misperceptions about the problem, or limiting what is seen to be possible by way of improvements;

■ feel comfortable with ambiguities and uncertainties, as you will never have full information;

■ 'make sense of' the problem situation, diagnosing it thoroughly so that you feel that you have an understanding of what is 'really' happening – the key issues in the situation, the factors which contributed to their becoming issues, and the causal relationships involved, and/or the likely effects of recent and possible future action;

■ given this understanding, work out what needs to be done;

■ convince anyone who needs to be convinced that this is indeed the appropriate course of action;

■ make sure that all those involved in this action are committed to the action and are enabled to implement it.

Case study work should enable you to become better all these aspects of dealing with complexity, whether on your course, or, more importantly, at work. The next section looks at perhaps the hardest aspect, which will permeate all your Master's studies and, even more so, your life as a manager. This is how to overcome our natural reluctance to deal with complexity and uncertainty.

Dealing with complexity

Case studies are not reality – more of their limitations in this respect shortly. But they are a pretty good halfway house. They are complicated, and difficult to make sense of, and the difficulties they present allow you to develop the conceptual skills which feature in the list above. Of these, that loosely called 'making sense' is perhaps the hardest of all. Working out what the issues are, when faced with a seeming 'mess' of information, feelings, different perspectives and interpretations of 'the problem' presents major challenges. The same is true of working out the causal factors and relationships involved.

Good problem solving depends upon adequate diagnosis. Whether you are following the rational Universal Management Paradigm (UMP), or taking a more creative or organic approach, you need to understand what is creating the difficulties experienced. 'Define the problem' may seem an obvious and simple first step, but it can be the hardest thing of all if there is any degree of complexity involved.

People do not like complexity and uncertainty. There seems a strong human tendency to simplify, make assumptions and move on to solutions. Kepner and Tregoe (1965) identified this tendency when they observed problem-solving groups and found that

→ Ch 11
they acted highly irrationally, leaping to discussing solutions before exploring the nature of the problem. Figure 11.3 showed an example of the sort of discussion they observed.

There are probably good evolutionary reasons for this rush to solution: if a lion is prowling outside, or a flood rushing upon you, deep explorations of causes are unlikely to help you survive. But it does not make for good decisions in the face of the sorts of complexity encountered at work. One of the reasons that consultants sometimes have a bad name is that many of them have a single 'product' or approach that they apply to almost every problem. If they have been selected carefully for relevant expertise this may not matter. But if the problem for which they are called in is not one to which their stock solution is appropriate, they may cost the company significantly more than their (considerable) fees.

The frustrations you encounter in dealing with the complexities of cases on your course should contribute to making you more effective as a consultant, whether on a course consultancy project or in real life. You will learn the importance of holding back and exploring all the themes in a problem, and you will see how applying as wide a range as possible of concepts and theories gives different views of the situation. These different views, each partial, will add up to a far richer understanding than your immediate reactions. You will also, once you start to listen, realise that team members who disagree with you may do so because they are adopting a different perspective from your own, and making different assumptions. Their perspective may highlight features in the situation you had not appreciated, or cause you to value differently ones you *had* identified. It may also make you aware of some of your own assumptions, and how they are affecting your perception and interpretation of factors in the situation.

Critical application of ideas

Much of the academic content of your course will consist of ideas intended to *help* you make sense of organisational complexities. Case studies give you something to make sense *of!* One skill not explicitly mentioned above, though implicit in 'making sense', is choosing suitable frameworks and ideas to help with this. The ideas taught in your course will not in any sense be 'solutions'. But by using them in a situation, you may find that they lead you to suggestions that will improve things. This point was nicely made by one of my students recently, when he said:

> What is different about this course is that all my previous management training has purported to give answers: this one is giving me the questions.

Different ideas are of more or less use in different situations. You need to be able to work out which will be useful in any particular situation, and then to derive benefit from using them. A framework is useful in a particular context if it prompts you to ask questions that generate useful information about the situation and/or helps you to make sense of the answers and other evidence generated. You are likely to be faced with new theories and concepts throughout your life, and will need to be able to critically evaluate these, too. Are they logically consistent? Are they based on reasonable evidence? When are they likely to be useful? In what ways? When are they likely to be of little value? Working critically with theories in the contest of case studies will develop your ability to evaluate ideas that you meet long after your course has finished.

By now you should see the importance of those features of case study work that are most likely to drive you to despair – complexity, uncertainty, information unreliability and/or overload, and 'woolliness' of what you are being asked to do. These are precisely the features of real working life that are most difficult to cope with as a manager. It is these aspects of cases that will help you develop the necessary conceptual skills.

Groups, assumptions and communication

The potential value of case study work goes far beyond the purely conceptual. If used in the group context described above, cases simulate real contexts well enough to give you the opportunity to practise *all* of the managerial skills listed earlier. The group is important – your group work on the case allows simulation of the teamworking and negotiation with colleagues that you would need in dealing with complex problem situations in reality.

Communication skills will be practised in two ways. You will obviously need to communicate with members of your team while working on the case. There will usually be a great deal of heated discussion about interpretations and significance of information, and the virtue of different courses of action. Your ability to make your points in a way that others can understand, and to argue clearly and coherently, will be important. The skills addressed in the previous chapter will be vital. Furthermore, through presenting your analysis and conclusions, orally and/or in a written report, you will develop the communication skills that you would need if you were to gain approval for a particular proposal. (These skills will be addressed in subsequent chapters.)

→ Ch 11, 15, 16

Some of your most heated debates are likely to stem from different underlying assumptions and values, whether about the specific case situation, about organisations in general or about life as a whole. One of the greatest areas for potential learning is becoming aware of such assumptions, your own and those of others. The previous chapter made clear how assumptions can have a profound effect on how you perceive and interpret information. Your assumptions will affect how you conceptualise problems and evaluate solutions. Yet, if you are unaware of these assumptions, and you probably *are* unaware of them, the negative effects can go far beyond shouting matches. You may come up with views of a situation that do not correspond to those of any other stakeholder, and 'solutions' which aggravate the situation. Or you may fail to realise the potential of a whole set of possible options.

Contextual awareness

There is one more area of potential learning. The importance of context was stressed above, and the context is part of the case. Managers often focus on internal aspects of a situation, when the significance of these depends upon things *outside* the organisation. Your analysis of any particular case will develop your understanding of the importance of specific contextual features. By studying a large number of cases you will also develop an appreciation of the range of contexts that exist, and their characteristics. It will not give you the same understanding as you would gain from working in a wide range of different organisations. But that option is not open to everyone, and takes time even for those who can do it. Cases are a shortcut to broadening your understanding of the world of business, of the sorts of situations that can be problematic, the kinds of factors likely to be relevant to these, and the wide range of possible options that might be considered.

Limitations of cases

The above may have suggested that cases are the perfect route to management learning. It is important, however, to be aware of their very real limitations. The most obvious is that cases are simplifications. They have been filtered by the case author, who chose what to include, and what to exclude, and how to describe what was included. The greatest challenge to managers in real life often comes from the parts that are 'simplified out'. The messy interactions between people, resistance to change, power and its manifestations, the amount of time needed for communication – the list of such things is endless. But if you become better at dealing with those aspects that are a frequent feature of cases you should have more time and energy to deal with these other, trickier aspects.

'Filtering' by the author can also be frustrating because inevitably you will find that there is no information on things that you feel are important. You are then forced to base your analysis on assumptions about key aspects. Alternatively, you may be swamped with an oversupply of data (though remember that developing the skill to select relevant information from such a mass is important in real life). Such frustrations, while annoying, can actually enhance your learning, so are not therefore really limitations of the approach.

More worrying is the way in which cases are sometimes taken as a 'model' of how things should be done (and the common practice of giving 'solutions' may enhance this). Such equating of case with reality is positively dangerous. Case descriptions are biased snapshots of a point in time, or perhaps a period up to such a point. The bias may lead you to a particular interpretation that would not have been valid even in that situation, and may be even less so in seemingly similar situations.

The 'historic' nature of cases adds to the problem of using cases as 'models'. Success may be widely publicised at the time, but prove transitory. It is fairly tempting to analyse the factors contributing to a favourable situation and assume that you have found a universal recipe for success. But what is successful one year may fail the next. We once made a marketing course where every 'exemplary' firm we filmed for the accompanying video was in serious, and public, trouble, even before the first students saw the video! Nor were we unusually unlucky or ill-advised. Clutterbuck and Kernaghan's (1990) study of organisational failure included a throw-away comment in the foreword to the effect that within three years of a study of successful companies (Goldsmith and Clutterbuck, 1984) one-third of the companies from which the authors developed their formula for success were in severe difficulty. Any 'answers' or 'recipes' you are tempted to derive from case studies should therefore be treated with extreme caution!

One of the reasons tutors like teaching with cases is that they are often in possession of the 'solution', and can reinforce their credibility with students by offering it to students at the end. But the above shows the dangerous nature of 'solutions' that may be offered. First, even if the solution consists of what the organisation actually decided, you are not to know if it was the right decision. This is the difficulty with complex situations. There are so many things you do not know. In real life a decision may have rapid disastrous consequences that suggest that the decision was *wrong*. But this does not mean that given the information and probabilities facing the organisation at the time it was wrongly taken! Normally the outcomes are more ambiguous: the changed situations may be deemed better by some, acceptable by others and not as good as the original by a few. In such cases it is very difficult to evaluate the decision. Since so many organisational situations are of this kind, it can be argued that a further limitation of case studies is that they can give students the idea that it is appropriate to seek 'the solution' to a messy organisational problem.

A final potential limitation of case learning is that not all tutors have the necessary skills to use them effectively. Although students do a lot of the work themselves, and need to accept the responsibility for managing their work and their learning, tutors can make a huge difference. To help students learn from cases a tutor needs to be able constantly to 'diagnose' progress, and give inconspicuous direction, and then to draw all the potential learning points out of student experience. The following method for coping with cases will help you to maximise your learning whatever the degree of support on offer.

COPING WITH CASES

It should by now be clear that analysing any substantial case is likely to present a wide range of challenges. These include:

- rapid reading;
- managing and interpreting large amounts of information;
- living with ambiguity;
- working effectively in a team;
- using abstract ideas to help with analysis and synthesis of something approximating messy reality;
- coping with time pressures;
- presenting information orally and in writing;
- managing your own learning, to a greater or lesser extent.

The links to most of the chapters in this book are fairly obvious. Most will help you in case study work. This chapter looks at two aspects of cases not dealt with elsewhere, the emotional dimension and the problem of where and how to start when faced with a forbiddingly complex situation.

Earlier it was hinted that case study work can generate a high level of negative feelings, often caused by a sense of failure. This may be because you feel you have 'got nowhere' with the case. If so, the 'method' offered shortly should help. It may, however, be a sense of having done less well than other groups, of having 'lost' some kind of contest. Because the emotional dimension of learning is often underrated, you need to be aware of the possibility of such feelings, and to understand where they come from. You should then be able to avoid them, and instead see failure as a valuable learning opportunity.

Failure and dissatisfaction

Most managers seeking a qualification seem to have a high need to achieve, and are also fairly competitive. Many also feel that getting things 'right' constitutes achievement, and giving a more impressive presentation than another group constitutes 'winning'. But note the caution given earlier about whether 'right' answers *can* exist for complex cases. And think about why you are working with a case. It is *not* (except in an examination) to come to a right answer. It *is* to develop all the skills listed earlier, that is, about *learning*. And learning requires practice, feedback and reflection.

So, use case studies to experiment with different ways of using course ideas to sort out a case. And remember that your learning comes not only from your own work and group experience, but also from seeing what others achieved that perhaps you did not. You need to reflect on what worked, and on what didn't work for the group, and on why others may have reached different conclusions.

A sense of failure can get in the way of learning. Defensiveness sets in. 'Scapegoating' can occur, with one group member (or perhaps the tutor) blamed for the 'failure'. This will prevent any learning. Alternatively, the group may indulge in a kind of 'groupthink', deciding that they *did* do brilliantly, despite what people said about their analysis – others just did not understand its merits! It is important that you are alert to the possibility of these responses. And if you start reacting in these ways, or see the group reacting thus, try to stand back and ask the following questions:

- What were we doing anyway – why does it *matter* to be best?
→ Ch 10   ■ How can we learn from what we have done?

If you can address these questions with your group, you will be able to transform your experience of the exercise, and also the extent to which you learn from it. What you initially felt to be a failure can become a very real learning success.

A METHOD FOR APPROACHING CASES

There are three strands to the method for approaching cases. The first strand concerns practical aspects of managing the task and materials facing you. The second is more conceptual, and concerns the best way to deal with complex problems. The early, diagnostic stages of analysis are discussed below: they are absolutely vital. Resist any temptation to skimp them and get on to the 'real work'. The third strand is that of
→ Ch 11   working effectively in a group. This was dealt with in Chapter 11, so is not discussed in

detail here, but you need to be fully aware of the task and process management aspects of teamworking and refer to that chapter where necessary.

The stages below are important in almost any group work on a case.

1. Preparation

One practical issue concerns the sheer volume of many cases. If you are issued with a case in advance of the session at which it will be discussed, avoid the temptation to put it to one side and forget it. Plan enough time to familiarise yourself with the case and its contents. Allow time for a solo pass through at least the 'understanding' and 'scanning' stages described below. If you do not do this, your learning, and that of fellow group members, will suffer, and they may see you as a passenger, and resent this.

2. Understanding the task

One of the first things you need to do is understand what is being asked of you. Are you supposed to adopt a particular perspective, or slant your analysis towards a particular 'client'? What sort of outcome is being asked for? Is it an evaluation of something that has happened, or recommendations as to what *should* happen? If the latter, how far down the path to a detailed action plan are you expected to go? Are there particular parts of the course you are supposed to draw on, or particular techniques you must use? What form of presentation is asked for? Are there constraints on this – word or time limits for example? How long do you have to work on the case?

→ Ch 15

If you are unsure about the meaning of words in the question, consult the glossary at the end of Chapter 15 (Helpfile 15.1). If you are still unsure, or other aspects of the brief are unclear to you, talk to the person who assigned you the case. Misunderstandings about what you are expected to do are in no one's interests. Once you are working in a group, you need to check whether your understanding of the task matches that of others in the group: it is essential that you reach a shared (and correct) understanding of the task.

3. Scanning the case

Once you know what you are meant to be doing, you need to get a 'feel' for the situation in the case. Speed-read the case, trying to get a general idea of what it is about, and the sort of information with which you are presented. If any questions occur to you at this stage, or points 'jump out' as significant, or course concepts seem relevant, jot them down when you get to the end.

→ Ch 9

Having done this, go through the case slightly more slowly, using a highlighter or taking notes of points which seem important. If there are sets of figures, try to see what they might mean in general terms. (Effective reading techniques, covered in Chapter 9, will be invaluable in case study work.)

4. Description – exploring the situation and identifying themes

When scanning you will inevitably start to impose structure on the situation by judging that some things are important and others are not. But try to do this as little as possible. It is far easier to narrow your scope later than to widen your perspective once you have imposed limits. If you are by now working as a group, you will find rich pictures (*see* Chapter 10) to be really useful in helping you to come to a shared perception of what is going on. (Relationship diagrams do this too, but tend to be less fun, and you will learn more if you are enjoying it.)

→ Ch 10

Try to identify and represent all the things that could possibly be relevant to the situation. From these you will be able to construct the web of interrelated issues that cause the situation to be worthy of analysis. Make sure that you look at factors outside the immediate problem context, as these may be significant. If different views emerge, try to find out the reason for differences. Have some people seen things in the case that others have missed? Or do they bring different sets of assumptions to the group? Either may be important.

Once you can agree on a fairly broad representation of the situation, look for 'themes' – linked sets of factors that seem to contribute to one aspect of the situation. For example, there might be one strand to do with perceived poor quality, another to do with changes in competitor behaviour. Within each such strand there might be groups of sub-issues.

Useful pre-diagnostic questions:

- Who thinks there is a problem, and why?
- What is the evidence upon which they are basing this opinion?
- What is (or is not) happening, and when and where?
- What related things are not problematic, and why not?
- What is the wider context within which the situation exists?
- Who, or what, can influence the problem situation?
- What other stakeholders are there?
- What constraints are there that restrict the 'solution space'?

At this stage you are looking for a useful way of *describing* the situation. If you are looking at a problem situation it may help to think of what you are doing as analogous to a lawyer interviewing a client, or a GP asking a patient, 'What seems to be the trouble?' Note the word 'seems'. You are looking for presenting symptoms. What is actually happening? You have not yet worked out what *is* the problem. Much less are you ready to think about solutions! Beware of falling into that common trap.

Finding out what is happening may involve some fairly deep digging into the information provided. Are there any trends in figures? Graphs may help show these. Avoid digging too deep, however. Until you have moved into the next stage, and worked out *why* things are happening, too much detail can cloud the issue, or you may spend time on things which your subsequent diagnosis shows to be marginal. A degree of moving back and forth between this stage and the next (diagnosis) may be necessary. This is called *iteration*, and you may need to backtrack in this way at any stage. As you find out more information about the problem, your ideas of important factors and relationships will become clearer. As they do, you will realise that you need to look more deeply at some of the information to clarify your ideas about what is actually happening. Some of your investigative work may take considerable time and effort. You may need to plan how to divide it between sub-groups, and how and when to share their findings.

5. Diagnosis – working out why things are as they are

As noted earlier, proper diagnosis is the real challenge. The diagnosis stage is probably the one to which you should devote most of your effort, though its success will depend upon the adequacy of the previous stages – an unclear task can thwart you, as can an imperfect or overly narrow grasp of the situation concerned.

You need now to start imposing structure on the mass of information in the case. There are several approaches to structuring, the most important being to use course ideas and frameworks. One useful way to bring these in is to take each of the themes you have identified and brainstorm potentially relevant course concepts. This will provide a useful reference list in the heat of later moments.

Another way of forcing you to look at concepts from an early stage (and of ensuring that you look at all the layers of the problem) is to structure issues vertically, from those concerning individual employees, through the group or section, to the organisation as a whole, and finally to its wider environment. You can thus produce a matrix of main issues, and their related problems, and think about relevant concepts for each 'layer'. You may wish to add a final column for implications and/or recommended actions, but, if you do so, this should not be filled in until later (a version is available on the **website**). (*See* Fig. 12.1.)

	Issues	Concepts	Implications/actions
Individuals			
Groups			
Organisations			
Wider environment			

Fig. 12.1 'Layer matrix' for case study analysis

12

Case studies, complexity and consultancy

This approach can be somewhat mechanistic – an apparent attraction if you are faced with a big and messy problem. The danger is that it may lead to a somewhat superficial investigation of causes, because of the limitations of space on the matrix, and premature categorisation. However, it can act as a useful prompt to look at all these layers. Do not, though, try to fit everything into cells on a tidy matrix like that in Fig. 12.1. For example, you may be offered several frameworks for looking at the wider environment – the classic one is 'STEP' (also known as STEEP, PEST, STEEPV, PESTLE . . .). This highlights key aspects of the environment (sociological, technological, economic, (green) environment, human values and political (including legal) factors) which may be significant. It acts as a useful checklist for exploration, but you would be hard pressed to fit it into a matrix like that above.

Another classic framework you will almost certainly encounter is Porter's (1980) model of the five forces driving industry competition. This would cause you to look at the threats posed by new entrants to the market and of substitute products, and the bargaining power of suppliers and buyers, and the degree of rivalry among existing firms. Again, this might be a useful way of looking at one aspect of a situation, but would be hard to fit into the simple matrix in Fig. 12.1.

→ Ch 10

One useful strand of your diagnosis is to explore how a situation arose. What were the contributory factors? Drawing a multiple-cause diagram (*see* Chapter 10) is an excellent aid to this, and such diagrams are invaluable for diagnosis. They help you to broaden your thinking away from 'obvious' diagnoses, and into the layers of interrelated causes that are a feature of most organisational situations.

If you are trying to explore relationships between parts of an existing problem situation, try using relationship diagrams or systems maps. Both can help you to gain a clearer view of the situation from different perspectives.

The more diagrams you draw, and the more frameworks you can use to provide 'shopping lists' of things to explore, the richer will be your diagnosis. This will minimise the risk of jumping to premature and simplistic conclusions. If you deliberately use as many 'tools' in your diagnosis as possible you force yourself to confront some at least of the complexities in the situation.

→ Ch 9

Use the predictive power of theories, too. For example, if the case involves poor motivation you could draw upon Expectancy Theory (Chapter 9). This suggests that motivation depends upon the perceived links between effort, performance and reward. Using this model would lead you to look at these *links*, paying particular attention to where they may be weak, and at the *values* staff place on the rewards associated with performance. The theory would predict that the problem would lie in weakness in one or more of these areas.

Remember to go back to the case information, and look more carefully at things that become important as your diagnosis proceeds. You will need to produce *evidence* to support your diagnosis. (Evidence-based practice is now seen as important in a wide range of professions, and you will need to think carefully about evidence in any project or dissertation you are required to produce.)

Use the data provided. What *information* can you derive from the data? Are there any apparent trends? Where are they leading? Are there discontinuities in trends? If so, what are they associated with? Are some figures out of line with others, for example are your selling expenses out of line with those of your competitors, or is one product line contributing much more (or less) than others? You may need to do some calculations in order to turn data into information which answers the sorts of questions you are asking. The data will seldom be given in the form you want!

Throughout your diagnosis make a deliberate attempt to sort out evidence from assumptions, and to ask both how sure you are that your assumptions are correct, and how important it is to your diagnosis that they are. If others in the group have different assumptions this is easy. If you are all sharing similar assumptions it is harder to identify and then question them.

Above all, try to avoid thinking about 'solutions' at this stage. As your ideas evolve it is good, even necessary, to move between the third and fourth stages of tackling cases (scanning the case and describing it). But to move on to solutions before you are sure what the problem is risks a 'solution' to something which is not the problem, and which may even exacerbate it.

6. Production of a problem statement

It is very helpful at this stage to produce a written statement of your perception of the key problems. This will act as a reference point during future discussions. It will also form a basis for improved statements of problems if your understanding of the situation deepens during subsequent discussions, and will be useful in preparing your subsequent presentation. It is surprising how often in the heat of discussions you can forget what it is you are trying to achieve, and wander off in some different direction. Even if this is a productive redirection, which has come about because your perceptions have become clearer, it can be confusing if not everyone knows what the redirection is. If it is an inadvertent redirection, the scope for misplaced effort is enormous. A clearly written problem statement can be an excellent way of avoiding this.

In consultancy projects it is even more vital to produce an agreed statement of the problem to be addressed, and of the way in which it is to be approached. Without an agreed project proposal, a consultant may at some point find it difficult to gain necessary access to information, or may be criticised for failing to achieve something that was not part of the agreed brief. An agreed statement can protect against both these problems.

If you have more than one problem, it is helpful to prioritise them. If you have time to tackle only some, it would be sensible to focus on those with highest priority. Useful criteria for selection include:

- **importance** – what will happen if the problem is not addressed?
- **urgency** – how quickly must this problem be solved?
- **hierarchical position** – to what extent is this problem the cause of other problems?
- **solvability** – can you do anything about it anyway?

7. Deciding on criteria for a solution

It may seem out of order to consider how you will choose between solutions before you have thought of any, but there is a serious reason for this. It derives from the power and attractiveness of solutions, and the need to counteract this. Once you have thought of even one solution, there is a danger of becoming wedded to a particular idea, and slanting your criteria for choice in favour of this particular one. This point is discussed further in Chapter 19, in the context of dissertations and theses, where similar considerations apply.

→ Ch 19

It is, therefore, safer to think about criteria for solutions as soon as you are clear about the problem structure. In one sense criteria follow from this. If the deepest problem identified is to do with culture, for example, then solutions must be likely to influence this for the better. But if there are also financial problems, then there will be criteria associated with these as well. Indeed, whatever the problem, financial criteria are likely to be important.

If you list the characteristics of a 'good' solution at this stage, you will have a set of yardsticks against which to measure your options, yardsticks that relate to your identification of organisational needs, not merely to your particular set of options. As well as identifying the positive aspects to be sought from a solution – the ability to reduce costs, or to generate capital, or whatever – it is also worth looking at the constraints that will limit the possible option range. Is there an absolute budget for a project? Are there national union agreements that must be honoured? Are there legal constraints? By identifying these as well, you will have mapped out the field within which solutions *must* lie, as well as the part of the field in which it is most *desirable* that they fall.

8. Generating alternatives

Once you have a clear idea of your objectives, have decided upon the problem areas that you wish to address and are reasonably sure you have analysed their root causes, you will need to think about possible ways forward. What are the options? You will again need to draw heavily on course concepts to suggest better ways of operating. Other useful sources of ideas might be information you have gained from other case studies, from reading the business press or from each other's past experience. This last source is perhaps your richest resource of all, and in your discussions you should always be aware of what other members have to offer, and ensure that their contributions are encouraged where they can be of value. However, it is crucial to link experience to the concepts and theories you are using.

You may also find it helpful to use creativity techniques: the broader the range of options you generate, the better. You will probably be familiar with brainstorming already. This is one of the longest-established techniques habitually used by managers. Although you may already be using it at work, and will almost certainly cover it at some point in your course, a very brief description is included here in case you are not familiar with the approach and need it soon. If you have been taught other creativity techniques, use these too.

Brainstorming

Brainstorming is often used loosely to refer to any attempt at coming up with ideas. However, it was originally designed as a specific method for disabling the censors which habitually operate within our subconscious, suppressing ideas unworthy of attention before they ever surface. The method aims to create a climate within which silliness and unserious behaviour are the norm, thus freeing participants to voice those normally suppressed ideas. Among these may be the germ of a totally new approach which offers a way out of an existing deadlock. Furthermore, one person's silly idea may spark off a new train of thought in another person, which may itself lead somewhere.

Thus, in running brainstorming sessions you try to create a climate of fun, and to free people from their inhibitions. You also aim to capture and display *all* ideas voiced so that they can act as a stimulus to further thought, as well as being available for further consideration after the exercise.

To reduce inhibitions, the group must agree to voice *no* criticism of any idea expressed, and contribute *all* ideas that occur to them, no matter how bizarre. The weirdest ideas may be the most valuable. To get the group into the mood, start the session by spending a few minutes brainstorming a manifestly silly topic, such as what to do with a dead parrot or how to terminate an endless visit from your in-laws.

To ensure that all ideas are captured and displayed, it is normal to work in a room with writing surfaces all round, whether whiteboards or sheets of flipchart paper stuck to the walls. One of the group members writes down all ideas as they are called out, using writing large enough to be easily read by everybody.

The group then agrees on the topic to brainstorm, and starts shouting ideas. The only allowable criticism is that of people voicing criticism! The group continues until it runs out of steam. Only then is any attempt made to evaluate the collected ideas. This is often done by a smaller group, who may group ideas, look for totally impossible ones and see how they might be made possible, or merely look for the best among the bunch. Your group could decide on the best way of handling ideas, given the task in hand.

Other techniques

Some idea-generation techniques try to ensure that all group members make a contribution; sometimes quieter members may not give all their ideas. Nominal Group Technique, for example, involves a rather bureaucratic taking of turns in contributing ideas, and voting on the best. This is not likely to reduce inhibitions, however, so where a totally new solution is sought it is probably not appropriate.

Other approaches make conscious use of analogy and metaphor or forced associations, perhaps to random objects provided by a facilitator, or words selected at random from a dictionary. Thus, you might think of the problem 'as if' it were something else, or consciously look for similarities and differences between your problem and something completely different as a way of stimulating your thoughts out of their habitual channels.

However you choose to become creative, it is important that you do generate a sufficiently broad range of options. You are unlikely to walk out of a chain store with an

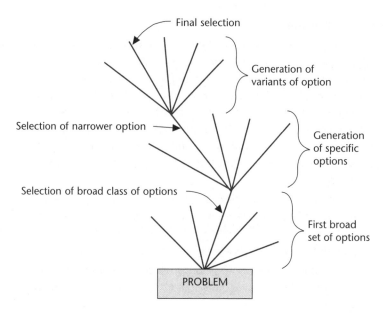

Fig. 12.2 Option selection by successive divergence and choice

exclusive designer suit; your chosen option can never be better than the best among those you generate.

You may need to go through successive cycles of divergence and convergence in generating options. The first pass may generate a huge variety of widely different possibilities. After focusing on one broad class, you can be creative again in deciding on options within that class, narrow down, broaden out at the next level, and so on. This is a common way of approaching product design, but is also applicable to the design of organisational solutions, though with the proviso that the interrelatedness of organisational problems may sometimes mean that the extremes of focusing which this method produces can be insufficiently holistic.

Figure 12.2 shows how the method can be thought of as the generation of part of a tree, along which you travel by way of ever smaller branches and twigs. It is important if you are using this method that you ensure that each set of branches or twigs consists of mutually exclusive options. If not, by choosing one path you may be neglecting whole areas that might be highly relevant.

9. Evaluating options and selecting the most appropriate

If the solution tree approach described above is adopted, you will be exercising choice even while at the generation of options stage. With other methods there should usually be a variety of options generated, as few problems have a single possible solution. The next stage is, therefore, to evaluate the options, in order to see which option, or combination of options, is likely to be most effective.

In evaluating options you will need to consider their likely effect, not only on the focal problem, but on the situation, and indeed the organisation, as a whole. If these

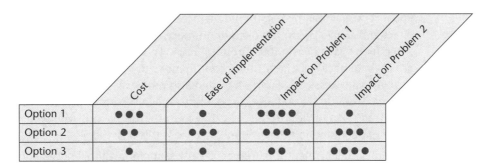

Fig. 12.3 Schematic for a '*Which?*'-type approach to option comparison

relationships are not understood, and the possible implications of each option thoroughly teased out, there is a risk that the cure will be worse than the disease. Since forecasts are always guesses, it is important to have an idea of how likely your forecast outcomes are. And, as before, it is important to know how sensitive your forecasts are to your assumptions.

Once you have teased out the likely effects of your options, you can test these against the criteria you decided upon earlier. If there is a single criterion the process is relatively simple. If there are several criteria which you feel to be important, then you may wish to weight these, giving more emphasis to the most important criteria. If you are using quantitative criteria, then it may be sensible to multiply scores on each criterion by the weighting factor, and derive an overall weighted score. If more qualitative factors are important (and qualitative factors should never be excluded merely because they are harder to deal with in analysis) you will need to find some other way of handling the different aspects of your predicted outcomes. One fairly robust technique is to construct the sort of table found in *Which?* magazine, where goods are rated on a number of criteria, being given dots, rather than a number score. Figure 12.3 gives an example of this technique. This allows an 'at a glance' evaluation to be made of the table. The use of dots rather than numbers avoids giving a spurious impression of accuracy. This tabular approach is just as effective with policy options as it is with washing machines.

10. Designing an implementation strategy

In real consultancy you would be thinking about implementation issues as you worked through your analysis, even if this was not strictly within your remit. In case study analysis within a course, you may not be required to consider this aspect. After all, you will not usually be in a position to implement any of your recommendations. Nevertheless, it is important that recommendations are implementable, and you may well be asked to produce an action plan as part of your assignment. Successful action is much more likely in real life if implementation has been considered from the earliest stages. Whether or not you are strictly required to make recommendations for implementation of your chosen option(s) it is, therefore, worth at least thinking about how they might be implemented.

For successful implementation in general, it is important that those who will be affected feel involved in the decision to make changes, rather than the changes being something wished upon them from on high. This is not just good PR. Those involved are likely to have genuinely useful contributions to make to the decisions, as they will have relevant knowledge and understanding not available elsewhere. In a real project you might set up consultative mechanisms to achieve participation. With a case study you clearly cannot do this, but it is still worth thinking about who would be involved, and what contribution they might make were this possible.

The other vital element is extremely careful planning, with all necessary steps taken into consideration. It is no use planning a highly sophisticated new information system, and forgetting to plan for the considerable staff development needed to make it work. This would have to involve not only those inputting data, but also those intended to benefit from the outputs, and is absolutely essential if the system is to be of any real value. Such planning *can* be done in the context of a case study, and if you are required to do it, should be given due emphasis. It is all too easy to see the decision itself as the important thing, and not to plan time to allow for thought as to how this decision can be made effective. Critical path analysis may well be helpful, but the real work will lie in thinking about the decision in relation to the organisation. What are its different implications for all those involved? This will enable you to identify the steps that will be needed to ensure that positive effects are fully achieved, and as many of the negative ones avoided as possible.

11. Presenting your findings

In presenting your findings you will want to convince your audience that you have thoroughly understood the problem, that you have obtained all the necessary information to reach a decision, that you have analysed this information in a sensible fashion, and that the conclusions you have reached are to be trusted. These conclusions should be presented clearly, so that your audience is convinced that your recommendations should be followed.

→ Ch 16   For class-based discussions, it is likely that you will need to make an oral presentation. Chapter 16 deals with the basics of making an effective presentation to a group. You should work your way through this before making (or critiquing) your first case study presentation, unless you know you are already an expert in this field.

→ Ch 15, 17   In real-life consultancy, you may often be called upon to make a presentation, but you will *always* need to make a written report on your findings. If you are analysing the case for assessment, then, too, you will need to produce a written version of your findings. Chapter 15 deals with written reports, and Chapter 17 touches on case study-based answers in examinations. You should refer to these as appropriate.

Guidelines for case study analysis

- Clarify task requirements.
- Skim-read.
- Read more slowly, highlighting issues.
- Explore the case and its context, identifying themes.
- Formulate problem statements.
- Identify solution criteria and constraints.
- Identify tasks and allocate to individuals or sub-groups.
- Analyse, using course concepts to help find root problems.
- Work out recommendations.
- Craft analysis and recommendations into a clear presentation.

EXERCISE 12.1

Work through the 'What Should Chris do?' case on the **website**. Note, answers are posted on the **website** rather than at the end of the chapter.

FROM CASES TO CONSULTANCY

As already indicated, analysing a case requires many of the same skills as consultancy. You can practise these skills by acting as an internal consultant on small projects. Analyse aspects of your own organisation as if it were a case, seeking to use a range of concepts and techniques to cast light on situations and suggest how they might be improved. Distance learning students may find that they are often set assignments requiring them to carry out such internal analyses.

Once you have become confident with analysing complexity in cases and at work, you may wish to go on to practise acting as an external consultant. Many face-to-face Master's programmes include a consultancy project to ensure that students leave with at least a little practice in this area. You will need, however, to go on and develop a wider range of skills if you are to become fully effective. The complexities of an unfamiliar real situation will be far greater than those represented in a case. And you will need to seek out most of the information you need, rather than being provided with it. There will, too, be the dimension of liaising with your client, and ensuring that you understand his/her objectives for the project, and that you retain your client's trust throughout. (This aspect is a feature of many projects so is discussed further in Chapter 19.) You will need a high level of interpersonal skills to maintain a good relationship with the client organisation. And if you plan to live by consultancy, you will need marketing and other skills.

→ Ch 19

SUMMARY

- Case studies are a vehicle for practising the application of skills, knowledge and techniques learned in courses to quasi-real situations.
- They can also increase awareness of the business context in which students are likely to eventually operate.
- Group interaction, time-management and presentation skills can be developed at the same time as conceptual/analytical skills.
- Difficulties are encountered because typically students are given more responsibility for managing their own learning than they are used to.
- Further difficulties arise because tasks may be somewhat unclear, and because case studies frequently contain an overabundance of information. Group dynamics may also hinder progress.
- It is essential to devote sufficient attention to diagnosing the real causes of a situation: this is despite a tendency to leap to solutions rather than explore the complexity of the problem.
- The complexities within a case can be usefully approached by the use of relevant course concepts, together with an overall structure based upon a national approach to problem solving: explore situation; define problems; decide criteria; generate options; evaluate options; present recommendations.
- Case study analysis is useful preparation for consultancy work, but it is important to remember that real life is more complex than cases, and seldom allows of clear 'solutions'. Consultants need, too, to employ a far wider range of skills.

Further information

- Easton, G. (1992) *Learning from Case Studies* (2nd edn), Prentice Hall.
  This gives much more detailed guidance on case study analysis than is possible here.
- Kneeland, S. (1999) *Thinking Straight*, Pathways.
- Pidd, M. (2003) *Tools for Thinking: Modeling in Management Science* (2nd edn), Wiley.

→ 13 Using numbers

INTRODUCTION

Much of the information managers use is presented as numbers. If you can 'read' these numbers, if you can understand what they mean, and do not mean, you will be at an enormous informational advantage over colleagues who cannot. You will be asking relevant questions, pinpointing fatal flaws and spotting trends or imminent threats that no one else sees. They, meanwhile, will be jumping to misguided conclusions, or accepting fallacious reports because they look 'scientific'. If you can go further, and take raw data and turn it into useful information which you then communicate to colleagues you will have a powerful weapon at your disposal. Being comfortable with numbers, being able to extract meaning from them, and being able to communicate that meaning are essential managerial skills.

Most management-related Master's programmes aim to develop your ability to turn numbers into information; many assume a basic level of numerical competence from the outset. This chapter is intended for those of you who fear that you do not have this basic level. It aims to set mathematics in context, and to show that playing with numbers can be easy, even fun, rather than tedious or difficult. It shows you how you can extract meaning from numbers, and communicate this, whether graphically or otherwise. It shows you how statistical techniques can help you assess how significant the messages are. And it covers basic mathematical skills so that you can use equations to answer questions.

If you are already confident of your mathematical ability and comfortable with basic statistics you do not need this chapter (though you might like to check your assessment of this by working through Exercise 13.1 below). Use your time on other topics with which you are less happy. If you were once able to do maths, but have forgotten how, a quick scan of the chapter will refresh your memory and remove any anxiety.

If you are seriously worried, use this chapter to develop your skills and help to build your confidence. I have tried to mix 'easy' material with the more difficult. If things start to get difficult, continue. Things will shortly get easier again. You will find some very basic 'remedial' maths in the Helpfile at the end of the chapter: it may be helpful to work through this early on.

Most people find pages of numbers remarkably hard to 'read'. Yet graphs or other pictorial representations of numbers make it easy to see 'patterns'. Even if some of the 'harder' maths in the chapter is more than you want to engage with, you should still work on the parts which help you turn numbers into diagrams. You will find this invaluable if you are trying to make a point in a presentation, a report or a meeting. The picture will communicate the 'message' that the numbers contain. You also need to be able to avoid being misled by pictures cunningly constructed to make a point that they do not really support. If you understand how to represent numbers pictorially, using techniques such as bar charts or the sort of graph you drew in maths at school, you will be well on the way making some sense of numbers, and communicating this sense. If you are very worried about your number skills you might like to scan the chapter fairly quickly, selecting only those parts that seem easy to study in detail. At a second pass you may find some of the rest is easier too.

DIAGNOSING YOUR CURRENT SKILL LEVEL

The first thing that you need to feel comfortable with is the set of symbols that constitute the 'code' of mathematics. Whatever your confidence level, try Exercise 13.1 to check your memory of the basics. It is important to work through the whole exercise, doing as much as you can, *and writing down your own answers* before you look at the answers at the end of the chapter. If you find it difficult or impossible, don't worry. Turn to the end of the chapter, pour yourself a drink and/or do some deep breathing, and work your way through the Helpfile, 'Cracking the code'. You should find that it is really quite simple, and that by the time you have worked through the chapter you can return to the exercise and complete it with relative ease. If you feel in need of more practice, further exercises can be found in sources such as Morris (2000), suggested at the end of the chapter, and on the **website**.

EXERCISE 13.1

(a) Write the following as decimals:

  ¾   ⅖   1⅓   1⅗   ⁵⁄₁₁   ⅝

___ ___ ___ ___ ___ ___

→

(b) Write the following as percentages:

2 $\frac{3}{4}$ $1\frac{1}{3}$ $\frac{19}{11}$ $\frac{1}{4}$ $\frac{2}{3}$

___   ___   ___   ___   ___   ___

(c) What is the value of:

2^3 14^2 3^4 $3^2 \times 3^2$ 12^3 1^4 6^0

___   ___   ___   ___   ___   ___   ___

13

Using numbers

(d) Write as a power of a single number:

$2^2 \times 2^5$ $3^4 \div 3^2$ $10^3 \times 10^5 \div 10^8$ $17^5 \times 17^3$ $21^{21} \div 21^3$ $x^3 \times x^2$ $x^y \div x^2$ $z^{2x} \times z^{2y}$

___   ___   ___   ___   ___   ___   ___   ___

(e) Use your calculator to work out the following writing your answers using only two places of decimals:

$\sqrt{16}$ $\sqrt{144}$ $\sqrt{36}$ $\sqrt{38}$ $\sqrt{2}$ $\sqrt{10}$

___   ___   ___   ___   ___   ___

(f) Write as a power of a number (or letter):

$\sqrt{2^{16}}$ $\sqrt[4]{10^4}$ $\sqrt[3]{3^2}$ $\sqrt{(x^2y^2)}$ $\sqrt[7]{z^{14}}$

___   ___   ___   ___   ___

(g) If $x_1\ x_2\ x_3,\ \ldots\ x_r$ represent the numbers 1, 2, 3, ... r, what is the value of $\sum_{r=1}^{3} x_r$?

_____

(h) Represent the following information graphically (use a separate piece of paper, if not drawing from a spreadsheet):

Sales volume:	0	1000	2000	3000	4000
Production cost ($):	5000	10 000	15 000	20 000	25 000
Sales revenue ($):	0	7500	15 000	22 500	30 000

(i) Which of the following are true?

(i) $7 \neq 7$ (ii) $3 \geqslant 1$ (iii) $5 > -5$ (iv) $3 < -5$ (v) $x^2 > x$ when $x = 1$

___   ___   ___   ___   ___

(j) Write the following without the bracket:

$2(x + y)$ $3(x - y^2)$ $-3(x - y)$ $(x - y) - (x - y)$ $(x - y) - (x - 2y)$

___   ___   ___   _____   _____

(k) which of the following is true?

   (i)   A result with p > 0.05 is more significant than one where p < 0 .05.
   (ii) Statistical tests can tell you if your predictions are correct.

(l) Work out:

$5 + 2 \times 4$ $3 \times 6 - 5 + 4$ $x + x \times x \div y$ $1.2 \times 3.4 - 1.2 \div 6.1$

_____   _____   _____   _____

Additional exercises are given on the companion website **www.booksites.net/cameron**

CAUSES OF DIFFICULTY

Often, worries about mathematics are unfounded. Perhaps this exercise was easier than anticipated; if so you may wish to reconsider whether you need to study this chapter at all. But if you found most of the above questions difficult, it is worth thinking about *why*.

A few people suffer from the number equivalent of dyslexia. Far more are the victims of poor teaching. Children are really good at working out 'fair shares' or how long it will take to save up for something. Yet somewhere along their educational road, this becomes 'mathematics', and 'difficult', or even emotionally threatening. If you have an emotional reaction to numbers, and feel panic setting in at the sight of an equation, you will need to address it. It is a very real reaction, and one which will interfere with your learning. Try taking deep breaths, consciously relaxing, or even a modest intake of alcohol before working with the difficult bits. Do as much practice of simple 'sums' as you can, and only move on to harder things when you feel confident. Success will reduce the fear. And keep reminding yourself of how your work as a manager would be improved by feeling more comfortable with numbers and basic mathematics.

ACTIVITY 13.1

Think about the numbers that have passed across your desk/screen during the last week. Give yourself a score out of 10 for the extent to which you felt confident that you could understand, interpret and use these numbers. ☐

List uses you might have made of them if you had been happier in dealing with them.

_____

_____

I have been faced recently with current and past student registration figures, the results of a market research survey, financial models showing likely income from a new programme at different fee levels and different student numbers, budget figures for the last (and previous) financial year, and assorted statistics at the end of research papers. I wanted answers to questions such as, 'Is it worth our while, financially, to develop the new programme?', 'Are we currently operating as effectively as in recent years?', ' Do these results support the author's theory?' Your own list is likely to be somewhat different. But you may have referred to similar needs to calculate the value of something you wish to know, to work out whether variations in your findings are likely to be meaningful, or referred to the need to answer 'what if?' questions.

ACTIVITY 13.2

Think about your experience with maths at school. How do you think your teacher rated your ability?

_____

_____

Highlight any of the following which you felt confident about doing when at school:

simple arithmetic; simple algebra; plotting graphs; working out averages; working with fractions; differential equations, basic statistics and probability tests.

Underline any which you think you have forgotten by now, and double-underline any you never knew.

The above two activities, together with Exercise 13.1, should have helped you get a feel for the size of the task facing you in coming to terms with the maths you will need to use to benefit from your course. Use the information to work out how much time you will need to devote to this topic, amending your study plan if necessary.

ACTIVITY 13.3

Aim to become more aware of the potential uses of numbers, and of mathematics, at work. Construct a section in your learning log in which you note all the 'numbers', statistics and equations (which may be built into spreadsheets) which pass across your desk and/or are available to you (perhaps on an intranet) when making decisions. Include any numbers for which you do not at present see a use and explore the uses to which they are put by others. This will help you make sense of your coursework, and alert you to techniques which are in common use in your own organisation, and information sources you could learn to use better.

Assess your own abilities in making effective use of the information, and develop an action plan for developing any necessary skills.

I hope that the activities in the chapter thus far have convinced you, if you needed convincing, that it _is_ worth trying to become more competent at using some basic mathematical techniques. These will enable you to make better use of numerical information at work, as well as to gain good marks on your course.

DESCRIPTIVE EQUATIONS

Some of your difficulties may come because of the way equations are sometimes introduced for purely descriptive purposes. Mathematical expressions used in this purely descriptive way are not intended to provide 'solutions', or answers to specific questions, but rather to clarify (if you are lucky), or spuriously impress (if you are not). After a complex description, an equation will appear. Sometimes the equation may be even more complex than the description, involving lots of mathematical symbols and lots of different letters, the meanings of which have to be explained in a lengthy key. Unless the equation is the first step in constructing a model, or does indeed clarify the argument, you can probably ignore this kind of equation. If the author's intention was merely to make an argument look more convincing and scientific by using equations, then the equation deserves no further attention.

So if you find an equation you don't understand, rather than putting down the paper with a feeling of failure, ignore the equations, and see what you can derive from the text alone. You will be in good company in this approach. Roger Penrose, a mathematics professor at the University of Oxford, suggested if you encounter a formula:

> a procedure that I normally adopt myself when such an offending line presents itself. The procedure is, more or less, to ignore that line completely and to skip to the next actual line of text! Well, not exactly this; one should spare the poor formula a perusing, rather than a comprehending glance, and then press onwards.

(Note at the start of *The Emperor's New Mind*, Oxford University Press, 1989.)

Lucy Kellaway (2000) expresses her view of such things in another formula, which you may enjoy!

$F + M = P * R$ *where* F = *formula*, M = *management*, P = *pretentious and* R = *rubbish!*

It does make the point that there are a lot of spurious equations around in the literature. (Though of course there are some extremely useful ones too.)

MODELLING

While I have much sympathy with Kellaway's view, once you go beyond purely descriptive uses, equations can, properly used, provide an invaluable *modelling* tool.

A model is something which has enough key aspects of the real thing to allow you to answer questions about it, but more easily or economically than by experimenting with the thing itself. Thus an architect might construct small simplified models of alternative designs (easily done on a computer) which allow a client to gain an impression of each in order to make a choice.

Similarly, a manager might 'model' a situation by using equations representing relationships between key variables. Such a model might allow you to work out the expected return on different mixes of products, at different prices, different fixed and variable costs and/or with different levels of sales, or the impact on profitability of different levels of absenteeism, or perhaps the expected returns on different investments given prevailing interest rates (or with a range of possible interest rate changes over the period for which money will need to be borrowed). The equation will not tell you what sales figures will be, nor what will happen to interest rates, but it will tell you the likely *results* of different values of these, always assuming that you have chosen an appropriate equation to model the relationships between the factors in question.

If you want to work out the cost of compound interest on a loan of €266 000, borrowed at an annual interest rate of 8% over five years, you will need only slightly more complex techniques, which will be introduced later. If you want to work out the optimum product mix under varying conditions of labour demand, materials costs, profit margin, etc. you will need more complex techniques still. Mathematics can provide whatever degree of complexity you are likely to want, though for complex uses it may not be cost-effective to learn the techniques yourself. If a problem requires PhD-level expertise in Linear Programming, it is probably better to hire an expert, rather than try to master the higher reaches of the subject yourself. It *will*, however, help considerably if you know enough to have a broad understanding of what he/she is doing.

UNDERSTANDING PROBABILITY AND STATISTICS

Before going further, there is one idea that you need to understand, because I shall start to draw upon it before we get much further. This is the idea of *probability*, that is, of the likelihood of something happening. (If you gamble, you probably have a fairly clear idea of this anyway.) If something is certain to happen, it is said to have a probability of 1. If it is impossible, of 0. Thus if I have a bag of white balls, and I put my hand in and pull one out, there is a probability of 1 (p = 1) that it will be white, and of 0 that it will be black. If the bag (and we assume that it is an opaque bag, I am choosing by feel alone, and all the balls feel the same) contains two balls, one black, one white, the probability of choosing the white one is 0.5. The probability of choosing the black one is the same. If there are four balls, three white, you can probably guess the probability of each – for white p = 0.75, for black, p = 0.25. Lots of the numbers you deal with in management *could* have been influenced by chance. And this is where statistics comes in.

'Statistics' means both '*sets of data*' and also '*the branch of mathematics concerned with making inferences from such data*'. When Disraeli referred to 'lies, damned lies and statistics' he was presumably referring to the invalid inferences that may be drawn, and indeed are still frequently drawn, from sets of numbers. Statistics in the second sense deals in *probabilities*.

Imagine, for example, that two selection methods are compared. Of the 200 candidates selected by one method, 150 are rated as excellent by their bosses five years later, 10 are satisfactory, and the rest have left. Of 100 selected by another method, 50 are rated as excellent, 25 as satisfactory, two as unsatisfactory, and the rest have left. We have no reason to believe that the two groups were treated any differently once they joined the organisation, nor that the pool of applicants was any different in either case.

Most people would be fairly ready to believe, from the above figures, that the first selection method was better. But it is not something about which we can be *certain*. Odd things can sometimes happen purely by chance.

Suppose you spend a day tossing coins, and carefully noting in a small notebook the result of each throw. By evening you will have many sheets of paper covered with rows of things like HHTHTTHTTT... There will have been some stretches when you had a run of heads, and other stretches when you got mostly tails. Of course most of the time they will be fairly mixed, but if you picked two sheets at random you might, purely by chance, get one with far more heads than tails, and another where the reverse was true. Someone not knowing your method of generating the results might be convinced that the two pages referred to quite different situations.

Selection of potential employees is not an exact science. We can expect a degree of random variation to enter into it, even if it is not as random as tossing a coin. Has this random variation accounted for the difference in the results of the two selection methods?

It is hard to answer that question, because we are very bad at assessing probabilities unaided. How likely do you think it is, for example, that in a class of 32 schoolchildren at least two will share a birthday? How likely is it that if you toss a coin just six times you will get either six heads or six tails?

In fact, the chances of shared birthdays are about three to one, i.e. it is three times as likely that there is a shared birthday as that there is not. And although if you got HHHHHH many people would accuse you of using a weighted coin, the chance is as high as 1 in 32. So if your class all tossed six pennies, you would not be at all surprised if one of them *did* get six alike.

If straightforward things like this are hard to assess, it is clear we need techniques for assessing the probabilities of more complicated results, so that we know how much significance to attach to them. How likely is it is that the differences between the two selection methods described above were caused purely by chance? A vast battery of statistical techniques exists, and you will almost certainly be introduced to some of them during your course. Later in the chapter some of the simpler ideas of distribution, probability and correlation are introduced.

It is worth noting, however, the one lesson that has stayed with me since studying statistics as an undergraduate. Even if you know something about statistics, check any research plans with a competent statistician who can advise you on the size of sample you need, and on the sorts of statistical tests you should use to decide whether your results are significant. (This will be particularly important when planning data collection for your dissertation. Many students ignore this advice, and their results are worth very little in consequence, despite their hard work.)

Much organisational research pays scant regard to statistical considerations, and therefore produces results of dubious validity. But these results are often treated as sound, thus possibly leading the organisation to take unwise decisions. Probability and statistics can never tell you what *will* happen. But they can tell you how likely various outcomes are under different assumptions about the environment. Before getting on to this, however, there are simpler ways of making sets of numbers 'speak'.

MAKING DATA MORE MEANINGFUL

Much of the data with which you will be faced, whether at work or generated by your research for a dissertation, will be in the form of strings or tables of numbers. Most of us find it difficult to make any sort of sense of a large set of numbers. This is why you often need bar charts, graphs and other ways of presenting sets of data so that aspects of those figures can be seen at a glance – these will be covered soon.

13

Using numbers

Measures of the centre

First, let us look at ways of summarising a set of numbers without graphical aid.

You can describe a set of numbers using:
■ mean – the average – the sum of values divided by the number of values
■ median – the middle value if values are ranked according to size
■ mode – the value which occurs most often.

Suppose as chair of an Exam Board I noted that the two markers used had given the following scores:

Marker 1: 20, 70, 80, 83, 50, 55, 75, 60, 61, 30, 95, 55, 54, 51, 40, 57, 69, 70, 75, 81.
Marker 2: 40, 43, 47, 60, 49, 55, 51, 60, 63, 49, 42, 70, 75, 50, 46, 41, 49, 67, 60, 42.

It is very difficult to make sense of these figures when they appear like this. Harder still if you have 10 markers, each marking 150 scripts, as is often the case with the course I chair. In order to start to draw conclusions, you need to organise the figures in some way. The simplest is to provide a summary of the scores, by giving the *average*, or *mean* score. To do this, you add the marks awarded by each marker, and then divide by the number of scripts marked.

EXERCISE 13.2

Find the mean score for each marker above using a calculator:

Marker 1 _____   Marker 2 _____

Sometimes, if the distribution is a bit odd, a mean score can be misleading, and you will find some other measure of the 'middle' of the group useful. One of the two most commonly used is the *median*, which gives you the size of the middle value if you order all the measurements by size and then take the value of the measurement which is in the middle of the list. Thus the median value of 1, 1, 4, 5, 7, 10, 10, 10, 11 is 7. There are 4 values bigger than this, and 4 smaller. The other measure is the *mode*, or the value which occurs most often. The mode for the list above is 10.

EXERCISE 13.3

Find the mean, median and mode for each of the following sets of values:

(a) 5, 5, 3, 2, 6, 7, 9, 11, 1   mean _____   median _____   mode _____

(b) 1, 3, 1, 10, 13, 2, 7, 8, 4   mean _____   median _____   mode _____

To get a better 'feel' for the effect of different sorts of distributions on these measures of central tendency, experiment with writing lists where mean, median and mode all have different values. Try to construct at least one list where the differences are substantial (no answer is given for this part).

Range

The mean (or median or mode) may be all you need to know, but you can see that you lose a lot of information by merely giving the average. One group has a much wider spread of scores than the other, and the average gives no indication of this. One simple way of adding this information is to supplement the mean with information about the *range*, the spread from the highest value to the lowest. In the earlier example, the range for Marker 1 would be 20–95, for Marker 2, 40–75. You can see that Marker 2's scores are more bunched together.

Interquartile range

The range can be misleading if you have a maverick outlying score. Suppose you were looking at absenteeism in two departments. Most sick absences might be for two or three days. But one department might have someone who was terminally ill, and had been absent for months. This would make both the mean and the range in that department far higher than the figure for the other department. For this reason a measure called the *interquartile range* is sometimes used. You remember that in order to work out the median you ordered the data and counted up until you reached the middle value. Quartiles are worked out similarly, but having ordered the data you count up to the quarter point and the three-quarter point. The interquartile range is the distance between these two points, that is, the range within which the middle half of your observations lie.

EXERCISE 13.4

Work out the interquartile range for Markers 1 and 2 above.

By extension, if you have large sets of data it can be helpful to identify deciles or even percentiles. The bottom 5th percentile would represent the 5% of the population with the smallest values – for example ergonomists typically ignore the top and bottom 5th percentile. Thus if (like me) you are shorter than 95% of the population you may find work surfaces too high in kitchens, or have difficulty reaching the control pedals in a car.

DISTRIBUTIONS AND HISTOGRAMS

Mean and range together tell you something about the data, but there may be other important features not conveyed. Suppose Marker 1 gave one student 20, one 80 and all the rest 50, whereas Marker 2 gave half the students 20 and all the rest 80. In this case, mean and range would be the same for both groups, yet if you described the markers only in terms of means or ranges you would be failing to communicate the fact that the scores were actually very different. For a start, Marker 2 is failing half the scripts, whereas all save one of the scripts seen by Marker 1 are gaining a pass. In many cases it is helpful to see how scores (or values) are distributed within different groups. You can get an idea of this at a glance from the numbers given in the example above, as I have deliberately exaggerated the distribution. But suppose the differences, though real, were less extreme, and that each marker had dealt with 500 scripts. You would not be able to see the *distribution* of the scores at a glance, and would need the figures to be summarised in a way which showed the pattern more clearly.

A primitive and simple technique, the tally, can be very useful. To produce a tally, you divide your measures into a number of categories. Here five categories might be chosen: say 0–20, 21–40, 41–60, 61–80, and 81–100. If you had a larger number of scripts you could afford to use smaller bands. Then for each score you put a tally mark in the appropriate band, as below. (Adding the fifth mark as a diagonal slash across means the groups of five stand out more clearly, and makes adding up afterwards much easier.)

Marker 1

81–100	///
61–80	⤤ //
41–60	⤤ //
21–40	///
0–20	/

EXERCISE 13.5

Complete the tally for the actual marks given earlier by Marker 2 – ignore the hypothetical and bizarre distribution described subsequently (no answer given):

Marker 2

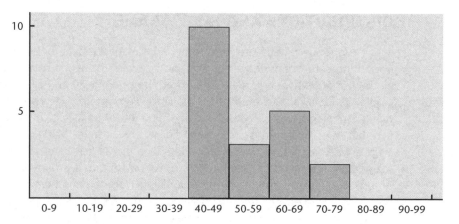

Fig. 13.1 Histogram for Marker 2 scores

Often, instead of tally marks, a bar of an appropriate length is drawn. These bar charts, which show how often different values occur, are called *histograms.* As the categories on a histogram should cover all possibilities, with one category starting as the other finishes, the bars are usually drawn as adjacent. They can be drawn horizontally or vertically. Figure 13.1 shows a vertical histogram for Marker 2's scores.

These diagrams are an extraordinarily useful way of summarising data. They are easy to draw, whether by hand or by computer, and give a clear picture of how results are distributed. The only thing you need to beware of is the occasional practice of using categories of different size. In the tally example given, each band was 20 marks. But if you wanted, for example, to amalgamate 0–20 and 21–40, to give a band twice as wide, you would need to adjust the height so that the *area* of the bar still corresponded to the number of instances. When 'reading' bar charts, remember this – looking at the height if categories are not of equal width is potentially misleading.

Normal distributions

One distribution is of particular interest. This is called the 'normal distribution' or, because of its shape, a bell curve. Figure 13.2 shows some examples of normal curves with different central points and different spreads. The normal curve is a theoretical one, but, for many different variables, if you were to take a large sample and plot them in infinitely narrow bars, you would come up with a curve like this. Imagine that you measured the IQ scores of 20 000 people, and drew a histogram with bars only one mark wide. You would get something very close indeed to a normal curve. Many variables are distributed 'normally'. The height of adult men (or women) would show a similar pattern, or even the weight of loaves of machine-produced bread. Perhaps more importantly, as many statistical tests depend upon this, the arithmetic means of large samples from a single population are normally distributed.

You can see that the normal distributions shown vary in their means and their ranges, but are all symmetrical. This means that for any normal distribution the mean, median

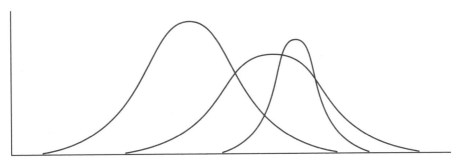

Fig. 13.2 Examples of normal distributions

and mode will be the same. If you know the mean of the distribution you know a lot about it. If you also know its 'spread', you know all there is to know. This 'spread' is described by something called a *standard deviation.*

Standard deviation

If you have done any statistics at all, you will have heard of standard deviations. They are widely used in a variety of situations as an indication of how figures are distributed. A median, or the interquartile range, will tell you where a certain proportion of your values lie – that was how you worked them out! If you have a normal curve, the standard distribution will also tell you how much of the distribution lies within a certain part of the curve. (For a normal distribution, 68% of values will lie within one standard deviation of the mean, and 95% within two standard deviations.)

Figure 13.3 shows this graphically.

It is not particularly difficult to work out a standard deviation. The box on page 250 shows the necessary stages.

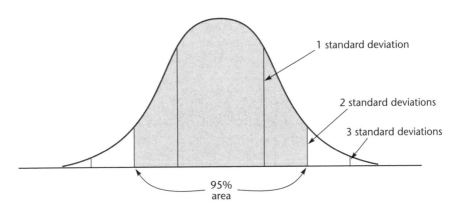

Fig. 13.3 Standard deviations and the normal curve

To calculate a standard deviation

- find the average or mean value of your observations ($\bar{x}$)
- work out the difference between each value and this mean
- square all of these differences (this means that the values are all positive)
- add all these squares together
- find the mean value of the square (called 'variance') by dividing the sum of squares by n where n is the number of observations
- take the square root of this average – this is the standard deviation.

Using an equation to express this (and it shows that even a slightly nasty looking equation *can* be useful – it is easier to remember than the set of instructions above):

$$\text{Standard deviation} = \sqrt{\frac{\Sigma(x - \bar{x})^2}{n}}$$

Or by working out the bracket and cancelling the 'n's that result:

$$= \sqrt{\frac{\Sigma x^2}{n} - \bar{x}^2}$$

The second way of writing this is much easier to work out when you want to insert your values of x and n.

This gives you the standard deviation of a whole population. But usually you will have measured only a smallish sample of that population, and this formula will give you a smaller value on such a sample than you would have obtained if using the whole population. If you have a small sample, a better estimate of the standard deviation of the 'parent' population is obtained by dividing by ($n - 1$) rather than n. For a large sample the difference will be insignificant – dividing by 89 rather than 90 will make little difference. For a sample of 9, dividing by 8 rather than 9, say, will make a noticeable difference.

Note that while each of the above ways of representing data (means, medians, range, standard deviation and so on) tells you *something* about how sets of data compare, you need to be very careful about drawing conclusions about the *significance* of differences between the sets, and even more careful about the reasons for these differences. And this is where you start to need statistical techniques.

Statistical significance

In Exercise 13.2 you found that Marker 1 awarded a higher average score but that this could be the result of a variety of things. It might be merely random variation. On the next set of scripts there might be no difference, or the difference might be in the opposite direction, even if all other things were equal. Statistical tests call tell me the probability of the difference being due to chance alone. Some of the figures that pass across my desk are printouts telling me means and standard deviations of different markers, whether they are marking low or high, and whether this difference is significant.

Beware, though. Even if tests strongly suggest that there *is* a significant difference, they will not tell me whether it is the marker or the students marked that are different. While it is indeed possible that Marker 1 was more generous than Marker 2, this is not necessarily the case. The probability generated by statistical tests may tell me that it is highly unlikely that such a difference arose by chance. But it won't tell me what the non-chance factor was. At my own exam boards I need to know whether there are obvious reasons for differences between markers' scores before drawing such a conclusion. Perhaps one marker has marked a high proportion of scripts from overseas exam centres where many of the students may have English as a third or fourth language, and do less well in exams because of this.

Even if I am fairly sure that there are no obvious reasons for expecting a difference in the students, and the statistics suggest a real difference, they do not *prove* Marker 1 was applying different standards. Normally if a result is such as would arise only one time in 20 the result is described as 'significant' ($p < 0.05$). If it were to be expected only once in a hundred times the difference would be deemed 'highly significant' ($p < 0.01$). But note that, even if the difference is highly significant, the statistics have not 'proved' anything. They make it a reasonable assumption, and I would normally adjust the 'severe' marker's score accordingly. But I need to remember that, one time in a hundred, my reasonable assumption can be expected to be wrong!

Some of the significance of the standard deviation now becomes clear. You can see that the points indicated by the 2nd and 3rd standard deviation distances in Fig. 13.3 relate directly to significance. For a normal distribution, points lying more than 2 standard deviations from the mean are 'significantly different' and those more than 3 standard deviations away are highly significantly so. (This is assuming you are testing for any difference. Results would be twice as significant if there were only one direction in which a difference, if it existed, could be expected.)

BAR CHARTS

In case your nerves are slightly frayed by now, let us take a step away from continuous curves, and back to bars. A histogram is a special form of a bar chart. Bar charts have many uses beyond depicting frequency, and because of this are one of the standard diagram forms easily produced from a spreadsheet. If you have a number of sets of data on different features of something, bars are helpful. You might have annual rainfall and average temperature for major cities around the world, or various production figures for a number of different plants. You cannot draw graphs of rainfall or production because there is no particular way of ordering the different sets of data. Lima could come before London because it was earlier in the alphabet, or with other South American cities, before or after Europe, or wherever you choose to put it. The bars or sets of bars are therefore drawn as separate from each other, although if there are several bars for each town, plant or whatever, these bars will often be drawn as touching each other, as then they are more clearly distinct from the other sets of information. The goal is clarity. It would be misleading to imply continuity of data in the same way that it exists on a histogram. Several different types of information can

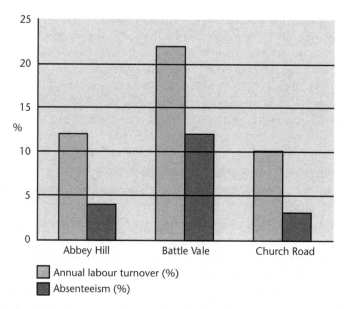

Fig. 13.4 Bar chart showing absenteeism and labour turnover rates at three sites

be clearly shown on the same bar chart by using different colours or different forms of cross-hatching to distinguish between the bars, and a key to show what these represent. Figure 13.4 shows an example of a bar chart.

EXERCISE 13.6

Represent the following information on a bar chart:

Business school	% entrants with degrees	% women
Aston	62	13
Bradford	88	19
City	88	30
Cranfield	82	11
Durham	71	32
LBS	97	22

(The above figures are for 1983, and taken from Hussey (1988). Sadly the percentage of women does not seem to have risen as much as one might hope, given that research suggests that an MBA has a bigger impact upon a woman's future salary than upon a man's.)

Note: Because of the difference in range of the two sets of figures you may find it helpful to use two scales, one covering the full range for the percentage with degrees, one covering a much smaller range, therefore allowing a wider spread within that range for the percentage of women. Experiment to see what gives you the clearest picture.

It can be a tremendous advantage to use different scales to increase clarity. For example, if all the values you are plotting lie between 90 and 95, differences will be barely perceptible on a 1–100 scale. But if you use the same distance to represent from 90 to 95, the variations will be much more apparent. Be careful though. Once you stop using 0 as the bottom of your scale a bar that is twice as high as another no longer means that the value is twice as much.

Sometimes it is necessary to use each interval on the scale to represent an increase in size gained not by adding, but by multiplying. This is known as a *logarithmic* or *exponential* scale. It allows you to represent a much wider range of values on a single scale than would be possible with an interval scale, yet still to see how things at the small end relate to each other. You will see an example of such a scale when you come to the next diagram.

You will see that great care is needed in interpreting bar charts, as the use of different scales can be misleading if the differences and their implications are not clearly understood. Using different scales may make your diagrams much clearer, but if the reader is careless in reading them, you may not communicate. If you are using other than a normal interval scale starting at zero, you may wish to point this out in your text to be doubly safe. Sometimes scales seem to have been chosen almost with the intention of misleading. Look at the chart in Fig. 13.5, which is similar to one that appeared in a reputable scientific periodical. What, at first glance, is most likely to kill you?

It is only when you stop to think that surely lightning *can't* be so much more dangerous than smoking that you realise that the scale is dealing in risks, expressed in such a way that unlikely things get a taller bar than likely things. Think: a 1 in 10 chance is much *bigger* than a 1 in 100 chance, yet it comes lower on the scale.

Sometimes bars are used to show proportions. In this case the height of each bar will be 100, with a part of each bar devoted to the different quantities that go to make up that whole. Again you will need to differentiate the parts with colour or shading. For

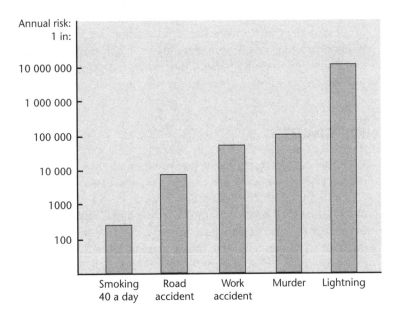

Fig. 13.5 Risk of some causes of death

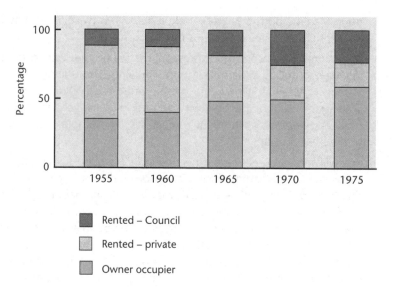

Fig. 13.6 Types of dwelling in a village

example, a survey of a small village over a number of years might show the proportion of owner occupation rising. This could be represented as in Fig. 13.6.

You cannot tell from the chart how *many* of any type of dwelling existed in any year, as you could from the type of bar chart described before. In fact the village was growing quite significantly over the period in question, but there is no way of telling this from Fig. 13.6. All that you can say is how the total in any one year was divided between the three categories. You need to be very careful not to draw conclusions about whether actual *numbers* in any category are increasing or decreasing. Although the proportion of privately rented accommodation decreases, the overall growth in housing provision might well mean that the actual numbers of privately rented dwellings are increasing, albeit more slowly than the overall rate of increase. Again you need to be careful when reading the diagram.

PIE CHARTS

The other type of representation commonly used to show proportions of a total in different categories is the *pie chart*. Again, the ease of generating such diagrams on a PC has led to a proliferation in their use, often in a multiplicity of colours, sometimes in mock 3D. Such charts have obvious attractions. They *look* good, and are prettier than simple bar charts. They are easy to understand, even by those who are uneasy about fractions. While some people might struggle to explain how proportions of ⅙, ⅓ and ½ relate to each other, it is immediately obvious with a pie chart, as Fig. 13.7 shows.

However, pie charts become less useful when there are many 'slices'. We are not very good at judging fine differences between angles by eye, and it can be quite hard to tell whether some of the 'slices' are bigger than others. The picture can be further

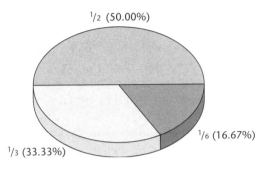

Fig. 13.7 A very simple pie chart

confused by the 3D effect, professional though this may look. It then becomes necessary to print the percentage on each slice, and to label it, which rather negates the intended advantage of visual impact, as in Fig. 13.8. When there are more than four or five 'slices' you may find using a bar chart is much clearer.

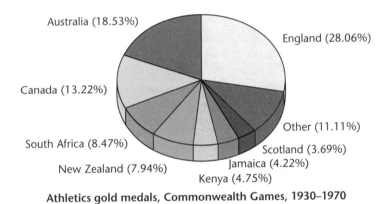

Athletics gold medals, Commonwealth Games, 1930–1970

Fig. 13.8 A pie chart with too many slices

EXERCISE 13.7

Convince yourself of the advantage of bar charts by representing the pie chart (in Fig. 13.8) in bar chart form. You will see how much easier it is to compare the size of the different parts).

Note that, while bar charts can be used to show either a range of values, or, by fixing the height of the bar at 100%, to show proportions, a pie chart can *only* be used for proportions. It is totally invalid to use it to show, say, sales figures for a number of years.

GRAPHS

One common way of showing how two variables are related is to draw a graph. The basic principles of coordinate geometry allow you to plot a point using two 'coordinates'. You will be familiar with this if you use maps much. Suppose I am planning to join a walk organised by the Long Distance Walkers Association. Rather than rely on verbal directions on how to get to the meeting point, I look in the programme for the map grid reference, in this case 'Landranger 175 GR 772817'. Having found the map and opened it, I look along the map for the 77 line on the grid, and follow it up until it meets the 81 line running across. I know that the point I need is a bit to the right, and rather more up from this, and sure enough, there is the car park, and I can work out the best way to get there.

On a map the dimensions are purely geographical : E ↔ W and N ↔ S. You are more likely to be interested in rather different variables, and in a series of points rather than a single one. Again each 'axis' – the horizontal line and the vertical line – has meaning, but the dimensions might be anything. Height, weight, number of observations, value of sales, temperature – it will depend upon the data. For example, you might be interested in how costs are related to volume of production. If so, you would want to plot the cost for each production level.

Your first decision is which axis to use for which. Note that costs would *depend* in some way upon number of units produced. At school, you probably talked about an 'x' axis and a 'y' axis. Typically, the independent variable is referred to as 'x', and is plotted along the horizontal, or 'x' axis, and the dependent variable is plotted along the 'y' or vertical axis. (Note, this is easy to remember if you think "x is 'a cross'".) So if cost depends upon production, it is dependent, and needs to be plotted on the y or vertical axis. You also need to think about appropriate scales for each axis, so that the 'picture' is as clear as possible.

EXERCISE 13.8

Plot the graphs representing each of the following sets of figures:

(a)
Month:	Jan	Feb	Mar	Apr	May	Jun	Jul	Aug
Sales (€K):	57	60	99	95	110	90	95	79

(b)
Production	<100	100+	200+	300+	400+	500+	600+	700+
Cost/unit (€)	2.5	2.25	2.0	1.5	1.25	1.0	1.0	1.0

In Exercise 13.8, you could see clearly how production costs were related to the volume of production. In this case the relationship was not linear, i.e. in the form of a straight line. Presumably there were minor economies of scale over the first part of the range (a slightly more significant one at the 300 point than the rest, perhaps by using a different machine). Beyond 500 there seemed to be no further room for improvement, at least within the range considered.

Note that in plotting a graph you need a *scale* for each axis, in contrast to a bar chart where the order of the bars does *not* matter, say rainfall in various capital cities, and you have a scale along one axis (say, cm) but not along the other axis. There, you

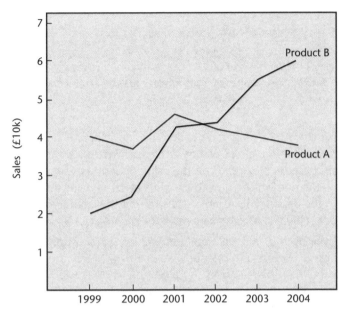

Fig. 13.9 Graph showing sales for two products

merely have a number of labelled points or bands. (Sometimes you will see the top of such bars joined together to give a *graph* but this is not really valid. A graph should always represent the relationship between *two* variables.)

Of course, as with bar charts, you can show several things on a single graph. You can see from Fig. 13.9 that a rough visual comparison can be made of the two sets of figures shown. This would be much more difficult if you were working just from the sets of raw figures.

Graphs and equations

A graph is a good way of showing how two different things are related. The figures in Exercise 13.8 were presumably worked out from a knowledge of the different costs involved. Sometimes you may have this knowledge in the form of an equation. Suppose that you know that cost of production consists of a fixed element and a variable element, or

$$C = F + nV,$$

where C is total production cost, F is the fixed cost (for example workshop rental), n the number of units produced and V the variable cost (for example, labour and materials) per unit produced. You might also know that you can sell a unit for £P. If so, you could express sales revenue (S) as

$$S = nP$$

Do not worry if you are puzzzled by these equations. Read fairly quickly to get the general sense. There is more on equations later. You can revisit this section once you have read that.

EXERCISE 13.9

If fixed costs are £50 per week, variable costs £1 per unit, and units sell for £2, plot the lines showing how both costs and income increase as production increases. From this, deduce the number of units which must be produced and sold if you are not to lose money on the enterprise!

Exercise 13.9 should have shown several things. First, note that the equation is an example in the classic form $y = nx + c$, where y is the 'dependent' variable. It is called this because it depends on the value of another variable, or the 'independent' variable, i.e. the one which you choose to fix at some value in order to see what effect this has on the dependent variable. Thus to plot this graph you would work out the value of y for each value of x, make a mark for each pair of x,y values, and join the dots.

If you do this, you will note that $y = nx + c$ is a straight line: this is because it does not include squares or higher powers of x or y. (If y had been a function of x^2 then the line would have been curved. Try plotting $y = x^2 + 1$ for values of x from -4 to $+4$ to prove it!) Thus every change in x will produce a proportional change in y. The slope of the graph will depend upon the number in front of x. If this is a 2, then for every unit increase in x, y will increase by 2 units. And so on. You can find out the value of the constant term, c, by looking at where the line cuts the 'y' or vertical axis. (Look at the graph in the answers to Exercise 13.1 for another example, and check that your $y = x^2 + 1$ curve indeed cuts the y axis at 1.)

It should now be clearer how you can use graphs to answer questions. From the graph in Exercise 13.9 you could work out the level of sales beyond which (assuming you sell all you make) you will go into profit. (This point is known as 'breakeven'.) This was the reverse of finding where to meet for the walk! To find the value of x you drew a vertical line down from that point until it met the x axis, and to find the corresponding y value, you drew a horizontal line from the point across to the y axis. Reading off the values gave you the solution.

EXERCISE 13.10

Plot the graphs for the following two equations for values of x from -3 to $+3$:

a) $y = 2x^2 - 1$

b) $y = 4x + 3$

c) Use the graph to identify possible values of x and y if both equations apply.

Fitting lines to data points

In the examples in Exercise 13.10 you knew the equation. Often you may have merely a collection of observed pairs of values (say essay marks and exam scores for a group of students, or value of sales made and number of outlets visited by the salesman that month). In this case you can still plot the values, but it might not make a lot of sense to join up the dots – if you have a lot of values, there might be a mass of zig-zags. But look at the pattern made by the dots themselves. Sometimes you may see a clear pattern emerging. If so, you will want to know whether there is indeed a relationship (correlation) between the variables, and if so, what that relationship is, what is the best line you can draw to represent the set of points, and what is the strength of this relationship. The stronger the relationship between the two variables, the easier it will be to fit the line to the data visually.

EXERCISE 13.11

Draw the line that you think best fits the data in the scattergraphs below:

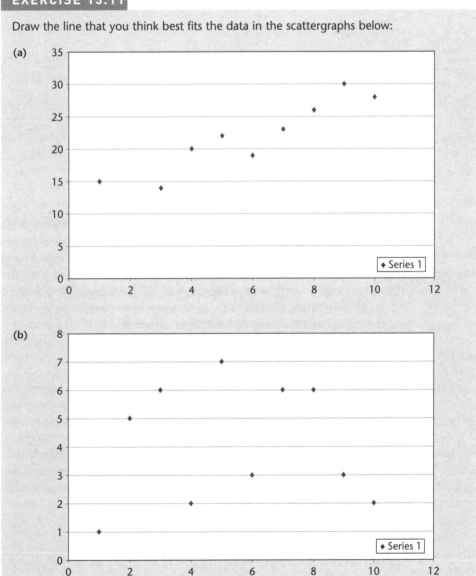

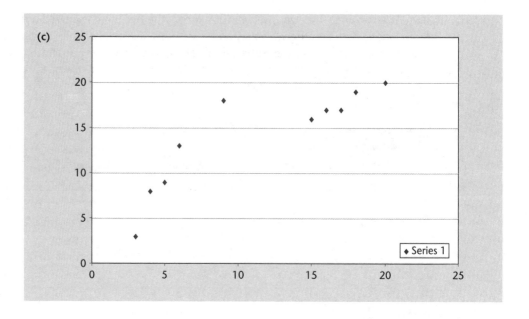

You probably experienced a lot of uncertainty when trying to fit a line to the set of points in scattergraph (b) above. But because this is a very common problem, a statistical technique has been developed that will allow you to assess both the strength of the relationship and the line of 'best fit'. Note that this only works for straight lines of the form $y = nx + c$. If the dots look as if they would better fit a 'U' shape or some other non-straight line, then the approach is not appropriate. Scattergraph (c) above is a case in point. While it is fairly easy to fit a line to the whole set of points, visual inspection suggests that two different lines would give a much better fit.

Linear regression

The mathematical technique for fitting lines is called 'linear regression'. You could, with patience, draw a series of possible lines, and work out how best each fitted the points by working out the sum of the (vertical) distances from each point to your line (see Fig. 13.10). (These distances between actual value and the value on the curve you have fitted are called residuals.) Or better, as when working out the standard deviation, you could get rid of the problem that some distances are negative by working out the sum of the squares of the distances. Your best line would be the one for which the sum of these squares of residuals was least.

Fortunately, given that this trial and error process would normally be tedious in the extreme, it is possible to work out what line is best from the numbers themselves. Each 'dot' on your scattergraph can be thought of as having an 'x' and a 'y' value. Thus continuous assessment might be thought of as x, and exam score as y, and the line you are trying to draw would represent the best equation of the form 'exam score = function of continuous assessment + constant'. (In my experience exam scores tend to be 15% lower, so there would be a negative constant.)

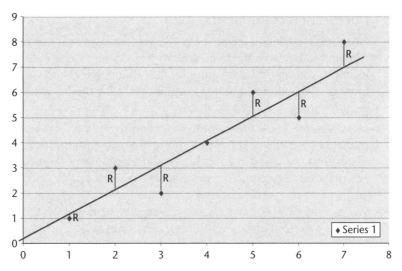

Fig. 13.10 A fitted line showing residuals

If you ever want to work out a regression line, use the procedure outlined in the box below. This may seem a long process, but is much quicker and more reliable than trial and error! (*Note: See* the Helpfile if the Σ and $\bar{x}$ symbols puzzle you.) Using Excel is even better.

Process for working out a regression line of the form $y = a + bx$:

- work out the average value of x ($\bar{x}$) (i.e. x multiplied by mean x)
- work out the average value of y ($\bar{y}$) (i.e. y multiplied by mean y)
- for each point, work out $(x - \bar{x})$ – call this diff$x$, and $(y - \bar{y})$ – call this diff$y$, and multiply them together to give diff$x$.diff$y$
- add together all the (diff$x$.diff$y$)s to give Σ (diff$x$.diff$y$)
- square each (diff$x$) and add these squares together to give (Σ(diff$x$)^2)
- divide Σ(diff$x$.diff$y$) by Σ(diff$x$)^2; this gives you 'b'
- $a = \bar{y} - b\bar{x}$

If you find it easier to work from a formula:

$$\text{If } y = a + bx$$

then

$$b = \frac{\Sigma(x - \bar{x})(y - \bar{y})}{\Sigma(x - \bar{x})^2}$$

Do remember, though, that this makes sense only if the data points look as if a straight line would be the best fit to the data. If when you plot them the scattergraph you get suggests a curve of some point, you will need different techniques to work out the best fit.

13

Using numbers

Correlation coefficients

Once you have found a line of best fit, you may well want to know how strong the relationship between the two variables actually is. Is the correlation significant? For example, you might have figures for advertising spend and sales at different points in time. Or the figures might be for outlets visited and sales as described above.

Clearly if the points were pretty close to your line of best fit (i.e. the residuals were small) you might be confident that the two things were related. A *correlation coefficient* (denoted by *r*) indicates the strength of the relationship. It is a way of describing how much of the variation in your data is explained by your regression line. Or conversely, how much is unexplained – how big are the residuals? Or, to get away from the positive/negative problem, how big is the sum of the squares of the residuals? (Now you can see why '*r*' may have been chosen to represent it.) If the coefficient is +1, the points are perfectly related. As *x* increases, *y* increases, and all points lie exactly on the line. If *r* is −1 then again the relationship is perfect, but as x increases, y decreases. Figure 13.11 shows approximate values of *r* for different sets of data.

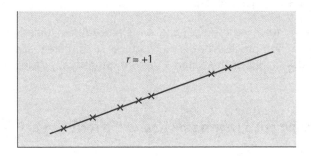

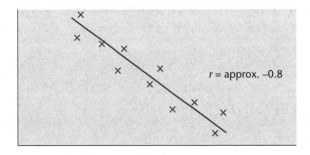

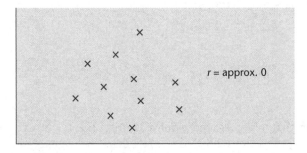

Fig. 13.11 Approximate correlation coefficients for different data sets

The formula for calculating r looks very similar to that for b above – indeed, the top, or numerator, is the same. But the denominator is the square root of what you get when you multiply $\Sigma(x - \bar{x})^2$ by $\Sigma(y - \bar{y})^2$. There is a nice symmetry here. Thus:

$$r = \frac{\Sigma(x - \bar{x})\,(y - \bar{y})}{\sqrt{\Sigma(x - \bar{x})^2\,\Sigma(y - \bar{y})^2}}$$

However, Excel has a built-in correlation function, so you should not need to work this out for yourself.

The size of r does not in itself tell you how significant the relationship is. The more data points you have, the more significant is a correlation of a certain size. There are statistical tables in which you can look up the minimum size of r needed for different levels of significance for the number of observations you have. But remember, even if you have decided to call one variable a dependent variable, a correlation between this and the independent variable is not evidence of *causality*. There might be a third variable that influenced both the things you were looking at. Or there might be a causal relationship, but in the opposite direction from that you imagine – instead of A causing B as you assume, B might be causing A.

The correlation coefficient described above was worked out by Pearson, and assumes you are using a real measurement scale to get your values, for example number of visits and volume of business. But often in management research you may only be able to rank things rather than measure them. If so, you will need different, 'non-parametric' statistics.

Forecasting

But to return to something simpler and more obvious. Graphs are frequently used to show trends over time. Indeed, graphs (and regression lines) can be used to provide simple forecasts. By continuing the graph in the direction it seems to be heading, you can estimate future values. As most graphs will show a degree of variation about what seems to be the general direction, you will need to beware of continuing just in the direction of the last section of the graph, as a slightly odd last value might mislead you significantly – this is where regression lines help. But try to forecast the future direction of the following graphs by eye.

13

Using numbers

EXERCISE 13.12

Extend, or *extrapolate from*, the following graphs to provide an estimate of future trends, putting a dot where you think the next point is most likely to be:

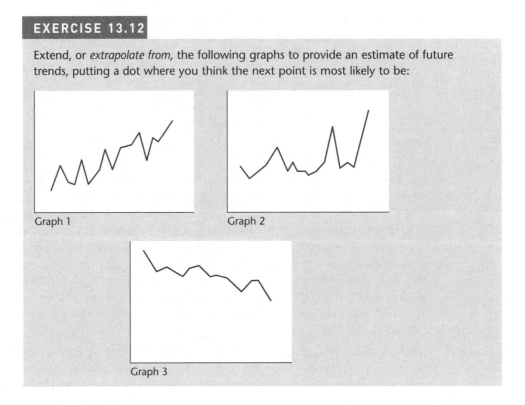

Graph 1

Graph 2

Graph 3

In the discussion above the main emphasis has been on showing data in a way that makes visual sense. These techniques are likely to be extremely useful to you. But it was also clear that to extract the full sense you may well need to supplement them by doing simple sums, or working with equations.

ESTIMATING

You have already seen how a calculator can make things much easier for you, but that it has its weaknesses. Some of these may not be obvious, as the calculator may still give you an answer. For example, the four calculators in our house, when we tried to add 50% to 100 by pressing ☐1☐☐0☐☐0☐☐+☐☐5☐☐0☐☐%☐ gave 200, 300, 250 and 150. Calculators do not know, either, when you have pressed a wrong button – which is all too easy in a long set of figures. It took me many tries at working out the markers' means in Exercise 13.2 before I got the same answer a second and third time! You therefore need to have a rough idea in your head of what the answer should be so that if it comes out wildly different you know that something is wrong.

The technique for doing this is called *estimating*. For example, if you are adding up 10 numbers in the range 700 to 900, you can estimate that the answer will be somewhere about 8000. If it is more than 9000, or less than 7000, you have done something wrong. Whatever the calculation that you are doing, it is worth getting a ballpark figure in your head, so that you know if some extra noughts have crept in somewhere, or you have pressed a $+$ somewhere instead of a $-$.

EXERCISE 13.13

Estimate the value of the following before doing the calculation on your calculator:

	Estimate	Answer
(a) 2734 + 5955	_____	_____
(b) 40 569 ÷ 9	_____	_____
(c) 25% of 39 400 113	_____	_____
(d) 95 + 15% of 113	_____	_____

ROUNDING

To estimate, you are probably working to the nearest hundred or thousand to get a rough idea of what the answer will be. This technique, called *rounding*, is very important. You will remember that when you used your calculator to work out 1⅔ it filled up its display with '6's. You will seldom wish to work to so many places of decimals. Total accuracy is often not particularly important. To work to lots of places of decimals is not only inconvenient: it implies a spurious accuracy, casting doubt on your grasp of what your results really mean.

Suppose that your project involved using a questionnaire to obtain a measure of job satisfaction. Respondents were asked to rate a number of aspects of their jobs on a scale from 1 to 5. If you wanted to work with average scores in this case it would be totally absurd to give these to much more than one decimal place, as the ratings themselves are subjective, and the scale crude.

When rounding, you increase the last number you are using by 1 if the first number you are discarding is greater than 5, leaving it alone if the number you are discarding is less than 5. Opinions vary as to whether you should round up or down if it is 5. It doesn't really matter which you do, but whichever you prefer, you should do this consistently. Thus, 1.5326719 would be 1.5 to one decimal place, or 1.533 to three decimal places.

EXERCISE 13.14

Round the following to two places of decimals:

1.6324   3.9995   7164.2294   51.1111   1.6556

_____   _____   _____   _____   _____

You will see from this exercise that rounding to, say, two decimal places does not provide a consistent level of accuracy. A better measure is the number of *significant figures* in the answer, i.e. the number of digits between the first digit which isn't zero and the number which you round (inclusive). Thus 7 268 893.4 is 7 269 000 to four significant figures, and 0.006038215 is 0.00604 to three significant figures.

When you are including sets of figures in reports, think carefully about the number of significant figures needed to convey your message with most force and clarity. Too many digits can obscure the picture; too few might be misleading.

FRACTIONS, PERCENTAGES AND RATIOS

While you probably studied fractions at school, you may have paid less attention to ratios. You will encounter a number of key ratios in your accounting and business policy courses, and will need to be happy with the concept. Ratios are a sort of fraction, and fractions will also appear in other contexts, so a quick revision of how to deal with fractions is appropriate. The need for fractions will have already emerged if you have worked through 'division' in the Helpfile. Fractions can be expressed in three forms: as one number divided by another; as a decimal; or as a percentage.

EXERCISE 13.15

To refresh your memory, try the following. Your garage is offering tyres at 80 per cent of their original selling price. You decide to buy two, which would normally cost £100. You also have a company card, entitling you to a 5 per cent reduction on anything you buy. What should you end up paying, and should you ask for your 5 per cent discount before or after the promotional discount is deducted?

Fractions

With a calculator it is easy to turn fractions into decimals and then to work with them just like any other number. Unfortunately we cannot leave it at that, as many of the equations you will encounter will include letters, and your calculator cannot decimalise those. There are other times when you will not *wish* to turn a fraction into a decimal. Therefore, you need to know a few basic rules for dealing with fractions. Sometimes they will make a calculation so easy that you can dispense with your calculator anyway.

Rule 1 You can multiply or divide top and bottom of a fraction by the same thing, be it number or letter or mixture, without changing the value of the fraction.

Imagine cutting a cake into 2, or 4, or 6, or 10, or 12 pieces. What would be half the cake in each case? Clearly, $\frac{1}{2} = \frac{2}{4} = \frac{3}{6} = \frac{5}{10} = \frac{6}{12}$.

Similarly, $\frac{2(3 + y)}{3(3 + y)} = \frac{2}{3}$

as you can divide top and bottom by $3 + y$. This operation is called *cancelling*, and is very useful in simplifying fractions, so that a sum becomes easier to do.

EXERCISE 13.16

Simplify the following fractions by dividing top and bottom by the same thing, i.e. a factor common to both:

(a) $\frac{20}{30}$ _____

(b) $\frac{75}{100}$ _____

(c) $\frac{6}{9}$ _____

(d) $\frac{22}{11}$ _____

(e) $\frac{16}{12}$ _____

(f) $\frac{3x}{4x}$ _____

(g) $\frac{4(x + 1)}{8(x + 1)}$ _____

Rule 2 To multiply a series of fractions you multiply all the numbers (or letters or brackets) on top to get the 'thing on top' (the *numerator*) in your answer, and multiply all the things underneath to get the *denominator* or 'the thing on the bottom' in your answer.

Thus, $\frac{2}{3} \times \frac{4}{5} = \frac{8}{15}$, and $\frac{1}{2} \times \frac{3}{4} = \frac{3}{8}$. You can now see how cancelling comes in very handy. You can cancel out numbers, or letters, or whole brackets, that appear on both top and bottom in a string of things to be multiplied, even if they do not appear in the same fraction. Thus $\frac{1}{2} \times \frac{4}{5}$ can be written as $\frac{2}{5}$, for you can divide both the 2 on the bottom, and the 4 on the top, by 2.

EXERCISE 13.17

Multiply the following sets of fractions, using cancelling to make the sum easier:

(a) $\frac{2}{3} \times \frac{3}{4} \times \frac{4}{5} \times \frac{1}{2}$ _____

(b) $\frac{1}{(n + 1)} \times \frac{(n + 1)}{3}$ _____

(c) $\frac{1}{xy} \times \frac{x}{(1 + y)}$ _____

(d) $\frac{1}{2} \times \frac{50}{100}$ _____

(e) $\frac{2y}{14} \times \frac{7}{xy}$ _____

(f) $\frac{2}{15} \times \frac{3x}{4y} \times \frac{y(y + 1)}{x}$ _____

(g) $\frac{y}{x} \times \frac{7}{y} \times \frac{x^2 y}{14}$ _____

13

Using numbers

Note that whether or not the bottom line of a fraction is written with a bracket round it, you must treat it as if it had one. It would be quite correct to write $1 + y$ in (c) above, i.e. without a bracket, but you could not divide it by any y that might be in the top line, as this would not go into the whole phrase '$1 + y$'.

Following this same rule, you can see that to square a fraction you square the number on the top and the number on the bottom to get numerator and denominator. Thus ½ squared is ¼, ⅔ cubed would be $\frac{2 \times 2 \times 2}{3 \times 3 \times 3}$ or $\frac{2^3}{3^3}$, or ⁸⁄₂₇. You can either write the index number against top and bottom figures in a fraction you wish to raise to a certain power, or put a bracket around the whole fraction, and write the index number against the top of the closing bracket. Thus the fifth power of ⅔ could be written as $(⅔)^5$, or the nth power of $\frac{x}{y}$ as $\left(\frac{x}{y}\right)^n$.

EXERCISE 13.18

Write out the value of $\left(\frac{x}{y}\right)^n$:

(a) where x is 1, y is 2 and n is 3   (b) when x is 2, y is 6 and n is 2

_____   _____

Rule 3 To divide something by a fraction you turn the fraction upside down and multiply by the inversion.

Well, obviously you have to do *something* different: $4 \div 2$ *can't* be the same as $4 \div ½$. And it makes a sort of sense. If $4 \div 2$ means dividing it into two equal parts, then $4 \div ½$ could be seen as dividing it into half a part. You would get 8 halfpenny pieces (if they still existed) from 4 pence, but only two 2p pieces.

$$\text{So } 4 \div ⅓ \text{ becomes } 12, \quad ½ \div ¾ = ⁴⁄₆, \quad \frac{(2x + 1)}{3} \div \frac{2}{(x + 1)} = \frac{(x + 1)^2}{3} \text{ etc.}$$

Because you are converting a division into a multiplication by inverting it, you can string together multiplications and divisions without problem, provided you remember to write all the divisions upside down and then multiply. So:

$$½ \times ¾ \div ⁵⁄₇ \times ¹⁄₁₄ \div ⅗ \quad \text{can be written as}$$

$$½ \times ¾ \times ⁷⁄₅ \times ¹⁄₁₄ \times ⁵⁄₃ \quad \text{which cancels down to } ¹⁄₁₆.$$

Similarly,

$$\frac{(x + y)}{(2y + 3)} \times \frac{3}{x} \div \frac{2(x + y)}{(2y + 5)} \quad \text{becomes} \quad \frac{(x + y)}{(2y + 3)} \times \frac{3}{x} \times \frac{(2y + 5)}{2(x + y)}$$

which, as you can divide both top and bottom by $(x + y)$, cancels down to

$$\frac{3(2y + 5)}{2x(2y + 3)}$$

EXERCISE 13.19

Work out the following combined multiplications and divisions. Leave the brackets in as was done in the example above. Don't worry that we have not yet learned how to multiply them out.

(a) $\dfrac{1}{2} \times \dfrac{2(x + y)}{3} \div \dfrac{3(x + y)}{2}$ _____

(b) $\dfrac{x}{y} \times \dfrac{y}{x} \div \dfrac{x}{y} \div \dfrac{2}{3}$ _____

(c) $4 \div (x + 1) \times \dfrac{3}{4} \div \dfrac{(x + 2)}{(x + 4)}$ _____

(d) $\dfrac{3}{4} \div \dfrac{3}{5} \div \dfrac{x(x + 1)}{(y + 1)}$ _____

(e) $1\dfrac{1}{2} \times \dfrac{3}{4} \div \dfrac{y}{x}$ _____

Rule 4 You can add or subtract only fractions which share a common denominator.

Percentages

Go back to your cake. It makes sense to *talk* about '$\frac{1}{2} + \frac{1}{3}$', but would be clumsy to include this expression in, say, a string of multiplications. You cannot say that $\frac{1}{2} + \frac{2}{3}$ is $\frac{3}{2}$, or $\frac{3}{3}$, or $\frac{3}{5}$, because it isn't. In order to write the addition as something with a single number on top and bottom, we need to turn each fraction into the same sort of thing. $\frac{1}{2}$ can be written as $\frac{3}{6}$, and $\frac{1}{3}$ as $\frac{2}{6}$. These we *can* add, to give $\frac{5}{6}$. Similarly, $\frac{1}{2} - \frac{1}{3}$ could have been described as $\frac{3}{6} - \frac{2}{6}$, or $\frac{1}{6}$. You can do the same if you have letters in your fractions. If you wish to add $\frac{3}{5}$ and $\frac{5x}{y}$ you can turn both into fractions with $5y$ on the bottom line, by multiplying top and bottom of the first one by y, and top and bottom of the second by 5. This will give you the sum $\frac{3y}{5y} + \frac{25x}{5y}$ or $\frac{(3y + 25x)}{5y}$. When dealing in percentages you are reducing everything to hundredths, so you have a common denominator and can add and subtract.

Note that you *cannot* cancel between different terms in an addition in the same way that you could for a multiplication. Note also that you cannot cancel between *part* of the numerator and the denominator. You cannot get rid of either the 5 or the y in the answer above by dividing the $3y$ by y or the $25x$ by 5. You have to be able to divide every term on the top line by something on the bottom line to cancel. Thus if the top line had been $5y + 25x$ you would have been able to cancel out the 5 in the bottom line, as the top could have been written as $5(y + 5x)$ and the 5 could have been cancelled with the 5 on the bottom line.

EXERCISE 13.20

Write the following as single fractions:

(a) $\frac{3}{4} + \frac{7}{8}$ _____

(b) $\frac{3}{x} + \frac{4}{y}$ _____

(c) $\frac{5x}{y} - \frac{2(x+1)}{y}$ _____

(d) $\frac{2}{3} + \frac{3x}{5}$ _____

(e) 50% of $\frac{3}{4}$ _____

(f) $\frac{y(5x+1)}{x} + \frac{xy}{(5x+1)}$ _____

(g) $\frac{5}{(x-1)} - \frac{3}{(x-2)}$ _____

Ratios

Now that you have the basic rules for dealing with fractions at your fingertips, whether these fractions are expressed in letters, numbers or a mixture, we can move on to ratios, which are a form of fraction.

You use ratios when you are more interested in the relative sizes of things than in the absolute differences between them. To say that Part A costs 20p more than Part B may be more or less impressive depending on how much they both cost. If Part A costs £200.20, the difference is less striking than if Part A costs 40p. In the second instance it costs 100% more than Part B, or 200% as much, whereas in the first instance it is 0.1% more, or 100.1% of the Part B price.

Ratios are obtained by dividing one thing by another. Thus in the above, with Part A at 40p, the ratio of the cost of Part A to Part B is 2 : 1, or $\frac{2}{1}$, depending on how you prefer to write it. You obtain the ratio of A to B by dividing A by B. Thus the ratio of Part B's cost to Part A's is 1 : 2, or $\frac{1}{2}$. The thing you are finding the ratio of is written first, or on top. The thing you are finding the ratio of it to is written second, or underneath. So if there are 500 students on a course and 10 tutors the staff : student ratio is 1 : 50 or $\frac{1}{50}$. The advantage of the fraction way of writing it, rather than the colon, is that you can then include the ratio in an equation if you want to, and deal with it like any other fraction. Since percentages are just another way of writing fractions, you can, of course, express ratios in percentages, too.

EXERCISE 13.21

Imagine your departmental budget is £40 000, of which £12 800 is spent on advertising.

(a) What percentage of your budget is spent on advertising? _____

(b) What is the ratio of your advertising budget to your total budget? _____

(c) What is the ratio of your advertising budget to your budget for everything else? _____

Any accounting and finance course will introduce you to many ratios. This is because ratios deal in relative values rather than absolutes and so allow you to make meaningful comparisons between operations of different size. Certain key ratios are used to compare an organisation's performance from year to year, and to identify emerging trends.

A key financial ratio which you will encounter is 'Return on Capital Employed' (ROCE), sometimes known as 'Return on Investment' (ROI). While an MBA course will take you through the process of working out which figures should be used in calculating this ratio, you can practise working with ratios by calculating ROCE in a variety of cases.

$$\text{ROCE (or ROI)} = \frac{\text{Operating profit (pre-interest and tax)}}{\text{Capital employed}}$$

EXERCISE 13.22

Calculate ROCE (as a percentage) in the following cases (figures in £000):

	Operating profit	Capital employed	ROCE
(a)	500	4000	_____
(b)	164	83	_____
(c)	4.3	13	_____
(d)	(10)	256	_____

Because capital employed may vary, it is common to calculate an average value, using net assets at the year start and end.

EXERCISE 13.23

Calculate ROCE as a percentage, using average investment:

	Operating profit	Assets at year start	Assets at year end	Mean investment	ROCE
(a)	45	335	300	_____	_____
(b)	330	120	160	_____	_____
(c)	2200	7800	8000	_____	_____
(d)	(55)	5600	5500	_____	_____

Profit margin (the ratio of profit before interest and tax to sales) is clearly a major factor in determining ROCE. The other important factor is asset turnover. Asset turnover is a measure of how well the fixed assets and working capital of the firm are utilised. Profit margin multiplied by asset turnover gives ROCE.

EXERCISE 13.24

Asset turnover must be the ratio of *what* to net assets? (That is, if asset turnover is x : net assets, what is x?)

Another important ratio which can be used for practising working out ratios is liquidity, which shows the extent to which short-term claims by creditors are covered by assets which are likely to be converted into cash within the same timescale. One measure of this, called the 'Current Ratio', is the ratio of current assets : current liabilities. It is more likely to be given as a decimal number than as a percentage.

EXERCISE 13.25

Calculate the current ratio in the following cases (figures are in £000):

	Current assets	Current liabilities	Current ratio
(a)	10 000	5 000	_____
(b)	40	35	_____
(c)	2	3	_____
(d)	3 500	2 000	_____

You will learn many more ratios, and how to interpret them, on your course. Sometimes you will be faced with whole pages of figures from which you will be required to derive the ratios before interpreting them. This may at first sight seem forbidding, but in most cases, as the above exercises go some way to show, all you will need by way of mathematical skill is the ability to add, subtract, multiply and divide appropriate numbers, using a calculator or spreadsheet. The greater problem is to keep a clear head! The sums are not very important. What *is* important is to be able to look at the figures and see what they *mean*. Where do things seem to be changing, or where do there seem to be potential problems? And then you have to think about possible explanations for what you have observed, and what these mean. These explanations may often be found by using other numbers, but it is a logical, not a mathematical exercise.

USING EQUATIONS

In earlier examples you were using equations to find values, simply by substituting numbers for letters. But equations can allow you to do more than this. Take the simple(?) example of compound interest. Suppose you borrow £1000 for five years, at 15% interest p.a., and instead of paying the interest, add it to the amount you owe. Thus at the end of the first year, the amount you owe will be £1000 plus 15% of £1000. That is, the debt at the end of year one (call it D_1) will be 1.15 × the sum borrowed.

Your debt at the end of year two will be 1.15 × D_1, or 1.15 × 1.15 × the original £1000.

13

Using numbers

EXERCISE 13.26

Use your calculator to find the debt at the end of year two. Then calculate the debt at the end of year three.

Year two_____ Year three_____

Now you can see why it is useful to replace numbers by letters. It enables us to write a general, all-purpose formula for how to calculate the amount owed, without specifying the actual figures. We can say that after any number of years, call it n, the balance outstanding will be $(1.15)^n$ × £1000. If you want the debt after 10 years, it will be $(1.15)^{10}$ × £1000, and so on. If you have a sufficiently sophisticated calculator you will have a key which allows you to do this directly, but otherwise you will need to multiply repeatedly. Of course, you could also use Excel!

We can make the formula more general by using a different letter, say A, for the amount originally borrowed, and even more general by using a further letter, say r, for the percentage interest rate. Thus if we use D_n to indicate the debt at the end of year n, we have a completely general formula:

$$D_n = A(1 + r)^n$$

Using this formula we can work out the debt for any sum, any interest rate, any sum borrowed, and any length of time, merely by replacing the letters by the numbers that we wish to use in a particular case, and then working out the answer.

EXERCISE 13.27

Work out the amount that will be owed:

(a) at the end of one year on a loan of £2000 at 13% _____

(b) at the end of two years on a loan of £1500 at 25% _____

(c) at the end of five years on a loan of £10 000 at 15% _____

In this instance we are dealing with the simple case of substituting values in the formula to work out the amount owing after a given period with compound interest. It is simply a question of plugging in the right numbers, as the quantity you wanted, D_n, was sitting neatly by itself on one side of the '=' sign. Often it will be less simple. The value you want, traditionally referred to as x, may be mixed up in the middle of an equation, and you may need to move terms around to get it to itself. Or worse still, you may want to find several terms (x, y and z?) which are all mixed up in the same equation, in which case you will need to work with several equations at once to find solutions.

Another common calculation you will need to do is in a sense the reverse of compound interest. Suppose you are considering an investment, say buying a machine. You are assuming that this machine will generate a certain amount of income over a number of years. Is it worth investing? Presumably only if the income gained is more than what you would get by investing the same amount in an investment of equivalent risk over the same period. You can see from the way that compound interest grows that future income has to be quite a lot if it is to be more than your investment would generate, particularly if interest rates are high. To bring future income in different years back to a common 'present value' you divide the projected income for year n by $(1 + r)^n$ and all these values together. (The discount rate, r, will reflect prevailing interest rates, and the risk involved.) The *net present value* is what is left when you subtract the original investment from the sum of the present values. If positive, you might well decide to invest.

Note that, although classical algebra traditionally dealt in 'x's and 'y's, you can use any letters you choose, and you will usually find it much easier to choose a letter which relates in some way to what it describes, as when we chose D for debt, and r for rate in the example above. This makes it much easier to remember what the equation is all about, and which term relates to which. Indeed, if you are struggling with an equation where the author has steadfastly refused to do this, you can sometimes make more sense of it by translating the 'x's and 'y's into letters that have a more obvious meaning. (If you are quoting a standard equation in an assignment or examination, you should, however, always use the 'official' letters.)

With some equations you will be able to find an answer. In other cases, you may have sets of variables and formulae where there is no answer as such, but where you can learn techniques which will allow you to maximise, or optimise, results. You will learn these when you study courses on Operations Research. Key among these techniques are use of the calculus (differential equations), discovered in the seventeenth century, and linear programming techniques, which date from the Second World War.

Don't panic. Differential calculus will be introduced (briefly) later in the chapter. The main point to note here is how easily you can move terms around in a fairly simple equation. Since the principle is the same, you should now be able to approach the more complex manipulations, which you will doubtless be taught, with more confidence.

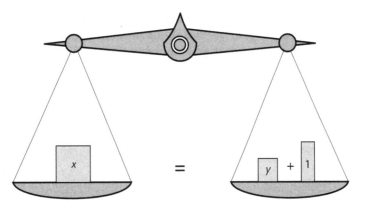

Fig. 13.12 An equation as a balance

An equation can best be visualised as two sets of things which are in balance. For example, look at Fig. 13.12.

In Fig. 13.12 x, and $y + 1$, can be weighed in the pans and found equal, and we can thus write $x = y + 1$. Visualising it in this way makes it very easy to see what you can and cannot do to an equation. Clearly you could add the same quantity to each side, and the scales would still balance. Thus in the above case you could write $x + 1 = y + 1 + 1$, or $y + 2$, and it would still be correct. Similarly, $x + z = y + z + 1$ would also be true. You could also take the same quantity away from each side and leave the scales in balance. Thus you could write $x - 1 = y$, or $x - y = 1$.

You could multiply the two sides by the same thing, too. Doubling each side would still produce balance, as would trebling, or anything else. So $2x = 2(y + 1)$, $10x = 10(y + 1)$, or $zx = z(y + 1)$. By the same token, you can divide each side by the same thing. Taking half of what is in each pan will still balance the scales, as will dividing by anything else. Thus:

$$\frac{x}{2} = \frac{(y + 1)}{2}, \text{ and } \frac{x}{z} = \frac{(y + 1)}{z} \text{ and } \frac{x}{(y + 1)} = 1$$

Indeed, whatever you do, as long as you do it equally to both sides, you will be left with a valid equation. What you cannot do is to do something to one side, and do it to only part of the other side. Multiplying all of the right-hand side by a quantity, but multiplying only some of the left, would not be valid. Thus you could not write $2x = 2y + 1$ in the above example. (To remember this, you will need to put brackets round each side of the equation if you start multiplying or dividing.)

This is the main rule for manipulating equations. Once you have grasped it, you will be well away. Thus, suppose that you were working with the debt example we used earlier, but you knew the amount owed at the end of the period and the interest rate at which the money had been borrowed. What you did not know, and wanted to find out, was the original debt. Suppose that after four years at 20% the debt was £4147. You *could* experiment by trying different original loans, and working out the debt in each case. When you got too big a debt you could try a smaller loan; if that came out too small you could try a bigger one, getting closer to your £4147 debt each time.

Alternatively, you could rearrange the equation so that the term you wanted, A, was on the left of the '=', all by itself, and then work out the figure you wanted directly. You do this by using the fact that you can do something to both sides of the equation without affecting its validity.

The original equation was:

$$D_n = A(1 + r)^n$$

Don't worry that this is much more complicated looking than the $x = y + 1$ type of example used above. The principle is exactly the same. In this case, we want to stop the A from being multiplied by $(1 + r)^n$. If you had $2A$ and wanted to have only A you would divide by 2. It is exactly the same here. If we divide $A(1 + r)^n$ by $(1 + r)^n$, then the two $(1 + r)^n$'s cancel out, and leave us with A. But remember, if we did something to one side of the equation, we had to do it to the other, so we must divide the D_n by $(1 + r)^n$ as well. Thus we get the equally valid equation:

$$A = \frac{D_n}{(1 + r)^n}$$

This is a much more useful arrangement of the equation if A is what we are looking for. We know the values of D_n and r and n, so can put these into the equation, giving $A = £4147 \div (1.2)^4$, which your calculator should tell you is near enough £2000. This should be a much quicker, as well as more accurate, way of getting the answer than the trial and error method. (Note, however, that there will be occasions when trial and error is your only option, so do not underestimate that method's potential!)

To use a different equation, suppose you wanted to find x, and you knew $y = 7 + 3x + \frac{1}{y}$. You will remember from earlier that the first thing you could do would be to subtract $7 + \frac{1}{y}$ from each side of the equation, leaving you with $y - 7 - \frac{1}{y} = 3x$. Then, since we usually write what we are trying to find on the left of the '=' sign, we could swap the sides over to give $3x = y - 7 - \frac{1}{y}$. We then need to get rid of the 3, so we divide both sides by 3, giving us:

$$x = \frac{(y - 7 - \frac{1}{y})}{3}$$

If this were to be included in a longer equation, and there might be some chance of further cancelling, we might wish to sort out the rather messy $(y - 7 - \frac{1}{y})$ into a single fraction. To do this we need to express it all in 'y'ths, that is, as something over y. Just as 2 is $\frac{4}{2}$, so y can be written as $\frac{y^2}{y}$, and 7 as $\frac{7y}{y}$, so the whole phrase inside the bracket could just as well have been written as $x = \frac{(y^2 - 7y - 1)}{y}$, or the whole equation written as:

$$x = \frac{(y^2 - 7y - 1)}{3y}$$

If you know y, it is now easy to work out the value of x. For example,

$$\text{if } y = 2, \ x = \frac{(4 - 14 - 1)}{6}, \text{ or } -\frac{11}{6}$$

EXERCISE 13.28

Rearrange the following equations to get x on the left, then work out the values of x if:

Value of x:

(i) $y = 2$ (ii) $y = -3$ (iii) $y = 0$

(a) $2y = x + 5$ $x =$ _____ _____ _____ _____

(b) $y + 1 = 3x - 2$ $x =$ _____ _____ _____ _____

(c) $y + 2x = y - x + 12$ $x =$ _____ _____ _____ _____

(d) $\dfrac{y}{4} = \dfrac{x}{2} + 3$ $x =$ _____ _____ _____ _____

(e) $xy = 3$ $x =$ _____ _____ _____ _____

(f) $\dfrac{x}{y} = y + \frac{1}{2}$ $x =$ _____ _____ _____ _____

(g) $\dfrac{y}{(x + 3)} = 4$ $x =$ _____ _____ _____ _____

(h) $\dfrac{x}{(y + 2y + 1)} = y + 4$ $x =$ _____ _____ _____ _____

13

Using numbers

WORKING WITH BRACKETS

In the above, you have often needed to use brackets because this is a way of reminding you either that everything on the top and everything on the bottom of a fraction must be multiplied or divided by the same thing if the fraction is to stay the same, or that everything on each side of an equation must be treated in the same way if the equation is to remain valid. In the exercise above, you could work with the brackets by substituting numbers and then working out the value of the bracket before dealing with it further, but sometimes you will need to work with brackets when you cannot do this. You have already seen that a simple multiplication, say $2(a + b)$, means multiplying *everything* in the bracket, here by 2, giving you $2a + 2b$ in this case. If you want to multiply *two* brackets, you need to multiply everything in the first bracket by everything in the second. Thus

$(a + b)(c + d)$ will give you $ac + ad + bc + bd$

Note that if two brackets are written side by side it means they are to be multiplied. There is no need to use a 'x' sign to show this. Work out the value of the above where $a = 1$, $b = 2$, $c = 3$ and $d = 4$, and then check that this is the same as if you multiplied 3 by 7.

EXERCISE 13.29

Work out the value of:

(a) $2a(3b + 2c)$ _____

(b) $\dfrac{x(6y - 4z)}{2}$ _____

(c) $3r(s + 2t) + 3s(2r + t)$ _____

(d) $(2x + y)(y + 2)$ _____

(e) $\dfrac{(3z + 4y)\,(2y + z)}{2(4y + 2z)\,(a + b)}$ _____

DIFFERENTIAL CALCULUS

I mentioned that this was one of the things you might need during your course, and it is one of the most alarming looking. However, as with much of maths, the basic operations are pretty simple. If your nerves can stand it, it is worth having a brief look before leaving this chapter. You may well have studied calculus at school, and brief revision will bring it back.

Think back to earlier work on drawing graphs and on using equations to answer questions. You used a plot of an equation to discover a breakeven point, and you used intersections between two curves to find possible solutions to *simultaneous* equations, where you needed both equations to be able to answer a question. (See Answer to Exercise 13.10).

The differential calculus is another approach to using equations to provide answers to questions. In particular it allows you to work out the rate at which a value is changing at a certain point on a curve, and the point where the value is highest (or lowest).

For straight lines, the rate of change is constant, but for curved lines, the rate is changing all the time. This rate is shown by the *tangent* to the curve, the line which just touches the curve at that point, and reflects the direction of the curve at the point of contact. (If drawing a tangent of a circle, you would draw the radius at that point, i.e. the line from the centre of the circle to the point where the tangent is being drawn. The tangent would be at 90° to that radius, i.e. at right angles to it. If you are drawing a tangent by eye, it can be useful to try first to draw the line that cuts your curve at right angles.)

If you were to plot average day length per week for every week of the year you would find that it would start to increase from the winter solstice and continue increasing until the summer solstice when it would decline. And the line would not go straight up and then straight down, but would be in the shape of a wave. It would be flat at the solstices, then start gradually to curve up. The line would be at its steepest at the equinoxes before it started to flatten off towards the next solstice. The angle of the line would reflect the rate of change in day length. (If your diary shows sunset and sunrise, try this for yourself.) At the highest and lowest points on the curve, the curve would be effectively horizontal.

The process of *differentiation* allows you to work out the rate of change of a curved line at any point. Where this rate is zero, the line is changing direction, passing from negative to positive or vice versa. So a zero rate of change will mean the point is a maximum or minimum value. Rather than going into the theory, and in keeping with the approach throughout the chapter, the box which follows gives a purely pragmatic approach to differentiation. It will get you started, and allow you to work out simple things. For anything complex, you need another book.

Idiots' guide to differentiation

- The slope of a line plotting values of some variable y against known values of x is called (usually) 'dee why by dee ex' and written (usually) 'dy/dx'. The process of working it out is called 'differentiation of y with respect to x'.

- If y is some function of a power of x, the dy/dx will be a function of one power lower of x. Thus if y is a function of x^2, dy/dx will be a function of x. If y is a function of x cubed, dy/dx will be a function of x squared.

- This function includes the *number* of the power of the x in the original equation. Thus if $y = x^2$, $dy/dx = 2x$. If $y = 4x^3$, $dy/dx = 12x^2$.

- If you have several different powers of x in one equation, you apply the same rule to each term. Thus if $y = x^4 + 2x^3$, $dy/dx = 4x^3 + 6x^2$.

- Remember that x is really x^1, so if $y = x$, $dy/dx = 1$. And if $y = 7x$, $dy/dx = 7$.

- Remember, too, that x^0 is 1, so any constant terms in your equation, i.e. any terms that do not depend on x, can be thought of as an 'x to the nought' term, and will be multiplied by zero when you differentiate. They therefore vanish. The fixed costs on your breakeven chart are a constant. If you were to differentiate that line they would vanish. And indeed they do not affect the slope of the total costs line.

- To find the maximum or minimum of a curve, work out dy/dx and then find the value(s) of x for which this is zero.

- Although it is traditional to use y and x, you can obviously differentiate an equation expressed in any letters, as long as one letter expresses the value of the equation expressed in terms of the other letter. (If a term appears on both sides you will need to sort out the equation before you can differentiate.)

- You can work out a second-order derivative by differentiating dy/dx. This would give you the rate at which the rate of change was changing. It is usually called d^2y/dx^2.

- Higher-order derivatives are similarly possible.

- Integration reverses the process. But remember that constants vanish when you differentiate, so you cannot reconstitute the original equation. There will be an unknown constant which you cannot specify, so you will need to insert a letter to indicate this. Thus the 'integral' of $2x^2$ ($\int 2x^2$) will be $\frac{2}{3}x^3 + K$.

- The integral of a curve at a given point indicates the area under the curve to the left of that point. Thus the integral at x on a frequency graph of heights of males in a population would tell you what proportion of the population was 'x' or shorter.

SOFTWARE FOR DEALING WITH NUMBERS

I have already indicated that calculators, whether handheld or on your computer, can be invaluable, and have mentioned also using spreadsheets. In fact computers make dealing with numbers easy in many ways. A number of statistical packages are available, which can greatly facilitate analysing the results of research; SPSS (Statistical Package for the Social Sciences) and SAS (Statistical Analysis Software) are in common use. You still need to understand the basic principles of statistics, or else you will not use such packages to good effect. And you will need to be sure that you are going to generate a sufficient volume of data to make the effort of learning to use the package worthwhile. But if you are planning a project which will generate quantities of data, then explore what your institution provides by way of licences for software and instruction in their use.

Even if you do not intend a major research programme, you will need as a manager to be familiar with the two forms of software you are likely to already have at your disposal, software for generating spreadsheets and software for handling databases. Spreadsheet software is likely to be the most useful. The Microsoft version is called Excel, but other integrated office software packages will have an equivalent component.

A spreadsheet is an arrangement of 'cells', i.e. spaces, arranged in rows and columns, into which you can enter text, numbers and equations to calculate values using the contents of other cells. If you open Excel you will be offered such an array of empty cells. Thus, as Fig. 13.13 shows, I might want to enter last year's course registrations on different courses in the first column, this year's in the second column, and instruct the computer to calculate the ratio of this year's figures to last year's figures, expressed as a percentage.

We can use a cell to enter: **a title** (see top row), a **number,** or a **formula** (see column D and row 6).

We can alter the numbers whenever we like, and the formula will automatically calculate the totals and percentages and enter the result in the appropriate cells. The column and row titles I have chosen will make it clear what the numbers that appear mean, as the formulae will not be shown when the spreadsheet is run and the results appear on screen or are printed out.

	A	B	C	D
1		**Last year**	**This year**	**Percentages**
2	Accounting	100	109	= (C2/B2)* 100
3	Business studies	230	218	= (C3/B3)* 100
4	Computing	200	242	= (C4/B4)* 100
5	Design	50	46	= (C5/B5)* 100
6	**Total**	= B2+B3+B4+B5	= C2+C3+C4+C5	= (C6/B6)* 100

Fig. 13.13 Example of a spreadsheet

> **EXERCISE 13.30**
>
> Open a spreadsheet, and enter the numbers and formulae in Fig. 13.13. Then highlight the actual figures, and experiment with using the charting facility. (No answer given)

You can see that once you have set up a spreadsheet, which can be fairly time consuming, it saves a lot of time. As in the above example, equations can be set up to reference cell positions rather than particular values, which means that these equations can be copied and pasted and the spreadsheet re-used with different sets of data. The time needed to set up a spreadsheet has been reduced by many shortcuts that are now standard features of the software. For example, the need to total a column or row is so common that Excel provides an 'Autosum' function which allows you to instruct a total to appear at a single mouse click. It is also extremely straightforward to calculate percentages, ignore negative values, round numbers to a given level, provide an average, or compute the rate of return on an investment, if you know present and future value. I referred earlier to the facility to calculate correlations.

A further advantage is that you can use the facility the spreadsheet offers to draw bar charts, pie charts, scatter diagrams and graphs. (Excel provides a 'chart wizard' to make this easy.)

Rather than writing a further chapter (at least) on how to use Excel, when you perhaps have a different package, I shall leave it at this. You should, early in your course if not before, become familiar with using spreadsheets, using whatever training resources are at your disposal. (There is a wealth of material available on the Web, if you have no printed material to hand. Some starting points are suggested in the Further information at the end of the chapter.)

FURTHER SKILLS DEVELOPMENT

The above treatment has, I hope, given you an idea of some of the things you can usefully do, once you are more familiar with numbers and basic mathematical techniques, and introduced the basics of the subject. There is no real substitute for practice if you are to become familiar with the techniques involved. Additional exercises can be found on the **website**. Alternatively, make up further equations for yourself, and try using equations you have made up to solve problems. What equation can you construct to tell you how far a car will go on g gallons of petrol if it does 56 mpg? How many miles to the litre will it do if there are 4½ litres to the gallon? There are any number of such small equations that you can construct. Or you can obtain Graham and Sargent, *Countdown to Mathematics* (*see* Further information), a GCSE maths revision book or Morris (2000) to provide further examples. Check that your chosen book provides answers, as you will need feedback on your work. If you do feel particularly weak in this area, and you have time to spare before starting your course, this is one form of preparation that will pay huge dividends. Good luck!

SUMMARY

- Simple techniques such as bar or pie charts or graphs can enable you to represent sets of data in such a way as to make them more meaningful, allowing visual comparison between sets of figures, or the estimation of trends.

- Ratios, fractions or percentages can be used to indicate how parts relate to each other, or to the whole.

- Ratios are particularly important in accounting and finance.

- Ratios or fractions can be multiplied by multiplying numerators to give the new numerator, and multiplying denominators to give the new denominator. They are unchanged if top and bottom are multiplied by the same thing. They can be added or subtracted only if the denominator is the same in all cases.

- Equations can be used to find unknown values, or to provide a general formula from which values can be calculated in specific cases.

- Equations can be simplified, or rearranged, using the basic rule that an equation remains valid no matter what you do to one side, provided you do the same thing to all of the other side as well.

- Statistical techniques can be used to provide estimates of the probability of sets of results arising because of random variation, rather than because of a systematic difference. They will tell you only the probability of something, not whether it is true or not.

- Graphs can be drawn to show patterns and to answer questions.

- Differential calculus can help to answer questions about rates of change, maximal and minimal points on a graph, and areas under a curve.

- Spreadsheets can make it very easy to calculate dependent variables, once you have set up the table.

- Spreadsheets also make it very easy to produce graphical representations of data.

Further information

- Graham, L. and Sargent, D. (1981) *Countdown to Mathematics*, vol. 1, Addison-Wesley with Open University Press.
  This covers much the same ground at greater length, and provides many more examples for you to work through, with answers.

- Huff, D. (1991) *How to Lie with Statistics*, Penguin.

- Moroney, M.J. (1951) *Facts from Figures*, Penguin.
  This is a classic but accessible introduction to statistics.

- Morris, C. (2000) *Quantitative Approaches in Business Studies* (5th edn), FT Prentice Hall.

- Morris, C. and Thanassoulis, E. (1994) *Essential Mathematics – a Refresher Course for Business and Social Studies*, Macmillan.

- Oakshott, L. (1998) *Essential Quantitative Methods for Business, Management and Finance*, Macmillan Business.

- Powell, J. (1991) *Quantitative Decision Making*, Longman.
- Rowntree, D. (1987) *Statistics Without Tears: a Primer for Non-mathematicians*, Penguin.
- Sprent, P. (1991) *Management Mathematics*, Penguin.
- Stutely, R. (2003) *The Definitive Guide to Managing the Numbers*, Pearson.
  Useful information on spreadsheets and finance for those who are worried about this part of a programme.

13

Using numbers

HELPFILE 13.1
Cracking the code

This section takes you, very gently I promise, through the basic symbols you may find in mathematical equations.

You will know that in 5 + 3 the '+' is telling you to take the *sum* of 3 and 5, or what you get when you add them together. If you had trouble doing the sum, or would have done if it had larger numbers, you can easily get the answer from your calculator, by pressing the obvious buttons. Here you would need 5, +, 3, =. Note that, for additions, the order of the terms does not matter. 5 + 3 is the same as 3 + 5.

You will also know already that 5 − 3, or 5 minus 3, means what you get when you take 3 away from 5. Again, you can easily do subtractions by pressing the obvious calculator buttons. Note that subtractions are more complicated than additions in two ways. First, the order *does* matter. 5 − 3 is *not* the same as 3 − 5. If you have £3000 in the bank and take out £5000 you are *not* in the same situation as if you have £5000 and take out £3000! In the second case you will have £2000 left, and your bank manager will be happy. In the first case you will have an overdraft of £2000, and unless you cleared this with the bank first, they will probably *not* be happy. You will have −£2000. This may be written as (£2000) in some sets of accounts.

Second, there is the interesting question of what to do when you want to take away an amount that is already negative, i.e. has a − sign in front of it. To 'take away' your overdraft, someone would have to *give* you £2000, and indeed to take away a number that is already negative you *add* that number. Thus 5 − (−3) is 5 + 3, or 8. Note that basic calculators can't do this for you; you have to apply this rule of signs yourself before you press the buttons.

This indicates multiplication. 5 × 3 means 5 lots of 3, or 15. Again, the obvious calculator buttons will produce the answer if you have forgotten your tables. And, as with addition, order does not matter. When dealing with negative numbers, you need to count the number of '−' signs in the string of numbers you are multiplying. If you have one, or indeed any odd number of minuses, the answer will be negative. For example, if you owe 5 weeks' garage rent at £3 per week, you have 5 × (−3), or − £15.

If you are multiplying two negative quantities, or any even number of negatives, the answer will be positive. A cheap calculator will not be able to handle a string of mixed signs in a multiplication. When you put in a − it will start to subtract. So you will have to treat the numbers as positive, and again add the right sign yourself, once you get the answer.

Part of the reason for difficulty in working with mixtures of signs on a calculator is that in a string of things to add, subtract, multiply and divide, the signs have different *strengths*. If you see 5 + 3 × 2, this means that you should work out the 3 × 2 *first*, before adding the 5. Thus you get 11, *not* 16. Multiplication and division signs are stronger than addition and subtraction signs, so must be worked on first. Sophisticated calculators are progammed with this rule, but cheap ones are not.

÷

This indicates division. 5 ÷ 3 means what you get when you divide 5 into 3 equal portions. If the second number goes into the first with no problems, for example in the case of 6 ÷ 3 where the answer is 2, life is simple. If it does not, because the first number is not capable of being produced by multiplying the second number by a whole number, you start getting into *fractions*. If I produce five cakes, my three children will know that they will get less than two each, because there are fewer than six cakes, and more than 1½. To be sure they are happy, I could divide each cake into three equal parts and give them a part of each cake. The *fraction* of each cake that they would get would be ⅓.

Figure 13.14 shows how one share is 5 times ⅓, which could be assembled into 1⅔ cakes. You could write the '1⅔' as ⅝ if you liked. You will see in a minute why this can sometimes be useful.

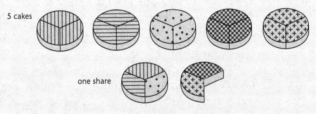

5 cakes

one share

Fig. 13.14 When you have five cakes and three children ...

.

This is a decimal point. You will be used to seeing figures written in decimals. 1.5 means 1½. The decimal point divides the whole number from the fraction. Adding fractions can be quite difficult, but if they are expressed as decimals, the sum can be easily done. Press 5, ÷, 3, = on your calculator to see what 1⅔ is in decimal notation. The same sort of system works to the right of the decimal point as to the left. You will know that the first place to the left of the decimal point represents units, the next tens, the next hundreds, and so on. As you move one place to the left, you multiply by 10. Once you move to the right of the decimal point, exactly the same applies. But because you are now travelling right instead of left, each shift away from the decimal point means a *division* by 10. Thus 1.5 means 1 and ⁵⁄₁₀, 1.05 means 1 and ⁵⁄₁₀₀, etc.

It is very easy to work with decimals on a calculator, as they work in exactly the same way as whole numbers. As long as you remember to insert a decimal point at the right place in each number, the calculator will do the rest. You merely have to remember that your calculator will not be able to cope with a mixture of additions and multiplications if it is a cheap one, and you will have to work out the multiplications or divisions first, before inserting the result into the sum you give to the machine. If you are working in decimals without your calculator, you must remember to line up the decimal points. Thus in adding 101.75 and 1.003 you will get:

$$101.75 +$$
$$\underline{1.003}$$
$$102.753$$

In this way, you are adding units to units, $\frac{1}{10}$ths to $\frac{1}{10}$ths, and so on.

If you want to add a string of fractions on a cheap calculator, you will again start to confuse it. To get around this, use the memory. Each time you work out a fraction as a decimal, add it into the memory. The button usually says $\boxed{M+}$ for this. If one of the fractions is to be subtracted, press the $\boxed{M-}$ button. When you have finished, you can access the result with the memory recall, probably $\boxed{MR}$, button.

$\boxed{\%}$

Percentage, or per cent. This is a fraction expressed in $\frac{1}{100}$ths. Thus 1 is $\frac{100}{100}$ths or 100%, half is $\frac{50}{100}$ths or 50%, etc. This is very similar to working in the first two numbers to the right of the decimal point, and has the same advantages as does using decimals. It is very hard to see how $\frac{11}{13}$, $\frac{27}{31}$, and $\frac{6}{7}$ relate to each other. If you express them as percentages it is very easy to see which is biggest, or to add or subtract them. Use your calculator to find out what a variety of fractions are in percentages. You will probably be able to do this by pressing say $\boxed{1}$, $\boxed{\div}$, $\boxed{4}$, $\boxed{\%}$ to get $\frac{1}{4}$ as a percentage. Start with something you know first, like $\frac{1}{2}$, to check that these are the right buttons.

$\boxed{=}$

You will have been happily using the $\boxed{=}$, or 'equals' button on your calculator if you have been trying out simple sums as suggested above. Equations always contain an equals sign. It means that everything to one side of it is the same as everything to the other side. More of this later.

$\boxed{2}$

The power of two, or squared. Little numbers up in the air to the right of a number or letter mean that it has been multiplied by itself, the number of terms in the multiplication being given by the number. Thus 2^2 means 2×2, and 3^2 means 3×3. We call this 'squared', or 'to the power 2'. If the little number is a 3 we call it 'cubed', or 'to the power 3'. 4^3 is $4 \times 4 \times 4$. 10^3 is 1000. After this we run out of special terms, and are reduced to speaking of 'to the power 7' or whatever. What do you think you get when you multiply two powers of a single number? Try it with $10^2 \times 10^3$. You will find you get 100 000, or 10^5. This always works. You can simply add the powers together if you are multiplying two powers of a single number. Remember this, as it has all sorts of uses. By the same token, you can *divide* a power of a number by another power of that number by subtracting the second index from the first. Thus $2^3 \div 2^2 = 2$, or $10^{12} \div 10^8 = 10^4$.

There are two funny indices, the power 0 and the power 1. Try to work out what these must mean, remembering that to *multiply* powers you *add* the indices. Raising a number to the power 1 must therefore mean using the number as it stands. 5^3 must be the product of 5^1 and 5^2. But you know that 5×5^2 is 5^3, so 5^1 must be 5. By the same token, $5^0 \times 5^2$ should be 5^2. But the only thing that you can multiply 5^2 by to get 5^2 is 1, so 5^0, or indeed anything to the power nought, must be 1.

$\boxed{\sqrt{}}$

Square root. This is the number which multiplied by itself gives you the number you first thought of. Thus $\sqrt{9}$ is the number which, when squared, gives the answer 9, i.e. 3. Press $\boxed{8}$,$\boxed{1}$,$\boxed{\sqrt{}}$ on your calculator to find the square root of 81. You should be able to work out what the index number, or power, of a square root is. Stop for a minute and try.

If you are stuck, remember that to multiply two powers you *add* the index numbers. And the index for a number itself is 1. This will only work if each index is ½. Thus $\sqrt{4} \times \sqrt{4} = 4 = 4^{1/2} \times 4^{1/2}$.

Just as you can find squares, cubes, fourth powers, etc. so you can find cube roots, fourth roots, etc. Cube roots are written as $^3\sqrt{x}$ or $x^{1/3}$, fourth roots as $^4\sqrt{x}$ or $x^{1/4}$, etc. Work out $^4\sqrt{16}$ on your calculator.

You will not have found a '$^4\sqrt{}$' key, but you knew that a fourth root is the square root of a square root, so if you could not do the sum in your head, you could press $\boxed{1}$,$\boxed{6}$,$\boxed{\sqrt{}}$,$\boxed{\sqrt{}}$, giving the answer 2.

If you still feel a bit bemused you will find it helpful to find squares, and square roots, and cubes and fourth powers of a variety of numbers, writing down each number with its square or whatever, until you get the feel for how such numbers relate. You can check your squares by finding their square roots to see that these are what they ought to be, or your square roots by multiplying them by themselves.

This exhausts the signs on a cheap calculator. Scientific calculators have a much wider range of keys, offering all sorts of facilities, including the ability to do calculations involving mixed additions and multiplications without getting muddled. Even better are the financial calculators, which allow you to derive values for things like net present value at the press of a button, instead of sweating blood working these out by hand as did earlier generations of students. You will doubtless want to invest in one of these calculators once you start your MBA accounting courses, but while you are just gaining confidence, you might actually be better off with a simple cheap calculator: there is less to confuse you.

Other mathematical signs you will frequently encounter include the following.

$\boxed{x}$

x or indeed any other letter. This is referred to as a variable, and appears in an equation to indicate something that can take a number of values, or whose value you do not know. Although some people are put off by the appearance of a letter in an equation, in fact you treat it just like a number, and can move it around in the same way. Of course, if you want, say, to multiply it by 2, you can't write in a new number, but you can work with, say, $2x$, quite happily. Indeed it is often very much simpler to play with letters in an equation than with numbers, which explains their popularity. When we deal with equations in more detail you will see why.

13

Using numbers

This means the mean value of x, the value gained by adding all values of x and dividing by the number of such values.

The Greek letter sigma, used to indicate the sum of. You will often see something of the form $\sum_{n=1}^{r} x_n$. This indicates that there are a series of values of x, which have been called for convenience x_1, x_2, x_3, all the way up to x_r. You are to add all these values for x_1 through to x_r. Thus you could express a year's sales figures as the sum of the monthly totals, x_1 to x_{12}, written as $\sum_{n=1}^{12} x_n$, or the second quarter's total as $\sum_{n=4}^{6} x_n$. The notation may look clumsy and forbidding, but is often an economical way of expressing something in an equation.

$\int (\ldots)\, dx$ denotes integration with respect to x. (The symbol for an integration is an s, because integration is essentially summation.)

This means 'function'. If we say $y = f(x)$ we mean that y varies in some way as x varies, or it is a *function* of x. It could be $2x$, or $x + 10\,000$, or anything else involving x. You could, for example, write $v = f(l,b)$ to indicate that the volume (v) of a room depends upon its length (l) and breadth (b). (It also depends on its height, which you are choosing not to mention.) This is one of the favourites among those who like to repeat their text in equation form. Unless they specify what the function *is*, their complicated-looking expressions are unlikely to communicate more than their verbal description.

This simply means 'not equal to'. If you write $x \neq y$, you are saying that x *cannot* take the same value as y.

This means 'less than'. If $x < y$, then x is less than y.

This means 'greater than'. If $x > y$, then x is greater than y. It is easy to remember which is which, as in both signs the wider part of the wedge is pointing to the larger number.

$\boxed{\leqslant}$

This means 'less than or equal to'. If $x \leqslant y$, then x cannot be greater than y, though it could be the same value, or smaller.

$\boxed{\geqslant}$

Obviously this means 'greater than, or equal to'.

$\boxed{(\,)}$

Brackets. These are very important in equations. If things are in a bracket, it means that they must be treated as a whole. $2(7 + 6x + y)$ means that you must multiply *everything in the bracket* by two, for example. Here you would get $14 + 12x + 2y$. Also, $(5+3) \times 2$ tells you to do the addition first.

Answers to Exercises

Exercise 13.1

(a) 0.75, 0.8571428, 1.3333333, 1.7142857, 0.8181818, 0.75.

(b) 200%, 75%, 133%, 91%, 25%, 67% (taking the nearest whole percentage as the answer).

(c) 8, 196, 81, 81, 1728, 1, 1.

(d) 2^7, 3^2, 10^0, 17^8, 21^{18}, x^5, x^{y-2}, $z^{2(x+y)}$.

(e) 4, 12, 6, 6.16, 1.41, 3.16 (giving answers to two decimal places).

(f) 2^8, 10^1, $3^{\frac{3}{4}}$ x^1y^1 (or xy), z^2.

(g) 6.

(h)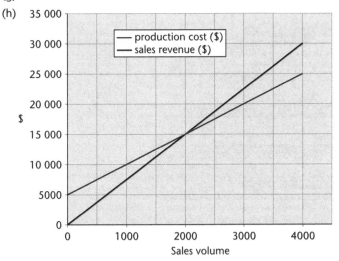

(i) ii, iii.

(j) $2x + 2y$, $3x - 3y^2$, $3y - 3x$, 0, y.

(k) neither

(l) 13, 17, $x + \dfrac{x^2}{y}$, 3.88 to two places of decimals.

If you had more than one or two (careless) mistakes you should take time to work through relevant parts of the Helpfile. You will also know which parts of the chapter will need most attention.

Exercise 13.2

61.55, 52.95.

Exercise 13.3

(a) mean 5.44, median 5, mode 5

(b) mean 5.44, median 4, mode 1.

13

Using numbers

Exercise 13.4

Marker 1, ranked scores: 20, 30, 40, 50, 51, 54, 55, 55, 57, 60, 61, 69, 70, 70, 75, 75, 80, 81, 83, 95
Marker 2, ranked scores: 40, 41, 42, 42, 43, 46, 47, 49, 49, 49, 50, 51, 55, 60, 60, 60, 63, 67, 70, 75.

Note: when there is no single mid-point you usually average the two mid-points (highlighted above) to give a median or quartile value. Thus the interquartile range for Marker 1 is 52.5–75, and for Marker 2 is 42.5–60.

Exercise 13.6

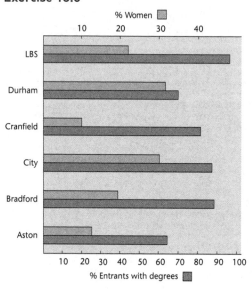

The chart shows one possibility. But it does give a false impression of the percentage of women, so you might have preferred to use the same scale for both. It would depend on whether you were primarily interested in the differences in each type of percentage *between* the schools, or the differences between the two percentages in each case.

Exercise 13.7

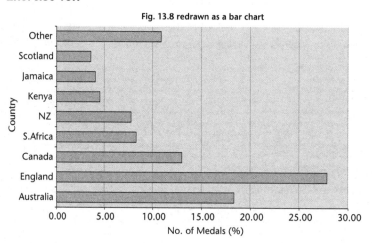

Fig. 13.8 redrawn as a bar chart

Exercise 13.8

(a)

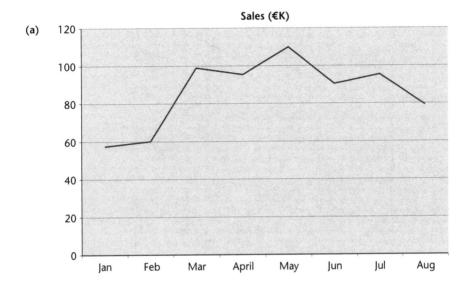

(b)

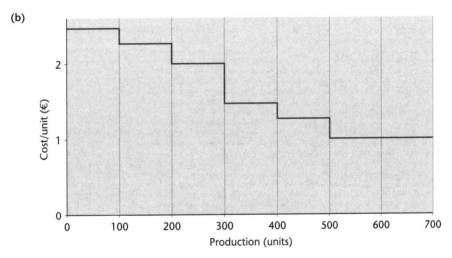

Exercise 13.9

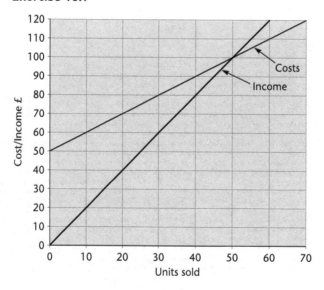

You can see from this that you will break even when you sell 50 units.

(If you sell n units, income is $2n$, while costs are $n + 50$. Thus you break even when n is such that $2n = n + 50$. Subtracting n from each side of the equation shows that this must be when $n = 50$.)

Exercise 13.10

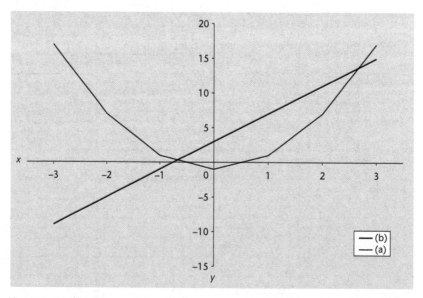

You can see that there are two solutions, one somewhere near $x = -0.7$ and $y = 0.5$, and another around $x = 2.7$ and $y = 13.5$. (Note: line (a) would ideally be a smooth curve, getting smoother the more values of x – i.e. intermediate fractions – you plotted).

Exercise 13.11

(a)

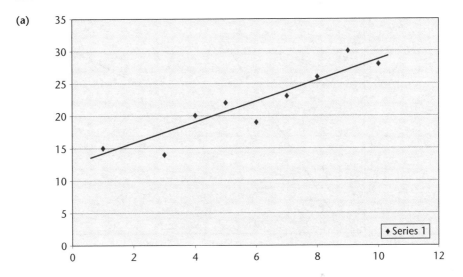

(b)

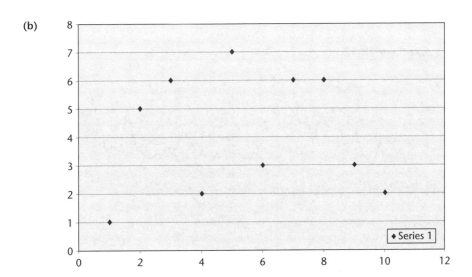

No line is shown: these data points do not appear to lie on a line

13

Using numbers

(c)

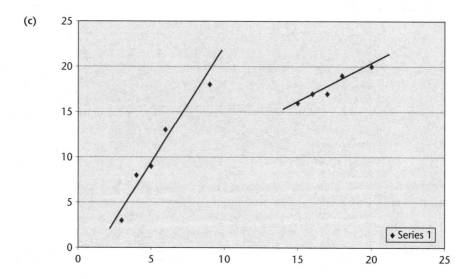

While a single line **could** be fitted to these points, visual inspection suggests two lines are more appropriate, as shown.

Exercise 13.12

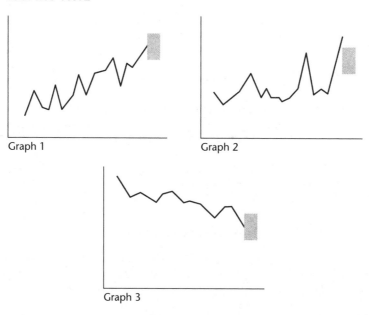

Graph 1

Graph 2

Graph 3

The shading in the graphs shows the broad areas that are reasonable. If the end of your line lies outside this area, you should ask yourself whether you have been unduly influenced by recent variations in the graph.

Exercise 13.13

(a) My rough guess was 8600. Actual figure, 8689.
(b) My rough guess was 4100. Actual figure, 4507.7.
(c) My guess was 10 000 000. Actual figure, 9 850 028.3.
(d) My guess was 107. Actual figure, 111.95.

Perhaps your guesses were better!

Exercise 13.14

1.63, 4.00, 7164.23, 51.11, 1.66.

Exercise 13.15

£76. It doesn't matter which way round the discounts are calculated. You pay £0.95 × 0.80 × 100 (or £0.80 × 0.95 × 100), and it makes no difference what order numbers appear in a multiplication.

Exercise 13.16

(a) $\frac{2}{3}$　(b) $\frac{3}{4}$　(c) $\frac{2}{3}$　(d) 2　(e) $\frac{4}{3}$ or $1\frac{1}{3}$　(f) $\frac{3}{4}$　(g) $\frac{1}{2}$

Exercise 13.17

(a) $\frac{1}{5}$　(b) $\frac{1}{3}$　(c) $\dfrac{1}{y(1 + y)}$　(d) $\frac{1}{4}$　(e) $\dfrac{1}{x}$　(f) $\dfrac{(y + 1)}{10}$　(g) $\dfrac{xy}{2}$

Exercise 13.18

(a) $\frac{1}{8}$　(b) $\frac{1}{9}$

Exercise 13.19

(a) $\frac{2}{9}$　(b) $\dfrac{3y}{2x}$　(c) $\dfrac{3(x + 4)}{(x + 1)(x + 2)}$　(d) $\dfrac{5(y + 1)}{4x\,(x + 1)}$　(e) $\dfrac{9x}{8y}$

Exercise 13.20

(a) $\frac{13}{8}$ or $1\frac{5}{8}$　(b) $\dfrac{(3y + 4x)}{xy}$　(c) $\dfrac{(3x - 1)}{y}$　(d) $\dfrac{(9x + 10)}{15}$　(e) $\frac{3}{8}$

(f) $\dfrac{y(5x + 1)^2 + x^2y}{x(5x + 1)}$　or　$\dfrac{26x^2y + 10xy + 1}{x(5x + 1)}$　(g) $\dfrac{[5(x - 2) - 3(x - 1)]}{(x - 1)\,(x - 2)}$　or　$\dfrac{(2x - 7)}{(x - 1)\,(x - 2)}$

Exercise 13.21

(a) 32%　(b) 32:100 or $\frac{32}{100}$ (or 0.32:1)　(c) 47% or 0.47:1 (or 128:272)

Exercise 13.22

(a) 12.5%　(b) 198%　(c) 33.1%　(d) (4%) – a negative return

Exercise 13.23

	Mean investment	ROCE
(a)	317.5	14%
(b)	140	236%
(c)	7900	28%
(d)	5550	(1%)

Exercise 13.24

Sales.

Exercise 13.25

(a) 2   (b) 1.14   (c) 0.67   (d) 1.75

Exercise 13.26

$D_2 = £1322.50$, $D_3 = £1520.87$

Exercise 13.27

(a) £2260   (b) £2343.75   (c) £20 113.57

Exercise 13.28

(a) $x = 2y - 5$ (i) -1 (ii) -11 (iii) -5

(b) $x = \dfrac{(y + 3)}{3}$ (i) ⅔   (ii) 0   (iii) 1

(c) $x = 4$ (i) 4   (ii) 4   (iii) 4

(d) $x = \dfrac{y}{2} - 6$ (i) -5 (ii) $-7\frac{1}{2}$ (or $-\frac{15}{2}$)   (iii) -6

(e) $x = \dfrac{3}{y}$ (i) ½   (ii) -1 (iii) infinity (or undefined)

(f) $x = y^2 + \frac{1}{2}y$ or $y(y+\frac{1}{2})$ (i) 5   (ii) $7\frac{1}{2}$ (iii) 0

(g) $x = \dfrac{y}{4} - 3$ (i) $-2\frac{1}{2}$ (ii) $-3\frac{3}{4}$ (iii) -3

(h) $x = (y + 4)(3y + 1)$ (i) 42   (ii) -8 (iii) 4

Exercise 13.29

(a) $6ab + 4ac$

(b) $3xy - 2xz$

(c) $3rs + 6rt + 6rs + 3st$, or $9rs + 6rt + 3st$

(d) $2xy + 4x + y^2 + 2y$

(e) $\dfrac{(3z + 4y)}{4(a + b)}$ (note it was possible to divide top and bottom by $2y + z$)

Exercise 13.30

	A	B	C	D
1		Last year	This year	Percentages
2	Accounting	100	109	109
3	Business studies	230	218	94.78261
4	Computing	200	242	121
5	Design	50	46	92
6	**Total**	580	615	106.0345

SKILLS FOR ASSESSMENT

14 Scoring well in assessment

Learning outcomes

By the end of this chapter you should:

- understand the objectives of your assessors in setting assignments
- appreciate some of the key differences between UK assessment systems and those in some other countries
- be aware of the most common causes of student failure
- have strategies for avoiding these hazards
- understand basic principles of communication in the context of assessent.

INTRODUCTION

Thus far you have concentrated on developing a range of skills which will help you to benefit from your studies, and which will transfer easily to work. Learning to be better at your job is arguably the most important outcome of your studies. But you will also want to pass your courses, perhaps with distinction. Gaining a qualification was probably your initial, and most powerful motive! While you are unlikely to pass a course if you do not learn anything, learning does not, conversely, ensure a pass. You have to be able to *demonstrate* to your examiners that you have learned what they intended!

The aim of the next few chapters is to help you to gain grades that are at least as high as your learning deserves. To do this you need to understand the viewpoint of those who are assessing you, and the characteristics of the types of assessment with which you may be faced. You also need to develop some fairly specific skills in being assessed, although even these may be relevant in some work situations as well.

This chapter looks at general aspects of assessment. It covers the purposes of assessment, the particular challenge of work-based assignments, the common causes of failure on Master's programmes in management, and the general principles of communication which underlie all types of assessment. It looks briefly at the particular challenges faced by graduates from abroad who are studying at Master's level in the UK. Subsequent chapters will deal with more specific types of assessment: written reports; oral presentations; examinations; portfolios and assessment centres; and producing a thesis or dissertation.

CHALLENGES FOR STUDENTS FROM OTHER COUNTRIES

If you gained your degree in a different country from your postgraduate study, under a different educational culture, assessment can present real challenges. You may have language problems – it is one thing to read and understand in the peace of a library, quite another to be able to write an answer to an exam question at speed. There may be less obvious differences that create even greater difficulties. Education systems differ in the way that they expect students to behave. One of the biggest differences is in the degree of critical thought expected. (The idea of critical reading was introduced in Chapter 9.) Master's-level study in the UK typically requires substantial independent study, and independent thinking about what you read. This may be a shock if you come from a country where very little independence of thought is required for first degrees – memory being seen as more important then anything else. If you studied under such a system, you may find assessment in a country like the UK very difficult at first. This chapter should give you a first understanding of the way that assessors' minds may work, and what they are looking for. Read this and the following chapter carefully. You will probably also need to refer frequently to the glossary of terms used

→ Ch 9, 15   in assessment at the end of Chapter 15 (Helpfile 15.1). If you can, take advantage of your tutors' willingness to explain things, and if you do poorly in the first pieces of work you submit, try very hard to get detailed feedback on how you need to change your approach.

Above all, do not feel ashamed if you find this way of working difficult. You are undertaking something extremely challenging in studying in an unfamiliar system. So be open about your difficulties and seek help, whenever and wherever possible. Of course, it makes excellent sense to have done all you can to develop your language skills beforehand, and to have taken full advantage of any induction courses offered. But throughout the course you are likely to find that if you make your needs known, you can get the support you need, from fellow students, from tutors and from others within the university community. And the effort will be worthwhile. Your understanding at the end of the course will have grown far more than will have that of local students. And you will, at the same time, have made a significant contribution to their understanding of the wider context of management.

ASSESSMENT IN CONTEXT

Assessment is a complex area, with many influences acting upon it. The ways in which you are assessed will depend upon the nature of the programme in which you are involved, what it is trying to teach and the views about learning that underpin its design. The approach to assessment may also depend upon where the institution is trying to 'position itself' in the management education market.

Critics of current forms of management education see assessment as a vehicle for policing both tutors and students in a system which demands a high level of conformity from both. From a less critical viewpoint, assessment is both a vehicle for learning and a necessary means of demonstrating that standards are being maintained.

Institutional objectives for assessment

In choosing your course the likely value of the qualification will have been a factor. You would not want to work hard for a degree from an institution which was seen as third rate. Reputations of academic institutions depend upon 'standards' being visibly maintained. Institutions do not wish their graduates to bring the institution into disrepute by their subsequent incompetence or ignorance. Their first objective for assessment is therefore to ensure that their graduates have reached a standard worthy of the qualification awarded.

Second, this concern with standards must be *perceived* by others. Academics want colleagues elsewhere to respect the place where they work. More importantly, institutions want to gain, or keep, a 'seal of approval' from one of the major accrediting bodies: AMBA, EQUIS and the AACSB are the main bodies for MBAs. Recognition by one of the main professional institutions may be equally important for specialist Master's degrees. The recent explosion in postgraduate management education, and in the number of institutions providing it, has made this concern even more pressing. One of the generally accepted ways of maintaining standards, and thus meeting both these objectives, is to have a rigorous structure of assessment, including unseen examinations, with a system of external examiners to maintain comparability between institutions.

There is a third, and perhaps even more important, objective for assessment. Properly designed it can be an 'engine of learning', driving students to exert effort that they would not otherwise exert, providing both carrots (the glow of satisfaction from a good grade) and sticks (the risk of not being allowed to proceed towards a qualification). If the assessment is well designed it will direct that effort into activities that will enhance learning and increase understanding. If students are given detailed feedback on their efforts they will gain understanding of their strengths and weaknesses and will be able to do better in future.

You may curse the assignment that keeps you up until after midnight to meet a deadline, but the pressure may have been necessary to get you to do the work at all. You may hate getting a fail grade on the first piece of work you submit, but will thank it later, when you have remedied whatever weakness caused it, and gone on to do far better next time. (I received one thank-you e-mail which started, 'You may not remember me, but [three years ago] you gave me 38 on my first assignment. I've just got a distinction on my final MBA course. . .'.)

What is assessed

Traditionally examinations were the most important form of assessment. Where teaching is seen as transmitting knowledge, they are an efficient way of testing that students can remember key information, concepts, techniques and theories. This is a common feature of many educational systems. Exams are also good at assessing the ability to construct a reasoned argument from evidence. This tends to be important in UK Master's degrees, but does not feature in all undergraduate examinations, particularly in those emphasising the 'knowledge' aspect of education. Whether intentionally or not, written communication skills are also assessed.

Exams were supplemented by a thesis or dissertation, which allowed research skills and a higher level of analytical skills to be assessed, as well as presenting a greater test of writing skills, and other challenges including time- and project-management.

→ Ch 2

Both these forms of assessment are still widely used today (and have subsequent chapters devoted to them). But as programmes have moved away from the purely 'academic', and become more concerned to develop the range of skills outlined in Chapter 2, the scope of assessment has correspondingly increased. Thus, you may be required (if studying while working) to apply what you have learned to situations you encounter at work. Indeed, many programmes ask for an internal consultancy project rather than a thesis. In either case, 'own-organisation' based assessment presents very specific challenges, dealt with in the next section. You may be required to work on some assignments in a group, perhaps 'meeting' electronically to do this, and be assessed either on your contribution to the effort, or as a whole group with a single mark. Your competence as a manager may be assessed via a portfolio of work-based evidence. Some assessment may be computer based, with automatic scoring of multiple-choice questions.

Thus, 'what is assessed' is changing in two ways. The range of skills which business schools seek to teach, and which therefore needs to be assessed, is widening. The range of ways in which schools attempt to assess these skills is changing in consequence.

Work-based assessment

→ Ch 8

Now that part-time students are in the majority, work-based assignments are common. They allow assessors to test not only your familiarity with concepts and models taught in the course, but your ability to *apply* these concepts appropriately and constructively. This requires a higher level of skill than the writing of an academic essay. Many of these concepts are remarkably simple in themselves. But *using* these concepts to make sense of a complex and confusing situation, and to come to creative conclusions as to what to do about it, may be a real challenge. A key part of that challenge is being sufficiently selective.

Being selective

In compiling a case study (even one that seems huge), the author will not have written down more than a fraction of what *could* have been written. Points will have been selected to be relevant to the intended analysis. In a work-based assignment, however, you may feel you are floundering in a sea of potentially relevant, though perhaps not easily accessible, information. Furthermore, you may be emotionally involved, and there may be things you simply do not 'see' because you take them for granted. It is very difficult to stand back and think dispassionately. You will frequently experience many uncertainties as to what to consider and what to ignore. 'Hard' information from company records may turn out to be surprisingly unreliable. 'Softer' information from interviews or other sources may be biased or present problems of interpretation.

Another problem with own-company work is that it is harder to think up creative options than for a case study. In the case study you will be blessedly unaware of most of the constraints that would apply in reality. In your own organisation you are likely to be all too aware of what has already been tried and failed, or is considered as quite out of the question by significant members of the organisation. Yet, your assessors will still be looking for the ability to come up with such options.

Most management courses at Master's level are concerned with developing strategic skills in a manager. A prerequisite for successful strategy is sensitivity to the wider environment. Your assessors will therefore require you to demonstrate the ability to look beyond your organisational boundaries. You may need to adopt the perspective of a more senior manager in the organisation using information about the environment to inform decision taking. If so, it may help if you check out your perceptions with someone at that level of seniority. If you are doing an in-company project you may need to find someone in such a position who is prepared to be your 'client'. In either case you will develop skills for operating on a different level.

Work-based assignments, especially projects or dissertations, may be longer term than much of the older style of assessment. This, together with the conflicts generated by part-time study, means that you will need highly developed time-management skills.

The shift in emphasis from examinations to assessment based on work-relevant skills demands an even broader range of skills than your assessors may have intended. Convincing your assessors that you can *apply* your learning appropriately to tackle managerial problems in a creative and sound way requires many skills of vital importance to a manager. This will be the case even if these skills are not themselves directly assessed.

COMMON CAUSES OF FAILURE

Outright failure is relatively uncommon on most management-related Master's programmes. It is more common for students to withdraw from a course without completing it. Such withdrawal is another form of failing to meet your original objectives, so it will be considered here. Figure 14.1 (p. 304) shows the pattern of interrelated causes most commonly contributing to either form of failure.

ACTIVITY 14.1

Add to Fig. 14.1 any additional factors which you feel might threaten your own course completion.

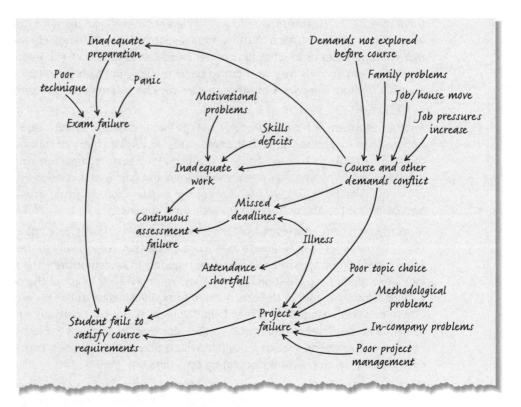

Fig. 14.1 Multiple-cause diagram exploring causes of student failure

Highlight any of the factors on the original diagram (Fig. 14.1) which you feel might be particularly relevant to you.

The factors on the diagram, and presumably any you have added, can be divided into those you can do nothing about, those which with the aid of this book or other assistance you *might* be able to influence, and those where there *is* a remedy, albeit a long-term one.

Environmental changes

In the 'probably unavoidable' category are illness, sudden totally unanticipated change in job demands, redundancy and relationship breakdowns. In some of these cases your studies may themselves be a causal factor. While there is usually little you can do to prevent these disasters, you should take immediate action if they *do* strike. Even if your course is the least of your worries you should inform the college of your problems as soon as they happen.

To minimise the effect of problems:

- keep ahead of schedule
- seek advice at once
- work out coping strategies
- keep tutor informed
- manage your stress.

If warned of problems *before* deadlines are missed, tutors are far more likely to be sympathetic, and may well be able to help you find a way of staying with the course despite your problems. If not, they will probably be able to keep the door open for you so that you can resume your studies when problems are resolved. Most tutors will go to almost any lengths to support and aid students. But they are not psychic, and if the student does not alert them to problems, there is little they can do to help. Keep your tutors fully informed as soon as problems begin to surface.

Some 'avoidable' events you may choose *not* to avoid. Finding a better job, moving to a better house, getting married, or adding to your family are events which put enormous stress on a part-time student, stress which is often underestimated beforehand. If you seriously wish to complete your course, and especially if you want to do well on it, you should think very carefully before risking making life more difficult for yourself. Obviously, you may still wish to go ahead, but do not underestimate the increase in pressure which will result.

Unfortunately(?), the mere fact of studying may increase your chances of a better job, whether in your own organisation or outside. I *have* known students negotiate a delay in promotion until they have finished their course, while others have deliberately suspended their habit of looking at job advertisements, but not everyone wants to do this: think carefully about the strategy that is right for *you*.

If things happen to put extra pressure on you, and you want to continue studying, you should seek advice straight away. The longer you delay, the fewer the options that may be open to you. And keep your tutors informed of the situation. If you have worked out a coping strategy with them, they will want to know that this is the right one, and that you are (or indeed are not) in control of the situation.

Skill deficits

One of the commonest causes of failure, especially in the stress of an examination, is the inability to 'answer the question'. By this, I mean the particular question asked, all parts of that question and the right number of questions. This can also apply with continuous assessment, though usually less catastrophically. If you have developed critical reading skills, such misinterpretation is less likely. You can further increase your chances of answering what is intended by following the advice in this section. (Written

→ Ch 15, 17 assignments are dealt with in the next chapter, and examinations in Chapter 17.)

Difficulties with time-management and communication, achieving a good balance between theory and 'reality' and dealing with numbers, though slightly more problematic, can be overcome. There are suggestions on all these areas within this book, and if you are worried about your writing ability or other personal skills you should devote some time to developing these, preferably before the course starts.

If you have not yet started to study, and are planning to enter a postgraduate programme on the strength of your managerial experience rather than your educational qualifications, you may be worried about whether you will cope. There may be courses locally available that could help you develop the necessary skills. Before committing yourself, however, check with your intended college as to skill levels they think are required. You may find that you are worrying unnecessarily: their expectations may be far lower than you think.

In the unlikely event that your educational background does turn out to be more of a handicap than you anticipated, and makes it impossible to get passing grades, it is very important that you see this as merely a failure on assessment criteria, not failure as a manager. The point has already been made that institutions are as yet a long way from being able to assess competence with much reliability. I have known several excellent managers fail courses, even in areas of their own special expertise. Personnel managers have failed human resource management courses, senior marketing managers have failed marketing courses.

This in no sense meant that they were less than good at their job. Rather, they had problems in areas specific to Master's-level assessment, usually either exam technique or with developing an argument from evidence and theory and communicating this argument clearly in writing. In the first area, there is clearly no relationship between this and on-the-job performance. The inability to argue from evidence might be a serious skill deficit in many jobs, but not every managerial role demands it, so it may not be interfering with their current job performance.

If you find that your chosen programme is too much of a challenge, you might wish to think about transferring to a course at a lower level. This might develop your assessment-related skills at a more leisurely pace and prepare you to for successful post-graduate study.

You may decide to persevere with your course, despite initial difficulties, in the reasonable hope that your skills will develop as you go along. If you fail in the end, disappointment will be inevitable: you have not gained your initial objective. But gaining a Master's is not everything and there is no need to feel a sense of personal failure. Instead, dwell on what you have *gained* from your studies. You may well have learned more than some of those who passed.

So do not let fear of failure cause you to drop out silently if the course turns out to be tougher than expected. Instead, discuss any such fears with your tutors and, if appropriate, with your employer. Once you know all the options open to you it will be easier to see what is the best course of action for *you*, the one which will have the greatest beneficial effect on your personal development as a manager.

Dissertations/projects/theses

As you can see from Fig. 14.1, dissertations are a particularly high-risk part of the programme, with many different factors capable of contributing to failure in this aspect. Even students who have coped well with the earlier part of the course may find difficulty with the greater freedom and longer timescales involved, and the need for a high level of independence in directing their work.

Projects based on in-company research are singularly vulnerable to changes within the company concerned which are outside your control. In the extreme case you can lose your job halfway through your research, thereby losing access to further data. Equally devastating to the project, if not to yourself, is the discovery that the part of the organisation you are researching is under threat, or about to close. Other threats occur if your in-company 'client' leaves, and is replaced by someone antagonistic to the project, or if your project topic suddenly becomes highly sensitive.

→ Ch 19   The risk of many of these happening may be minimised by careful topic selection. This is dealt with in Chapter 19. If, despite care at this stage, things go wrong, then you should follow the earlier advice of seeking guidance from your tutor or supervisor at once.

Motivation

The remaining major cause of failure is loss of motivation. You might find that it requires far more effort than you expected to get the grades you want. Or the prospect of giving up your free time for two or three years may become increasingly unattractive. Once the immediate excitement of starting the course has worn off, there may seem to be few rewards along what is a very long path.

Full-time students can find their motivation is flagging at times, but it is generally less of a problem for them. They are eating, sleeping (if not a lot) and breathing their MBA or other course, surrounded and supported by other students and faculty. Much of their learning takes place through group work. The course is shorter. The conflicts are simpler, usually between work and sleep, not between work, job and family.

Part-time students are faced with a longer course of study, much of which may be done in isolation. There will be pressures and conflicts every day, these being subject to unpredictable variation. If these pressures mean that you cannot study as much as you anticipated, and that you are getting lower grades than you hoped, these grades will be disincentives to further work, rather than rewards.

Motivational resources:

■ your teachers

■ fellow students

■ yourself.

The three main sources of motivational 'recharging' are your teachers, fellow students and yourself. Institutions vary enormously in the amount of support and contact they offer students, and in the extent to which contact with fellow students is encouraged or even possible. As both types of contact can be great boosts to enthusiasm, ensure that you take full advantage of what *is* available. Make the effort to attend all face-to-face sessions on offer, even if the quality of the lecturer's input is variable: there are other benefits in terms of contact with your fellow students. In any case, merely voting with your feet will not bring about improvements. Remember, you (or your employers) will have paid a considerable sum for your course. If you do feel you are not getting value for that money, you should make your feelings known.

If you are dissatisfied with any aspect of your programme, make that dissatisfaction known. This will allow the institution to do something to improve the situation. Many colleges are still poor at training lecturers and monitoring the quality of their work. Unless students complain, there will be no way for a problem to come to light.

If your institution provides you with a personal counsellor or academic adviser (terms vary), then this person can help with motivational as well as other problems. You should feel no inhibitions about seeking help. This will not be held against you, nor affect your grades in any way other than positively; if you encounter real problems this adviser can argue for these being taken into consideration when your final marks are decided.

The value of self-help groups

→ Ch 11

If at all possible, try to develop informal contacts with other students. Informal study groups, often called 'self-help' groups, are one of the most powerful antidotes to 'motivation droop'. Such groups were discussed earlier, and your institution may be able to help in various ways, such as by releasing student names or giving guidance on how to run such groups. There was a very simple list of such guidelines given at the end of Chapter 11.

Self-help groups are particularly valuable for management students. Much of the excitement of the course will come in seeing how the ideas can make sense of organisational situations, and from seeing how many more options there can be in a situation than you realised. By learning more about other organisations you can broaden your awareness considerably. Other students can be a source of more information on these things than the official course material, so do try to 'exploit' this source.

Discussing the application of course concepts with fellow students will make the ideas come alive in a way that relying on your own experience may not. It can also be reassuring to find that, when you experience difficulty with a part of the course, you are not alone. A commiseration session when the going gets tough can be highly encouraging, as well as cathartic.

If group members come from different specialisms, you will have a range of help on offer. For example, MBA groups often contain students with backgrounds in accounting, marketing, HR and several other areas. As part of such a mixed group, you can receive (and offer) supplementary tuition in areas of need and expertise. Thus when you do hit a problem and perhaps cannot contact a lecturer for help, you have access to a friendly coach.

If there are no other willing students locally, you may be able to gain some of the benefits by starting a discussion group with interested colleagues at work. They will gain second-hand benefit from your studies, while giving you valuable motivational support. If you are being supported by your employer, your training manager may be interested in setting up such a group, as a way of increasing the return on their investment in your course fees. If not, you might be able to make informal arrangements with other managers with whom you feel comfortable.

→ Ch 11

If you are on a distance learning programme, your course will probably use on-line discussion groups of some form, so distance will be no obstacle to interacting informally with fellow students. Such discussion can be immensely useful, and the ability to share experiences across continents can be a major advantage of such a programme. Chapter 11 offers ideas for effective virtual group work.

The final source of help for drooping motivation lies within yourself. This may sound about as helpful as the suggestion to a depressive that he 'snap out of it', or advice to use your bootstraps for self-elevation, but it *is* feasible. The algorithm shown in Fig. 14.2 summarises the procedure involved. The item 'Analyse possibilities for improving situation' is the key.

Obviously, the way you go about improving your motivation will depend on the underlying problem. Common problems are:

Problem: You have been working far too hard, allowing no time for exercise or relaxation, and are physically and mentally jaded.

Remedy: Build in 'treats', and schedule time off, some of it for enjoyable exercise.

Problem: You have received lower grades than you had hoped, and your ego feels somewhat bruised.

Remedy: Reassess your objectives. If passing is your main objective, middling grades will get you the qualification just as well as high ones. Consider what else you were achieving in that period that was competing with your studies for your time. Applaud yourself for the full range of your achievements during the period.

Problem: Your studies seem to stretch forward into the distant and dismal future, and you really don't know whether you are making any progress.

Remedy: Assess progress to date. Look at early assignments and see how much better you could do now. Review your study log/personal development file if you have been keeping one. (If not, start such a log.) Set interim targets for the course.

Problem: You can't see what the course has to do with your job.

Remedy: Talk to your tutor and your training officer, mentor or superior in your organisation. Make active efforts to find links. Talk to other students to see whether they have the same feeling.

Problem: You are being sabotaged by resistance, overt or covert, from colleagues or family.

Remedy: Consider whether you are collaborating in the sabotage. If so, think again about why *you* want a Master's degree, and be firmer about sticking to your goals. Discuss the problem in a positive way with the sources of the resistance. People may be unaware of it, or of the strength of their feelings. You may be equally unaware of the demands you are making on them, or of other changes in your attitudes.

Motivational problems are among the hardest to solve, but provided your original objectives are still valid, it should be possible to regenerate at least some of your original enthusiasm.

14

Scoring well in assessment

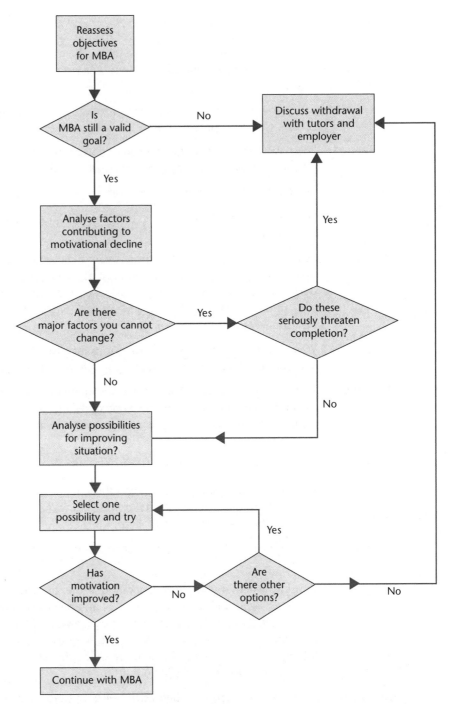

Fig. 14.2 Algorithm for tackling motivational problems on an MBA (or other course)

ASSESSMENT AS COMMUNICATION

In doing an assignment or an examination the effectiveness with which you communicate will affect your grade in two ways. First, because communication is an important aspect of management, you will be penalised if you show weakness in this area. Second, your tutor can only give marks for what you succeed in communicating. If you fail to demonstrate the extent of your knowledge and understanding because of communication problems, you will not gain marks for it. It is therefore important that you understand the principles governing any form of communication. You also need to take steps to develop your skills in those types of communication most necessary for Master's-level study. This will be particularly important if you know (or discover) your communication skills to be weak.

No assessor will be unduly concerned with your literary skills. Examiners are not looking for an ability to use a wide vocabulary or complex grammatical forms, or to evoke depths and nuances of emotion in your reader. And if it is clear that English is not your first language, tutors will normally be very tolerant of spelling and grammar faults. But your language must allow you to put across the message that you intend, in a manner suitable to your target audience. You need understandable, plain English, supplemented by whatever visual aids will strengthen your message. This point is developed in Chapter 15.

→ Ch 15

ACTIVITY 14.3

Think of the last time that you were unhappy with the effectiveness of a communication you either sent or received. Jot down the aspects which contributed to your lack of satisfaction.

_____

_____

_____

_____

_____

_____

The chances are that your dissatisfaction concerned either the substance of the communication, or the manner in which it was communicated. This distinction is worth bearing in mind. It is also worth remembering that there are two distinct parties to any communication, the sender or originator of the message, and the receiver or intended audience. Figure 14.3 shows these aspects.

Figure 14.3 is a simple, even simplistic diagram. But it illustrates the way in which such simple frameworks can act as a sort of shopping list, ensuring that you direct your attention to all of the relevant aspects of a situation. Thus the diagram makes the point that, in planning an effective communication, you need to pay attention to these four

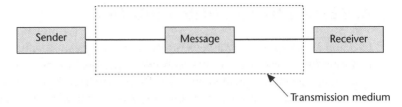

Fig. 14.3 The elements of communication

elements. It does not tell you what to do about them, but can act as a starting point for generating relevant questions. Some examples follow.

Sender

What are your objectives? Unless *you* are clear as to these, they are unlikely to be achieved. Is your goal to impress, inform or influence, or a combination of these? What characteristics or attributes do you have that are relevant to the situation? For example, are you much better at face-to-face spoken communication or writing? Do you tend to overcomplicate matters, assume more knowledge in your audience than is reasonable, or antagonise others without intention? Are you particularly good at explaining the meaning of figures, or making implications of a situation clear, or bringing others to see your view? Once you know your own strengths and weaknesses you can use that information to make your communication more effective.

Receiver

What are the receiver's objectives? Are they congruent with yours, or in conflict with them? Is the receiver happier with some forms of communication than others? At work you may have subordinates who do not read easily, or a boss who insists you put everything in writing. There may be an organisational style of report writing your boss will expect you to follow. Different lecturers will have preferences for one style over another. Is there a constraint on the length of a communication? Many busy managers refuse to look at anything that cannot convince them in a one-page summary that it is worth their time. Assignments may have word limits. Some audiences may have very short attention spans.

The message

Is what you have to communicate simple information, or is it an interpretation of information? If the latter, how compelling is that interpretation? Do the facts 'speak for themselves'? If so, how many of the facts are necessary to achieve this effect? How important is quantitative information as part of the message? Can it be presented in a way that increases its significance? Are relationships a key part of the message? In this case diagrams will probably be necessary.

In any course assessment you need to remember that the overall message must be that you have absorbed relevant concepts, techniques and information, and can use these appropriately to perform well as a manager, or at least to take sensible decisions in a real or simulated managerial situation. Check that you have made your use of course concepts sufficiently explicit.

The channel

→ Ch 18

For course assessments, the communication channel will normally be prescribed: a written document of a certain length; an oral presentation; or a written or viva voce examination. These may sometimes be supplemented by examples of work you have produced in your job (*see* Chapter 18), where the prescription may be more general. In communication at work, the range of options may be much greater. If you are unhappy with a superior's decision, do you raise the matter 'in passing', in the course of other discussions, send a brief e-mail saying you are unhappy about certain aspects and would like to discuss them, or write an extensive analysis of why the decision is faulty, sending it to everyone in the organisation right up to the chairman? (This is assuming that you do not deem it wiser to keep quiet!)

Whatever your choice, you will need to bear the characteristics of your chosen channel in mind. It is worth recalling that however they are transmitted, messages tend to lose something in the transmission. You probably played 'Chinese whispers' as a child. Any ambiguity in the message received (due in that case to the difficulty of hearing the whisper) will be acted upon by predispositions in the receiver, with additional distortion at each link in the chain. Similar distortions can accumulate at work. If new working arrangements are communicated in over-sophisticated language by a boss, they may be interpreted by the audience as another attempt to screw the workers, whatever the actual message intended. A message 'cascaded' through several layers of management may be subtly transformed at each stage.

Unfortunately this carries through into assessment. The lecturer faced with an assignment or exam paper presented in poor handwriting or with lots of keying errors, and in unclear English, is likely to put down an ambiguous statement to failure to understand a key point. The same ambiguity in a correctly typed, well-laid-out piece of work might be interpreted much more charitably, with the marker feeling sure that the student *really* knew it, but hasn't made it quite clear.

It is essential to be aware of the ease of losses in transmission, and to adopt strategies for avoiding these. For example, underlining key words, including diagrams of key relationships, and making a clear *brief* statement of a complex point before you immerse yourself in the full complexity, can all help to reduce such losses for written messages. Signposting the structure of your argument at the outset and supplementing spoken messages with visual materials can also help. These may be transient, for example displayed slides, or permanent handouts or notices.

If you are aware of the elements that must be considered if you are to communicate successfully, and if you are absolutely clear about your objectives and those of your audience before you start, and if you *plan* your assignments with as much attention to these factors as to the specific points required in each assessment, you should find that your grades are much improved. Subsequent chapters address points specific to particular forms of communication, such as written reports and oral presentations.

14

Scoring well in assessment

SUMMARY

- Your assessors will wish to be convinced that you have absorbed, and can appropriately use, information, skills and techniques taught by the course.

- This means that you will need to do more than merely reproduce things from memory, even if this was the focus of assessment on your first degree.

- They will want to know that you can identify significant factors in a situation or its environment, and use what you have learned to solve managerial problems, generating and evaluating a sufficiently broad range of options and making sensible recommendations.

- They will want to be assured that you can communicate your arguments in a clear and convincing fashion, using appropriate communication forms.

- Above all, they will not want to give you a qualification if they feel that your competence at the end of the course is so low as to cast doubt on the credibility of their teaching, or of the qualification in general.

- Student failure is uncommon, and more often due to failure to complete the course than failure on assessment.

- If problems do occur, whether caused by external factors, or those arising from your own characteristics, discuss these with your tutor at once, and possibly with your superior or training manager too.

- If you have difficulty sustaining motivation, analyse the reasons and seek all the support you can, from your tutors, your organisation, and, most importantly, from fellow students.

- In the highly unlikely event of your deciding to withdraw or failing on a component of assessment, it is important to see this as something specific to the course, and in no way as casting doubt on your managerial abilities or potential.

- Plan all your assessed work from the perspective of seeking to communicate successfully, bearing in mind your own objectives and characteristics, those of your audience and characteristics of the message intended, and the channel by which it is to be communicated.

→ 15 Writing assignments and reports

Learning outcomes

By the end of this chapter you should:

- appreciate the importance of clear written communications
- understand the importance of clarifying requirements for an assessment
- recognise plagiarism, and know how, and why, to avoid it
- know how to generate a range of initial ideas
- be able to structure these to produce an initial outline of your report, with appropriate subheadings
- be able to expand these into a first draft, using clear English, ways of showing numbers clearly and diagrams where appropriate
- be able to develop this into a well-presented final draft
- be improving your spelling and grammar, if these are problematic.

INTRODUCTION

Written communication skills are crucial for managers: they are likely to contribute significantly to your future career success. Documents you have written (whether paper based or electronic) may be widely circulated. A good report is likely to impress both superiors and clients. Much of your assessment is likely to be based upon what you write, so your skills in this area will have an equally strong influence on your success in your course.

Assignments need to fully address the question and be:

- in appropriate style and format
- well structured
- clearly argued
- evidenced
- based on theory
- your own work.

To do well in written assignments you need first to understand precisely what is being asked. Then you need to construct an answer which is well structured, is clearly argued, covers the necessary ground and is in an appropriate style and format. Reports are still the most common form for substantial management communications, and some of your assignments will probably need to be produced in this format. Even where a report is not asked for, you are likely to find that a similar, clear structure will greatly improve your work.

This chapter covers the interpretation of questions. It deals with assignment planning, written communication in general and the use of a report format. For those finding written assignments particularly challenging there are several supplementary Helpfiles at the end of the chapter. A glossary of terms commonly used in assignments is given as Helpfile 15.1. Helpfile 15.2 covers the basics of spelling, and Helpfile 15.3, punctuation and grammar. Helpfile 15.4 is specifically for non-native English speakers. Turn to the appropriate Helpfile if you know that your grammar or spelling is prone to 'wobble', if tutors or other readers complain that they are not sure what you mean, or if your grades on written assignments seem lower than you feel you deserve.

→ Ch 10, 12   Other chapters are also highly relevant to producing good written work. These include those on use of diagrams and on working with case studies. For group assignments the chapter on working in teams will be relevant. For substantial reports, in the context of
→ Ch 19   dissertations or projects, you will also need Chapter 19.

ASSIGNMENT PLANNING

To plan, you need to be clear about the administrative side of what is required: for example, the submission deadline, the word limit, the required format. But there is a more substantive side to requirements. What actually is it that you are asked to write? What is the question that you are to address? Success demands that you identify both these aspects of your objectives, and then plan carefully to ensure that you have the time, resources and so on needed to meet them. Guidelines for such planning are outlined below, and discussed in more detail in the text that follows.

Assignment planning guidelines

- Identify 'administrative' requirements.
- 'Deconstruct' the question to identify precisely what is required.
- Identify 'strands' or themes.
- Identify theory/concepts relevant to themes.
- Work out a structure for answer.
- Plan time and other resources.
- Identify interim targets/review points.
- Follow your plan!

Administrative requirements and constraints

It is usually simple to identify administrative requirements, but this does not mean they are unimportant. As many marks are lost because of failure to submit work on time, to keep within word limits, writing an essay when a report is asked for, or submitting work to the wrong place, as are lost because of academic shortcomings.

So make sure that you have identified such requirements. *Note assignment deadlines in your diary, or electronic or wall calendar to ensure that you do not forget them.* Then plan the actions needed to meet them. Such planning will be equally important for written assignments at work, so it is a good habit/skill to develop. Remember the 'planning fallacy' – projects tend to take longer than you think. Plan generously when setting aside time to carry out the actions.

Content planning

The first stage here is again to look at what is required. It is not always immediately obvious what a question is asking. What *seems* obvious may be only a small part of what is required. You need to 'deconstruct' the question carefully, making sure you have identified *all* its constituent parts, *and* worked out precisely what is required in answer to each part. Take a question I have recently been marking. In essence, the question was:

> As part of a review of your organisation's management and use of information, and the effectiveness of technology use in this, write a report which describes your own use, as a manager, of information, and evaluate your organisation's system in terms of meeting your needs.

This is a messy one. First there is an administrative point – a report is asked for. This means identifying a suitable recipient and bearing your specified audience in mind as you write. (More detail on report formats is given shortly.) But there are other potential traps which are far more dangerous than failing to use the specified report format. The first is the clear specification of perspective. Students were asked to write about their *own* use of information. Many wrote about the organisation in general, without mentioning how they fitted into it, or giving any idea of what information they used. Second, the main thrust of the question was about management and *use* of information, not about technology. Technology was clearly seen by the question-setter as part of a wider 'information system'. Yet many students wrote exclusively about technology. Not surprisingly, there was little evaluation. (See Helpfile 15.1 at the end of this chapter if you would not have been sure what the word meant in this context.) If students did, exceptionally, evaluate something, they tended not to do this from their perspective as a manager. As a consequence, many students were surprised at the low marks they received.

So how might they have done better at identifying what was required? Deconstructing the question they would have realised that the first part – *As part of a review of your organisation's management and use of information, and the effectiveness of technology use within this* – gave important contextual information, but was not the essence of the 'instruction'. Note, though, the strong hint here that a wider *information system* was being considered, with the IT involved being seen as only a part of this wider system.

What students were actually required to do was, using report format, *describe their use of information* and *evaluate their organisation's [information] system* from the perspective of their own use of, and therefore need for, information.

Several other parts are implicit. You cannot easily evaluate something without making clear just what it is that you are evaluating, and against what criteria you are evaluating it. So in order to evaluate your organisation's information system, you need to say what it *is*. Some sort of definition or other representation is called for. Later in the instructions students were recommended to use diagrams where possible, and this is an instance where a systems diagram would be very useful. Then some sort of criteria are needed against which it can be evaluated. Clearly these needed to be derived from the manager's own information use and needs.

If students had tried to take the question apart in this way – to 'deconstruct' it – before planning their answers, they would not have so cheerfully submitted detailed descriptions of organisational IT systems, with virtually no comment as to their appropriateness. Of course it was important to include consideration of IT as part of 'the system', but a wider perspective and evaluation was clearly called for.

To take another, rather simpler example, again of an assignment which I have recently marked:

Evaluate your organisation's approach to recruitment and selection.

ACTIVITY 15.1

Before reading further, take a couple of minutes to think about the parts of which this question is made. You might like to sketch these out in the form of a mind map on a separate piece of paper. Don't worry about the fact that you have not yet studied the course for which this was an assignment. Aim at a level of detail similar to that in the example above.

Again, this was a question where many students missed much of the point. They *described* – often at great length – the detail of their organisation's procedures, though often only those for selection. But for good marks, far more was expected. The question was designed to test the students' ability to relate the theory which they had been taught on this topic to their own situation. To answer it well, students needed to demonstrate that they understood what recruitment and selection were intended to achieve, and the distinction between the two terms. (Evaluation implies testing against some sort of standard.) They needed to relate this to the organisation's overall objectives and its staffing plan. They then needed to describe key features of their organisation's policy and practice in this area, evaluating these against relevant legislation and prescriptions of good practice taught in the course. It was important to show an awareness both of the difficulties of implementing that good practice in the real context, and of the problems likely to arise from ignoring it.

There are, thus, many invisible parts to a seemingly simple question. All too often, students seized on the opportunity to describe their organisation's practice at inordinate length, even down to the names of those who sent out letters to candidates or were on interview panels. This more than used up the allowed word limit. Inevitably, amid all this detail there was no reference at all to the effectiveness of this practice in organisational terms, nor to any considerations of equal opportunities legislation, nor indeed to anything else that their course had covered.

As a marker I was not particularly interested in the intricacies of the particular organisation. Privately, of course, these glimpses of organisational life were fascinating, but students' awareness of such detail was not what was being assessed: there were no marks to be gained from mere description. Where the marks *would* have been available, should the students have chosen to seek them, was in a demonstration of their *understanding* of the relevant course concepts.

To show this understanding, they needed to use the concepts to describe and evaluate organisational practice. If the students in question had taken more trouble to clarify what was really required, and had understood their audience's objectives more clearly, they would not have fallen into this trap. Their marks might then have been a pleasant surprise, rather than the reverse. Use the glossary in Helpfile 15.1 at the end of this chapter to help you work out what an assignment requires. If at any point you are unsure, or seem to be interpreting an assignment differently from other students, check your understanding with the tutor who set it. Misunderstanding the task is in no one's interest, so most tutors will welcome such checks.

→ Ch 14

Of course, the need to clarify requirements is not limited to course assignments. Communication depends upon an understanding of the characteristics of the receiver, as the previous chapter discussed. Any business document must be written with a clear understanding of your audience's objectives, as well as your own. These are often not what they may appear at first sight. So explore the context of a request for a report, if you possibly can. Although the request may come from your boss, he or she may be planning to circulate your report, under your name or theirs, to a much wider audience. Knowing this, and understanding the debates to which your report is intended to contribute, you can direct your efforts far more effectively. Time spent clarifying requirements is seldom wasted; indeed it may *prevent* considerable subsequent waste of time and effort.

Once you have a clear understanding of your remit, including any elements not explicit in the original, write down the expanded version. You will need to check progress against objectives at intervals during your work. You do not wish to forget elements that you have so carefully worked to establish.

Identify themes and relevant concepts

When you 'deconstruct' a question some themes will already be starting to emerge. You probably found this in the previous activity. Your next stage is to develop these further, and identify any you have missed. Once you have themes you will have 'hooks' on which to hang concepts. But also, concepts can suggest themes, so at this stage it is worth being fairly open to ideas about both. Individual brainstorming is a good way of coming up with a wide range of possible candidates for inclusion.

If you have been given a group assignment, you should have been working as a group on agreeing objectives, and will obviously be able to do the brainstorming together as well. Even for an individual assignment it can help to do the brainstorming with others, perhaps your self-help group. A group brainstorming will generate many more ideas than an individual one. By bouncing your ideas off other people, and exploring the differences between your views in a constructive way, you will also become more aware of some of your own assumptions and prejudices. Thus, a group can help you to take a broader view of the situation than if you are limited to your own perspective. For work-based assignments, collaboration with colleagues has obvious potential benefit. They will probably hold essential information to which you will need access, and their (different) perspectives are an important part of the situation.

Whatever your approach, make sure that you look at the whole situation, including its context, rather than focusing narrowly on 'the problem'. It is usually easier to narrow down from a broad base than to expand on a narrow one. Breadth of approach, though not superficiality, is one of the things MBAs in particular are trying to develop.

It is important to look as broadly as possible at relevant course concepts. These are just as important as candidates for inclusion as are aspects of the situation under consideration. Many of the frameworks and theories which you will be taught in your course will provide the basis of a 'shopping list' of potential factors, and of significant relations between them, for inclusion in your analysis. These might include the 'four (or seven) Ps' (or 'Cs') in marketing, or the STEP (STEEP, STEEPV, or PESTLE) framework for analysing the competitive environment and business planning, or Expectancy Theory if the topic concerns motivation.

Ideally, your jottings should be in a form which you can manipulate when moving on to the next stage of trying to impose structure. Computers make this is easy: you can rearrange your headings by cutting and pasting, or use mind-mapping software. Restickable notes or cards which you can move around a large sheet of paper are good low-tech alternatives – some people find that more tangible approaches work better at the early draft stage. This is particularly the case if you are planning a group assignment. Whatever you choose, your aim at this stage should be to assemble your jottings in such a way that you can absorb them all easily, and build up a picture of what is potentially relevant. You can then try various arrangements of this picture to see which way it makes most sense.

→ Ch 10, 12 This is very similar, if not identical, to the approach suggested for the early stages of case study analysis, and similar diagramming techniques, as described in Chapter 10, are relevant. When the basic structure of what is required is fairly obvious, mind maps are particularly useful. They will enable you to develop this structure by drawing sub-themes out of main ones. Thus, your structure generates further ideas, rather than being imposed, perhaps uncomfortably, upon those ideas once they have been produced.

There is a slight danger that you will not be sufficiently experimental with mind maps if structure is *not* self-evident. They can still be extremely useful if you are prepared to experiment with a variety of sets of branches, drawing many possible mind maps before deciding on the best. But if you become prematurely wedded to the first set of major branches that come to mind, the whole of your subsequent work may be locked into an inappropriate structure. Unless you feel no qualms whatsoever about throwing a large proportion of your diagrams into the bin, you might be safer to reserve mind maps for the next stage.

Rich pictures are much safer. Because they look childish you are less likely to take them seriously. But you may have difficulty in representing many course concepts in this format, and need to resort to rather more words than would be ideal. Provided you retain the advantage of being able to absorb your whole picture more or less at a glance, this should not be too much of a disadvantage. Figure 15.1 shows three

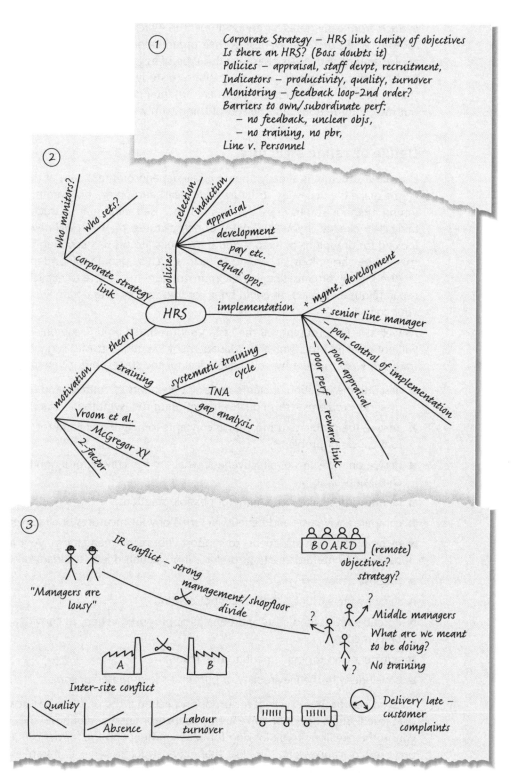

① Corporate Strategy – HRS link clarity of objectives
Is there an HRS? (Boss doubts it)
Policies – appraisal, staff devpt, recruitment,
Indicators – productivity, quality, turnover
Monitoring – feedback loop-2nd order?
Barriers to own/subordinate perf:
 – no feedback, unclear objs,
 – no training, no pbr,
Line v. Personnel

15

Writing assignments and reports

Fig. 15.1 Three specimens of early student assignment notes: 1. Brain dump approach; 2. Mind mapping; 3. Rich picture

extracts from early notes for an assignment in which first-year MBA students were asked to assess the effectiveness of their organisation's human resource policy. (I apologise for the over-emphasis on this type of assignment, but it is likely to be easily understandable whatever you are planning to study, and even if you have not yet started your course.) These diagrams are not intended as models for a good answer, but merely to demonstrate the sort of thing with which you might like to experiment.

Define or refine structure

How far a structure is already apparent will depend on the nature of the question (some make the necessary structure fairly clear) and on the diagramming or other jotting methods you have used thus far. If you used mind maps, structure should be fairly clear already. If you used notes or rich pictures, then you will now need to start looking for groupings of factors. You may choose to group according to problem themes, by chronology, according to factors such as geography or department involved, or by organisational level. Your structure may relate to explicitly stated separate question parts, or could be according to conceptual frameworks suggested in your course.

As well as these groupings, if the assignment is based around a problem situation you will normally find the 'Universal Management Paradigm' (UMP) suggests a useful framework. You should by now have a feel for the stages, but to remind you:

- describe the situation, including relevant elements of context, and indicating why it presents problems – this equates to exploring the 'symptoms' of a problem;
- analyse the problem, using course concepts to help understand (or diagnose) the root causes of problems;
- decide on measures of effectiveness: what are the criteria for a good solution; what constraints exist;
- identify and describe the range of possible solutions;
- compare likely costs and benefits in terms of your measures of effectiveness;
- recommend, with arguments to support your recommendations, your preferred solutions (some organisations prefer a more action-oriented variant on this);
- propose action;
- say why the existing situation cannot continue;
- describe anticipated costs and benefits of proposed action, to convince the audience of its merit;
- outline a plan for implementing the action;
- conclude with the inevitability of pursuing the proposed action.

Such an approach is excellent for producing action if the problem has been correctly diagnosed. But it does not make it easy to incorporate the diagnosis and analysis that your tutors are likely to be looking for in assignments, so the former is normally preferred for coursework. It is clear that either structure provides a framework for arguments. These arguments are at the heart of what you are aiming at.

It may help to think of yourself as a lawyer, making a case for the 'guilt' of aspects of the present situation, and then defending your recommendations, or as a doctor making a diagnosis, convincing the patient that the diagnosis is correct, and recommending treatment. Within either framework you can work through the evidence presented by the situation, using relevant concepts as an aid to interpreting these.

Of course, at this preparatory stage your arguments will be tentative and skeletal, as you will not have gathered the evidence to support them. Indeed, if a lot of research is needed, as in major projects, you may be looking for no more at this stage than themes to pursue. But it is well worth starting to think about structure long before you have all the evidence you need. You may find the argument mapping techniques → Ch 9   introduced in Chapter 9 are useful, even at this stage.

There is a serious danger, especially with work-based assignments, of falling into the 'trees hiding the wood' trap. A rough idea of structure before you leap into the details will guard against this. At the same time, it will enable you to be more selective in your information gathering. This is *not* an invitation to limit yourself to information supporting your argument. This would produce a biased case, and unreliable recommendations. But you should direct your effort towards gathering information relevant to your identified themes, rather than collecting a mountain of data in the hope that it might come in useful. There is a powerful reluctance in most of us to discard something on which we have expended effort. You will often *need* to do this in order to sharpen your focus, but there is sense in minimising the necessity.

Check against requirements

Once you have devised an adequate outline structure, your planning stage is well under way. At this point you should check back against the objectives as clarified earlier. Does your proposed structure seem appropriate given the requirements for the assignment? Be as critical as you can in this evaluation. If there are weaknesses in your structure, it may be disappointing to have to rethink it. But it is far better to identify problems at this stage and revise your structure than to have to rewrite a substantial report halfway through. Very occasionally this will be necessary, because new information or blinding insight will so alter your perceptions that you can see an infinitely better way of proceeding. But it should not be necessary simply because you were insufficiently critical of your own work at an early stage.

Plan the timing of your work

→ Ch 19   There is a more detailed treatment of project planning in Chapter 19. For dissertations it constitutes a major consideration. Refer to this if you think planning is a weak point, or if you are uncertain as to your ability to meet deadlines. Otherwise, merely bear in mind that you must plan for 'dead time', such as waiting for replies to letters or getting hold of references to books or articles you do not have in your possession. And do not underestimate the time taken to write at least two drafts of your report, preferably more. (Redrafting takes significant time, but can hugely improve the quality of your work if you are prepared to approach your latest draft as a (ruthlessly) 'critical bystander'.)

Once you have submitted a number of assignments, you will be better able to make accurate estimates of time requirements. Until you have this experience, allow a large contingency factor. To make sure that you keep to your plan, set yourself clear interim targets for all save the shortest pieces of work, and treat these as real deadlines. (Chapter 6 is relevant here.)

→ Ch 6

Time planning, and keeping to your plans, is crucial. Many undergraduates survive by working all night when an assignment is due. As a practising manager you cannot afford this luxury. Furthermore, Master's-level assignments are often so substantial that a single night would not suffice. You will find that your job will develop a nasty habit of peaking in its demands just when you were planning a major assignment effort. This will not be a catastrophe if you have allowed slack time for just such contingencies and reserved it for genuine emergencies.

'I work best under pressure' is no excuse for relying on last-minute efforts. Part-time students are *always* under pressure. Your aim is to prevent this pressure from becoming impossible, by careful planning and good time management.

DEVELOPING YOUR MATERIAL

Once you have a skeleton structure, and know how much time you have available, you should have a clear idea of how to start developing the substance of your assignment. Remember, however, that your structure was intended to provide a firm base for *starting*, not a concrete cast. It may well need to be amended considerably in the light of the evidence you collect and the way your thoughts about the situation develop as you work on your assignment.

You should not feel discouraged if you do find that you need to change your approach. It does not mean that your initial planning was wasted, but rather that this planning has started a process of conceptual development that is now leading you away from the obvious and into producing a much better assignment. The structure, together with your course concepts and the information you have collected, is leading you to a more creative or penetrating perspective on the situation in question. So treat your initial structure as a working tool which you can deliberately modify (though not inadvertently ignore) when this will lead to better work.

The following guidelines, though by no means exhaustive, may be helpful in your work. The rest of the chapter expands upon them.

Guidelines for assignments

- Develop clear arguments.
- Use theory where possible.
- Seek evidence as widely as possible.

- Use diagrams where appropriate.
- Avoid assertions and opinions.
- Avoid plagiarism.
- Start drafting as soon as possible.
- Redraft for clarity and conciseness.

In preparing the substance of your report, you need to be sure that all your arguments will be substantiated. Avoid assertions (e.g. 'So-and-so is true', or 'everybody knows that . . .') or opinions (e.g. 'I think . . .'). No matter how confidently you state these, they are unlikely to impress either superiors or tutors. Sadly, as a marker (or indeed as your manager) I am not interested in your opinions just because they are yours. You might or might not know what you are talking about. I want to know how you reached that opinion, what it is that the facts and the theory suggest. So your position needs to be supported by reasoning, based on evidence or accepted theories, or preferably both. Argument mapping is really helpful at this stage.

→ Ch 9

Your report is intended to convey a position. You have taken relevant information, using course ideas to suggest what information is relevant and to make sense of that information, you have organised this information and these arguments so that a picture emerges, conclusions become obvious and it is relatively easy to develop a set of recommendations from these. At no point should your reader be wondering why you have said something, or whether what you said can be believed. And especially, your conclusions should not come as a surprise. You should be building towards these throughout your report or essay.

Avoid plagiarism

→ Ch 19

There is more of this in Chapter 19, but for any assignment you need to be aware of the importance of submitting work that is *your own*.

Submitting material written by other people as if it were your own is *plagiarism*. Universities regard this as a serious offence, and it attracts severe penalties. You may be 'asked' to leave a programme if you are found guilty of plagiarism, so it is important to understand the different sorts of plagiarism and the ways in which you may risk committing it. You may realise that it is cheating to copy the work of another student. You may be less aware that you are also deemed to be 'copying' if any material you use is essentially the same as the original. Such use is plagiarism if you do not make explicit which material is not your own, and credit the original author. This is true even if you make minor changes in your text. Rearranging paragraphs, or changing a few words is not enough to render the material your own. Whether you are using another student's work, a text, or material you find on the Web you are plagiarising whenever you have not made it absolutely clear and explicit that the material is not your own. You need to put text you have chosen to use in its original form in either italics or quotation marks. If you are adapting slightly, then you need to show which text of yours is essentially an adaptation. And in both cases you need to say clearly where you found the original material (how to reference is discussed later in this chapter).

There are many possible reasons for plagiarism. Some of the common ones are that students:

- get behind, have no time to write an assignment, so 'borrow' one from a friend or colleague;
- get low grades, so submit work from a better student or material copied from the Web;
- are lazy – it is easier to use someone else's work;
- misunderstand what is required – in some educational systems reproducing the (appropriate) original material is acceptable, but in the UK and many other systems it is not;
- are not sure whether they understand an idea so copy the original rather than putting it in their own words;
- give credit for an idea, but fail to show which words are taken unchanged from the credited author.

Remember: using others' words, without saying that you are doing so, counts as plagiarism. You can be severely penalised for this, perhaps even asked to leave!

Plagiarising, or copying, is *never* acceptable in the UK. Take the following steps to avoid it. Wherever possible, use your own words. So if you are explaining a concept encountered on your course, rephrase it in your own words; this demonstrates understanding. *Always* give a reference to the person who originated the concept (see below). If you want to quote exact words, which is perfectly acceptable in moderation, indeed sometimes necessary to make a point, use either quotation marks or italics to distinguish that which is in someone else's words, and give a *full* reference, including the page quoted from. If you want to use words found on the Web, again, show that they are a quotation and give your source. Never 'borrow' things that other students have written. (The exception, of course, is a group project, but you may even then be asked to make clear which group member is responsible for what contribution.)

If you are unsure of your ability to write good English, the temptation to reproduce, rather than rephrase, may be strong. Resist it at all costs. You will learn little, and may pay a heavy price if you are discovered. Discovery is becoming more common as many universities use sophisticated software to detect plagiarism.

Seek your evidence as widely as possible

Obviously, the relevant evidence will be determined by the question. For work-based assignments evidence may come from information gathering within your own organisation. As suggested earlier, discussions with colleagues can generate relevant information (and be surprisingly enlightening, too). An important aspect of many problem situations is that they may be viewed in very different ways by different key people in that situation. Such differences of perspective may be a significant element in a problem.

Subordinates may prove happy to co-operate in your work. Indeed you may be able to make it into a developmental experience for them. This will also serve to reduce any resentment that may be developing towards your course. Superiors or mentors, if they are supporting you in your studies, can also derive benefit from helping you with your assignments. Such help might be in the form of discussions, suggestions as to further sources of information or comments on ideas and drafts. Being involved will enable them to use your assignments as a form of in-house consultancy, as well as making sure that your learning experience is as rich as possible, increasing the return on their investment in your course. (If you wish to convince them further that such help is a good idea, you might point out that good 'customised' company MBAs or other programmes tend to be much more expensive than an off-the-shelf model. By supporting you in your work-based assignments they are, in a sense, doing their own customising, in a way that is both cheap and highly effective.)

Examples of evidence that might be appropriate in an organisation-based assignment include: results of interviews with key company personnel; company data; records from your own part of the organisation; survey data collected in-company by other consultants; external information such as published market intelligence, government statistics or trade surveys. Relevant literature on the topic culled from management journals, books or even newspapers will also be needed in most cases, together with any course material or lecture notes relevant to the assignment.

→ Ch 19

Remember that evidence is usually less than perfectly reliable, and you should assess the extent of the unreliability of all the evidence on which you draw. There is more on this in Chapter 19. Look at this if you are planning an assignment based on evidence you need to gather from your company or the environment.

Use theory as much as possible

Some assignments may be purely theoretical. Others may require you to use theory to analyse a case study. In either case, theory use should be explicit. If writing an in-company report, however, you will normally need to be careful to use this theory *inconspicuously*. You will thus gain its benefits in making a complicated situation clearer, but will avoid antagonising your readers. Colleagues may feel threatened if your arguments assume theory or knowledge that they lack. They may feel genuinely irritated by unnecessary jargon, or profess irritation as a form of defence if threatened.

When writing assignments intended primarily for course assessment you need be less restrained. Remember that the point of your programme is to equip you with a set of conceptual tools and techniques. You are being taught to apply these in a variety of organisational situations in order to cut through complexity and reach valid conclusions as to the best of the strategic alternatives available and how to implement it. The same theory which might irritate superiors in an internal report is likely to be just what your tutors are looking for. They need it to check that you have absorbed and can use theory appropriately. Thus, theory will almost certainly need to be *explicit* in any report you write for your course.

By the end of your course, theory should have become second nature, and *implicit* in everything you do. You are most likely to achieve this if you take the opportunity to experiment with different ways of using the conceptual tools, and of obtaining feedback from your tutors on this, via your use of these tools in assessment. Many of the marks for assignments may well be allocated to correct use of appropriate theory, so what is good for your learning will also be good for your grades. Part of your preparation for an assignment will therefore be to explore potentially relevant theories and concepts, and experiment with them to determine their usefulness in your particular context.

Use diagrams where possible

If you are analysing a problem situation to see how it arose, *multiple-cause* diagrams are invaluable, and can often be usefully incorporated in your report. By working back from the event or situation of interest, through contributory factors and factors contributing to those and so on, multiple-cause diagrams can communicate a clear understanding of the web of relationships involved, and allow your reader to see the relevance of a much wider range of possible interventions than are immediately obvious.

→ Ch 10

Appreciation of important interrelationships will enable your reader to see why you have avoided some recommendations. It will be clear that they risk producing unintended consequences worse than the original problem. (These are not as uncommon in real life as you might think!) *Relationship* diagrams will help you to achieve the same benefits for more static situations. Don't forget the basic organisation tree, or organigram, familiar to everyone. It can represent one form of relationship very clearly. And, of course, *mind maps* and *fishbone* diagrams have fairly obvious uses, both as frameworks for generating evidence, and for organising evidence into coherent arguments once generated.

Organise the materials you generate as you go along

If your materials are disorganised, you will spend a lot of time later trying to sort them out, or to find documents that you know are 'somewhere'. Your outline structure will provide a framework for this, but it is useful, additionally, to keep a log of what you have collected and how you have filed it, and of what is still outstanding, so that you can assess progress at a glance. Such a log serves the important function of giving you a feeling that you are making progress, thus keeping your motivation high, even if the assignment is a long one.

It is particularly important to keep a full reference with your notes on each idea or piece of evidence you might use (referencing is discussed later in the chapter). It is all too tempting to omit this. It seems impossible, at the time, that you could forget where you got something from. There is a strong temptation to 'do all the references properly at the writing-up stage'. (I have wasted *countless* hours in looking for articles or quotations that were not in the publication I 'remembered'. Indeed, some sources seemed to have mysteriously ceased to exist since I last read them!)

As you are unlikely to be able to afford to waste *any* time in this way, organise your information from the start. Keep references with the relevant material, and full details

Organise materials better by:

■ planning the materials you will
need

■ logging progress in acquiring them

■ checking progress against deadlines

■ organising materials as you collect
them

■ clearly distinguishing 'quotations'

■ filing full references.

→ Ch 19

in a separate file. If you have extracted chunks of original text, distinguish this clearly from your own notes. Similarly, record all possible details about interviews, letters sent, group discussions held, sources of company data, etc. You need to *know* the mailing list for different letters, or the participants in a particular discussion, not to have to reconstruct these from memory.

Start drafting as soon as possible

This need is discussed more fully in Chapter 19, but briefly, the sooner you start to draft, the clearer you will become about your remaining information needs. Just as moving on to the evidence-gathering stage may have thrown up deficiencies in your structure, so can drafting make you more aware of gaps in evidence. It is, therefore, a mistake to wait until all your evidence is complete before starting your first draft. You should be starting a skeleton draft at the planning stage, developing it as your thoughts become clearer and you gather more evidence. Decisions on major subheadings should be possible by the time you have half your evidence, even for a major assignment requiring substantial research.

DRAFTING WRITTEN ASSIGNMENTS

→ Ch 6, 7

Getting started should present few problems if you have followed the guidance offered so far. By setting interim deadlines, and starting rough drafting while still collecting evidence, you should be starting your first full-length draft with plenty of time in hand, a clear idea of what you are going to write and adequate material to hand. The dreaded 'writer's block' should, therefore, be no threat. Indeed, if you have been developing your time-management skills at work and in your studies, even the more common, though potentially equally damaging, vice of procrastination should be much diminished.

Drafting guidelines

■ Prepare outline structure at outset.

■ Refine structure when possible.

■ Set manageable interim targets.

■ Start a rough draft very early indeed.

■ If stuck, do other study for a (short) while.

■ If still stuck, consider discarding recent work and changing direction.

■ If still stuck, seek tutor's help.

■ Check progress against targets.

■ Complete draft in time to revisit and redraft.

15

Writing assignments and reports

You may occasionally, for some reason, find it difficult to start, or difficult to restart after a break in your work. Thoughts about the absolute necessity of fixing the roof, cleaning the oven, digging the potatoes or any other preferred displacement activity, may start to surface, deterring you from starting work on your draft. If so, you have two weapons at your disposal.

First, you must remind yourself that this is only an early draft. It is not the finished product, it does not have to be perfect, and you do not have to start at the beginning and work through to the end. Many people find writing much more stressful than they should because they try to get it right first time, rather than seeing drafting as a process of successive refinements.

Sometimes you will only find out what you want to write by starting. What emerges may be quite a surprise. But once something has emerged, however scrappily, there is something to work with. Redrafting can allow this to be worked up into a piece that is infinitely better than the original. However, unless you *allow* yourself to produce something that you know to be imperfect as a starting point, the process will not be able to take place. If you know yourself to be a perfectionist, remind yourself constantly that imperfection is a necessary part of the process. A sculptor may saw wood into roughly the right shape before starting detailed carving. Those first rough cuts, unimpressive in themselves, produced something which could be developed into a masterpiece.

A second help, if you are in difficulty, is to start with the part of the report with which you feel most comfortable. Introductions are never the best place to start in any case, as it is impossible to introduce a report until you know what that report contains. So start with your evidence, or even your conclusions, if that suits you better. This is only a first draft, and you can modify your initial sections to take account of the content of earlier parts of the report once you get to your second draft.

Sometimes, the resistance to writing stems from the size of the task with which you are faced. If so, draw on time-management techniques, and set very easy targets at first. If you really cannot get started, set the task of drafting any two pages, and schedule this for a specific time. Once you have those two pages, force yourself to stop and indulge in some detailed planning of what parts you will write when. If you set yourself eminently achievable tasks at first, you can get into the habit of writing. Each time you complete a writing task you should find that the resistance to starting work is less next time, until you find you are enjoying the chance to get back to work. This momentum

→ Ch 6

will be sustained only if you treat your report as an 'elephant', and write a little of it every day.

If you are an extreme case, and a mere two pages is enough to induce caffeine poisoning, then you will need an even easier task. Your resistance even to picking up a pen or switching on a PC must be overcome. Start with writing something pleasurable, such as a letter to an old friend, or rude thoughts about your course, before moving on to drafting the assignment. (It is highly unlikely that you will need such tough measures if you have worked through the Handbook thus far.)

If you suddenly become stuck in mid-draft, rather than chewing pencils or playing electronic patience, stop what you are working on and start work on a different part of the report. You could even do some other coursework as an alternative. But make a point of coming back the next day, or soon after that, to the place at which you blocked, and try to discover the cause of your difficulty. You will often find that the problem has arisen because you took a wrong turning earlier in your report, but are unwilling to face up to this because it will mean scrapping some of the work you have done. Go back to the last point at which you are totally happy with your draft, and think about how you need to modify it thereafter. You probably know already, if you are honest with yourself!

Be concise

In preparing your final draft (and two or even three redrafts can usually improve your work if you have time) pay particular attention to whether you could say the same thing in fewer words. Many assignments have word limits, and if you are unnecessarily 'wordy' you will not fit the intended content into the limit and lose marks as result. I frequently find myself writing comments like 'you need to discuss this in more depth' on assignments that are up to – or even over – the word limit. The student will say 'but I didn't have room'. If they had cut out all the unnecessary verbiage they would have had plenty of room. There is more on writing clear English later, but the need for concise expression is of over-arching importance. Be ruthless and cut out all phrases that do not earn their keep. If you develop the habit of writing to the point in your assignments it will stand you in good stead when writing exam answers under pressure.

ACTIVITY 15.2

The following is an example of a (weak) student's 'diagnosis' of a rather complex situation. The student is a professional, an employee of a company providing services via a customer (Y) to a consumer (X) with whom the student is in near daily contact. Read it, and consider how you might have rewritten it more concisely. Note any other comments that you might wish to offer the student.

> What is clear from my diagnosis is that whilst I could certainly apply the rules and procedures regarding specifications and costs for a project that seemed appropriate to me, as within my job description I have the right and authority to do so, I do not have the means to enforce them against [X], other than advising [Y] of any variance and that [X] was responsible for it. This could be very damaging to the current relationship between me and [X], but also possibly between [Y] and the firm I work for given that I would be seen to be 'pointing fingers' and demonstrating a lack of control, which would not instil confidence in our performance as a company, and risk us losing the contract, as well as the tendency it would have to make my company doubt my competence. This calls for definition of the Terms of Engagement, an immediate short-term intervention that would assist everyone involved in understanding exactly what I am responsible for, and how far my authority extends. This brings me back to my original idea of using the agreement of a strategy as a dialogue in which all the stakeholders with a perspective can

engage to understand the other's perspective. This does of course rely on each stakeholder attempting to understand the other's point of view! I think that this is highly unlikely to ever happen given the personalities concerned. Reflection on this, as well as the time taken to reach the current position in the project, has made me question who is to be persuaded as part of this strategy, me or [X].

Comment

This is an extremely difficult task, not least because the student is not at all clear what evidence has been gathered to underpin this 'diagnosis', nor what theory had been used to drive whatever data collection and interpretation had been undertaken. (This was an example of a report receiving a fail grade.) It is harder because the overall meaning is very hard to deduce. My best attempt is below. Maybe yours is better. (Note that it is very easy to be critical of someone else's writing. The real challenge is to be equally harsh on your own.)

I am authorised to specify and define budgets for projects according to set procedures, but lack the authority to ensure that [X] will observe these. I can only advise [Y] of any subsequent variance against budget and the reasons. However, to blame [X] explicitly could damage the working relationship between us, highlight my own lack of control and threaten the company's credibility with [Y].

A better approach might be to define and agree 'Terms of Engagement' that clarified [X's] and my own responsibilities. Ideally this would take place through a dialogue between the stakeholders on our overall strategy and how best to achieve it, given our different perspectives.

Reflection on progress thus far has made me question the validity of my own assumptions about the problem, and suggested that I may actually be a part of it.

This uses only 50% of the words of the original. I leave you to judge whether it conveys more or less meaning, and whether your own redrafting is better. I hope that your redraft retained or enhanced the impact of the stunning insight in the final point.

USING REPORT FORMAT

Students are sometimes inhibited by the need to write a 'report'. You may feel that there is some mystique to report format, some secret formula that you are not privy to. There are two reasons for the emergence of report formats. The first is the logical necessity to structure your arguments, the second is that the structure is intended to help your readers find their way around what may be a substantial document. Knowing the general order to expect can help.

Some organisations seek to maximise this effect by having a standard format for all company reports. If this is the case in your own organisation, make sure that you have a copy of the rules, or one or two reports to act as models, before you start. Your lecturers may also have clear ideas about the structure required, and obviously if your

Reports should normally include:

- title page, with author, addressee and date
- acknowledgements (if appropriate)
- summary
- contents list (if any length)
- introduction
- main and subsidiary sections, appropriately titled and numbered
- conclusions
- recommendations
- references (or bibliography)
- appendices (if needed).

report is for assessment purposes you should meet their requirements.

The following discussion covers what might be seen as the broad range of normal practice. Follow this in the absence of organisational or business school guidelines or prescriptions. Normally a report includes a summary, a title page giving report title, date, addressee and sender, a list of contents, an introduction, a main body which may be divided into numbered sections and subsections, conclusions, recommendations, references and appendices. The function of each will be discussed in turn.

Title page

Any report is written, and must be read, in a specific context. It is vital, therefore, that at the start of the report you make clear who has originated the report, to whom it is addressed, and the date. The report also needs a title, and this should normally be as descriptive as possible. This information is frequently presented on a title page, giving a professional look from the start. An example is given in Fig. 15.2 – in this case students were asked to write the report as if addressed to their superior.

In deciding upon a title for a report at work, think about how it will be used. Is the title going to appear in any listings of reports? If so it will need to indicate the sort of report and coverage in a way that will enable a potential reader, browsing through the list, to know whether your report is worth obtaining. Are there other reports on similar topics in your organisation? If so, you will need a title that distinguishes your report from theirs.

Date is a vital part of the context of a report. Information usually has a short shelf-life. It may be important for people to know whether your report was written before or after some major event having impact on your topic, or before or after another report. It is, therefore, essential that all reports be clearly dated, usually on the front page, as this may be the first thing a reader will wish to know.

In indicating addressee and sender, it is usually worth indicating a person's title, if this is relevant to their part in the report. Thus, you might be a senior marketing manager but have generated the report in your capacity as chair of a working party on restructuring the organisation's marketing capacity. In that case, it would be the latter title that would be important, and it should be included, with your job title if that is important too.

Contents list

The contents list should show your major and minor section headings, preferably numbered, and appendices. Figure 15.2 shows a contents page for a student assignment in report format.

You will see that the contents list provides a clear indication to the intending reader of the structure of the report to follow, as well as acting as an index for anyone wishing to refer directly to a specific part of the report, rather than read the work in its entirety. The numbering system shows clearly what is a major (e.g. 2) or minor (e.g. 2.1, 2.2) heading. Shorter reports will usually not need further division. If you need sub-subsections for a longer report you could use a further level of numbering (e.g. 2.1.1, 2.1.2). Some organisations number paragraphs, rather than pages. This allows easy reference to any paragragh but has the disadvantage of confusing any system for numbering major and minor sections. Since the latter is such a powerful aid to indicating the structure of your report, you may prefer to use section numbering if given a free choice.

Section and subsection titles should be as descriptive as their short length allows. This further helps the reader to understand how the report is structured, and allows easy reference to sections of most interest.

Appendices are usually numbered in a different way from parts of the report proper – you can use letters or roman numerals. Again, descriptive titles are useful.

It is helpful to give page numbers as an aid to this index function, although with a short report it is not essential.

The summary is normally regarded as outside the report, and does not therefore feature on the contents list.

Acknowledgements

If you have written a substantial report, perhaps on your main project, you may want to acknowledge any significant help you have had, perhaps from a supervisor, or client organisation. Think carefully about the purpose of this part of your report. It can give great pleasure for example to supportive family to include them. You may feel strongly

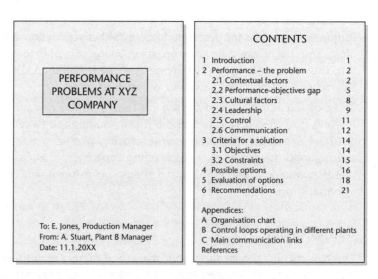

Fig.15.2 Example of student title and contents pages

about references to divine help. Neither is likely to lose you marks. Failure to acknowledge your supervisor, while mentioning your goldfish, may however subconsciously influence the marking process. Failure to acknowledge contributions of key members of a client organisation may have an equally negative effect.

Summary

For any lengthy document a summary or abstract is useful. Practice varies as to whether this should be at the end of the report, at the front, even before any contents page, or an introductory part of the report. Many organisations insist on a one-page summary at the very front, arguing that it is possible for a busy manager to decide on the basis of this whether to invest any further time in the report. A similar summary is often required for a thesis or dissertation.

An introductory summary serves as orientation to the reader. It will be much easier to make sense of a complicated argument if you know the overall shape of the report in advance. Putting the summary at the end reflects its purpose of reinforcing key points of the document just read, and probably stems from the fact that it is likely to be the last thing you write. For assignments, the summary should normally be a summary of the whole report, rather than just of recommendations. You should, therefore, include a brief statement of the original problem, and of the main arguments or evidence that have led you to your conclusions. In assignments with a tight word limit a good summary (which would not normally be counted against the word limit) may mean that the introduction has less to do, and can therefore do it more effectively within the words allowed.

Introduction

This is a crucial part of your report. Although an initial summary, and your contents page, will have started the process of reader orientation, the introduction is where such orientation is mainly achieved. If you are not prefacing your report with a summary your introduction will be particularly crucial. Your reader will usually come to the report with a number of questions:

- Why is this topic important?
- What was the remit of the report writer?
- What is the main argument in this report?
- On what evidence is this argument based?
- How is the argument structured?
- What are the implications of the argument?

If your introduction can answer these questions, at least in outline, your reader will be in a much better position to read the subsequent report with interest, and will follow your developing argument with greater ease. Of course, if you have included an initial summary, some of these questions will have been answered already, and you can concentrate in your introduction on the significance of the topic and the aims of the work reported.

It is a great pity, given the above, that many students use their 'introduction', whether in assignments or examinations, to do no more than restate the set question. It *is* important that the remit be established, but you will usually have 'deconstructed' a question to discover the various parts implicit in it or otherwise developed your understanding of the question. At the very least, this expanded version should be included in your introduction. Preferably your introduction should go beyond this, as suggested above.

Unfortunately, the only extension of the introduction offered by many students is the inclusion of background information. Again, there is a degree of justification in this. In establishing the significance of the topic, you need to describe the context to some extent. But the introduction should not be seen as 'introduction and background', as it clearly often is. Any detailed background which you feel might be of interest to those reading the report should form a separate section, preferably in an appendix. The only background information which should appear in your text is that essential to understanding your argument.

Main section(s)

As already suggested, you will normally need several major subsections within your main section. These can often be mapped moderately closely on to the stages of the UMP. Thus, you might include a more detailed exploration of the background to the problem (this is *not* the same as background information on the organisation), the relationship between the problem and other factors, constraints and so on as suggested earlier in the chapter. Sub-topics within each main topic (the twigs on the branches, if you used a mind map) will usually have subheadings, their numbers relating to that of the major heading, as was the case in Fig. 15.2. Take care that headings and subheadings clearly indicate the content of each major and minor section.

Think carefully about what should be included in main text, what relegated to appendices. Normally your aim is to make your main text as clear, compelling and interesting as you can for your readers, to increase the chance that they will understand and accept your arguments. It is these considerations that should influence your decision on what to include. Appendices should be seen as supplementary support, rather than essential to your argument. They are in a sense optional extras. The text should be capable of standing alone, if the reader chooses not to look at the appendices.

Diagrams frequently serve the function of supporting or clarifying your text, and should therefore be included at the appropriate point. Not only will they reinforce your argument, but they will make the text look less dense and forbidding, and thus help in sustaining your readers' interest. It is also extremely inconvenient for the reader to have to be continually turning between text and appendices in order to follow an argument.

Diagrams which should be relegated to the appendix include any extremely detailed diagrams which only the most dedicated or critical reader would wish to refer to, and any working diagrams produced in the process of developing those which *are* in the text (if it is appropriate to include these at all). Your tutor, though not your organisation, may be interested in the thought processes which the latter reveal. When you *do* feel the need to append diagrams, you should always refer to them, and to where they may be found, at the appropriate point in your text. There is nothing more irritating to the reader than to spend a long time thinking about a point, or wanting more evidence on it, only to find, 30 pages later, that the material is in fact there.

Much the same arguments apply to tables or diagrammatic representations of evidence such as graphs or bar charts. Where they are an important part of your argument, they should be in the text. In the appendix you should put the more extensive information summarised in your in-text tables or charts, and any detailed mathematical argument. Those sceptical about your arguments can refer to the full information on which they are based, while those who are happy to accept your condensed representation of the data will be able to follow the main thread of your argument without interruption.

To summarise, your main section should be self-standing, capable of being understood without reference to appendices. However, those not prepared to take your summaries of evidence at face value will find supporting detail in the appendices.

Within the main body of your text, if the report is a long one, you can orient the reader at intervals by including a short introduction to each main section. The structure of the report as a whole should follow the 'Say what you are going to say, say it, then say what you've said' principle. The same form can usefully be followed within each major section.

Throughout the main body of your report you should be aiming to develop arguments, based on evidence, which build up to your eventual conclusions. It is worth checking at intervals that this is what is happening. If you *cannot* summarise each section in these terms, you should think again about what you have written. It may be that some of the evidence which you have included does not contribute to your argument, or that part of your argument is not substantiated by evidence.

Note: while 'Introduction' and 'Recommendations' are reasonable section headings, 'Main section' is *not*. In this part of the report your headings will be chosen to describe the particular themes you have decided to cover in your report (*see* Fig. 15.2 for an example).

Conclusions

Your conclusions section should follow naturally from what you have written thus far. There should be no new material introduced at this stage, but rather a drawing together of the arguments you have developed earlier so that their implications can be spelled out. Students often have difficulty in distinguishing between conclusions and recommendations, and indeed the distinction can be a fine one. It may help to think of the conclusions as being more to do with logic, while the recommendations deal with the implementation of these conclusions. Thus, in an essay you might have 'conclusions' but not recommendations. In a report with a tight word limit and a requirement to 'recommend . . .' you might omit conclusions, and include brief logical justification for your recommendations within the recommendations section.

Recommendations

As with the summary, there is debate as to the best location for recommendations. The more action oriented prefer them at the front, as in the second framework suggested earlier. This is the response of the manager who says, 'Tell me what you want me to do, and then convince me'. There is a lot of sense to this in many work contexts. Your evaluation of an argument is much helped by the knowledge of the end to which that argument is leading. On the other hand, recommendations cannot be made until the logical process of analysis and conclusion has been gone through, so there are equally powerful arguments for recommendations appearing at the end, and in academic contexts this will usually be the required order.

Perhaps the best compromise is to have an introductory summary which includes a brief statement of recommendations, and then to have the fuller statement of recommendations, together with any additional arguments needed to justify them, at the end. Check with those requiring the report as to their preferred position.

> **Recommendations should:**
> - flow obviously from analysis
> - be clear proposals for action
> - be sensible and realistic.

Wherever you choose to position them, your recommendations should be clearly prioritised, and the priorities justified. Those evaluating your report will be checking that these priorities are appropriate, and that the recommendations are consistent with prevailing conditions in the organisation and its environment. For example, recommendations which call for a massive investment at a time when the organisation has cash flow problems and is already having difficulty in raising money will not be highly regarded. Similarly, if recommendations give a high priority to an interesting but not essential development, and a lower priority to something needed to ensure the continued survival of the organisation, there is likely to be little respect for the writer of the report.

References and/or bibliography

A list of references at the end of a report (but before appendices) gives the full details of all sources you have specifically referred to in the report. A bibliography includes not only sources which have been specifically mentioned but also those which have influenced what you wrote in a more general way, or are otherwise relevant to the topic covered. Whether or not you include a full bibliography will depend upon the circumstances. For most reports, references are all that is required. For a thesis, a fuller bibliography may be appropriate. Check with your tutors.

So why is referencing deemed so important? Some of your evidence will be in the form of secondary data, information collected by others. You will also be drawing (I hope) on concepts which have been introduced in your courses. In both cases, your readers might wish to reassure themselves that you are making appropriate use of information or theory. To do so, they would want to look at the information personally, to check that you are not misquoting it, or using it out of context, or go back to the author responsible for the theory you used, to see that you have really represented the concepts correctly.

More positively, your reader might be so fired with enthusiasm by your report as to be inspired to research the topic further, taking up where you left off. In either case, the reader needs to be able to find your sources. You need, therefore, to have made very clear in your text what source you are using at any point, and to include a list, usually at the end, with the full reference to the material in question. Most academic institutions recommend use of the Harvard referencing system or slightly abbreviated form. This is the system adopted in this book, so you can use it as a model. If following this system, when you mention an author in the text you would say 'Handy (1985)', while in your references you would say:

Handy, C.B. (1985) *Understanding Organizations* (3rd edn), Penguin.

The full Harvard style also gives place of publication before publisher. There are other styles of giving references, but this is the most widely used in academic circles. You will see that the title of the book is distinguished by the use of italics, but could equally well have been underlined. If you are quoting a journal article, then usually the article title is given in quotation marks, and the journal title is italicised or underlined. In the latter case you will also need to show volume and issue numbers of the journal, and the page numbers on which the article appears. Thus:

Hendry, C. and Pettigrew, A. (1986) 'The practice of strategic human resource management', *Personnel Review*, 15, 5, pp. 3–8.

If you are referring to more than one publication by an author in a single year, you normally distinguish these by the use of letters, e.g. Handy (1985a), and Handy (1985b).

References should normally include only those sources which have been directly referred to in your text. If you wish to include other items which might be of interest to the reader, but to which no direct reference has been made, the list is normally entitled 'Bibliography'. For direct quotations, as for example when you want to reproduce a whole paragraph from one of your sources, you should always include reference to the page from which the quotation is taken.

Where you have quoted from materials found on the Internet you should include the copyright statement of the Web page or website, and any citation instructions, and to note the date on which you last visited the Web page. For example,

http://www.leeds.ac.uk/library/training/referencing/goldenrules.htm (accessed 04/04/07) provides an excellent tutorial in referencing using the Harvard style.

Appendices

It has already been indicated that appendices (sometimes called annexes) are where you include supporting information and/or evidence for those wishing for more detail, or those wanting more information before they are prepared to be convinced by your argument. Thus, you might append a copy of a questionnaire, or an interview schedule, or the monthly production figures for all departments and sites which you have summarised in tabular form in your text, or detailed organisation charts for the organisation you are studying, rather than put all this in the text.

Appendices are sometimes used by students as a way of getting around the word limit, as it is generally assumed that appendices do not count against this. While this *may* be true – and you would need to check with your tutor – it is not a good stratagem. Material essential to your argument should *not* be in an appendix. If including it in your text makes you go over the limit, you should consider whether your style is too verbose, or whether the scope of your report needs to be narrowed slightly.

As was mentioned in the context of diagrams, any material in your appendices should be referred to at the appropriate point in your text, so that the reader who *does* wish to refer to the supporting evidence knows that it exists, and where to find it.

WRITING CLEAR ENGLISH

Even students who are native English speakers lose marks because their use of the language is inadequate. Their meaning is unclear, and their marker fails to realise what they are trying to say. Grammatical and spelling errors may be serious enough to cost marks. Students for whom English is a second or subsequent language often (though not always!) have greater problems.

In either case, it is worth paying attention to your use of language. If you have doubts about your abilities in this respect, you should study the following section. After all, the credibility of any report you write at work will be reduced by poor expression. Grammatical or spelling mistakes may create doubt as to your competence in other areas. Lack of clarity in the way you write implies a lack of clarity in the way you think. Neither will improve your promotion prospects.

Clearly, it is beyond the scope of this chapter to teach you the full complexities of the English language if you are not a native speaker. Helpfile 15.4, at the end of this chapter, gives some suggestions, but if your English is weak, you should probably take a language course before starting postgraduate study in English. Inadequate language skills cause many overseas students to fail, so it is important to ensure that you will be able to benefit from a programme. (Ask your institution what level you should score on a standard test if you are worried.) But if the problem is minor, the following basic guidelines and short explanations of how punctuation can be used may help. Helpfiles 15.2 and 15.3 will help too – they include a list of words commonly misspelled or misused in management assignments.

The following guidelines should help you to improve the style of your assignments, or other reports, at least in terms of increasing the clarity of your communication.

Go for simplicity

While it is possible, if you are thoroughly confident in your use of English, and can keep control of a whole sequence of subordinate clauses, some of which may describe elements of the main clause, others of which may describe phrases which are already subordinate clauses themselves, without forgetting which verb belongs to which clause, or omitting verbs altogether, to construct a sentence that is grammatically correct, the overall effect is usually far from satisfactory, as the reader soon starts to lose track of the main idea, which may have been introduced several lines earlier, and by the end of the sentence it is extremely likely that he will have lost the thread altogether. Is that clear? Probably not! Perhaps you had to read the sentence several times to get the meaning. Yet, many students get close to such complexity in their assignments. Often they do *not* keep their grammar under control.

Imagine how much harder the sentence above would have been if it had used long words! If you have a predilection for multisyllabic words, habitually utilising these in preference to equivalent, albeit briefer terms, possibly intending significantly to enhance the impressiveness of your communication by demonstrating the extensiveness of your vocabulary, the capacity for obfuscation is multiplied significantly. So don't indulge yourself! Use short words, and short sentences. Your meaning will almost certainly be far clearer.

If you want to gain a rough assessment of your likely clarity in terms of how you score on these two aspects, there is a measure called the *Fog Index* which you can calculate. Take six sentences at random from what you have written. This is probably best achieved by deciding in advance *which* sentences, e.g. second, fifteenth, twenty-eighth, etc. or by throwing a die to generate random numbers. If you look at the text while selecting, the process will not be random. Count the number of words in the selected sentences, and the number which have three or more syllables. Express this as a percentage. Divide your total number of words by six to give average sentence length. Add this average length to the percentage of long words, and multiply by 0.4. If your answer is greater than 12, your writing is 'foggy'. (If you want to work out the Fog Index for a shorter passage, use the whole passage, and adjust your sentence length calculation accordingly.) Your word processor can probably be set to show readability statistics. If you want to go even further than this, I have seen an advertisement for software that not only checks your grammar, but also tells you how close your style comes to one of a number of preferred models ranging from Hemingway to an insurance policy!

EXERCISE 15.1

Calculate the Fog Index of the first two paragraphs after the heading 'Writing clear English', and compare it with the index for the first two paragraphs under 'Go for simplicity' using all the text, rather than a sample, in each case.

ACTIVITY 15.3

Find a piece of writing which you did recently, and calculate your own Fog Index. Check it occasionally in future work.

Shorter sentences will almost certainly make your writing clearer. Activity 15.3 probably demonstrated this. You will be far less likely to violate grammatical rules; shorter sentences are much easier to control. With a long sentence you may inadvertently omit

Improve clarity with:

- shorter words
- shorter sentences
- shorter paragraphs
- one idea per paragraph.

a verb, either from the main part of the sentence or from one of the clauses within it. Or you may use a singular form of verb when it should be plural, or vice versa, because you have forgotten the actual subject of the verb. In a short simple sentence such an error would be glaringly obvious.

There are, therefore, clear arguments for keeping words and sentences short. Similarly, you should avoid over-lengthy paragraphs. Paragraphs serve to break a piece of writing into units which the reader can absorb at one go. Ideally, a paragraph will be 75–100 words long. More importantly, it will relate to a single topic or idea. Combining disjointed ideas into a single paragraph will confuse your reader, who will be expecting, and therefore unsuccessfully seeking, connections between them.

Be careful, however. If paragraphs are *too* short, it can make your writing seem disjointed. Check whether the paragraph needs to be expanded, or whether other short paragraphs are in fact devoted to the same idea and could therefore be combined. If not, do not worry too much. The occasional short paragraph will do no harm. Indeed, it can be used to emphasise a point. But if your entire report consists of very short paragraphs, you might wish to rethink the whole thing. Perhaps you are not developing your ideas sufficiently.

If paragraphs are too long, text can seem forbidding and dense, and the reader may find it heavy going. See whether you can split very long paragraphs into shorter ones. The carving-up process requires you to think carefully about the points you are making within that section of text. This may generate significant improvements to your draft. When you think about what you were *really* trying to say, you often find ways of saying it better.

I once spent a year as sub-editor of a student newspaper, and most of my job consisted of carving large paragraphs into smaller ones. A report can stand much longer paragraphs than a newspaper, but that year has given me a ruthlessness which I lacked before, and which has stood me in good stead ever since.

However you split your paragraphs, it is a good idea to *link* them so as to avoid disjointedness. The first part of the previous sentence constitutes just such a link (see how many more you can identify in previous paragraphs). It relates the idea of linking back to the earlier idea of splitting. Linking needs to be done with a light hand. You do not wish to spend half of each paragraph covering ground covered just before.

At the same time, you want to avoid the floating 'this'. I mean the 'This means . . .', or 'This is . . .' type of link, where it is totally unclear whether the 'this' is the whole previous paragraph, the last sentence or the subject (or even the object) of the last sentence. Whether you use 'this' to link sentences or paragraphs, you should always check that it is firmly 'anchored', i.e. that it is absolutely clear to the reader what 'this' is, with no ambiguity possible.

I have a strong suspicion that students are often tempted to use long words, sentences or even paragraphs because they feel that this is the expected academic style. Others think that a simple idea may be made more impressive in this way. There is also a feeling that jargon is necessary. Sadly, these feelings are well grounded. There was a depressing piece of research which showed that the same paper given to academic audiences was rated much more highly when the presenter used a high Fog Index delivery rather than a low one. You may, indeed, in the course of your studies, come to the conclusion that many of the 'difficult' papers you read in journals are expressing remarkably simple, even unoriginal, ideas, once you manage to penetrate the language in which they are written. It *is* part of the academic culture to write in a 'learned' style. And you *are* expected to use jargon, to the extent that it expresses course concepts directly relevant to the assignment set.

However, most management-related Master's courses aim to develop written communication skills needed at work. If your course has this goal, you will need to avoid the more academic style. Of course, I am not suggesting that you use only words of one syllable, sentences of no more than five words, and exclude *all* jargon. But try to use the simplest language consistent with expressing your ideas adequately, and only those jargon words that are necessary to demonstrate your ability to apply course concepts to problem situations. Almost all tutors, and most managers, will be more impressed by clarity than by unnecessary complexity.

Even with short sentences you may be prone to grammatical errors. If you suspect this to be the case, work your way through Helpfile 15.3 at the end of this chapter. This covers punctuation and its role in generating grammatically correct sentences, together with other common grammatical mistakes.

Avoid sensational or emotive language

While you want what you write to be as interesting as possible, it is best to avoid sounding like a cheap newspaper. For example, if you had surveyed the observance of health and safety guidelines in an organisation and found many shortcomings, it would be in order to describe the situation as 'worrying', 'thoroughly unsatisfactory' or 'in breach of legislation'. It would not be appropriate to talk of 'a downright disgrace', 'a thoroughly immoral situation', or 'another example of capitalist managers exploiting the oppressed workers'. It is possible to make your meaning perfectly clear while using slight restraint in your language. Indeed, you may make your point *more* forcibly in this way, as you will avoid reducing your credibility through inappropriate language.

Use the first person with care

You will need to check what the expectations of your audience are on this. For example, I have used the first person in this book, in common with many Open University texts. The views in it are personal, and I wanted also to avoid sounding too distant. Having cut my writing teeth in the OU context, I find 'the author' sounds pretentious. In any case, much of the text is intended to replace the tutor to whom you may not have ready access, offering the same sort of support. It is not intended as academically authoritative, and suggestions are offered for you to use as you please. 'I' seemed more appropriate therefore. But writing in the first person may not be the approved style for assignments, and may be totally inappropriate in organisational reports. Check before using it.

Check what you have written

Better still, if your spelling or grammar 'wobbles' on occasion, get someone else to check it for you. Your main sources of help are:

- **A dictionary** – keep it on your desk and consult it whenever in the slightest doubt.
- **The spellchecker on your word processor** – this will highlight non-existent spellings and mistypes, but unfortunately will not be smart enough to spot your mistake if your misspelling has generated a valid word, such as 'there' when you meant 'their'. Because of this difficulty a list of common misspellings (common in student assignments at least) is given in Helpfile 15.2 at the end of this chapter. This focuses on words where the misspelling is a valid (if unintended) word, and therefore unlikely to be picked up by the spellchecker.
- **A secretary** – if you still have one. Many (alas not all) secretaries have excellent command of English. If so, they may be willing to check your assignments before you hand them over. (Of course, if you dictate, the problem does not arise, though having a secretary who takes dictation is an increasingly rare facility.)
- **Anyone else** – it is always a good idea to ask someone else to read an important draft. This will enable you to check that your intended meaning is clear throughout, and to see what reaction it produces. Again, make it clear that you would *welcome*, rather than be offended by, corrections to grammar or spelling, and do not become defensive if corrections are offered.

The power of English

The clarity of your English depends partly on its correctness. And clarity will have a major impact on *all* your written communications. It will help you get good grades for assignments, will make a marked difference to your exam scores and will influence the way people react to reports that you write at work. While content is important, it is not sufficient. The way in which that content is expressed will influence both how much of it is actually communicated, and the way in which readers react to it. This is why your writing skills are so important.

Try the following exercise. If you miss some of the possible improvements, work through Helpfiles 15.2 and 15.3 at the end of this chapter, and then try some of the additional exercises on the **website**, to see whether your grasp of grammar and spelling has improved. During your course, pay careful attention to feedback from tutors on your writing style. Look for other sources of feedback on your writing, too, both during your course and thereafter, and try, where possible, to critique your own work.

EXERCISE 15.2

Improve the following text:

The problem in many organisations where labour turnover and absenteeism are high are that their is low moral and the affect of this makes workers less happy. This makes recruiting expences high, looses valuable skills from the organisation, and the staff remaining, who's moral then drops further. This is a viscious circle centred about a deepseeted problem. Yet, the managements' disinterest often means that there staff are caught in this trap for year's. This insures a constant decline in affectiveness. Personal departments are powerless to, if senior management support is absent. There as frustrated as everyone else are – and everyone knows what that means!

While it is easy to make mistakes, it is not difficult to improve the clarity, and correctness, of your writing. If you bear in mind the points covered in this chapter, refer to the Helpfiles where necessary, and always read what you have written, the production of written work for assessment can be a stimulating challenge. It need not be stressful, a chore to be postponed, and something which gives you little satisfaction and low grades, although for too many students this is sadly the case. Instead, each assignment can be both a vehicle for learning, and an enjoyable and satisfying task.

WRITING FOR THE SCREEN

I am not suggesting a change of career here. But many universities now ask you to submit your assignments electronically, and while everything in this chapter applies to assignments however they are submitted, there are a few additional points which can improve assignments that are to be submitted – and marked – electronically.

I speak with a certain amount of feeling, having just finished marking a batch of electronic assignments which, with appendices, were anything up to 70 pages long. I did not print off hard copy – that would have meant death to half a forest, and would have cost a lot in ink. This is a tutor's eye view of marking such assignments – the implications for you in preparing such assignments should be fairly clear.

The seven 'secrets' of successful electronic submission

1. **Be compatible** – with the system and my computer. You will usually be told what 'the system' requires. Even if this seems absurdly archaic to you, obey these instructions. Remember that universities are less likely to be using state of the art machines, or the very latest software. So use the version they say. Anything more sophisticated may not work on the assignment handling system and/or your tutor's machine. (A student recently submitted a beautiful-looking report, but the words in all the diagrams – which were essential to understanding her argument – appeared in what looked like Korean script on my machine. I could not give credit for what I could not read.)

2. **Keep within limits** – the system my own university uses has a maximum limit on file size. If you are scanning in materials, or appending highly formatted or very long organisational documents, you may be at the limit, and tutors' comments may push you beyond it so that the script cannot easily be returned through the system. So keep your file size well within the prescribed limit.

3. **Be legible** – or rather pity the tutor's eyesight. One of the great advantages rightly claimed for moving away from handwritten assignments was legibility. But reading from a screen is not always that much easier. A sans serif font like Arial or Verdana is much clearer on a screen than a fancier one like Times New Roman. (Avoid really fancy ones like *Harlow solid italic* at all costs, no matter how strong the temptation!) Font sizes below 11 (in Arial) may be difficult for anyone with less than perfect vision.

4. **Take care with your summary** – I find it particularly difficult to grasp a long report when reading it one screen at a time. A good summary which gives me the big picture of the whole report is an invaluable aid.

5. **Leave good margins** – the Word 'insert comment' facility is invaluable to tutors. It allows them to identify precisely the text to which a comment applies, and to insert that comment in the margin at an appropriate point without affecting your pagination. If your margins are miniscule, this doesn't work so well. Not all tutors will use this facility – some may intersperse their comments with your text, but you should at least give them the chance!

6. **Make 'navigation' easy** – in a paper assignment it is relatively easy to flip back and forth between a point in a report and the relevant appendix. With an electronic assignment this is harder, unless you use hypertext to allow linking. To the tutor this is a godsend, provided you also provide a 'back' button to allow easy navigation back to the relevant point in the assignment.

7. **Look at what your tutor says** – not all tutors will comment extensively. But if they do they may be as devastated as I was to learn that one student – a weak student whose work had prompted comments almost as long as her original – had been unaware that I was commenting at all. She had not bothered to look at the assignment again.

SUMMARY

- Written assignments need to be carefully planned, with the requirements of the intended audience fully considered.
- You need to be extremely careful to avoid plagiarism, using your own words rather than 'borrowing' those of others unless you give them due credit.
- Seemingly simple questions need to be broken down into their constituent, if implicit, parts.
- Diagrams can be useful in the early stages of planning content and structure.
- Plans need to be checked against requirements at regular intervals.
- Time management is essential if deadlines are to be met.
- Assignments may be asked for in a variety of formats. Clear structure and judicious use of subheadings will almost always improve clarity, even if a 'report' is not required.
- A report should be seen as essentially an argument based on evidence. This

evidence includes information about a situation and relevant theory. Your goal is to get your readers to accept your argument and consequent recommendations.

■ The drafting process should be started as soon as possible rather than left until evidence collection is complete. Several drafts will be needed, so early drafts can be amended in the light of subsequent findings.

■ Reports are normally in a format which includes: a title page with sender, addressee and date, as well as title; a summary; a list of contents; an introduction; the main body of the report, broken into major and minor subsections; conclusions; recommendations; a reference list; and any necessary appendices. Organisations may have house styles varying slightly from this.

■ Whatever the format, an appropriate style and correct use of English will enhance the clarity of your arguments. Simplicity of language is usually an advantage, and spelling and punctuation are important.

■ Where possible, diagrams and results important to your argument should be included in the text. More detailed supporting evidence should be included as appendices.

■ If you are asked to submit your assignments electronically, pay particular attention to appropriate presentation for reading from screen.

Further information

■ Blamires, H. (2000) *The Penguin Guide to Plain English*, Penguin.

■ Bowden, J. (2004) *Writing a Report*: 7th edn, Howtobooks.

■ Forsyth, P. (2006) *How to Write Reports and Proposals*, Kogan Page.

■ Giles, K. and Hedge, N. (1994) *The Manager's Good Study Guide*, The Open University.

■ Gowers, E. (1954) *The Complete Plain Words*, HMSO.
  Now available in Penguin. This is the classic work on use of English. It has been regularly updated even since the author's death, and is well worth acquiring.

■ Seely, J. (2002) *Writing Reports*, Oxford University Press.

■ Truss, L. (2003) *Eats, Shoots & Leaves: The Zero Tolerance Approach to Punctuation*, Profile Books.
  An amusing defence of appropriate punctuation.

■ http://www.leeds.ac.uk/library/training/referencing/goldenrules.htm

15

Writing assignments and reports

HELPFILE 15.1
Glossary of terms used in examination and assessment questions

If you are not used to answering assignment questions in social science subjects, the following interpretation of terms commonly used may help you to be sure that you are meeting the requirements of the question.

Analyse

This means to examine part by part. Thus, if you are asked to analyse a problem situation, you would be looking for the roots of the problem, rather than merely describing the symptoms which are presented. You would normally be expected to draw heavily on ideas and frameworks in the course being assessed in order to identify the root causes. The analysis may be the basis for suggesting possible ways forward and deciding between them.

Comment

This terse instruction may appear after a quotation or other statement. You are required to respond in a way that shows that you understand the topic to which the statement refers. Thus, you might need to define any terms contained, explain the significance of the statement and possibly evaluate it (*see* below), or state the extent to which you agree and disagree, and give your reasons for this.

Compare

This means look for both similarities and differences between the (usually) two things mentioned. It is very easy to forget one or the other, and safest always to think of 'compare' as shorthand for 'compare and contrast'. You would normally be expected to describe the similarities and differences, and perhaps come down in favour of one or the other. Sometimes it is possible to do this comparison using a table, with one column for each of the things being compared perhaps with a third column for comments.

Contrast

This is a subset of compare. You are expected to focus only on the differences between the things mentioned.

Critically appraise/evaluate

This means to discuss the strengths and weaknesses of a proposition or theory (*see* 'criticise' and 'evaluate' below – you will need to incorporate elements of both) in terms of its logic and the evidence on which it is based, and would need to identify any hidden assumptions.

Criticise

This means to judge the merit of a statement or theory, making clear the basis for your judgement. This might be in terms of the evidence on which a theory is based, or the internal consistency of that theory, or the theoretical, logical or factual underpinning of an opinion.

Define

This means to state precisely the meaning of a concept. Normally this will be a definition that you have been given in your course. Sometimes there may be competing definitions, in which case you may need to give both (or all, if more than two), and to discuss the differences between them. You will often be asked to include examples of the thing to be defined, but even if not, doing so may help to establish that you understand the meaning of the term in question.

Describe

This means give a detailed account of the thing referred to, again with a view to establishing that you know what is being referred to, and understand its significance. Diagrams can often help you to describe something, and should be included if they add something to the words.

Discuss

This means to extract the different themes in a subject, and to describe and evaluate them. What are the key factors/aspects? What are the arguments in favour of and against each aspect? What evidence is there in support and against? What is the significance of each aspect?

Evaluate

This means to say what something is worth. If a theory were to be evaluated, you would look at the evidence supporting the theory, and the usefulness of that theory to managers. You will often need to first establish the criteria against which something is to be evaluated.

Explain

This can mean to make something clear or to give reasons for something, depending on the context. Frequently you would need to do both to answer a question. Remember that your explanation, as with all assessment, is intended to demonstrate your understanding of the concept to your assessor.

Identify

This normally means you are to decide what the important factors are, and describe them briefly.

Illustrate

This sometimes means use a diagram or other graphic aid, but more frequently means give examples to show that you know what you are talking about.

Interpret

This normally means make sense of something, make it clear, usually giving your judgement of the significance of the thing to be interpreted. You might be asked to interpret a set of figures or a graph, in which case you would need to describe in words the significant features, or 'messages' contained therein.

List

This needs to be treated with caution. Strictly it means to give single words or phrases. But sometimes the assessor really means you to give a brief description rather than merely a single phrase. If in doubt with written assignments, ask. If in an exam, make a reasoned guess from the number of marks allocated to this part of the question.

Outline

This means give a brief description of key features of whatever.

. . . ?

By this I mean those questions which seem to invite the answer 'Yes' or 'No', e.g. '. . . Do you agree?' or 'Are budgets an adequate control mechanism?' It is very rare for the assessor to require a simple yes or no. It is far more likely that you are expected to discuss the statement, and evaluate it.

HELPFILE 15.2
Spelling (the right word)

Because spellcheckers and dictionaries exist, I make no attempt here to list all the words which appear misspelled on assignments. Instead I concentrate on those which occur wrongly so often that the student clearly has no doubts about their correctness, and which are valid words in themselves. They would therefore not be picked up by a spellchecker, and presumably do not cause the student to reach for the dictionary. I am assuming that you *do* use the spellchecker! It is an easy and vital tool, even if sometimes irritating.

advice–advise

The noun has a 'c', the verb an 's'. It is clear from the pronunciation which is which in this case, though people still make mistakes. You can use this pair as a model to help you decide in the case of other pairs, e.g. practice–practise, where the pronunciation is no help. Or use 'ice is a noun' to help you remember.

affect–effect

To 'affect' something is to change it, or to have an *effect* on it. As a noun, 'affect' is used by psychologists to mean mood. As a verb, 'to effect' something means to bring it about. Thus, 'In order to affect the way recruiters treat minority groups, it may be necessary to effect new legislation. The effect of the legislation should be to make discrimination illegal.'

councillor–counsellor

'Councillors' are elected local authority representatives (among other things). It is 'counsellors' who give advice, or counsel.

disinterested–uninterested

'Disinterested' means impartial or unbiased. If you mean someone shows no interest in something you need 'uninterested'. This mistake is *extremely* common, but highly irritating to more sensitive readers.

ensure–insure

To 'ensure' means to make sure. 'Insure' means to take out an insurance policy.

hear–here

'Hear' has to do with ears, 'here' means in this place (Beatles fans may fondly remember 'Here, there, and everywhere . . .').

imply–infer

'Imply' means to hint at. The speaker or writer implies. 'Infer' means to draw a conclusion, or inference, from something, and is done by the reader or listener.

i.e.–e.g.–etc.

The abbreviation 'i.e.' means 'that is', i.e. another way of saying the same thing. The abbreviation 'e.g.' means 'for example', so it is only a part of the same thing. If you mean 'and so on', you should use 'etc.'. But it is sloppy to use etc. more than sparingly. It can suggest that you haven't bothered to think an argument through. There is a fairly common school of thought (especially among editors) that none of these abbreviations should be used unless absolutely necessary.

it's–its

This is by far the commonest mistake I encounter. More than half of students seem to get it wrong. 'It's' is short for 'it is' – the apostrophe stands for the missing letter. 'Its' means 'belonging to it'. The confusion arises because in old English the possessive form used to be 'John his coat', or whatever. So when this was shortened to John's coat, the apostrophe was representing the missing letters. But now it just means belonging to, and its origins are forgotten. Check that you are in the minority who can use 'its' and 'it's' correctly.

lead–led

The metal is 'lead' (as in lead pipes), so too is the *present* tense of the verb, as in 'I lead the parade every day'. 'Led' is the past – 'Yesterday I led it, as usual'.

loose–lose

'Loose' means 'to unfasten', or 'not tight'. 'Lose' refers to misplacing something, or not coming first in a race.

moral–morale

This is another *extremely* common confusion. When you are talking about job satisfaction, you mean 'morale'. Every time 'moral' is used in this context it conjures up visions of defrauding the customer, or carryings-on behind the filing cabinets.

oral–aural–verbal

'Oral' has to do with the mouth, so refers to speaking (or taking medicine); 'aural' has to do with the ears; while 'verbal' means to do with words, which might be written or spoken. (Apparently ear drops labelled 'to be taken aurally' are often misapplied.)

personal–personnel

'Personal' means 'belonging to you', or 'private': if you mean 'employees', you need 'personnel'.

principal–principle

'Principal' means most important, or the head of something. 'Principle' means an idea, or truth. Or if you are into morality, it can refer to a code of conduct. So 'The principal consideration is . . .' or 'the Principal of the College ..', but 'An important principle when marking assignments is . . .'.

stationery–stationary

You buy envelopes – stationery – at a stationers. A car can be stationary.

their–there–they're–theirs

'There' is the place. (Remember 'Here, there and everywhere . . .'.) 'Their' indicates possession. 'They're' is short for 'they are', with the apostrophe indicating the missing letters again. Note, too, no apostrophe in 'theirs' (as in 'the car was theirs').

to–too–two

The only times you *don't* use 'to' is if you mean excessive ('too'), or the number ('two'). So 'Two of us are going to be too late'.

were–we're–where

'Were' is the past tense, 'we're' is the shortened version of 'we are', 'where' is the place (think of it as getting the answer 'there', which is only one letter different). So 'Over there, where we were, we're almost there'.

who's–whose

Another muddling case, like 'its', where the apostrophe indicates omission not possession. So 'who's' is short for 'who is', and 'whose' means 'belonging to whom'.

your–you're

And again, 'you're' means 'you are', while 'your' indicates 'belonging to you'.

You will see that by remembering the simple rule that an apostrophe stands for letters left out, you can cure many of the misspellings. For the rest, you will either need to learn the correct spellings by rote, or use mnemonics. For all other words that cause you doubt, use your dictionary. If you find it embarrassing to consult one openly, get an electronic one!

HELPFILE 15.3
Punctuation and grammar

Once your spelling is under control, the only thing left to worry about is getting the punctuation right. Punctuation can totally change the meaning of a sentence. Grammar checks on your word processor are some help here, but the following comments might also be useful. If you keep your sentences short, you will need very few types of punctuation, but are likely to want to use at least the following.

Full stops (.)

You will need one of these at the end of each of your (short) sentences. Check that your sentence is complete before putting the full stop. It might be a single word, such as 'No'. But if the sentence is longer, check that it makes complete sense. It will usually only do this if it has at least one verb (a 'doing' word, like 'write' and 'go') and a noun (person or thing) to do whatever it is. If the verb needs an object, i.e. is done *to* something, then the object must be in the sentence too. If you do indulge in long and complicated sentences, check that each verb has subjects and objects as required.

A full stop is also used to indicate an abbreviation, as in co., though is not needed if the abbreviation includes the last letter of the shortened word, as in Dr or many other titles. Remember the earlier caution about the use of abbreviations, however.

A series of three full stops, '. . .' can be used to indicate either that you are breaking off before finishing something or that you are omitting a section of a quotation. (This is called an 'ellipsis'.)

Question marks (?)

These are used instead of a full stop at the end of any sentence which asks a direct question, such as 'What are your objectives in seeking to gain an MBA?' But they are not needed if the question is reported, such as, 'Many students wonder why they are working for an MBA'.

Exclamation marks (!)

These can be used (sparingly) to denote excitement, or amazement, or to indicate humour or sarcasm.

Commas (,)

These are used to split up parts of a sentence to make the meaning clearer and allow the reader to draw mental breath. They may split strings of nouns, such as 'MBA students need time, self-discipline, organisation and motivation'. You could have added a comma before the '*and*'. In a longer list this would be preferable, for a short one it is less important.

Commas may split other lists, such as adverbs or verbs. For example, 'You need to work quickly, efficiently, thoroughly, and with extreme concentration', or 'You will need to think, plan, set deadlines, and monitor your progress'.

Commas are essential to split up more complex sentences with several parts. I shall not give an example, as this book is full of them: my husband says I have an unfortunate tendency towards baroque sentence construction!

When using commas it is essential to check that you have not inadvertently split a verb from its subject. You must not, for example, write 'The courses I am studying, include accountancy and marketing'. In this case *courses* is the subject, and *include* its verb. Similarly, avoid writing 'Panda eats, shoots and leaves'. (But do read Truss (2003) for more about commas.)

Inverted commas ("..."), or ('...')

Use these whenever you are quoting, whether speech or a section of text. You can use single or double inverted commas (if there is a rule, few people are aware of it), but should be consistent. You may sometimes have a quote within a quote. For example a passage of text you are quoting may itself include a quotation. If so, use double quotation marks to distinguish this if you normally use single, or vice versa. Quotation marks may also be used to denote titles of books or articles, although it is equally common to underline these or use italics to distinguish them.

Apostrophes (')

As already indicated, these indicate where a word has been shortened by omitting letters, e.g. 'didn't'. An apostrophe is also used to indicate possession, when s is added to a normal word, as in 'a dog's breakfast'. For plurals, when an s is there already, the apostrophe is added *after* the s, as in 'eight weeks' work'. Note that for odd plurals, where you *do* need still to add an s to indicate possession, as in men's, or women's, then the apostrophe is *before* the added s. Remember that where there is a special word to indicate the possessive, there is no need for an apostrophe. After all, you would never write hi's, so should not use one with its, yours, theirs, hers. Despite this, the use of *it's* to mean the possessive is probably the commonest grammatical mistake seen in assignments. Remember, 'it's' means 'it is'. The apostrophe is standing for a missing letter.

Brackets

These are used to separate off something that is an addition or insertion (such as an aside which casts light on what you have said). When they occur as the last part of a sentence, close the bracket *before* the full stop. (When a bracket encloses a complete sentence you should put the full stop before the bracket.)

Dashes (–...–)

These can be used instead of brackets to separate off the same sort of thing, or used singly to indicate a break in the train of thought – those occasions when inspiration strikes in mid-sentence.

Semi-colon (;)

This is a weaker form of a full stop. It is used to separate things that could be separate sentences, but which are closely linked, thus making the writing less abrupt. Always check before using a semi-colon that what follows it could stand as a sentence in its own right; if it does not, you should probably have used a comma. You also use semi-colons to separate the items in a list, when you started the list with a colon. You can use it before the final item in the list, even if this follows 'and'. You will need many resources for successful study: access to a good library; a place to work in peace; sufficient time; sympathetic family; and a supportive employer.

Colon (:)

This can be used to introduce a list, as in the example above, or in a way similar to a semi-colon, to link two clauses that could stand as sentences in their own right. You would tend to prefer the colon if the second clause explained the first, if you wanted to highlight a strong contrast between them, or if you wanted to draw particular attention to the connection between them. For example, 'He had no trouble getting on to the course: his father was head of department.'

Capital letters

These are used at the start of each sentence, or for names of people (John Smith), places (Paris), months (May), or adjectives derived from these (Elizabethan, French, Parisian), and for the first and major words in a title (The MBA Handbook).

Other common mistakes

The first is mixing singular verbs with plural subjects, or vice versa. So you should say 'one of the students *was* (not 'were') late', and 'the group *was* annoyed'. 'Data' is strictly a plural, but these days it is acceptable among all but extreme purists to refer to it in the singular, 'data is available . . .'. To say 'a data' still grates, and should be avoided. Talk about a piece of information if you don't like to use 'datum', the correct singular.

Another fault is using incorrect prepositions. It should be 'different *from*', not *to* (though 'to' increasingly seen), and 'centre *on*', not *round*.

Confusing 'shall' and 'will' is also common. You should say 'I shall', or 'we shall' when talking normally about the future. 'Will' is used only to denote strong determination. Thus: 'I shall sit my exam next month. I will work very hard beforehand'.

You should also avoid confusing 'can' and 'may'. 'Can' refers to being able to, 'may' to being permitted to. I *can* swim, as placed in water I shall not drown. I *may* swim here, because it is a public beach. 'May' can also mean that something is moderately likely to happen. It may rain tomorrow. 'Might' means less likely, but still possible. There might be a flood, but I should be very surprised.

Confusing 'due to' and 'owing to' is also frequent. 'Owing to' means because of, and usually comes at the start of a sentence. 'Due to' means caused by, and usually comes after the verb 'to be'. Owing to confusion over meanings, words are often used incorrectly. This is often due to poor teaching of English at school.

HELPFILE 15.4
If English is not your native language

If you are about to study in English for the first time, you may be worried about your abilities. This worry is reasonable, but may not be justified. Many students who are non-native English speakers write far better English than my native speakers! However, even if your chosen institution does not insist upon it, it is worth taking one of the standard English tests available to check that you are likely to be able to cope with Master's-level study in the language.

Three areas of competence will be important:

- **Reading** – you will need to read, and understand, a considerable volume of fairly difficult materials.
- **Speaking** – you will need to be able to follow, and contribute to, group discussions.
- **Writing** – you will need to be able to express yourself in written English in assignments, and, under pressure, in examinations.

I shall focus here on written English, although improving this will impact upon speaking and writing too, and one of the ways of improving your writing is to read as extensively as possible. For more detailed treatment of these points, see Giles and Hedge (1994), from which much of what follows is drawn.

To improve your written English you need to improve your vocabulary, and your grammar.

VOCABULARY

Although students often worry about vocabulary, the problem is seldom that the students do not use a wide enough range of words. More often, the words are used in a way that leaves their meaning ambiguous. Part of the reason for this lies in the difference between *active* and *passive* vocabulary. Words which you understand when read in context, but which you do not readily use, are part of your passive vocabulary. Those you use easily are active. (A similar distinction applies to grammatical structures.) It is likely that you will need to extend and consolidate your active, and perhaps also your passive vocabulary.

To focus your efforts you need to concentrate on frequency, speciality and utility of words. Clearly, words which you encounter frequently in your reading and in lectures are ones which you need to know, and probably need to be able to use easily. Log any such words where you are unsure of the meaning, check with dictionaries and native speakers to be sure that you do understand, note down and learn them!

Words which appear in assignments are of particular importance. You must be absolutely sure that you understand what the assignment requires. The glossary in Helpfile 15.1 is a good starting point, but always check any word in an assignment if you are unsure as to exactly what it means. And make sure that you *learn* the meaning of such words. They may well appear in examinations.

Beware of terms that resemble words in your own language. For example, the common word 'sensible' in English now means 'showing good sense' (as in 'sensible shoes', i.e. ones that are comfortable for walking in). Yet, the similar-looking Spanish or Italian '*sensible*' means 'sensitive', a meaning which the English word lost shortly after the time of Jane Austen. If something is not making sense it may be because you are assuming an equivalence that no longer exists.

Dictionaries are not a lot of help, however, for colloquial English. Some assignment writers revel in using such terms, perhaps in the interests of making a scenario sound 'real'. For example, a recent reference to 'mothballing' a factory (closing it down, but in a way that it can be opened later if there is a need for it) – puzzled one of my (French) students. If the dictionary offers no meaning which makes sense, you have no option but to ask a native English speaker for help.

Many of the words or phrases you encounter will be specialist terms. Some will have originated in the study of management or related subjects but most will be everyday words that are given a specific meaning when combined (such as transaction costs, or value chain). Normal dictionaries are of limited use here – but you should be given definitions for such terms, and you will be on an equal footing with other students, as such specialist terms will be new to them too. You may well not know the equivalent term in your own language (though if you have a management text from home you should easily be able to find it).

To extend your vocabulary, Giles and Hedge suggest the following:

- Write down words and phrases rather than merely repeating them in your head – this will help them stick in your memory.

- Try to learn vocabulary in context, so write new words and phrases into a sentence to learn the way they are used.

- Try to group new words with other words that frequently occur with them – for example 'personnel' might be grouped with: personnel manager; personnel department; military personnel; 'all personnel should receive health and safety training'.

- Set aside regular 'slots' in your study schedule for learning vocabulary. Don't make these too long. Little and often is more effective.

- Work out a system for recording your new vocabulary – for example 'groupings' could be shown diagrammatically on cards, to be easily carried around.

- Read for language acquisition – this is different from reading for information (also important). Identify problematic words, check the meaning, and if they seem important (in terms of frequency or utility) ensure that you have a correct definition and start a 'grouping' card for them.

- If your course has not yet started, use an introductory management text, together with an interesting book by a 'guru' and the *Financial Times* and/or *The Economist* as the basis for your 'reading for language acquisition'.

GRAMMAR

English grammar is complex and somewhat beyond the scope of this book. It is poorly understood by many in the UK who were educated in the 1970s and 1980s, when in state schools grammar was seldom taught. Hints are given earlier in the chapter. Study these. If possible, ask someone who is good at English to read your assignments before you submit them. Where they think grammar could be improved, make sure that they explain (if they can) what is wrong and why, so that you understand how to improve things. And ask tutors for as much feedback as possible. Some are reluctant to correct grammar for fear of seeming petty, but will do so if you show that you genuinely want their help.

If you are uncertain about your grammar it is particularly important to keep the structure of your sentences simple.

Answers to Exercises

Exercise 15.1

(If my counting is right)

Writing clear English:

Words: 151

Words of three or more syllables: 16

Percentage of such words: 10.6 (a)

Sentences: 10

Average sentence length: 15.1 (b)

Fog Index = 0.4(a + b) = 10.3 (OK)

Go for simplicity:

Words: 232

Words of three or more syllables: 45

Percentage of such words: 19.4 (a)

Sentences: 7

Average sentence length: 33.1 (b)

Fog Index = 0.4(a + b) = 21 (not OK).

Exercise 15.2

The problem in many organisations where labour turnover and absenteeism are high *is* (subject is 'the problem') that *there* is low *morale*. (This sentence is easily split here.) The *effect* of this is to make workers less happy. (You could argue that this is merely repeating the morale sentence . . .) *High labour turnover* (otherwise it is not at all clear what 'this' is) makes recruiting *expenses* (I know this word wasn't included in Helpfile 15.2: Spelling, but that doesn't mean you shouldn't look it up in a dictionary if unsure) high, *loses* valuable skills from the *organization* (either this American spelling, or the English *organisation* is acceptable in most cases, but be consistent) and *puts pressure on* (otherwise this part of the sentence lacks a verb) the staff remaining. (Another place where the sentence can be split, but if you chose not to, I hope you wrote *whose*.) Their *morale* then drops further. This is a *vicious* (dictionary again) circle, centred *on* (*stemming from*, or *caused by* would be better) a *deep seated* (*deeply rooted* better?) problem. Yet the *management's* (presumably only one management is being discussed in each case) *lack of interest* (surely they are hardly unbiased in this, merely unaware) means that their staff are caught in this trap *for years* (nothing belongs to the years). This *ensures* a constant decline in *effectiveness. Personnel* departments are powerless *too* (or perhaps *to act*, depending on the intended meaning), if senior management support is absent. *They're* (but *They are* would be much better) as frustrated as everyone else *is*. (Omit the rest, as the style is inappropriate, and in any case it adds nothing.)

It still is hardly incisive, or elegant, but it is better …

→ **16** # Making presentations

Learning outcomes

By the end of this chapter you should:
- understand the requirements for an effective presentation
- be aware of the faults which commonly reduce effectiveness
- realise the importance of delivery technique
- be able to structure a presentation
- know how to use visual aids effectively
- appreciate the uses and limitations of PowerPoint
- be confident in handling questions
- be able to control 'nerves'
- know how to produce a good 'poster' presentation.

INTRODUCTION

Most managers need to stand up in front of a group of people and make a prepared presentation occasionally in their careers. Some managers do it frequently. Presentations, like reports, are high-risk, high-visibility activities. Success, and failure, can have a significant effect on your career. Some managers rise to the challenge and thoroughly enjoy speaking in public. Others suffer agonies beforehand, and worry afterwards that they did themselves less than justice.

It is common for MBA and other management-related Master's courses to involve frequent group work, and for group members to take turns in presenting their group's results to the whole class. Such presentations are sometimes assessed, sometimes not. Even those who make frequent presentations at work usually have scope for improvement. Those with little experience of talking to groups may be so nervous about making a presentation that it interferes with both enjoyment of, and learning from, the exercise concerned, and may reduce marks gained for the work done.

At conferences, in addition to the main spoken presentations there will often be the opportunity for 'poster presentations' – or these may be a feature of in-course presentations. Many of the rules of oral presentation apply, but there are additional considerations.

While it is beyond the scope of this book to turn you into a *brilliant* speaker, or 'poster presenter', becoming *good* should be well within your reach. Although *bad* presentations abound, and you will doubtless have experienced many, the basic principles of effective presentation are remarkably simple. By following them, you should be able to create a professional impression that will serve you well on your course and in your job.

THE RISKS OF PRESENTING

There are many similarities between written and spoken presentations: both are designed to communicate in an ordered way. Spoken presentations carry additional risks, because speaking to an audience takes place in real time. You cannot try different versions, or go back and correct something you do not like. You cannot afford to go blank. And you have an audience there who will let you know if they do not like what you are saying. If someone starts to read a report that turns out to be inappropriate, they can put it down and waste no more time on it. If they are captive in the middle of a row in a roomful of people, they are more or less forced to hear the presentation through. They may feel strong resentment if it turns out to be a waste of time.

ACTIVITY 16.1

Think of an unsatisfactory presentation that you have attended recently. (Lectures are fair game here!) List the factors contributing to your dissatisfaction.

_____

_____

_____

_____

_____

If your experience mirrors mine, you may have listed factors selected from the following list: the speaker was inaudible; slides, OHTs or PowerPoint projections were illegible; the speaker's voice was a hypnotic monotone which had the entire audience asleep; the entire address was read; content was so muddled that it was impossible to follow; the speaker jumbled his or her notes, and spent most of the time trying to find out where they were; half the slides were upside down or out of order; you knew the content already; you didn't *want* to know the content; the room was hot, cold, stuffy or otherwise uncomfortable. The possible list is almost endless, but the above are common faults.

I still remember being subjected, at a society's national conference, to a speaker who gave as his speech a word for word replay of a paper of his that had appeared in the last issue of the society's own journal. I know this, because I had read it during the train journey there. (This speaker had been flown back to the UK at some expense to do this.) There was another splendid occasion when the speaker *read* his speech to a hundred people, all of whom had been handed copies beforehand. He was drowned out at intervals by the combined rustle of the audience turning pages in unison.

The working hours lost through audiences sitting through inappropriate or ineffective presentations must be beyond counting. Yet by attention to the principles of communication already covered in Chapter 14, and to the additional factors peculiar to oral presentation, all this could be avoided.

→ Ch 14

As before, it is essential to be absolutely clear about your objectives, and to have researched these to make sure that they are appropriate to your intended audience. If you are trying to do the wrong thing, it matters little how well you do it.

Presentational problems:

- content inappropriate to audience
- pace inappropriate to difficulty
- poor delivery
- location uncomfortable/ difficult for audience
- poor visibility of visual aids.

Once you have avoided the risk of shooting at the wrong target, you can think about your aim. Your delivery must be appropriate to your audience's knowledge and abilities. Your own manner is critical. You must avoid distracting or antagonising your audience by your mannerisms or style of delivery. Instead you must use your manner to make your message carry a force beyond that possible with the written word. You must pace your delivery so that your audience can easily absorb what you say. If you go slowly through the obvious, your audience will start to yawn. If you rush through complex arguments, those still awake will be totally confused. So adjust your speed to the difficulty of what you are communicating.

You must also work to minimise the problems presented by the location itself. There may be acoustic problems which work against you. You will need to find ways around this, whether by changing the seating pattern, or talking more loudly than usual.

Visual aids can be a problem. Slides may be under the control of someone with whom it is difficult to communicate. An OHP may be so elderly that fine detail or poor contrasts on a slide will be totally lost. PowerPoint projections can be very hard to see in a strong light. (Sunny rooms without blinds present real problems.) You will need, again, to adapt to what is available, as good visual aids can be invaluable.

Presentational strengths:

- clear structure
- appropriate content
- interesting delivery
- good illustrations of points
- audibility and visibility
- awareness of audience reaction
- keeping to time.

The most significant threat is also an opportunity. This is the possibility of audience interaction. Once you have written a report it stays written, even if it does not suit the audience. A live audience can give you many cues as to how well your presentation is going. Are they asking stimulating questions, or aggressive ones? Are they leaning back with their arms folded, or forwards, hanging on your every word? Are they *awake*? Audience interaction can become totally disruptive, making it impossible for you to present in a structured manner unless it is controlled. Carefully handled, though, it can make the whole event really stimulating for all concerned.

The remainder of this chapter is devoted to showing you what is necessary if you are to avoid the risks presentations involve, and make the most of the opportunities that they offer.

STRUCTURE

Remember that you are making a presentation for a *purpose*. There is something you want to say, and that the audience needs (you think) to hear. You have a story to tell, and want to tell it effectively. Because an audience cannot turn back the page and check what you wrote earlier, it is very easy for them to lose the thread of your spoken argument. Structure is therefore even more important in presentations than it is in written reports, and needs to be emphasised at frequent intervals. The old advice of 'Tell them what you are going to say, say it, and then tell them what you have said' still holds good. You will note the parallel, in a written report, of using an introductory summary, the main report, and then conclusions. It is possible to break these three broad sections down further.

Introductory section

Introduce yourself, explain your objectives, say how long you will be talking for, indicate the main points you will be making and how you will structure these. Make clear the ground rules concerning questions (for example, you may be happy to be interrupted with requests for clarification, but would prefer to take more substantial questions at the end).

Main section

Just as when writing a report, you need to clarify the problem situation which you are addressing: what are the significant factors in both situation and environment, and the evidence that change is needed? What was your remit, and how did you go about the work on which you are reporting? Describe the measures of effectiveness to be used in evaluating options, and how options score on these measures. Make clear what you are recommending.

When presenting orally, you will need to give additional pointers to internal structure within your main body. When you have finished dealing with one point, signal this by a brief summary of the point just made, and then a short statement of the point you are about to start on. Visual aids can be useful for this.

Conclusion

Summarise your key points, again using visual aids if appropriate, emphasise your recommendation or conclusion, thank your audience for their patience, and invite questions.

You will find that a simple and clear structure makes audiences much better able to follow a talk.

DELIVERY TECHNIQUE

Whenever you encounter a particularly good speaker, study their technique. See if they are doing things that would be of benefit to your own delivery. If you have yet to meet one, the following commonsense principles, adopted conscientiously, should improve your performance.

Aim to form a relationship with your audience

Try when you introduce yourself to sound human rather than too impersonal. Look at members of the audience. Check at intervals that you are on the right lines. Was that point clear? Can everybody see this slide? Treat questions with courtesy, and thank people for the points they make. Any attempt to make a member of the audience look inadequate will rapidly produce antagonism.

Make it easy for people to hear and understand

Speak clearly, without gabbling, and vary your tone. Avoid dropping your voice at the end of each sentence. Don't turn your back on your audience while you are speaking (blackboards are a hazard here). Use short sentences and straightforward language, using jargon only when absolutely necessary. Use the sorts of words and phrases you use for speaking, not those you would use in writing (the large difference between the two explains why it is often so difficult to follow a speaker who is reading).

Try to be interesting

Use visual aids (more on these shortly) to sustain interest, and vary your pace. Relevant jokes can be effective if used sparingly. Avoid jokes completely if you have any doubts at all about your skill in telling them. Bad jokes *may* have a place in an after dinner speech, but they are seldom useful in a course or work presentation.

Use detail sparingly

It is far harder to take in a mass of detail from a spoken presentation than from a written report. If detail is important, have a written handout for distribution before or after (*not* during) your presentation, to be used in much the same way as an appendix to a report. Handouts distributed *during* your talk will lose you your audience. It doesn't matter how many times you tell them not to read a handout until later: the temptation will be irresistible. If you do not believe this, try it once, on an occasion when it isn't all that important to hold your audience.

Keep any notes brief

It is reassuring to have notes, especially if you are nervous. Then you know that there is no risk of your 'drying up' completely. But keep them brief, and number them clearly so that if you *do* drop them in your anxiety, or they mysteriously rearrange themselves, you can reorder them easily. Cards are easiest to handle. Resist the temptation to squeeze as much on to each card as is physically possible. You need to be able to refer to your notes at a glance. You do not want to spend minutes peering at them to find where you are.

Mark the point at which you will be using each visual aid. Otherwise it is all too easy to leave one out. If someone else is presenting slides, you will then start getting them out of synch. Some speakers like to use overheads in lieu of notes. While this is frowned upon by purists, and certainly is not very creative, it can help clarify structure provided key points only are included, and thought is given to ensuring that they are useful to audience as well as speaker. However, there is a risk of giving a very dull presentation, and talking to your computer screen rather than your audience (*see* the discussion of PowerPoint below).

If you are afraid of 'freezing' completely, it may help to write out your entire speech. But keep it in your briefcase. Its mere existence (together with the other preparation you have done) will make it highly unlikely you will need it!

Watch the body language

If a glazed look of incomprehension is dawning in the eyes of your audience, you may not be explaining enough. Drooping eyelids may mean that you are going too slowly, or the audience knows the material already, or that your voice is too monotonous. If feet or fingers are tapping with restrained force, you are being highly irritating. If you do not know why people are starting to show such signals, *ask* your audience. And adapt your presentation accordingly. This is much safer than assuming you know the answer, and making things even worse.

You need to consider your own body language, as well as that of your audience. Are you distracting them by expansive gestures or over-exuberant pacing the floor? Are you showing signs of nervousness (thus reducing the authority of your presentation) by fiddling with hair, clothes, or contents of your pockets? You can reduce the chances of this by minimising the opportunities – tie back hair you might otherwise be fingering, don't wear jewellery, remove jangly objects from pockets. If you worry that this may be a weakness of yours, ask a friend to signal you if you are starting to distract your audience.

Don't try to fool people

It seldom works. If you know there is a weakness in your case, admit to it, rather than hoping that nobody will notice. (But do make sure that you have minimised such weaknesses by adequate preparation.)

16

Making presentations

Allow time for questions

Don't regard this as time which you are free to use by over-running your intended time. Not keeping to your allotted time is a sure sign of ineffectiveness. It is fine to extend into question time if your audience genuinely wishes this, but you should be disciplined about your contribution. Above all, you should avoid over-running the stated time for the session as a whole. Audiences plan their time, and do not like to have these plans disrupted.

VISUAL AIDS

From anyone but a highly gifted speaker, a presentation that consists of straight unbroken talk is hard to take. To maintain your audience's interest, some sort of variety is needed. If you are presenting a group's work, then it may be possible for different members to be responsible for different parts of the presentation. Visual aids, skilfully used, can provide this.

Visual aids can:

- reinforce key points
- clarify meaning
- aid retention
- keep your audience awake.

Also, there are some things that can be conveyed far better visually than by words alone. Relationships can be more clearly diagrammed, trends clearly shown via graphs. Video clips can be enormously effective in giving visual impressions of what you are talking about. An object waved in front of the audience can make a point. A faulty item will say a lot about quality. A pile of thick reports and a sheaf of computer printout will help you convince people that there is too much data and not enough information.

If your presentation is a lengthy one, say in excess of half an hour, then it is worth varying your aids. For example, if I am making a presentation to potential sponsors about our MBA programme it is important to give a flavour of how distance learning actually works. A set of graphs and bullet points cannot do this. So I show examples of video sequences, and of printed course units, examples of tutorial programmes and of pages of student assignments with tutor comments. This communicates important points, as well as varying the pace and maintaining interest.

You may wish to use a mix of diagrams: some could be on prepared slides, others drawn on a board or flipchart at an appropriate point in your talk to vary the pace. Handouts that you *do* want people to look at while you talk, such as a detailed table that you wish to discuss at length, can usefully be distributed as people take their seats.

It may sound obvious, but it is important that people can *see* your visuals. Even experienced speakers frequently get this wrong. The two commonest problems are barriers between some of the audience and the visual aid, and lack of clarity in the aid itself. Avoid being a barrier yourself. The speaker who obscures half the screen is all too common. Other barriers such as pillars and equipment may be a problem. You may need to ask people to move to where they can see, at least while you are using the screen. This is not ideal, but better than their sitting in comfortable blindness.

Overloading slides is an even commoner problem. All too often a speaker will project whole tables of figures or pages of text from a book or report, without a hope of any of the audience being able to read them. Your slides need to be capable of being read from the back of the room by someone who is just about ready for a new pair of glasses. This means that any words or numbers need to be *big*, so you will not be able to use many on a single slide. When using colour, be careful that this does not reduce contrast. (I have in my possession some professionally produced slides in tasteful shades of blue on blue. With a small room, and a really powerful projector they are nearly legible . . .)

Limit your visual aids to what is appropriate. For a short presentation you should need very few. The ease of generating slides on a computer (*see* below) leads some presenters to use far too many slides so that their audience retains nothing but a blurred impression of an endless series of visuals which they have had no time to absorb. They will have been so busy trying to read these at speed that they will have heard nothing the presenter has said. It is hard to look and listen at the same time, particularly to different words. Allow reading time, or read the same words, then expand upon them. And above all be selective. Use slides only when you need to.

Using PowerPoint

Computers make it remarkably easy to produce impressive overheads either for direct projection or for printing on transparencies. Few managers would contemplate giving a presentation without computer-generated overheads, usually using PowerPoint. It offers a number of significant advantages, particularly professional appearance, and flexibility. You can revise your presentation at the last minute, and easily tailor it to a particular audience. You can incorporate relevant tables and graphics (though *see* the caution above on complextity and overload). If you are carrying your laptop anyway, you do not need to carry anything additional. If not, or as a safeguard against loss, you can e-mail your presentation to whoever is organising the event. You can produce a handout with reduced versions of your slides and room for notes, at the press of a button.

Clearly these advantages mean that you do need to be familiar with the basics of using this, or a similar programme. You will not be credible if not. But it is probably only the basics that you need. PowerPoint can do far more than you are likely to need. You can produce fancy backgrounds, and all sorts of animations at the touch of a button, and it is easy to carried away by this. But beware – few of these elaborations help! Fancy backgrounds distract, and reduce clarity. Animations may look impressive, but are similarly distracting. While it is sometimes extremely useful to build up a picture a bit at a time, you should restrict use of the facility to such times. Words continually flying in from left and right will seldom help your audience to grasp and retain the points you are making. And now that everyone can use PowerPoint, being expert in its use is less impressive than once it might have been. Remember at all times that you are trying to communicate effectively, and use the tools at your disposal to this end alone.

There are less obvious, but perhaps more serious hazards with PowerPoint in terms of the way that it can easily constrain your presentation to an endless series of bullet points. As Naughton (2003) pointed out, it was conceived in a software sales environment. So it tends to turn everything into a sales pitch. There was a version of the Gettysburg address doing the e-mail rounds a while ago that demonstrated this limitation (*see* **www.norvig.com/Gettysburg**). But Tufte, a Yale professor and expert on visual communication, goes further in his criticism, arguing (in 'The Cognitive Style of PowerPoint', available, at the time of writing, from **www.edwardtufte.com**) that PowerPoint's ready-made templates tend to weaken verbal and spatial reasoning and corrupt statistical analysis. He attributes the loss of the space shuttle Columbia to a slide that led Nasa to overlook the destructive potential of the crucial loose tile.

This is not to argue for refusing to use anything but the hand-scrawled, barely legible exhibits that are still often used. They have their place in 'transient' presentations, for example on group work, where all you are seeking is to convey your thought processes to fellow students. But they would be inappropriate for a formal presentation to a client. (*Note*: a caution is still in order here. If using a photocopier, be sure to use special photocopying acetates – the normal 'write-on' acetates will melt their way into the machine's innards. Your institution will not thank you for causing them to call out maintenance staff.)

If you have no access to PowerPoint and projector, or an OHP, or want to vary pace, prepared flipchart sheets, or ones drawn as you talk can be used in the same way. Again, principles of simplicity and clarity apply. If you want to draw any diagrams as you go along, remember to leave blank sheets at appropriate points. An accomplice is useful if you are forced to use a flipchart. Turning the sheets quickly and elegantly is difficult: if you do it yourself it is bound to interrupt your flow.

HANDLING QUESTIONS

Questions can be enormously helpful, or can wreck a presentation entirely. Normally it is safest to restrict questions *during* your presentation to those seeking clarification, reserving more substantive questions to the end. It is all too easy, otherwise, to be sidetracked from your main argument, and to lose both direction and any chance of sticking to your planned timetable. Be sure that in postponing your answer you do so in a positive, courteous way. A questioner who feels 'put down' may go on to be disruptive. If you are holding a question until the end, make a note of it so that you do not forget to deal with it later, or ask the questioner to ask it again at the end.

The most important thing is to understand what is being asked. This is not as easy as it sounds. Careful listening is difficult when you are nervous, and questioners often ask multiple questions, or express themselves less than clearly. It is worth noting down the key parts of the question as it is asked, so that when you come to the end of dealing with the first part you are spared the sickening realisation that there was more, but you have totally forgotten what it was. If you are uncertain as to the meaning of the question, clarify it with the questioner. This will normally be taken as a serious attempt at meeting his or her needs, rather than evidence of your stupidity.

If a question challenges what you have said, resist the temptation to become defensive, or to attack the questioner. Take the contrasting point of view seriously. Unless you are completely sure that the questioner has misunderstood you or is misinformed, look for ways in which you can use it to *develop* your position. If they have misunderstood, and simple repetition or correction will not resolve the difference quickly, it is better to offer to discuss it in greater depth *after* the presentation, rather than get into an argument which few of the audience will find interesting.

People ask questions for many reasons, and you are likely to encounter some questions intended to display the questioner's own expertise rather than add to your presentation. Where this is the case, the simplest method is to praise the questioner's knowledge or understanding, agree with as much of the 'question' as you can, and thank the person for their contribution.

Where questions are pointing to a genuine weakness in your presentation, it is usually better to acknowledge, indeed share, the concern, rather than pretend that the problem is less than the questioner rightly thinks. It may, in this case, be helpful to ask the questioner, or other member of the audience, for suggestions as to how the problem might be resolved. You will need, at the same time, to ensure that a small problem is not allowed to grow out of proportion to your main argument.

DEALING WITH NERVES

Most people are nervous the first few times they have to stand up in front of a group of people and talk. Good speakers always retain a slight tinge of nervousness; they find this gives an edge to their performance. Complacency can lead to flatness and boredom all round, so a degree of nervousness helps. But you need to reduce it to a level that will enhance rather than detract from your performance. The factors which can help you here are practice, exposure to other similar situations, relaxation techniques and thorough preparation.

If you are in the minority who view presentations with extreme trepidation, take every chance, whether it be at work, in your leisure activities or on the course, to force yourself to talk in front of people. It really does get easier the more you do it.

→ Ch 5   Relaxation techniques were discussed in Chapter 5. They can be enormously helpful immediately prior to a presentation. If you have not practised such techniques, you may need to fall back on chemical substitutes such as a *small* drink or medication. If the latter, experiment beforehand to ensure that it does make you better able to perform. Drugs can have variable effects, and are best avoided if at all possible.

Increase your confidence in presenting by:
- frequent practice
- relaxation techniques
- thorough preparation.

Most important, though, is to be confident that you are well prepared. Knowing exactly what you are trying to convey and how you are going to tackle it, that you have thoroughly researched the topic of your presentation and have supporting evidence and examples at your fingertips, are the best possible antidotes to nerves. Look at the presentation not as a problem occasion but as an opportunity for doing something really interesting and worthwhile, as a challenge rather than a threat. If it is to fellow students it is an opportunity to develop skills, and any shortcomings will constitute a learning opportunity, for you, and for your audience.

To get you over a possible initial onrush of nerves, make sure that you have memorised your introductory remarks. Take a sip of water and a deep breath, go through your introduction, and by then you should be calm enough to enjoy yourself.

 ## PREPARATION

This is the key to successful presentations. You can *never* afford to cut corners here. It is essential to have researched your audience and the requirements for the presentation so that you are absolutely sure that you are aiming in the right direction. It is vital to have thought carefully about what to include and how to structure it, and about how best to add force to your arguments. It is important to have prepared the most professional-looking visual aids that circumstances allow. It is very helpful, as just suggested, to have learned your introduction by heart.

Unfortunately the necessary work goes beyond this. It is important to rehearse your arguments many times, so that you feel confident in expressing them. Some of this can be done piecemeal. You can work on sections while jogging, or *sotto voce* in the dentist's waiting room. But for an important presentation you *must* allow at least one full-scale rehearsal in conditions as close as possible to the actual presentation.

Arrange furniture to resemble the area from which you will be speaking. Visualise the audience layout. Position a dummy flipchart/OHP/computer (or whatever aids you will be using) as they will be placed on the day, and go through the motions of using them. Look at your non-existent audience, introduce yourself to them, and go through your entire presentation exactly as you plan to do it in reality. Only thus can you be sure that your proposed presentation will fit the time available. If at all possible, find an audience. Family, friends, colleagues or fellow students might oblige. Ask for their comments. Failing that, a tape-recording could give you insight into strengths and weaknesses of your proposed presentation. This may all seem like overkill, and for small informal presentations it may be. But if you are giving an important formal presentation and it matters that you perform well, and if you do not have a lot of experience, then the effort will be justified.

Another important part of preparation involves arriving at the location early enough to check *everything*. Are seats positioned so that people will be able to see all they need? Is the OHP or data projector set up and working and focused? Does your presentation work on the computer provided, if you have not brought your own? (This can be a real problem if you are using a laptop which 'speaks a different language' because you have travelled.) Is the video, if used, working and set up? Are tapes wound to the right point? Are flipcharts correctly positioned, and are there enough working pens? 'If anything *can* go wrong it *will*' applies as much to presentations as to anything else. It is unwise to leave anything to chance.

Finally, though this is often omitted, it is worth coming to an arrangement, perhaps on a reciprocal basis, with a colleague or fellow student, whereby they will give you honest feedback on your performance. Preferably you should schedule this for soon, though not immediately, after the presentation. Immediately after the event you may be in a state unsuited to the receipt of constructive criticism.

POSTER PRESENTATIONS

Thus far the chapter has addressed formal presentations to a (normally) seated audience. At conferences it is common to supplement the formal presentation programme with less formal poster presentations. You may, as part of your course, be asked to prepare such a presentation. Typically a large area will be made available for such presentations, and each presenter will be allocated wall space for a poster. The audience will wander round the room, looking at the various displays and stopping to discuss those of particular interest with the 'presenter', who will be standing by the poster ready to answer questions.

This allows participants access to a much greater number of presenters than would otherwise be the case, and is often used to allow students to present their research. If you are doing a dissertation, you may have the opportunity to take part in a poster session at an external conference. This sort of presentation is also sometimes used in organisational contexts, for example at meetings between members of different project groups, so it is worth extending your presentation skills to include this format. In either case the poster presentation tends to be aimed primarily at peers.

Poster presentations present their own communication challenges to the presenter. The 'talking' part tends to be less intimidating: you are talking to people individually or in very small groups. On the other hand these conversations are equivalent to the 'questions' part of a formal presentation, which is in many respects the most challenging as much of the control passes to the questioner.

The real challenge for most, however, is in poster design. Typically, you will have a space 1 m high, and 1.5–1.75 m wide. This space has to work hard for you. Obviously, (as with any communication) your first task is to clarify your objectives. What do you want it to achieve? Clearly this will depend on what you are presenting upon, and the context in which you are presenting. Are you simply aiming to inform as many participants as possible? If so, what are the key points you are trying to get across? Are you trying to sell yourself or your research and if so, to whom? Are you aiming to engage colleagues in conversation? If so, what would you particularly like to talk with them about? Are you seeking like-minded people from other universities with whom to network? If so, what would be most likely to interest such people? This is not an exhaustive list. It merely indicates the sort of objectives you might have. You need to be absolutely clear of your objectives on each occasion.

Posters aim to:
- attract
- inform
- start conversations
- advertise your work
- summarise achievements.

Clarity is paramount because 1.5 sq m is not very big, and anything within this space has to be visible from around 1.5 m. So every word needs to count, and you need to use pictures (or graphs or whatever) as much as possible. Aim to 'show' rather than 'tell'. A good rule of thumb is 20% text, 40% graphics and 40% space. This last 40% is not a 'waste of precious space'. You could cram more into it, but the overall effect would be far less than the impact of what you can communicate via the 60% if it is well laid out.

Given this limitation on what you can effectively include, there are some important questions to answer.

Sheila Cameron The Open University	LEADERSHIP: THE ANSWER TO EVERYTHING?

Introduction		Title C
xxxxxxxxxxx		xxxxxxxxxxx
xxxxxxxxxxx		xxxxxxxxxxx
xxxxxxxxxxx		xxxxxxxxxxx
xxxxxxxxxxx		xxxxxxxxxxx
xxxxxxxxxxx		xxxxxxxxxxx
xxxxxxxxxxx		xxxxxxxxxxx

Title A	Title B	Conclusion
xxxxxxxxxxx	xxxxxxxxxxxxxxxxxxxxxxxxxx	xxxxxxxxxxx
xxxxxxxxxxx	xxxxxxxxxxxxxxxxxxxxxxxxxx	xxxxxxxxxxx
xxxxxxxxxxx	xxxxxxxxxxxxxxxxxxxxxxxxxx	xxxxxxxxxxx
xxxxxxxxxxx	xxxxxxxxxxxxxxxxxxxxxxxxxx	xxxxxxxxxxx
xxxxxxxxxxx	xxxxxxxxxxxxxxxxxxxxxxxxxx	xxxxxxxxxxx
xxxxxxxxxxx	xxxxxxxxxxxxxxxxxxxxxxxxxx	xxxxxxxxxxx

Sheila Cameron The Open University	LEADERSHIP: THE ANSWER TO EVERYTHING?

Context	2	4
xxxxxxxxxxxxx	xxxxxxxxxxxxx	xxxxxxxxxxxxx
xxxxxxxxxxxxx	xxxxxxxxxxxxx	xxxxxxxxxxxxx
xxxxxxxxxxxxx	xxxxxxxxxxxxx	xxxxxxxxxxxxx
xxxxxxxxxxxxx	xxxxxxxxxxxxx	xxxxxxxxxxxxx
xxxxxxxxxxxxx	xxxxxxxxxxxxx	xxxxxxxxxxxxx
	xxxxxxxxxxxxx	xxxxxxxxxxxxx
	xxxxxxxxxxxxx	xxxxxxxxxxxxx
	xxxxxxxxxxxxx	xxxxxxxxxxxxx
		xxxxxxxxxxxxx

1
xxxxxxxxxxxxx
xxxxxxxxxxxxx
xxxxxxxxxxxxx
xxxxxxxxxxxxx
xxxxxxxxxxxxx
xxxxxxxxxxxxx

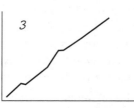

5
xxxxxxxxxxxxx
xxxxxxxxxxxxx

Fig. 16.1 Possible layouts for poster presentations

- What are your (very few) key points?
- How can you convey these graphically?
- How can you lay these out on a poster so that they will communicate to someone walking past at a distance of up to 2 m?

Remember, you may be in competition with many other posters, and participants will not look in any detail at more than a small proportion of these. You will not have time to talk to everybody even if you attract them. So how can you ensure that you engage those people with whom you are likely to have the most profitable conversations, prime them to ask the most useful questions, and leave a favourable impression both of you personally and of the work that you have done?

If you Google 'poster presentations', you will find a wealth of information on how to lay out posters for maximum impact. The essential messages are:

- You need to say who you are, where you come from, and the topic covered by your poster – IN VERY LARGE WRITING.
- You need to have a clear 'path' through the poster so that people can follow the narrative easily.
- You cannot afford to waste a single word – '**Findings**' or '**methodology**' do not convey much information by themselves. But something like '**80% misunderstand age legislation**' carries a message. Think newspaper headlines here. Writ large, and with bar charts or other simple graphics to support them.
- You need a way of continuing the exchange when you have 'engaged' someone's interest. At very least show your e-mail address clearly on the poster. Even better, have a handout expanding on key points, with your e-mail on it. Safest of all, particularly if your key aim is to network, to have people write *their* e-mails (or write it for them) and e-mail a more substantial document – the text behind the headlines – a couple of days later, with a note saying how much you enjoyed talking to them.

Figure 16.1 shows two possible layouts for poster presentations for a standard research presentation. You may be able to be far more creative – but do remember the need for clarity from 1.5–2 m. Messy and cluttered does not on the whole attract.

This chapter has introduced the basic requirements for effective verbal and poster presentations. You can use knowledge of these, together with practice, and reflection on that practice, to bring about considerable improvements in your performance, and this should be more than adequate for your course. If presentation skills are crucial to your job, you may need more help than this chapter can give. Try everything suggested, and get feedback from colleagues, but, also, you might consider asking your employer whether you could go on one of the many excellent short courses on the topic. There, with intensive video feedback and tutor support, you should be able to develop your skills to a high level.

16

Making presentations

SUMMARY

- Effective presentations depend on thorough preparation.
- You need to be clear about what you are trying to do, and what your audience needs.
- Structure is even more important than with written reports.
- Good visual aids are easy to produce and very effective.
- PowerPoint can be an asset, but you need to be careful it does not 'drive' your presentation in ways that are unhelpful.
- Audibility, visibility and ability to pace your delivery to suit your audience and content are very important.
- For poster presentations similar considerations apply, but you need to maximise your use of limited space.
- Questions can be an asset but must not be allowed to be disruptive in a face-to-face presentation.

Further information

- Bradley, A. (2006) *Successful Presentation Skills* (3rd edn), Kogan Page.
- Collins, J./Video Arts (1998) *Perfect Presentations,* Marshall Publishing.
- Conradi, M. and Hall, R. (2001) *That Presentation Sensation,* FT Prentice Hall.
- Leech, T. (2001) *Say it like Shakespeare,* McGraw-Hill.
  This gives an interestingly different slant on presenting.
- Manchester Open Learning (1993) *Making Effective Presentations*, Kogan Page.
- Naughton, J. (2003) 'How PowerPoint can fatally weaken your argument', *The Observer,* 21 December.
- Williams, J.S. (1995) *The Right Way to Make Effective Presentations*, Eliot Right Way Books.
- http://www.ncsu.edu/project/posters/NewSite/ (accessed 15.04.07).
  There are many useful websites on poster presentations, but try this one.

→ 17 Passing examinations

Learning outcomes

By the end of this chapter you should:

- understand the purpose of examinations
- realise the importance of preparing, and following, a sensible revision plan
- know how to prepare yourself physically for the exam
- be able to control nerves during the exam
- recognise the best questions to answer
- understand the necessity for time management during the exam
- be able to answer your chosen questions fully and effectively.

INTRODUCTION

Examinations are generally recognised as an unsatisfactory way of assessing most of what management education is trying to achieve. Many institutions now regard continuous assessment, together with an element of organisation-based project work, as better indicators of student learning. But examinations have virtues of convenience, ease of standardisation and the ability to ensure that what is assessed is indeed the student's own unaided work. Distance institutions, in particular, find it hard to develop an acceptable substitute for this kind of assessment. It is much harder for them to ensure that students do not receive help with continuous assessment, and an examination is therefore necessary to prevent students gaining undeserved qualifications. Examinations are also still seen as important by accrediting bodies.

In my experience, examination boards go to extraordinary lengths to *pass* students. But sometimes they cannot help feeling that the student has perversely gone to a similar amount of trouble to thwart their efforts. This chapter examines the main reasons for exam failure, suggests ways in which you can prepare for examinations, and introduces techniques which you may be able to use in the examination itself to ensure success. The focus is on written exams. Other forms of examination and assessment, including *viva voce* examinations, are covered in the next chapter.

→ Ch 18

TYPES OF WRITTEN EXAMINATION

Probably the commonest form of written examination is an unseen paper of two or three hours' duration, which you are required to answer without access to books or notes. Thus, you will be drawing upon your memory of what was in the course. This can seem quite daunting if you have not sat such an exam for some years, and you may worry about whether your memory is as good as it once was. If you prepare as suggested in the next section, you should have fewer problems than you fear.

Three other forms of written examination are reasonably common. These are computer-marked papers, 'open-book' exams and exams based on case studies issued in advance of the exam. Each presents hazards which may not be apparent at first sight. They are therefore discussed briefly here.

Computer-marked exams

Although these are more popular at lower levels of study, they are sometimes used at Master's level. They are good at checking factual recall, if carefully constructed can test understanding, and are cheap to administer and mark.

There are two key points to note if you want to do well. First, 'wrong' answers may be penalised. If this is the case, it may be safer to miss a question than to guess. Find out what rules are being operated in your case, and adjust your strategy accordingly.

Second, questions may be fairly complicated, and possible answers cunningly chosen to catch you out if you have not fully appreciated what is being asked. (If you have a certain kind of twisted mind, it can be great fun setting such questions!) You therefore need to read questions very carefully indeed, making sure you understand the significance of every word, and to think carefully before answering. Obvious answers can be wrong.

If you are not given lots of practice in the sorts of questions you are likely to encounter try to get hold of past questions and spend some time trying to work out how the examiner's mind was working.

Open-book exams

In these exams you are allowed to bring course materials and notes into the examination. This may seem infinitely preferable to relying on memory, but beware the following:

1. Any time spent looking things up in your materials will mean less time for writing. If you have a lot of materials and a small exam desk, you may spend so long searching for that elusive section that you write very little indeed. To avoid this, you still need to be extremely familiar with the course content, so that you need to make minimal reference to materials. It can also help to have a note of where key diagrams or equations can be found.

2. Anything you merely copy from materials will gain you zero marks, demonstrating little more than the legibility of your handwriting. You therefore need to keep

quotations to an absolute minimum, giving brief summaries of key points, perhaps with references, rather than extended quotes or reproductions of diagrams. Reserve the bulk of your time for actually *answering* questions, as outlined in the remainder of the chapter. If you have not sat an open-book exam before, it is particularly important to do a practice exam under normal time constraints and conditions. This will help you become more aware of how easy it is to fall into the traps outlined, and be more aware of how to avoid them.

3. A good index, prepared with the exam in mind, is essential for an open-book exam and, even then, aim to make minimal use of the book, resesrving most of the time for writing.

4. Remember that open-book exams do *not* reduce the need for revision. While it may be useful to refer to the book for a detailed formula which you will then *use*, the normal time constraints of an exam will mean any other use of books will be severely restricted.

Seen case studies

In these exams you are given a case study in advance of the exam, to enable you to study it. You are not, however, usually given the questions that will constitute the exam. You may or may not be able to bring the case into the exam. If you are, there may be limits placed on the amount of annotation allowed. It is important to find out what will be allowed, and work out how best to exploit this. It is possible to write quite a lot in margins, and underlining can be crucial. Cross-references to ideas or other relevant cases could be added.

Whether or not you can take anything in to the exam, spend as much time as possible familiarising yourself with the detail of the case, analysing it, thinking about which course concepts are relevant, predicting possible questions and trying to answer these. You may be able to work with others on case discussion. If so, exploit this. It is probably worth setting each other unseen questions and then marking each other's efforts. This can give you useful insight into the examiner's mind, and into what is meant by 'exam technique', as well as showing aspects of the case that you may not have fully appreciated.

COMMON CAUSES OF FAILURE

Almost all student failure can be put down to a limited number of causes. Some of these are remarkably simple to remedy, others far more difficult.

Not knowing enough

This is the reason students imagine to be most likely to cause them to fail, but it is fairly uncommon for this factor alone to be responsible for failure. It is usually possible to pass an examination with very limited knowledge, certainly knowing far less than the whole of a course being examined, provided that what you *do* know is relevant and put to good use. Conversely, you may 'know' a great deal – in the sense of being able to reproduce it – but gain few marks if you do not understand what it means, why it is important, or how to use it. If you devise a revision plan, as suggested later, there should be little chance of your entering an exam not knowing or not understanding enough to pass.

Poor time management

Common causes of failure include:

- poor time management
- answering too few questions
- missing out parts of questions
- not actually answering the question
- not using course ideas.

This is by far the commonest apparent cause of failure. In most exams you will be expected to answer a set number of questions. The marking scheme will allocate marks accordingly, and your scriptmarkers will abide by this scheme. The familiar 80 : 20 rule applies. You can expect to get 80% of the marks with only 20% of the effort that full marks would require. So the pursuit of perfection is a certain route to failure. It is essential that you spend a reasonable time answering each question required. Even if you feel you know nothing about your last choice, still spend time on it. You are likely, despite your ignorance, to gain more marks by attempting it than by spending the time polishing another answer. *Never* inadvertently leave yourself no time to answer one or more questions. Always work out how much time you can afford for each question, and keep a close watch on the clock to ensure that each question gets its fair share. Heavily weighted questions should, of course, receive a time allocation in proportion to the marks they are worth.

To illustrate the importance of this, imagine that you have to answer four equally weighted questions. (This means that each question is worth up to 25 marks of your final score, but markers may well mark each out of 100 and then scale down.) It will be fairly easy to get 30% (i.e. 7.5 marks toward your overall score), even on a question about which you are very unhappy. If you do not attempt it, you will get zero. The same time spent working on another question *might* have raised what was already a 65% to a 73% (i.e. add two marks to your overall score) but would be highly unlikely to bring it up to 95. If your overall performance is marginal, the difference between the 7.5 marks gained by the first strategy, and the additional 2 marks by the second strategy might easily make all the difference between pass and fail.

In working out your time budget, you must allow sufficient time for reading the paper and thinking about which questions to answer. Also you will need time to plan your answer. Writing time is therefore very restricted. Do not expect to be able to write a lot. And do *not* feel you have to go beyond your time budget because your answer does not look long enough. Some of the highest marks go to short answers, provided they are relevant and well structured.

Failing to answer the question asked

Of course, those whose time management is awry will fail to answer the question. But there is another significant group of students who allow sufficient time for a question, but then proceed to write what seems to be an answer to something completely different. As examiners will usually be marking to a scheme which allocates so many marks to each sub-part of a question, an answer bearing little relation to what was expected will gain few marks. The only exception to this is when a student has found an original, but still valid, interpretation of the question. Then, if the marker is sufficiently alert to realise that this *is* valid, it may be marked on its merits. There is no guarantee, however, that such an answer will be accepted, so you are not advised to aim for originality.

→ Ch 15

It is absolutely crucial that you spend some time making sure that you understand what the question is asking for, and identifying all the different parts which may be hidden within a seemingly straightforward question. This is not always easy under exam conditions. It is worth checking, too, that you are not straying away from the question during the course of your answer. Re-read the question at intervals while you are writing your answer, to make sure that you are not drifting away from the main point, or omitting important sub-points. You may find it helpful to refer to the glossary of terms commonly used in exam and assignment questions given in Helpfile 15.1 (at the end of Chapter 15).

Panic

A tiny minority of students find themselves in a state of total panic in the exam. If you are prone to this, you should consult your doctor well in advance, so that the problem may be both registered and addressed. You should also devote time to learning breathing and relaxation exercises, and practise these as much as possible before the exam. Such exercises are also helpful if you do not suffer from outright panic, but are still nervous enough in the exam for it to affect your performance.

Illegible script

Markers may be faced with 100 or more scripts to mark in a very short period. If they can barely read your writing, they may miss many of the points you thought you had made. You will receive disappointing marks in consequence. If your writing problem has a medical cause, consult your tutor to see whether it would be possible for you to type or dictate your answer. If your writing is simply difficult to read, you should practise writing legibly at speed, well in advance of your first exam.

Other problems

You may anticipate other problems, or encounter them unexpectedly. Perhaps you fall ill shortly before an exam, or suffer a major problem at work or home. If so, as with other problems, it is imperative that you let your tutor or someone else in authority know about the problems, and that your exam performance has been affected in consequence. You should inform appropriate people as soon as it is at all possible. Most institutions will make allowances for such things if they know about them. They cannot take problems into account if they are unaware that anything is wrong.

While there is a range of potential problems, it is important not to get these out of perspective. Each is unlikely, and may never happen to you. It is merely important to know what you should do in the unlikely event that disaster strikes. However, most students on most MBA and other management-related Master's courses pass their exams. With only a little attention to the rest of this chapter you should be able to end up in that large majority.

EXAM PREPARATION

→ Ch 9 In one sense, your exam preparation starts when you begin to study the course. If your note taking was done with revision requirements in mind, then subsequent preparation will be much easier. However, at some point prior to the exam you will wish to focus more specifically on revision, and on developing a strategy for gaining good marks in your exam. As with many of the techniques suggested in this book, the action required is simple and straightforward. But it does require time and planning, and the discipline to start working towards the exam early, well in advance of it being sufficiently imminent to cause anxiety.

To prepare effectively:
- identify what is required
- plan your revision time
- revise actively
  - summarise
  - diagram
  - test knowledge
  - practise answers
- keep fit.

You will probably find you use your time more effectively if you go through the following stages as you start your exam preparation.

Identify requirements

It will not surprise you that, as with any other project, you need to know as much as possible about what is required. It should be possible to obtain past exam papers and analyse these for the sorts of topic covered and the type of question asked. Try to put yourself in the examiner's position. It is not easy to think of suitable questions that can be answered in 45 minutes (or whatever the time allocation) under exam conditions. It is even harder to devise questions which will allow students to show that they know, understand and can use parts of the course covered. Some topics will be much easier to write questions on than others. These will naturally predominate. Other topics are so central to understanding a subject that they are almost certain to be needed.

Look at the format of the paper. How many questions are there to choose from? How many topics does this mean you can afford not to revise? With a little research you should be able to identify those areas of the course that it would be dangerous not to know, those which look useful and those which look less important. You should also have a clear idea of the absolute minimum you must know to have even a chance of passing, the amount that would be fairly safe and what would give you a comfortable margin of error.

Find out from your tutors what *level* of knowledge is needed. Is it fine detail or broad principles? It is a waste of time learning the finer details of employment legislation if all you are required to know is the broad categories covered. But if you *will* be required to know precisely under what conditions a claim of unfair dismissal can be brought, then broad principles will not be enough. Find out, too, the balance of theory to practice which is required. Many of these finer points will vary from course to course, so you will need to gain information on each course for which there is an examination.

Make sure that you know what, if anything, you can take into the exam room. For some courses you are allowed to bring your notes or a limited amount of printed information. Check whether any case studies issued in advance of the exam should be brought in. If so, their margins may be usable for other notes too – check whether this is allowed. Programmable calculators provide interesting possibilities; again, institutions have different policies as to whether these are allowable. Palmtops are unlikely to be allowed. If the course has totally open-book exams, check you have read the caveats earlier in the chapter. Such examinations are dangerous if you are unused to them.

Prepare a revision plan

This is possible once you are clear about requirements. Decide how much of each course you wish to cover in depth, which parts you will give slightly less attention to, and what, if anything, you are going to omit. Think about the time you realistically have available for your preparation, and allow a contingency factor for the disasters that are all too common at critical points like exam time. Think about *how* you wish to work. Do you want to go through the course once, or several times? How *will* you go through it? Clearly you do not have time to read all the books again. Will some parts take longer than others because they do not come easily to you? If you have got into the habit of planning your work earlier in the course, this stage should be almost second nature to you now.

Prepare a chart, showing when you will work on each part of the course. Remember to allow time at the end for overall preparation, and practising with past papers. And do not rely on the night before the exam. That is better used for purposes other than revision. Your chart should have spaces for you to tick off each piece of work completed. Although this is not strictly necessary, you will find that it helps motivation enormously. Sustaining motivation may be important if you are starting to revise well in advance of the exam.

Revise actively

Once you have allocated your time for preparation, use this time so as to gain maximum benefit. Merely reading through your books and notes in a passive way is unlikely to be of value. As you tackle each topic, you need to bear in mind the following questions:

- What do I need to *learn* (e.g. formulae and diagrams)?
- What do I need to *know* and *understand* (e.g. principles and techniques)?
- What do I need to be able to *do* with the above?

Your exploration of requirements should have put you in a position to answer these questions.

Keep these questions in mind as you work through your materials. You may find it helpful to keep two sorts of notes, those on facts you must learn, including key references, and those on more general points. Even if you followed the advice of taking your course notes with revision in mind, you should still take notes as part of your exam preparation. Condensing your original notes, perhaps progressively, is an excellent way of absorbing material.

I have seen some excellent one-page summaries of entire courses, and students often circulate these electronically. Recipients express almost ecstatic gratitude. This may be misplaced. They do not realise that although such summaries are an invaluable culmination of hours of revision they are no substitute for it. Their value depends upon having gone through the process of producing them. Thus while they will help the person who produced them enormously, their value to others may be very little.

En route to producing such a summary, aim to interact with the materials in as many ways as possible. Draw diagrams of text. Describe course diagrams in words. Try to represent relationships with equations. List possible uses of different techniques. Figure 17.1 shows an example of some notes which have incorporated some of these different things.

Some of your summarising can be done as a kind of test, without looking at materials. You can then go back and see whether there is anything significant that you have left out, or anything you have misremembered. You can also test yourself by inventing possible exam questions when you have finished a summary, and then (after a decent interval) trying to answer them. Use past exam papers too, sketching out skeleton answers. Practise going through the following routine:

→ Ch 14

- analyse the question to see what it is *really* asking, underlining key words (*see* Chapter 14);
- identify key parts of the course which are relevant;
- identify relevant concepts, techniques, theories and examples from that part of the course;
- sketch out the way in which these could be used to answer the question.

Aim to do this fairly quickly. It will save it from becoming tedious, and will give you valuable practice in organising your thoughts rapidly. Then go back to your course materials to check that you have not omitted other relevant ideas or examples, and that those that you *thought* were relevant do indeed contribute what you thought they would. By *working* on materials in this way, you will find that revision is not boring, and that you will retain material much better.

Of course, you will still probably have to *learn* a limited number of things using old-fashioned rote learning, unless you were wise enough to identify such things during your course and learn them as you went along. It can be helpful to write such things on index cards so that they are easily portable, and to carry them about with you so that you can learn them on buses, in the bath or whenever else your brain is not otherwise occupied.

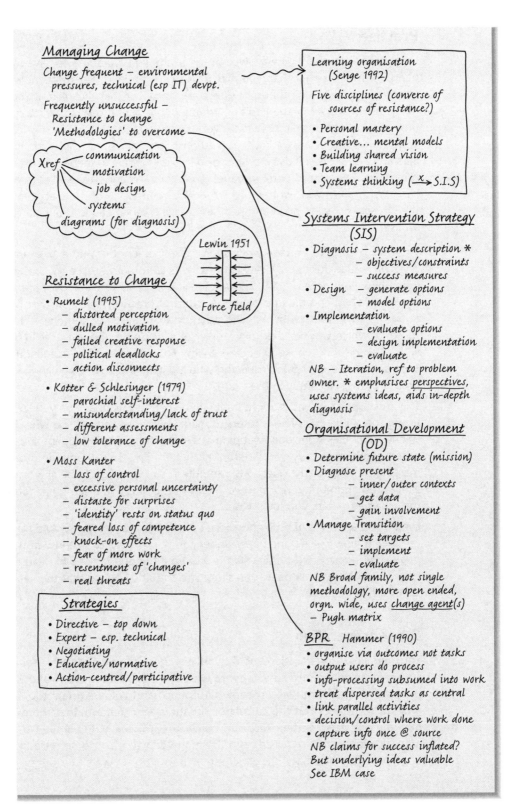

Managing Change

Change frequent – environmental pressures, technical (esp IT) devpt.

Frequently unsuccessful – Resistance to change 'Methodologies' to overcome

Xref — communication
— motivation
— job design
— systems
— diagrams (for diagnosis)

Lewin 1951
Force field

Resistance to Change

• Rumelt (1995)
  – distorted perception
  – dulled motivation
  – failed creative response
  – political deadlocks
  – action disconnects

• Kotter & Schlesinger (1979)
  – parochial self-interest
  – misunderstanding/lack of trust
  – different assessments
  – low tolerance of change

• Moss Kanter
  – loss of control
  – excessive personal uncertainty
  – distaste for surprises
  – 'identity' rests on status quo
  – feared loss of competence
  – knock-on effects
  – fear of more work
  – resentment of 'changes'
  – real threats

Strategies

• Directive – top down
• Expert – esp. technical
• Negotiating
• Educative/normative
• Action-centred/participative

Learning organisation (Senge 1992)

Five disciplines (converse of sources of resistance?)

• Personal mastery
• Creative... mental models
• Building shared vision
• Team learning
• Systems thinking ($\xrightarrow{X}$ S.I.S)

Systems Intervention Strategy (SIS)

• Diagnosis – system description *
  – objectives/constraints
  – success measures
• Design – generate options
  – model options
• Implementation
  – evaluate options
  – design implementation
  – evaluate

NB – Iteration, ref to problem owner. * emphasises perspectives, uses systems ideas, aids in-depth diagnosis

Organisational Development (OD)

• Determine future state (mission)
• Diagnose present
  – inner/outer contexts
  – get data
  – gain involvement
• Manage Transition
  – set targets
  – implement
  – evaluate

NB Broad family, not single methodology, more open ended, orgn. wide, uses change agent(s)
– Pugh matrix

BPR Hammer (1990)
• organise via outcomes not tasks
• output users do process
• info-processing subsumed into work
• treat dispersed tasks as central
• link parallel activities
• decision/control where work done
• capture info once @ source
NB claims for success inflated?
But underlying ideas valuable
See IBM case

Fig. 17.1 Example of summary notes

17

Passing examinations

Practise

Unless word processors are allowed in the exam, you are going to have to sit, pen in hand, for much longer than you may have done for years. Many students are now so unused to putting their thoughts directly on to paper that they can no longer do this freely. If you are out of the habit of writing with a pen, it really is worth spending some time getting back into it. Otherwise you may find that there is an unwelcome block which inhibits your answering the questions. So start by practising writing anything at all, with a pen! Keep a diary, send old-style paper *letters* to friends, or experiment with using Julia Cameron's 'morning pages' technique as suggested earlier (*see* Chapter 6). Do a first draft of your written assignments by hand. Any of these activities will reopen the channel between brain and pen, and make it much easier to answer questions in an exam.

→ Ch 6

The next thing is to practise writing for the sort of length of time an exam will take. This will reduce the risk of developing writer's cramp, and make you better able to judge how your time is going without looking at your watch all the time. This practice is probably best combined with the next sort of practice, that in answering real exam questions. You can start by working on individual questions, some of which could be those for which you sketched out answers earlier. Some, though, should be questions which you have not looked at before. Allow yourself an appropriate length of time for each question. Build up to answering whole papers if possible, again working to the time limit that will apply in the exam.

This exercise will be much more useful if you can get feedback on your performance. Ideally, persuade one of your tutors to mark your work and tell you where you went wrong. Alternatives include swapping attempts with a fellow student and marking each other's work, or putting your attempt away for a few days, then trying to work out a marking scheme for the questions attempted. You will need to be very careful to allocate an appropriate ration to *each* part of the question attempted. You can then use the scheme to mark your own work.

Even if you are short of time and cannot do all the practice you would like, it is essential that you write one paper under conditions as close to those of the real exam as you can manage. Not only will this give you a good idea of what you can do within the time, but it will habituate you slightly to the situation, so that the nervousness you suffer will be reduced.

Other preparation

Your remaining preparation should concern more physical matters. You will need a supply of pens that are easy to write with and not likely to go wrong when you most need them. You will probably find pencil and colours useful too, and a ruler and rubber. Check out the calculator situation. Find out whether there is anything else you will need in the exam and make sure it is ready. Remember to take any identification that is required. And if you are allowed to take in refreshments, consider whether a flask of coffee and a snack might revive you during a long exam.

Make sure you know exactly where an exam is to be held: double-check this. You might be sure and *wrong*. A friend recently arrived late and breathless at an exam, having run two miles across town from the hall where he had sat *other* exams.

Some of your preparation should concern getting yourself in shape for the exam. Working all the hours there are for the weeks before the exam and keeping yourself going on black coffee is not the way to enter the exam with a functioning brain. The additional stress of being in the exam room may be enough to completely disintegrate you. Very occasionally students will work so hard before the exam that they are barely able to write their names on the paper. This is a tragic waste of effort. It is far better to enter the exam slightly underprepared, but with your brain fresh enough to make good use of what you do know.

So include exercise in your revision plan, and make sure that the night before the exam you get some more exercise, do something relaxing and go to bed early rather than indulging in last-minute cramming. I remember feeling terribly guilty just before my finals, because I encountered one of my tutors when I was out on a long walk. But much to my surprise, rather than condemning my laziness, she praised my common sense. I have since come to see that she was right. Exams are not about suffering, but about how best to achieve a desired level of performance.

After all this, it remains only to get to the examination in good time. This means allowing for the worst that the road or rail system can do to you, and for fog, flat tyres, etc. In other words, allow plenty of time, and then some. It can do dreadful things to your concentration if you rush into the exam at the last possible minute, knowing that you have left your car on a double yellow line, and still sweating from the exertion of running to the exam hall.

DURING THE EXAMINATION

If you have followed your revision plan, and prepared yourself adequately for the exam, you should be keyed up enough to give your best performance but not over-anxious. The following guidelines for the day itself may be useful.

Use time before the exam to relax

If you arrived early, as suggested, go for a walk, or get a coffee. Try consciously to relax. Visualise yourself sitting calmly, feeling clear-headed and in control, writing fluently and confidently.

Read the paper carefully

If you have a choice, much will depend on your choosing the best questions. You will need to read the paper carefully and think about how you might answer each question before making your choice. If there is a compulsory question, you may prefer to answer that first, and then take a coffee break while you think about the rest of the paper. Or you may feel that reading the paper may give you ideas about how to answer the compulsory part. Much will depend on the nature of the paper. It is often useful to highlight the separate parts of compound questions, to ensure that you do not accidentally miss some out.

Work out your time allocation for each question and monitor time usage

You *must* be disciplined about this. The results of poor time budgeting have already been described, and it is essential that you avoid these. Note the time at which you will cease working on one question and move to the next, and keep to these times. Allocate time within questions according to the likely marks allocated to the different question parts. You can work these timings out before the examination if the format is known. When doing your calculations remember to allow some time for reading the paper. Sometimes you will see a question with different weightings attached to each part. Ration your time accordingly. If some questions carry a heavier weighting than others, allocate time accordingly. During the exam make sure that you move to the next question on schedule. If this does not allow you to finish an answer, jot down key points still to make and leave space. You can come back later if you save time on another question. This is a safer strategy (80 : 20 rule) than aiming to finish but getting behind schedule.

Read each selected question very carefully

It is essential that you understand exactly how the examiner wants the question approached. Do not choose a question simply because you know a lot about the topic to which the question refers. Students often give the impression that they have learned a topic, and then taken the question as the excuse to write down everything they have learned, rather than making their answer relevant to the question asked. Consider the following question (it may be nothing like the sort of questions you will encounter, but the principles remain the same).

> *To what extent do accounting techniques provide adequate control mechanisms for an organisation?*

This is a seemingly simple question, but consider how much is potentially contained within it. What sort of control mechanisms does an organisation *need*, and what does control *mean* in this context? What is the nature of accounting-based controls? (You would need to give some examples to demonstrate your point.) What, therefore, are their strengths in terms of organisational control? What are their weaknesses? What sorts of problems might arise if control depended solely on accounting techniques?

You can see that a student who wrote down all the accounting techniques he or she knew, complete with all the formulae, would gain few marks. They would have demonstrated that they knew all the techniques, but not that they understood their implications, nor anything about the context in which they were used, which was what the question was all about.

In choosing your questions, it is more important that you understand what the question is driving at, than that you can remember all the details of the topic in question. If the question relating to your pet topic puzzles you, resist the temptation to answer it anyway, unless there is nothing else on the paper that you understand. Avoid what seem to be totally open-ended questions in favour of those that are themselves clearly structured, thus indicating the structure expected in your answer. The former question type may *look* as if it doesn't matter how you approach it, but it is in fact dangerous to assume this. The examiner may have very clear ideas about what is required. Look at the **website** for additional questions to 'deconstruct'.

Spend time planning your answer

It is usually essential to spend time thinking about how you will tackle your answer. Mind maps can be very useful here, as they will build on whatever structure is suggested by the question to provide a skeleton for your answer. By following this structure, you will be able to write coherently, and to the point. Time spent planning and making notes is seldom wasted. You may have less time to write your answer, but that time will be used far more efficiently. (There was a student who wrote three pages of notes and half a page of answer, but that is the only time I have known someone suffer from spending too much time planning. He appealed against his fail grade claiming that he had put a note on the exam paper explaining to the examiner that he had run out of time, and that his failure to answer the questions should not therefore be held against him!)

If you are running short of time, never cross out your notes until you are sure that you have covered everything in them. It is safer not to cross them out at all. Make notes on a separate page, clearly labelled 'Notes' and leave them there. Examiners are supposed to ignore any work that has been crossed through. However, if they are desperately seeking the extra mark you need to pass, they *may* be more charitably inclined if it is clear from your notes that you had a good grasp of the issue and merely ran out of time.

Use a clear structure

As in your written assignments, you will find subheadings make the structure of your argument clearer. This is particularly important if your *writing* is hard to read. Diagrams can also usefully be included as part of your answer. Be careful though. This is an area where pursuit of perfection is particularly dangerous. Drawing a beautiful diagram can take ages. Aim for quick clarity rather than anything too artistic. Your examiner will expect no more.

If a question asks for a particular form of answer, say a report, make it look right. For a report you will gain easy marks by saying who it is to and from, and titling it, and giving a list of contents (fill these in at the end, having left space). And if it asks for calculations, show your working as well as the result. In this way you will pick up marks for doing it in the right way, even if stress causes you to make an error.

Check at intervals that you are still on course

This applies not only to your time usage, but also to the way that you are answering each question. Once you have worked out what the question is asking, you need to check at intervals that you are still answering this. It is all too easy to get carried away by your flow, and wander off the point. Re-reading the question at intervals, and checking that you are still on target, is essential. A skeleton answer prepared at the answer planning stage helps prevent such wandering, as well as increasing your chance of answering *all* of the question.

Remember what you are trying to do

To do well in exams:

- budget time carefully
- choose questions you understand
- identify all parts of a question
- plan your answer
- use diagrams where possible
- move to next answer on schedule.

Above all, in writing your answers follow the same rules as you would for continuous assessment. Remember that you are trying to show that you *know*, *understand* and can *apply* the concepts taught in the course. Avoid unjustified assertions, go for reasoned argument instead. Build your argument from evidence and texts you have studied. Quote key authors when using concepts, preferably with a date. And even when an essay is required, rather than a report, use *introduction* and *conclusions* sections in your answer, and use other subheadings where they help make your structure clear.

If, despite your best intentions, your time management goes awry, force yourself to stop the question you are working on, even if not complete, in order to spend 15 minutes jotting down notes on the question you have not had time to answer. Again, it is important to give examiners something on which to exercise their charity, if you are needing it.

Above all, don't worry too much about examinations. As was said earlier, the great majority of students pass, so even if you do not take the advice in this chapter your chances are pretty good, and better if you don't lose sleep worrying. If you do plan your preparation, and follow a sensible strategy during the exam, you should be almost certain of success.

SUMMARY

- Examinations test a narrow range of skills but have many practical advantages.
- It is important to plan your exam preparation, starting well in advance of the exam date.
- This preparation should be aimed at ensuring that you are physically, as well as academically, in good shape for the exam.
- Active revision is far more effective than passive.
- Use past exam papers if at all possible.

- During the exam it is important to budget time carefully, to read questions thoroughly and only attempt those that you are sure you understand. You should check at intervals that your answer is still relevant.
- If you *do* encounter problems that interfere with your preparation or examination performance, let your college know at once.
- Take heart from the fact that most students at this level pass their exams.

→ 18 | # Other forms of assessment

Learning outcomes

By the end of this chapter you should:

■ understand why alternative forms of assessment may be used

■ appreciate your assessors' objectives in each case

■ be in a position to work out a strategy for satisfying those objectives, whether assessment is by oral examination, via an assessment centre or portfolio based

■ be starting to assemble material for a portfolio 'just in case'.

INTRODUCTION

Traditional examinations are designed to assess *knowledge*. But management education has been steadily moving away from mere transmission of knowledge, and towards the development of competence, and the ability to apply knowledge to make sense of real situations. With this move has come increasing use of alternative types of assessment, although examinations *are* still used, particularly in institutions concerned to gain or retain accreditation. Written assignments are common, and have also already been covered. Projects and dissertations are equally prevalent, particularly so with specialist Master's degrees, and are dealt with in the next chapter. But you may well encounter a range of other forms of assessment on your programme, and these are dealt with here.

→ Ch 19

The first, portfolio-based assessment, is increasingly used by professional bodies as part of a case for gaining, or retaining, membership of the profession. Even if your course does not use it, you may need to compile a portfolio in other contexts. Personal Development Files are one form of such a portfolio. The second form, the assessment centre approach, is more commonly used as a selection tool within organisations, so, again, the skills concerned are highly transferable. The third type of assessment, the face-to-face or viva voce examination, is probably the oldest form of examination. In some counries it is still the prevalent mode. It is increasingly being seen as a necessary supplement to newer forms of assessment. It is also widely used in its traditional roles of defending a thesis or dissertation, and when additional evidence is needed in the case of borderline students.

Obviously, you will need to select those parts of the chapter which are relevant to your own programme (or to assessment encountered in your job). Whichever parts of the chapter you are using, you will find an emphasis on the likely objectives of your assessors. If you understand these, you are more likely to be able to satisfy them and to do well, whatever the form of assessment.

THE REASONS FOR ALTERNATIVE APPROACHES

There have been several references already to the dissatisfaction felt with traditional forms of assessment. To be acceptable, assessment needs to be reliable, valid and cost effective, and must contribute to the learning process.

It must be reliable

If the assessment is repeated, or if different assessors are involved, the result should be the same. You would be unhappy if you felt that your exam score or portfolio grade depended upon who marked it, or on whether you took the course this year or last. (Unfortunately, even examinations are seldom as reliable as you might suppose: few institutions are brave enough to double-mark papers blind, i.e. with neither marker knowing what the other gave.)

It must be valid

The assessment must measure what it purports to measure. An assessment on a course which depended more on your ability to write coherently than on your understanding of the important parts of the course would hardly be satisfactory. More than *being* valid, it is important that the assessment is *seen* to be valid. If you were assessed by a method that was, in some absolute sense, valid, but which nobody believed to be so, your qualification at the end of the day would be worth very little.

It must be cost effective

You would not want the cost of your course to be doubled by the use of an enormously sophisticated assessment process.

It should contribute to the learning process

Even an exam does this by providing you with the motivation to work intensively on the course over a finite period. This can help the integration of the concepts taught, as you will be forced to hold them in your brain at the same time. Other forms of assessment are better at contributing to learning. For example, doing a project for assessment can be highly developmental.

The unease with current forms of assessment on management courses does not stem from inside information concerning inter-marker *reliability* on assignments or examinations, although it well might. It stems from a much deeper questioning of the purpose of management education. If the purpose is not merely to impart knowledge but to develop *competences*, then traditional examinations, which are aimed firmly at testing knowledge, are not *valid*. Competence is more than knowledge. It includes a mixture of skills and attitudes as well. Some form of assessment which tests these is needed.

This argument is clearly very important at lower levels of management. There are basic management skills, such as the ability to interview someone for a job or to chair a meeting effectively, which it would be reasonable to expect of anyone with a management qualification. It is possible to ask a student to write about drawing up person specifications or constructing interview plans. Someone who displays understanding of the processes involved should be in a better position to interview effectively than someone who does not. But it would be quite possible to know what should be done and still be absolutely hopeless at selection interviewing.

Similarly, while an understanding of the principles of running meetings is helpful, it does not ensure effective chairmanship. If assessment is to be *valid*, therefore, some way of assessing such skills is essential. If it is accepted that management education should have a skills development element, then valid ways of assessing skills must be found.

PORTFOLIO ASSESSMENT

Some management programmes are now designed around the performance standards drawn up for National Vocational Qualifications (NVQs) in management. Although this is more common at Certificate and Diploma level, part at least of your chosen programme may be assessed in this way. More generally, graduates of Master's programmes are expected to be able to demonstrate 'a range of cognitive and intellectual skills together with techniques specific to business and management. They should also demonstrate relevant personal and interpersonal skills'. These will need to be assessed. Some, including 'critical thinking' or 'the capability to identify assumptions, evaluate statements in terms of evidence, detect false logic or reasoning, identify implicit values, define terms adequately and generalise appropriately' or 'numeracy and quantitative skills including the use of models of business situations' can be assessed by conventional methods. Others – such as 'managing creative processes in self and others' or 'personal effectiveness: self-awareness and self-management; time management'; 'sensitivity to diversity in people and different situations'; 'the ability to continue learning' or 'learning through reflection on practice and experience' – will be better served by some form of portfolio and or personal development file assessment.

The NVQ approach of splitting management skills into a number of discrete generic competences does present difficulties, and is perhaps less popular now within management than 10 years ago. But the claim that portfolio assessment is more valid, and more reliable, than traditional assessment is still common. Working through a set of standards or competences, reflecting on your strengths and weaknesses, and thinking about suitable evidence of your ability can be a stimulus to considerable learning.

A major drawback of this form of assessment, however, is that it is extremely expensive. There are no economies of scale. Candidates need individual support. Portfolios can take hundreds of hours to assemble, and many hours to assess. And there may be a need to supplement portfolio assessment with observation of behaviour in the workplace, or in a simulation thereof, and by questioning in order to check that the candidate has the necessary understanding and knowledge of the job areas covered.

If you are not currently working as a manager, or are in a very specialist role, you may be able to draw on experience outside work, for example in a voluntary organisation, but many part-time students find they have no time for such experience! While simulations may be carried out as part of your course (e.g. a role play of a grievance interview) to provide some evidence, portfolios relying heavily upon simulated evidence are not encouraged.

However, if you are a practising manager and part of your course is based on an NVQ framework, with assignments designed to generate evidence for a portfolio, this can be a useful added bonus. If so, or if you think you may later need to compile a portfolio for professional purposes, it is worth understanding the approach and thinking about the sorts of evidence that you already have access to. You can then ensure that you preserve it.

Constructing a portfolio

In order to develop a portfolio, it is essential that you know the standards against which you will be assessed. This presents problems if you are constructing an anticipatory portfolio! If your course involves portfolio assessment, ask your business school as soon as possible for a copy of the relevant standards. If you are developing a portfolio or a personal development file for a professional institute, approach them for details.

If you have only a broad idea of the skills that are relevant, you could still start to think about how a 'just in case' portfolio might be assembled. If you have the full list of competence elements and the associated performance criteria, you can plan in more detail the evidence you should collect.

Ask yourself first whether you think you have each skill in question – you will need to do this for a personal development file. Then consider when and how you use it. If your portfolio is for personal development, you then need to write down an action plan for any further skill development needed, and log the development process. If your goal is to prove you already have the requisite skill, think about what *evidence* you could produce to demonstrate this.

The sort of evidence you consider might include, among other things: business plans you have drawn up; policy statements you have drafted; budgets you have constructed; staff development plans you have made; interview plans or records (or even tape-recordings of the interviews); reports you have written; or letters you have sent. DVDs you have made, either intended as communications or specifically as a record of some activity such as chairing a meeting, might be suitable evidence. The list is almost endless.

For each piece of evidence, note the competence(s) it relates to, and any context helpful for an assessor. Thus, to an interview plan, you could add a note saying what it was about the candidate's application form that made you want to concentrate on these points, or include the form itself, removing any identifying features to protect confidentiality. You could also include the person specification for the job. Indeed, if you were responsible for drawing up the person specification yourself, comments giving your reasons would again be helpful. If an activity such as a training session were the basis for demonstrating your skills, you could include not only your plan for the session, and a justification for this, but feedback

Evidence for assessment should:

- be carefully selected
- demonstrate relevant skills
- be indexed to relevant standards
- address each of the standards
- have accompanying explanatory narrative.

forms from candidates, and a note as to how future sessions would be modified in the light of feedback.

You can see how a portfolio will rapidly become fairly bulky, if you are keeping hard copies, but also how it can help you to reflect upon your effectiveness in your job, and how its compilation may be developmental and rewarding, rather than a chore. (If you are compiling an 'ePortfolio' within a virtual learning environment, storage may still be an issue if document files are large.) If the portfolio is primarily for developmental purposes, it can be highly motivational to include evidence that your action plan has been successfully carried out, and you are using the skill developed. Conversely, if you are keeping a learning diary or study log as suggested earlier, this might usefully be incorporated into your portfolio to demonstrate your ability to learn by providing a comprehensive record of skills development and application.

In addition to your supplementary notes, you might think about the ways in which you could prove that work is indeed your own. If you have a sympathetic superior, you might be able to get a signed note saying that work was done by you, or under your supervision. You may occasionally receive a letter thanking you personally for your efforts in a particular endeavour. Add all such evidence to your portfolio.

If you are constructing a 'just in case' portfolio, you should be careful about going to great lengths in generating *new* materials. Your efforts might be misdirected. But there is good reason to think about everything you do, about the skills that it demonstrates, and what, if anything, you could preserve as evidence of that skill. (Remember to remove sensitive pieces of information.) You can then draw on your 'evidence' whenever the need arises, whether for MBA assessment, for use in your annual appraisal, or in support of a job application. You will also be able to retain useful materials should you change jobs.

There should be a secondary and fairly significant benefit. While thinking about the skills you are demonstrating, you may realise that there are skills that you are *not* demonstrating, either because you do not have them or because your job limits what you can do. In either case, the information should help you to work out your own personal development plan, if possible in discussion with your training manager or your appraiser.

If you have a gap before your course starts, beginning to plan a portfolio with your training manager or appraiser might be an excellent form of preparation, particularly for a more skills-based course.

ASSESSMENT CENTRES

Many organisations use assessment centres as a way of identifying development needs in their managers, or for selecting staff for rapid career progression. Assessment centres put groups of employees through a number of activities, many of which simulate the sort of behaviour that will be required at work. Group problem-solving exercises and in-tray activities are obvious examples. Management games, fact-finding exercises, analysis and presentation (akin to a case study) and simulated (and real) interviews are also used. Trained assessors rate participants against set criteria, and decisions are taken, and feedback is given, on the basis of these ratings. Similar methods may also be used by colleges as an adjunct to more conventional assessment forms, and as a supplement to portfolio assessment.

You can see that assessment centres are expensive to run. They are therefore mainly used for staff likely to reach senior levels. But apart from the expense, there are problems of validity. Often only sketchy attempts have been made to validate the process, and train assessors. Thus, the criteria used, and any judgements made, are questionable. Are they relevant and fair? Do they merely replicate existing management styles, thus entrenching exactly those styles and practices that need to be improved?

If judgements of your performance at an assessment centre can profoundly affect your career, as when 'failing' forever bars you from promotion, these concerns are extremely important. Where such centres are used as one of several sources of information which is used to construct a development plan for an individual, possible weaknesses in the system may be less critical.

Preparing for assessment via simulation

As already indicated, assessment centres are widely used in industry, and on the more competence-based Management programmes. If your own programme uses such assessment, it should not present you with any serious problems. It will probably consist of observations of your performance in the sorts of activities to which you have become accustomed during your course, and indeed your career. However, as much of the debate about assessment centres concerns the validity of the criteria against which assessments are made, you would be well advised to do as much research as you can into the sorts of criteria which will be used in your particular case.

For in-company assessment centres, criteria are often derived after consultants have interviewed senior managers in that organisation. From these interviews they extract criteria which are felt to distinguish successful managers within that organisation, as perceived by those senior people. Particularly in an organisation with a strong culture, this may be a reasonable way of proceeding.

'Old faithfuls' are in-tray exercises and leaderless group discussions, planning exercises, where there is access to an overabundance of information requiring the ability to select from this what is needed, simulated consultancy exercises and computer-based management games.

It is difficult to prepare yourself specifically for assessment centre-type assessment, beyond doing all you can to find out as much as possible about the organisation and its culture, and about what is being assessed. If possible, practise the skills identified. You may find that your self-help group can be a useful source of feedback on any group work activities to which you may be subjected. Apart from that, the only preparation you can undertake is the more general preparation described in Chapter 17, aimed at ensuring that you are in good physical and mental shape for the assessment.

→ Ch 17

VIVA VOCE EXAMINATIONS

Oral assessment is the earliest assessment form of all. It is still frequently used to help examiners decide upon borderline examination scores and for theses and dissertations. It is also used for assessment which is heavily portfolio based, as a way of checking those areas where the portfolio left doubts either about the candidate's current understanding in an area of competence, or about the extent to which the work is entirely his or her own. Because one-to-one oral examinations can be tailored to each individual candidate, they are more flexible than mass examination, although normally more expensive for an institution to provide.

Preparing for a viva voce examination

You may be given a viva because of a borderline mark in a written examination. Or it may be because your exam mark does not properly reflect your ability, perhaps because you were ill when you sat it. Some institutions routinely examine by viva everyone who submits a dissertation. Some do this only if examiners have concerns about the work. The first thing you need to do is to find out *why* you are being given a viva.

If it is to give you the chance of improving on a mark gained in a written examination, then you should do the same sort of revision that you would normally do for a written exam. You will be tested on your depth and breadth of understanding of the course in question. You could usefully also reflect on what you did in the exam, and any weaknesses that you know you displayed there. It is likely that your examiners will have looked at your paper. If you are already aware of what was wrong with it, it will be a mark in your favour. If you have paid special attention to remedying any weaknesses identified, and are now in full command of the material where you were weak before, you should be in an excellent position. Do not limit your revision to such areas, however, as you may well be asked about other areas of the course as well, and would not wish to reveal weaknesses of which the examiner was not already aware.

If your oral is a routine one, required of all students in support of a project or dissertation, then apart from making sure that you can remember what is in the dissertation (and given that you will have sweated blood in writing it, it is unlikely that you will have forgotten) little preparation is needed. You might wish to think again about your 'reflections' section and what you learned, and about any areas where you know your research to be weak and how you can explain or defend these. Examiners are fond of focusing on both areas.

But, usually, a routine viva for a dissertation will be aimed mainly at assessing whether the work is your own. This will be done by testing your understanding of both methods and results. The existence of enough in-depth knowledge to confirm your involvement is normally established very quickly. The exam then usually turns into an interesting discussion on the finer points of your research, presumably a topic dear to your heart.

If the project viva is a non-routine one, find out all you can about the reasons why you have been selected. Your project supervisor should be able to help here. It may be that there are weaknesses of which you are all too aware in your report. If so, think of ways in which you can strengthen your position in the oral. These are likely to involve explaining why the weaknesses were unavoidable, if this was not gone into in depth in your report. Be prepared to say how, if you were starting the project with the benefit of hindsight, you would avoid these weaknesses in future work. Avoid excuses, and instead focus on taking a constructive approach based on the lessons your project has taught you.

Finding out weaknesses

Clearly you will need to know what the weaknesses were felt to be. Check with your supervisor that your list is complete! The weaknesses which you don't know about are the most dangerous! It is important to find out what these are, and to think about how you can strengthen your position. Students often expect to be questioned only about their results, but examiners are equally interested in their methods. Make sure, therefore, that you pay due attention to any weaknesses in your methodology, as well as thinking about your analysis and results.

Whether you are asking your supervisor to identify areas of weakness, or answering questions in your oral, it is very important not to be defensive. If your examiner thinks that something about your report is weak, you will not succeed in changing his or her mind by denying the weakness. Nor will you get all the information out of your supervisor that you need if the first hint of criticism causes you to bristle and reject all the points made. It may be hard to accept that the work over which you have laboured so long and so hard is not perfect in every respect. It is particularly hard if you feel insecure about your own qualities, and cannot handle the idea that weakness in your product implies weakness in yourself.

Although avoiding defensiveness *is* particularly difficult if you feel at all insecure, it will be hard to make progress if you cannot accept that there are areas where progress would be a good idea. So try very hard to accept that, since *nobody* is perfect, there is no need for *you* to be. And because writing a dissertation is enormously challenging, some things can be expected to go wrong. Remembering this will make it easier to accept a weakness when the examiner points it out. You can then give further background information on what went wrong, and do everything you can to demonstrate that any weakness in the project has been a source of learning.

You may find it helpful to bring to the examination examples of work you did, or data you obtained, that did not feature in your report. Again, your aim will be to demonstrate not only that this is your own work, but that you went about it in a well thought out manner, and responded to any setbacks in a positive way, so that you learned from the experience.

Although you need to avoid defensiveness, you should not accept any unwarranted criticisms. Sometimes an examiner will not have had time to read your report in as much depth as he or she should, and may have misunderstood, or not grasped, key points. If this is the case you *should* defend your position. But where a criticism is deserved, there is seldom much to be gained in pretending that this is not the case. It casts doubt on *your* understanding of what you have done, as well as contributing to an uncomfortable atmosphere in the examination.

If your oral examination is in conjunction with a portfolio rather than a dissertation, the same considerations should still apply. The check could again be on understanding or on authenticity. Again, it will help to take a constructive approach to areas of known weakness. Again, your preparation could usefully include further thought on these areas. And the following comments apply equally to all types of oral examination.

You should always listen very carefully to the questions the examiner asks. This may sound so obvious as to be not worth saying, but it can be surprisingly difficult if you are nervous. There is a strong tendency to start thinking about your answer before the examiner has finished asking the question, and thus miss part of it. Or to fail to consider all the possible implications of the question. To be fair, some examiners are particularly poor at formulating clear questions. If you are not sure of the meaning, avoid guessing. Instead, ask for clarification before proceeding. And stop to think about your answer, if you feel this is necessary. No examiner should mind a short pause while you gather your thoughts. This is far better than giving an irrelevant answer, or one that is only partial.

A sensitive issue concerns how formal you should be during the examination. You will need to take your cues from your examiner, but on the whole anything you do to help the *process* of the interview will not go amiss. Therefore, you should not avoid the occasional smile if the occasion arises, and need not avoid the examiner's eye. The occasion is one for *communication*, and anything which helps communication will help you. So check that the examiner has understood what you say, as well as checking that you have understood the examiner. It may be that there is something else that you could say which would entirely satisfy your examiner, but unless you check whether or not this is needed, you will probably not add it.

SUMMARY

■ When a programme's emphasis shifts from knowledge to competence, assessment methods may alter to reflect this.

- Portfolio assessment is based on evidence drawn from the workplace, and organised according to the competences required.
- Evidence that might be useful can be assembled even before a list of competences is available, and taken with you if you change jobs.
- Assembling a portfolio is a useful developmental experience in its own right.
- It is closely related to your learning file activity.
- Portfolios may be supplemented by assessment of simulated activities.
- Assessment centres allow you to demonstrate a range of relevant behaviours.
- Oral (viva voce) examinations might be a supplement to either of the above, or used in conjunction with more conventional assessment forms.
- Whatever the form of assessment, it helps to be as clear as possible about the assessors' objectives, and the criteria being used.
- It is also helpful to accept any areas of weakness and attempt to build on these, rather than becoming defensive, and denying that they exist.

18

Other forms of assessment

→ **19** Projects, theses and dissertations

INTRODUCTION

Your dissertation or project can be the highlight of your studies, allowing you to apply much that you have learned during your studies to a real and fascinating problem. Or it can be a source of endless worry and potential cause of failure. This chapter aims to ensure that it is the former, by helping you to select an appropriate topic and approach, to manage your project work effectively and to write your report in an appropriate and timely way.

Master's-level programmes in any subject traditionally involve a substantial project, thesis or dissertation element. (The words are sometimes used interchangeably, but if a distinction is to be made, 'project' more commonly refers to work where the practical application predominates, 'thesis' to longer and more academic research-oriented work, and 'dissertation' to something intermediate. I shall normally use 'project' when referring to applied work, and 'dissertation' when points refer to any point on the theory–application spectrum.) In management subjects, project work is an important way of allowing you to demonstrate deep learning, and the ability to relate what you have learned to real problem situations. This chapter will address some of the challenges of application of theory to real contexts.

→ Ch 11

As well as allowing you to practise the application of concepts and skills developed during your studies and show 'deep learning', a dissertation offers you the chance to work on a topic dear to your heart. Potential benefits are high: you may gain useful insights into your own organisational context. To do so will require you to demonstrate both interpersonal skills (vital to any consultancy work) and investigative skills.

This Handbook cannot provide detailed coverage of research methodology or statistics – each would take a book in itself, and most programmes will include one or more modules which cover these topics. Instead I shall try to highlight areas which students typically find problematic, and suggest steps you can take to minimise the risks, and maximise the potential benefits attached to your dissertation.

Because project work is far more independent and self-driven than studying taught modules, this part of the programme allows you to develop the important skills required for self-management. Indeed, if your self-management skills are weak, the project will be a high-risk part of the course, particularly if you are under significant pressure from competing demands.

To summarise, the potential benefits of project work are great. You might find solutions to a long-standing organisational problem and thus bring yourself to the favourable attention of senior management in your own organisation. If you are acting as consultant to another organisation you may increase your chances of ultimately working there. You will almost certainly develop a wide range of skills (personal, interpersonal, and investigative) that will be invaluable throughout your career. But work-based projects also present context-specific risks. Things may change in your target organisation and/or with the sponsor of your project, which may result in withdrawal of cooperation. It is important to be aware of such risks when choosing a project, and to take steps to manage them, as well as choosing a project which will develop your skills to the full.

Many of the steps described should be taken well in advance of the research itself. Choice of topic, negotiations with your organisation and careful planning are critical, and should be commenced *at least six months* in advance of the 'official' dissertation period.

CHARACTERISTICS OF MANAGEMENT RESEARCH

Research is a process of finding things out in a purposeful and systematic fashion, in order to increase knowledge. Management research is like all research in this respect. But there are some features which distinguish it from many other forms of research.

You may find it helpful to think about these if your background is in a different academic area.

Saunders *et al.* (2007) suggest that management research:

■ is *transdisciplinary*, i.e. it draws on a range of disciplines to generate insights that could not be gained by separate use of these disciplines;

■ is intended to have *practical use*, thus either needs to point to some form of action or to take account of the practical consequences of the findings;

■ involves, therefore, a *reflexive* process whereby theory and practice inform each other. Thus, the problems addressed should grow out of this interaction between theory and practice;

■ requires organisational sponsors of research to be convinced both of the potential use of findings and that the demands of cooperation are likely to be justified.

Your own research is likely to fall into one of three categories:

■ A project addressing a real organisational problem – typical of part-time MBA programmes which allow students to do their research within their own organisation, often on a topic closely related to their own responsibilities. Such research might evaluate some aspect of an organisation's performance in the light of theory, or address a practical organisational problem, culminating in a set of recommendations in a report to that company. Some projects may go as far as implementing recommendations.

■ A consultancy-type project – more common on full-time programmes, either as part of a work placement or for a local organisation that supports your institution by offering project facilities. Aims might be similar to those of the previous category, and indeed in some own-organisation projects you may be acting as an internal consultant to another part of the organisation.

■ An experimental or library-based project of more academic interest, and not requiring liaison with an organisation – typical of specialist Master's programmes or full-time programmes without opportunities for consultancy or placements.

If your research addresses an issue in a real organisation, all of the characteristics suggested by Saunders *et al.* have implications for your choice of topic, and for what you need to do to carry out research successfully. In particular they emphasise the need for sufficiently broad topic choice, and for significant interaction with your client organisation. The discussion which follows is primarily directed towards such research. If you are carrying out a more academic management-related project you may still find the issues relevant. Whether you are an MBA student addressing a very practical problem, or on a specialist programme and researching a narrower issue in a more academic fashion, you will normally need to find the right balance of theory and practice to satisfy course requirements. Neither pure theory nor theoretic problem solving is likely to be satisfactory.

Finally, there is clearly a range of practical issues to be considered in terms of gaining organisational and institutional support for your research. This raises the important issue of stakeholders in your research.

STAKEHOLDERS IN YOUR DISSERTATION

There are at least four important stakeholders in your dissertation, as shown in Fig. 19.1. (If you are doing a group project, then fellow group members will constitute a fifth important category.)

As with any complex situation, it is worth exploring the different perspectives and objectives of these stakeholders. If you understand these objectives, and possible conflicts between them, you are most likely to be able to minimise such conflict, and maximise your chances of meeting requirements.

Your institution

Your institution is a major stakeholder in your research. A dissertation plays a key role in meeting the educational aims of your programme. Your work is likely to be viewed by external examiners and other quality assessors, and it may contribute to ongoing research within the department. There will be published requirements for the dissertation. You will find it much easier to meet these requirements if you understand the reasons for them.

Institutions vary in their priorities, so find out as much as you can about your chosen institution's aims and objectives as soon as possible. Generally, educational aims include developing the following skills and abilities in students:

- the ability to carry out investigative work in organisations and arrive at valid results;
- the consultancy skills expected of MBA holders (including building and maintaining a good relationship with a client);
- the ability to manage a substantial piece of work with only minimal guidance;
- analytical skills;
- report-writing skills;
- the ability to integrate and apply what has been learned on a variety of courses;
- the ability to find relevant literature beyond that included in past courses, and to use this to good effect;
- the ability to assess the value and limitations of information in deciding on future courses of action;

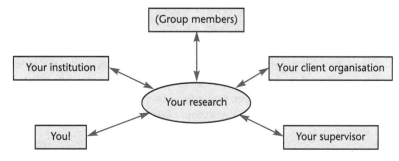

Fig. 19.1 **Stakeholders in a dissertation**

- the ability to approach real problems at a strategic level;
- the ability to reflect on the investigative process and on the student's own strengths and weaknesses during this, and learn from it;
- research skills that will enable students to progress to a PhD if they so require.

Institutions will have the related aims of generating high-quality projects so that they can convince quality assessors of the excellence of their teaching, and satisfy sponsoring organisations.

To meet the educational objectives of most programmes the chosen topic will need to be broad enough to allow interesting analysis and use of a wide range of theory.

The sponsoring organisation

Assuming that you are able to find an in-company project, the objectives of your 'client' will be important. Many of these will be specific to the topic you finally choose, but there are some non-topic-specific considerations also.

ACTIVITY 19.1

Consider what objectives the organisation might have for your project, regardless of the topic chosen. List these here:

_____

_____

_____

_____

_____

Comment

If researching your own organisation, your list might, for example, have included a desire to involve certain people in an initiative for developmental purposes, or even to test your own capabilities in a particular direction. Other objectives might be to minimise use of company time, to be seen to be supporting management development, to support some other company initiative, and to minimise the risk of upsetting anybody. Whether the likely objectives are overt or fairly well hidden, you are more likely to be able to come to a mutually acceptable topic if you are alert to these factors.

If your client organisation is used to sponsoring projects of this kind, they may well have goals that are easily met by your research project. But if they do not have such experience you may need to be very careful to ensure that their objectives are consistent with those of the other stakeholders. This is discussed in more detail later in the chapter.

You!

Ideally your client company will be giving you considerable support in your project. Even so, the main effort will necessarily be your own. Too often students settle on a project topic on the 'Well, I've got to do *something*' principle, and then spend a depressing six months or more working on something which does not interest them at all. Before considering topic choice in more detail, it is worth thinking about your own general objectives, ones that might be served by a well-chosen project. These might include, for example:

- a desire eventually to specialise in a particular area
- a desire to work in a particular part of the organisation
- the wish to incorporate a leisure interest more closely into work.

More project-specific objectives might include the desire to address a problem that impacts directly upon your own work.

ACTIVITY 19.2

List any personal objectives that your project *might* be made to serve:

_____

_____

_____

_____

_____

Group members

If you are doing a group project, then it is important to think about the objectives of all group members, and if possible ensure that you are working with fellow team members who share your objectives. It is important that they want to do as well as you do, and are prepared to put in similar levels of effort. (It is highly frustrating to feel that you are the only one in the group who is prepared to do any work! On the other hand, it may feel uncomfortable to realise that everyone else is contributing far more than you.)

As well as ensuring that your personal objectives are consistent with those of other team members, you need to pay particular attention to making sure that all group members are absolutely clear and agreed concerning the *project* objectives. This agreement will need constant communication and checking to ensure that you keep working towards the same aims. And, of course, you will need to apply all your team-working skills (*see* Chapter 11). Indeed, group projects are an excellent way of developing such skills. And because it is a more complex activity, project management (*see* later) will require even more attention than it does for individual projects.

→ Ch 11

19

Projects, theses and dissertations

Your supervisor

Although you are expected to work fairly independently at this stage in your studies, you will almost certainly be allocated a supervisor for your project. This role is interpreted differently by different institutions, and by different supervisors and those supervised within them. But in all cases your supervisor's objectives are for you to pass! And they will do what they can to achieve this. In the best case, your supervisor can be an invaluable source of expertise, guidance, support and encouragement, and make a major contribution to your eventual success. But this depends upon your developing a good relationship with your supervisor and maintaining that contact and relationship until your dissertation has been submitted. Even if you are completing your research after you have finished the taught part of your course and have gone elsewhere, continued contact is important. E-mail makes it easy to keep in touch, and send draft material for comment, no matter where you are completing your work.

Some institutions (wisely) *require* you to meet your supervisor a certain number of times, and to agree certain key points such as project proposal, data plan, report outline and at least one draft chapter. Even if this is not required, you might discuss whether you and your supervisor could usefully aim to reach such agreements, and set target dates for these.

Contact is not enough. You also need to take feedback seriously. Supervisors normally have a much clearer idea than you do of the work a proposed topic will involve, and the likelihood of eventual success, given your progress at any point. If they express reservations about your choice or your drafts, *take heed*. Over the years I have examined many dissertations where students have either not been required to have these contacts with supervisors, or have ignored advice they have received. The results have been heartbreaking for all concerned. The dissertations have looked beautiful; they were nicely bound and demonstrated excellent wordprocessing and graphic skills. They have been dedicated to the family and friends who had clearly made considerable sacrifices to sustain the student through the enormous labour involved. But all this effort and sacrifice was wasted because the dissertation failed.

Project topics were not realistic, data were inadequate and the style of writing often quite inappropriate. One student was seeking to improve the social and economic position and health of women in her home country. Another had become carried away by the economic history of his country, totally failing to address the strategic issues for finance institutions that were the alleged topic of the dissertation. Another had described a (painful) change initiative in his organisation in full and fascinating detail, but with no analysis or even mention of theory. Another had interviewed a number of friends and drawn sweeping conclusions about a completely different group of managers from those the friends represented. Yet another had incorporated huge sections of text culled from the Internet, without acknowledging he was not the author, and was facing disciplinary action for plagiarism.

In each case the failure will have caused the student and his or her family immense distress. Yet, this could have been avoided if the student had sought and heeded their supervisor's advice throughout the process, and made use of supervisor comments on draft material.

So if it is at all possible:

- Agree key milestones with your supervisor, even if this is not required by your institution.
- Check your progress at each of these stages: repeated checks are important because if you become deeply involved in a project for its own sake you may well start to meet your personal objectives at the expense of meeting academic requirements.
- Take your supervisor's feedback very seriously – if you disagree, try to work out why you find it difficult to accept.
- If disagreements cannot be resolved, or for some reason you cannot get the level of support that it is reasonable to expect from a supervisor, see whether it is possible to change supervisors. This should not be done lightly, but occasionally may be the only way to get the help which you can reasonably expect.

TOPIC CHOICE

An ideal project:

- interests you
- is of use to your client
- meets academic requirements
- is feasible
- will be valuable *whatever* you find
- offers learning opportunities
- is low risk.

Research can usefully be thought of in terms of a question which you are trying to answer, and when thinking about topics, it is helpful to formulate your ideas as questions. You are seeking a question that is *worth* answering, that you *can* answer within the constraints of resources (primarily time, money and access), and that will enable you to *meet dissertation requirements.*

Some students, sadly, do a poor dissertation on an excellent topic. The converse is harder: it is almost impossible to do a good dissertation on an unsuitable topic. While some refinement of topic as you progress is possible, even desirable, major change becomes increasingly difficult as your work progresses. It is therefore vital that you start with a suitable topic area, and refine it into something that your supervisor agrees will allow you to do a good dissertation.

Time spent on considering possible projects is a wise investment. In fact you may need to be prepared to start work on a project and then revise or totally revisit your choice as you find out more about what it will involve. This may seem inefficient and time consuming, but it can save you hundreds of hours of depressing work on a poorly chosen topic. There is nothing more depressing than realising that the best you can hope for, and that this is far from certain, is a barely adequate result, because of limitations in your original objectives. In considering possible topics, there will be several factors you will need to evaluate.

Interest

Perhaps the most important criterion is that the topic be of interest to yourself and, if the project is organisation based, to your client organisation. You will be putting considerable and extended effort into the project, and the organisation will be bearing not only the significant cost of any working time employees (including you) devote to it but also additional costs such as travel, duplicating, phone calls, postage, information searches, etc.

If you and your organisation (and that usually means an individual within the organisation with the status to act as client for the research) are not equally interested in the topic, there are likely to be problems. If it is *your* interest that is weak, motivation is likely to slump during the dissertation period, and you will find it an enormous effort to do the necessary work. If your *client* is not interested, then he or she may not provide you with the support you need, whether this is in terms of refining your project plans, facilitating access to information needed or sponsoring your final report so that it is taken seriously at an appropriate level within the organisation.

If you are not genuinely interested in a possible topic, therefore, or if you detect a lack of real interest on the part of your likely client, you should keep seeking alternative topics until you do find one of concern to you both.

Scope

It is also important that your chosen topic is potentially broad enough and deep enough for you to exhibit the range of skills your institution will expect. Because the dissertation is expected to develop generalisable investigative skills, you will be expected to evaluate possible research methods or approaches as part of your project work, selecting an appropriate one and justifying your choice in your final report.

On a more specialist Master's course, a fairly narrow topic, studied in considerable depth, may be required. For an MBA you will normally be expected to take a reasonably broad perspective and to show the strategic awareness that the programme is supposed to develop. You will need to research your topic in such a way as to demonstrate an awareness of the organisational context in which the problem is situated. You topic will therefore need to be broad enough to allow you to demonstrate both methodological awareness and strategic thinking.

Thus, if your employer asked you to find alternative suppliers of packaging materials and recommend the cheapest, this would not be a suitable research topic. If you had been asked, however, to review the effectiveness of the packaging operation as a whole, and make recommendations as to ways in which it might be redesigned so as to better serve organisational objectives, there would be much more scope. There would be real questions about what constituted measures of effectiveness in this case, and about suitable investigative methods and sources of information. There would need to be a clear understanding of the operation of the rest of the organisation, and its requirements if appropriate recommendations were to be made. Aspects of studies on accounting, operations management, human resource management and other ideas such as benchmarking could be used to inform the research.

Educational and employers' definitions of 'project' may be a long way apart. Your employer may imagine that a course project is the same as other 'projects' in the organisation – that is, any piece of practical work to be done to meet organisational objectives. You may need to spend some time making clear that there are educational objectives to be met too, and explaining what these entail, before you, your college and your organisation can come to a mutually acceptable topic.

Symmetry of research outcomes

This is a less obvious, but important criterion. It means that your research results should be interesting no matter how they turn out. Research to 'prove a point' should be avoided. First, you are likely to bias the result in your attempt to get the answer you want. There is surprisingly large scope for the unconscious introduction of bias into research. Careful design is needed to minimise this, as biased results are naturally worthless. Second, if you succeed in designing your research so that bias is eliminated, and then do *not* prove your point, the result will be of little interest.

To take an unlikely example, you might have a hunch that, contrary to popular wisdom (and research), gaining an MBA does not improve career prospects. You might carefully design a research study, comparing career patterns of matched groups of managers, the only difference being that one group gained an MBA five years ago and the other didn't. If, as a result, you found that an MBA did nothing to improve career prospects, or positively harmed them, this would be interesting. If you found, however, that those with MBAs did progress faster, the general response might be 'So what?' Demonstrating the obvious has little value on the whole, unless it is an assumption which has *never* been put to the test.

Because overturning received wisdom can be a highly desirable, newsworthy and publishable outcome, you may wish to take risks of this kind. If so, do it with due consideration, and build in enough additional information collection that your resulting thesis will be of interest even if the original assumption was wrong. In this case, what aspects of the MBA were helpful? Which types of career progression were most common or fastest? Is there variation between different types of organisation or different jobs? Is there an age or gender effect? Does the effect depend upon whether senior staff in the organisation themselves have an MBA? Supplementary questions of this kind could provide the material for an acceptable thesis even if the main question was a risky one and did not turn out as you expected. Of course, it is better to select a main question which itself is characterised by equal interest in possible outcomes.

Feasibility

This is obviously a critical consideration for any proposed project. Attempting the impossible shows lack of judgement, and is a recipe for stress and disappointment. Significantly less is possible within the time and resource constraints of a Master's dissertation than many students optimistically assume. If at any time you feel your ideas might be slightly ambitious, stop at once. They are probably wildly unrealistic! All projects have a way of expanding to fill at least twice the time allotted to them, so always aim to undershoot, and allow large margins for the unexpected.

As well as checking that the proposed project looks possible within the time constraints of the dissertation, you need to check it against other resource constraints. These include finance and availability of information. If your project looks as if it will incur costs which neither you nor your sponsor is prepared to bear, then it is unlikely to be feasible unless some other sources of finance can be found. The following also call into

19

Projects, theses and dissertations

question the feasibility of a proposed project: it requires access to classified, or even sensitive, information; you will need information which cannot be obtained without a major investment which neither you nor others in the organisation are prepared to make; it requires the cooperation of those outside the organisation who are highly unlikely to see any reason for cooperating (or of those within the organisation who are unwilling for political or other reasons to support the research).

Risks

The scope for things to go wrong is closely related to aspects of feasibility and this 'catastrophe factor' should be just as carefully considered. Your research is likely to involve a timescale over which considerable change may take place in your client organisation (and indeed in your own life). It is important to consider how vulnerable your potential project is to such changes. It is of course impossible to find a totally risk-free project. If you are promoted into a job on the other side of the world, or indeed, if you are made redundant, you will have more pressing concerns than whether you will still have access to the information you need to complete your dissertation. You cannot guard against the wide range of possible, but highly improbable catastrophes that just *might* happen. But you can think about those things that are fairly *likely* to happen within any organisation, and which can seriously impede a project. These include political or personnel change, increase or decrease in workload, and restructuring. You should attempt to assess the probability of such events within your organisation and their likely effect on any proposed topic. Only then can you decide whether the risk is an acceptable one.

If the risks are high, could they be reduced by reformulating the topic? You cannot prevent a department being shut down at 24 hours' notice when you are in the midst of collecting information on it. But you can reduce the chances of such disruption by avoiding as a subject for your research any part of the organisation under serious threat.

'Real time' projects, involving ongoing implementation of change or of evaluation of such change as it happens, are particularly vulnerable. Any change to the timescale of the subject of the research can have disastrous effects on a tight project plan. And if the project starts to go wrong, people may start to withold information. It is far safer to select a topic where data sources already exist. You can then draw upon these within a timescale to suit your project requirements.

Politically sensitive projects are particularly dangerous. If the political climate within the organisation shifts, you may find that cooperation is withdrawn and confidentiality restraints are placed upon your eventual report.

The above list of factors which should influence your choice of topic will be common to most situations, and should be supplemented by any criteria deriving from your personal list of objectives above.

ACTIVITY 19.3

List any personal criteria which are important to you in your choice of topic:

_____

_____

_____

_____

_____

→ Ch 12

It may seem premature to be thinking about criteria for evaluating project topics before generating possibilities to evaluate, but there is sound methodological sense in this. The argument was outlined in Chapter 12, but will be briefly restated here. If you think about possible options first, and then think about ways of evaluating them, your choice of criteria may be influenced by the characteristics of the option which you at first sight prefer. The unwitting bias that results removes the advantage of taking a systematic approach to the choice of option. Many problem-solving methodologies therefore explicitly recommend that measures of effectiveness are specified *before* options are generated, and this is the approach suggested here. You should follow the same pattern in your research if your chosen topic involves recommending a small number of options chosen from a wider range.

Learning opportunities

Project work offers the opportunity for many different types of learning and skill development. Some aspects – time and project management – will be common to all topics. But some topics may offer particular opportunities for you to develop skills that you know would be helpful to your chosen career path. It is worth thinking about how to maximise your personal development through choice of a project that will 'stretch' you in the required directions, or cause you to learn things that are particularly relevant to your hoped-for career.

GENERATING POSSIBLE TOPICS

You may have a long-standing and burning desire to investigate a particular topic, and regard your dissertation as a heaven-sent opportunity to indulge this wish. If so, you may see topic choice as irrelevant. You know what you want to do so it would be a waste of time to generate a range of options which will inevitably be rejected. Put such thoughts aside! You may find that there is more value in the exercise than you think. Indeed, having such a strong determination to address a pet topic can be positively dangerous. While it is certainly important that a topic interests you, it is equally important that it is of interest to your client, that it will meet your institution's requirements, and that it is 'do-able' within the constraints operating. Your own enthusiasm for a topic may blind you to its shortcomings in these areas, or cause you to underestimate their importance. By forcing yourself to take the generation of alternative topics seriously, and to evaluate your preferred topic against these, you may become more aware of potential hazards. You can then find ways of improving your preferred topic by modifying it to incorporate elements of other options.

You may, however, belong to the larger class of students for whom despair sets in at the prospect of having to find a suitable topic. Perhaps you feel your organisation offers no suitable opportunities, or that your boss is antagonistic to the whole thing, or perhaps you still do not really have a clear idea of what is required. Those in this second, despairing, category have a strong temptation to put off all thought of the project for as long as possible. Perhaps they hope that inspiration will occur at some future point.

While this *may* happen, it is fairly unusual for a suitable topic to surface by itself. You are far more likely to find yourself in the uncomfortable position of having to choose a project topic in a rush, with your research due to start and no time for proper thought or for discussion with your supervisor and organisation. This bodes ill. It is likely that your chosen topic will not be totally satisfactory to any stakeholder, and that you will have difficulties throughout your research in consequence.

If, therefore, you are unhappy about project choice, start work *at least six months* in advance, giving yourself extra time for this stage, rather than reducing the time available by procrastination.

Sources of ideas:

■ own interests

■ client concerns

■ current work problems

■ past dissertations

■ media

■ academic literature

■ brainstorming

■ ideas notebook.

→ Ch 12

In any problem situation, your chosen solution will be no better than the best option generated. (It can, of course, be worse, if you choose the wrong one!) Your aim at this stage should therefore be to generate as wide a range of possibilities as you can. There are several different things that can help in this. Brainstorming and other creativity techniques were introduced in Chapter 12, and you may have learned more about them during your course. If so, use them!

You can carry out brainstorming of possible topics with fellow students, with colleagues at work, or, ideally, with both. Each group is likely to produce very different options, and by amalgamating two disparate lists you will widen the range. From the lists you can select any item that seems to have in it the germ of a possible project and discuss the most likely with your possible client, perhaps using the successive branching and narrowing approach shown in Fig. 12.2.

ACTIVITY 19.4

List the most promising topic areas generated by your brainstorming or other creativity techniques:

_____

_____

_____

_____

_____

_____

Another immensely rich source of possible ideas is the store of past dissertations. It is customary for universities to keep successful ones in their libraries. These can be referred to on demand. They form excellent material on which you can practise your scanning and rapid reading techniques. The best ones will give you an idea of how much can be achieved in a dissertation. You may find this inspiring or profoundly depressing! The weaker ones will demonstrate the minimum that is acceptable. If the first category depressed you, this should make you feel better. However, it should not make you complacent. The minimum may be surprisingly low in some institutions, but it would be dangerous to aim for this lowest acceptable level. There may have been extenuating circumstances, or the student may have been extremely lucky to have passed.

Even if the minimum pass standard is surprisingly low, you are unlikely to gain much satisfaction from poor work. But knowing the range of acceptable standards may make the project less threatening: many students find dissertation work unnecessarily stressful because they are aiming for a standard more appropriate to a PhD than a Master's.

Perusing past dissertation titles and their abstracts should give you a field of possibilities from which it is possible to select a small number of suitable areas for subsequent development, to be added to those drawn from your brainstorming.

ACTIVITY 19.5

Draw a mind map or other diagram to represent the field of recent dissertation topics, showing broad areas and sub-areas into which these can be classified.

ACTIVITY 19.6

List dissertation titles which suggest projects that might be possible within your own context:

_____

_____

_____

_____

Existing dissertations can also be used to provide an alternative slant to your search by giving you insight into what it is that makes a project interesting for you.

ACTIVITY 19.7

Select dissertations which do _not_ strike you as potentially applicable in your own context, but which still look extremely interesting. Analyse these to see whether they have any features in common, or in other ways indicate what your definition of 'interesting' implies. List these features:

_____

_____

_____

_____

_____

Finding a client

For in-company projects on part-time programmes you will normally be expected to find a client within your own organisation. This can present problems if you are between jobs, or know that during the course you are likely to change jobs, or that your organisation is likely to undergo major change. If for any of these reasons you think that you do not have an obvious organisation to work with, you should discuss alternatives with your tutors immediately – they may be able to suggest an organisation willing to host a project, or be able to help you to explore possible avenues you have not thus far considered. Some students do projects with voluntary organisations, others gain access to organisations they have worked with in the past, or have had contact with in other ways. Some choose a topic for which they can 'capture' the necessary data before reorganisation or job change makes access impossible. Others may gain permission for a project not based on a specific organisation.

Once you have identified your client *organisation*, the next set of activities involves mapping the organisation and potential areas a project might address and finding a 'client' or sponsor within the organisation. The ideal internal client understands what you need, is supportive of your studies, has some good ideas about potential projects within his or her area of control, is open-minded about how things might turn out, has access to the internal resources you are likely to need, and is someone with whom you feel you can communicate relatively easily.

If you are not the first student from your organisation, you may find considerable in-company expertise in the selection of suitable topics. Previous clients of the research and past students will both be good sources, and constitute a valuable resource which you should exploit to the full. If you are breaking new ground and therefore lack this resource, you will need to explain dissertation requirements very carefully to those who will need to approve your plans and to any others whose cooperation will be important.

There are obvious advantages in involving potential clients in topic choice if this is at all possible. They are after all key stakeholders, and may be able to suggest topics that are of particular interest to them. If potential clients feel that they were largely responsible for the choice of topic, they will have a much stronger commitment to making the project a success because of their feelings of ownership. There are, however, risks associated with client-selected projects and these need to be recognised and steps taken to minimise them. Some risks stem from the very strong organisational meanings attached to 'project', or 'research', meanings which as already indicated may be very different from those prevailing in your institution. You may, therefore, have topics pressed upon you which offer too little or perhaps too much scope for meeting dissertation requirements. You may have topics offered with a ready-made solution to which the client is strongly attached. Apart from the high risk that the 'obvious' solutions is not the right one, in such cases the client is unlikely to support the diagnostic work that may be required by your course. This is why it is essential that these requirements are made absolutely clear at the outset of discussions, and that your client understands that the topic chosen must be acceptable to you and your thesis supervisor.

These initial discussions are absolutely crucial to future success. As with any consultancy, building a good relationship with your client is essential. Your client needs to have confidence in your ability to do something of use within the organisation, and to do this without causing any negative effects. You can help to build this confidence by preparing carefully for every meeting with your client, having a clear idea of what it is that you would like to achieve in the meeting, and using your talking and listening skills to the full. You need to be able to have an open and honest conversation about what you need, and to air any concerns either of you may have. If these are addressed at the outset, they can usually be resolved to both of your satisfaction. If they are hidden, only to emerge later, resolution can be difficult or even impossible.

→ Ch 11

Many of your discussions will be with superiors, or with an in-company mentor if you have one, or with your training department. However, do discuss your search for a topic with colleagues at the same level as yourself and subordinates. They may be able to suggest additional possible topics, and can comment usefully on ideas you already have. The following activities are relevant if you are planning to do a project in your own organisation.

ACTIVITY 19.8

List three problems of which you have been aware during the last six months, either within your own part of the organisation, or elsewhere:

_____

_____

_____

_____

_____

Use separate pieces of paper to construct multiple-cause diagrams showing contributory factors in each case. Identify common themes between problems, and main causes within each. For each cause or theme, construct a mind map expanding the cause into as many areas as possible. List any project areas suggested by this mapping exercise:

_____

_____

_____

ACTIVITY 19.9

Similarly, think of three changes, either within the organisation or to its environment, which you think will affect the way your job will, or should, be done in the next 12 months. List these:

_____

_____

_____

ACTIVITY 19.10

Again, use a mind map to explore related areas for each potential change, and consider whether any of these areas or groups of areas might prove a useful starting point for research. List any which have potential:

_____

_____

_____

An example of a mind map and subsequent thoughts on a possible project in an organisation where it was felt that there might be an absenteeism problem is shown in Fig. 19.2. (Figure 10.4 showed how the related form of diagram, a relevance tree, could be used in much the same way.)

→ Ch 10

If you are seeking a more academic dissertation it is worth keeping an ideas notebook throughout your programme, jotting down topics and questions that you find

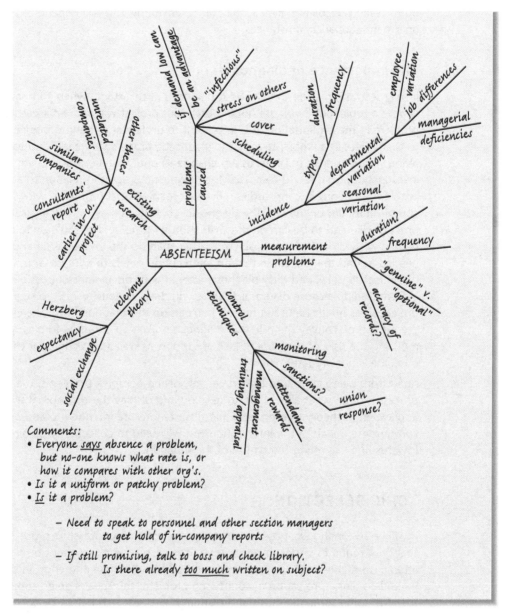

Fig. 19.2 Student's mind map and subsequent thoughts on a possible absenteeism topic

particularly interesting. These might occur during lectures, or while you are reading, or result from assignments during the progrramme. This notebook can then provide a starting point for topic generation. You may also find that you can adapt the above activities to help you to produce a mind map of related questions for these topic areas.

Once you have selected a range of possible topic areas, you need to select a small number for further exploration. As your first attempt to assess possibilities against these criteria will necessarily be fairly rough and ready, you should be able to keep anything up to seven possibilities 'live' at this stage. Obviously, this will depend to some extent on organisational circumstances.

The importance of diagnosis

It may seem premature to talk about diagnosis at this stage, when you have yet to choose a topic. But if you are hoping that your project will address a particular problem in the organisation, it is important to understand the importance of diagnosis to the project as a whole, to start the diagnostic process very early, and to continue to refine your diagnosis (or if necessary change it) until you are well into your

→ Ch 12   investigation. Chapter 12 discussed the diagnostic process in relation to addressing problem situations in case studies. For real organisational problems, with their complexities and unknowns, the diagnostic challenges may be much greater, and the process will need to be carried out over a longer time. It is all too easy to accept other people's assessment of 'the problem', rather than do the investigation and analysis needed to find the real cause that an intervention needs to address. You need to carry out at least a quick and dirty diagnosis early in your discussions of possible topics with a client. Multiple-cause diagrams such as you drew in Activity 19.8 to suggest potential project areas might be useful here. If you can do this diagnosis with the client, and at the same time convey the role that diagnosis is likely to continue to play, you will be reducing the risks of subsequent lack of support as well as making clear that the outcome is not predetermined.

Apart from being central to the process of solving complex problems, the diagnostic process is often what allows you to develop and display the conceptual skills and application of theory that projects and dissertations are intended to address. Furthermore, much of the information you will need to collect may be directed towards understanding the nature of the situation.

TOPIC SELECTION

It will be becoming clear by now that topic selection is an iterative process, i.e. one that goes round in circles, progressing a little each time. You cannot be *totally* sure that a topic is suitable until you have invested considerable time and effort in developing your ideas. For a project on a work-based problem, this means going some way towards doing some diagnosis and planning your research before being sure that this is a suitable topic. If at the end of this process you find that the topic is *not* suitable, you may feel you have wasted a lot of time and effort and are back to the start. Sometimes this will have been unavoidable. But a 'quick and dirty' early assessment may be enough to identify topics as *likely* to turn out to be unsuitable.

It therefore makes sense to do a very broad-brush evaluation of a number of projects in parallel, before proceeding to a more detailed evaluation of a smaller number. Part of this evaluation may be a very hasty provisional diagnosis. After this you will be in a better position to select the option with which to proceed. If you run with enough options at each stage you will have a reasonable chance of at least one looking promising by the end of the more detailed pass. Then even if a number of possibilities turn out to be unsuitable you will have made progress at each stage.

Figure 19.3 shows a basic algorithm for project choice. This shows the process as a series of yes/no decisions for a single topic, which, together with a process of refinement if possible, will enable a single topic to be developed into something which is at least a possibility, or else to be rejected.

If using the suggested broad-brush, multi-topic approach, you would need to use the algorithm on each topic, but of course several topics could be discussed in a single meeting with a potential client.

An alternative approach, or one which could be used to select from those topics which survived the algorithmic approach, would be to construct a *Which?* type diagram (*see* Fig. 19.4), in which you list possible topics and rate them, say from one to five, on each of the criteria which you are using, totalling the points for each option. If you are using such a table *without* using the algorithm first, then you would need a symbol for 'fails to meet criterion', say X. Any option with one or more X's would be rejected, regardless of its 'point' rating.

Two aspects of which you must be particularly aware are real-time dependence and political sensitivity as each can lead to a high 'catastrophe factor'. If a topic depends upon something happening in real time, avoid it if there is any risk at all that time slippage might occur. It is far, far safer to investigate a situation which already exists.

Be alert, too, to potential political sensitivities. These are harder to spot. Political structures within an organisation may not be immediately obvious, and may change. Think carefully about whether your potential findings could be perceived as a threat by anyone. If so, could this result in difficulties being put in your way at some point during your investigation? Do the people concerned have the power to block access to information or resources, or even to close down your project?

For your second pass you will need to put much more detailed thought into your planning. It is only once you have started to develop an idea into a research project that you will be able to see how feasible it is likely to be, given the constraints under which you will be working.

At this stage you will need to be clear, for each possible topic, who would be your client within the organisation. You will need to have detailed discussions with each client, in order to clarify their objectives for the research, and the resources and other support which they could make available to you for your research.

You will also need to have thought fairly seriously about your research method. It can be extremely helpful to have a written brief from your client at this stage. You will need

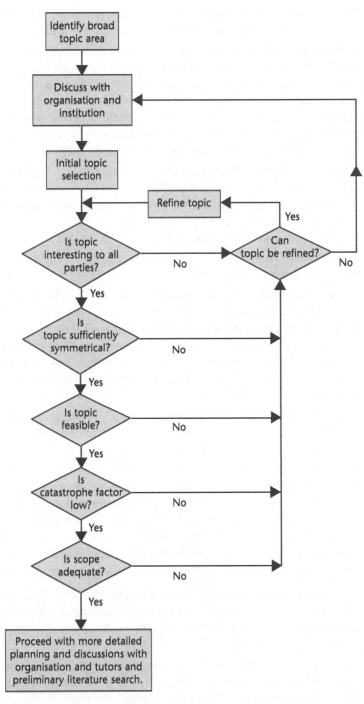

Fig. 19.3 Algorithm for project choice

Criteria	Topic 1	Topic 2	Topic 3	Etc.	
Project interests me	● ●	● ● ● ●	● ● ● ● ●		
Client supports project	● ● ●	● ●	● ● ●		
Adequate breadth of topic	● ●	● ● ●	● ● ● ● ●		
Availability of resources	● ● ● ●	● ●	● ● ●		
Absence of political sensitivity	●	● ● ●	✕		
Low reliance on real-time events	●	● ● ●	●		
Etc.					

Fig. 19.4 Example of part of a project evaluation table

to make it very clear, however, that you are still at the planning stage, and it may be necessary for the brief to be amended by mutual agreement.

Once your client's objectives are clearly understood, check these with your project supervisor to ensure that a brief of this kind would also allow you to meet institutional objectives. You can then analyse the possible topics in more depth. A useful framework for this analysis is to aim to produce a short project proposal for each topic. Such proposals are typically 1000–1500 words long, but your institution may specify a different wordcount.

Your proposal should aim to cover:

- **Problem description** – background to the problem, its context and its significance.

- **Project aim** – the purpose of the project, its scope and its limitations – this is where thinking in terms of research questions is a useful start to developing more concrete and SMART project objectives.

- **Value to the organisation** – it is important to establish why the organisation needs to know what the project is intended to establish.

- **Likely project design** – possible research methods, timescale and the skills likely to be employed.

- **Data requirements** – what information will be needed, how this will be obtained and what analysis will be carried out.

Obviously, there will be scope to alter and develop this proposal as the project develops. Much of your early work will involve detailed consideration of possible methods of carrying out the research to answer whatever question the topic poses and exploring sources of possibly relevant data. But unless you have thought in some detail about these topics at the selection stage you may hit an unexpected block in mid-project. To decide upon a final topic in which to invest your hundreds of hours of work you need to know how the possibilities are likely to compare on the issues described above.

19

Projects, theses and dissertations

I have not addressed the need for originality in the above discussion. While good research *is* original in the sense of covering new theoretical or experimental ground – and a PhD thesis would be expected to show considerable originality – this criterion is less important with research at Master's level. Obviously, you would not meet your stakeholders' objectives by merely repeating research already carried out or plagiarising someone else's discussion of methodology, but theoretical originality is not usually expected. The narrow constraints under which you will be operating make it unlikely (though not impossible) that you will be able to devise and demonstrate some totally new theory of organisational behaviour. An MBA or specialist management-related thesis is much better seen as showing creative use of existing theory and techniques to solve a real organisational problem, and this chapter is slanted towards this type of research.

If your final choice of option seems rather less than theoretically revolutionary, but your supervisor is happy with it, you should not therefore worry. Your chances of success will be the greater. And there will almost certainly be sufficient challenge in applying existing theory to produce a valid answer to a real problem.

Once you have decided upon a project proposal that is acceptable to your supervisor and your client and of interest to yourself, you should, if at all possible, obtain written agreement to the proposed research and to the necessary access to information required. This may seem unnecessarily legalistic, but it can be a useful precaution. Your client may be wholeheartedly behind your proposal, but there is no guarantee that your client will remain in a position to support you throughout your project. Personnel move, and you might find that someone less sympathetic to your aims takes over. A written agreement will not prevent all the problems this may produce, but can strengthen your case. It is also a useful protection against claims from some quarters that your research is in some sense a failure because it fails to meet the objectives of the complainant. If these were not the agreed objectives of the research, then you will again find the written agreement useful. Even if you hit no such snags, the agreed brief will serve as a useful reference point for yourself, a standard against which you can test any necessary modifications to your plans.

LITERATURE SEARCH

Whatever the type of project you are doing, you are likely to need to make *several* searches of relevant literature. The first has already been alluded to. In deciding on a suitable topic, you will need to do a fairly superficial trawl of relevant literature. As you start to define your topic more narrowly you will need to do more focused, 'in-depth' searches. You will need first to clarify your research question. Then you will need to work out how to approach your own research (this is likely to include searching both the topic and literature on research methodology). Finally, it is important to set your research in context when writing your report – what you do needs to be interpreted in the light of what others have done and found in the area.

How far you need to go will depend upon the type of project you are undertaking. The closer you move to the 'academic' end of the spectrum, the more substantial will be the expected literature review part of your dissertation. Similarly, more in-depth discussion will be expected of how your findings relate to this literature. How far you *can* go will depend upon the resources at your disposal.

Your first problem is knowing where to start, and how. A good first step is to get to know your library and the resources it offers. Libraries contain a wide range of information sources, both traditional print and electronic. This information is systematically and consistently organised and there will be people there who are only too happy to explain the systems to you, and help you to make good use of them. If you are studying part-time, particularly if this is by distance learning, find out what electronic resources you can access remotely, and what support is available to you in learning to make use of them. Find out, too, what your local public library offers, and whether there is a convenient university library – students at one university can normally negotiate reader privileges at other university libraries.

Parameters and keywords

Once you have at least a rough idea of the question you intend to investigate you can start to set some parameters to help define your search area. You will probably need to know:

- the broad subject area, e.g. marketing, motivation, health and safety legislation;

- the language of your search. Note that American and English are different languages! Many words are either completely different (car/automobile) or spelt differently (behaviour/behavior). This is important in electronic searching;

- the business sector in which you are interested, e.g. manufacturing, not-for-profit, defence;

- how far back you want to search, e.g. five years;

- the type of literature you want to search, e.g. refereed journals only, government publications.

You then need to generate a list of *keywords* to drive your search. These are the words you will look up in indexes, or use with an on-line search engine. Think about the sorts of words that authors might have used in the title of the kind of article you want to read, together with the names of significant researchers in the area. A recent review article can be really helpful here, as can the bibliography of a past dissertation in a similar area. Tutors can also be extremely helpful! Try using brainstorming, either individually or with a group of other students or colleagues, to generate possible keywords and phrases. Once you have something to start with, you can use that to generate other possible terms. Suppose you have used a keyword and found a useful-sounding item on the database. If you then display the full entry, it will normally show you 'subject headings' or 'descriptors', or some other term relating to the index terms used. Among these may well be other potentially useful keywords.

→ Ch 10   Another good technique is to construct a relevance tree (*see* Fig. 10.4). As you draw this, teasing out possible sub-areas, you will be able to think about which you need to search immediately, and which may become the main focus of your research. It can be helpful to highlight each category in a different colour so that you can easily distinguish the 'immediate' from the 'important'.

You can use such a relevance tree as a working document. As you read, you will inevitably refine your thinking about your topic. Update your relevance tree to reflect different ways of looking at the subject which emerge, or new issues which emerge as potentially important.

Types of sources

Sources can be thought of as primary, secondary or tertiary. A primary source is one where a work appears for the first time. Primary sources include reports, conference proceedings, theses, some government publications, company reports, and unpublished manuscripts such as letters or committee papers. They may be difficult to locate, and not all dissertations will need to make use of them.

Secondary sources are more accessible, and likely to form an important part of the literature you search. Journals, particularly academic refereed journals (print or electronic), which offer a degree of 'quality assurance', are likely to be crucial. Books, professional journals, newspapers, other government publications, and items found on the Internet are also good secondary sources.

Tertiary sources, including indexes, abstracts and catalogues, are designed to help you locate other sources, or to give you an introduction or overview of a topic. These are likely to be your starting point, via your library and/or the Internet.

Using tertiary sources

Indexes. Enter a keyword (subject or author name) and the index will suggest relevant journal articles or other sources, giving you the full reference for each so that you can look it up, or request it if the library does not own a copy. As well as indexes to academic journals, there are on-line indexes to newspapers and business reports which you may find useful, together with searchable archives of newspapers.

Abstracts are indexes which give you not only the reference, but also a brief outline of the content of the article. This may enable you to decide that you do not need to look at the full article!

Citation indexes are particularly useful if you find a relevant article and want to know how the ideas in it have developed since. A citation index will tell you all the subsequent articles which have referred to that original. (The reference list at the end of the original will give you all the papers which the author used, so between the two you should have good coverage right up to the present.)

You will normally need to use several indexes and abstracts to ensure complete coverage. Consult your librarian if possible over those most likely to be useful.

Print indexes can normally be searched by one word or phrase only. This may produce a frighteningly long list unless your word is newly coined.

Electronic indexes, whether on CD-Rom or via the Internet, offer you the chance to be much more refined in your search, producing a more manageable list of articles, most of which should be relevant provided you have chosen your words and *link terms* carefully.

Link terms and logic

These link terms, derived from Boolean logic, allow you to narrow your search. The terms are AND, OR and NOT (though your system might use '+' and '−' to indicate the same thing, or even some other convention). Figure 19.5 is a pictorial representation of the relationship between these terms. The other useful symbols are '*' and '?'. 'Motiv*' would allow you to pick up all words with that start, e.g. motivate, motivation, motivating. ? allows the gap to be filled in different ways to allow for different spellings, e.g. behavio?r would pick up both behaviour and behavior. (Note that these conventions are not yet standardised, so check your chosen index for the symbols used.)

Thus, to take the example shown in Fig. 19.5, you could ask for 'pay AND appraisal' (or '+' or whatever) and be offered only references containing both terms, a much shorter list than either 'pay' or 'appraisal' alone. Asking for 'appraisal NOT financial' might spare you hundreds of references on financial appraisal, but still give you a lot of other kinds of appraisal. You might wish to use OR if alternative terms are used for the topic in question, e.g. 'downsizing OR redundancy'. Internet searches can take hundreds of hours, and throw up a large proportion of commercial sites, so indexes and abstracts can be a more efficient route. They were designed with user needs in mind, and tend to include only reputable sources.

As well as indexes to academic journals there are on-line indexes to newspapers and business reports which you may find useful, together with searchable archives of newspapers.

Catalogues, whether provided by libraries, publishers or booksellers, can be extremely useful. Examples include the British Library Public Catalogue, Pearson's own website, and Amazon's UK and US sites. (Sample URLs are given at the end of the chapter. For a fuller list, *see* Saunders *et al.* (2007).)

On-line searches

Internet searches will almost certainly also be necessary, however. Some up-to-date sources may be accessible only by this route. Be disciplined, though: avoid pursuing things just because they sound interesting, unless you have hours to spare. And be

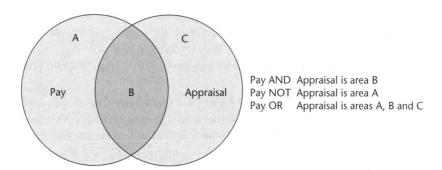

Fig. 19.5 The Boolean logic of searches

cautious about the reliance you place on Internet sources. While some (e.g. government sources) are likely to be excellent, others most certainly are not. The Internet is a great noticeboard, and many consultants use it to advertise their wares by means of 'snippets' of information on management topics of current interest. While some of these may be based on solid information, many are not.

If you are not yet proficient in searching, on-line tutorials are available. *See* references at the end of the chapter for examples. Important tools in Internet searches will probably be search engines, and information gateways and subject directories.

Search engines

A search engine ranges across the Web and comes up with links to sites which include mention of your specified search word(s). General search engines, such as Google, allow you to access over three billion documents. A more specialised seach engine such as that of the UK (or other) government will limit its links to central and local government websites and government agencies. Meta-search engines will run searches simultaneously over several engines. In 2005, researchers from two US universities worked with Dogpile to carry out research on the results of different engines, using 10 000 user queries. They found that across the three top search engines, only 3.2% of first pages of results were the same! (Dogpile is one of a range of 'meta-search engines' which have been developed. These run simultaneous searches over several engines.) The findings above make a clear argument for using a meta-search engine to make searching more effective.

Information gateways

Search engines wander around the Web looking for your word(s) but information gateways and directories are more organised, checking sites at regular intervals and structuring them to allow more systematic browsing. This can save a lot of time, though may miss the occasional 'gem'. You can think of a search engine as giving you access to a mountain of jumbled books, journals, junk mail and even personal diaries, while a gateway is more akin to an ordered library. Again, examples are listed at the end of the chapter.

Saving information from the Internet

A major benefit of accessing materials electronically is that you can easily save them, which sounds far better than having laboriously to take notes. But it is easy to feel the job is done simply by copying. Unfortunately, you may assemble a forbidding mountain of undigested files. So notes are still useful. And it may be better to bookmark sites you may or may not need, rather than keeping unnecessary information.

It will save you a lot of time if you save references in appropriate directories (keeping annotated lists of contents). Otherwise you may end up with a long list of HTML files which are time consuming to search. When saving resources from the Internet, remember to include not only the site address (URL) but also the copyright statement of the page or website and any citation instructions and to note the date on which you last visited the page. You need to give this in your references. If you will be collecting a large number of references, it is much easier if you use a bibliographic software package to help you organise these. (Ask your librarian for advice on this if you are not already familiar with such packages.)

Using what you have found

→ Ch 9

When you have selected likely sources, and accessed them electronically, or obtained them through a library, you need to remember why you are reading them (*see* Chapter 9), and read, copy and take notes appropriately. If you are planning to include a major literature review section, your notes will need to be fairly detailed. You should normally aim for your literature review to establish current understanding of an area, showing why your research question is worthy of attention.

You will normally need to start your review with general statements of the topic area and an overview of key ideas, before narrowing down to discuss in more detail the work most relevant to your specific research objectives. Look at academic papers and choose good examples as models, and ask your supervisor to suggest past dissertations which had particularly good literature searches for you to look at.

In addition to the report section specifically addressing your literature review, you will use the fruits of your search at intervals during your report. They will be particularly important in your discussion and conclusions sections. Here you will be aiming to show the significance of your own findings in relation to those of others, and may be able to draw on other authors in support of your recommendations. Being aware of these uses while you read will enable you to take more useful notes.

You may find it helpful to use the following checklist for evaluating your review (derived from Saunders *et al.* (2007)).

Literature review evaluation checklist

Does your review start at a more general level before narrowing down? ☐

Is it clear how the research covered relates to your research question and objectives? ☐

Have you covered the main relevant theories? ☐

Have you covered at least a representative sample of the relevant literature on the topic? ☐

Have you highlighted issues where your project will provide new insights? ☐

Have you included up-to-date literature? ☐

Is your evaluation of the literature objective and balanced? ☐

Have you clearly justified your own ideas? ☐

Is the review coherent and cohesive? ☐

Does it lead clearly into subsequent sections of your report? ☐

19

Projects, theses and dissertations

Avoiding plagiarism

→ Ch 15

The importance of avoiding plagiarism was stressed in Chapter 15, but is so important that the key points are reinforced here. Plagiarism seems particularly common in project reports and dissertations. It is tragic when students fail to gain their Master's, having passed all their other courses, because they are found guilty of deliberate – or even inadvertent – plagiarism. Plagiarism is any attempt to pass off the writing of others as your own. In academic circles this is seen as theft of intellectual property and deceit, and is severely penalised. Because it is easy to cut and paste electronic text, plagiarism appears to be on the increase, and universities are becoming seriously concerned about this.

Some students, under pressure to complete their dissertations or mistrusting their own drafting ability, insert large fragments of text from other sources without acknowledging that fact. Literature reviews seem particularly prone to this. While it makes excellent sense to save text in the original if you are going to draw on it heavily, you need to be very careful to be clear in your own information storage what is your text and what is copied. And while it is good practice to quote other authors occasionally, you need to make it crystal clear in your report which sections are direct quotes, and attribute these quotations. Use quotation marks or italics to define the text quoted, and give the reference immediately after. Most of the time, however, you need to use your own words, and draw together and critique several authors, rather than relying on a single text. Mere reproduction of other people's words does not display the critical and evaluative skills that dissertations are designed to test.

Some students clearly feel that 'borrowing' text found on the Internet is safe – given the myriads of possible sites, they are unlikely to be found out. But this is far from the case. There are usually very obvious stylistic differences between plagiarised text and that genuinely written by the student. Furthermore, universities are increasingly using software which helps them to detect instances of work borrowed from other students. Where plagiarism *is* detected academic penalties may be severe: students may be removed from a course, or even asked to leave the university without a qualification.

PRIMARY DATA COLLECTION

Before going on to consider issues of methodology, it will be helpful to have an understanding of some of the commonest approaches to collecting primary data to inform a project or dissertation. Three approaches are popular, though there are others. You will need to read a text devoted to management research, or follow a course on methodology to become competent, but the discussion in the rest of this chapter will make more sense if you have at least started to think of some of the practical considerations involved in gathering your own data. I shall look at interviews, questionnaires and focus groups as these are frequently used in the context of a dissertation. Note, however, that there are many other ways of generating data, and these may not be appropriate, or only marginally so, for your own chosen topic.

Interviewing for information

One of the most popular ways of collecting information is to conduct a series of interviews. This requires you to use the talking and listening skills developed earlier, but you need additionally to know a little about the potential hazards of collecting data in this way.

→ Ch 11

Interviewing may seem simple. You merely ask some questions, either standard ones or (you may think) even better, anything that on the spur of the moment you are inspired to ask. Provided these fall under a set of fairly broad headings, this can be called a 'semi-structured' interview. You record the results, analyse them and you have the answer to your research question. Alas, it is rather more difficult to collect useful data. Although you can learn a great deal from merely talking to people, provided you listen carefully, it is difficult to put together what each person tells you and make collective sense of it. There is also a possibility that they will misunderstand your questions or you will misunderstand their answers. They may even tell you only what they think you want to hear. Even worse, you may hear only what fits in with your preconceptions and biases.

Skilful interviewing therefore requires that you add to your talking and listening skills certain other abilities. You need to be able to:

■ formulate unambiguous questions which do not indicate, even subtly, the 'right' answer;

■ avoid giving any other hints as to what you want;

■ use a style which encourages a person to answer questions freely and to the best of their ability;

■ probe and clarify if the answer is not sufficiently full or clear;

■ record interviewees' answers accurately for subsequent analysis.

Of course, as with everything else, you also need to be absolutely clear about what it is that you want to know. And you need to have thought about the number of people to ask and how to choose them, given the question which your project is trying to answer.

Interview types

Before you can do this, you need to think about the type of interview which best suits your purpose:

■ **Structured** interviews are those where you work out a set of questions before you start and ask each interviewee exactly the same questions, in the same order, and even in the same tone of voice, so as not inadvertently to bias your results.

■ **Semi-structured** interviews are those where you 'know what you want to know', that is, you have a set of themes, issues or topics which you want to explore. But you 'go with the flow' to some extent, approaching these issues in an order that seems appropriate, given the way the conversation is going, dropping issues which seem inappropriate with a particular respondent and adding others which the conversation suggests may be important.

■ **Unstructured** or in-depth interviews are even more informal and non-standardised. The interviewee is given free rein to talk about a topic in depth.

The appropriate type of interview will depend both on what you are trying to find out and on where you are in your investigation. At an early stage, while your thoughts are developing, unstructured interviews are likely to be most useful in suggesting issues that seem to be important to the people concerned and relationships that seem to exist between these issues. Having this information could help you to formulate a set of questions for a structured interview. While you can gain strong impressions from such interviews, and they may uncover whole areas you had not seen as relevant, they are very difficult to analyse in any systematic way.

If you want to be able to describe tendencies or patterns in a group of responses, structured interviews tend to be preferred. They allow you to compare the responses of different groups to the same questions and explore whether responses to one set of questions are related to responses to others. Analysis is usually easy: there is normally only a limited range of answers to any of these questions. You may be able to code answers while the person is talking. Several people can do the interviewing and their sets of answers are easily amalgamated. A structured interview is really a questionnaire which is administered by someone else. It has all the advantages of a questionnaire (*see* the next section, where question design for either is discussed). But if you use an interview, you are more likely to get answers to *all* the questions and a higher response rate – questionnaires go into the bin all too often. For example a senior manager may agree to be interviewed, but might throw away a questionnaire.

Despite the rather cynical comment earlier, semi-structured interviews can be extremely useful. For example, if you are trying to find out *why* a structured interview gives you certain patterns, you are likely to need a semi-structured interview. Suppose you had used a questionnaire to find out how satisfied people were with their jobs and whether they had applied for jobs elsewhere. You might have found that in most departments people were satisfied, but in two they were not. In one of these unhappy departments everyone was applying for jobs elsewhere, in the other they were not. To find out both why they were unhappy and why they were behaving differently with respect to other jobs, a semi-structured interview could be useful.

Types of question

The exact way in which you phrase your question can have a significant effect on the answers you are given by the interviewee. For semi-structured and unstructured interviews you will need to rely on three main types of question: open, probing and closed.

Open

Open questions allow the interviewee to decide what it is important to include in an answer. Questions which are *too* open can produce long and sometimes irrelevant answers. 'What do you think about the recent redundancies?' might produce anything. 'What methods has your organisation used to make people redundant?' would produce a more focused answer (assuming that it was methods that interested you). 'What', 'who', 'when', 'where', 'why' and 'how' are among the words useful for open questions.

For effective interviewing:

- use active listening
- set the scene carefully
- ask simple, neutral questions
- probe if necessary
- minimise closed questions
- close the interview carefully
- record data immediately.

Closed

Closed questions are those which tend to generate a 'yes' or 'no' answer, for example: 'Were recent redundancies handled well?' This type of question might be very useful either as a starting point, or as a follow-up to clarify your understanding. 'So on balance do you think that the methods chosen were appropriate?' could be useful as a check on your understanding of part of an answer to a more open question. Use such questions sparingly, though. If you use closed questions too early you risk closing a topic before you have found out what you want. If you use them too often your interviewee will tend to give shorter and shorter answers.

Probing

Probing questions are used to explore answers in more depth. If you want to know more than the interviewee has given in an answer, you can say something like: 'That's interesting. Could you tell me more about the reasons for ...?' or '... why the relationship between ...?' or whatever it is that you wish to be expanded. Probes are very useful if you realise that you have inadvertently asked a closed question!

Once you have selected your respondents, gained their agreement, know what you want to find out, and the sorts of questions you need to ask, there are some basic points to note. These will help you to generate valid data:

Guidelines for interviewing

- Practise active listening and observe body language.
- Manage the start of the interview very carefully – it is crucial to its success. You need to make the person feel comfortable. Thank them for their help and explain again the purpose of the interview and how long it is likely to take. You need to stress confidentiality, making clear whether anyone else will have access to the results of the interview. It usually helps to make clear that the interviewee will not be identifiable in the final report (unless of course they have agreed to be identified). You need to indicate what will happen to the results of your investigation. It is helpful, too, to give an idea of the sort of responses you want (e.g. brief or more discursive, immediate or considered). And you need to explain how you are recording answers (normally notes or tape recorder) and make sure that the person is happy with this.
- Keep questions as short and as simple as possible. If you roll three complex questions into one, it will be hard for your interviewee to make sense of what is required. It will also be hard for you to make sense of what they say! Also, if your question is rambling, your respondents will tend to follow your lead and speak at great length without saying very much. This makes both recording and analysis difficult.
- Use language that your interviewee will understand. It is pointless to use jargon or over-intellectual language with people who are unused to such words.

- Ask neutral questions. It is extremely easy to bias answers by using negatively or positively loaded words in describing some of the options.
- Use closed questions sparingly, only when you mean to.
- Start with questions that the interviewee will find easy, interesting and non-threatening. This will allow them to settle and to feel comfortable with you. Later in the interview you can ask more challenging questions, or touch on sensitive issues, with a good chance of getting a valid response. These sensitive questions might elicit very little early in an interview.
- Conclude by thanking the interviewee and giving them the chance to raise any concerns they may have as a result of the interview.
- Record your data as soon as possible after the interview. If you have made notes, sort them out and do any necessary classifying of responses while the interview is still fresh. If you are making audio recordings, do not let these accumulate. Transcribing/analysing takes ages and is best done as you go along in most cases. You may wish to modify later interviews in the light of early responses. It is therefore important immediately you finish to think about how the interview has gone. Note any problems and new thoughts that it prompted that seem important, particularly if you are near the start of your interviewing programme.

(This is available on the **website**.)

FOCUS GROUPS

Thus far the discussion has covered interviews with individuals. But you may want to gather information from a group of people. If so, it can be helpful to use focus groups. Many organisations use this technique, particularly as a way of finding out what is important to customers or potential customers.

To hold a focus group you assemble a small group (usually 6–10 people) whose views are relevant to your research. The group is asked to discuss your chosen topic. The aim is to allow group members to develop their own ideas through unstructured interaction. This can throw up ideas that the research has not considered, and show that other issues are more, or less, important than anticipated.

As the researcher, you facilitate the group. This should be a fairly passive role once the topic has been introduced. You are trying merely to encourage interaction within the group, not to steer it. If the discussion flags, you can ask supplementary questions such as 'What about . . .?' If one person dominates, you may need to gently subdue them. If some people do not contribute you may need to encourage them. If the discussion veers totally off the point, you may need to gently redirect it. You need to avoid steering the discussion too firmly because this will reduce your chances of finding out anything that you do not already know. In industry, focus groups are often run by trained psychologists, but the group-working skills you developed in Chapter 11 should help you to make a reasonable job of it.

→ Ch 11

You will need to keep a careful record of the discussion. This can be recorded for later analysis. Alternatively, or additionally, notes are taken. If at all possible, find someone to help you with this. It is very hard to take adequate notes while doing a good job of facilitation.

Focus groups can be extremely useful at the start of a project, when you are trying to identify important issues or research questions. But they have the same drawback as informal interviews. The sample is likely to be too small for reliable conclusions. The process of making sense of what was said is also highly subjective, with the researcher struggling to extract meaning from a fairly free-ranging discussion. You will normally need to build on your focus group findings with a more systematic investigation.

QUESTIONNAIRES

Surveys requiring respondents to complete a questionnaire are a popular way of collecting information for all sorts of purposes. You may have received various 'market research' questionnaires through the post or been sent a questionnaire after you bought something or made use of a service. Although you can include open-ended questions on a questionnaire, the fact that you cannot probe or clarify responses can make analysis of responses to these quite difficult. The main strength of questionnaires is that they allow you to identify and describe the extent of variation in answers on particular topics and to look for relationships between positions on one set of questions and positions on another. Thus, you could use a survey to establish factual things like the educational qualifications of users of a particular sports facility, or frequency of usage, or attitudinal aspects such as their satisfaction with the various sports on offer. You could also look for relationships, such as between level of education and preferred sport and/or satisfaction levels.

Questionnaire design is crucial, particularly if the respondents are supposed to fill in the questionnaire themselves. (Sometimes questionnaires are administered over the phone or face to face in a structured interview.) You need to have a very clear idea of what you need to know, to ask it in a totally unambiguous way and to make clear how the respondent is to reply.

ACTIVITY 19.11

Imagine that you work in a medical centre and you want to collect information from patients on their alcohol usage. Think about the way in which you and people you know might respond to the following questions and how much information this is likely to give the practice. If possible, ask a few people, using only one of the questions below, followed by informal discussion to check what it means, then ask others all three, in the order shown.

A Does alcohol play a part in your life? _____

B Would you describe yourself as a light, moderate or heavy drinker? _____

C How many drinks do you have a week on average? (count a half pint
of beer, one small glass of wine or a single of spirits as '1') _____

| 0–1 | 2 -3 | 4–7 | 8–14 | 15–21 | 22–35 | 36–42 | 43+ |

You need to be very careful in interpreting answers, as your follow-up discussion may have shown. Question A (taken from a real questionnaire) presumably elicited both 'yes' and 'no' from people with very similar levels of drinking. B may well have elicited some 'light' responses from people who consume rather more than those who see themselves as 'moderate' drinkers. The range of possible drinking levels given in C may make it easier for people to admit to drinking, say, 22 units than if the scale had stopped at 22+, as it makes them appear well within the range on offer, rather than at the extreme. For areas that are often under-reported, like drinking and smoking levels, this may be an important consideration.

You can perhaps see from this why it is important to pilot a questionnaire with a small number of people – try it out and then look at the answers that are given. Do some questions produce the same answer from everybody? If so, they may not be generating much information. Do some questions get omitted? This may be because people do not realise that they must turn the page, or because the question looks like part of the instruction, or because it is not clear what the question means or how to answer it. Talk to those who filled out the questionnaire about whether they had difficulty with any of the questions and probe the meaning of their answers to check that you will be interpreting them correctly. Check, too, that your layout and the way the questions are to be answered make it as easy as possible to analyse the results.

Response rates

It is really important to get a reasonable response rate. What constitutes reasonable will depend on the size of your sample, the complexity of the analysis you want to do and the randomness or otherwise of the 'sample within a sample', those people who *do* fill in the questionnaire.

ACTIVITY 19.12

Suppose that you send a questionnaire to 100 people. You write a pleasant covering letter, explaining what you are doing and why, as well as why their participation is important and that responses will be treated confidentially, but you receive only 10 replies.

Think of reasons for people not replying, and what this means about the usefulness of the 10 you get back. Think too about how you might be able to increase the response rate. If possible, discuss this in a group, drawing on your own responses to questionnaires you have received.

You probably came up with reasons such as 'questionnaire looked too long and time consuming', 'first few questions were difficult/intrusive/boring/incomprehensible so didn't go further', 'why should I pay for a stamp to give them information?', 'meant to but somehow didn't get around to it' and so on. The best way of increasing the response rate will depend on the reasons – a well-designed, appealing questionnaire will address the first two, use of e-mail or a stamped addressed envelope the third. Small incentives such as a prize for the lucky reply and a better prize if the questionnaire is returned within seven days will address two reasons and reminders are also helpful.

It is vital that you *do* ensure a better response rate than this. If you send out 100 questionnaires and get 10 back, you will have very little data to analyse. Worse, you will not know if the 10 were reasonably typical of the 100, or the only 10 who were different in some significant way. For example it might be that the only people who reply to a questionnaire about the quality of nursing care during a recent hospital stay are the tiny minority who had a really bad experience and are still angry enough to want to tell someone about this when the questionnaire arrives. If you assumed they were typical, you could be seriously misled about the quality of care that most patients at the hospital receive.

If you use questionnaires, you are facing a minefield. Plan to spend some time reading about questionnaire design and sampling, or consult an expert, before designing your questionnaire, and never use a questionnaire without first piloting it. Try it out on several people and afterwards ask them to interpret their answers, and comment on any uncertainties or difficulties they had in answering any questions.

RESEARCH METHODOLOGY AND APPROACH

Many dissertations have a 'methodology' section. Strictly speaking, 'methodology' is the theory of how research should be undertaken. It includes the theoretical and philosophical assumptions on which the research is based and what these assumptions mean for choice of approach. Thus, a full 'methodology' section would discuss your position on how knowledge is generated, the extent to which you believe you are an impartial observer of 'fact' or seeking to make sense of a socially constructed reality in which you are a participant. You would also need to discuss your position on the use of *deductive* testing of a hypothesis in a highly structured and 'scientific' way, as opposed to *inductive* building of theory from observations in a more flexible way. The latter approach would probably use qualitative data and recognise that, as observer, you are yourself part of the research process.

The extent to which you will need to discuss such issues will depend partly upon where your research lies on the academic–applied continuum. While it is always worth spending a little time thinking about your own position on these issues, sometimes a fairly straightforward justification of 'methods' rather than discussion of methodology will suffice. You will always, however, need to develop a clear research strategy fitted to your research objectives. Your chosen approach, or mix of approaches, needs to be such as to provide a believable, i.e. reliable and valid, answer to your research question, within the constraints operating.

While some questions can be answered from existing literature, you will probably want to supplement this by generation of further data. This may be by planning experiments, or, more commonly, by conducting some sort of survey, whether by interview or questionnaire, or exploring a specific case, either to test theory or to generate new ideas. The discussion in the previous section should have given you an idea of what this can involve. Whatever method you decide upon there will be further questions. For example, if you are planning a questionnaire, issues will include: how many people you need to gain information from; which kind of people need to be represented; whether to use a paper or electronic questionnaire; which questions to include; whether a less structured approach using interviews or focus groups might be a better starting point for informing questionnaire design.

Whichever approach you choose, you will need to be able to justify it in terms of its appropriateness to your chosen research question, that is, in terms of whether the data generated are reliable and provide a valid answer to this question. Thinking about the data you need to generate is therefore a vital early stage.

Data planning

Detailed and realistic project planning is essential, and should begin as soon as you are happy with your project choice, certainly well before you are due to commence your research. This is because you cannot fully assess the feasibility of your proposal until you have a detailed plan of what will be involved. Only then can you start to put timescales to these activities.

No matter how carefully you have done your first two selections, it is still possible to discover snags in a proposed project once detailed planning is carried out, and you need time to go through a third cycle of project choice and develop your second or third choice of option if your first starts to look too risky or is not as feasible as it seemed. Most snags at this stage can be handled by modifications to the proposal, but in the unlikely event of finding that you need to abandon a topic altogether, you do not want this to happen well into the research time. By then it will be a disaster. If it happens before the project is officially due to start, because you are well ahead on your planning, it may be frustrating and annoying, but it is far from catastrophic.

Before you can draw up bar charts or other detailed schedules, you will need to think in considerable detail about your data requirements. For most projects, the bulk of the 'work' consists of data collection and analysis. In conducting your research you will be aiming to collect evidence on the basis of which you can draw convincing conclusions. If your information is deficient, if you do not have enough, if it is not the information you actually need to address your particular issue, or if your information is biased or inaccurate, any subsequent analysis and conclusions will be worthless.

Obviously, the data you need will depend upon your chosen topic. Part of your course should be directed towards enabling you to understand how to go about detailed analysis of data requirements; for example, where you can go to find different sorts of data, how best to design a questionnaire that will tell you what you need to know, how big a sample you need in order to obtain a statistically valid result, and so on. However, you may not learn these things until you are starting your research. This may be too late to allow the detailed planning which depends on an understanding of data needs. This section therefore aims to indicate, very briefly, the sorts of issues which are important. Suggestions are given for further reading which will allow you to make a more detailed study of data requirements and possibilities if timescales, or the content of your particular course, lead you to feel that this is necessary.

Two important distinctions in considering the data you will need concern primary versus secondary and quantitative versus qualitative data.

Primary data are those that you collect yourself. This might be by direct observation, by interview, by application of a questionnaire or by other means. Primary data can be tailored to your particular requirements. You can design a questionnaire to give you answers to precisely the question of concern to you, administer it to an appropriate sample and know exactly under what conditions it was administered. You know how accurate the data are, and should have a clear idea of any ways in which inaccuracies might have crept in. Unfortunately, you pay a significant price for all these advantages. Collecting valid data tends to be very time consuming.

Secondary data are those collected by others. These might be the results of surveys carried out by others, government statistics, in-company statistics or records, etc. By using secondary data you will have access to far more information than you could possibly collect yourself, and much more rapidly. But you may not know how much reliance to place upon the data, particularly if they were gathered for purposes very different from your own. Even data that might be expected to be perfectly straightforward and reliable, such as a section's weekly production figures, may have been manipulated by those responsible for their compilation. Local managers often produce such figures as it will keep senior management off the back of the section head. The overall total might be right, but it is fairly common for some output from a good week to be 'stockpiled', and used to raise output figures in poor weeks. If your purpose was to explore correlates of variations in output, the figures would be of little use. It is important to be aware of the possible limitations of any data which you have not collected yourself, and to check, if at all possible, what factors may have influenced the figures. You also need to bear possible unreliabilities in mind when drawing conclusions.

When talking of data it is *quantitative* data, those involving numbers, which readily spring to mind. But important factors in a situation may be very hard to quantify. Attitudes and feelings may be important. Variations in perceptions, for example the different ways in which different groups of participants in a situation would map the relevant (for them) factors in a situation, may be highly significant. Because techniques for structuring such *qualitative* information, and deciding on the reliance to be placed upon it, are less well known than the techniques of basic parametric statistics, such factors may be omitted altogether. If not, numbers may be attributed to them, and totally invalid ways of interpreting those numbers attempted.

This may be clearer if you consider data using the classification usually applied in discussions of research. *Textual* data refers to verbal description, for example quotations from an article or an interview. Such data can be a splendid source of ideas and create a vivid picture for the recipient. An interviewee might tell you in all too graphic terms precisely what is wrong with his or her boss, or the organisation, or anything about which you choose to ask. He or she might describe precisely what should be done to solve the organisation's problems. But it is very difficult to know what reliance to place upon this information. Does this interviewee have some axe to grind? How common is this perception? There *are* occasions when such text can itself provide the basis for a more quantitative analysis, for example in examining the commonest sequences of moves in a large sample of transcripts of negotiations, but this involves fairly specialist techniques. If you are planning to make heavy use of textual data you should consult your thesis supervisor to make sure that you will be using them in a way that will be acceptable to the institution. Some of the qualitative data you will need may well be of a textual kind, until you find some way of at least partially quantifying the information.

Where you stand on qualitative versus quantitative approaches will depend on your assumptions about the nature of management and how knowledge about it is generated. But you need to be aware that, while quantitative data can be more 'reliable' and may be more generalisable, they are often less informative and may generate fewer insights. If you are aware of the distinction you will not claim 'answers' that the data cannot, by their nature, support.

Nominal or *categorical* data refers to data where some classification has been made, e.g. into country of origin, or type of first degree held by graduate managers. It is possible to count the members of each category, but even if the categories are identified by numbers, for example you might label the category 'chemists' as 1, 'biologists' as 2, etc., it is impossible to relate categories mathematically. Two chemists would in no meaningful sense equal one biologist!

Again, some of the qualitative information you seek may be capable of being categorised in a nominal fashion.

Ordinal or *ranked* data are those where it is possible to make some comparisons between different categories. Interviewers might, for example, categorise applicants into highly suitable, probably good, acceptable, would need significant training, and non-appointable. If highly suitable was 5 and non-appointable 1 then showing the distribution between the rankings at different appointment panels would carry some information. But you could not suggest that the difference between a '5' candidate and a '4' candidate was in any sense 'equal' to the difference between a '1' and a '2', nor that a '4' was twice as good as a '2'. Equally, it would be invalid to use any sort of statistics that assumed that this was what the numbers meant.

Interval data are those where it *is* possible to assume that differences between numbers mean something. The difference between 25 degrees Celsius and 35 degrees is the same as that between 45 degrees and 55. But there is no real zero on this scale. It was mere convenience that determined that the freezing point of water should be designated zero. So 40 degrees is not twice as hot as 20 degrees. Questionnaire scores on attitude questionnaires might, for example, be capable of being treated as interval data, though more usually they would be ordinal.

Ratio data are those where not only are intervals meaningful, but there is a real zero as well, so that ratios also make sense. Forty people out of work is twice as many as 20. An inflation rate of 12% is three times that of 4%, and it is meaningful to make such a statement. Ratio data are the only ones on which you can use any mathematical technique you wish. Even with ratio data you may not be able to use all statistical techniques, however, as some are more sensitive than others to the distribution of values you are likely to find in the sample you are looking at. With statistics, if you are not an expert it makes excellent sense to discuss your plans with someone who is!

Whatever the type of data you are planning to collect, you need to feel confident that the data will be accurate, relevant and reliable.

How accurate and reliable are the data?

Would a different observer obtain the same result? Indeed, would you get the same result if you repeated the exercise? If there could be a bias, in which direction are the results likely to be influenced? Are all relevant incidents (e.g. accidents) being recorded? If not, are omissions random, or most likely to occur in one particular direction?

Does the sample used warrant the conclusions drawn from it?

Refer to your statistics course notes to decide what size of sample you need if you are planning quantitative data. Remember that you may well end up with fewer data than you initially think. The return rate on questionnaires usually falls far short of 100%. Interviews may be cancelled at short notice, and so on. Allow for a reasonable rate of attrition, and plan your data collection so that your sample, even after this, is large enough.

It is also important that your sample is *representative.* You would be unwise to predict the election results on the basis of a survey of home-owners, for example. Yet, students all too frequently survey one very narrow section of their organisation, and on the basis of their findings go on to make sweeping recommendations concerning the entire organisation, if not the world. A dissertation I examined recently reported unstructured interviews with six people, all of whom had a distinctly partial view of the issue in question. On the basis of their expressed opinions the student made recommendations for a complete restructuring of the national sector of which their organisation was a part. This sample was so small, and so unrepresentative of the full range of people affected, that the dissertation demonstrated an ignorance of the rules for drawing conclusions from evidence so staggering as to constitute an academic crime.

Do the data actually measure what they purport to measure?

If you have devised a questionnaire, does it really measure what you think it does? How can you check? Are in-company data to be taken at face value? If at all possible talk to those responsible for putting the figures together. I still remember the difference between the wage clerks and management as to how a bonus scheme actually worked at one of the sites I visited in the course of a research project. I was attempting to answer what I thought was a simple question as to how much people were paid. Supervisors told me that there was a bonus scheme. The clerks involved insisted that the better you worked, the less you were actually paid. Further investigation suggested that the clerks were right! So try to find some way of checking any information you gather. For example, if you ask interviewees to describe an organisation's appraisal scheme they may all tell you that appraisals are carried out annually. Ask them to show you their last appraisal report, or to tell you the date at which their last appraisal interview was carried out, and a very different picture may emerge.

In considering your data requirements you will need to bear all the above factors in mind, and relate them to the particular question which you are trying to answer. This is a difficult task, and one in which you should take advantage of all the help you can get, whether from your project supervisor, fellow students who understand statistics or those within your organisation in a position to know what information may be available and how it might be obtained.

ETHICAL CONSIDERATIONS

In planning your research and data collection you will need to consider the potential impact of your research, particularly on your subjects. You may need to complete an ethics form for your organisation or university, or make a case to an ethics committee. Honesty, openness, lack of coercion and confidentiality are key ethical issues, as is privacy, if you are proposing to initiate contact with individuals. Your research should not cause harm or distress to anyone involved, or embarrassment of any kind to subjects or stakeholders. Pressure should not be exerted to gain participation or access to information. Concealing the purpose of the research as a whole, or of a specific interview or observation, may not be ethical. Breaking a promise of confidentiality certainly is *not* ethical. If you have promised that respondents or organisations will not be identifiable from your report, then you need to be absolutely certain that no clues to their identity are left. And if you have made other promises such as to provide a copy of the ultimate findings you need to follow through on this. It is in everyone's interests (your institution, which may rely on support from a sponsoring organisation, those in the organisation sponsoring your research, those cooperating in providing information, and above all your own, as your reputation is at stake) that you behave ethically at all times, and with courtesy and professionalism.

PROJECT MANAGEMENT

A detailed project plan will be the key element in your project management. It will provide the standard against which you will monitor your progress for the duration of your research, and through to the point of submitting your completed dissertation. Many dissertations go wrong because of faulty control, yet the use of simple project management techniques, which will almost certainly have been covered in your course, should prevent this. The use of such techniques should provide a fairly tight schedule of tasks, thus avoiding the 'I don't know where to start, so I won't' syndrome that afflicts some students.

Your plan should provide you with a series of planned completion dates for the various tasks involved. This will enable you to be aware immediately of any time slippage, and to take steps to remedy this, seeking help from your thesis supervisor if necessary. Many students *not* using project management techniques realise that something is seriously wrong only when it is far too late to do anything to repair the damage. Interim target dates will do more than merely reassure you that you are on course. They will have a major effect in sustaining your motivation, as each target met will be a source of satisfaction. If the only date towards which you are working is your final submission date, it is all too easy to feel that you are making no progress at all on the project, and to become demotivated in consequence. This is a splendid example of a vicious circle, with failure as the most likely outcome.

Identifying necessary activities

Once you have clarified the aims of your research through discussions with your client and supervisor, and thought in detail about your likely data requirements, you are in a position to think about the activities which will be needed in order to acquire and analyse the data, and to schedule these so as to allow you to complete your dissertation within the time allowed.

You will need to draw up a list of the activities necessary to achieve your objectives. You then need to think about the order in which these will need to be carried out. For example, if your plans include the design and use of a questionnaire, then necessary activities will include informal discussions with a small number of people in order to refine your ideas about the design of the questionnaire, and drafting a first version of this. Piloting the draft on a small sample will provide a check that there are no ambiguities, that the questions are interpreted as you intended (you can check this by interviewing the people involved after they have filled in the questionnaire), and that the thing can be completed within a reasonable time. You will also need to analyse results, and cannot do this until questionnaires have been completed and returned. And it may be necessary to send out reminders to increase the response rate.

Possibly in parallel with this, you will have to decide on the size of sample needed and how this should be selected. Once this has been decided you may need to gain organisational approval to your approaching the sample. Then you will probably wish to notify your sample in some way that your research is under way and explain its purpose so that you are more likely to get questionnaires returned and completed in an honest way. You will need to set up some mechanism for distributing and collecting questionnaires, you will need to have your final version duplicated in sufficient quantities, and so on.

Critical path analysis

You can see from the above that there may be fairly complicated sequencing problems. A useful technique for sorting these out is constructing *network diagrams*. By the time you come to do your project you will probably have covered these in your course, but, in case you are thinking about it before this, Fig.19.6 shows an example of a network. (This is hand drawn, but software is easily available to enable you to construct such diagrams, identify critical paths, and schedule activities efficiently.)

In Fig. 19.6, activities are identified by a number (a key – not shown – will show what each number represents). You read the diagram from left to right. The duration of the activity is shown not by the length of the arrow, but by the number in the semi-circle hanging below the line. The dotted lines are dummy activities, a device used to show that a separate chain of activities will also need to have been completed prior to the start of the next activity. Thus they normally do not have a duration. You can see, therefore, that in the case of Fig. 19.6 you cannot do the activity numbered 8 until you

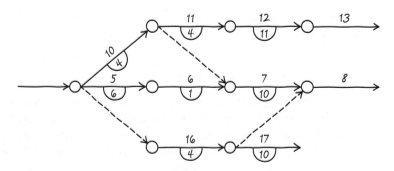

Fig. 19.6 Part of a hand-drawn network

have done 7 and 16, and you cannot do 7 until you have done 5, 6 and 10. You can also see that it will be at least 17 days (if the units of time are days) before you can start 8, and longer if you have not been able to do activities 10 and 16 in parallel.

Note that, although this is an example of a common way of drawing network diagrams, there are variants. If you have been taught a different convention, use that. The important thing is to use your chosen convention consistently so that the meaning of the diagram is clear.

Your diagram will only be useful if your estimates of how long it will take to do activities are reasonably accurate, and of course this can be quite difficult. Ask for advice, and then add a margin for error! The golden rule of projects is that things always take longer than you think. Make sure that you have allowed for 'dead time' – for example the time between sending out a questionnaire and gaining a response, or between writing to an organisation and being granted access. Aim to schedule activities in parallel to exploit this dead time. To plan the best use of your time you need to make use of the ideas of 'critical path' and 'float'. The critical path is the minimum time a project can take, i.e. the longest path through the network. It is critical because any delays on this path will delay the project. Activities on non-critical paths could be delayed if necessary. This scope for delaying is called 'float'. To calculate it you work backwards, from right to left, subtracting activity durations from the time of the event they feed into. Thus, it would not matter if you took 10 days for activity 16, provided you started it at least 10 days before activity 8 was due. (You can identify the float in Fig.1.1 by the dotted boxes.)

→ Ch 1

Drawing up a realistic schedule

Once you have drawn up a network, you need to think, too, about the time you have available. If you are working you need to make reasonable allowance for times when you know that you will be unusually busy in your job, and set yourself a lighter project workload at these points to compensate. Build in some slack for unexpected conflicting demands, too. If your initial schedule cannot be made to allow for such slack then you should revise your objectives to something more modest.

If using a PC for your scheduling you will be able to print out bar charts and revisions of bar charts with relative ease. If scheduling 'by hand' it is still worth the effort of drawing a bar chart. It provides a visible prompt to activity, and an overview of the pattern of your activities. It shows where slippage is possible and where it is critical that it does not occur. As it is almost inevitable that you will need to reschedule, and to add in activities that you omitted first time, it is worth leaving room at the end for extra activities, and then running off a number of blanks before you add the bars. This will make rescheduling less of a chore. Alternatively, you can use re-stickable paper for the bars. Whichever labour-saving device you use, it is important that you can draw up new schedules without wasting time when the need arises. It is not efficient to work from an out-of-date schedule, or one altered beyond the point of legibility.

Figure 19.7 shows an example of part of a hand-drawn schedule. Note that scope for slippage is indicated by the dotted areas after the bars. This should not, however, be taken as a licence to use the slack whenever you feel a little tired. The knock-on effects of this in terms of unreasonably high workloads in subsequent weeks would make a nonsense of all your planning and seriously threaten your success. Even deliberate slack should be saved for genuine emergencies rather than minor reluctance to work. If you use up your slack early in the project because of slight illness or mild overload at work, there will be none left when the real disaster hits you later on.

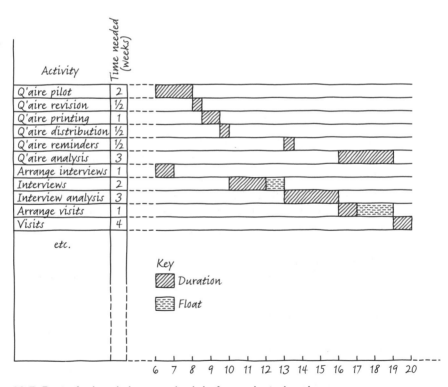

Fig. 19.7 Part of a hand-drawn schedule for project planning

ACTIVITY 19.13

Work out a bar chart (either hand drawn or on your PC) for your proposed project. Once it is complete, perform the following checks:

1. Starting at the end, check that you have included *all* the activities that must take place prior to the end activity. Work back through the chart checking that for *each* activity all the necessary preceding activities are represented.

2. Check that you have indeed scheduled these preceding activities *before* the activities that require their prior completion.

3. Check that you have built any necessary waiting time (e.g. for return of questionnaires, duplication or data processing by others) into your schedule.

4. Check the workload for each week, to ensure that the total is never excessive.

5. Check that your schedule is compatible with expected peaks in job or other conflicting demands.

6. Look at all activities where the float, or capacity for slippage, is small or non-existent, and check that your time estimates for these activities are realistic.

Comment

If the above activity gives you any cause for concern you should consult with your client and your project supervisor about ways in which the scope of the project could be reduced slightly, to make it more likely that you will be able to complete it successfully within the constraints operating.

Once you have a schedule which seems realistic to you and covers all that you think will be necessary, with sufficient slack for the later inclusion of things that you will subsequently realise are needed or for problems encountered elsewhere, you have your main project control tool. All that you need to do now is to *use* it.

It may be helpful to highlight major milestones in your research, and the dates by which these must be reached. You may have already passed two – topic choice and completion of planning! It is likely that others will be completion of your literature search, collection of information, completion of analysis, first draft of your thesis and final submission date. Highlight these points on your chart. (Some students show *only* these activities on their project plans, but such a lack of detail is virtually useless. I hope that the above discussion and activity led you to draw up a far more detailed chart.)

Add any milestones which are important to your particular institution. You may be required to submit revised plans or draft chapters at intervals. If so, submission dates for these should be noted. If possible agree to meet with your supervisor at appropriate milestones.

Now draw a large version of your chart and put it above your desk and make a smaller version for your diary. Refer to your chart at least once a week to ensure that you are on, or ahead of, target. The whole process can be made more fun, and can provide you with the satisfaction of a visible record of progress, if you colour in activities as they are completed.

If you do encounter an unexpected block, then use your chart to see where you could get ahead to compensate, so that the time scheduled for project work during the period you are blocked is still put to effective use.

Managing group projects

It is vital, with group projects, to set milestones for each member's work, and to meet regularly to review progress. It is almost inevitable that one member of the group will find it difficult to meet deadlines, either because of unanticipated problems outside the course, or because a task turns out to be harder than expected, or just because they find it difficult to work to a schedule. The group needs to know as soon as slippage starts, and to decide how to manage the situation so that the final deadline can be met.

Because some people are optimistic, assuming that undone work will be magically easier 'tomorrow', it is prudent to require members to circulate copies of what they have achieved at regular intervals, rather than relying on reports of 'progress'. (Call me cynical, but I find this is essential for group projects at work, as well!) If slippage is occurring on a critical path, or it is towards the end of the project and there is not much float left, then prompt corrective action will be needed. All this will be easier if the group has been communicating frequently throughout, members understand each other's strengths, weaknesses and situations, and an open and supportive way of working closely together has been developed.

> **Example of student experience on a group consultancy project**
>
> *This project gave me experience of working with a real-live client, gathering relevant information and managing both the client relationship and the project team. I learned a lot about group dynamics, as this was the first time we had needed to work as a team on a major project of real importance. There was a lot of conflict, some of it because aims were different. One person only wanted to pass, four wanted distinctions (though one of them didn't seem to want to do any work to achieve it).*
>
> *So only three of us were making a real contribution, which put a lot of pressure on us, and this got worse when one of us had to go home for her mother's funeral just as we were preparing the report and presentation. No one seemed prepared to take the initiative, so in the end I felt I had to try to 'lead' the group. I became rather autocratic, and allocated work to each member, making clear that it was their responsibility to do it by the deadline. This upset the more 'relaxed' members, and I had to put up with some very negative comments, but they did make some sort of attempt to do the work, even if it needed to be 'improved' after.*
>
> *Things which contributed overall to our success were regular meetings, taking decisions by consensus, keeping minutes of meetings, having a range of specialisms in the team, trying to accommodate external pressures on members, and defining tasks and responsibilities very clearly.*

The whole experience was a real roller-coaster ride: sometimes the pressure was enormous. But I now feel much more confident of my leadership abilities, and have decided to become a consultant. I have already developed an action plan for further development of the necessary skills. And yes, we did get our distinction!

Writing the first draft

One activity which can usefully be brought much further ahead than you probably realise is the first draft of parts of your thesis. It may seem absurd to start this while data collection is only just beginning and you have little idea of what your conclusions will be. But if you write a skeleton draft, using guesses at what results might be, you will often discover a need for additional data, as even if results *do* turn out as expected, they will support only a weak argument. By trying to construct that argument it becomes clear where additional pieces of information would strengthen your case enormously. If you are finding this out while still at the data collection stage, you can alter your plans and produce a much better piece of research in consequence. By the time you are officially 'writing up', it is usually too late for this.

Thus, the project choice phase is not the only one that should be seen as an iterative process. As with any complex problem-solving activity, a constant process of thought, experiment and refining your thought is necessary. This point is made explicit in many of the systems methodologies, some of which you may be taught during your course. → Ch 8   The process also reflects the Kolb learning cycle introduced in Chapter 8. We cannot make sense of complexity all at once. But we can make a little sense of it, work with our new ideas, see ways in which they can be improved, try the new ideas, see further weaknesses and ways forward, and so on. Thus step by step we come to an improved understanding.

A Master's-level project will almost certainly fall into this category of making progressive sense of complexity. You should, therefore, be aware at all times of the possible need to go back and slightly revise earlier thoughts. It is usually by such apparently backward steps that true progress is made. Similarly you should try to make experimental steps forward, for example, by trying an early draft, or analysing dummy material, to check out your ideas while there is still time for change.

Many problem-solving methodologies recommend several loops around the whole problem-solving cycle before a satisfactory solution is likely to be reached. You are likely to be operating under such tight time constraints that repeated iterations will not be possible, but you can approximate to this by doing 'quick and dirty' mini-studies to check on your intended directions, and by the sorts of jumps ahead suggested.

Keeping a project log

As well as your chart and its colour scheme, you should keep a more detailed record of progress in the form of a project log. In this you should record all project activity, times taken, details of what happened, snags encountered and insights gained. This can be enormously helpful to you when you come to write up your work, as it can be surprising how easily things which seemed burned into your memory at the time fade into oblivion. Your log can be a source of observations made at the time and eminently quotable at appropriate points in your dissertation. Furthermore, many students are asked to submit their reflections on lessons learned, and comments on how with hindsight the project could have been improved. This is intended to demonstrate that you have indeed learned something about the process of this kind of research, and how to be critical of such investigations. (It can also be a valuable source of necessary marks for the student for whom everything has gone wrong.) Your project log will be invaluable in writing such a 'reflections' section.

→ Ch 15

Either in your log or on your computer or somewhere else extremely safe, you should keep a full record of *all* sources referred to. Chapter 15 highlighted the enormous amount of time which can be wasted by having to hunt for part of a reference which you omitted to note (*which* journal was it in?) or a reference that you had on a piece of paper which somehow seems to have vanished. Even if it seems unlikely that you will need to refer to something, if it is remotely possible that you could use it, note it. It may turn out to be extremely relevant once you have developed your ideas.

With your schedule, your interim dates and your coloured pens, you will have every chance of keeping on target, and of avoiding the stress or distress which many less organised students experience. But things can still go wrong. You may encounter unexpected resistance at work, the organisation may hit a crisis, or you may have to face major problems at home. If anything like this happens, shout for help at once. Discuss your best course of action with your project supervisor, and keep him or her continually informed of the situation. Keep your client informed too. It is not a sign of weakness to admit to things turning out differently from anticipated. The weakness lies in refusing to admit that this has happened until it is too late for plans to be revised or other remedial action taken. A small amount of optimism may be justified. Things *may* look better tomorrow. But if they are still looking equally dire the next week, tell your supervisor without further delay!

WRITING UP

Many students dread writing their dissertation, feel oppressed that it is looming ever closer on the horizon, and postpone it as much as they dare (which is often far too much). Because they have left it too late, some parts are ill thought out, there is no time to obtain feedback on draft material from the supervisor or to revise parts that don't seem to work. The resulting dissertation is equally depressing to student, supervisor, client and examiner.

If you have followed the suggested practice of writing skeleton drafts at an early stage, and are reasonably competent at word processing, the drafting process can be relatively painless. You will know that revisions are easily made, your skeleton drafts can be amended and made use of, your references will be already on the computer, and you will presumably be using your PC for some, at least, of your data analysis, probably using a package which means that figures and graphs can be easily integrated into your report.

→ Ch 15 Your dissertation will need to follow the basic principles of report writing covered in Chapter 15. You may find it helpful to refer back to this. The section which follows discusses additional drafting points specific to dissertations and theses.

Who is the audience?

The first, and crucial point is to find out the required audience for your report. Are you expected to submit a report addressed to your client, to the academic examiner, or in some way to blur the issue and write a sort of multi-purpose report? This latter approach would need to steer a delicate course between 'useful ideas' and 'jargon'. Your organisation, after all, will primarily want to know what to do about something that is bothering them. They are not really concerned about the extent to which you have adopted a position that could be described as 'weak logical positivist', or how appropriate a 'grounded theory' approach is to the problem. But you would probably need to convince your examiners that you *do* understand such methodological considerations, and that you have thoroughly searched the relevant literature to find theories and techniques and data relevant to your chosen problem.

Analysis will present fewer conflicts. Both audiences are likely to need convincing that your analytical techniques are appropriate to the type of data you have collected and to the questions in which you are interested, and that you have used them correctly. Both will want to know that the data you have collected form an adequate basis for the conclusions that you are drawing. And both will require that your presentation is clear, your arguments are logical, and your recommendations sensible, unambiguous and ordered according to reasonable priorities.

Both will probably also appreciate suggestions as to future steps to be taken in order to implement your recommendations, though your examiners are likely to be the only ones concerned with your reflections on the progress of the project and the lessons that you learned.

Obviously, it is important that your submitted thesis is written for the prime benefit of your examiners. If they do not require the submission of a client report, then you should probably consider 'versioning' your thesis for company use. With a word processor this is a minor task, and well worth the slight effort if you wish your recommendations to be acted on by the organisation, and your own image to be enhanced. (If you are writing a more specialist and academic dissertation you may instead wish to version it for publication.)

The following broad framework is likely to be appropriate for your examiners:

Title page

1–2 page summary – *you may be required to submit this separately, rather than binding it with the thesis*

Preface and acknowledgements

List of contents – *numbering should usually reflect major and minor sections, e.g. 4, 4.1, 4.2, etc.*

List of tables, figures, etc. – *if appropriate*

Numbered sub-titled sections – these should normally include an initial statement of project aims, a short statement of major findings and recommendations, and then detailed descriptions of relevant literature, chosen research approach (with justification), data collected, analysis, conclusions and probably reflections

List of references

Additional bibliography – *if needed*

Appendices

Style should be clear, avoiding the use of unnecessary jargon, but using academic concepts where appropriate. Avoid being over-colloquial, and making unsupported assertions. It should be very clear how results are derived, and any shortcomings in the data should be discussed. A short introduction to each section can help make the structure of your arguments clearer to your reader, and the inclusion of relevant diagrams and tables (unless these are very complicated) will help your reader by clarifying points and by breaking up the text. Very detailed or complex information should be included as an appendix. It would interrupt your argument if it was in the main text.

If you can afford it, use good quality paper, as it improves the overall impression given by the report. Pay attention to diagrams, too. These should be either computer generated, or very carefully drawn by hand. Scrappy diagrams do not contribute to a good overall impression. And make sure that you know what type of binding is required. If none is specified, think carefully about the most appropriate and durable way of binding your dissertation.

Do check your spelling. Repeated spelling mistakes detract from the overall impression created, and in extreme cases a dissertation can be referred for corrections. Check, too, that you have not made mistakes when typing numbers, as errors here are more serious.

Even if you are not *required* to submit a draft of part of your thesis, the point was made earlier that your supervisor's comments on such a draft can be invaluable. It is important to check that your style, level of analysis and use of academic sources is what is required by the institution. There may be simple ways in which major improvements can be made, and you should find out about these at an early stage if at all possible.

If you start your drafting early, have developed your report-writing skills earlier in your course and are reasonably competent at word processing, the drafting of your thesis can be one of the most satisfying parts of your whole course. You are creating a substantial piece of work based on your own findings, and are seeing this take shape before your eyes. Far from a chore, this can be enormously exciting.

SUMMARY

- Management research is usually directed whether directly or indirectly towards real organisational problems.

19

Projects, theses and dissertations

- You should start work on your initial planning months in advance of the official project start.
- Topic choice is critical, and should be an iterative process involving yourself, your project supervisor and, if doing an applied project, your organisational client.
- Diagnosis of complex organisational problems is both challenging and crucial.
- You will normally be expected to show that you can make good use of literature and information sources beyond those introduced in earlier courses.
- You should take full advantage throughout your project of the support and expertise your supervisor can offer.
- A good topic is interesting to all parties, gives sufficient scope, exhibits symmetry of outcomes, is feasible and not too prone to catastrophe.
- Interviews, focus groups or questionnaires are often used to generate primary data, but care needs to be taken to ensure that these data are valid, and properly interpreted.
- Detailed project planning is essential, and cannot be undertaken until you have a clear idea of how you will proceed and the data that will be required.
- Networks and bar charts are invaluable for project control.
- Work should be as iterative as possible, with dummy analyses of data carried out and skeleton reports drafted well before data collection is complete.
- Analysis should be appropriate to the type of data collected.
- You should ensure that you avoid plagiarism by clearly identifying and attributing all text and diagrams that were originated by others.
- The final report should be clear, well presented and directed towards the right audience.

Further information

- Bryman, A. and Bell, E. (2007) *Business Research Method* (2nd edn), Oxford.
- Coghlan, D. and Brannick, T. (2005) *Doing Action Research in Your Own Organization*, Sage.
- Glaser, B.G. and Strauss, A.L. (1967) *The Discovery of Grounded Theory, Strategies for Qualitative Research*, Weidenfeld & Nicolson.
  This is a classic text on qualitative approaches.
- Howard, K. and Peters, J. (1990) 'Managing Management Research'.
  This is a special issue of *Management Decision* (Vol. 28, No. 5). It provides a clear, fairly brief coverage of different types of management research, what is involved, and a short but useful bibliography.
- Jankovicz, A.D. (2005) *Business Research Projects* (4th edn), Thomson.
  This gives excellent practical guidance on projects from undergraduate through to Master's level.
- Lee, T.W. (1999) *Using Qualitative Methods in Organizational Research*, Sage.
- Oliver, P. (2003) *The Student's Guide to Research Ethics*, Open University Press.

- Rudescam, K.E. and Newton, R.R. (2001) *Surviving your dissertation* (2nd edn), Sage.
- Saunders, M., Lewis, P. and Thornhill, A. (2007) *Research Methods for Business Students* (4th edn), Financial Times Press.
  This contains considerably more detail on the topics covered here.
- White, B. (2000) *Dissertation Skills for Business Students*, Continuum.
- Young, T.L. (2006) *Successful Project Management* (2nd edn), Kogan Page.
- http://comparesearchengines.dogpile.com/OverlapAnalysis.pdf (accessed 04/04/07).
  For a comparison of search engines and argument in favour of meta-searching.
- **www.direct.gov.uk**
  Searches UK government and related websites.
- **www.dogpile.com**
  Or for UK site, .co.uk, a good meta-search engine.
- **www.google.com**
  A good general search engine.
- **www.intute.ac.uk**
  This is a free on-line service which says it provides you with 'access to the very best Web resources for education and research. The service is created by a network of UK universities and partners. Subject specialists select and evaluate the websites in our database and write high quality descriptions of the resources'.
- **www.lights.com/publisher**
  Links to major publishers' websites.
- **www.netskills.ac.uk/TONIC**
  A UK on-line course in Internet-related skills.
- **www.scholar.google**
  For academic references.
- **www.surfwax.com**
  Another useful meta-search engine.

19

Projects, theses and dissertations

→ # AFTERWARDS

Beyond your Master's . . .

By the end of this chapter you should:

- have considered how to sustain the learning habit
- have a clear idea of your objectives for the next five years
- appreciate the range of options open to you
- have decided upon your preferred option
- be starting to work towards implementing that option
- know how to go about researching a job opportunity and making an effective application, if this is necessary.

INTRODUCTION

If you have now finished, or are about to finish, your Master's degree, congratulations are due. It is a considerable achievement, the more so if you have been studying part-time, and balancing the demands of job and course.

You have two last tasks, if you are to gain the full benefit from your studies. The first is to think about how you can sustain the 'learning habit' into the future. In a rapidly changing world, lifelong learning is far more than a politician's slick phrase. Your continued career success, and the success of any organisations you work for, will depend upon it. A manager who is prepared to reflect on his or her personal practice, identify areas for improvement and take steps to bring that improvement about will become more and more effective (and impressive) as an individual. The same open and questioning attitude is likely to question organisational practices and seek improvements there too.

→ Ch 8   The discussion in Chapter 8 of how managers learn may well have caused you to develop the learning habit already. But if it didn't, and you have been relying upon your formal studies to guide your learning thus far, now is the time to re-read that chapter, and think about how to ensure that you will continue to learn after your degree.

Your second task is to review your life objectives, and think about what further steps you can take now you have gained your qualification. Again, you may already have been doing this at intervals during your programme. If not, this chapter offers a framework for doing so, and suggestions as to how to implement your chosen strategy. It covers the range of options that may now be open to you, and how to choose between them. There is also guidance on researching job opportunities, preparing an application and making a good impression during an interview.

In going through this process you will in a sense be treating yourself as a live case study, and putting into immediate practice skills which your course will have developed. Furthermore, this will be in a context of obvious personal relevance and importance.

LIFELONG LEARNING

You may feel your brain has been stretched for too long, and by now you just want a rest. Or you may be 'addicted' to the excitement of learning, to the 'high' which comes on suddenly making sense of a situation in a new way because of a theory or concept, or of knowing that you have done something better than ever before because of improved skills. In either case, you need to continue to learn. If you have developed the habit of reflective practice it will not feel like work. But even if you are still at the stage where it is an effort to establish the habit, you probably cannot *afford* simply to stop.

As lifelong careers (*see* later in the chapter) have become less common, responsibility for management learning has tended to shift from the employer to the individual manager. Your future employability will depend on your continued learning, so it is very much in your interest to accept this responsibility.

Lifelong learning

This requires continued, systematic:

■ reflection on experience

■ development of new concepts

■ testing of these against experience

■ practice of skills.

■ seeking of new challenges.

The learning skills you have developed while studying may therefore be among the most valuable things gained from the programme, and it is worth thinking about how to carry these forward into your future. Without the discipline of your course, and the goad of assignments and examinations, it is easy for the pressure of everyday work to drive out all else. You then become trapped in the 'experience' part of the Kolb learning cycle, and do not go through the other stages necessary for continued learning.

To avoid this, you need to find ways of continuing to reflect on your experience, so that you can develop your repertoire of useful concepts, and test these against the radically changing world in which you are likely to be working. The following elements are crucial to a sustained learning habit.

■ **Having experiences** – this will be happening to you constantly at work and/or on your course – but you may want to think about how you can extend the experiences you have (see the end of this list). You need also to stand back and observe your experiences and your reactions to these.

- **Reflection**. Time needs to be scheduled for this thinking about your observations, whether daily, weekly, at the end of each significant assignment or all of these. If you have been keeping a learning journal, as suggested earlier, you will find it useful to continue this. If not, starting such a journal may go some way to replacing the course experience. Some reflection can usefully be done in discussion with colleagues. A key strand in the emerging discipline of knowledge management is the need to make tacit knowledge explicit. (Tacit knowledge is what we know, but have not yet put into words, even for ourselves.) Knowledge that is explicit can be more easily retained and shared within the organisation. If this is to be achieved, the process needs to be recognised as important, and time scheduled for the necessary thinking and discussion.

- **Theorising**. You then need to interpret/make sense of your experience. Your course will have introduced you to a wide range of theories and concepts. Try to continue the habit of applying these to your work experience, using them in new contexts as part of your process of making sense of what is happening in your organisation, and what you are doing in response to this. Expand your repertoire by judicious reading, surfing, discussion with colleagues and attendance at professional meetings and conferences. (Remember to keep exercising your critical skills: many management books, papers and presentations are fairly superficial and/or based on inadequate evidence or dubious assumptions.)

- **Testing**. As you encounter new ideas, and develop your own, continue the process of deliberately testing them against your experience as a manager. Only thus can you develop an improved portfolio of conceptual tools.

- **Practice**. In the above you will be practising your learning skills, and some of your critical ones. There will be more concrete skills which you can continue to practise, too. There is probably still room to develop your communication skills in various contexts, for example, or expand your analytical skills.

- **Seeking new challenges**. Your job will probably throw up many new challenges – particularly if you now have the confidence to see situations as opportunities to put your competence to the test. If not, it is worth actively seeking such opportunities. Learning comes from stepping beyond what is 'safe', and stretching yourself.

 It is worth taking time to think about skills you would still like to develop, as well as how to ensure that your 'reflective practitioner' skills are sustained. Use the following activity as the basis for doing this, deciding on targets and review dates, and noting the latter in your diary. Or you may like to use the proformas on the **website**.

ACTIVITY 20.1

→ Ch 7

1. If you have not been keeping a learning journal as part of your personal development file, revisit the section in Chapter 7 on this. Decide on a form, and take any necessary steps to assemble a framework.

2. Identify suitable times for regular reflection, and those key events which should also prompt reflection. Identify occasions that would be suitable for group reflection. Take steps to ensure that such reflection takes place.

20

Beyond your Master's . . .

3. List skills which you would like to develop further, and develop a plan (with actions and target dates) for this development. You might usefully discuss this with your manager, perhaps in the context of an appraisal interview. (Remember the importance of feedback on performance in developing skills.)

4. List areas of interest, where you would like to find out more, and think about ways in which you can achieve this, again developing a plan with target dates. (Update this regularly, as new areas become important.)

5. Whether or not you are keeping a learning journal, make sure that you schedule regular sessions (perhaps monthly) for consolidation of what you have learned, and further reflection on the effectiveness of your ongoing learning.

REASSESSING OBJECTIVES AND OPTIONS

Your life objectives, and the subset of your career objectives, have probably changed significantly as a result of your studies. Your perspective will have broadened, you will have made new contacts, and you will be aware of a wider range of options. Unless you actively revise your objectives in the light of your experiences you are missing out on a significant potential benefit of study. It may be more interesting to work from a blank sheet, here, rather than consciously trying to develop objectives trees such as you constructed earlier. If you prefer a tabular format see the **website**.

ACTIVITY 20.2

→ Ch 3

Construct a new set of objectives trees showing your goals for the next five years. Do not restrict yourself at this point to career objectives. Start with the wider set of life objectives and nest your career objectives within these. When you have finished, you may like to compare your new trees with those you did at the start of your studies.

Exploring options

Your trees should have clarified your medium-term objectives and the shorter-term goals needed to meet them: now you can think about ways of achieving these. Your options are likely to be highly personal and any discussion here will be necessarily general, but it may act as a prompt.

You may well have broadened your appreciation of the paths available through discussions with fellow students. Perhaps they are in jobs which sound interesting, but which you had never previously considered. You will by now realise that it is important that you generate as wide a range of options as possible, so you need to go beyond this chance suggestion of possibilities. You should by now be well aware of the advantages of brainstorming as a technique for doing this. As with so many of the topics in this book, working with a small group of others can be extremely helpful in encouraging creativity and ensuring breadth of approach.

When checking your brainstormed options, you may find it helpful to compare the range of ideas produced with the whole potential field. Logically, the field of options can be divided into:

- making no change;
- staying with your present organisation but doing something different, either within your present job or in a different job;
- doing a similar job with a different organisation;
- doing a different job with a different organisation;
- doing something completely different.

It might be well worth looking at all these categories of option to see whether they have potential in relation to your objectives as redefined. Even if you are sure that you *know* the obvious next step for you, it can stimulate your thinking to try to find ways in which, for example, doing something completely different might be made to satisfy your objectives. Sometimes the obvious next step is not on the shortest path to where you ultimately want to be.

Staying with your own organisation

If you favour making no change, do not feel guilty about being unenterprising. If your job is fully satisfying and continues to provide you with all the challenges that you need, then why not stay with it? Provided that your choice is a positive one and not the result of nervousness about the unfamiliar or inability to think of anything different, it can be viewed as a positive course of action.

If your choice is to seek a change in responsibilities within your organisation, you will need to think carefully about the changes that you would ideally like and consult with others in the organisation (perhaps your mentor, a training manager, your own manager and a senior manager in the area you would like to move to) about the best ways in which the desired changes might be brought about. Your focus should be, first, on what it is you want to achieve, given the increased skills and altered perspective gained from your course. Second, you should look at how these might be taken advantage of by your organisation. Only then should you consider specific posts which might be suitable.

It can be fairly limiting to restrict your choice to jobs that are currently vacant, choosing the best among them. A better route to job enhancement might in many cases be offered by adding additional roles to your current job. You might wish to think about whether getting involved in management development as a trainer offers you scope for using and further enhancing your skills. Are there any major in-company projects starting up in which it would be interesting to be involved? If so, could you persuade your organisation that you could make a worthwhile contribution to one of these? Is there a problem which you know of, and which you might be able to tackle as an in-company consultancy exercise? Would a secondment offer opportunities? This could be to another part of your own organisation or to a different organisation.

Moving to a new organisation

If you think that you would like to move to another organisation, then a similar approach to deciding just what you want, and finding the best way of getting it, should be adopted. Again, this is normally preferable to merely scanning vacancies, although there is no reason why you should not do the latter in parallel. You will recognise the arguments from the discussion of how to approach case studies and project work. It was argued there that it was important to look at objectives and measures of effectiveness *before* looking at possible options. Otherwise, a particular option might slant your thinking and limit your choice in consequence. What was important for a case study is even more so when your future is in question.

Your main sources of information about alternatives will be the Internet and the press (including relevant specialist publications), and personal contacts. Be careful, though. Much of the information you gain may be somewhat unreliable.

It is not easy to assess the advantages and disadvantages of a potential job. Job descriptions in further particulars you receive may be highly edited. The impression given at an interview may be carefully rose-tinted. Many organisations are primarily concerned with selling the vacancy to potential applicants, not realising that lack of honesty at recruitment can lead to expensive labour turnover soon after. You will therefore need to be creative and devious in order to find out about what an organisation is like to work for. Are jobs frequently advertised? If so, is growth sufficient to account for this high rate? Do you know anyone who works there, or can you get to speak to someone who does? It is surprising how helpful switchboard operators can be in suggesting people you might like to talk to, and how informative these same people can be when you phone them up as a total stranger, explaining that you are considering applying for a job. The person vacating the advertised job is obviously an excellent source of information, if available for questioning. Can you interact with the organisation as a potential customer and gain insight in that way? Are visits offered to potential candidates? Does the job advertisement or further particulars invite you to contact a named individual? If so, take advantage of the offer.

What is the economic strength of the sector in which the organisation is operating and the market position of the organisation? Jobs have been advertised in organisations when preliminary discussions about redundancies were already taking place. Is the organisation ripe for a takeover? Your studies should have put you in a position to assess the company much more effectively than before.

Doing something completely different

In thinking about the possibilities of doing something completely different, you should include consideration of as wide a range of potential areas as possible. What about doing a PhD? Many universities (including the Open University) now offer opportunities for doing research 'at a distance', so that this could be done without threat to your full-time employment. You might, of course, *wish* to do research full-time, either with your organisation's sponsorship or with the aid of a mature student grant or research fellowship. Again, there is a range of possibilities.

What about writing a book, or at least a series of articles for publication? Your dissertation, if you wrote one for your course, may have distinct possibilities for 'versioning' for other audiences. There may be areas where you realised that you knew more about the topic than your lecturers. What is the potential for using this knowledge in some way?

If you enjoyed working in groups and making presentations on your work, or found the academic side of the work really stimulating, what about starting to teach management studies? As with research, you do not need to give up your full-time job: given current academic salaries you might well not wish to. Part-time and distance management education programmes may well be seeking part-time teaching staff. Contact your local college(s) and the major distance learning institutions to see what opportunities are available. Your own recent study experience and your qualification should make you an attractive applicant. (You would of course need to check with your employer that such 'moonlighting' was not in breach of your contract, but many employers welcome the continued development opportunities offered by such leisure activities.)

What about consultancy? Again, your qualification would be highly relevant and working for a large consulting organisation would rapidly expose you to a wide variety of different organisations and their problems. The breadth of experience so gained could stand you in excellent stead if you wished after a few years to take another managerial job. You might even wish to set up in business on your own as a consultant, although this option can be fairly lonely and carries a high risk. (It is possible to insure against some of this, and you would need to do so, which can be expensive.) You may need to devote a large proportion of your time to marketing your skills, and your ability to handle the work you generate will be necessarily restricted. You might consider forming a loose network with others in the same position so that you can help each other out if overload occurs, as well as offering each other support.

If you prefer working with individuals at a personal level, coaching (both business coaching and life coaching) seems to be a growth area at present. Business journalism, broadcasting and voluntary work are other examples of possibilities. While the suggestions above may not attract you, they give some indication of the range of options available.

The fairly radical restructuring of organisations during the 1990s forced many managers into a 'portfolio' lifestyle, at least for a part of their career. Such a portfolio might consist of a mix of activities from the above list. It can offer variety, opportunities for personal development and a more balanced risk than working in a single area.

ACTIVITY 20.3

Try to think of at least three further options which differ radically from those already suggested, to ensure that you are casting your net sufficiently broadly:

_____

_____

_____

MAKING AN EFFECTIVE JOB APPLICATION

Whether you are looking for internal promotion, seeking a job in another organisation or aiming to work at something completely different but still as an employee, you are likely to need to make a job application. Your course may have covered this, but, if not, you should take this aspect seriously.

Over the last few years, I have dealt with hundreds of job applications from managers, many with MBAs. A significant number of these applications were rejected almost cursorily on the grounds that the applicant did not appear to be serious enough about the job to take a minimum amount of trouble over the application. In the past I have rejected applicants for one or more of the following reasons:

- Application form was full of errors and failed to address the person specification.

  Reaction: this is a person who can't be bothered.

- The required application form was not submitted – the applicant merely sent a CV that looked as if it was prepared some time previously, and was not tailored in any way to the job in question.

  Reaction: this person doesn't particularly want this job.

- The application came in after the deadline (and no reason was offered).

  Reaction: we have plenty of applications already that *were* in on time. Anyway, it looks as if this applicant is not organised.

- There was no supporting CV and no letter giving reasons for the application and highlighting strengths in relation to this particular job.

  Reaction: this person misses opportunities.

- No references were given, or referees failed to respond (it is important to check that your referees are willing to give you a reference and will be in the country at the required time).

  Reaction: we don't interview/appoint without good references being received.

- Reference was unfavourable.

  Reaction: if even the referee thinks so poorly of this person ...

  (This one is difficult, as people are often unwilling to say that the reference they are agreeing to write will be less than glowing – ask them outright if you have doubts.)

- The applicant did not seem to have fully understood the nature of the advertised job.

  Reaction: either this person has taken no trouble with their application or they are not very bright.

- The applicant seemed to have given no *thought* to what the organisation was looking for, and how they could deliver this.

  Reaction: this person has not taken their application seriously, or they are not good at analysing problems.

- The applicant was late for the interview.

  Reaction: if they can't manage to get to an interview on time ... (Note: we did recently make an exception for a man who rang to say a tree had fallen across the road right in front of his car, and he and another motorist thought it would take them a couple of hours to shift it – so ring to let the selectors know if something arises which you could not have foreseen.)

- The applicant was dressed inappropriately for the interview. (One person I interviewed for a job involving contacts with senior managers in client organisations showed up wearing jeans!)

Reaction: this shows lack of judgement. Besides, the effect on clients/ subordinates/superiors would be bad.

- The candidate gave one-word answers and did not look at the interviewers once.

Reaction: this candidate lacks presence/communication skills/interpersonal skills.

- The candidate spent the interview talking incessantly without letting the interviewer get a word in edgeways. (You would be surprised how common this is.)

Reaction: this person can't listen/understand what is required. They would be exhausting to work with.

- The candidate put all their energies into proving what a brilliant person they were rather than demonstrating how their skills matched job requirements.

Reaction: may be good at selling themselves, but hasn't thought about the job or analysed what is required.

- When asked at the end of the interview if they had any questions the only one was something like 'When will I hear?'

Reaction: this person has not thought much about the job – Note: this would not lose you a job if you were well ahead in other respects, but if you are very close to another candidate a penetrating question showing understanding of the likely challenges on taking the job might be a useful differentiator, showing you had really thought about the implications of working there.

To apply successfully:

- thoroughly research job and organisation
- 'version' your application
- highlight your strengths for *this* job
- prepare carefully for interview
- consider any potential weaknesses
- behave professionally in the interview
- listen carefully, and think before speaking.

I appreciate that it is bad practice to give advice in negative form, but these are all examples that have made a powerful impression on me when selecting. From the above it is fairly clear how you can increase your chances of making a successful application, provided you want the job sufficiently to put in the necessary homework beforehand. First, it is essential to research the job and organisation as thoroughly as possible. You will have started this process when you were deciding whether or not you wished to apply. Once decided, it is necessary to take it further. Once you *know* enough about the job and the organisation, you need to *think* about how you can use this knowledge to strengthen your application.

Considerable effort needs to be put into preparing your initial application. The impression created must be of a thoughtful, organised applicant, who really wants the job and who can argue for his or her strengths as a candidate succinctly and powerfully. It helps to say something somewhere that makes you stand out from what may be hundreds of other applicants. A

20

Beyond your Master's . . .

slightly original turn of phrase in describing your leisure activities might catch the selector's eye. Or there might be something different in the way you argue why this is precisely the job to which you can make a significant contribution. An application checklist is available on the **website**.

Qualities needed in the application

All aspects of your application should show evidence of judgement and selectivity, with everything you write, whether on application form, CV or supporting short letter, tailored to the job in question.

You should 'version' your CV for each job application, emphasising your most relevant experience. Aim to go beyond merely listing jobs you have held, with key responsibilities which you had in each. It is far more impressive if your CV highlights the aspects of each job, and the skills which you exercised or developed in consequence, that are particularly important for *this* job. Always give more emphasis to more recent experience than to things you did a long time ago, unless early experience is singularly relevant.

Keep working at improving your CV if you are not being shortlisted. Although you may be aiming at unrealistic jobs (and it is worth asking if this is the case), it may be the way you are applying. (A friend made numerous unsuccessful applications before seeking advice on his CV. I made fairly minor changes in line with the above guidance and he got an interview – and the job – with his next application.)

Interview preparation

If you are invited for an interview, you will wish to find out even more about the job and the company. Possible sources were listed above. If there are any that you did not approach earlier, or others that are now offered, take advantage of these. You want to know as much as possible about the job, the organisation and the market in which it operates.

Before the interview you will obviously be thinking about your strengths in relation to the job. But consider, too, areas where you are less strong. You may well be asked about these, and will create a much better impression if you have clearly thought about them, and worked out a strategy for dealing with them as soon as you are in post. If you honestly think you are the perfect candidate, you can describe 'weaknesses' that interviewers may well interpret as strengths: 'I have a tendency to become *too* involved in my work'.

Research suggests that selection decisions are often taken within the first few minutes of an interview. At this point the selector has little to go on beyond appearance, so it is important that you take steps to ensure that your appearance works in your favour. Part of your research should cover the dress code within the organisation. You need to fit this 'model' and to look as if you have taken trouble with your appearance.

It is worth arriving early enough to repair any ravages of travel in the cloakroom. And to avoid carrying a lot of clutter into the interview, leave bags and coat at reception or in a secretary's office rather than dragging them into the interview room. Again, you will look far more professional without them. If you wish to take in examples of your work that you feel strengthens your application, pack materials in the order you would wish to present them in a neat case (but see the caution below).

If you are inexperienced at job interviews, or know that you tend either to clam up or to babble nervously, practise beforehand. Think of possible questions, and persuade someone to role-play the interviewer and feed you with the questions. Ask them to give you feedback on the impression you created. Record the interview and play it back. You should gain two benefits from this. First, you will be able to spot habits or weaknesses that impair your performance, and work on reducing these. Second, you should become less nervous with practice, and find that you have the courage to stop and think before replying, and that your replies become more coherent and fluent as well.

Interview techniques

During the interview it is important to listen very carefully to the questions asked, and to think about how to answer them before opening your mouth. If you are unclear as to what the interviewer wants, ask for clarification. If you want thinking time, ask for it. 'That's a really good/interesting/challenging question. May I think for a minute?' Try not to get bogged down in minutiae. If asked for an example of needing to operate a disciplinary procedure, don't go into what Fred was wearing and what Maisie had been saying for months, and where they were when you finally caught him at it. Instead give only as much detail as is necessary to show that you acted appropriately and in accordance with sound principles and organisational policy.

In the sort of job you are likely to be seeking, interviewers are likely to be looking for the ability to think clearly, to select relevant factors from a situation and to take appropriate decisions in the light of available information. Getting into blow-by-blow discussions of things that have happened will not help you to convince them of your strategic ability!

In most managerial jobs interpersonal skills are important. You should have developed such skills during your studies, but remember to apply them in the interview. Eye contact with your interviewer is important, and occasional smiles can work wonders, though excessive smiling at inappropriate times can be off-putting. You need also to be aware of your body language. Remember the importance of first impressions and walk in confidently, smiling at any panel member whose eye you catch. Sit down in an 'open and interested' posture. Avoid leaning back, crossing your arms, or otherwise looking defensive and, of course, avoid nervous fidgeting. Watch the interviewers' body language too for cues that you may be talking too much, or otherwise not responding as they want.

Sometimes, particularly if large distances are involved, interviews may be held by video-conference link or phone. If interviewed by video-conference, avoid rapid movements. Low band-width can make you look as jerky as an early movie star. Instead, sit in as relaxed a manner as possible, do not fidget or gesticulate, and look directly at the camera. Extremes of sound may be similarly exaggerated by the technology, so avoid these too.

20

Beyond your Master's . . .

INTERNET RECRUITMENT

Jobs are now normally advertised on-line. Even those in the paper will give a Web reference and often expect an electronic application. This is quicker and cheaper than paper systems, and may attract applications from a wider and/or different field.

The basic principles of making a successful application are the same whether paper or electronic. But you may need to tailor your approach slightly to suit the medium. There are also some points where electronic application protocol is as yet unclear.

In the case of e-mail applications you may be uncertain as to the level of formality expected. E-mails tend to be less formal than memos or letters. Should your application be similarly informal? While opinions on this vary, unless the advertisement itself is clearly informal it is probably safest to err on the side of greater formality, composing your e-mail as if it were a normal letter of application. However, as the span of 'electronic attention' is often slightly less than that for paper material, it is worth paying even more attention than usual to clarity and brevity. Remember that your application may be read either from screen or print-out, so make sure that it will work equally well in either case.

Try to ensure that both your electronic CV and application form are clear and focused and use relevant key words. The first sift may be electronic if large numbers of applications are expected, so ensure that the evidence of how you meet essential requirements is clearly signposted. Avoid 'padding'. This is undesirable with any CV, but it is claimed that electronic CVs are usually scanned (if by humans) for a maximum of three minutes. This means that your relevant experience needs to make an impact on the selector well within that time.

GOING FORWARD

You should now have clarified your goals, at least for the next few years, and have thought about how to start moving towards them. You should be aware of your strengths and weaknesses as a potential candidate for a range of jobs, and have an idea of how to go about making yourself more marketable. The SWOT framework, which you will probably by now know all too well, may be useful here. Pay particular attention to your strengths and how to exploit these – therein will lie your particular competitive advantage.

As with all other types of management, your career management will be helped if you schedule regular, if not necessarily frequent, reviews of your objectives and progress towards these. Only thus can you ensure that you are in control of your career, and directing it towards the objectives which are of greatest importance to you, even when time or experience causes those objectives to change.

It remains only for me to wish you the very best of luck in travelling your chosen path. I hope that this Handbook has been of help to you in gaining your qualification, and that the skills you have gained on your course will assist you in attaining your more important life objectives.

SUMMARY

■ The skills and approaches you learned on your MBA are equally applicable to the 'case' of planning your own career progression.

■ It is important to be clear about your objectives, and about how you will measure progress towards these.

■ Consider as wide a range of options as possible before choosing.

■ Staying in your present job can be a positive choice.

■ If you are looking for another job, it is important to research possibilities thoroughly.

■ If you are applying for another job, it is important that your application is carefully compiled, relates to the particular job and is such as to make you stand out from perhaps hundreds of other applicants.

■ In interviews your interpersonal skills are being assessed, as well as your other qualities relevant to the job. Again, careful preparation is important.

■ Once you are in the job you want, continue to apply what you have learned on your Master's, not only to your job content, but to your own career management and achievement of your life objectives.

Further information

■ Bridges, W. (1997) *Creating You & Co: Be the Boss of Your Own Career*, Nicholas Brealey.

■ Bryon, M. (2007) *How to Pass Graduate Psychometric Tests* (3rd edn), Kogan Page

■ Clutterbuck, D. and Dearlove, D. (1999) *The Interim Manager: A New Career Model for the Experienced Manager*, Financial Times/Pitman Publishing.

■ Comfort, M. (1997) *Portfolio People: How to Create a Workstyle as Individual as You Are*, Century.

■ Hornby, M. (2000) *3 Easy Steps to the Job You Want* (2nd edn), Pearson Education.

■ Robinson, J. and McConnell, C. (2003) *careers un-ltd*, Pearson.

20

Beyond your Master's . . .

References and Bibliography

Adair, J. and Allen, M. (2003) *The Concise Time Management and Personal Development.* Thorogood.

Allen, D. (2001) *Getting Things Done*, Piatkus.

Andreas, S. and Faulkner, C. (1996) *NLP: The New Technology of Achievement*, Nicholas Brealey.

Back, K. and Back, K. (1999) *Assertiveness at Work* (3rd edn), McGraw-Hill.

Baguley, P. (1992) *Teams and Team-Working*, Teach Yourself Books, Hodder & Stoughton.

Barker, A. (2002) *How to Manage Meetings*, Sunday Times/Kogan Page.

Baumann, B. (1992) 'Master ohne Wert', *Forbes*, 10, pp. 68–72.

Belbin, R.M. (1981) *Management Teams*, Heinemann.

Belbin, R.M. (1993) *Team Roles at Work*, Butterworth-Heinemann.

Bickerstaff, G. (ed.) (2006) *Which MBA? A Critical Guide to Programmes in Europe and the USA* (18th edn), The Economist Publications/Pearson Education.

Bird, P. (1998) *Teach Yourself Time Management*, Hodder & Stoughton.

Bishop, S. (2000) *Develop Your Assertiveness* (2nd edn), Kogan Page.

Blamires, H. (2000) *The Penguin Guide to Plain English*, Penguin.

Bowden, J. (2004) *Writing a Report*: 7th edn, Howtobooks.

Bolton, G. (2001) *Reflective Practice: Writing and Professional Development*, Sage.

Booles, R.N. (2004) *What Color Is Your Parachute?* Ten Speed Press.

Bradley, A. (2006) *Successful Presentation Skills* (3rd edn), Kogan Page.

Bridges, W. (1997) *Creating You & Co: Be the Boss of Your Own Career*, Nicholas Brealey.

Bryan, M., Cameron, J. and Allen, C. (1998) *An Artist's Way at Work: Twelve Weeks to Creative Freedom*, Pan.

Bryon, M. (2007) *How to pass the GMAT*, Kogan Page.

Bryon, M. (2007) *How to Pass Graduate Psychometric Tests* (3rd edn), Kogan Page.

Bryman, A. and Bell, E. (2007) *Business Research Method* (2nd edn), Oxford.

Bryson, J.M., Ackermann, F., Eden, C. and Finn, C.B. (2004) *Visible Thinking*, Wiley.
This shows a range of ways in which diagrams can be used to make sense of situations and develop strategies for dealing with them.

Butler, G. and Hope, T. (1995) *Manage your Mind: The Mental Fitness Guide*, Oxford University Press.

Buzan, T. (2003) *Use Your Head*, BBC Publications.

Buzan, T. (2003) *The Speed Reading Book*, BBC Publications.

Buzan, T. and Buzan, B. (2003) *The Mind Map Book: Radiant Thinking – Major Evolution in Human Thought*, BBC Publications.

Carter, R., Martin, J., Mayblin, B. and Munday, M. (1984) *Systems, Management and Change: a Graphic Guide*, Harper & Row, in association with the Open University.

Caunt, J. (2000) *Organise Yourself*, Kogan Page.

Checkland, P. (1981) *Systems Thinking, Systems Practice*, John Wiley and Sons.

Clegg, B. (1999) *Instant Time Management*, Kogan Page.

Clegg, B. (2000) *Instant Stress Management*, Kogan Page.

Clutterbuck, D. and Dearlove, D. (1999) *The Interim Manager: a New Career Model for the Experienced Manager*, Financial Times Pitman Publishing.

Clutterbuck, D. and Kernaghan, S. (1990) *The Phoenix Factor*, Weidenfeld & Nicolson.

Coghlan, D. and Brannick, T. (2005) *Doing Action Research in Your Own Organization*, Sage.

Collins, J./Video Arts (1998) *Perfect Presentations*, Marshall Publishing.

Comfort, M. (1997) *Portfolio People: How to Create a Workstyle as Individual as You Are*, Century.

Conradi, M. and Hall, R. (2001) *That Presentation Sensation*, Financial Times Prentice Hall.

Cramer, S. (2000) *The Ultimate Business Library: 75 Books that Made Management*, Capstone.

Deal, T. and Kennedy, A. (1982) *Corporate Cultures: The Rites and Rituals of Corporate Life*, Addison-Wesley.

Easton, G. (1992) *Learning from Case Studies* (2nd edn), Prentice-Hall.

Entwistle, N. (1996) 'Recent Research on Student Learning and the Learning Environment', in 'The Management of Independent Learning', J. Tait ad P. Knight (eds), SEDA, Kogan Page.

Fayol, H. (1949) *General and Industrial Management*, Pitman (translated from the 1916 original in French).

Forster, M. (2006) *Do It Tomorrow: and Other Secrets of Time Management*, Hodder & Stoughton.

Forsyth, P. (2006) *How to Write Reports and Proposals*, Kogan Page.

Frost, V. (2006) 'Can Your Manager Manage?', *Guardian*, Work 2, pp. 1–2.

Gibson, R. (ed.) (1998) *Rethinking the Future*, Nicholas Brealey.

Giles, K. and Hedge, N. (1994) *The Manager's Good Study Guide*, The Open University.

Glaser, B.G. and Strauss, A.L. (1967) *The Discovery of Grounded Theory: Strategies for Qualitative Research*, Weidenfeld & Nicolson.

Glynn, J.J., Murphy, M.P. and Perrin, J. (1998) *Accounting for Managers* (2nd edn), International Thomson Business Press.

Goldsmith, W. and Clutterbuck, D. (1984) *The Winning Streak*, Penguin.

Goleman, D. (1998) *Working with Emotional Intelligence*, Bloomsbury.

Gowers, E. (1954) *The Complete Plain Words*, Penguin.

Graham, L. and Sargent, D. (1981) *Countdown to Mathematics*, Vol. 1, Addison-Wesley with Open University Press.

Greising, D. (1998) *I'd Like the World to Buy a Coke. The Life and Leadership of Roberto Gorzueta*, Wiley.

Handy, C. (1999) *Inside Organisations*, Penguin.

Hardingham, A. (1995) *Working in Teams*, Institute of Personnel Development.

Herzberg, F. (1966) *Work and the Nature of Man*, World Publishing Company.

Honey, P. and Mumford, A. (1986) *The Manual of Learning Styles*, Peter Honey.

Hornby, M. (2000) *3 Easy Steps to the Job you Want* (2nd edn), Pearson Education.

Howard, K. and Peters, J. (1990) 'Managing Management Research', *Management Decision*, Vol. 28, No. 5.

Huczinski, A. (1996) *Management Gurus. What Makes Them and How to Become One*, International Thomson Business Press.

Huff, D. (1954) *How to Lie with Statistics*, Penguin.

Hussey, D.E. (1988) *Management Training and Corporate Strategy*, Pergamon Press.

Israel, R., Whitten, H. and Shaffran, C. (2000) *Your Mind at Work: Developing Self Knowledge for Business Success*, Kogan Page.

Jankovicz, A.D. (2005) *Business Research Projects* (4th edn), Thomson.

Jantsch, E. (1967) *Technological Forecasting in Perspective*, OECD.

Kakabadse, A., Ludlow, R. and Vinnicombe, S. (1987) *Working in Organisations*, Penguin.

Kellaway, L. (2000) *Sense and Nonsense in the Office*, Financial Times Prentice Hall.

Kelly, F.J. and Kelly, H.M. (1986) *What They Really Teach You at the Harvard Business School*, Grafton.

Kepner, C.H. and Tregoe, B.B. (1965) *The Rational Manager*, McGraw-Hill.

Kind, J. (1999) *Accounting and Finance for Managers*, Kogan Page.

Kline, N. (1999) *Time to Think*, Cassell Illustrated.

Kneeland, S. (1999) *Thinking Straight*, Pathways.

Kolb, D.A., Rubin, I.M. and MacIntyre, J.M. (1984) *Organizational Psychology* (4th edn), Prentice-Hall.

Lataif, L.E. (1992) 'MBA: Is the Traditional Model Doomed?', *Harvard Business Review*, Nov–Dec, pp. 128–40.

Lawler, E.E. and Porter, L. (1967) 'Antecedent Attitudes of Effective Managerial Performance', *Organizational Behaviour and Human Performance*, Vol 2, pp. 22–42.

Lee, T.W. (1999) *Using Qualitative Methods in Organizational Research*, Sage.

Leech, T. (2001) *Say It Like Shakespeare*, McGraw-Hill.

Lifeskills International (1999) *Staying Healthy at Work*, Gower.

Lucas, B. (2001) *Power Up Your Mind*, Nicholas Brealey.

Luthans, F. (1988) 'Successful Versus Effective Real Managers', *Academy of Management Executive*, Vol. II, No 2.

Moon, J.A. (1999, reprinted 2005) *Reflection in Learning and Professional Development*, RoutledgeFalmer.

Morgan, G. (1986) *Images of Organisation*, Sage.

Moroney, M.J. (1951) *Facts from Figures*, Penguin.

Morris, C. (2000) *Quantitative Approaches in Business Studies* (5th edn), Financial Times Prentice Hall.

Morris, C. and Thanassoulis, E. (1994) *Essential Mathematics – a refresher course for Business and Social Studies*, Macmillan.

Morris, S. and Smith, J. (1998) *Understanding Mind Maps in a Week*, Institute of Management.

Naughton, J. (2003) 'How PowerPoint Can Fatally Weaken Your Argument', *The Observer*, 21 December.

Neenan, M. and Dryden, W. (2004) *Cognitive Therapy: 100 Key Points and Techniques*. Routledge.

Nutz, K. and Freiberg, J. (1997) *Southwest Airlines Crazy Recipe for Business and Personal Success*, Orion Business Books.

Oakshott, L. (1998) *Essential Quantitative Methods for Business, Management and Finance*, Macmillan Business.

The Official MBA Handbook 2003/2004 (19th edn) (2003), Financial Times Prentice Hall with the Association of MBAs.

Oliver, P. (2003) *The Student's Guide to Research Ethics*, Open University Press.

Pidd, M. (2003) *Tools for Thinking: Modeling in Management Science* (2nd edn), Wiley.

Pizzey, A. (1998) *Finance and Accounting for Non-Specialist Students*, Financial Times Pitman Publishing.

Porter, M.E. (1980) *Competitive Strategy*, Free Press.

Powell, J. (1991) *Quantitative Decision Making*, Longman.

Robinson, J. and McConnell, C. (2003) *careers un-ltd*, Pearson.

Robinson, P. (1994) *Snapshots from Hell: the Making of an MBA*, Nicholas Brealey.

Roberts, B. (1999) *Working Memory: Improving Your Memory for the Workplace*, London House.

Rose, C. and Nicholl, M.J. (1997) *Accelerated Learning for the 21st Century*, Piatkus.

Rowntree, D. (1987) *Statistics Without Tears: a Primer for Non-mathematicians*, Penguin.

Rudescam, K.E. and Newton, R.R. (2001) *Surviving Your Dissertation* (2nd edn), Sage.

Russell, L. (1999) *The Accelerated Learning Field Book*, Jossey-Bass Pfeiffer.

Saunders, M., Lewis, P. and Thornhill, A. (2007) *Research Methods for Business Students* (4th edn), Financial Times Press.

Seely, J. (2002) *Writing Reports*, Oxford University Press.

Sprent, P. (1991) *Management Mathematics*, Penguin.

Stutely, R. (2003) *The Definitive Guide to Managing the Numbers*, Pearson.

Thompson, G. (2005) *Stress Buster*, Summersdale Publishers.

Truss, L. (2003) *Eats, Shoots & Leaves: The Zero Tolerance Approach to Punctuation*, Profile Books.

Tuckman, B.W. (1965) 'Developmental Sequence in Small Groups', *Psychological Bulletin*, Vol 63, pp. 384–99.

Tufte, E. 'The Cognitive Style of PowerPoint, www.edwardtufte.com.

Tyler, S. (2004) *The Manager's Good Study Guide* (new edition), Open University.

White, B. (2000) *Dissertation Skills for Business Students*, Continuum.

Williams, J.S. (1995) *The Right Way to Make Effective Presentations*, Eliot Right Way Books.

Young, T.L. (2006) *Successful Project Management* (2nd edn), Kogan Page.

http://comparesearchengines.dogpile.com/OverlapAnalysis.pdf

A comparison of search engines.

www.abs.ac.uk

UK Association of Business Schools.

www.austhink.com/reason/tutorials

Explains argument mapping.

www.cipd.co.uk/subjects/health/stress/stress.htm

Site of the Chartered Institute for Personnel and Development.

www.direct.gov.uk

UK government sites.

www.dogpile.com

A meta-search engine.

www.edwardtufte.com

On the cognitive style of PowerPoint.

www.google.com

A general search engine.

www.helpself.com

Basic EQ test and material on leadership.

www.intute.ac.uk

Resources for education and research.

www.leeds.ac.uk/library/training/referencing/goldenrules.htm

Tutorial in Harvard-style referencing.

References and Bibliography

www.lights.com/publisher
   Links to major publishers.
www.mba.hobsons.com
   Information on various courses.
www.mbaworld.com
   Site of the Association of MBAs.
www.ncsu.edu/project/posters/NewSite/
   On poster presentation.
www.netskills.ac.uk/TONIC
   On-line course in Internet-related skills.
www.scholar.google
   For academic references.
www.similarminds.com/personality_tests
   Free personality tests.
www.surfwax.com
   A meta-search engine.

Index